HISTORY OF ANCIENT INDIA

History of Ancient India

Rama Shankar Tripathi

MOTILAL BANARSIDASS
INTERNATIONAL
DELHI

Reprint Edition: Delhi, 2026
First Edition: Delhi, 1942

ISBN : 978-93-48911-21-6 (Paper)
ISBN : 978-93-48911-82-7 (Cloth)

Also available at
MOTILAL BANARSIDASS INTERNATIONAL
H. O.: 41 U.A. Bungalow Road, (Back Lane) Jawahar Nagar, Delhi - 110007
4261 (Basement) Lane # 3, Ansari Road, Darya Ganj, New Delhi - 110002
12/1A, 2nd Floor, Bankim Chatterjee Street, Kolkata - 700073
Shop #. 6, 241, Luz Ginza Complex, Luz Corner, Mylapore, Chennai - 600004
Stockist : Motilal Books, Ashok Rajpath, Near Kali Mandir, Patna - 800004

Printed in India by
MOTILAL BANARSIDASS INTERNATIONAL

TO

THE SWEET

AND

EVER-CHERISHED MEMORY

OF

MY DEARLY BELOVED WIFE

HEMAVATĪ DEVĪ

"A perfect Woman, nobly planned,
To warn, to comfort, and command;
And yet a Spirit still, and bright,
With something of angelic light."

PREFACE

The object of this volume is to provide within a moderate compass a compendious account of the history, institutions, and culture of ancient India from the dim ages of antiquity to the establishment of Moslem rule. It has not been planned to meet the needs of any particular class of readers. Its primary purpose is to serve alike students, scholars, and all others, interested in the study of ancient Indian history, as a book of ready use and reference. How far I have succeeded in striking a happy balance in my narrative to suit the requirements and tastes of each one of these groups that approach history from widely divergent angles, it is for competent critics to judge. But suffice it to say here that in the pages which follow every attempt has been made to avoid presenting a mass of the dry bones of historical fact or over-burdening the account with intricate discussions on knotty problems of history, on the one hand, and giving a mere general and readable survey of India's long and fascinating past, on the other. I have endeavoured to tap and utilise properly the available sources of information, literary, epigraphic, and numismatic, and also to embody and set forth in a consistent manner the results of up-to-date researches on different topics and epochs. All the materials have been patiently sifted and critically examined with the sole desire to arrive at historical truth and scientific accuracy; and the unfortunate tendency, manifest in some modern publications, to extol or decry without warrant any of the manifold aspects of India's panoramic story, has been scrupulously eschewed. It is my firm conviction that the historian cannot take sides in a controversy.

For he is neither a propagandist of ideas nor a panegyrist of the exploits of ambitious dynasts of old. He must, as far as possible, eliminate the subjective element, and hold up the mirror of his mind to reflect facts plainly without the least distortion or colouring. Besides, he cannot afford to be dogmatic in his statements, specially in ancient Indian history, where gaps still yawn and the evidence is not only vague, uncertain, and incomplete, but also at times conflicting or contradictory. Such being the nature of the data at our disposal, even the historicity of some kings is indeed a matter of doubt and controversy at this distance in time. Our scepticism, however, appears natural, when we remember that our ancient predecessors as well had a fair measure of it. We may aptly recall here the words of *Viṣṇu Purāṇa*,[1] which run to this effect: "I have given this history. The existence of these kings will in future become a matter of debate and doubt as the very existence of Rāma and other august kings has become today a matter of doubt and speculation. Emperors become mere legends in the current of time—the Emperors who thought and think "India is mine." Fie on Empires, fie on the Empire of Emperor Rāghava."

The idea of the work originated a few years ago, but, for reasons which need not be detailed here, it could not materialise earlier. Even now I have not been able to write a chapter on Greater India and another on the general features of our history. I hope, however, to add both in the second edition when it comes out. I have not also been able to give maps and illustrations owing to the forbidding prices of printing materials.

My debt to all those who have written before me on the history of ancient India is heavy. I have studied their works with care and profit, and have drawn upon

[1] Bk. IV, Ch. 24, vv. 64-77.

them where necessary. I owe special obligation to my esteemed friend, Prof. B. L. Sahni, who very kindly went through the proofs at much personal inconvenience, and ungrudgingly gave me the benefit of his scholarship and experience. To my valued colleague, Dr. A. S. Altekar, I am grateful for going through the MS. and making some useful suggestions. Lastly, my thanks are also due to Mr. Ram Sumer for helping me in the preparation of the Index.

The system of transliteration adopted in the text is the one followed in my earlier work, 'The History of Kanauj.' To illustrate, we may mention: Bāṇa, Rāṣṭrakūṭa, Śaśigupta, Soma, Candra, Coḷa, Aṅga, Rigveda, etc. But, as a rule, I have not used diacritical marks in the case of modern place-names and other popular forms.

In conclusion, I crave the readers' indulgence for any blemishes and errors of omission and commission, which may still be discovered by the discerning eye, although no pains have been spared to make the account lucid, accurate, concise, and comprehensive. The subject dealt with here is vast and complicated, and while writing I was often reminded of the well-known lines of Kālidāsa:

क्व सूर्यप्रभवो वंशः क्व चाल्पविषया मतिः
तितीर्षुर्दुस्तरं मोहादुडुपेनास्मि सागरम् ॥

Vaiśākhī Pūrṇimā
April 30, 1942

RAMA SHANKAR TRIPATHI

LIST OF ABBREVIATIONS

Ep. Ind.—Epigraphia Indica.
S. I. I.—South Indian Inscriptions.
C. I. I.—Corpus Inscriptionum Indicarum, Volumes I, II & III.
R. E.—Rock Edict of Aśoka.
M. R. E.—Minor Rock Edict of Aśoka.
P. E.—Pillar Edict of Aśoka.
M. P. E.—Minor Pillar Edict of Aśoka.
Ind. Ant.—Indian Antiquary.
J. R. A. S.—Journal of the Royal Asiatic Society.
J. B. O. R. S.—Journal of the Bihar and Orissa Research Society.
Jour. Ind. Hist.—Journal of Indian History.
Jour. U. P. Hist. Soc.—Journal of the U. P. Historical Society.
J. B. H. U.—Journal of the Benares Hindu University.
Jour. Dept. Lett.—Journal of the Department of Letters.
J. N. S. I.—Journal of the Numismatic Society of India.
J. A. S. B.—Journal of the Asiatic Society of Bengal.
Mem. As. Soc. Beng.—Memoirs of the Asiatic Society of Bengal.
Proc. As. Soc. Beng.—Proceedings of the Asiatic Society of Bengal.
Proc. 1st. Or. Conf.—Proceedings of the first Oriental Conference.
Proc. Ind. Hist. Cong.—Proceedings of the Indian History Congress.
Ann. Bhand. Inst., or A. B. R. I.—Annals of the Bhandarkar (Research) Institute.
Ind. Hist. Quart., or I. H. Q.—Indian Historical Quarterly.

Rep. Arch. Surv. West. Ind.—Report of the Archæological Survey of Western India.
Arch. Surv. Ind., or A. S. I.—Archæological Survey of India.
A. S. S. I.—Archæological Survey of South India.
Arch. Surv. Ann. Rep.—Archæological Survey Annual Report.
Arch. Surv. Ind. Rep., or A. S. I. R.—Archæological Survey of India Report.
Mem. Arch. Surv. Ind.—Memoirs of the Archæological Survey of India.
Prog. Rep. A. S. W. C.—Progress Report of the Archæological Survey Western Circle.
Prog. Rep. Arch. Surv. Ind.—Progress Report of the Archæological Survey of India.
Cam. Hist. Ind., or C. H. I.—Cambridge History of India, Vol. I (Rapson).
Cam. Sh. Hist. Ind.—Cambridge Shorter History of India.
E. H. I.—Early History of India (Vincent Smith).
Ox. Hist. Ind.—Oxford History of India (Vincent Smith).
E. H. D.—Early History of the Dekkan (R. G. Bhandarkar).
Anc. Hist. Dec., or A. H. D.—Ancient History of the Deccan (J. Dubreuil).
Pol. Hist. Anc. Ind.—Political History of Ancient India (H. C. Raychaudhuri).
C. C. G. D.—Catalogue of the Coins of the Gupta Dynasties (John Allan).
Dy. Hist. North. Ind.—Dynastic History of Northern India (H. C. Ray).
History of Kanauj—History of Kanauj to the Moslem Conquest (R. S. Tripathi).
Bom. Gaz.—Bombay Gazetteer.
K. C. B. I.—Kṣatriya Clans in Buddhist India (B. C. Law).
Invasion by Alexander—M'Crindle, Ancient India, Its Invasion by Alexander the Great.

Ancient India—M'Crindle, Ancient India as described in Classical Literature.
G. B. I.—The Greeks in Bactria and India (W. W. Tarn).
Hc.—Harṣacarita.
Hc. C. T.—Harṣacarita (English Translation by Cowell and Thomas).
G. O. S.—Gaekwāḍ Oriental Series.
Sachau—Alberuni's India (English Translation).
Watters—On Yuan Chwang's Travels.
Beal—Buddhist Records of the Western World.
Life—Life of Yuan Chwang (Samuel Beal).
Stein—English Translation of Kalhaṇa's Rājataraṅgiṇī.
Elliot—History of India as told by its own Historians.
Briggs—History of the Rise of the Mahomedan Power (Tārīkh-i-Firishta).

CONTENTS

Chapter III

THE RIGVEDIC AGE

Chapter IV

LATER VEDIC PERIOD

Chapter V

THE SŪTRAS, EPICS, & THE DHARMAŚĀSTRAS

Section A

CHAPTER X

I—THE BRAHMAN RULERS

II—KING KHĀRAVELA OF KALIṄGA

Chapter XI

I—THE EPOCH OF FOREIGN INVADERS

II—THE "DARK" INTERVAL

PART III

Chapter XII

I—THE IMPERIAL GUPTAS

Chapter XIII

CIVILISATION UNDER THE GUPTAS AND RISE OF NEW POWERS

Section A

Chapter XIV

HARṢAVARDHANA OF THĀNEŚVAR AND KANAUJ

Chapter XV

POST-HARṢA AND PRE-MOSLEM NORTHERN INDIA

(From *c.* 647 A.D. to *c.* 1200)

Chapter XVIII

THE STATES OF THE SOUTHERN PENINSULA

CHAPTER XIX

INTRODUCTORY

PART I

CHAPTER I

INTRODUCTORY

Sources

Absence of History

Ancient Indian literature, varied and rich in many respects, is singularly deficient in history. There is no work in all the literary treasures of the Brahmans, Buddhists and Jains comparable to the *Book of Kings* or the *Annals* of Livy or the *Histories* of Herodotus. This is not because India's past is barren of deeds worthy of remembrance. On the other hand, the ages were filled with heroic achievements, great upheavals and dynastic vicissitudes, but, strangely enough, these events did not find any systematic record with due regard to chronology. Whether this curious neglect of an important branch of literary activity was due to a lack of proper historical sense, or to the indifference of the religious orders, that controlled and developed the literatures, towards the fleeting mundane affairs of life, there is no gainsaying that the historian of ancient India suffers greatly from the initial difficulty of the want of genuine works of historiography.[1]

[1] cf. Alberuni: "The Hindus do not pay much attention to the historical order of things; they are very careless in relating the chronological succession of things; and when they are pressed for information and are at a loss not knowing what to say, they invariably take to tale-telling" (Sachau, *Alberuni's India*, Vol. II, p. 10).

The sources of early Indian history may broadly be divided into two classes, literary and archæological, which are either indigenous or foreign.[1] Let us first take up the former.

Literary sources

Non-Historical Works

The earliest literature of India is purely of a religious kind. The patience and industry of a multitude of scholars have, however, succeeded in extracting from it useful bits of history. For instance, the *Vedas*—specially the *Rigveda*—have furnished us with fragments of historical information relating to the progress of the Aryans in India, their internal divisions and wars with the "Dasyus" and other cognate topics. Similarly, the *Brāhmaṇas* (e.g., *Aitareya*, *Śatapatha*, *Taittirīya*) and the *Upaniṣads*, like the *Bṛihadāraṇyaka* and *Chāndogya*, as also the Buddhist *Piṭakas*, *Nikāyas*, *Jātakas*, etc., and Jain canonical works (e.g., *Kalpa Sūtra*, *Uttarājjhayana Sūtra*) incidentally embody historical traditions that may be utilised with profit. Modern research has further demonstrated how such non-historical sources as the *Gārgī-Saṁhitā*, an astronomical work, or the dramas of Kālidāsa and Bhāsa, or even the chance illustrations of grammatical rules by Pāṇini in the *Aṣṭādhyāyī*, or by Patañjali in the *Mahābhāṣya*, sometimes afford us welcome light on dark corners of history. But valuable and trustworthy as these casual references are, they are far too meagre to satisfy our curiosity.

So-called Historical Literature

We must, therefore, turn to such works as contain what we may call the rudiments of history. The two

[1] See *The Imperial Gazetteer of India*, Vol. II, (Oxford, 1909), pp. 1 f.

Epics—the *Rāmāyaṇa* and the *Mahābhārata*—represent the first notable attempts of the ancient Hindus in this direction. No doubt, they give interesting pictures of the then religious and social conditions, but as chronicles of political events they seem lamentably full of tale-telling and chronological aberrations. Next come the *Purāṇas*, eighteen in number, which are said to have been recited by the *Sūta* Lomaharṣaṇa or his son (*Sauti*) Ugraśravas. Normally, they should deal with five set subjects, *viz.*, (*a*) *Sarga* (primary creation), (*b*) *Pratisarga* (re-creation after periodical dissolution of the universe), (*c*) *Vaṁśa* (genealogies of gods and *Riṣis*), (*d*) *Manvantara* (groups of *mahāyuga* "great ages" in a *Kalpa* or æon, in each of which the first father of mankind was Manu), (*e*) *Vaṁśānucarita* (histories of old dynasties of kings). Of these, the last topic alone is important for the purpose of history, but it is found in the *Matsya*, *Vāyu*, *Viṣṇu*, *Brahmāṇḍa*, *Bhāgavata* and *Bhaviṣya* only out of the extant Purāṇas. Thus, most of these "collections of 'old world' legends" have got no historical value whatsoever. Even the rest contain much that is manifestly mythological and altogether confused from the chronological point of view.[1] They sometimes treat contemporaneous dynasties or rulers as successive, or omit some of them entirely (e.g., the *Purāṇas* are silent about the Kushans, Indo-Greeks Indo-Parthians, etc.). No dates are given, and even names of kings are not unoften inaccurate (cf. the list of Andhra kings). Notwithstanding these defects, the *Purāṇas* certainly transmit scraps of historical data, and it would not be fair to disparage their authority roundly. Among other early productions relevant to our purpose, we may particularly mention Bāṇa's

[1] One may aptly recall here Goethe's observation: "The historian's duty is to separate the true from the false, the certain from the uncertain, and the doubtful from that which cannot be accepted"—*Maxims*, No. 453.

Harṣacarita, Sandhyākaranandi's *Rāmacarita*, Padmagupta's *Navasāhasāṅkacarita*, Bilhaṇa's *Vikramāṅkadevacarita*, and Jayaratha's *Prithvīrāja-vijaya*. Unhappily, however, these works preserve very little historical matter, and are more of literary pieces, being full of elaboration, metaphor, and imagery. The only work in Sanskrit, which can be described as a near approach to history, as we understand it, is the *Rājataraṅgiṇī* of Kalhaṇa. It was begun in 1148 A. D., and is based on writings of previous chroniclers as well as on royal charters and laudatory inscriptions. Kalhaṇa's account of Kashmir for a few centuries immediately preceding his time is quite reliable, but for the earlier period he too is unfortunately subject to strange lapses. In addition to these, we cannot omit to consider the evidence of some southern, chiefly Tamil works (e.g., the *Nandikkalambakam*, Oṭṭakkūttan's *Kulottuṅgaṉ-Piḷḷaittamiḻ*, Jayagoṇḍār's *Kaliṅgattu-pparaṇi*, *Rājarāja-śoḻan-Uḻā*, *Colavaṁśa-caritam*, etc.); the Ceylonese chronicles, the *Dīpavaṁśa* (fourth century A.D.), and the *Mahāvaṁśa* (sixth century A.D.); and such Prakrit compositions as Vākpati's *Gauḍavaho* and Hemacandra's *Kumārapālacarita*; all of which demand a cautious and critical use.

Foreign Writings

Not less valuable than the above sources are the accounts of foreign writers or travellers, whose knowledge of India was based either on hearsay or on actual stay in the country for a short time. To this category belong men of several nationalities—Greek, Roman, Chinese, Tibetan, and Moslem. The earliest reference to India is made by Herodotus who deposes to the political connection of North-western India with the Achæmenian empire in the fifth century B. C. Next, Alexander's hurricane campaign in the Punjab and Sind formed the subject matter of a number of Greek and Roman works by Quintus Curtius, Diodoros Siculus, Arrian, Plutarch, and others; and the value of their testimony can best be judged from the fact that but for them we should have known nothing about the Macedonian invasion, so thoroughly have Indian writers maintained silence regarding this memorable episode. The *Indika* of Megasthenes, the Seleucid ambassador at the Maurya court, is another important source of information about the institutions, geography and products of India. It is now lost to us, but fragments are still preserved in the form of quotations by later authors, such as Arrian, Appian, Strabo, Justin, etc. Similarly, the *Periplus of the Erythrean Sea* and Ptolemy's *Geography* furnish geographical data of interest.

Like the classical (Greek and Roman) works, Chinese literature is also of great help in reconstructing ancient Indian history. There are numerous notices in it regarding the movements of the predatory Central Asian tribes that profoundly affected the destinies of India; and above all, we have the excellent narratives of Fa-hian (399-414 A. D.)[1], Yuan Chwang (629-45 A. D.)[2], and I-tsing (*c.* 673-95 A. D.)—three of the most distinguished pilgrims, who visited India in search of knowledge and with the desire to worship at the sites hallowed by the memory of the Buddha. Further, the works of the Tibetan Lāmā Tārānātha, the *Dulva* and *Tangyur*, etc. may also be profitably consulted.

Then come the Moslem authors, who inform us how step by step the armies of Islam conquered India and introduced another vigorous factor into Indian polity. The most celebrated of such writers was Alberuni, a man of versatile intellect and a scholar of Sanskrit. He followed in the train of Mahmūd's invasions, and wrote in 1030 A. D. the *Tahkīk-i-Hind*,

[1] cf. The *Fo-kwo-ki.*

[2] cf. The *Si-yu-ki.*

a mine of information on India and her peoples. Still earlier Moslem writers were Al Bilāduri, Sulaimān (*Silsilat-ut-Tawārīkh*), and Al Mas'ūdi (*Murūj-ul-Zahāb*). Among other Moslem works, we may mention : Hassan Nizāmī's *Tāj-ul-Maāsir*, Mīrkhond's *Rauzat-us-Safā*, Khond Mīr's *Habīb-us-Siyar*, Firishta's *Tārīkh-i-Firishta*, Nizāmuddīn's *Tabaqāt-i-Akbarī*, Minhājuddīn's *Tabaqāt-i-Nasīrī*, Al Utbi's *Tarīkh-i-Yamīnī*, Ibn-ul-Athir's *Al-Tārīkh-ul-Kāmil*.

The observations and writings of these foreigners are particularly valuable not only for the light they throw on the political events, society, manners, geography, and religion of ancient India, but also because they establish synchronisms in the troubled sea of Indian dates. Indeed, the identification of Sandrakottos with Candragupta Maurya has been regarded on almost all hands as the sheet-anchor of Indian chronology.

Archæological sources

Inscriptions

Where the literary sources are reticent or obscure, inscriptions fortunately come to our rescue. Many thousands of them, the earliest belonging to about the fourth or fifth century B. C.[1] have been unearthed, and perhaps a large number still await the archælogist's spade. They are found engraved on rocks, pillars, stone tablets, metal plates, caves, etc., and are couched in the languages current at different periods and localities—Sanskrit, Pālī, mixed dialects, or the languages of Southern India, *viz.*, Tamil, Telugu, Malayālam, and Kanarese. Some of them are of considerable literary merit too, being either in prose or verse or a combination of the two. The majority of inscriptions are in the Brāhmī script, written from left to right; but a good

[1] cf. the Piprāwā (Basti district) Vase *Stūpa* inscription (*J.R.A.S.*, 1898, pp. 573-88), and the Baḍali (Ajmer) inscription.

number are also incised in Kharoṣṭhī running, like Arabic and Persian, from right to left. Their decipherment, which is a marvel of scholarship, reveals that their object is to record a donation, public or private, or to commemorate a great event, or the exploits of a conqueror. The edicts of Aśoka, containing his ethical exhortations, are, of course, a class by themselves. The subject-matter of inscriptions is indeed very varied. There are even Sanskrit plays (e.g., at Dhār and Ajmer) and musical rules (e.g., at Kuḍimiyāmalai, Pudukotta State) recorded on stone. The importance of these documents can hardly be over-emphasised. They are extremely useful in fixing dates, and often regulate and supplement what we learn from literature and other sources. For instance, in the absence of such epigraphic evidence the veil of oblivion would hang heavily even on rulers like Khāravela or Samudragupta[1], and our knowledge of the mediæval Hindu dynasties would be altogether incomplete. Sometimes foreign inscriptions, too, unexpectedly lend us aid. Thus, the Boghaz-Koi (Asia Minor) inscriptions, which mention Vedic gods, probably testify to the movements of Aryan tribes. We have elsewhere referred to the contact of India with ancient Iran, and curiously it is confirmed by inscriptions discovered at Persepolis and Naksh-i-Rustam[2]. Similarly, inscriptions throw a flood of light on the political and cultural relations between India and the Far East in early times.

Coins

The next guides, we may appeal to, are coins. Like the inscriptions, they corroborate the information

[1] They are respectively known only from the Hāthīgumphā and the Allahabad Pillar inscriptions.

[2] The Behistun record does not, however, include India in the list of provinces ruled by Darius.

derived from literature, and often modify or amplify it. They are of various metals—gold, silver, copper, or alloy, and contain legends or simple marks. Those with dates are doubtless very valuable for the framework of Indian chronology, but even undated and anonymous ones yield fruitful results when we carefully consider their fabric and type. Coins are almost our sole evidence with regard to the Indo-Scythian and Indo-Baktrian kings—Indian authors having completely ignored the latter except Menander. Coins shed remarkable light on the existence of *gaṇas* (autonomous communities) in ancient India, and also on the religious predilections of certain monarchs (e.g., of Kaniṣka) and their personal accomplishments (e.g., of Samudragupta). The purity of the metal undoubtedly reflects the economic conditions of the time, and the provenance of the coins helps us in fixing the limits of a kingdom. But the latter must be applied cautiously. For the discovery of Roman coins in South India would by no means indicate an extension of Roman power or political influence in India. It only recalls the famous lament of Pliny over the drain of Roman gold to this country in exchange for articles of luxury and spices, etc.

Monuments

Last, but not the least, are the monuments. They are not directly concerned with political history, but these temples, *Stūpas*, and monasteries (*vihāras*) vividly depict the artistic achievements and religious devotion of the people and princes alike. The monumental remains in foreign lands open to us a rather unknown chapter of India's ancient glory. Shrines, dedicated to Śiva, on the Dieng plateau (Java), and the vast panorama of bas-reliefs on the walls in the colossal temples at Boro-Bodur and Prambanam (central Java), as also the remarkable ruins at Angkor Vāṭ and Angkor Thom (Kambuja), reveal the hand of Indians, and show that they had migrated to the Far East and spread their power and culture there.[1] Even for purposes of chronology, the evidence of monuments cannot be entirely despised, for experts have demonstrated how important conclusions follow a close study of the stratification of buildings. Further, it may not be out of place to add here that sculptures and paintings (e.g., at Ajantā) occasionally illumine our path where we might otherwise have walked with faltering steps.

Conclusion or Main Features

Such, in brief,[2] are the sources for the resuscitation of India's early past. The most striking feature, when compared with modern history, is the meagreness of our materials and the wide range over which they lie scattered. Accordingly, the historian must work like a miner with the pick and shovel of his perseverance and critical judgment to get at the gold of facts without the dross of courtly exaggerations and poetic embellishments. Quite often rocks intervene in the shape of conflicting claims, utter absence of dates, or prevalence of several eras at different periods and places,[3]

[1] See Dr. R. C. Majumdar, *Ancient Indian Colonies in the Far East*, Vol. I, Champa; *Suvarṇadvīpa*; and publications of the Greater India Society; Dr. B. R. Chatterji, *Indian Cultural Influence in Cambodia* (Calcutta, 1928); *India and Java* (Calcutta, 1933); H. G. Q. Wales, *Towards Angkor*; and works of French and Dutch scholars.

[2] Literary works and inscriptions, referred to above, are merely illustrative. All the available sources, ancient as well as modern, have, however, been discriminately utilised by us.

[3] See Cunningham, *Book of Indian Eras*. We know of about a score of ancient systems of reckoning.

and it is only after overcoming these difficulties that we can achieve the object of building a connected and consistent account of ancient India. And here we must also bear in mind that the North is the predominant factor in our history, having been the centre of large empires that rose like waves in the sea and soon broke up into nothing. Aspirants to supreme dignity turned longing eyes across the Vindhyas, but never did India *completely* come under one sovereign umbrella, and even in the heyday of the Mauryas the extreme South remained outside the Imperial ambit. This lack of political unity in ancient India, despite the fact that she was indisputably a geographical and cultural unit[1], is the weakest point of her history, and, therefore, dynastic wars and territorial aggrandisements absorb our interest and attention to a greater degree than her achievements in the domain of religion, art, and literature.

[1] Dr. R. K. Mookerji, *The Fundamental Unity of India* (Longmans, Green & Co., 1914).

CHAPTER II

SECTION A

PALÆOLITHIC AGE

The story of the early man in India is largely shrouded in mystery. The common belief is that the remotest past represented the *Satyuga*—an age when man lived in an ideal state of happiness, free from misery, want, and decay. Sober history unfortunately does not know of any such golden period. On the other hand, all indications point to the fact that primitive man was sunk in the darkness of ignorance and barbarism, and that he marched towards the light of civilisation only by slow stages. So far as our evidence goes the earliest inhabitants of India were perhaps the palæolithic (derived from Greek words signifying 'old stone') men. They were a savage people who sought shelter under trees and in natural caverns.[1] They had no idea of cultivation, and probably did not quite know how to make a fire. They could not turn out pottery, and were ignorant of the use of metal. They lived on the chase and on nuts, roots, and fruits afforded by nature. Their implements for purposes of peace and of war against wild beasts and other denizens of water and forests were chipped in stone, and were of crude workmanship.[2] It is noteworthy that a majority of them are

[1] Certain caves in the Karnul district are believed to have been tenanted by palæolithic men (V. Rangacharya, *Pre-Musalman India*, Vol. I, p. 48).

[2] Palæolithic implements have been divided into ten classes—axes, arrow-heads, spears, digging tools, circular hurling-stones,

made in a peculiar kind of rock known as quartzite. Of course, where this material was not available other hard rocks were used. Besides some sites in the Dekkan, the districts of Madras, Cuddapah, and Chingleput in South India have yielded a rich harvest of such tools.[1] Sometimes they were also made of bone and wood, but being perishable they have all disappeared. Lastly, these men did not construct tombs to bury their dead, who were perhaps left to be devoured by animals and birds.

Section B

NEOLITHIC AGE

The next stage in the progress of man in India, as elsewhere, was reached when the use of the rough stone implements was not quite discarded, but most of them were carefully dressed and polished. They were now turned into highly finished objects of diverse and complex forms to meet a variety of requirements[2]. These neolithic (from a Greek word meaning 'new stone') men had made considerable advance towards civilisation. Apart from natural shelter in rocks, they constructed dwellings, perhaps "huts of wattle and thatches, daubed with clay," for themselves. They knew how to produce a fire and the art of cooking. They occupied themselves with fishing and hunting,

choppers, knives, scrapers, cores, hammer-stones and (probably) strike-a-lights (?), *Ibid.*, pp. 52-53.

[1] *Catalogue of Pre-historic Antiquities in the Government Museum, Madras* (1901); *Notes on the Ages and Distribution of Indian Pre-historic Antiquities* (Madras, 1916). Col. Bruce Foote has made a special study of Pre-historic artifacts in India. See also Panchānan Mitra, *Pre-historic India*, (Calcutta, 1923); A. C. Logan, *Old Chipped Stones of India*, (Calcutta, 1906); P. T. S. Aiyangar, *The Stone Age in India*; V. Rangacharya, *Pre-Musalman India*, etc.

[2] For their numerous types, see *Pre-Musalman India*, I, pp. 124-25.

tended flocks of domesticated animals, and also began the cultivation of land. Their food was simple, consisting of game, forest produce, vegetables, milk, honey, wild grains, etc.; and the dress of these neolithic men was probably leaves, barks of trees, and skins. They made pottery, at first by hand, but afterwards the wheel was used. The earthenware were either plain or painted and decorated with representations of flowers, leaves, etc. The neolithians chose the tough trap rock for their weapons of offence and defence, but things of domestic use were made of other materials of various colours. They buried their dead and erected tombs, as is evident from some pre-historic skeletons discovered in the district of Mirzapur. On the other hand, the finds of funeral urns, meant for the ashes of the dead, would show that cremation too was not unknown. Presumably they worshipped spirits of nature as embodied in trees and stones, and propitiated them by bloody sacrifices and offerings of food and drink. Further, in the caves of the Vindhya hills, there are neolithic "cup-marks" and "ruddle drawings," which give us some idea of the artistic efforts of these men. All these features indicate that the palæolithic and neolithic men must have been separated by a wide gap, maybe of centuries. Indeed, some scholars even deny that the latter were the descendants of the former. But our evidence being imperfect, it would be better not to dogmatise on this point. It is, however, certain that the neolithic culture was *widespread*, as remains of this period have been found almost all over the country, particularly in Bellary, Salem, Karnul, and other districts of the Madras Presidency.

Section C

I. THE ADVENT OF METALS

After many centuries, perhaps, the neolithic man

in India learnt the use of metals. Gold was probably his earliest discovery, but it served as a material for ornaments only. His implements and weapons were made of other harder metals. The remarkable finds in a large number of ancient sites prove that in South India stone was directly superseded by iron, whereas in North India axes, awls, swords, spearheads, daggers, harpoons, etc., were at first made of copper, and it was in turn followed by iron. Hoards of such copper implements have been discovered "all across Northern India almost from the Hooghly to the far side of the Indus, and from the foot of the Himālayas to the Cawnpore District." The times when the use of these metals became general are known as the Iron and Copper ages. It is, however, important to remember that, unlike other countries, there are no traces in India, except in Sind, of a Bronze Period intervening between the Neolithic and Iron ages. Bronze, which is an alloy of copper and tin,[1] is harder than pure copper, and is doubtless better suited for the manufacture of weapons, but the early men in India somehow did not make it the ordinary material for use. The few implements of this metal, that have been discovered in Jubbulpur, were, in the opinion of antiquarians, either experimental or of foreign origin. And bowls and other objects, found in South Indian cemeteries, were simply articles of luxury meant for domestic purposes, and would hardly indicate the existence of an age when bronze tools were commonly used.

II. THE DRAVIDIANS

The Dravidians, so called from the Sanskrit term Draviḍa, were one of the earliest cultured races of India.

[1] Generally, the ratio of alloy in bronze is nine parts of copper and one of tin.

Unhappily, the problem of their origin is still a puzzle, almost defying any definite solution. A number of scholars strongly affirm that they were the descendants of the primitive inhabitants of India, who in course of time had ascended up the ladder of civilisation. On the contrary, others are of opinion that they were foreign immigrants into this country from the Tibetan plateau or from the "Turanian homeland of Central Asia." Western Asia is, however, generally supposed to have been their original abode, and the similarity of the Dravidian and Sumerian ethnic types undoubtedly lends some colour to this view. In this connection we must not omit to take into account Brāhūī, the island of Dravidian speech in Baluchistan. It is believed that it represents the tongue of those who lingered on behind, while the main body advanced towards Hindustan through the mountain passes. This looks plausible enough, although sometimes a different conclusion is drawn from the existence of Brāhūī that there was a Dravidian over-flow from India into Baluchistan. Whoever the Dravidians may have been,[1] it is certain that they were an important element of population both in Northern and Southern India. Their languages still predominate in the South, but "Dravidian characteristics have been traced alike in Vedic and Classical Sanskrit, in the Prakrits or early popular dialects, and in the modern vernaculars derived from them."[2] The Dravidians were conversant with the use of metals, and their pottery was of an improved type. They knew agriculture, and were perhaps the earliest people to build dams across rivers for irrigation purposes. They constructed houses and fortifications, and their villages were ruled by petty chiefs.

[1] Many western scholars favour the view that the Dravidians belonged to the Mediterranean race. See e.g., Mr. J. Kennedy, *J.R.A.S.*, 1898, pp. 249, 261.

[2] *Cam. Hist. Ind.*, Vol. I, p. 42.

As observed by Dr. L. D. Barnett, Dravidian society was "to some extent matriarchal," and their religion was generally "dark and repulsive"[1]. They worshipped the Mother Goddess and a host of spirits, often with bloody human sacrifices, and the emblems of generation. Presumably, the Dravidians were identical with the "Dāsas" or "Dasyus" of the *Rigveda*; and we shall, therefore, hear more about them when we come to the period of the Aryans.

SECTION D

CHALCOLITHIC AGE

Importance of the New Discoveries

So far we were almost groping in the dark. We now see the twilight of Indian civilisation. The remarkable archæological discoveries at Harappa in the Montgomery district and Mohenjo-daro in the Larkana district, besides other sites in the Punjab, Sind (like Canhu-daro, Jhūkar-daro), and Baluchistan (e.g., Nāl, Kelat State), make it abundantly clear that several centuries before the period of the *Rigveda*, there were busy centres of life and activity along the course of the river Indus. They show that the people possessed a high degree of culture, which was similar to, and in many respects more advanced than that of contemporary Mesopotamia, Elam, and Egypt. Chalcolithic is the name usually given to this age—an age "in which arms and utensils of stone continue to be used side by side with those of copper and bronze." To get a glimpse into this remote past, we must take note of the relics unearthed at Mohenjo-daro,[2] which are essentially akin to those found at other

[1] *Antiquities of India*, p. 4.

[2] Sir John Marshall, *Mohenjo-daro and the Indus Civilisation* (3 volumes); K. N. Dikshit, *Pre-historic Civilisation of the Indus Valley* (Madras, 1939); N. Law, *Ind. Hist. Quart.*, March, 1932 (Vol. VIII,

places. The picture may be dim, but the outlines are sufficiently firm.

Buildings

Mohenjo-daro or the 'City of the Dead' is at present a heap of ruins. It is difficult to surmise what brought about its destruction. Earthquakes, inundations, the Indus altering its course, climatic changes—any of them may account for its final abandonment or disappearance. But it is evident from the excavations, which have been carried out down to the subsoil water, that the site must have been occupied for centuries. It was a prosperous city, well-planned and having wide streets and lanes at regular intervals. The buildings, considerably varying in size, appear to have been plain but dignified[1] Stone not being easily obtainable, walls were raised of burnt brick, laid in mud or in both mud and gypsum mortar. Crude or sun-dried bricks were reserved for foundations and terraces, where the elements could not do much damage. There were stairways leading to upper storeys, and windows and doors for admitting light and air. Bath-rooms and circular brick-wells were important features of most houses. The system of drainage, public or private, was remarkable. Dust-bins and rubbish chutes indicate the extreme care taken in matters of conservancy. On the whole, the people were flourishing, and even ordinary dwelling houses were provided with necessary conveniences. The larger structures were perhaps public property. One of them, a spacious pillared hall of the Intermediate

no. 1), pp. 121-64; Dr. Mackay, *The Indus Civilisation*; *Mem. Arch. Surv. Ind.*, nos. 41 and 48. On Harappa, see M. S. Vats, *Excavations at Harappa*, Vols. I & II, (1940).

[1] Was this lack of ornamentation in houses due to simplicity of tastes? Or, did the owners deliberately avoid outward marks of possessing wealth to escape the burden of extra taxes?

Period, may have been a shrine, although no images have been found there. The most striking of all remains is, no doubt, a vast hydropathic establishment—a brick Bath, 39 ft. × 23 ft. × 8 ft., with water-tight walls and flights of steps at the ends and other subsidiary verandahs, galleries and rooms. It was filled with water from a well nearby. Its drain with a corbelled roof, more than six feet in height, deserves particular mention. Another accessory to the great Bath is probably a *hammām* or hot-air bath, pointing to the existence of "a hypocaustic system of heating."

Agriculture

Little do we know about the agriculture of the Indus peoples, although the existence of such big cities as Mohenjo-daro and Harappa clearly indicates that food must have been available in an ample measure. Perhaps the grains they cultivated were wheat and barley, specimens of which have been found there. It is uncertain whether the plough had replaced the hoe, or the latter was still in use. Scholars believe that in olden times Sind received copious rainfall,[1] and this, as also the presence of a great river,[2] must have made the problem of irrigation easy of solution.

Food

Besides the above cereals and dates (stones of which have been discovered), it appears from half-burnt shells and bones and offerings to the dead that the Indus people used as food pork, beef, mutton, poultry, fish, and the flesh of other water animals. Perhaps milk and vegetables were also included in the dietary.

[1] The elaborate system of drainage and the use of burnt bricks for the exposed parts of buildings point to the same conclusion.

[2] Indus. Besides, there was the Mihran, which dried up in the 14th century A.D.

Animals Known

They knew several kinds of domesticated animals, of which bones of bull, sheep, pig, buffalo, camel, and elephant have been recovered; while those of the dog and horse, having been found near the surface, may belong to later times. The wild animals familiar to them were rhinoceros, bison, monkey, tiger, bear, hare, etc., which are depicted on seals and copper-tablets.

Use of Stones and Metals

Stone was rare in this region. It had accordingly to be imported from other places for door-sockets, saddle querns and mullers, statuettes, cult objects, etc. The metals known to the Sindhu people were gold, silver, copper, tin, and lead, which were used for a variety of purposes. The discovery of bronze in the earliest layer at Mohenjo-daro proves beyond doubt that it was then in use there. Iron has, however, not been found.

Ornaments

Ornaments, chiefly necklaces, ear-rings, anklets, and girdles of beads, were commonly worn by men and women of all classes. The rich made them of gold, silver, ivory, faience and other semi-precious stones like lapis lazuli, jasper, carnelian, agate or onyx; whereas those for the poor were made of copper, bone, shell, and terra-cotta.

Household Articles

Copper and bronze seem to have superseded stone as material for household implements and utensils. Mostly, however, they were earthenware. Quite a large number of such bowls, dishes, cups, saucers, vases, basins, and stone-jars of different forms have been discovered. Generally the pottery was wheel-made, and was painted and sometimes "glazed."

Weapons

Likewise copper and bronze had replaced stone for weapons of war or of chase. People were acquainted with maces, axes, daggers, spears, bows, arrows, and slings. Defensive weapons like shields, helmets, and armour were perhaps unknown, nor is there any trace of the sword.

Games and Weights

Stones were also used for weights, marbles and dice, which are among the most remarkable relics discovered. It is interesting to note that, like the Vedic Aryans, the Indus people were fond of dice. The smaller weights, of chert or slate, are cubical, whereas the heavier ones are conical in shape. It is said that they are made with "greater accuracy and consistency than those of Elam and Mesopotamia."

Toys

Generally they were clay models of birds, animals, men and women, rattles, or representations of carts. These playthings are sometimes useful as depicting the actualities of life.

Spinning and Textile

Spinning must have been freely practised in the houses of Mohenjo-daro, as would appear from the large find of spindle-whorls. Those of the rich were made of faience; the poor used the cheaper pottery and shell. Wool was used for warmer textile, and cotton for the lighter one. The latter, found adhering to a silver vase, appears on careful examination by experts to resemble the present-day coarser Indian variety with its "typical convoluted structure."

Dress

The dress of the people, like their personal features, must have varied. A statue, for instance, represents a male figure wearing a long shawl, drawn over the left shoulder and under the right, so as to leave the right arm free. The nude statues must not be taken to indicate that nudity was prevalent. They may have been meant for religious purposes.

Religion

Our scanty knowledge of the religion of these early peoples is derived from the seals, copper tablets, and figurines of metal, terra-cotta, and stone. The most prominent deity is the Mother or Nature Goddess,[1] whose worship was so common in ancient times in all countries from Persia to the Ægean coasts. This cult found a fruitful soil in India, and out of it developed the worship of Śakti with all its elaborate rites. Further, a seal portrays a highly conventionalised figure of a three-faced male god, seated *Yogī*-like, with animals on each side, who has been recognised as the prototype of the historic Śiva. If this conjecture be correct, Śaivism may legitimately claim to be the oldest living religion. That the worship of the phallic emblems—the *liṅga* and the *yoni*—was also prevalent is clear from the discovery of scores of aniconic objects of stone together with ring-stones, whereas the existence of

[1] From immemorial antiquity, India is the home of the worship of *Prakriti* or later *Śakti*, goddess *Prithvī*, and a host of *Grāmadevatas* (*Ambā*, *Mātā*, etc.)

ree-worship and Zoolatry or Animal worship is
ridenced by certain representations on seals. Popular
induism of today contains many of these elements,
ıus furnishing a remarkable proof of the extraordinary
ontinuity of Indian culture through the ages.

isposal of the Dead

An examination of the data available, both at
[ohenjo-daro and Harappa, shows that probably there
ere then three methods of disposing of the dead: (*a*)
omplete burial, (*b*) burial after exposure of the body to
rds and beasts, (*c*) cremation followed by burial of the
hes. The discovery of cinerary urns and jars, goblets
: vessels with ashes, bone, and charcoal may, however,
ıggest that during the flourishing period of the Indus
ılley culture the third method was generally in vogue.
t Mohenjo-daro, about a score of skeletons, some in
ıblic streets and others in a room, have been un-
.rthed, but there is no trace of a cemetery or burial
ace. At Harappa, on the other hand, a cemetery has
:en brought to light in the plain level ground near the
ounds. It is noteworthy that the remains of the dead
the latter site are associated with a distinct type of
ottery decorated with vegetable patterns and peculiar
ıimal designs.

nowledge of Writing[1]

One of the most interesting items of information
e get about the Indus people is in regard to their
quaintance with some sort of writing. Of course,
) regular documents on stones or baked clay tablets
ıve been found. But a large number of seals

[1] See Dr. G. R. Hunter, *Script of Harappa and Mohenjo-daro*
)34); Rev. H. Heras, "The Story of two Mohenjo-daro Signs,"
B.H.U., Vol. II, no. 1, pp. 1-6.

and sealings,[1] having excellent representations of unicorns and bulls and other objects, have inscriptions in a script, which belongs to the same order as Proto-Elamite, Sumerian, Minoan, and Egyptian. Its decipherment has so far defied the ingenuity of scholars. The view, commonly held, is that it represents a pictographic system of writing, each sign[2] standing for a particular word or object. A late stage of development is indicated by certain strokes and marks, which were perhaps vowel signs. It is believed that the direction of writing is from right to left, but in some cases it is *boustrophedon*, i.e., from right to left in the first line and left to right in the second. Nothing can yet be postulated about its connection with the later Brāhmī. Very likely the Indus script did not extend to other parts of India, or survive long.

Art

The Indus people appear to have made great progress in the ceramic art. They were fond of painted pottery, and some specimens of delicate workmanship and colour have come down to us.

Again, sculptures in the round, of stone and bronze, display great merit and anatomical faithfulness. The figure of a dancer standing on the right leg with the left leg raised in front is beautifully executed, and the pose is so full of movement that there is hardly any parallel to it even among the sculptures of the historic period.

But by far the most remarkable are the engravings on the numerous seals and sealings. The treatment of animals, specially the bull, is superb and full of realism. These figures leave no room for doubt that

[1] See also L. A. Waddell, *The Indo-Sumerian Seals Deciphered* (London, 1925).

[2] A list of no less than 396 signs has been prepared.

the Indus people, like the ancient Greeks, possessed artistic skill of a high order, and could delineate with vigour and effect.

Who were the Authors?

The skeletal remains as well as the sculptured heads[1] indicate that the population at Harappa and Mohenjo-daro was of a cosmopolitan character, consisting at least of four distinct ethnic types, viz., Proto-Australoid, Mediterranean, the Alpine and the Mongolian branch. Which of these races was the prime author of the Indus valley civilisation ? Diverse answers have been given to this query. It has been suggested that they were the pre-Vedic peoples (probably Dravidian), whose culture the Aryans destroyed. Some look upon the latter as the authors of this civilisation, pushing thereby the date of their (Aryan) domination in India considerably back. Others regard the Indus people as the kith and kin of the Sumerians or some allied race, and the common features between the civilisations of Sumer, Elam, and the Indus valley, despite their individual characteristics, no doubt, lend support to this view. Cultural evidences and arguments based on physical types are, however, shaky; and we cannot, therefore, be dogmatic over this problem until more conclusive clues are forthcoming.

Extent and Origin

Besides Mohenjo-daro and Harappa, archæological explorations reveal that there were a number of other sites in lower and upper Sind (e.g. Jhūkhar-

[1] But this evidence must be used with caution. For, as has been well pointed out, artists were by no means anthropologists; and the number of skulls discovered is too small to allow of any "safe generalisations" regarding the existence of several racial types (*Hindu Civilisation*, p. 28).

daro, Canhu-daro), South Punjab and Baluchistan (e.g., Nāl in Kelat State) belonging to the same Chalcolithic culture. As yet no traces of it have been found in the Gangetic valley, which in later times played an important part in the cultural and political history of India. Wherefrom, then, did the Indus valley culture originate? Was it an independent growth on Indian soil? Or, was its development due to the contact and impact of the ancient civilisations of Elam, Mesopotamia, and other Western lands? To these questions, a definite answer one hesitates to give at this stage of our knowledge.

Date

We do not know how long this culture flourished in the Indus valley, but from the stratification of buildings at Mohenjo-daro, where have been unearthed seven strata—three of the Late Period, three of the Intermediate, and one of the Early, leaving aside such as are submerged under the sub-soil water—it has been assumed, assigning roughly 500 years to each of the layers, that the period of its occupation fell approximately between 3250-2750 B.C. Of course, the beginnings of its civilisation may go earlier still, for Mohenjo-daro and its complex city life was a product of centuries of evolution. Moreover, a comparison of its finds with Mesopotamian and Elamite relics shows resemblances, which could not be merely fortuitous. If, as has been supposed, they prove that there was intercourse between these countries the Indus valley civilisation may be rightly taken to be "contemporary with the early culture of Sumer and with the later Pre-diluvian culture of Elam and Mesopotamia."

CHAPTER III

THE RIGVEDIC AGE

Origin and Home of the Aryans[1]

The twilight slowly brightened into dawn, and the sun of Vedic culture rose on the horizon of Indian history. Who were its progenitors, and wherefrom do they emerge into our historical view? Questions like these have been a bewildering source of controversy. Some Indian scholars, attaching great importance to the Paurāṇic evidence, strongly maintain that the Aryans were autochthons of the land. But their arguments do not find a wide support. Others with equal emphasis aver that the original Aryan home was the Arctic Circle (B. G. Tilak); or Bactria (Rhode); or the Pamirs. The general opinion, however, is that the Indo-Aryans, as also the Avestan Iranians, were a branch of the ancient "Indo-Germanic" (Indo-European) peoples or the *Wiros*,[2] and before their eastward migration, perhaps due to divisions, dissensions, or overgrowth of population in a circumscribed area, they occupied for long a common habitat, which has been variously located in Central Asia (Max Müller); European Steppes, north of the Black Sea (Benfey); Central and Western Germany (Geiger); or Austria, Hungary and Bohemia (P. Giles). This belief rests on grounds of the close similarity between the speech

[1] See Dr. Isaac Taylor, *The Origin of the Aryans*, London, 1889; G. Childe, *The Aryans*; A. C. Das, *Rigvedic India* (Calcutta, 1927); B. G. Tilak, *Arctic Home in the Vedas* (Poona, 1903); Lachhmī Dhar, *The Home of the Aryans* (Delhi, 1930).

[2] P. Giles uses the term 'Wiros,' meaning 'men' in most of the early languages (*Cam. Hist. Ind.*, Vol. I, p. 66).

as presented in the *Rigveda* and the Avestan and the "Indo-Germanic" tongues spoken by most European nations[1]; and also on the flora and fauna known to them and the likeness of their culture as inferred from the meagre data available[2]. Language and common peculiarities of life are, however, no certain proofs of consanguinity, for they can be adopted by one community from another. Nor are the anthropological researches of any particular help. They simply show that there is a physical type in India, which in many respects is akin to certain European races. Thus, though we cannot be sure that the blood of Europe runs in Indian veins, it is conceivable that the Indo-Aryans were at some stage not altogether isolated from the forefathers of the Western peoples.

The Rigveda

The earliest work, which the Aryans have left to posterity, is the *Rigveda*. It is a collection of 1017 hymns, supplemented by 11 others called *Vālakhilyas*, and is systematically arranged into 10 *maṇḍalas* or books. The hymns represent compositions of different periods,[3] and are of varying degrees of literary merit, being productions of priest-poets—mostly men and two or three women—of various families.[4] Excepting a few

[1] cf. e.g., Sanskrit *Pitri* with Zend *Paitar*, Latin *Pater*, Greek *Patir*, Celt *Athir*, Teuton *Fadar*, Tocharian *Patar*, and English *Father*; or Sanskrit *Dvau* with Latin *Duo*, Irish *Dau*, Gothic *Twai*, Lithuanian *Du*, and English *Two*; or Sanskrit *Asti*, Latin *Est*, Irish *Is*, Gothic *Ist*, and Lithuanian *Esti*.

[2] cf. *Cam. Hist. Ind.*, I, Ch. III, pp. 64-76.

[3] The *Rigveda* itself speaks of older and later *Riṣis* and their compositions. Winternitz thinks that there must be a gulf of centuries between the different strata of Rigvedic hymns. Great care was taken to preserve its textual purity by a number of devices like *Pada-pāṭha*, *Krama-pāṭha*, *Anukramaṇis*, etc.

[4] Orthodox tradition, however, regards the hymns as revelations to the *Riṣis*.

hymns, they are all invocations to the gods, conceived as personifications of the powers of Nature, to bestow spiritual and material favours on the worshippers. It is only those that are not directly addressed to the deities, which incidentally throw some light on princely liberality and tribal wars, as well as on the life and habits of the people. The information, scanty no doubt, is all the more valuable in the absence of any other material remains for giving us a glimpse into this distant age.[1]

Geographical Background of the Rigvedic Aryans

The *Rigveda* does not preserve any memory of the early movements of the Aryans, or how they entered India. Indeed, their geographical horizon appears from certain allusions to have been limited to an area extending from Afghanistan to the Gangetic valley. That the former region was occupied by the Aryans is obvious from the mention of rivers like the Kubhā (Kabul), the Suvāstu (Swat), the Krumu (Kurram), and the Gomatī (Gomal). The vast stream of the Sindhu (Indus) is well known, so also are its five tributaries—the Vitastā (Jhelum); Asiknī (Chenab); Paruṣṇī, later Irāvatī (Rāvī); Vipāśa (Beas); and the Śutudri (Sutlej). Similarly, the Driṣadvatī (Chautang) is named, but the Saraswatī, now lost amid the sands, evokes many a fervent song. From these references, one may reasonably infer that the Aryans were spread over all the tracts watered by these rivers, and they probably composed the bulk of the hymns here.[2] The Gaṅgā

cf. ऋषयो मन्त्रद्रष्टारः ; and also न हि छन्दांसि क्रियन्ते, नित्यानि छन्दांसि ।

[1] See A. C. Das, *Rigvedic Culture* (Calcutta, 1925).

[2] The hymns to the goddess *Uṣas* were apparently inspired by the glorious dawn of the Punjab. But those referring to the "strife of the elements" and the phenomenon of thunder and lightning were, according to Keith, composed "in the country round the Saraswatī river, south of the modern Ambālā" (*Cam. Hist. Ind.*,

(Ganges) and the Yamunā (Jumna) are mentioned only twice or thrice, which shows that though Aryan bands had advanced towards the Gangetic Doab, it was still an unfamiliar land. The sea was unknown to them, the word *samudra* being used to denote large expanses of water. The Himālaya or Himavant mountains are alluded to, but not the Vindhyas or the Narmadā river. Evidently, therefore, the Aryans had not yet established settlements in the southern direction. Other evidences are also in accord with the conclusions stated above. Thus, for instance, the *Rigveda* mentions the lion, but not the tiger, the denizen of the swampy jungles of Bengal. That the Aryans had not yet advanced to the eastern regions is further proved by the absence of any mention of rice. We must, however, urge caution against undue emphasis on such *argumentum ex silentio*, and as an illustration of its dangers it may be pointed out that salt, although abounding in Northern Punjab, is not even once mentioned in the *Rigveda*.

Tribal Divisions and Wars

The Rigvedic Aryans were not a homogeneous lot. They were divided into several tribes, the most important having been the five allied ones, viz., Anus, Druhyus, Yadus, Turvasas, and Purus, who dwelt on either side the Saraswatī. Besides these, mention is also made of the Bharatas (later merged into the Kurus), Tritṣus, Śriñjayas, Krivis, and other minor tribes. Quite often, they were fighting among themselves, and one of the notable events of Rigvedic history was the great battle on the Paruṣṇī, in which Sudās, king of the Bharatas, defeated with heavy losses the confederate tribes led by ten kings under the guidance of Viśvāmitra.

I, p. 79).

The victory is celebrated by his family priest, Vaśiṣṭha, but we do not know if Sudās attempted any consolidation of his conquests. Close upon the heels of the attack by the above-mentioned five allied tribes and by those of the North-west, *viz.*, Alinas, Pakthas (cf. modern Pakhthun or Pathans), Śivas, Bhalānases, and the Viṣāṇins, he had to face another crisis on the eastern side of his kingdom. Sudās, however, overcame it by successfully repulsing his assailants under the leadership of Bheda near the Jumna. The latter was perhaps a non-Aryan chief, as the curious names of the three tribes—Ajas, Śigrus, and Yakṣus—under him suggest.[1] Thus, besides inter-tribal warfare, the Aryans were engaged in struggles with the "Dasyus" or "Dāsas". They were carried on with unceasing relentlessness, for the two peoples had strong differences, both racial and cultural. The Aryans were tall and fair, and the "Dasyus" were dark-skinned and of short stature. Their features were uncouth, being flat-nosed (*anāsaḥ*). They did not believe in Vedic gods (*a-devayu*), indeed reviled them (*deva-pīyu*), never performed sacrifices (*a-yajvan*) or any rites (*a-karman*), but worshipped the phallus emblems (*śiṣṇa-devāḥ*) and followed strange laws (*anyavrata*). Their speech was unintelligible (*mṛidhra-vāk*).[2] These characteristics indicate that the "Dasyus" probably belonged to the Dravidian stock, then occupying the parts over which the Aryans were seeking to establish their domination. The "Dasyus" fought valiantly in defence of their homes and herds of cattle, and they yielded to the superior might of the Aryans only when the destruction of their *puras* and *durgas*, towns and crude fortifications, made

[1] The *Rigveda* mentions other non-Aryan peoples like the Simyus, Piśācas, Kīkaṭas, etc. Among other prominent Dāsa chiefs, we hear of Pipru, Dhuni, Cumuri, Sambara.

[2] A. C. Das, *Rigvedic Culture*, pp. 157-58 (Calcutta, 1925).

further resistance futile. Many of the 'Dāsas' became slaves (*dāsa*=slave) of the conquerors, having been admitted in society as *Sūdras*, but others retired into the jungles and mountain fastnesses, where we still find their descendants living in primitive conditions.

Political Organisation

The family (*griha* or *kula*) was the ultimate basis of the Vedic state. A number of families, connected with ties of kinship, formed the *grāma*. An aggregate of villages made up the *viś* (district or clan), and a group of *viś* composed the *jana* (tribe). The tribe was under the rule of its chief or king (*rājan*), who was often hereditary, as would appear from several lines of succession mentioned in the *Rigveda*[1]. Occasionally the *Rājan* was elected by the *viś*, but it is not clear whether the choice was limited to members of the ruling house or was extended to other noble families. The king led the tribe in battle, and ensured their protection, in return for which the people rendered him obedience or gave voluntary gifts. Perhaps the king did not then raise any fixed taxes for the maintenance of the royal state. When free from fighting, he dispensed justice and performed sacrifices for material prosperity. The *Purohita*, besides the *Senānī* ('leader of the army') and the *Grāmaṇī*, was the most important member of the royal entourage. He received gifts and by spells and incantations prayed for his master's success in all undertakings. The king was by no means an autocrat; his powers were limited by the will of the people as expressed in the *Sabhā* ('council of Elders') and *Samiti* ('assembly of the whole people').[2] The states were usually small, but due

[1] cf. e. g., Vadhryaśva, Divodāsa, Pijavana and Sudās.

[2] The true import of these terms is not quite clear. According to Keith, the *Samiti* was "the assembly of the people for the busi-

to wars and the "Dasyu" menace the tendency to coalesce under an overlord, or evolve bigger territorial units, had already started.

Family Life

The Rigvedic Aryans had developed a healthy family life, in which the ties of wedlock were held sacred and indissoluble. Monogamy was the usual rule, though among the "upper ten" polygamy was not unknown. There are no traces of polyandry and child-marriage. Women[1] enjoyed a certain amount of freedom in choosing their husbands, under whose protection and care they lived after marriage. Their position was of greater honour and authority at that time than is perhaps the case now. They controlled the household affairs, and participated in the sacrifices and other domestic ceremonies and feasts, gaily wearing their bright apparel and ornaments. There was perhaps no segregation of females or restriction upon their movements. They were educated, some of them like Apālā, Viśvavarā, and Ghoṣā even composing *mantras* after the fashion of the *Riṣis*. The standard of morality was comparatively high, but occasionally we learn of cases of lapse.

Besides husband and wife, the family consisted of other members—parents, brothers, sisters, sons, and daughters, etc. Generally their relations were marked by cordiality and a spirit of mutual accommodation and help. Sometimes, however, disputes about

ness of the tribe," and, the *Sabhā* denoted "the place of assembly, which served besides as a centre of social gatherings" (*Cam. Hist. Ind.*, I., p. 96).

[1] cf. B. S. Upādhyāya, *Women in Rigveda*, 2nd ed., (Benares, 1941); See also Dr. A. S. Altekar, *The Position of Women in Hindu Civilisation*, (Benares, 1938); C. Bader, *Women in Ancient India*, (London, 1925); Indra, *Status of Women in Ancient India*, (Lahore, 1941).

property, specially relating to land, cattle, ornaments, etc., must have caused ill-feeling and even the break-up of the family.

Occupations

As described elsewhere, the Aryans were then engaged in continual warfare, which was as such one of their main occupations. They fought either on foot or on chariots, drawn by horses, but horse-riding apart, cavalry is nowhere mentioned. Coats of mail (*varma*) and helmets of metals (*śiprā*) were used for protection on the battle-field. The principal weapons were the bow (*dhanus*) and arrow (*bāṇa*), spears, lances, axes, swords (*asi*), and slingstones. The warriors fought to the accompaniment of war-cries and the music of drums (*dundubhi*).

One of the important means of living for the Rigvedic Aryans was cattle-breeding. Their wealth and prosperity depended upon the possession of a large number of cows, which they regarded as "the sum of all good." We can, therefore, well understand their extreme desire to multiply them. Among other domesticated animals were horses, sheep, goats, dogs and asses.

Agriculture was their next occupation. Ploughing appears to have been an old practice of the Aryans, for it is significant the root *kriṣ* occurs in the same sense in both Sanskrit and Irānian. The plough was drawn by bulls, and had a metal share to make furrows (*sītā*) in the fields (*kṣetra*). Water was led into them by means of channels.[1] The corn cultivated was *yava* (perhaps barley) and *dhānya*, and when ripe, it was cut with sickles, threshed and winnowed properly, and then stored in granaries.

The Rigvedic Aryans also practised hunting for

[1] Water was drawn out of wells or from rivers. Manure too, if used then, must have added to the fertility of fields.

sport as well as livelihood. Birds and wild animals were caught in nets and snares (*pāśa*), or sometimes they were killed with bow and arrow. Pits were also dug for capturing deer, lion, and other beasts.

There is no mention of fishing, and navigation was limited to rivers by boats of crude construction. The absence of anchor or sails indicates that the Rigvedic people did not dare into the open main.

Trade

Coins were unknown.[1] Accordingly, trade was carried on by barter and the cow was regarded as the standard of value. There are grounds to believe that haggling was known, but a bargain, once made, held good.

Life being still primitive and simple, the requirements of the people were few, and could be easily supplied by themselves. But evidence is not lacking to show that specialisation in certain crafts had already begun. The worker in wood was an important figure in Vedic society, as his services were particularly needed in the construction of chariots, both for war and the race. He was still carpenter, joiner, and wheelright in one, and the dexterity of his art is often compared to felicity in composing hymns. We also learn of the worker in metal, who forged weapons, ploughshares, kettles and other domestic utensils. The general name for metal is *ayas* (Latin *aes*), which may denote either copper or bronze or iron. Goldsmiths fashioned ornaments of gold to minister to the wants of the gay and the rich. Mention is made of the tanner, who tanned leather and made such articles as bow-strings and casks. The work of sewing, plaiting of mats with

[1] *Niṣka* was not a coin, as supposed by some scholars. It was probably a kind of ornament worn on the neck.

grass and reeds, and weaving of cloth was mostly done by women. What is most noteworthy is that during the age of the *Rigveda* none of these functions bore the stamp of inferiority, as was the case subsequently, and they were carried on by the free members of the tribe.

Other Features of Life

(*a*) It appears from the casual allusions to dress in the *Rigveda* that the people wore a lower garment (*nīvī*), another garment, and a cloak. Sheep's wool was used for weaving cloth. They were embroidered with gold and dyed in the case of the rich, who further adorned their persons with such ornaments as ear-rings, necklets, armlets, bracelets, garlands, etc. The hair was oiled and combed. Women wore it "plaited"; and some men, too, preferred coils on their heads. Shaving was known, but beards were the norm.

(*b*) *Food*

The Rigvedic Aryans took both animal and vegetable food. The meat of sheep and goat was freely eaten and offered to the gods. It was also customary to kill the fatted calf on festive occasions or to entertain guests, but the cow was "aghnyā"—not to be slaughtered, because of her usefulness. Milk was, however, the chief article of diet. Among its various preparations, *ghee* and *dahi* (curd) were most commonly used. Grain was powdered into flour and with milk and *ghee* made into cakes. Vegetables and fruits were also included in the *menu* of the Rigvedic Indian.

(*c*) *Drink*

Mere water and milk did not satisfy the tastes of

the age. People were almost addicted to fermented drinks. On religious occasions *Soma* was the favourite beverage,[1] but *Surā*, a spirit distilled from grain, was the ordinary drink. The priests, however, disliked its use owing to its intoxicating character. Sometimes it led to the commission of crimes, which were by no means rare then.

(*d*) *Amusements*

The Rigvedic Indian did not lead a dull and drab life. He was fond of merry-making and pastimes. Joyous occasions were marked by music and dancing,[2] the latter often not quite innocent. The musical instruments included the drum (*dundubhi*), the cymbal, the lute (*karkarī*), and the flute. Singing may also have been practised for aught we know of its later development in *Sāman* songs. Besides chariot-racing and horse-racing, gambling with dice was the most popular amusement. Despite the loss of fortune and consequent ruin, the gambling-hall was the most frequented place and offered irresistible attractions to the players.

Religion[3]

The religion of the *Rigveda* is essentially simple, though it has many gods. This is natural, as the hymns are the product of a long period of priestly effort, and represent the deities of the various tribes. Most of the objects of devotion are the personifications of natural phenomena. They may be broadly classed as (1) Terrestrial gods, like Prithvī, Soma, Agni; (2)

[1] The ninth *maṇḍala* of the *Rigveda* is devoted to a praise of the *Soma*. Its juice had exhilarating effects. All efforts to identify the plant have so far not met with success.

[2] Both sexes indulged in this form of amusement.

[3] Griswold, *Religion of the Rigveda*.

Atmospheric gods, like Indra, Vāyu, Maruts, Parjanya; (3) Heavenly gods, like Varuṇa, Dyaus, Aśvins, Sūrya, Savitri, Mitra, Pūshan, and Viṣṇu—the latter five forms being all associated with the different phases of the sun's glory. Among these deities, Varuṇa occupies the place of honour, and is extolled in many a sublime hymn. He is god of the sky, and with him is bound up the conception of *rita*, first indicative of the cosmic and then of moral order. Next comes Indra, the god of thunder-storm, whose majesty is another favourite subject of praise. He causes the rain to fall and thus relieves the dryness of the earth. His importance grew with the advance of the Aryans to regions noted for storm and seasonal rainfall. It must not, however, be supposed that any kind of hierarchy among the gods was in the course of formation. The poets at different times ascribed pre-eminence to different gods, as they had to serve many masters and needs. The *Rigveda* also mentions abstract deities, such as Śraddhā (faith) and Manyu (anger); and among goddesses Uṣas (goddess of Dawn) inspires much noble poetry.[1] To propitiate these gods, prayers and sacrifices or oblations of milk, *ghee*, grain, flesh, etc. were offered. The utmost stress was laid on the performance of the latter in order that the worshippers may enjoy all happiness and prosperity. There is also a tendency in a few hymns of the *Rigveda* to identify one god with others, or to group them in pairs (e.g., *dyāvā-prithvī*), and carrying it further the composers arrive at the great monotheistic doctrine that "the gods are one and the same, only sages describe them differently."[2]

[1] The *Rigveda* also refers to some minor deities like the Ribhus (aerial elfs) and Apsaras (water-nymphs). There is, however, no trace in it of Zoolatry and Totemism.

[2] cf. इन्द्रं मित्रं वरुणमग्निमाहुरथो दिव्यः स सुपर्णो गरुत्मान् ।
एकं सद्विप्रा बहुधा वदन्त्यग्निं यमं मातरिश्वानमाहुः ॥
(*Rigveda*, I, 164, 46).

Date

Here we may consider the date attributed to the bulk of the *Rigveda*, or the civilisation it represents. Jacobi and Tilak are of opinion, mainly on astronomical grounds, that the hymns were composed at least 4,000 years before Christ. But their view is not generally accepted. On the other hand, Max Müller, arguing backwards from the known date of the Buddha, whose religious system was a reaction against Brahmanism and pre-supposed the existence of the entire Vedic literature, divided the latter into four epochs—Sūtra (600-200 B.C.); Brāhmaṇa, Āraṇyaka and Upaniṣad (800-600 B.C.); Mantra (1000-800 B.C.); and Chandas (1200-1000 B.C.)—and thus arrived at 1200-1000 B.C. as the period of the beginning of Vedic hymns, assigning approximately 200 years for the development of each epoch of the Veda. The arbitrariness of the last assumption was, however, a serious flaw in Max Müller's argument. Another line of evidence is furnished by recent researches at Boghazkoi, where inscriptions recording treaties between the Hittites and kings of Mitani have been discovered. It is clear from these documents that Vedic gods were worshipped in Asia Minor at least as early as 1400 B.C.[1] Of course, this discovery may lead to different conclusions. Some think that here we stumble upon the Aryans on their progress eastward; and others, relying on the typically Vedic character of the deities, postulate that the inscriptions represent the westward migration of the Indian Aryans. Whatever the truth, the well-known Tel-el-Amarna inscriptions, belonging to the same time as the Boghazkoi records, also mention Sanskritic names like Arta-

[1] Indra, Varuṇa, Nāsatyau and Mitra, who are invoked as protectors of the contracts, are respectively mentioned as In-da-ra, U-ru-w-na, Na-ṣa-aṭ-ti-ia, Mi-it-ra,

tama, Tusratta, for Mitani princes; and even some of the Kassites, who ruled in Babylonia between *c.* 1746-1180 B.C., bore such names as Shurias (Skt. Sūrya) and Marytas (Skt. Marutas), etc. Considering all this evidence, it may be reasonably supposed, with some margin for error, that the beginnings of Vedic poetry and civilisation go back to about the sixteenth century B.C.[1]

Indus and Rigvedic Cultures Contrasted

It may be interesting to note the dissimilarities between the Indus and Rigvedic cultures. The Indo-Aryans were still in the village state, living in small thatched houses of bamboo. The Indus people, on the other hand, had developed a complex city life with commodious houses of brick, equipped with bath-rooms, wells, and sanitation. The metals known to the Rigvedic Aryans were gold, copper or bronze, and perhaps iron. The Indus people have left no trace of iron; they used silver more commonly than gold, and their utensils and vessels were made of stone—a relic of the Neolithic age—as well as of copper and bronze. The weapons of offence were almost the same in both the ages, but the defensive helmet and coat of mail, known to the Rigvedic people, were not a feature of the Indus civilisation. It appears from the numerous seals discovered at Mohenjo-daro that the bull was their most important animal, but during the Rigvedic period the cow takes its place. The horse was unfamiliar to the Indus valley people, whereas the Rigvedic Aryans had domesticated it. Further, in the Indus

[1] Mr. B. G. Tilak, however, believed that "the traditions recorded in the *Rigveda* unmistakably point to a period *not later* than 4,000 B.C., when the vernal equinox was in Orion, or, in other words, when the Dog-star commenced the equinoctial year" (*The Orion*, Poona).

valley the worship of the phallic symbols was current; the *Rigveda*, however, shows no trace of it. The Indus people knew some sort of writing, and in art they had made considerable progress. The Rigvedic age is, however, devoid of any tangible proofs of Aryan achievement in this direction. These points of difference are enough to show how wide is the gulf between the two civilisations. And it was not a hiatus in time only, for either hypothesis, that the one was the progenitor or the descendant of the other, would land us in a difficulty or dilemma. The only possible assumption, which may satisfactorily explain the divergent characters of the Indus and Rigvedic cultures, is that the latter, although later, was unrelated to the former and had an independent origin and development.[1]

[1] See also Sir John Marshall, Mohenjo-daro (Vol. I), Ch. VIII, pp. 110-12.

CHAPTER IV

LATER VEDIC PERIOD

Wider Geographical Outlook

We have to depend upon the *Saṁhitās* of the *Yajurveda*, *Sāmaveda*, *Atharvaveda*, the *Brāhmaṇas*, the *Āraṇyakas*, and the *Upaniṣads*, all religious works,[1] for the later Vedic period, which, roughly speaking, comes down to about 600 B.C. During this age the Aryan civilisation gradually extended towards the east and the south. The north-western parts of India, the home of the Rigvedic tribes, fade into unimportance, and even the customs of those still dwelling there are viewed with disfavour. The centre of culture shifts to Kurukṣetra; and Madhyadeśa, the land of the Yamunā and the Gaṅgā, comes into prominence. Kośala (Oudh), Kāśī, and Videha (North Bihar), rise as great Aryan centres in the east. Mention is also made of Magadha (South Bihar) and Aṅga (South-eastern Bihar), although these regions had not yet been Aryanised and

[1] The *Brāhmaṇas* are attached to the Vedas. They are theological treatises in prose, explaining in detail the value and efficacy of sacrifices. The important *Brāhmaṇas* are the *Aitareya*, *Śatapatha*, *Pañcaviṁśa* and *Gopatha*. The *Āraṇyakas* are the concluding portions of the *Brāhmaṇas*, so called because on account of their mystical character they had to be studied in the seclusion of the forest. The extant ones—e.g., *Aitareya*, *Kauṣītakī*, and the *Taittirīya*—form appendages of the *Brāhmaṇas* of the same names. The *Upaniṣads* discard sacrifices. Their theme is how to obtain *jñāna* and deliverance by the absorption of the individual soul in the world-soul. Besides छान्दोग्य and बृहदारण्यक there are ten other noted *Upaniṣads*, viz., *Taittirīya*, *Aitareya*, *Kauṣītakī*, *Kaṭha*, *Śvetāśvatara*, *Īsa*, *Kena*, *Praśna*, *Muṇḍaka*, *Māṇḍūkya*.

their inhabitants were regarded as strangers. We now hear for the first time of the Andhras and other out-cast tribes like the Puṇḍras of Bengal, the Śabaras of Orissa and C.P., and the Pulindas of South-western India. Vidarbha or Berar occurs in two late passages of the *Aitareya* and *Jaiminīya Brāhmaṇas*. Thus, nearly the whole of Northern India from the Himālayas to the Vindhyas, and perhaps even beyond, had now come within the ken of the Aryans.[1]

Settled Life

There is ample evidence to show that large cities had now sprung into existence, and the people enjoyed a more settled form of life. We learn, for instance, of Kāmpilya and Āsandīvant, the capitals of the Pañcālas and Kurus respectively. References are also made to Kauśāmbī and Kāśī; the latter is still a great living town.

Tribal Groupings

In addition to the above changes, we find a noteworthy change in the relative importance of the different tribes. The Bharatas of the *Rigveda* are no longer a mighty political unit; their place is taken by the Kurus and their neighbours and allies, the Pañcālas. It appears that the Bharatas and Purus were merged into the Kurus. The Pañcālas were also a composite clan, as their name, derived from *pañca*—five, shows. According to the *Śatapatha Brāhmaṇa*, they were formerly called Krivis, who may, therefore, have been one of the constituent tribes. Perhaps the earlier Anus, Druhyus, and Turvasas, that disappear now from history, were

[1] See N. K. Dutt, *The Aryanisation of India* (Calcutta, 1925); V. Rangacharya, *Pre-Musalman India* (Vedic India, Pt. I), Vol. II, Chaps. III f.

also comprised in the confederation. The Kurus and Pañcālas are held out in the texts as examples of good manners and pure speech. Their kings are model rulers, and their Brahmans are celebrated for learning. They (Kuru-Pañcālas) undertake military operations in the right season, and their sacrifices are performed with the minutest details and care.[1] Their close neighbours in the Madhyadeśa were the Śalvas on the Jumna, the Vaśas and the Uśīnaras, who did not play any conspicuous part. The Śriñjayas were another tribe, who seem to have been allied with the Kurus, as they had at one time a common priest. We also hear of the Matsyas, who were settled round about modern Jaipur and Alwar.[2]

Rise of Powerful States

The amalgamation of tribes and their wars of aggrandisement gradually led to the formation of bigger territorial units as compared with those of the Rigvedic times. The ideal of 'paramountcy' or "universal sovereignty" now began to loom large on the political horizon, and kings performed sacrifices like the 'Vājapeya', the 'Rājasūya' and the 'Aśvamedha' to symbolise the degree of success achieved in realising their ambitions. The *Aitareya* and *Śatapatha Brāhmaṇas* mention the names of some monarchs, who performed the 'Aśvamedha' sacrifice along with the 'Aindra Mahābhiṣeka,' such as Para of Kośala, Śatānīka Sātrājita, and Purukutsa Aikṣvāka, etc. As the kings extended their sway, their titles also changed. Thus, *Rājā* was used for an ordinary ruler, and *Adhirāja*, *Rājādhirāja*, *Samrāṭ*, *Virāṭ*, *Ekarāṭ*, and *Sārvabhauma* denoted various gradations of suzerains.

[1] *Śatapatha Brāhmaṇa*, iii, 2, 3, 15; see also *Cam. Hist. Ind.*, Vol. I, pp. 118-19.

[2] See also B. C. Law, *Ancient Mid-Indian Kṣatriya Tribes.*

The King

With the emergence of larger realms, the importance of the royal rank also grew. This is reflected in the importance attached to, and elaboration of, the consecration ceremony itself, in which figured prominently such state functionaries as the *Purohita*, the *Rājanya* (noble), the *Mahiṣī* (chief queen), the *Sūta* (charioteer or bard ?), the *Senānī* (army commander), the *Grāmaṇī* (village headman), the *Bhāgadugha* (collector of taxes), *Kṣattri* (Chamberlain), *Saṁgrahitri* (treasurer), *Akṣavāpa* (superintendent of dicing), and others.[1]

The king, whose position was commonly hereditary,[2] still led in war, although minor operations were entrusted to the Senānī. He (i.e., the king) punished the wicked, and upheld the Law, *Dharma*. He controlled, if not owned, the land, and he could deprive any individual of it. Misuse of the latter prerogative must have meant considerable hardship to the commoner. Popular assemblies like the *Sabhā* and the *Samiti*,[3] not quite defunct yet, are rather rarely heard of during this period. The growth in the size of the kingdom must have made their frequent meetings difficult, and in consequence their control or check over the ruler must have progressively decreased. The will of the people, however, sometimes asserted itself. Thus a king named Duṣṭaritu was expelled by his discontented subjects, but he was subsequently restored to the throne by his *Sthapati* Cākra.

[1] The *Ratnins* are fewer in number in the earlier texts.

[2] For instance, in the case of the Śriñjayas monarchy lasted for ten generations.

[3] It is significant that the *Atharvaveda* (vii, 12) describes the 'Sabhā' and 'Samiti' as twin-daughters of Prajāpati. cf. सभा च मा समितिश्चावतां प्रजापतेर्दुहितरौ संविदाने । During its period of prosperity, the *Sabhā* functioned as a place for discussing public business

Political Divisions and Events

Unfortunately our knowledge of the political divisions and events of the Brāhmaṇic period is very meagre. We can glean only a few facts from incidental anecdotes in sacerdotal literature and from other dubious references in the *Epics* and the *Purāṇas*. We have already seen that the Kurus were the most important tribe now, and with them were closely associated the Pañcālas. The first great Kuru king is the one mentioned in the *Atharvaveda*, Parīkṣit by name. During his time the people were happy and contented, and the kingdom almost "flowed with milk and honey." It roughly corresponded to modern Thāneśar, Delhi and the upper Doab with its capital at Āsandīvant, later Hastināpura. The next ruler of note was Janamejaya, who, according to the *Brāhmaṇas*, was a great conqueror and extended his sway as far north-west as Taxilā. The *Mahābhārata* deposes that sometimes he held his court there, and listened to Vaiśaṁpāyana's narration of the Kuru-Pāṇḍu conflict. He performed a *Sarpa-satra* (snake-sacrifice) and perhaps two horse-sacrifices. We further learn that Janamejaya had some dispute with the Brahmans, and his three brothers Bhīmasena, Ugrasena, and Śrutasena, had each to atone for killing them by performing the Aśvamedha sacrifice. Little definite is known about Janamejaya's successors. The kingdom was visited by such calamities as hail-stones, locusts, etc., and ultimately Nīcakṣu abandoned Hastināpura, on account of floods in the Ganges, in favour of Kauśāmbī.

With regard to the Pañcālas, our information is still more scanty. Some of their kings must have

and also as a court of justice. Then there are references to *Samiti* sometimes electing or re-electing a king. cf. ध्रुवाय ते समिति: कल्पतामिह (*Atharvaveda*, vi, 88,3); or नास्मै समिति: कल्पते (*Ibid.*, v, 19,15).

achieved notable victories, as they are said to have performed the horse-sacrifice, a sure indication of growth in political power. The *Upaniṣads* mention Pravāhaṇa Jaivali, a patron of learning, who used to hold intellectual tournaments at his court. These learned conferences (*Pariṣads*), in which they followed the method of debate and discussion to thrash out the truth, were then a potent factor in stimulating thought and diffusing knowledge. The capital of Pañcāla was Kāmpilya, and the kingdom roughly corresponded to modern Farrukhabad district and parts of Rohilkhand.

After the downfall of the Kurus, Videha rose into importance. It was almost identical with modern Tirhut, and its capital, Mithilā, though not mentioned in Vedic texts, is a well-known town in later literature. This region received the light of Vedic civilisation after Kośala, as is clear from the story of Videgha Māthava in the *Śatapatha Brāhmaṇa*.[1] The most notable ruler of Videha was Janaka[2], the royal scholar and philosopher of the *Upaniṣads*, who flourished not long after the destruction of the Kuru capital. Like Akbar, he encouraged philosophical discussions, and his court was adorned by intellectual celebrities of the type of Yājñavalkya.[3] Janaka was called *Samrāṭ*, and his power and fame even excited the jealousy of Ajātaśatru of Kāśī.

The last-named monarch belonged to the Brahmadatta line, perhaps Videhan in origin. He was also

[1] It is said that Māthava the Videgha went along with his priest, Gotama Rāhugaṇa, from the land of the Saraswatī to Videha after crossing the Sadānīra (Gandak), which formed the eastern boundary of Kośala. Beyond this river, Agni Vaiśyānara did not burn over the country i.e., it did not then come within the pale of Aryanism.

[2] The modern town of Janakapur still preserves in its name a memory of this great ruler.

[3] Among other learned men of the times may be mentioned Uddālaka Āruṇi, Śvetaketu Āruṇeya, Satyakāma Jabāla, etc.

a great patron of men of letters. Earlier than the Brahmadattas, Kāśī was ruled by a family that traced its descent from Purūravas, the great ancestor of the Bharatas.

Kośala[1] was another eastern kingdom, which roughly corresponded to Oudh. It was under the domination of the house of Ikṣvāku. For long, it remained the eastern limit of Aryan civilisation until the Sadānīra (Gandak) was crossed. The earliest capital of the kingdom was Ayodhyā, which was the seat of the epic hero, Rāma, too.

Other contemporary powers, mentioned in the *Brāhmaṇas* and the *Upaniṣads*, were :

Gandhāra extending on both sides of the Indus with Taxilā (Rawalpindi district) and Puṣkarāvatī (modern Chārsadda, Peshawar) as its principal towns; the Kekaya territory lying between Gandhāra and the Beas river; the Madras, whose country in Central Punjab corresponded to modern Sialkot and adjacent districts; the Matsya kingdom comprising parts of Alwar, Jaipur and Bharatpur; and the land of the Uśīnaras situated in Madhyadeśa. These states were generally prosperous and well-governed, and the people were left free to pursue the arts of peace. At the same time, too much stress should not be laid on such a vain boast as that of Aśvapati Kekaya, who, according to the *Chāndogya Upaniṣad*, claims that he had cleared his kingdom of all thieves, drunkards, debauches and illiterate men.[2] Magadha and Aṅga were still regarded with aversion. For in a text of the *Atharvaveda* fever is wished away to the peoples of these lands. The

[1] Jala Jātukarṇya is represented in a late passage as the *Purohita* of the Videhas, Kāśīs, and Kośalas. Does this show that the three kingdoms were once allied together?

[2] cf. न मे स्तेनो जनपदे न कदर्यो न मद्यपः
नानाहिताग्निर्नं चाविद्वान्न स्वैरी स्वैरिणी कुतः ॥
(*Chāndogya Upaniṣad*, v, 11).

/lagadhas are also contemptuously described as *Vrā-*
yas, outside the pale of orthodox Brahmanism, and peaking a strange unintelligible language.

'ocial Changes

Society did not remain unaffected by the changes ıat were taking place during this period. No doubt, ıe division into four classes is already referred to in a *ıte* hymn of the *Rigveda*[1] but it is a moot point whether it ears any other traces of familiarity with the institution f caste, apart from the clear distinction between the ırya and the Dasyu. Now the divisions became more ronounced, and the caste-system was well on its way ›wards crystallisation. Unfortunately, the causes of ıis development are obscure. The starting point of ıese distinctions was, of course, the "colour bar" etween the fair Ārya and the dark Dasyu. But the ›nstant wars of the Aryans, the growing complexities f life and political conditions, and the tendency towards ›ecialisation in labour, gradually resulted in the formaon of hereditary occupational groups. Thus, those 'ho possessed a knowledge of the sacred lore, offiıated in religious ceremonies and received gifts were ılled Brahmans; those who fought, owned land, and 'ielded political power were classed as Kṣatriyas; the eneral mass of people—the traders, the agriculturists, ıd the craftsmen—were grouped under the term 'aiśya; and the Śūdra, reserved for menial service, was enerally recruited from the conquered Dasyus. There 'as, however, still no unnatural rigidity of castes as in

[1] cf. the *Puruṣasūkta* (X, 90, 12), which states that Brahmans, ṣatriyas, Vaiśyas, and Śūdras originated respectively from the outh, arms, thighs, and feet of the Creator.

"ब्राह्मणोऽस्य मुखमासीद् बाहू राजन्यः कृतः ।
ऊरू तदस्य यद्वैश्यः पद्भ्यां शूद्रोऽजायत" ॥

(*Rigveda*, x, 90, 12; *Yajurveda*, vāj., 31, 11, etc.).

the succeeding age. For we know that Cyavana, a Brahman seer, married Sukanyā, daughter of Kṣatriya Śaryāta; Kṣatriya rulers like Janaka of Videha, Ajātaśatru of Kāśī, and Pravāhaṇa Jaivali of Pañcāla distinguished themselves in the knowledge of the *Brahman*; and Prince Devāpi performed a sacrificial ceremony for his brother, Śāntanu.[1] As local particularism and the influence of the Brahmans waxed, the system began to lose elasticity, and mobility or change of occupation was disfavoured. Further, the off-spring of the inter-marriages among the different classes,[2] being looked down upon, tended to form separate groups. This process continued on account of other causes, like the adoption of a new calling or craft, until society became a strange congeries of mutually exclusive entities bound by strict laws of connubium and commensality.

Position of Śūdras and Women

The Śūdras are no doubt recognised as a distinct order of society in later Vedic literature, but they were regarded as impure and not fit in any way to take part in sacrifices, or recite the sacred texts. Aryan marriages or illicit relations with Śūdras were severely condemned. They were also perhaps not allowed to possess property in their own right. Indeed, the *Aitareya Brāhmaṇa* at one place represents the Śūdra as "the servant of another, to be expelled at will, and to be slain at will."

Similarly, the position of women was not high in all respects. Instances of Gārgī Vācaknavī and Maitreyī, of course, prove that education was imparted to

[1] Such instances of Brahmans and Kṣatriyas apart, it is noteworthy Vedic literature does not record the case of any Vaiśya rising to higher social rank.

[2] Manu calls the crossings between the members of the different castes *Anuloma* and *Pratiloma* marriages.

females, and some of them attained to rare intellectual heights. Women could not, however, inherit or own property; and their earnings, if any, accrued to their fathers or husbands. The birth of a daughter was considered "a source of misery." Kings and the richer people practised polygamy, which must have caused considerable irritation in the family circle.

Occupations

During this period great progress in agriculture was made. The quality and size of the plough (*sīra*) was improved;[1] and the use of manure was well understood for increasing production. In addition to barley (*yava*), several other kinds of grain like rice (*vrīhi*), wheat (*godhūma*), beans, and sesamum (*tila*) were now cultivated in their due seasons.

The fertile plains of Northern India increased the material prosperity of the Aryans, and this gave rise to a variety of occupations to meet the needs of the people. We thus hear of charioteers, hunters, shepherds, fishermen, fire-rangers, ploughers, chariot-makers, jewel-workers, basket-makers, washermen, rope-makers, dyers, weavers, slaughterers, cooks, potters, smiths, professional acrobats, musicians, guards of tame elephants, and so on.

Astrologers and barbers now appear as important figures. The physician healed the sick, but his profession was for some reason stamped with inferiority. Women mostly engaged themselves in dyeing, embroidery, basket-making, etc.

Other Features

The growth of civilisation is further reflected in the knowledge of more metals. While the *Ṛigveda*

[1] Some ploughs were so heavy as to be drawn by a team of twenty-four oxen.

mentions gold and *ayas* of uncertain import, this period knows of lead (*sīsa*), tin (*trapu*), silver (*rajata*), gold (*hiraṇya*), red (*lohita*) *ayas* (copper) and dark (*syāma*) *ayas* (iron). Gold and silver were mostly used for making ornaments, bowls, vessels, etc. Gold was obtained from river-beds, or from the bowels of the earth, or from ore by smelting.

Regular coinage had not yet started, though the use of *Śatamāna*, equivalent to 100 *krisṇalas* or *guñja* berries, was leading towards it. Thus the cow as a unit of value was gradually being replaced.

The dress, amusements, and food remained almost the same as in the time of the *Rigveda*. In a hymn of the *Atharvaveda*, however, meat-eating and drinking of Surā are regarded as sinful acts. This may have been due to the doctrine of *Ahiṁsā*, which now begins to germinate.

The later Vedic period was also probably marked by the knowledge of writing. It has been suggested by Bühler and others that it was introduced in India by traders from Semitic lands about the 9th century B.C. On the contrary, some scholars[1] stoutly maintain its indigenous origin, for which they assign an earlier date. The problem has been a veritable battle-ground for scholarly ingenuity, and it will continue to defy solution until some new discovery is made, or we get some unexpected light from the decipherment of Mohenjo-daro seals.

Religion and Philosophy

The theology of the later Vedic literature does not fundamentally differ from that of the old hymns. The deities of the *Rigveda* reappear; only we notice a change in their emphasis. Prajāpati, "the lord of creatures," who is the main subject of Brahmanic speculation, does

[1] See *e.g.*, *MM.* G. H. Ojhā, *Prācīna-lipi*, Introduction.

not, however, attain the position of a popular god. The two deities that share universal veneration are Rudra and Viṣṇu, still dominant in modern Hinduism. In the *Rigveda*, Viṣṇu is a mere form of the Sun-god; his worship by no means takes precedence. So is the case with Rudra, who has now won the most prominent place in the Vedic pantheon. He is called the "great god", and he already bears the epithet Śiva, "propitious," current at the present day. What was his primacy due to? Was the fusion of cultures in any way responsible for this development? At any rate, a seal, found at Mohenjo-daro, depicting a male god, who, according to Sir John Marshall, "is recognisable as the prototype of the historic Śiva," raises a strong presumption in favour of this view.

But though religion continued to remain polytheistic, there was a vast change in the religious spirit. The older hymns were now becoming obscure and unintelligible, and the appreciation of the striking phenomena of Nature no longer inspired the poet-priests to spiritual flights. Thus, religion assumed a stereotyped form, and the Brahmans rose into such complete ascendancy that they came to be regarded as veritable "gods on earth." They laid stress on rigid formalism, and elaborated a most complicated and all-embracing ritualistic system.[1] Mystic significance was attached to sacrifices and everything connected with them was endowed with magical powers. Indeed, it was thought that the welfare of the sacrificer depended upon their careful performance, and if there was the least deviation from any of the complex and minute details, dire consequences were sure to follow. In short, the sacrifice assumes such importance in the *Brāhmaṇas* that

[1] There were now *Sattra*-sacrifices lasting from a few days to a year or years. The number of priests also increased with the growth of rituals. The Hotri, Udgātri, Adhvaryu, and Brahman had each several assistants.

it is no longer the means to an end, but an end in itself.

This is, however, only one side of the shield. The age was essentially one of intellectual ferment, and while the priests were firmly entrenching themselves behind the cult of the sacrifice, some of the best minds among both the Brahmans and the Kṣatriyas were turning away from it[1] and seeking peace and salvation in true knowledge (*jñāna*). Their bold philosophical speculations are embedded in the *Upaniṣads*, like the *Chāndogya* and the *Brihadāraṇyaka*, which later on gave rise to the principal schools of Hindu philosophy (*Darśanas*), *viz.*, *Sāṅkhya*, *Yoga*, *Nyāya*, *Vaiśeṣika*, *Pūrva* and *Uttara-mīmāṅsā*. Striving restlessly to solve the riddle of the universe and to grasp the nature of the Self, the Aryan mind enunciated the great doctrine that the ultimate reality was one, *Brahman*. True knowledge alone led to infinite bliss by the absorption of the individual *ātman* in the world *Ātman*.[2] The natural corollary of this doctrine was the theory of transmigration, and the belief gained ground that until release was obtained by *jñāna*, the soul remained a prey to endless births and deaths. These were regulated by one's own deeds—an idea, which marks the beginning of the doctrine of *Karma*, i.e., no act, good or bad, is ever lost, and it must bear its proper fruit in the cycle of existence.

Progress of Knowledge

The mental stir of this epoch led to progress of

[1] e.g., the *Muṇḍaka Upaniṣad* (i, 2, 7) dubs those devoted merely to ceremonies and ritual as fools. Similarly, the *Brihadāraṇyaka* compares one performing sacrifices to gods to an animal serving the needs or comforts of his owner.

[2] The pithy expression *Tat tvaṁ asi*, "That art thou," beautifully sums up the Vedānta position of the identity of the individual soul with the world Soul.

knowledge in other directions as well. The systematic and intensive study of Vedic texts and the practical needs of religion in due course resulted in the growth of such sciences as *Vyākaraṇa* (grammar), *Śikṣā* (phonetics), *Kalpa* (ritual), *Nirukta* (etymology), *Chandas* (metrics), *Jyotiṣa* (astronomy). These *Vedāṅgas* or "limbs of the Veda" aim at "explaining, preserving or practically applying the sacred texts."[1] In this group, the most interesting works are those dealing with sacrificial aspects, or with phonetics, derivation, and grammar. We may specially mention here the *Nirukta* of Yāska, which, apart from its value for exegesis and grammar, is "the earliest specimen of Sanskrit prose of the classical type." It was thus another development of the period that of the several dialects arising out of the old Vedic speech of the Punjab, the one current in *Madhyadeśa* assumed pre-eminence and became the standard vehicle of expression. It was styled Sanskrit, 'polished,' in contradistinction to the common vernaculars called Prākrits. Its form having been fixed by the labours of grammarians, particularly Pāṇini,[2] Sanskrit gradually tended to be limited to the learned classes of the community. Next, the beginnings of civil law may be traced to the attempts which were made to lay down rules for the conduct of an individual in relation to his gods, family, society, and the state. The new manuals had no literary merit or grace; they were composed in a peculiarly condensed and drab prose style suitable for the purpose of memorisation. Indeed, such emphasis and importance was

[1] Macdonell, *India's Past*, p. 58.

[2] The date of Pāṇini has been the subject of frequent controversy. Keith places him "not later than 300 B.C." (*Cam. Hist. Ind.*, Vol. I, p. 113; *Aitareya Āraṇyaka*, pp. 21-25); whereas Macdonell believes that Pāṇini "lived after, probably soon after, 500 B.C. (*India's Past*, p. 136). Sir Ramakrishna Bhandarkar, on the other hand, plausibly argues that Pāṇini flourished about "the beginning of the seventh century B.C. (*E. H. D.*, 3rd. ed., p. 16).

given to conciseness in the *Sūtras* that an economy of a syllable even was considered almost as important as the birth of a son.

CHAPTER V

GLEANINGS FROM THE SŪTRAS, EPICS AND DHARMAŚĀSTRAS

SECTION A

THE SŪTRAS

Sūtra form

The origin of the *Sūtras* may be traced to the practical needs of the time. As the mass of sacerdotal tradition was growing rapidly both in matter and volume, it became increasingly difficult to learn everything by heart and to save the texts from undergoing changes in the course of oral transmission. Accordingly, a new prose style, convenient to memory though exceedingly dry, was developed; and treatises, in which rules were just strung together (*sūtra*=thread), were produced. Their merit consisted in the use of the fewest possible words. It is believed that "the general period of the *Sūtras* extends from the sixth or seventh

Age

century before Christ to about the second century."[1] Whatever one may say regarding this latter limit, the oldest *Sūtras*, at any rate, "seem to go back to about the time when Buddhism arose."[2]

Pāṇini and his great Grammar

We have already referred in a footnote to the controversy regarding the date of Pāṇini, and there is no doubt that Yāska was anterior to him. A native

[1] *Cam. Hist. Ind.*, Vol. I, p. 227.
[2] *India's Past*, p. 57.

of Śalātura in the north-west, Pāṇini is chiefly known for his work on grammar, the *Aṣṭādhyāyī*, which is a monument of thoroughness and "algebraic brevity." Incidentally, however, he gives bits of information useful for historical purpose.[1] During his time, the Aryans were probably unfamiliar with the Dekkan, for whereas he mentions Kaccha (Cutch) in the west, Kaliṅga in the east, and Avanti in the south, no name of a place beyond the Vindhyas occurs in his Grammar. The states (*janapadas*), of which he knew about twenty-two, were called after their peoples, like the Gandhāris, Madras, Yaudheyas, Kośalas, Vrijjis, etc. He also speaks of such territorial units as *Viṣaya* (province or division), *Nagara* (city) and *Grāma* (village). Monarchy was the norm, but there are references to *Gaṇas* and *Saṁghas* too. The king was the supreme head in all matters, and below him, as shown by Dr. R.K. Mookerji,[2] were the *Pāriṣadyas* i.e., members of the *Pariṣat* (council), *Adhyakṣas* (heads of departments), *Vyāvahārika* (Law-officer), *Aupāyika* (literally, one who devises ways and means. Was he in charge of finance?), *Yuktas* (officers in general), and other functionaries of administration. Further, we get a few details about the economic life of the people as well. It appears from Pāṇini that the main sources of livelihood were agriculture, service (*Jānapadi vritti*), profession of arms and labour. Trade and business (*kraya-vikraya*) flourished, and loans were advanced on interest. Among the crafts, he mentions weaving, dyeing, leather-working, hunting, carpentry, pottery-making, etc. He also records the existence of craft-corporations or guilds (*pūgas*). These organisations must have helped specialisation and promoted a sense of discipline and respect for law.

[1] Dr. R. K. Mookerji, *Hindu Civilisation*, Ch. VI, pp. 120 f. It is a book full of useful information.

[2] *Ibid.*, pp. 121-27.

The Sūtras Proper

As already mentioned, one of the six Vedāṅgas is *Kalpa*, which covered "the whole body of Sūtras concerned with religion." It is divided into three classes. Of these, the *Śrauta Sūtras* convey nothing historically valuable; they primarily deal with the great Vedic sacrifices of *Havis* (oblation) and *Soma* and other religious matters. They were, so to say, a continuation of the ritual side of the *Brāhmaṇas*, but they were never regarded as revealed or sacred. Later perhaps than the Śrauta manuals are the *Grihya Sūtras*, treating of domestic ritual. They embody minute rules for the performance of the various ceremonies marking every important epoch of an individual's life from conception to cremation. The most interesting of these sacraments (*Saṁskāras*) were *Puṁsavana* (ceremony for having an issue); *Jāta-karma* (birth-rite); *Nāmakaraṇa* (naming ceremony); *Cūḍā-karma* (tonsure); *Upanayana* (Initiation for study as a Brahmacārī); *Samāvartana* (rite of return home); *Vivāha* (marriage), of which no less than eight forms were known;[1] regular daily performance by every householder of the five great sacrifices (*pañca-mahāyajña*), besides other offerings on special *tithis* like new and full-moon days, etc.; and finally *Antyeṣṭhi* (funeral rite). In one of these treatises, the *Kauśika Sūtra*, are also dealt with medicinal formulas and magical practices for averting disease and disaster. Thus the *Grihya*

Śrauta Sūtras.

Grihya Sūtras.

[1] They were as follows: Brāhma, Daiva, Ārṣa, Prājāpatya, Āsura, Gāndharva, Rākṣasa, Paiśāca.

cf. ब्राह्मो दैवस्तथैवार्षः प्राजापत्यस्तथासुरः ।

गान्धर्वो राक्षसश्चैव पैशाचश्चाष्टमोऽधमः ॥ (*Manu-Smriti*, III, 21; *Yājñavalkya-smriti*, I, 58-61). See also *J.B.H.U.*, Vol. vi, no. 1, pp. 1-22.

ūtras give us an excellent insight into the ceremonies nd superstitions associated with home-life in ancient ndia.

Dharmasūtras

The next class of Sūtras is that of the *Dharmasūtras*, which are chiefly concerned with society rather than with he family. They deal with social usages and customs of every-day life. In them we see the beginning of civil and criminal law. Of course, they treat more exhaustively of the religious, but touch only lightly on he secular, aspect of law. The principal *Dharmasūtra* uthors are Gautama, who "can hardly date from later han about 500 B.C."[1] and Baudhyāyana, who is supposed to have belonged to Southern India. Next come Āpastamba, assigned by Bühler to about 400 B.C., and Vaśiṣṭha who certainly flourished after Gautama. Āpastamba appears to have belonged to the South, perhaps the Andhra country, but Vaśiṣṭha was doubtless a Northerner. Lastly, we may mention the not extant *Mānava-dharma-sūtra*, on which is based the metrical *Mānava-dharma-śāstra*, still considered the most authoritative work on law and an individual's conduct in life.

Social Orders

According to the Sūtras, *Varṇāśrama-dharma*[2] was a firmly established feature of society. They describe the duties and obligations of the "Dvijas"—Brahman, Kṣatriya, and Vaiśya—as well as of the Sūdras. We are also told that a "Twice-born" must pass through four stages (*Āśramas*) in life, viz., *Brahmacarya* (period of studentship), *Gārhastha* (married or householder's state), *Vānaprastha* (state of reclusion), and *Sannyāsa*

[1] *A History of Sanskrit Literature*, p. 260. Gautama's manual is wholly composed in prose aphorisms.

[2] See *Infra* for more details.

(hermit's life)—the last two being marked by the practice of ascetic exercises and retirement from worldly concerns. Tremendous emphasis was now laid on the purity of social orders (*varṇas*), which was possible only if the rules of marriage and interdining were meticulously observed. It was essential to avoid eating defiled food and coming in contact with what was unclean. There were strict injunctions regarding these matters, although differences of opinion do exist among the various authorities on certain points. Indeed, the older ones appear to be more lax in their views. For instance, Gautama allows a Brahman to take food offered by a "Dvija," and in need even that given by a Śūdra. In marriage, too, a good girl, though low-born, was sometimes accepted by a Brahman, it being definitely understood that she would occupy an inferior position, and the progeny of such union would be legally considered mixed. Marriage within the same *gotra* and within "six degrees on the mother's side" was prohibited, but the *Dākṣiṇātyas* or Southerners, on the other hand, had the curious custom of marrying the daughter of a maternal uncle. Thus, differences in the *Dharmasūtras* were to some extent due to local customs and conditions. Generally, however, their outlook was narrow, and this conclusion is further supported by their interdiction of sea voyages and learning the language of "barbarians" i.e., foreign tongues.

Royal Powers

The *Dharmasūtras* indicate the duties of the king. He was to afford full protection to his subjects from danger and molestation, and to chastise the evil-doers; to provide means of subsistence to learned Brahmans or *Śrotriyas*, students, and the disabled and infirm, who were not fit to work; to dispense justice; to reward the good; to lead in battle and fight with courage and resolution. He lived in a magnificent building (*veśma*), which was located in the town (*pura*). Besides, there were other halls to entertain guests and to serve as assembly houses (*sabhā*). Loyal and honest men were appointed to guard the people in towns (*nagara*) and villages (*grāma*) from thieves and robbers, and they had to make good the loss suffered by a person if the culprits remained untraced and stolen property could not be recovered.

Taxes

For purposes of administration and maintenance of the royal state, people paid taxes, which varied from one-sixth to one-tenth of the produce of land. The king could also, according to Gautama, take "one day's work per month from artisans, one-twentieth on merchandise, one-fiftieth on cattle and gold, and one-sixtieth on roots, fruits, flowers, herbs, honey, meat, grass, and firewood."

Law

The fountain of law was not the king; its source was the body of the sacred texts—the Vedas—and the tradition and practice of those who knew the Vedas[1]. Further, it is stated that the administration of justice should be regulated by "the Vedas, Institutes of the sacred Law, the Vedāṅgas, the *Purāṇas*, the (special) laws of countries, castes, families (not being opposed to the sacred records), the usages of cultivators, traders, herdsmen, money-lenders, and artisans."[2] Thus, the customs and usages of the various groups (*vargas*) and guilds (*śreṇīs*) were respected by the king.

The *Dharmasūtras* also throw some light on the laws of inheritance and the status of women, who, it appears, could not, on their own account, offer sacrifices or inherit property. Another unwholesome fea-

[1] Gautama, *Dharmasūtra*, XI, 19-21.
[2] *Ibid.*, I, 1, 2.

ture was that the idea of equality before the majesty of law was not well developed in the *Sūtras*, for caste considerations and the status of individuals had then much to do in the determination of punishments; and for a similar offence a Śūdra was heavily fined, whereas a Brahman was leniently treated.

SECTION B

THE EPICS

Origin of Epic Poetry

The beginnings of epic poetry in India may be traced to the *ākhyānas*, *gāthās*, and *nārāśaṁśīs*, mentioned in the *Brāhmaṇas* and other later Vedic texts.[1] They were recited by professional rhapsodists at certain ceremonies, and were considered very pleasing to the gods. In course of time these "songs in praise of men" developed into epic poems of considerable length, but of these only two are extant in Sanskrit. The *Rāmāyaṇa* and the *Mahābhārata* thus embody a mass of floating legends and bardic lauds recounting the triumphs and reverses, in war and love, of ancient heroes and heroines.

The Rāmāyaṇa : Its Main Story

The *Rāmāyaṇa* has been called *ādikāvya*, as it is the first example of a narrative poem written in *Śloka* metre in accordance with the rules of poesy. It contains 24,000 verses in all, and is ascribed, according to orthodox tradition, to the sage Vālmīki. Briefly its story is as follows :

There was a king of Ayodhyā named Daśaratha,

[1] These and the *Atharvaveda* also mention *itihāsa* (story) and *purāṇa* (legend), which may accordingly be regarded as the literary precursors of the Epics.

whose son was Rāma by Kauśalyā. After the young prince was married to Sītā, daughter of king Janaka of Videha, his father expressed a desire to make him *Yuvarāja* or heir-apparent. The announcement evoked universal joy, but it was soon turned into sorrow, when his step-mother, Kaikeyī, demanded in lieu of two boons, she had kept in reserve, that Rāma should be immediately sent into fourteen years' exile and that her own son, Bharata, be installed in his place. Accordingly, Rāma went to the forest followed by his devoted wife, Sītā, and his third brother Lakṣmaṇa. The subsequent adventures of the royal exiles in the course of their wanderings, the forcible carrying away of Sītā by the "demon-king" of Laṅkā, Rāma's anxious search of her, alliance with Sugrīva, war against Rāvaṇa, return to Ayodhyā after Sītā's recovery, and accession to the throne are then delineated with considerable skill and effect. The *Rāmāyaṇa* is superb indeed both as regards form and matter, and it portrays ideal characters in almost all aspects of human life.

Age of the Rāmāyaṇa

According to modern critics, the entire *Rāmāyaṇa* is not the product of one hand. Their investigations have demonstrated that apart from minor interpolations in other portions, the first and seventh books were definitively added afterwards. For here occur statements in conflict with those in later books and Rāma is transformed into an incarnation of the universal god Viṣṇu, whereas in the original poem (II-VI) he is merely a human hero. This process of deification must have taken some time, and it may even be that the genuine and spurious parts are divided by centuries. Now, to what period are we to assign the epic kernel itself? There can be no doubt from the insertion of the *Rāmo-*

pākhyāna in the third book of the *Mahābhārata* that "the poem of Vālmīki must have been generally known as an old work before the *Mahābhārata* assumed a coherent form."[1] Besides, it is significant that the *Rāmāyaṇa* does not refer to Pāṭaliputra, founded by Udāyin; the capital of Kośala is still called Ayodhyā, and not Sāketa, which was its name in Buddhist and other later works. Buddha is mentioned only once, and that too perhaps in an interpolated verse, and the political conditions indicate the paternal rule of kings, exercising sway over small states. A consideration of all these and other points has led Dr. Macdonell to suppose that "the kernel of the *Rāmāyaṇa* was composed before 500 B.C., while the more recent portions were probably not added till the 2nd century B.C. and later."[2]

Is the Rāmāyaṇa Historical?

The approximate determination of the date of the *Rāmāyaṇa* does not, however, solve the difficulty of the chronological setting of its heroes. This problem, of course, does not disturb the average Hindu. To him, Rāma is a divine figure, who lived "once upon a time," and the account of his deeds is a source of inspiration as well as a mine of absolute historical facts. But the critical reasoning of the historian is unable to find much useful information of the latter class. Indeed, some scholars even doubt if the narrative contains any history at all. For instance, Lassen and Weber take the *Rāmāyaṇa* to represent allegorically "the first attempt" of the Aryans to conquer the non-Aryan South, and spread their culture there. Macdonell and Jacobi, on the other hand, believe that it is a fanciful creation based on Indian mythology. According to this inter-

[1] *A History of Sanskrit Literature*, p. 306.
[2] *Ibid.*, p. 309.

pretation, Sītā is the personification of the furrow-goddess; Rāma stands for Indra; and his conflict with Rāvaṇa may be traced to the old Indra-Vritra myth of the *Rigveda*. Without labouring the point further, it amply illustrates how the story of the *Rāmāyaṇa* offers a fruitful ground for speculation. There is no doubt that it is thickly interwoven with mythological fiction, but to discredit the historicity of Rāma altogether appears too wide an assumption. He is mentioned in the Buddhist *Daśaratha Jātaka*, where we see him in his normal form divested of divine attributes. It is also known that Kośala was an important kingdom in *Madhyadeśa* ever since Aryan expansion eastwards. What, therefore, may be taken as the nucleus of fact is that Rāma was a real person, who belonged to the royal Ikṣvāku house of Ayodhyā, and whose achievements both in war and peace left a deep impression upon the popular imagination. The epoch of Rāma's beneficent rule is, however, as uncertain as the contemporary political condition of Northern or Southern India.

The Mahābhārata : Its Age

The *Mahābhārata*, which at present consists of over 100,000 verses (शतसाहस्रीसंहिता), has the rather doubtful honour of being the bulkiest epic known to literary history. It is divided into 18 (eighteen) books (*parvans*) of unequal size with the *Harivaṁśa* as a supplement. According to orthodox tradition, Dvaipāyana Vyāsa was the author of this stupendous work, but the essential lack of uniformity in its language, style, and contents clearly indicates that it is not the production of one brain or of one period. It is a gradual growth from an epic kernel,[1] which was in course of time

[1] Macdonell believes that the original epic kernel of the *Mahābhārata* consists of about 20,000 *Ślokas* or verses (*A History of Sanskrit Literature*, p. 283). He postulates three stages of its de-

thoroughly remodelled, extended, and enriched by Brahmans with an enormous amount of mythological, philosophical, religious, and didactic matter.[1] The *Āśvalāyana Grihyasūtra* furnishes the oldest evidence for the existence of the *Mahābhārata* in some form, and a land-grant of about 500 A.D., where it is definitely called "a collection of a hundred thousand verses," shows that by this date, or some time—say a century—earlier, it already existed in its present shape. Thus the beginnings, growth, revision, and interpolations of this tremendous compilation[2] are to be ascribed to this long interval between the fifth century B.C. and 400 A.D. *roughly*.

The Story in Brief

The framework of the epic deals with the great conflict between the Kauravas, the hundred sons of Dhritarāṣṭra, and the Pāṇḍavas, the five sons of Pāṇḍu. It was the culmination of their long-standing rivalry, which began thus :

After the death of Vicitra-Vīrya, the Kuru ruler, his younger son Pāṇḍu succeeded him, as the elder, Dhritarāṣṭra, was born blind. But owing to Pāṇḍu's premature death, Dhritarāṣṭra himself had to assume the reins of government within a short time. Being fond of his nephew, Yudhiṣṭhira, a man of rare virtue, he then nominated him heir-apparent. This aroused the jealousy of his eldest son, Duryodhana, who by his machinations compelled the Pāṇḍus to escape from the capital. During their wanderings they went to Pañcāla, where Arjuna won in a *svayaṁvara*

velopment. (*Ibid.*, p. 284).

[1] Extensive episodes and whole works, like the *Bhagavad Gītā*, have often been inserted to preach a moral.

[2] The Hindi *Prithvīrāja Rāso* of Cānd Bardāi has similarly been rehandled and expanded into its present bulky form.

the king's daughter, Draupadī, for himself and his brothers. This alliance proved a turning-point in their fortunes, for with a view to conciliating them Dhritarāṣṭra divided his kingdom, giving Hastināpur to his sons, and to his nephews a region of which Indraprastha became the capital. Here, too, the Pāṇḍavas were not allowed to reign in peace. Duryodhana lured Yudhiṣṭhira to play with him a game of dice, in which the latter lost everything—kingdom, wife, honour—and had to go in exile for twelve years. On the expiry of the period, he tried to get back the lost kingdom, but Duryodhana scornfully rejected Yudhiṣṭhira's terms. This led to a trial of strength. Hostilities lasted eighteen days on the famous battlefield of Kurukṣetra, and there was indescribable suffering and slaughter. Ultimately victory rested with Yudhiṣṭhira, who ruled gloriously for a brief period, and then retired to the Himālayas with his brothers, giving the care of the crown to the distinguished Parīkṣit.

Its Historical Value

In the main the story of the *Mahābhārata* is based on historical truth. Hastināpur and Indraprastha were doubtless real cities, and, despite their utter destruction by the ravages of time and the elements, their names still survive. The former is now represented by a hamlet of the same name on the Ganges in the Meerut district, and the latter is recognised in the small village of Indarpat on the Jumna, near modern Delhi. The traditional date, 3102 B.C.,[1] of the famous war between the rulers of the two places will hardly stand the test of criticism, but it has with some plausibility

[1] Mr. J. Rao thinks that the War took place in 3139 B.C., as according to a tradition Kriṣṇa passed away at the commencement of the *Kaliyuga* after the lapse of 36 years from the Mahābhārata war (*The Age of the Mahābhārata*, p. 5, etc.).

been placed about 1000 B.C.[1] For the *Śatapatha Brāhmaṇa* is familiar with the heroes of the epic, and it mentions Janamejaya as almost a recent personage. It is also known that the Kurus were a great people during the later Vedic period, although the Pāṇḍus do not at all figure either in the *Brāhmaṇas* or in the *Sūtras*. They first emerge into view with the later Buddhist literature as a mountain tribe. Does this show, as has sometimes been conjectured, that they were foreign immigrants, unrelated to the Kurus? At any rate, the theory is supported to some extent by their rude, uncourtly manners; practice of polyandry; and the name "Pāṇḍu," meaning "pale," which may perhaps indicate their Mongolian affinities. If the suggestion has any substance, the present text of the *Mahābhārata* gives an altogether garbled version of the actual origins and relations of the chief combatants. Similarly, it is difficult to accept its testimony regarding their allies. For instance, we learn that the Kuru hosts included the rulers of Prāgjyotiṣa (Assam), Avanti and Dakṣiṇāpatha, the Cīnas, Kirātas, Kambojas, Yavanas, Śakas, Madras, Kaikeyas, Sindhus, Sauvīras etc.[2] Apart from the fact that they were not all contemporaneous, it is doubtful whether these distant powers were interested in what was perhaps a local conflagration in Madhyadeśa. And surely they could not be called to arms as feudatories, for the nearness of the Kaurava and Pāṇḍava capitals itself shows that they did not hold an extensive sway. In short, there are undoubted deviations from historical accuracy in the *Mahābhārata*, but the central theme is authentic, and its characters,

[1] See also *Cam. Hist. Ind.*, Vol. I, pp. 276, 306-07. Another suggested date for the Mahābhārata war is 1400 B.C. (*Hindu Civilisation*, pp. 151-54; *Proc. Ind. Hist. Cong.*, 3rd. session, Calcutta, 1939, pp. 33-71).

[2] The allies of the Pāṇḍus were the kings of Pañcāla, Kośala, Kāśī, Magadha, Cedi, Matsya and the Yadus.

whose exploits were first popularised by story-tellers and minstrels, are by no means imaginary.

Gleanings from the Epics

The two Epics have not only many common phrases and fables but the conditions depicted in them are very much alike. We shall accordingly draw on both together for a picture of the life of the princes and the people. It must, however, be remembered that all the data do not relate to any particular period, as the Epics are a gradual growth, and were compiled and enlarged centuries after the events described.

(*a*) *The King*

The epic king was not an absolute despot satisfying his personal caprice only. He was amenable to the will of his brothers, councillors and the populace. He had also to recognise and respect the laws of different groups—*Kulas* (families), *Jātis* (castes), *Śreṇīs* (guilds), and *Pūgas* (communities). A wicked king was deposed or killed "like a mad dog." Even the immediate heir, if bodily defective, was not called to the throne. The king was installed and crowned with due ceremonies, and he was the leader of his people both "at home and in the field." He was expected to undertake expeditions with the advice of the ministers and the blessings of the priest, but in practice the king probably decided the matter himself in collaboration with his allies. The *Sabhā* had now become a mere body for consultation on military matters. The king lived amid pomp and splendour, and dancing-girls and women of easy virtue formed a part of his retinue. His chief recreations were music, gambling, hunting, animal fights, and wrestling contests. He meted out justice in the hall adjoining the palace. In old age he usually abdicated or retired in favour of his eldest son.

The capital was well protected with a surrounding wall, gates, towers, and moats, and supplied with the necessary amenities of life. There were music-halls, pleasure-gardens, well-laid out squares, beautiful buildings for the king and grandees of the court, and attractive booths for traders. The thoroughfares were lighted at night with lamps, and the dust-nuisance was allayed by watering them regularly.

(*b*) *Administration*

The king administered the realm with the help of a *Mantripariṣad* (ministry), which, according to the *Mahābhārata*,[1] consisted of four Brahmans, eight Kṣatriyas, twenty-one Vaiśyas, three Śūdras, and one of the Sūta caste. The Prime-minister and other councillors were men of the highest integrity, sagacity, and character. Besides, the king was assisted in the discharge of his duties by subordinate rulers (*Sāmantas*), the *Yuvarāja* (Crown-prince), the aristocracy, and such high officers as *Purohita* (Priest), *Camūpati* (Commander-in-chief), *Dvārapāla* (Chamberlain), *Pradeṣṭā* (Chief Justice), *Dharmādhyakṣa* (Superintendent of Justice), *Daṇḍapāla* (Presiding Judge of the Criminal Courts, or Chief Police Officer?), *Nagarādhyakṣa* (City-Prefect), *Kāryanirmāṇakrit* (Superintendent of Works), *Kārāgārādhikārı* (Superintendent of Prisons), *Durgapāla* (Warden of forts), etc.

The village or *grāma*, which was the lowest unit of administration, enjoyed considerable local autonomy under its headman (*Grāmaṇī*). Next, in the ascending scale were officers of ten (*Daśagrāmī*), twenty (*Viṁśatipa*), a hundred (*Śatagrāmī*), and a thousand villages (*Adhipati*). These officers collected revenue, detected crime, and maintained order within their jurisdictions, each being responsible to the next higher authority, and all even-

[1] *Śāntiparvan*, LXXXV, 7-11.

tually to the king.

(*c*) *The Army*

The king's army consisted of the Aryan nobles and commoners, who served as archers, slingers, rock-throwers, cavalrymen, chariot-drivers, elephant-riders, etc. The suggestion that fire-arms i.e., cannon and gunpowder were also used will hardly bear criticism. All that one may believe is that perhaps there were some "magically blazing" weapons like *Cakras* and arrows. It was deemed glorious for the warrior to die fighting. The Ksatriya fought for renown or for his chieftain. The king pensioned the widows of the fallen. Those captured in battle became the victor's slaves for a year at least. Sometimes, however, they were restored to freedom on certain conditions. Incidentally, it may be interesting to note that grass-eating was regarded as a sign of submission.

(*d*) *Gaṇas*

The *Śāntiparvan* of the *Mahābhārata* (Ch. 107, verses 6-32) also refers to the *Gaṇa* form of government i.e., the rule of the many. Its strength and prosperity depended on avoiding internal disunion, keeping counsels secret, obeying the leaders, and respecting established customs and usages. Sometimes a number of *Gaṇas* formed a sort of confederation (*Saṁgha*). For instance, chapter 81 of the *Śāntiparvan* represents Krisṇa as Head of the Andhaka-Vrisṇi league.

(*e*) *The People*

Caste was already a firmly-rooted institution. The nobles and the Brahmans had the upper hand in society, whereas the un-Aryan "Śūdras" were the under-dogs, and the slaves, "born to servitude," had no rights and possessions. The position of women had deteriorated as compared with what it was in the Vedic age. The custom of *Satī* is spoken of, and polygamy was practised. Going out veiled, sometimes referred to, was perhaps a court-custom. We also hear of *Svayaṁvaras*, i.e., self-selection of the bridegroom.

The bulk of the population lived in villages around forts (*durga*), perhaps of mud, tending cattle and practising agriculture. In times of danger, such as war and cattle-lifting raids, they took shelter inside these rude defences. The villagers were autonomous in ordinary affairs, but the king as the overlord administered justice and exacted taxes, which varied according to need and were perhaps paid mostly in kind. Merchants and others dwelt in towns. The former brought goods from afar, and paid customs duties. Townsfolk probably paid fines and taxes in money. The use of false-weights, sometimes alluded to, must have necessitated a careful supervision of the market-place by the state. The guilds of merchants and artisans wielded great influence, and, next to the priests, their heads (*mahājana*) were the objects of royal attention and solicitude.

The people were addicted to eating meat and drinking intoxicating liquors, although vegetarianism was gradually gaining ground on account of the doctrine of *Ahiṁsā*, stressed by the best minds of ancient times.[1]

(*f*) *Religion*

The worship of the striking phenomena of Nature was now left far behind. The Vedic deities had yielded precedence to the cult of the Hindu Trinity—Brahmā, Viṣṇu, and Śiva. New gods and goddesses, like Sūrya (Sun), Gaṇeśa and Durgā, arose, and it became a popular article of faith that Viṣṇu took on incarnation for establishing righteousness on earth. Along with this, the

[1] cf. *Chāndogya Upaniṣad*, III, 17, 4.

doctrine of transmigration was widely accepted. The Epics thus indicate that the foundations of modern beliefs had been well and truly laid.

Section C

THE DHARMAŚĀSTRAS

The Dharmaśāstras

The *Dharmaśāstras* represent the traditional teachings of certain Brahmanical schools on *Dharma* or civil and religious law. These texts, in *Śloka* metre, are the most important sources of Hindu law, and they throw a good deal of light on ancient Brahmanical institutions and civilisation. Of these codes, the principal ones are the *Mānavadharmaśāstra* belonging "rather to the time of our (Christian) era or before it than later;"[1] *Viṣṇudharmaśāstra*, which, though in Sūtra form, is decidedly posterior to the work of Manu, being largely based on it; *Yājñavalkyasmriti*, composed in Mithilā about the fourth century A.D.; and *Nāradasmriti* of about the fifth century A.D. Besides, there are minor *Smritis*, later *Nibandhas*, and commentaries, like the *Mitākṣarā*, which have also in course of time become authoritative.

Society : *Varṇas*

As in the *Dharmasūtras*, so in the *Dharmaśāstras*, caste-distinctions are the "frame" of society. Each of its limbs had its particular duties and privileges. Thus, according to Manu, the Brahman was to study and teach, perform *Yajña* and assist others in doing it, give alms and receive gifts; the Kṣatriya had to administer and to protect people, to spend money for advancing

[1] Hopkins, *Cam. Hist. Ind.*, Vol. I, p. 279.

knowledge and the cause of truth, to perform *Yajñas*, to study the scriptures, and above all, to fight bravely and fearlessly; the Vaiśya tended cattle, performed *Yajñas* etc., lent money on interest, and carried on trade and agriculture; and the Śūdra ministered to the physical comforts of the community, i.e., did menial service. The law-books also refer to "mixed castes," which originated from inter-marriages and illicit relations. Next, there were the non-Aryans, the *Mlecchas*, *Caṇḍālas*, *Svapākas*, etc., considered even lower than the Śūdras, almost beyond the pale of society.

The Stages of Life

The *Dharmaśāstras* mention the rules of the four stages of life (*Āśrama*), which applied to a *Dvija* or "Twice-born." The first, *Brahmacarya*, was the period of studentship. It began with the *Upanayana* ceremony, but the age of initiation often varied, as it depended on the circumstances and capacity of the youngster and the order to which he belonged. He learnt the Vedas and other sacred works or the Vedāṅgas and Darśanas etc., under the paternal care and guidance of teachers—Upādhyāyas and Ācāryas. The Brahmacārī's life was one of discipline and regular activity; he had to study diligently, worship daily and perform *Agnihotra*, beg alms, collect wood, and bring water etc., for his *guru* or teacher. Modern students may well take a leaf out of the book of their ancient compeers. After the completion of education, the *Brahmacārī* entered the *Gribasthāśrama* i.e., married and became a householder. A *Gribastha* was expected to give charity liberally and to clear the three debts he owed to gods, *Riṣis* and fore-fathers by *Yajña*, study and continence, and progeny respectively. In the third stage, *Vānaprastha*, an individual renounced all the "good things" of life and repaired to the solitude of the forest for calm contemplation, living there on the simplest fare, roots, and fruits, etc. Last of all was the stage of *Sannyāsa*, when all worldly connections were cut asunder and the body was subjected to mortification with a view to probing into the mysteries of existence and realising the ultimate Reality. The *Sannyāsī* subsisted on whatever he got by begging, and dedicated himself to the promulgation and dissemination of Truth and Righteousness. Such was the scheme of life enjoined on the upper three classes by the law-givers, but it is doubtful how far their injunctions were followed in practice. At any rate, it appears that *Sannyāsa* was generally meant for, and embraced by, the Brahmans only.

Position of Women

The *Dharmaśāstras* give us some idea of the position of women. At one place Manu says: "Where women are worshipped (honoured), the gods shower their blessings; but where they are not honoured, all acts are fruitless."[1] Curiously, however, in another verse he regards them as a source of evil leading men astray[2]. He does not also contemplate that a woman could ever be independent; she was to be under the tutelage or guardianship of her father in childhood, of her husband in youth, and of her sons in old age.[3] Further, according to Manu, women were of unstable temperaments, and they could not, therefore, be called as witnesses.[4] He countenan-

[1] cf. यत्र नार्यस्तु पूज्यन्ते रमन्ते तत्र देवताः ।
यत्रैतास्तु न पूज्यन्ते सर्वास्तत्राऽफलाः क्रियाः ।।
(*Manusmriti*, III, 56).

[2] cf. स्वभाव एष नारीणां नराणामिह दूषणम् (*Ibid.*, II, 213).

[3] cf. पिता रक्षति कौमारे भर्ता रक्षति यौवने ।
रक्षन्ति स्थविरे पुत्रा न स्त्री स्वातन्त्र्यमर्हति ।। (*Ibid.*, IX, 3).

[4] *Ibid.*, VIII, 77.

ces marriages of maidens when they are only twelve or eight years old;[1] but with regard to the sale of daughters he seems to express contradictory opinions.[2] A woman could be abandoned or divorced by the husband if she was barren or bore only daughters,[3] as also on the ground of unfaithfulness. Manu deprecates widow-remarriage and *Niyoga* (Levirate),[4] whereas Nārada permits both. *Strīdhana* apart, it is not made explicit by Manu if a widow was entitled to inherit her husband's property.[5] Nārada denies this right to her; Yājña-valkya, on the other hand, recognises a widow as her husband's heir. Although the custom of *Satī* does not obtain sanction till late, the lot of widows, debarred as they were from participating in auspicious ceremonies, must have been hard indeed. There is no mention of *Purdah*, and Manu admits that nobody could "guard a a woman by force." [6]

The State

The *Smritis* recognise monarchy as the normal form of government. Manu emphasises the necessity of having a king, for without him confusion would reign supreme all round (VII, 3). The king is attributed a divine origin. Manu says: "A king, though an infant, must not be despised because he looks a human being; verily, he is a great deity in human form."[7] He further adds: "Through his powers (*pra-*

[1] *Ibid.*, IX, 94.
[2] See *Manusmriti*, VIII, 204; III, 51; IX, 98.
[3] *Ibid.*, IX, 81.
[4] *Ibid.*, IX, 65.
[5] She could inherit the property of her issueless son (*Ibid.*, IX, 217).
[6] *Ibid.*, IX, 10.
[7] cf. बालोऽपि नावमन्तव्यो मनुष्य इति भूमिपः ।
महती देवता ह्येषा नररूपेण तिष्ठति ॥ (*Manusmriti*, VII, 8).

bhāva), he is Agni (Fire), Vāyu (Wind), Arka (Sun), Soma (Moon), Dharmarāṭ (Yama), Kubera, Varuṇa and Indra."[1] But at the same time it is to be noted that a king, though considered divine, is not represented as an absolute autocrat ruling with an iron hand for his own glory. He wielded the *Daṇḍa* only to maintain and enforce the *Dharma*. He was by no means regarded as above the *Law*. Indeed, it is said that *Law* destroys a king, who is indolent, sensual, tyrannical, and unrighteous.[2] According to Manu, the sources of *Dharma* are (*a*) the Vedas, (*b*) the Smritis, (*c*) *Ācāra* i.e., practices of pious men, and (*d*) self-satisfaction.[3] To these Yājñavalkya adds certain secondary sources, like deliberation, decision of *Pariṣads* and of learned persons, temporary needs not inconsistent with one's duties, royal edicts, special usages of guilds, corporations, etc., and local customs. Manu also refers to the laws of countries (*deśadharma*), of castes (*jātidharma*), of families (*kuladharma*), of heretics (*pāṣaṇḍas*), and of corporations (*gaṇas*).[4]

The *Dharmaśāstras* recognise a Kṣatriya alone as king, although history knows of kings belonging to other castes also. He led a well-regulated and strenuous life for the good and progress of his people and kingdom. In the discharge of his onerous responsibilities, he acted on the advice of a cabinet consisting of seven or eight ministers, and whatever orders the king gave were taken down, or passed on, by secretaries (*Sahāyas*). He received petitions from his subjects in the assembly-hall (*sabhā*), adjacent to the palace, and decided cases prescribing fines, religious expiations,

[1] *Ibid.*, VII, 7.
[2] *Ibid.*, VII, 17-28.
[3] cf. वेदोऽखिलो धर्ममूलं स्मृतिशीले च तद्विदाम् ।
आचारश्चैव साधूनामात्मनस्तुष्टिरेव च ॥ (*Ibid.*, II, 6).
[4] *Manusmriti*, I, 118.

and other penalties according to the nature of the offence and the status of the parties concerned. Besides the counsellors (*amātyas* or *mantris*), the king governed through a host of officials, high and low, *Mahāmātras* and *Yuktas*, assisted by spies (*cāras*), *agents provocateurs*, and other *instrumenta imperii*. The principal departments of state were those of (*a*) Espionage, which kept a strict watch everywhere and on everybody; (*b*) Finance, in charge of income and expenditure; perhaps it also supervised stores, working of mines, etc.; (*c*) Military, to preserve internal peace and repel foreign invasions; (*d*) Police, meant to apprehend criminals and maintain law and order; (*e*) Justice: it dispensed justice and settled disputes.

Lastly, a few words may be said about the divisions of the kingdom and local administration. The empire (*rāṣṭra*) comprised *deśas* or *janapadas* (regions or provinces), sub-divided into *viṣayas* (divisions), *nagaras* (cities) or *puras* (towns), and *grāmas* (villages). A *nagara* or city was placed under such a high officer as could inspire awe and confidence among citizens, and he was also given authority to deal with all matters concerning urban life (*Sarvārthacintakaḥ*).[1] A village was under the *Grāmika*, who was by way of remuneration daily supplied by the villagers with all the essential requisites of food, fuel, and drink (VII, 118). Over him were officers of ten villages (*Daśī*), who got one *kula* of land (sufficient to be tilled by six pairs of oxen); officers of twenty villages (*Viṁśateśa* or *Viṁśi*), assigned five *Kulas*; officers of a hundred villages (*Śateśa* or *Śatādhyakṣa*), allowed to have one village for their maintenance; and officers of a thousand villages (*Sahaśrapati*), remunerated with the revenues of a town.[2]

[1] *Manusmriti*, VII, 121.

[2] *Ibid.*, VII, 115, 118, 119. Viṣṇu omits the lord of twenty villages.

Justice

The *Smritis* generally enumerate eighteen causes of disputes, such as debts, sales without adequate title, fixing of boundaries, partition, non-payment of wages, breach of contract, partnership, adultery, violence, slander, larceny, robbery, etc. Thus, there were both kinds of cases—civil[1] and criminal. Those accused or suspected of theft had to prove their innocence by oath or ordeal, or sometimes both were combined. Manu mentions only two kinds of ordeal, fire and water (VIII, 114), but Yājñavalkya and Nārada add three more—scales, ploughshare, and poison—, and in the *Brihaspatismriti* the list mounts to nine varieties. Punishments inflicted or recommended are severe. For example, a cow-lifter had his nose cut off; and one who stole more than ten "kumbhas" of grain or silver or gold was executed (VIII, 320, 321). Any kind of treasonable conduct was usually visited with the death penalty. A Brahman, if found guilty, suffered excommunication, losing all right to inheritance. Indeed, Manu lays down that whatever crime a Brahman may commit, he should never be killed but only exiled (VIII, 380). At the same time, however, it may be observed that for a similar offence Manu prescribes a fine of one *Kārṣāpaṇa* only for a commoner and one thousand in the case of a king (VIII, 336). This was perhaps in accordance with the principle that the more eminent, influential, and knowing a man is, the heavier should his punishment be.

In civil law, the later *Smritis* treat of contracts and business partnerships—an idea not quite known to the earlier works and the *Sūtras*. Manu speaks only of religious partnership—Brahmans sharing fees (*dakṣiṇā*) by officiating together in a ceremony, but Yājñavalkya

[1] Not unoften civil litigation was avoided by arbitration.

mentions partners in trade and agriculture (II, 265). Similarly, Nārada and Brihaspati refer to them, and how their shares were to be determined. The law-books further show that loans were advanced, and the interests on them varied from fifteen per cent to sixty per cent according to the caste of the debtor. Usury is, however, generally discouraged; a Brahman specially was not expected to charge a high rate of interest.[1] If a debt could not be cleared, a Śūdra-debtor did some kind of labour in lieu of it. To enforce payment of debt, the practice of sitting and fasting unto death in front of the debtor's house was also sometimes resorted to.

Taxation

Taxes were intended to be light and equitable. The king is advised not to put too great a burden on the people, nor to resort to unrighteous and covetous methods. The *Mahābhārata*, for instance, exhorts him to gather taxes from his subjects like a bee sucking honey from flowers, or a calf drawing milk from the udders of the cow.[2] The great law-giver, Manu, allows a king to take from merchants one-fiftieth part of their profits in cattle and gold, and one-sixth, one-eighth, and one-twelfth of agricultural produce such as rice etc. (VII, 130); and also one-sixth of the profits in *ghee*, honey, perfumes, vegetables, fruits, roots, etc. (VII, 131, 132). Artisans, smiths, and labourers paid taxes in the form of a day's labour monthly (VII, 138). The *Śrotriyas* were, however, exempted from taxes (VII, 133). Others enjoying this immunity were the blind, the deaf, the lame, the aged, and those who helped the *Śrotriyas* (VII, 394). In conclusion, we may add that among other important

[1] Nārada altogether forbids Brahmans to practise money-lending (*Nāradasmriti*, I, 111).

[2] *Śāntiparvan*, Ch. LXXXVIII, 4-8.

sources of state-revenue were excise duties, customs or tolls, levies at ferries, etc.

Occupations and Trade

The *Smritis* indicate to some extent the material condition of the people by the crafts they mention. Thus, we hear of blacksmiths, goldsmiths, oilmen, dyers, tailors, washermen, potters, weavers, leather-workers, distillers, makers of bow and arrow, wood and metal-workers, etc. Besides, there were the mechanics and artisans, who were regarded as particularly useful members of society.

Agriculture was the mainstay of the mass of people, but trade, too, was not neglected. It was carried on by barter as well as by the medium of coins consisting of gold *Suvarṇas*, silver *Raupya māśakas*, *Dharaṇas*, and *Śatamānas*, and copper *Kārṣāpaṇas* (VIII, 135-137). The state fixed the prices of articles, and anybody guilty of adulteration or the use of false measures and weights was punished. It was prohibited to export grains in times of famine, or such goods as were under state-monopoly. There were well-known trade-routes, which occasionally were unsafe. Rivers were crossed by boats, and on land carts and animals conveyed merchandise to and fro.

PART II

CHAPTER VI

I. THE AGE OF THE BUDDHA

SECTION A

India just before the rise of Buddhism

The Buddhist and the Jain works are primarily devoted to the inculcation of religious ideas rather than the narration of political events. Occasionally, however, we obtain flashes of historical light from stories or anecdotes preserved in these books. It is thus incidentally that we learn of the sixteen great powers (*solasa mahājanapadas*), which must have existed in the seventh or the early sixth century B.C., as the list is given in the oldest Buddhist writings[1] and it does not exactly fit in with the conditions prevailing in the Buddha's time. These states were:

1. Kāśī with its capital of the same name, also called Vārāṇasī. It greatly prospered under the rule of the Brahmadattas. Aśvasena, father of *Tīrthaṁkara* Pārśva, is believed to have been one of the early kings of Kāśī.

2. Kośala: Its capital was Sāvatthi (Śrāvastī) or Saheṭ Maheṭh, in the Gonda district, during the Buddhist period. Prior to that, Śāketa and Ayodhyā had served as capitals. The rulers of Kośala and Kāśī were often

[1] See e.g., *Aṅguttara Nikāya* (I, 213; IV, 252, 256, 260). The Buddhist Sanskrit work, *Mahāvastu*, gives a slightly variant list. The names, as mentioned in the Jain text *Bhagavatī Sūtra*, are also different.

at war, and one of the former, Kaṁsa, uniformly styled "Bārānasiggaho" in Pāli works, eventually succeeded in annexing the latter kingdom. At any rate, it is known beyond doubt that Mahākośala, father of Pasenadi, exercised complete sway over Kāśī.

3. Aṅga: It lay to the east of Magadha with Campā, near Bhagalpur, as its capital. Some of the Aṅga monarchs, like Brahmadatta, appear to have defeated their Magadhan contemporaries. Subsequently, however, Magadha emerged supreme.

4. Magadha: It comprised the modern districts of Patna and Gayā, and the capital was Girivraja. Among the notable pre-Buddhist rulers of Magadha were Brihadratha and his son Jarāsandha.

5. Vajji: It represented a powerful confederation of eight clans, and was called after one of them. The other prominent clans were the Licchavis, the Videhas, and the Jñātrikas. In Buddhist literature, the Vajjis, like the Licchavis, are often located at Vaiśālī, which may accordingly be taken as the seat of the confederacy itself.

6. Malla: The territory of the Mallas was on the mountain slopes, probably to the north of the Vajjian confederation. They had two branches with their capitals at Kuśinārā and Pāvā. It is noteworthy that in Pre-Buddhist times the Mallas were a monarchy.

7. Ceṭi or Cedi: The land of the Ceṭis, identified with the Cedis of the older documents, lay near the Jumna, and roughly corresponded to modern Bundelkhand and adjacent tracts. Its metropolis was Suktimatī or Sotthivatī-nagara.

8. Vaṁsa or Vatsa: The country of the Vacchas was situated along the banks of the Jumna, to the north-east of Avanti, with its capital at Kauśāṁbī or Kosambī (modern Kosam, about thirty miles from Allahabad). It was Nīcakṣu who fixed his residence here after the destruction of Hastināpura. To this Bharata dynasty

belonged Parantapa, father of the Buddha's contemporary Udena.

9. Kuru: The Kuru realm was in the neighbourhood of Delhi. Among its towns may be mentioned Indapatta (Indraprastha) and Hatthinīpura (Hastināpura). The Kurus had now lost their political importance.

10. Pañcāla: This region roughly corresponded to modern Rohilkhand and a portion of the Central Doab. It had two divisions, Northern and Southern, the Ganges forming the boundary line. Their capitals were Ahicchatra and Kāmpilya respectively. One of the early Pañcāla kings, Dummukha (Durmukha), is credited with conquests in all directions.

11. Maccha or Matsya: The Matsyas ruled to the west of the Jumna and south of the Kurus. Their capital was Virāṭ-nagara (modern Bairāṭ, Jaipur State).

12. Śūrasena: The Śūrasenas were masters of a kingdom, of which Mathurā was the capital. It was here that the Yādava family played a great part.

13. Assaka: In the Buddha's time the Assakas were settled on the Godāvarī with Potali or Potana as their chief town, but when the list was drawn up their territory appears to have been between Avanti and Mathurā.

14. Avanti or Western Malwa: Its capital was Ujjain. The metropolis of its southern portion was Māhissatī or Māhiṣmatī (modern Māndhātā), where ruled the Haihayas in ancient times.

15. Gandhāra i.e., modern eastern Afghanistan: Its capital was Takṣaśilā (modern Taxilā, Rawalpindi district). The kingdom perhaps also included Kashmir.

16. Kamboja: The Kambojas also held sway in the north-west, being usually associated with the Gandhāras in epigraphic records and literature. We hear of

Rājapura and Dvārakā as its important towns.[1]

The list is curious in certain respects. It recognises Aṅga and Kāśī as still independent, and does not mention Orissa, Bengal, or any place south of Avanti.

Section B

INDIA AT THE TIME OF THE BUDDHA

(a) *Democratic or Autonomous Clans*

We learn from works in Pālī that at the time of the Buddha there were, besides monarchical states, a number of democratic or autonomous clans, some of little account, and others enjoying considerable power.[2] Amongst such communities we learn of the following :

1. The Śākyas of Kapilavatthu or Kapilavastu : They were settled on the border of Nepal and English territory, and their capital has been identified with the present Tilaurā-koṭ. They traced their descent from Ikṣvāku of the Solar race.

2. The Bhaggas of Suṁsumagiri : They were an ancient clan, being identical with the Bhargas of the *Aitareya Brāhmaṇa*. According to Dr. Jayasval, their seat of power was somewhere in or about the district of Mirzapur.[3]

3. The Bulis of Allakappa : Not much is known about them. They were located near the kingdom of Vethadīpa, presumably between modern Shahabad and Muzaffarpur.

4. The Kālamas of Kesaputta : The location of their chief town is uncertain. Has it anything to do

[1] See also Raychaudhuri, *Pol. Hist. Anc. Ind.*, 4th ed., pp. 81-129; *Cam. Hist. Ind.*, Vol. I, pp. 171-74; Rhys Davids, *Buddhist India*, pp. 23-29.

[2] See B. C. Law, *Kṣatriya Clans in Buddhist India* (1922); *Cam. Hist. Ind.*, Vol. I, pp. 174-78; *Buddhist India*, pp. 17-23.

[3] *Hindu Polity*, p. 49.

with the Keśins—a people mentioned with the Pañcālas in the *Śatapatha Brāhmaṇa*? Ālara, the great teacher of the Buddha, belonged to this tribe.

5. The Koliyas of Rāmagāma: They were to the east of the Śākyas, and the river Rohiṇī formed the dividing line between the two territories. Their relations were generally peaceful, but once the two clans came into conflict for the distribution of the waters of the Rohiṇī.

6. The Mallas of Pāvā, identified by Cunningham with Padraunā in the Gorakhpur district. Some, however, take Fazilpur to stand on the site of ancient Pāvā.

7. The Mallas of Kuśinārā, corresponding to modern Kasiā, where was discovered a small temple with a colossal statue of the Buddha in the *Parinibbāna* (*Parinirvāṇa*) posture.

8. The Moriyas of Pipphalivana: The identification of the capital is doubtful. They are said to have been a branch of the Śākyas, and were so called because their place ever resounded with the cries of peacocks (*mora*).

9. The Videhas of Mithilā (present Janakapur just within the Nepalese border). It is noteworthy that Videha, once ruled by Janaka of Upaniṣadic fame, was no longer under a monarchical government.

10. The Licchavis of Vaiśālī or modern Basārh in the Muzaffarpur district. They were an important people then. They were Kṣatriyas, and as such got a share of the Buddha's relics. They came into intimate contact with both Mahāvīra and the Buddha, and thus greatly profited by their exhortations and teachings. It is represented that the Licchavi oligarchy had a governing body comprising 7,707 Rājās. The Licchavis were noted for their full and frequent assemblies, and they carried on discussions in a spirit of confidence and concord.

Details about the Śākyas, etc.

The Buddhist works naturally give us more details about the Śākyas, as the Buddha came of this stock. We are told that at the helm of the state was the President, who bore the title of *Rājā*. It is uncertain whether he was drawn from one noble family only, and for what period he was elected. Thus, the Buddha's father, Suddhodana, was a *Rājā*, and we also hear of his cousin, Bhaddiya, holding this office. The business of the clan was carried on in the open assemblies in *Santhāgāras* or Mote-halls, where the young and the old, the rich and the poor alike were present. The Buddhist works give us a vivid idea of how deliberations were conducted in these assemblies, which were modelled on the religious *Saṁghas*.[1] We learn that there were regular meetings with proper seating arrangements made by a special officer called *āsanapaññāpaka* or *āsanaprajñāpaka*. Each meeting to be valid must have the requisite number of members present, but the chairman (*Vinayadhara*) was not counted for the purpose of the quorum. It was the duty of the whip (*Gaṇapūraka*) to complete the quorum by requisitioning the presence of members. The business began with the formal presentation (*sthāpanaṁ*) of the motion (*ñatti* or *jñāpti*), which was followed by a proclamation (*anussāvanaṁ*). Discussion related to the motion only, and all cantankerous and irrelevant talk was avoided and checked. A resolution (*pratijñā*) received one reading (*jñāpti-dvitīya-kamma*) and sometimes even three (*jñāpti-catuttha-kamma*). Silence of the members on the resolution was regarded as assent, but in case of disagreement they had recourse to various devices,

[1] See Jayasval, *Hindu Polity*, pp. 103-17; *Jour. U. P. Hist. Soc.*, Nov. 1934, Vol. VII, pt. II, pp. 59-69; B. C. Law, *Kṣatriya Clans in Buddhist India*, pp. 110-119.

like referring the matter to a committee, with a view to arriving at a unanimous decision. If no unanimity was possible, votes (*chanda*) were taken. Voting was by tickets (*salākā*), generally slips of wood, of various colours to indicate different views. The officer collecting votes was styled *Salākāgāhāpaka*, who was expected to show no kind of prejudice, malice, or fear. Voting was perfectly free and unfettered, and the majority view (*ye-bhuyya-sikaṁ*) prevailed. A question, once decided, was not to be re-opened. Records of proceedings also appear to have been kept by clerks. The procedure was thus truly democratic, anticipating in many respects the working of modern popular assemblies.

The clan subsisted on the produce of the rice-fields, and the cattle grazed in the village common or the forests. The villages were grouped together, and persons following particular crafts generally lived at one place. For instance, potters, smiths, carpenters and even those following priestly avocations had their own settlements. On the whole, the Śākyas were a peaceful community, and cases of theft or other crimes were rare. Perhaps they also had, like the Koliyas, regular police officers, who were distinguished by a special headgear, and who were notorious for "extortion and violence." When caught, the offenders were produced before a court of justice and carefully tried. The Vajjians, at any rate, had, as would appear from the *Aṭṭhakathā* or Buddhaghoṣa's commentary on the *Mahāparinibbāna-Sutta*, a very complicated judicial system; and punishments were awarded according to the Book of Precedents (*Pavenu Potthaka*), when the accused was uniformly adjudged guilty by a succession of officers, viz., Justices (*Viniccaya Mahāmātas*), Lawyers (*Vohārikas*), Doctors of Law (*Sūtra-dharas*), Council of Eight (*Aṭṭhakulakā*), the General (*Senāpati*), the Vice-Consul (*Upa-rājā*), and the Consul (*Rājā*). Each of these could, of course, let off the person charged, if considered innocent.[1]

(*b*) *Monarchical States*

During the lifetime of the Buddha the most important development in the politics of the country was the rise of the four kingdoms of Kauśāmbī (Vatsa), Avanti, Kośala, and Magadha.[2] They were now ruled by vigorous personalities, who had launched a policy of aggrandisement and absorption of neighbouring states. It inevitably led to conflicts among these powers, and, as we shall presently see, they were all ultimately welded into one mighty empire.

I. *The Vatsa kingdom*: Its capital was Kauśāmbī or Kosambī, identified with modern Kosam on the Jumnā, to the south of Allahabad. The Buddha's contemporary ruler of this land was Udena or Udayana, son of Śatānīka Parantapa, of the Bharata dynasty. Tradition has preserved many stories of Udena's love adventures and wars. For instance, the *Udenavatthu* informs us how once, after being captured—perhaps in war[3]—by Pajjota (Pradyota) of Avanti, Udena eloped by a clever ruse with his rival's daughter, Vāsuladattā or Vāsavadattā, and married her in his capital. Similarly, other legends mention the daughter of Dhriḍhavarman, whom he restored to the throne of Aṅga, and Padmāvatī, sister of king Darśaka of Magadha, as Udena's queens. Echoes of his *digvijaya* and victory in distant Kaliṅga, and enmity with a Kośala king come from later Sanskrit works like the *Kathāsaritsāgara* and the *Priyadarśikā*. It is,

[1] Rhys Davids, *Buddhist India*, pp. 20-23; B. C. Law, *K.C.B.I.*, pp. 120-21.

[2] D. R. Bhandarkar, *Carmichael Lectures on the Ancient History of India*, 1919.

[3] According to tradition, Udena, who was specially proficient in playing on the lute, fell into a trap dexterously set up by Pradyota. See also H. K. Deb, *Udayana Vatsarāja* (Calcutta, 1919).

no doubt, difficult to rely upon them implicitly, but that Udena was a powerful prince, who was at war with some of his contemporaries and formed matrimonial alliances with the ruling houses of Avanti, Magadha, and Aṅga, appears to be the substratum of truth.

We do not know whether his son, Bodhikumāra,[1] succeeded him. The *Kathāsaritsāgara*, at any rate, would have us believe that the kingdom of Kosambī was annexed to Avanti by Pālaka, son of Pradyota.

Lastly, it may be added that Kosambī became a centre of Buddhist activity from the time of the Buddha, who was himself often there. Udena was at first not favourably disposed towards the new teaching, but was subsequently much impressed by conversation with a celebrated Buddhist monk, named Piṇḍola.

II. *Avanti*: It was at this time ruled by Caṇḍa Pajjota (Pradyota), who had his capital at Ujjayinī. He had, as already noticed, matrimonial relations with Udena of Kauśāmbī and perhaps also with the Śūrasena king of Mathurā, called *Avantiputto*. Pajjota was a man of cruel disposition and inordinate ambition.[2] According to the *Purāṇas*, he had the "neighbouring kings subject to him." We have referred above to his clash with Udena, and his power apparently grew to such an extent that even Ajātaśatru had at one time to fortify his capital in expectation of an attack by Pajjota (Pradyota). His successors were weaklings, about whom history has not condescended to record anything of note. Of course, one of them, Pālaka, appears to have annexed Kosambī to his realm. He was over-

[1] A *Suttānta* of the *Majjhima Nikāya* is called after Bodhikumāra. As a *Yuvarāja* perhaps, he governed the Suṁsumagiri region, where he is said to have built a magnificent palace for himself.

[2] Pradyota was also known as Mahāsena on account of his large army (cf. तस्य बलपरिमाणनिर्वृत्तं नामधेयं महासेन इति (*Svapnavāsadattā*, V, 20).

thrown by Ajjaka or Āryaka, son of Gopāla, who did not ascend the throne in favour of his brother Pālaka. The *Purāṇas*, on the other hand, insert one Viśākhayūpa between the two.[1] Then followed Avantivardhana.

Avanti was another important centre of Buddhism. It was the home of several ardent adherents of the Buddha, like Mahākaccāna, Soṇa, Abhaya Kumāra, etc. Indeed, Dr. Rhys Davids suggests that Buddhism, born in Magadha, received its garb in Avanti, i.e., the Pālī canon was composed in the form of speech then current there.

III. *Kośala*: The rise of Kośala in the very centre of Northern India was an important feature in the political situation of the sixth century B.C. Already during the time of Kaṁsa, who was one of the predecessors of Pasenadi (Prasenajit), the Buddha's Kośalan contemporary, the long-drawn struggle between this kingdom and Kāśī had ended in the absorption of the latter. There are also references in Pālī literature indicating that the Śākyas had accepted the hegemony of Kośala, and Pasenadi is often described as "the head of a group of five *Rājās*." Besides, his sister's marriage with Bimbisāra, king of Magadha, must have further secured his position. But this very matrimonial alliance eventually became the cause of discord and conflict. For, as we shall see below, when Bimbisāra was starved to death by his son Ajātaśatru, the former's wife, Kośaladevī, died of grief. Pasenadi then confiscated the township of Kāśī, which had been conferred on her as pin-money (*nahāna-cuṇṇamūla*). This led to war between Kośala and Magadha, and it went on for some time with unvarying relentlessness but with varying fortunes. At last, a treaty was drawn up, and Pasenadi gave to Ajātaśatru the hand of his daughter, Vajirā, and also the revenues of the township of Kāśī in dispute.

[1] However, this appears to be a mistake.

Educated at Taxilā, Pasenadi was a large-hearted ruler. He gave lands on the royal domains to the Brahmans, and also donated groves and built monasteries for the Buddhist monks. His relations with the Buddha were specially cordial, and he often used to visit him and seek his advice in difficulties. Once Pasenadi expressed amazement at the way the great Teacher maintained peace within the Order (*Saṁgha*), whereas the former was sorely troubled by the depredations of robbers, like Aṅgulimālā, and by the machinations of his family and ministers. Indeed, Pasenadi lost his throne on account of the revolt of his son, Viḍuḍābha (Viruddhaka),[1] instigated by the minister Dīgha-Cārāyaṇa. Pasenadi invoked Ajātaśatru's aid, but before entering Rājagṛiha the Kośala king died of fatigue and anxiety at its gates. Ajātaśatru honoured him by a state-funeral, and wisely left Viḍuḍābha undisturbed.

Viḍuḍābha

Viḍuḍābha's reign is darkened by the terrible atrocity which he perpetrated on the Śākyas.[2] Apparently he did all that to avenge their treachery in marrying Vāsabha-Khattiyā, a slave-girl, to his father, but perhaps his real motive in invading the territories of the Śākyas was to destroy their autonomy completely. We do not know anything more about Viḍuḍābha or his successors.[3] When the curtain rises again, Kośala has become a part of Magadha.

[1] Other forms of the name are Viruḍhaka or Kṣudraka.

[2] Viḍuḍābha or Viruddhaka attacked the Śākyas and massacred a large number of them. This happened shortly before the Buddha's death, and it led to the dispersal of the Śākyas from their homeland.

[3] Their names are Kulaka, Suratha, and Sumitra: cf.
क्षुद्रकात् कुलको भाव्यः कुलकात् सुरथः स्मृतः ।
सुमित्रः सुरथस्यापि अन्त्यश्च भविता नृपः ।।

IV. *Magadha*: The land of Magadha, regarded with aversion in Vedic literature, first owed its political importance to the dynasty founded by Bṛihadratha. His son, Jarāsandha, who is the hero of many extravagant legends, appears to have been a powerful king. This line came to an end in the sixth century B.C., for when the Buddha lived and preached, Magadha was ruled by Bimbisāra of the Haryaṅka-kula.[1] He was the son of a petty chieftain, Bhaṭṭiya, and was also known as Seniya or Śreṇika. At first, he held his court at Girivraja, but later another capital, aptly called Rājagṛiha,[2] arose around his new palace.

Bimbisāra extended his influence in the beginning by a policy of matrimonial alliances. His principal queens were Kośaladevī, sister of Pasenadi; Cellanā, daughter of the Licchavi prince Ceṭaka; and Kṣemā, Madra (Central Punjab) princess. These marriages not only show the high position of Bimbisāra among his royal contemporaries, but they seem to have also paved the way for the expansion of Magadha. For instance, Kośala-devī alone brought as pin-money a part of Kāśī yielding a revenue of a hundred thousand.

Bimbisāra also enlarged his kingdom by his military skill. We learn that after defeating Brahmadatta, he boldly annexed Aṅga, which roughly corresponded to modern Monghyr and Bhāgalpur districts. That other territories were absorbed into Magadha during the reign of Bimbisāra is further clear from the estimate of its size given by the Pālī commentator Buddhaghoṣa, according to whom it had almost doubled itself during the interval between the Buddha and Bimbisāra's successor. The government was well organised, and the

[1] We have followed the Pālī version. The *Purāṇas*, on the other hand, make Bimbisāra a descendant of Śiśunāga. See *Infra*.

[2] Identified with modern Rajgir. The Cyclopean walls of the old capital are among the most remarkable finds in India. Rājagṛiha was on the outskirts of Girivraja.

activities of the high officers of the realm, called Mahāmattas (Mahāmātras), were strictly watched and controlled. The administration of criminal law was also severe.

Bimbisāra cultivated friendly relations with distant states, for he is said to have received an embassy from a king of Gandhāra, named Pukkusāti. Incidentally it shows that Bimbisāra must have flourished when Gandhāra was still an independent kingdom, i.e., prior to the Achæmenid conquest about 516 B.C. We can arrive at a closer approximation to truth by another method. According to the Ceylonese chronicles Bimbisāra's reign lasted 52 years,[1] and Ajātaśatru had ruled for 8 years at the time of the Buddha's death, which has been fixed by Geiger and other scholars in 483 B.C. Add to this sixty years (52+8), and we get 543-44 B.C. as the date of Bimbisāra's accession to the throne.[2] He was a patron of the Buddha from the very start of the latter's career, and as a mark of good-will Bimbisāra presented the famous Bamboo grove (Karanda-Venu-vana) to the *Saṁgha*. He also fed monks and exempted them from paying fares and ferry dues. But Bimbisāra made endowments in favour of other sects as well, and we cannot, therefore, be sure how far he progressed along the path. Indeed, the *Uttarājjhayana* (*Uttarādhyayana*) *Sūtra* and other Jain works even represent him as a devotee of Mahāvīra and having faith in his Law.

Ajātaśatru

Bimbisāra was succeeded by his son Ajātaśatru, also called Kuṇika, about the year 491 B.C. The latter was at first his father's viceroy at Campā, the capital of

[1] According to the *Purāṇas*, the duration of his reign was only 28 years.

[2] See also *Pol. Hist. Anc. Ind.*, 4th ed., pp. 184-86.

Aṅga, where he learned the art of government. Tradition says that at the instigation of Devadatta, a cousin of the Buddha and his rival to the leadership of the *Saṁgha*, Ajātaśatru imprisoned his father and starved him to death.[1] It is difficult to accept this story literally, but what appears probable is that Bimbisāra's end was tragic and perhaps due to foul play.[2] Afterwards, Ajātaśatru is represented in the *Sāmaññaphala-Sutta* as having expressed remorse to the Buddha for his heinous crime, and the great Teacher felt impressed by his penitence and exhorted him to "go and sin no more." Ajātaśatru's visit to the Buddha is also depicted in one of the Bhārhut sculptures of about the middle of the second century B.C.

The manner of her husband's death gave such a tremendous shock to Kośaladevī that she too died of grief. Pasenadi immediately confiscated the revenues of the Kāśī estate, which had been settled on her as 'pin-money', and this resulted in hostilities between him and Ajātaśatru. The duel was a prolonged affair, fortune favouring each combatant alternately. At last, they came to terms, and the Magadhan monarch got not only the disputed township of Kāśī, but also the hand of Pasenadi's daughter, Vajirā. Henceforth Kāśī was permanently absorbed into the kingdom of Magadha.

The next important event in Ajātaśatru's reign was his conflict with the Licchavis. Traditions differ regarding its cause. Any of these—Ceṭaka's refusal to surrender Ajātaśatru's half-brothers, Halla and Vehalla, who had taken shelter in Vaiśālī with certain prized objects, or an alleged treachery on the part of the Lic-

[1] This is alleged against Ajātaśatru, when his plot to kill Bimbisāra with a dagger miscarried, and the latter had abdicated in favour of him.

[2] The Jaina tradition, however, does not represent Ajātaśatru as a parricide.

chavis concerning a mine of gems—may have provoked war.[1] But the real motive appears to have been the destruction of the power of the neighbouring oligarchy, which was without doubt a thorn in the side of an ambitious potentate. Ajātaśatru took all possible precautions to ensure victory. He sent his trusted ministers, Sunīdha and Vassākara, to sow dissensions among the Licchavi chiefs. He organised his army carefully, and equipped it with powerful and destructive weapons. The war, though long and sanguinary, ended in favour of Ajataśatru, and the Licchavi territories passed under his rule. Perhaps after the conquest of Vaiśālī, he carried his arms further northward, and the regions up to the mountains accepted submission to him. Thus the annexation of Aṅga, Kāśī, Vaiśālī, and other surrounding lands made Magadha the mightiest kingdom in Northern India. It naturally aroused the jealousy of Avanti, and although we hear of Ajātaśatru fortifying his capital in anticipation of Pradyota's invasion, we do not know if it ever materialised in his time. According to Pālī works, Ajātaśatru's reign lasted 32 years, but the *Purāṇas* give 27 years only as its duration. The Jain works testify that he was a follower of their faith, but the Buddhist texts would have us believe that in his later days Ajātaśatru did honour to the Buddha and found solace in his ethical teachings. Thus, it was due to his regard for the Buddha that Ajātaśatru claimed a share of his relics, and enshrined them in a *Stūpā*.

SECTION C

RELIGIOUS MOVEMENTS

The sixth century B.C. is one of the cardinal epochs in human history. It was an age of extraordinary

[1] *Pol. Hist. Anc. Ind.*, 4th ed., p. 171.

mental and spiritual unrest in several regions widely apart. For instance, Zoroaster in Persia and Confucius in China were promulgating their teachings about this time. In India, too, ardent spirits were unusually active in quest of Truth, and the centre of this ferment was Magadha, where the Brahmanic influence was not yet so deep or potent. Already the *Upaniṣads* had marked a stage of revolt against cumber-some rituals and bloody sacrifices. The pretensions and caste-exclusiveness of the Brahmans, which were galling to the people in general, had further prepared the ground for new doctrines to germinate. A host of teachers went up and down the country preaching and propagating their solutions of the abstruse problems of God and Soul, and of how to escape from the endless misery of births and deaths by the light of knowledge or the rigours of self-mortification. Numerous reforming schools[1] thus sprang up, but most of them either died out or outlived their utility in course of time. Two of these, known as Jainism and Buddhism, however, proved strong enough to survive, and even today they profoundly influence the thought and faith of mankind.

Career of Mahāvīra

According to the Jains, their religion originated in the remotest ages of antiquity. They believe that Mahāvīra, the last *Tīrthaṁkara*, was preceded by twenty-three other prophets. Of these, the penul-

[1] The Pālī works mention that, when the Buddha began his ministry, there existed no less than sixty-two different sects (according to the Jain texts, their number was 363). Among these were the Ājīvikas, Jaṭilakas, Muṇḍa-sāvakas, Parivrājakas, Māgandikas, Gotamakas, Tedaṇḍikas, etc. The most prominent teachers of the time, besides the Buddha, were: Purāṇa-Kassapa, Makkhali-Gośāla, Nigaṇṭha-Nāṭaputta, Ajita-Keśakambalin, Pakuddha-Kacchāyana, Sañjaya-Belaṭṭhaputta.

timate, Pārśvanātha, appears to have been an historical personage, but the rest are all dim and shadowy figures, wrapped up in mythology. He was the son of king Aśvasena of Benares, but Pārśva abandoned the royal state in favour of a life spiritual. His main injunctions were: (1) non-injury, (2) non-lying, i.e., not to tell lies, (3) non-stealing, (4) non-possession. We do not know how far he progressed in his mission, but the next *Tīrthaṁkara*, Mahāvīra, who followed Pārśva after about 250 years, definitely placed the religion on a secure footing. Vardhamāna, as Mahāvīra was known earlier in his family circles, was born at Kuṇḍagrāma, near Vaiśālī. He was the son of Siddhārtha, Head of the Kṣatriya Jñātrika sect, and his mother was Triśālā, sister of the Licchavi chieftain, Ceṭaka, whose daughter was married to Bimbisāra. Vardhamāna thus had an aristocratic lineage, and this must have materially helped him in his ministry. We learn that after leading an ordinary householder's life till the age of thirty, he wandered away from home to become an ascetic. He practised severe meditation and subjected his body to the utmost self-torture for twelve long years. At last, he attained to omniscience (*kaivalya*), and was hailed as the 'Nirgrantha' (free of fetters), or the 'Jina' (conqueror), from which is derived the name of his followers. From this time onward till his death, thirty years later, at the age of seventy-two, Mahāvīra spread the tenets of his religion in Magadha, Aṅga, Mithilā, and Kośala. To the four virtues enjoined by Pārśva, he added a fifth, viz., strict chastity. He gave up clothing, and went about naked. Some scholars trace the division into Svetāmbaras and Digambaras to this new practice of Mahāvīra. But this view does not appear to be tenable, as the schism took place in the third century B.C. after the return of the Jains from South India, where they had retired owing to famine under the leadership of Bhadrabāhu. Mahāvīra passed away at Pāvāpurī (in the Patna district), perhaps in *circa* 527 B.C.[1] This, date, however, is open to certain objections.

Main Doctrines of Jainism

The Jains repudiate the authority or infallibility of the Vedas,[2] and do not attach any importance to the performance of sacrifices. They believe that every object, even the smallest particle, possesses a soul (*Jīva*), endowed with consciousness. A natural corollary of this principle was their scrupulous observance of *Ahiṁsā* or non-injury to any sentient being. Sometimes, however, its strict enforcement led to strange contradictions, for history records instances of Jain kings ordering the execution of persons guilty of killing animals. The Jains reject the conception of a Universal Soul or a Supreme Power as the Creator and Sustainer of the universe. According to them, "God is only the highest, noblest, and fullest manifestation of the powers which lie latent in the soul of man."[3] The Jain goal of life is to attain deliverance from the fetters of mundane existence. The cause of the soul's embodiment being the presence of *kārmic* matter, *Mokṣa* can be achieved, if and when a Jain gets rid of all *Karma* inherited from past lives, and acquires no new one. The way to this lies through the Three Jewels (*Triratna*) of right faith, right knowledge, and right conduct. The Jains greatly emphasise the practice of penances, such as *yogic* exercises and fasting, even to the point of death. The idea is that rigorous discipline gives strength to the soul, and keeps the lower matter subdued.[4]

[1] Another date suggested for Mahāvīra's decease is 546 B.C.
[2] The Jains have got their own Canon.
[3] Sir S. Radhakrishnan, *Indian Philosophy*, Vol. I, p. 331.
[4] See Mrs. S. Stevenson, *The Heart of Jainism*; Jagmanderlal

Life of the Buddha

Like Jainism, Buddhism also was founded by an illustrious Kṣatriya. His family name was Gotama, but he is better known by his spiritual title of the Buddha. He was born of Māyā in the Lumbinī garden (modern Rummindei or Rūpan-dehi), near Kapilavastu. His father, Suddhodana, was the "Rājā" of the proud Sākya clan. Fearing his son's reflective cast of mind, he married him to Gopā or Yaśodharā[1] at an early age, and surrounded him with all kinds of enjoyments and luxuries. But, in a world full of disease and misery, these did not offer any satisfaction to the meditative Gotama. He, therefore, escaped one night in his 29th year from the palace, leaving his wife and newly-born son Rāhula behind, to seek solace in the life of a recluse. Not getting any mental repose or calm from his studies under two distinguished teachers of the time named Ālāra Kālāma and Uddaka Rāmaputta, Gotama went to the sylvan retreats of Uruvela, near modern Bodhgayā, to practise the severest austerities. He subjected himself to such rigorous discipline that he was reduced to a mere skeleton. But he did not in any way advance towards the goal, and consequently he gave up the method of self-torture, so common then, as fruitless, and partook of milk-food offered by Sujātā, who had gone to worship the tree-deity. At last, one night, while he sat under an umbrageous *Pīpal* tree on a seat made of grass, the light dawned on him and he became the Buddha, the perfectly Enlightened One, at the age of thirty-five. After some misgivings whether people will understand its abstruse nature,

Jaini, *Outlines of Jainism* (Cambridge, 1916); Barodia, *History and Literature of Jainism* (Bombay, 1909); Radhakrishnan, *Indian Philosophy*, Vol. I, Ch. VI, pp. 286-340; C. L. Shah, *Jainism in Northern India*.

[1] Other texts call Gotama's wife Bhaddakacchā or Bimbā.

he decided to promulgate his message to the world, and accordingly he first turned the wheel of the Law in motion at Sarnath. His first converts were those very five *Bhikṣus*, who had abandoned his company in the forests of Uruvelā, thinking Śramaṇa Gotama to have deviated from the path of penances for the pleasures of the palate. For the next forty-five years his life was one of incessant activity. He preached to the people in their vernacular, and won their heart and mind by his noble teachings, kindness, moral grandeur, and deep sympathy. Princes and peasants, all extended their support to him, and within a short time his *Saṁgha* grew into a mighty organisation. Buddhism had a chequered career in India, and although it has now almost disappeared from the land of its birth, it is still a powerful religion in the East and Far East, and holds sway in various forms over countless millions of men.[1]

Date of the Buddha's Death

After a long and successful ministry, the Buddha passed away at the age of eighty at Kuśinagara, modern Kasiā in the Gorakhpur district, where some years ago a colossal statue of the Master was discovered in a reclining posture. It is difficult to determine exactly the date of this event, which may be regarded as one of the most important points in our system of chronology. Vincent Smith placed it in 486-87 B.C., but the year 483 B.C., as proposed by Fleet and Geiger on a thorough examination of the available data, may be accepted as very near the truth.[2]

[1] See E. J. Thomas, *The Life of Buddha* (London, 1927); H. Oldenberg, *Buddha* (London, 1882).

[2] Some scholars, on the other hand, take 543 B.C. to be the date of the Buddha's *Parinibbāna*.

His Teachings

The teachings of the Buddha were essentially simple and of a practical nature. He did not concern himself with the problems of God or the Soul, as he believed such discussions were of no help in one's moral progress. He declared that everything was transitory or impermanent (*sarvaṁ aniccaṁ* or *anityaṁ*). Like other teachers of his day, he regarded existence as an evil; but he was far more deeply stirred by the grim reality of sorrow and suffering. He, therefore, mainly addressed himself to analysing its cause and finding out a way leading to its cessation. These were the Four Noble Truths (*Cattāri-ariya-saccāni*), which he proclaimed with all his earnestness, *viz.*, sorrow (*dukkha*); cause of sorrow (*dukkha-samudāya*); cessation of sorrow (*dukkha-nirodha*); and the path leading to the cessation of sorrow (*dukkha-nirodhagāminī-pratipad*). According to him, the root of all human misery was 'desire' (*tanhā*), and its annihilation was the surest means of ending unhappiness. He held that death was no escape from it, as it led to rebirth and further suffering. The suppression of 'thirst' (*tanhā*) was possible if people followed the noble Eightfold Path, viz., (1) right belief, (2) right thought, (3) right speech, (4) right action, (5) right means of livelihood, (6) right endeavour, (7) right recollection, (8) right meditation.[1] The Buddha called it the Middle Path (*Majjhima-magga*) as it avoided both the extremes of gross luxury and grim austerity. Even those who were unable to retire from the concerns of life could obtain success by following it. The members of the *Saṁgha* were to strive after the attainment of *Nibbāna* or *Nirvāṇa*, or "extinc-

[1] *cf.* (१) सम्यक् दृष्टि (२) सम्यक् संकल्प (३) सम्यक् वाक् (४) सम्यक् कर्मान्तः (५) सम्यक् आजीवः (६) सम्यक् व्यायामः (७) सम्यक् स्मृति (८) सम्यक् समाधि ।

tion of personality"(?). They were exhorted to be strictly pure in thought, word, and deed. As an aid to this, he laid down ten commandments, of which the first five were to be observed by the laity also : (1) not to covet others' property, (2) not to kill, (3) not to use intoxicants, (4) not to tell lies, (5) not to commit adultery, (6) not to take part in singing and dancing, (7) not to use unguents, flowers, or perfumes, (8) not to eat at odd hours, (9) not to sleep on comfortable beds, (10) not to accept or keep money. The Buddha thus prescribed a severely practical code of conduct for his disciples, and discouraged philosophic speculation considering it unprofitable for one's spiritual advance. What was still more important is his healing declaration that all could partake of his message, irrespective of sex, age, or position in society.[1]

Relation Between Jainism and Buddhism

For a long time it was commonly believed that Jainism was only an offshoot of Buddhism or *vice versa.* It is, of course, now too late in the day to hold this opinion, although the similarities between the two systems are remarkable indeed. Both are indifferent to the authority of the Vedas, and deny the efficacy of rituals. Both ignored God, and decried distinctions based on birth. Both emphasised the principle of *Ahiṁsā* and the effect of *Karma* upon an individual's future life. Both tolerated popular superstitions and beliefs. These are no doubt striking resemblances, but their approach towards certain fundamental problems is widely different. For example, Buddhism propounds that everything lacks an ego (*Anātmavāda*),

[1] See T. W. Rhys Davids, *Buddhism* (London, 1877); J. H. C. Kern, *Manual of Indian Buddhism* (Strassburg, 1896); A. B. Keith, *Buddhist Philosophy in India and Ceylon* (Oxford, 1923); Radhakrishnan, *Indian Philosophy*, Vol. I, Chaps. VII-XI, pp. 340-703.

whereas according to Jainism every object or particle in this world is tenanted by a soul (*Jīva*). Jainism glorifies self-mortification. The Buddha, on the other hand, recommended the Middle Path, avoiding the extremes of sensualism and asceticism. Their conceptions about deliverance and salvation also are not quite similar. Being products of the same age and land, it was inevitable that Jainism and Buddhism should have some common features, but at the same time their differences were so marked that often there was a good deal of rivalry between them.

Section D

ECONOMIC CONDITION[1]

Village Organisation

The *Jātakas*, the *Piṭakas*, and other Pālī works furnish interesting information on the economic condition of India at the time of the rise of Buddhism. As at present, the bulk of the people then lived in villages. The population of a village (*grāma*) was concentrated within a relatively small area, as the dwellings (*gribas*) were all clustered together to ensure safety. Around the villages there were arable fields (*grāma-kṣetra*), divided into plots by channels for water or marked by a common fence. The holdings were usually small, but larger ones were not altogether unknown. The village folk had common rights over the adjacent forest (*vana* or *dāva* or *dāya*) and the grazing grounds, where the cattle belonging to various householders were sent under the charge of a collectively hired herdsman (*gopālaka*).

The rural economy was based on what may be

[1] Rhys Davids, *Buddhist India*, Ch. VI, pp. 87-106; *Cam. Hist. Ind.*, Vol. I, Ch. VIII, pp. 198-219.

called 'peasant proprietorship'. But no owner could sell or mortgage his part of the land without the consent of the village council. He cultivated the fields himself, but often employed labourers or slaves for the purpose. There were no big estates or landlords. The king received the tithes and his share, varying from one-sixth to a twelfth,[1] of the produce in kind through the headman (*gāmabhojaka*). The latter was an important person in the village. He carried on there the business of the government. At that time he was probably either a hereditary officer or was elected by the village council, which also helped him in maintaining local peace and security. The village residents were endowed with a sturdy civic spirit. They united of themselves in such undertakings as laying irrigation channels, building mote-halls, rest-houses, etc. The women extended their full co-operation in these works of public utility. On the whole, each village was self-sufficient, and life was simple and unsophisticated. There were few rich men and no paupers. Crime was rare, but people sometimes suffered greatly from famines occasioned by droughts or floods.

Cities

Very few cities (*nagaras* or *nigamas*) are mentioned in Buddhist literature. Of these, the most important were: Bārāṇasī (Benares), Rājagaha (Rājagriha), Kauśāmbī, Sāvatthi (Śrāvastī), Vesālī (Vaiśālī), Campā, Taxilā, Ayojjhā or Ayodhyā, Ujjeni (Ujjain), Mathurā, etc. Imperial Pāṭaliputra was yet to be founded. The towns were generally fortified, and the houses were built of wood and brick. The poor then, as now, lived in meagre dwellings, the rich in im-

[1] Manu says that the king should take as his share 1/50th of cattle and gold from merchants and 1/6th or 1/8th or 1/12th of the produce from cultivators (*Manusmriti*, VII, 130). Besides, we sometimes hear of special levies, forced labour and other exactions.

posing and sumptuous structures, well plastered and painted both inside and outside. In the cities the people enjoyed greater comforts and led a gayer life.

Arts and Crafts

The main industry of the people was, of course, agriculture. Besides, they had made considerable progress in such crafts as wood-work including cart-making and ship-building, architecture, leather-dressing, pottery, garland-making, weaving, ivory-work, confectionery, jewellery, and work in precious metals.[1] There were other occupations (*hīna-sippas*), e.g., tanning, fishing, hunting, dancing, acting, snake-charming, rush-weaving, etc., to which was attached a social stigma. It was the general tendency of young men to follow their fathers' callings, but exceptions are also recorded. For castes did not always determine crafts. Thus, we find a weaver turning an archer, Kṣatriyas working in the fields, and Brahmans taking to trade, carpentry, and even tending cattle.

Guilds

Persons following the same profession normally organised themselves into guilds (*śreṇī*), and often lived, or had their business centre, in one ward or street (*vīthi*) of the town. The *Jātakas* name at least eighteen such groups. Each had a President (*Pamukha*) or Alderman (*Jeṭṭhaka*), whose position was one of great responsibility and honour. Sometimes, to ensure greater cohesion different *vargas* or guilds perhaps combined together under a common head.

[1] The *Jātakas* often give a list of eighteen principal crafts. This included the Worker in wood (*Vaḍḍhakī*), Smith (*Kammāra*), Worker in stone (*Pāṣāṇa-koṭṭaka*), Weaver (*Tantu-vāya*), Dyer (*Raṅgakāra*), Potter (*Kumbha-kāra*), Barber (*Nahāpaka*), etc.

Trade and Trade-Routes

In those days trade, both inland and foreign, was fairly brisk. Merchants made fortunes by dealing in articles like silks, muslins, cutlery, armour, brocades, embroideries, rugs, perfumes, drugs, ivory, ivory-work, jewellery, etc. They went long distances up and down the great rivers of the country, and even undertook coasting voyages to Burma and Ceylon from Tāmralipti (Tamluk) on the east, and from Bharukaccha (Broach) on the west. There are also references to voyages as far as Bāveru (Babylon). Inland, the traders followed certain well-established routes, connecting the various parts of India. One of them ran from Sāvatthi (Śrāvastī) to Patiṭṭhāna or Pratiṣṭhāna (modern Paithān in the Nizam's dominions); another linked Sāvatthi with Rājagaha; a third skirted along the base of the mountains from Taxilā to Śrāvastī; and a fourth connected Kāśī with the ports of the western coast.[1] In crossing the desert of Rajputana the caravans were guided in the cool of nights by stars under the direction of 'land-pilots.' Brigands infested these routes, especially the less frequented ones, and looted merchandise when they could safely do so. Such dangers, coupled with the taxes and octroi duties paid in each state that was crossed, must have raised the prices of commodities very high.

Money

The age of barter was almost drawing to a close. Now the ordinary medium of exchange or transactions was a coin called *Kahāpaṇa* (*Kārṣāpaṇa*). It was of copper, 146 grains in weight, and marks were punched on it by merchants or guilds, guaranteeing its standard and

[1] These long routes had several intermediate halts, and there were ferries on the way for crossing rivers.

fineness. Other coins referred to in Pālī texts were *Nikkha* and *Suvaṇṇa* of gold. Smaller copper tokens are called *Māsaka* and *Kākanikā*. We also hear of instruments of credit and interest (*vaḍḍhi*) paid on loans.[1] Banks were then unknown, and surplus money was either converted into ornaments, or hoarded in jars and buried in the ground, or put in the custody of a friend and a written record was kept of it.

II. *Successors of Ajātaśatru*

According to works in Pālī, Ajātaśatru was succeeded by his son Udāyin or Udāyibhadra (cf. *Dīgha Nikāya*) about 459 B.C. The *Purāṇas*, however, insert after Ajātaśatru another king named Darśaka, whose historicity is also established by the *Svapnavāsadattā* of Bhāsa.[2] Some scholars suppose that the *Purāṇas* have wrongly placed him, and identify him with Nāga-dāsaka, the last ruler of the line of Bimbisāra. Udāyin is chiefly known for having founded the city of Pāṭaliputra on a spot where his father had built a fort to ward off an expected attack from the side of Avanti. It was strategically situated on the confluence of the Sone and the Ganges,[3] and was thus better suited to serve as the capital of a growing kingdom. Udāyin's successors, Anuruddha, Muṇḍa, and Nāga-dāsaka, were mere nonentities,[4] and although the story that all of them were parricides might not be true,[5] it is certain that their weakness or

[1] Money-lending (*Iṇa-dāna*) was, of course, regarded as a legitimate profession, but usury was strongly disfavoured.

[2] We are told that Darśaka was king of Magadha, and his sister Padmāvatī was married to Udena (Udayana) of Kosambī.

[3] The junction of these two rivers is now several miles up Patna.

[4] As shown below, the successors of Udāyin, according to the *Purāṇas*, were Nandivardhana and Mahānandin.

[5] Vincent Smith, however, refers to the analogy of Parthian history, which knows of three successive parricide princes, *viz.*, Orodes, Phraates IV, and Phraates V, (*E. H. I.*, 4th ed., p. 36, n. 2).

unpopularity must have gone a long way to enable Śiśunāga—a mere *amātya* (*minister*)—to seize the throne for himself. This king is represented in the *Purāṇas* as an ancestor of Bimbisāra, but the Ceylonese chronicles indubitably prove that the former came several generations after the latter.[1] After the *coup d'etat*, Śiśunāga is said to have made Girivraja his residence, placing his son at Vārāṇasī (Benares) as governor.[2] The most noteworthy achievement of Śiśunāga was the annihilation of the power of the Pradyotas, with whom a clash had become inevitable after their conquest of Kosambī. Probably the vanquished king of Avanti was Vartivardhana or Avantivardhana, and it is significant that the Pradyota dynasty disappears from the stage of history about this time. Thus, this triumph made Śiśunāga ruler of almost the whole of Madhyadeśa, Malwa, and other territories in the North.

The Nandas

About the middle of the fourth century B.C., the Śiśunāga dynasty was overthrown by an upstart named Mahāpadma,[3] who initiated a line known in history as that of the Nandas.

Origin

Traditions differ regarding his origin. According

[1] *Pol. Hist. Anc. Ind.*, 4th ed., pp. 178-79. Dr. H. C. Raychaudhuri's interpretation of the data available for the period seems to us most convincing.

[2] cf. वाराणस्यां सुतं स्थाप्य संयास्यति गिरिव्रजं ।

[3] Called Ugrasena in Pālī works. The name is in allusion to his huge army. Similarly, the name Mahāpadma perhaps indicates that his army was as big as could be arranged in the lotus fashion (*Padmavyūha*). Or, does it signify that he possessed wealth amounting to a *Padma*? Has the name Kālāśoka or Kākavarṇa anything to do with his dark complexion?

to the *Purāṇas*, he was born of a Śūdra woman, but in Jain works he is described as the son of a courtesan by a barber. The Greek writer, Curtius, gives a slightly different account. He deposes that Alexander's Magadhan contemporary was the son of a barber, who by his good looks had won the queen's heart, and who subsequently assassinated the reigning sovereign, perhaps Kālāśoka or Kākavarṇa, represented in the *Harṣacarita* to have been done to death with a dagger thrust into his throat in the vicinity of his capital.[1] Whichever version may be true, there is no doubt that Mahāpadma was low-born, and he owed his position to successful intrigue. At first, he pretended to be the guardian of the young princes,[2] but eventually he killed them also and seated himself on the throne.

Mahāpadma

Mahāpadma greatly extended the influence and the limits of the Magadha kingdom. He is said to have subverted many contemporaneous powers, like the Ikṣvākus, Kurus, Pañcālas, Kāśīs, Śūrasenas, Maithilas, Kaliṅgas, Aśmakạs, Haihayas, etc., and implacably uprooted the Kṣatriyas.[3] Perhaps it is in allusion to his conquests that the *Purāṇas* call him *Sarvakṣatrāntaka* like Paraśurāma, and an *Ekarāṭ* (sole suzerain), although the latter term exaggerates his real position. Of course, Magadha had already absorbed the neighbouring states in the earlier reigns, and the fall of Avanti in the time of Śiśunāga had left it without any rival in

[1] *Hc. C. T.*, p. 193.

[2] They were ten in number, and are believed to have ruled jointly.

[3] See also *Pol. Hist. Anc. Ind.*, 4th ed., pp. 187-90. cf. महानन्दिनस्ततः शूद्रागर्भोद्भवोऽतिलुब्धोऽतिबलो महापद्मो नन्दनामा परशुराम इवापरोऽखिलक्षत्रान्तकारी भविष्यति। ततः प्रभृति शूद्रा भूपाला भविष्यन्ति। स चैकच्छत्रामनुल्लङ्घितशासनो महापद्मः पृथिवीं भोक्ष्यति।

the North. We further know from a reference in the *Kathāsaritsāgara* to Nanda's camp that Kośala formed a part of Magadha, and the Hāthīgumphā inscription, which refers to the excavation of a canal by Nandarāja, identified with Mahāpadma, doubtless proves that Kaliṅga had come under its domination. Incidentally, this epigraph also sheds light on his religious predilections, for Nandarāja (Mahāpadma?) is represented as having removed to his capital a prized image of a Jain *Tīrthaṁkara*. Presumably, it was on account of their leanings towards Jainism that the Nanda monarchs had Jain ministers like Kalpaka, Śākaṭala, etc. Thus, Magadha had step by step emerged as the premier kingdom, and thenceforth its history was that of India itself for a pretty long period.

His Successors

Mahāpadma was followed by his eight sons,[1] of whom the last was the contemporary of Alexander. He is called Dhanananda in Buddhist literature, whereas the Greeks mention the name Agrammes or Xandrames (Augrasainya ?). He maintained, according to Curtius, a stupendous army, consisting of 200,000 foot, 20,000 horse, 2,000 chariots, and 4,000 elephants, and was reputed to be the possessor of immense riches.[2] But Agrammes or Dhanananda was avaricious, irreligious (*adhārmika*), and of tyrannical disposition, and this, along with his base ancestry, made him extremely unpopular among his subjects. Indeed, it was represented to Alexander by a chief named Phegelis

[1] They are mere names. The *Purāṇas* do not mention them except Mahāpadma's son Sukalpa or Sumālya (Sahalya). cf. तस्याऽप्यष्टौ सुताः सुमाल्याद्या भवितारः । तस्य महापद्मस्यानु पृथिवीं भोक्ष्यन्ति (*Viṣṇu P.*).

[2] Traditions of the fabulous wealth of the Nandas are preserved in the *Mahāvaṁśa*, *Kathāsaritsāgara*, Yuan Chwang's *Records*, and a Tamil poem.

(Phegeus) or Bhagala that if he had advanced further he would have easily defeated the Nanda ruler. After Alexander's departure Candragupta Maurya, who had met the Greek invader with a view to furthering his designs against the Nandas, took advantage of the situation, and destroyed the Nanda authority in Magadha with the help of the wily Brahman, Cāṇakya.[1]

Date

According to the *Purāṇas*, Mahāpadma ruled for 28 years[2] and his eight sons for twelve years only. The Ceylonese chronicles, however, mention 22 years as the length of the reigns of all the Nandas. The dynasty probably came to an end about 322-21 B.C.

[1] cf. *Viṣṇu Purāṇa*: ततश्च नवचैतान्नन्दान् कौटिल्यो ब्राह्मणः समुद्धरिष्यति ।

[2] The *Matsya Purāṇa*, however, gives him a long reign of 88 years, which is obviously an error for 28. If the former version be accepted, the duration of the Nanda dynasty, consisting of two generations, would come to 100 years. cf. महापद्मस्तत्पुत्राश्च एकं वर्षशतं अवनिपतयो भविष्यन्ति (*Viṣṇu P.*).

APPENDIX

Genealogical table of the Predecessors of the Nandas

(a) *Purāṇas*

No.	Name	Length of reign
I.	Śiśunāga	40 years
II.	Kākavarṇa	26 „
III.	Kṣemadharman	36 „
IV.	Kṣemajit or Kṣatraujas	24 „
V.	Bimbisāra	28 „
VI.	Ajātaśatru	27 „
VII.	Darśaka	24 „
VIII.	Udāyin	33 „
IX.	Nandivardhana	40 „
X.	Mahānandin	43 „
	Total	321 years

(b) *Ceylonese Chronicles*

No.	Name	Length of reign	Remarks
I.	Bimbisāra	52 years	Came to the throne in *circa* 543 B. C. at the age of 15.
II.	Ajātaśatru	32 „	The Buddha died in the 8th year of his reign.
III.	Udāyin or Udāyibhadra	16 „	
IV.	Anuruddha	8 „	Believed to have been parricides.
V.	Muṇḍa		
VI.	Nāgadāsaka	24 „	

(*b*) *Ceylonese Chronicles*—(contd.)

No.	Name	Length of reign	Remarks
VII.	Śiśunāga	18 years	Belonged to a new family. Before seizing power, he was only an *Amātya*.
VIII.	Kālāśoka	28 ,,	Had a tragic end.
IX.	His ten sons, the most prominent being Nandivardhana	22 ,,	Ruled simultaneously, perhaps under the guardianship of that adventurer, who became the first Nanda.
	Total ..	200 years	

CHAPTER VII

CONTACT WITH THE OUTSIDE WORLD

SECTION A

THE PERSIAN CONQUEST

Let us now turn for a while from Magadha and other eastern states to take a peep at what was happening in the north-western part of India. It was divided in the latter half of the sixth century B.C. into a number of petty principalities, and there was no great power to curb their mutual strifes and jealousies. Naturally it provided a strong tempting ground to the Imperialism of the Achæmenian monarchy, which had arisen in Persia about this time under the leadership of Kurush or Cyrus (*c.* 558-30 B.C.) He extended the bounds of his empire as far west as the Mediterranean, and in the east he conquered Bactria and Gadara (Gandhāra), but it is unlikely he advanced beyond the frontiers of India. His immediate successors, Kāmbujīya I (Cambyses I), Kurush II (Cyrus II), Kāmbujīya II (Cambyses II)—530-22 B.C.,—were too busy with affairs in the west to think of the east, but Dārāyavaush or Darius I (522-486 B.C.) appears to have annexed a portion of the Indus region, as evidenced by the inscriptions at Persepolis and on his tomb at Naksh-i-Rustam, mentioning the Hidus or the people of Sindhu (Indus) among Persian subjects. This conquest was made probably some time after 518 B.C., the assumed date of the Behistun record, which omits the

Cyrus

Darius I

Hidus (Indians) from the list of subject peoples, and long before 486 B.C., when Darius I died.

Herodotus tells us how Darius I essayed to achieve his object. He first sent an expedition some time after 517 B.C. under Skylax of Karyanda to explore the possibility of a passage by sea from the mouths of the Indus to Persia. He sailed down the Indus, and in the course of his voyage collected a good deal of information, afterwards utilised with advantage by Darius I. Herodotus also testifies that the conquered Indian territories, which perhaps did not include much of the Punjab, were constituted into the twentieth Satrapy of the Persian Empire; and it yielded the enormous tribute of 360 Euboic talents of gold dust, equal to about one million sterling. Obviously, these tracts were then very fertile, populated, and prosperous.

Xerxes

In the reign of Khshayārshā or Xerxes (486-65 B.C.), the successor of Darius I, Indian mercenaries, "clad in cotton" and bearing "cane bows and arrows tipped with iron," formed a part of his expeditionary force against Hellas, and so it is certain that he maintained Persian authority intact in the north-western part of India. Presumably it continued for some time more, but we do not know with certitude when the connection between Persia and India finally snapped. There is, at any rate, some evidence to show that Indian auxiliaries figured in the army of Darius III Kodomannos in his fight with Alexander.

Results of Contact

The political contact between the two countries was beneficial to both in several respects. Trade received a fillip, and perhaps the spectacle of a unified empire stirred Indian ambition to strive after a similar end. Persian scribes introduced into India the Armaic form of writing, which in Indian environments later developed into Kharoṣṭhī, written from right to left like Arabic. Scholars have even traced Persian influences in Candragupta Maurya's court ceremonial,[1] and in certain words and the preamble of the edicts and in the monuments, particularly the bell-shaped capitals, of Aśoka's time.

Section B

THE INVASION OF ALEXANDER

Alexander's cautious advance eastward

After the collapse of the Achæmenian power in the battle of Gaugamela or Arbela in the spring of 331 B.C. and the burning of the magnificent palace at Persepolis in 330 B.C., Alexander formed plans to realise his ambition of conquering India, and thus outrivalling Herakles and Dionysos whose achievements were the subject of many a popular song and legend. Accordingly, unmindful of the rigours of climate and the numerous obstacles presented in his progress by man and nature alike, Alexander set himself with his habitual foresight to the task of subjugating the lands that lay on his route in order to maintain free and uninterrupted communication with his distant base. He first occupied Seistan, and then burst upon southern Afghanistan, where "at a point commanding the roads" he founded a city called Alexandria-among-the-Arachosians, now represented by Kandahar. The following year, he appeared in the Kabul valley with his invincible hosts, but before he could direct his energies towards India he had to reduce Bactria and other adjacent territories to submission, which upheld

[1] cf. Lipi=dipi; Devānaṁ piyo Piyadaṣi Rājā evaṁ āha= Thātiy Dārayavaush Kshayāthiya.

the Persian cause under a prince of the blood royal. Alexander succeeded, with some difficulty, in subduing them, and when all opposition was laid low, he recrossed the Hindu-Kush in ten days and arrived at the strategic outpost of Alexandria—under the Caucasus, which he had founded in 329 B.C., two years before his hurricane campaign beyond the mountains. He then advanced towards Nikaia, situated "between Alexandria and the Kabul river";[1] here or somewhere "on the way to the river Kabul,"[2] Alexander divided his army into two sections. One was placed under the command of his trusted generals, Hephæstion and Perdiccas, with instructions to go ahead and construct a bridge over the Indus for the safe passage of his forces; and the other was led by Alexander himself against the warlike tribes and recalcitrant chiefs of the frontier.

The Aspasioi routed

The Aspasioi (cf. Iranian *Aspa* or Sanskrit *Aśva* = horse) of the Alisang-Kunar valley were the first to be subdued by Alexander, who captured 40,000 men and 2,30,000 oxen transporting the choicest among the latter to Macedonia for being employed in agriculture. Arrian (IV, 25), however, deposes that with these people "the conflict was sharp, not only from the difficult nature of the ground, but also because the Indians were....by far the stoutest warriors in that neighbourhood."[3]

[1] *Cambridge History of India*, Vol. I, p. 348. Smith locates Nikaia to the west of modern Jalalabad (*Early History of India*, 4th ed., p. 53), whereas Holdich puts it at Kabul.

[2] *Cambridge History of India*, Vol. I, p. 348, note 3.

[3] M'crindle, *Ancient India, Its Invasion by Alexander the Great*, p. 65. We have given full references in this chapter, because our account materially differs from the accepted interpretation of the evidence.

Nysa

Alexander next attacked the hill-state of Nysa, which probably occupied a site on the lower spurs and valleys of the Koh-i-Mor.[1] It was governed by a body of aristocracy consisting of 300 members, Akouphis being their chief. The Nysæns readily submitted to Alexander, and placed at his disposal a contingent of 300 cavalry. They claimed descent from Dionysos, and in proof of it pointed out that the ivy grew in their country and that the mountain near the city was the same as Mēros. This gratified the vanity of Alexander, and he, therefore, allowed his weary troops to take rest and indulge in Bacchanalian revels for a few days with their alleged distant kinsmen.

Defeat of the Assakenoi

Continuing his advance, Alexander defeated the Assakenoi (Sanskrit Aśvakas or Aśmakas, perhaps a branch of, or allied to, the Aspasioi), who opposed him with an army of 20,000 cavalry and more than 30,000 infantry,[2] besides 30 elephants.[3] Their main stronghold Massaga[4] was considered almost impregnable, being protected on the east by "an impetuous mountain stream with steep banks," while to the south and the west nature had "piled up gigantic rocks, at the base of which lay sloughs and yawning chasms".[5] These natural fortifications were reinforced by a deep ditch and a

[1] *Early History of India*, 4th ed., p. 57 note.

[2] 38,000 infantry, according to Curtius (VIII, 10, M'crindle, *Invasion by Alexander*, p. 194).

[3] Arrian, IV, 26, *Ibid.*, p. 66. The siege of Massaga is put before the capitulation of Nysa by Arrian, and after it by Curtius.

[4] Identification uncertain. Was it the same as Sanskrit Maśakāvatī? Vincent Smith places it "not very far to the north of the Malakand pass" (*E.H.I.*, 4th ed., p. 57).

[5] Curtius, VIII, 10, M'crindle's *Invasion by Alexander*, p. 195.

thick wall. The citadel appeared to baffle the military ingenuity of Alexander, but it could not hold out long after its Chief, Assakenos, had been killed by a chance shot.[1] Thinking further resistance useless, his wife, Kleophis,[2] surrendered herself to Alexander, and it is said that as a result of their romance she subsequently gave birth to a son bearing the name of the great conqueror.[3] It is interesting to note here the part played by nearly 7,000 Indian mercenary soldiers in the defence of Massaga. We learn that Alexander guarranteed them safe passage if they evacuated the city, but when they had actually retired to a distance he suddenly fell upon them and made "a great slaughter of their ranks" Diodoros says that the Indian mercenaries at first "loudly protested that they were attacked in violation of sworn obligations, and invoked the gods whom he had desecrated by taking false oaths in their name."[4] Thereupon, Alexander retorted that "his covenant merely bound him to let them depart from the city, and was by no means a league of perpetual amity between them and the Macedonians".[5] Undaunted by this unexpected danger, the Indian mercenaries fought with great tenacity and "by their audacity and feats of valour made the conflict, in which they closed, hot work for the enemy."[6] When many of them had been killed, or were in the agony of deadly wounds, the women took up the arms of the fallen and heroically defended the citadel along with the men. After fighting desperately they were at last overpowered by superior numbers,

[1] Arrian, IV, 27, *Ibid.*, p. 68.

[2] Curtius, however, calls Kleophis the mother of Assacanus, who is said to have died before Alexander invested Massaga (VIII, 10, *Ibid.*, p. 194).

[3] Justin, XII, 7, *Ibid.*, p. 322.

[4] Diodoros, XVII, 84, M'crindle's *Invasion by Alexander*, p.269.

[5] *Ibid.*

[6] *Ibid.*, p. 270.

and in the words of Diodoros "met a glorious death which they would have disdained to exchange for a life with dishonour".[1] The episode, no doubt, reveals to us that India had her own Joans of Arc in those bygone times, but it does not speak well of Alexander's chivalry and his sense of respect for agreements, and Plutarch rightly observes that it "rests as a foul blot on his martial fame."[2] After the fall of Massaga, Alexander advanced further, and in the course of a few months' hard fighting captured the important and strategic fortresses of Ora, Bazira, Aornos, Peukelaotis (Skt. Puṣkarāvatī, modern Charsadda in the Yusufzai territory), Embolima and Dyrta.[3]

Situation in North-western India

Thus, having subjugated the frontier regions and posted adequate Greek garrisons to maintain his authority there,[4] Alexander felt himself free to press onward. The odds were undoubtedly in his favour. The Punjab and Sind, which were to bear the brunt of his arms, presented the sorry spectacle of a disunited house. There was no towering personality of the type of Candragupta Maurya, who successfully repelled the invasion of Seleukos Nikator two decades after; on the other hand, North-western India was parcelled out into a number of states, monarchies as well as clan oligarchies, engaged in petty internecine

[1] *Ibid.*,

[2] Plutarch, Ch. LIX, M'crindle's *Invasion by Alexander*, p. 306.

[3] The identification of these places is not quite certain. Minor towns of the lower Kophen (Kabul) valley were occupied with the help of local chiefs named Kophaios and Assagetes (Aśvajit ?) —Arrian, IV, 28, *Ibid.*, p. 72.

[4] For instance, Nikanor was appointed satrap of the country to the west of the Indus, and Philippos was put in command of a garrison at Peukelaotiș (*Ibid*).

feuds and jealousies, in which some of them found their opportunity for seeking alliance with an alien aggressor. Indeed, the gates of India were, so to say, unbarred by the Rājā of Taxilā, who lost no time in proffering allegiance to Alexander, and who also rendered every assistance to the advance body of the Macedonians under Perdiccas in bridging the Indus and in securing the submission of the tribes and chieftains, like Astes (Hasti or Aṣṭakarāja ?),[1] whose territories lay on their route.

Taxilā and Abhisāra

About the beginning of the spring of 326 B.C. after offering the customary sacrifices and allowing his tired troops a short respite, Alexander crossed the Indus safely somewhere near Ohind (modern Und, a few miles above Attock), and was welcomed at Taxilā by Omphis or Āmbhi,[2] son of the deceased Taxiles, with rich and attractive presents consisting of silver and sheep and oxen of a good breed.[3] Gratified at these gifts, Alexander returned them, adding his own, and thus won not only the loyalty of the ruler of Taxila but also a contingent of 5,000 soldiers from him.[4] Similarly, Abhisares, the astute king of Abhisāra (Poonch and Nowshera districts), and other neighbouring princes, like Doxares[5], surrendered to Alexander of their own accord, thinking that resistance would be of no avail.[6]

[1] The capital of Astes was stormed by Hephæstion in thirty days, and his principality was given to one Sang-gaios (Skt. Sañjaya)—Arrian, IV, 22, *Ibid.*, p. 60.

[2] Sylvain Lévi, *Journal Asiatique*, 1890, p. 234.

[3] Arrian, V, 3, M'crindle's *Invasion by Alexander*, p. 83; Curtius, VIII, 12, *Ibid.*, p. 202.

[4] Arrian, V, 8, *Ibid.*, p. 93.

[5] *Ibid.*, p. 92.

[6] Diodoros would, however, have us believe that Embisaros (Abhisares) had made an alliance with Poros and was preparing

Poros

However, when the latter reached the Hydaspes (Jhelum) he found the great Poros (Paurava ?) on the other side of the river ready, no doubt, to meet him in response to his summons from Taxilā, but at the head of a vast army eager for the fray.[1] Alexander finds it difficult to cross the stream, and there ensues a battle of wits between the two august opponents. Ultimately, the invader decided "to steal a passage" (Arrian), which he did with about 11,000 of his picked men near a sharp bend several miles up the river from his camp in the dead of night when a severe storm accompanied with rain and thunder had abated the vigilance of Poros. Further Alexander camouflaged his intentions and movements by leaving a strong force under Krateros in his camp and another with Meleager midway between it and the place where the river was crossed.[2] Detecting that he had been foiled in his attempt to prevent Alexander from landing his troops on the eastern side of the Hydaspes, Poros despatched his son "at the head of 2,000 men and 120 chariots"[3] to obstruct the advance of his audacious adversary. The young Poros was, however, easily routed and killed by Alexander.

Alexander and Poros face each other

At last, Poros himself moved and opposed Alexander with 50,000 foot, 3,000 horse, above 1,000 chariots, and 130 elephants. In the centre, the

to oppose Alexander (XVII, 87, *Ibid.*, p. 274).

[1] Curtius, VIII, 13, *Ibid.*, p. 203.

[2] Guards were also posted all the way to ensure free communication.

[3] Arrian, V, 14, *Ibid.*, p. 101. According to Curtius, the detachment was commanded by Poros' brother, Hages (VIII, 14, *Ibid.*, p. 207).

elephants formed a sort of front wall, and behind them stood the foot-soldiers. The cavalry protected the flanks and in front of the horsemen were the chariots. As Alexander viewed the equipment of Indian forces and their disposition in the Karri plain,[1] he was constrained to remark : "I see at last a danger that matches my courage. It is at once with wild beasts and men of uncommon mettle that the contest now lies."[2] In the engagement which opened with the furious charges of Macedonian horsemen, Indians fought with great vigour, and, as Plutarch says, "obstinately maintained" their ground till the eighth hour of the day,[3] but eventually the fates turned against them. The main strength of Poros lay in the chariots, "each of which was drawn by four horses and carried six men, of whom two were shield-bearers, two, archers posted on each side of the chariot, and the other two, charioteers, as well as men-at-arms, for when the fighting was at close quarters they dropped the reins and hurled dart after dart against the enemy."[4] On this particular day, however, these chariots were of no use at all, for the violent storm of rain "had made the ground slippery, and unfit for horses to ride over, while the chariots kept sticking in the muddy sloughs formed by the rain, and proved almost immovable from their great weight."[5] Besides, owing to the slippery condition of the ground it became difficult for the archers to rest their long and heavy bows on it and discharge arrows quickly and with effect.[6]

Causes of Poros' defeat

[1] *E.H.I.*, 4th ed., pp. 69, 88.

[2] Curtius, VIII, 14, M'crindle's *Invasion by Alexander*, p. 209.

[3] Plutarch, Ch. LX, *Ibid.*, p. 308.

[4] Curtius, VIII, 14, *Ibid.*, p. 207.

[5] *Ibid.*, p. 208.

[6] Arrian deposes that the bow "is made of equal length with the man who bears it. This they rest upon the ground, and pressing against it with their left foot thus discharge the arrow having

Furthermore, the Indian army was far too unwieldy to withstand the masterful manœuvres of the mobile Macedonian cavalry, or the attacks of the disciplined phalanxes. And lastly, the elephants, on whom Poros had placed so much reliance, got frightened when the Macedonians began to hack their feet and trunks with axes and choppers. Thus the beasts fled from the field of battle "like a flock of sheep" and they "spread havoc among their own ranks and threw their drivers to the ground, who were then trampled to death."[1] Whatever may have been the causes of this disaster, Poros, a magnificent giant of over six feet in height, did not shrink from the stress of battle, or abandon the field like Darius III Kodomannos of Persia, but true to the injunction of Manu संग्रामेष्वनिवर्तित्वं (VII, 88) he stuck to his post in spite of the "nine wounds" he had received, and continued hurling darts at the enemy with dogged tenacity, perhaps thinking within himself:

> "With fame, though I die, I am content,
> Let fame be mine, though life be spent."

When Poros was ultimately captured and brought before Alexander, he was not at all "broken and abashed in spirit"[2] but boldly met him as one brave man would meet another brave man after a trial of strength, and made the proud demand: "Treat me, O Alexander! as befits a king."[3]

drawn the string far backwards: for the shaft they use is little short of being three yards long........" (*Indika*, Ch. XVI, M'crindle's *Ancient India as described by Megasthenes and Arrian*, p. 225.)

[1] Curtius, VIII, 14, M'crindle's *Invasion by Alexander*, p. 211.

[2] Arrian, V, 19, *Ibid.*, p. 109.

[3] *Ibid.* In a recent paper (*Proceedings of the Second Indian History Congress*, Allahabad, 1938, pp. 85-91), Dr. H.C. Seth of the Nagpur University has tried to show on the basis of a dubious passage occurring in the Ethiopic version of the *Life and Exploits*

Re-instatement of Poros

Justin informs us that Alexander "out of respect for his valour restored him (Poros) in safety to his sovereignty."[1] Perhaps the chivalrous instincts of Alexander were to some extent responsible for the generous treatment he accorded to Poros, but there must have been stronger reasons as well, for politics hardly knows of any such magnanimity. In the first place, the stout resistance of Poros, which is further apparent from the high casualty list,[2] must have conveyed its own lesson to Alexander. The latter also knew that as he was hailing from distant Greece it was impossible for him in the very nature of things to compel all the conquered lands to continue rendering him obedience without enlisting local loyalty, assistance and co-operation. Then, again, his ambition to found a permanent empire in the east largely remained unfulfilled, and it was, therefore, necessary for him to pursue a policy of conciliation, to adopt, so to say, the method of capturing wild elephants by means of tame ones. Accordingly, Alexander extended to Poros

of Alexander (E.A.W. Badge's Translation, p. 123) that the great invader received his first set-back in the battle of Jhelum and he sought peace with Poros. It is difficult to appreciate the force of the learned Professor's observations, for firstly, we do not know with certainty the date of the Ethiopic Text. Secondly, it utterly goes against the uniform testimony of the classical (Greek and Roman) authors, and there is no reason to believe that they deliberately conspired to record what was untrue. Thirdly, if Poros was the victor, as Dr. Seth would have us understand, how could then Alexander advance right up to the bank of the Hyphasis. A consummate general like him would never have done so, if at the very gate of India he had to bow to the arms of Poros.

[1] Justin, XII, 8, M'crindle's *Invasion by Alexander*, p. 323.

[2] Diodoros says that 12,000 men were killed and 9,000 captured (XVII, 89, *Ibid*, p. 276). According to Arrian, however, the loss in killed was 20,000 infantry and 3,000 cavalry and all the chariots were broken to pieces (V, 18, *Ibid.*, p. 107).

the olive branch of peace and friendship by reinstating him in his dignity and sovereignty. And in doing so, Alexander was not only acting in consonance with the dictates of diplomacy and statecraft, but, strangely enough, he was also following the traditional policy of Hindu conquerors, advocated by Manu[1] and Kauṭilya,[2] viz., the policy of placing either the vanquished monarch or some scion of his family upon the throne instead of resorting to direct annexation.

Foundation of two towns

Alexander then founded two towns. One was called Boukephala after the name of his faithful charger which died in India.[3] The other, Nikaia, meant to commemorate his victory, arose on the site of the battle with Poros.

Defeat of the Glausai and younger Poros

Next, having propitiated the Greek gods, Alexander marched into the territory of a nation called the Glausai or Glaukanikai (= Sanskrit Glaucukāyanakas(?) of the *Kāśikā*), taking thirty-seven of their cities "the smallest of which contained not fewer than 5,000 inhabitants, while many contained upwards of 10,000".[4] At this stage Alexander heard of revolts against him; Nikanor, Satrap of "India-west of the Indus," was assassinated and Sisikottos, i.e., Śaśigupta, too, who

[1] cf. Manu :

सर्वेषां तु विदित्वैषां समासेन चिकीर्षितम् ।
स्थापयेत्तत्र तद्वंश्यं कुर्याच्च समयक्रियाम् ॥

(vii, 202).

[2] Book VII, Ch. XVI, p. 313.

[3] Boukephala stood on the Hydaspes at a point where it was crossed.

[4] Arrian, V, 20, M'crindle's *Invasion by Alexander*, p. 112.

held the citadel at Aornos on behalf of Alexander, sent urgent messages for help. The neighbouring satrap, Tyriaspes, and Philip, 'Resident' in the kingdom of Taxilā, promptly responded and thus averted any immediate danger to Macedonian authority. After the arrival of Thracian reinforcements and the renewed submission of the ruler of Abhisāra, Alexander crossed the Akesines (Skt. Asiknī or Chenab) and subdued the younger Poros, nephew of the great Poros. His territory, known as Gandaris,[1] as also that of the Glausai, was added by Alexander to the kingdom of his quondam enemy—the senior Poros (Paurava).

Capture of Pimprama

By August, 326 B.C., the Macedonian arms penetrated beyond the Hydroates (Paruṣṇi or Irāvatī i.e., modern Rāvī), and Alexander won fresh laurels by capturing Pimprama belonging to the Adraistai (Ariṣṭas of Pāṇini ?).

Sangala stormed

Soon afterwards Alexander invested Sangala, the stronghold of the Kathaians (Skt. Kaṭhas), who "enjoyed the highest reputation for courage and skill in the art of war."[2] Strabo, quoting Onesikritos, informs us that among the Kathaians beauty was highly valued and "the handsomest man was chosen as king."[3] Every child was examined by public authority two months after its birth to determine "whether it has the beauty of form prescribed by law and whether it deserves to live or not."[4] Men and women among them chose

[1] cf. Strabo, M'crindle's *Ancient India*, p. 37.
[2] Arrian, V, 22, M'crindle's *Invasion by Alexander*, p. 115.
[3] cf. Strabo, M'crindle's *Ancient India*, p. 38.
[4] *Ibid.*

their own partners, and the women burnt themselves along with their deceased husbands.[1] These Kathaians fought with great dash and stubbornness, so much so that even Poros had to come to the aid of Alexander with "a force of 5,000 Indians".[2] At last, when the fortress fell, no less than 17,000 of the defenders gave up their lives and more than 70,000 were captured together with 300 waggons and 500 horsemen.[3] This resolute resistance of the Kathaians incensed Alexander to such an extent that he razed Sangala to the ground. Then with a view to guarding the rear he sent Greek garrisons to the conquered cities, and himself marched towards the Hyphasis (Beas) to realise his cherished dream of planting the Hellenic standards in the easternmost ends of India.

The Greek army refuses to advance

But when Alexander reached the river, a strange thing happened. His ever-victorious troops, which had braved many a danger and privation so far, suddenly laid down arms and refused to go further for the sake either of fame or of plunder.

Its causes

Before we follow the fortunes of Alexander in the course of his return journey, let us pause here to consider and analyse the causes of this unexpected change in the attitude of the Greek soldiers. What was it owing to which the war-drum failed to produce an echo in their hearts, and the impassioned entreaties and eloquent exhortations of their supreme commander and king evoked no response except streaming

[1] *Ibid.*
[2] Arrian, V, 24, M'crindle's *Invasion by Alexander*, p. 119.
[3] *Ibid.*

tears and loud lamentations?[1] What was it due to that all their enthusiasm and eagerness to establish Greek supremacy in distant lands at once melted away on reaching the Hyphasis? It is true the Greek soldiers were war-worn, home-sick, disease-stricken, and destitute;[2] and many of them were ill-equipped, for it was now increasingly difficult to transport and supply garments from Greece, and not a few were depressed because their friends had perished by disease or fallen victims to sanguinary battles. But was there any other ground for their conduct which doubtless savoured of mutiny? Plutarch gives us some clue to this mystery, for he indicates that even after the contest with Poros the Macedonian forces were considerably dispirited, and it was with reluctance that they had advanced as far as the Hyphasis at Alexander's bidding. He says: "The battle with Poros depressed the spirits of the Macedonians and made them very unwilling to advance farther into India. For, as it was with the utmost difficulty they had beaten him when the army he led amounted only to 20,000 infantry and 2,000 cavalry, they now most resolutely opposed Alexander when he insisted that they should cross the Ganges."[3] The Greeks had been impressed by the heroism and skill of Indian soldiers. Indeed, according to Arrian, "in the art of war they were far superior to the other nations by which Asia was at that time inhabited."[4] That is perhaps why the Greeks showed even after fighting against Poros that they had "no stomach for

[1] Plutarch, Ch. LXII, M'crindle's *Invasion by Alexander*, p. 310; Arrian, V, 28, *Ibid*, p. 127.

[2] cf. Koinos: "We have conquered all the world, but are ourselves destitute of all things"—Curtius, IX, 3, *Ibid*, p. 229.

[3] Plutarch, LXII, *Ibid.*, p. 310. Plutarch has here underestimated the strength of the army, and instead of the Hyphasis he has mentioned the Ganges.

[4] Arrian, V, 4, *Ibid.*, p. 85.

further toils in India." But when Alexander egged them on to march forward it was like putting the proverbial last straw on the camel's back. During their progress towards the Hyphasis Alexander's troops had heard all sorts of alarming rumours that beyond it there were extensive and uninviting deserts, impetuous and unfathomable rivers, and what was more disquieting, powerful and wealthy nations maintaining huge armies. Curtius represents Phegeus (Phegelis ?),[1] identified with Bhagala,[2] as giving the following information to Alexander: "The farther bank of the Ganges was inhabited by two nations, the Gangaridae, and the Prasii, whose king Agrammes kept in the field for guarding the approaches to his country 20,000 cavalry and 200,000 infantry besides 2,000 four-horsed chariots, and what was most formidable force of all, a troop of elephants, which ran up to the number of 3,000".[3] Similarly, Plutarch says that "the kings of the Gangaritai and Praisiai were reported to be waiting for him with an army of 80,000 horse and 200,000 foot, 8,000 war-chariots and 6,000 fighting elephants. Nor was this an exaggeration, for not long afterwards Androkottos who had by that time mounted the throne, presented Seleukos with 500 elephants and overran and subdued the whole of India with an army of 600,000 men."[4] The substantial truth of these statements is borne out by indigenous sources also, which tell us of the enormous riches and power of the Nanda monarch holding sway over the Gangaridai and Prasii nations.[5] Arrian's deposition, too, is much to the same effect, but he seems to refer to the country im-

[1] Curtius, IX, 2, *Ibid.*, p. 221.

[2] *Cam. Hist. of India*, Vol. I, p. 372.

[3] Curtius, IX, 2, M'crindle's *Invasion by Alexander*, pp. 221-22.

[4] Plutarch, LXII, *Ibid.*, p. 310.

[5] See Raychaudhuri, *Pol. Hist. Anc. Ind.*, 4th ed., pp. 188-91.

mediately beyond the Hyphasis. He observes: "It was exceedingly fertile, and the inhabitants were good agriculturists, brave in war, and living under an excellent system of internal government; for the multitude was governed by the aristocracy, who exercised their authority with justice and moderation. It was also reported that the people there had a greater number of elephants than the other Indians, and that those were of superior size and courage."[1] These details spurred the indomitable spirit of Alexander and made him all the more keen to advance into the heart of India. The Macedonians, on the other hand, as affirmed by Arrian, "now began to lose heart when they saw the king raising up without end toils upon toils and dangers upon dangers."[2] Indeed, the army held conferences "at which the more moderate men bewailed their condition, while others positively asserted that they would follow no farther though Alexander himself should lead the way".[3] Alexander made a fervent appeal to his comrades to divest their minds of these false rumours and follow him with "alacrity and confidence." He declared: "I am not ignorant, soldiers, that during these last days the natives of this country have been spreading all sorts of rumours *designed expressly to work upon your fears*, but the falsehood of those who invent such lies is nothing new in your experience".[4] This assurance was, however, of no avail. The troops persisted in their refusal to enter into further contests with the Indians beyond the Beas, "whose numbers," so answered Koinos, "though purposely exaggerated by the barbarians,

Alexander's appeal

[1] Arrian, V, 25, M'crindle's *Invasion by Alexander*, p. 121.
[2] *Ibid.*
[3] *Ibid.*
[4] Curtius, IX, 2, *Ibid.*, p. 223.

must yet, as I can gather from the lying report itself, be very considerable."[1] Alexander made his last desperate attempt to rouse the spirit of his soldiers by threatening to march on even if forsaken by them: "Expose me then to the dangers of rivers, to the rage of elephants, and to those nations *whose very names fill you with terror*. I shall find men that will follow me though I be deserted by you."[2] But the Macedonian troops were so struck by the energetic resistance and bravery of the Indians, whom they had met on the battlefields, and they were so unnerved and terrified by the reported military strength of the nations beyond the Hyphasis that even this threat, this grim prospect of Alexander plunging headlong into the depths of the enemy's country and, maybe, losing his life there, was simply met by silent tears. This brought the situation home to Alexander, who exclaimed in utter dismay: "I have all along been knocking at deaf ears. I am trying to rouse hearts that are *disloyal and crushed with craven fears*."[3] He then gave orders for retracing their steps homeward. Thus the cherished dreams of Alexander to found an eastern empire vanished, and that brilliant military leader and the hero of a hundred fights had to give way to the fears of his troops, although such fears were altogether foreign to his own indomitable nature. And when Diodoros Siculus informs us that the greatest nation in India was the Gangaridai, "against whom Alexander did not undertake an expedition, being deterred by the multitude of their elephants,"[4] we are not to understand that he himself had any misgivings about his strength, or reluctance to embark upon further

No response

[1] Curtius, IX, 3, *Ibid.*, p. 229.
[2] Curtius, IX, 2, *Ibid.*, p. 226.
[3] *Ibid.*
[4] *Ancient India as described in Classical Literature*, p. 201.

adventures, but it was chiefly due to the pusillanimous attitude of his troops that his progress was arrested and he was forced to retreat.[1]

Altars

It is said that with a view to marking the extreme point of his advance eastward Alexander gave directions for the construction of twelve colossal stone altars, dedicated to the chief Greek gods.[2] When these massive monuments were completed, Alexander offered sacrifices, accompanied with appropriate ceremonies, for a safe return home.

Retreat: Scheme of administration

The Macedonian storm, having swept over the Punjab, receded in September, 326 B.C., and probably beyond hearing its rumblings the peoples of the Gangetic plains knew nothing of its devastating fury. Soon Alexander reached the bank of the Hydaspes (Jhelum), which was the scene of his conflict with Poros. Here Alexander made proper arrangements for keeping the conquered parts of the Punjab under his subjection. He placed his new ally, Poros, in charge of all the tract between the Hydaspes and the Hyphasis, and Omphis or Āmbhi of Taxilā was given full jurisdiction over the Indus-Hydaspes Doab. Likewise, the ruler of Abhisāra had his authority extended over Kashmir with Arsakes of Uraśā (Hazārā district) as his vassal. And as a counterpoise to the rule of these Indian princes, Alexander stationed adequate Greek garrisons in cities founded by himself on Indian soil. These Greek settlers were meant to be the sentinels or guar-

[1] See also *J.A.S.B.*, New Series XIX, 1923, pp. 765-769.

[2] These altars must have been on the right bank of the Hyphasis and not on its left side, as Pliny would have us believe (VI, 62).

dians of his overlordship, so that no enterprising Indian monarch may be able to rise in revolt in order to shake off the alien yoke.

Sophytes

Alexander then made preparations for sailing down the rivers, but before the voyage actually began he cleared the path of all potential enemies by bringing about the subjugation of Sophytes (Saubhūti ?), whose kingdom had "a mountain of fossil salt which could supply all India."[1] He was thus the chief of the country of the Salt range.[2] Incidentally, it may be noted that according to Strabo the land of Sophytes had dogs of "astonishing courage" and mettle, and Alexander witnessed their fight even with a lion.[3] Curtius further avers that the people of Sophytes "excelled in wisdom, and lived under good laws and customs."[4] Like the Kathaians, they held beauty in great esteem and marriages were contracted not on considerations of high birth but of looks. They examined every infant medically, and if they found "anything deformed or defective in the limbs of a child they ordered it to be killed"[5]

Voyage down the river

Towards the close of October the signal for departure was given with the sound of the trumpet, and the Macedonian boats glided down the river in grand array, protected on both the banks by troops under

[1] Strabo, M'crindle's *Ancient India*, p. 38.

[2] According to Curtius, however, the kingdom of Sophytes was on the west of the Hyphasis (IX, 1, M'crindle's *Invasion by Alexander*, p. 219).

[3] *Ibid.*, p. 220; Strabo, *Ancient India*, p. 38.

[4] Curtius, IX, 1, M'crindle's *Invasion by Alexander*, p. 219.

[5] *Ibid.*

the command of Hephæstion and Krateros respectively, until they reached the confluence of the Akesines and the Hydaspes.

The Siboi and the Agalassians

Here Alexander disembarked to measure swords with the Siboi (Skt. Śivis), who were preparing to oppose him with an army of 40,000 infantry,[1] and the Agalassians (Agraśreṇis), who had mustered an equally great force of 40,000 foot and 3,000 horse.[2] The Siboi, who "dressed themselves with the skins of wild beasts, and had clubs for their weapons," were routed; but the Agalassians gallantly defended their capital and at first repulsed Alexander with serious losses. Curtius observes that realising their desperate position the defenders "set fire to their houses, and cast themselves along with their wives and children into the the flames."[3] Thus the Agalassians anticipated the mediæval Rajput custom of *Jauhar*.

The Malloi and the Oxydrakai

Close upon the heels of the Agalassoi operations followed Alexander's campaign against the Malloi (Mālavas) and the Oxydrakai (Kṣudrakas), the "most numerous and warlike of all the Indian tribes in those parts" who were ready to give him a "hostile reception" after "having conveyed their children and their wives for safety into their strongest cities."[4] Curtius says that these two nations were formerly at enmity with each other, but when the gravity of the peril threatening their liberty dawned upon them, they coalesced together and

[1] Curtius, IX, 4, *Ibid.*, p. 232.
[2] Diodoros, XVII, Ch. XCVI, *Ibid.*, p. 285.
[3] Curtius, IX, 4, *Ibid.*, p. 232.
[4] Arrian, VI, 4, *Ibid.*, p. 137.

gathered an army of 90,000 foot-soldiers, besides 10,000 cavalry and 900 war-chariots. The Macedonian soldiers, who had begun to think that they had come to the end of all hazardous tasks, were struck with "an unexpected terror" at the prospect of meeting fresh opposition, and in the words of Curtius "began again to upbraid the king in the language of sedition,"[1] saying that he had not ended war, but only shifted its theatre. Fully determined to prevent a repetition of the story of the Hyphasis, Alexander made a moving appeal to them "to permit him to return from India with honour, and not to escape from it like a fugitive."[2] This time it had the desired effect; the troops were galvanised into fresh activity and they rose to such a high pitch of war-frenzy that without giving any warning Alexander suddenly swooped down upon the Malloi, when they were working unarmed in the fields.[3] A large number of them were mercilessly slain, but this did not break the backbone of their resistance. Some of the Malloi shut themselves up within the city, but it was stormed and 2,000 persons lost their lives. Others took shelter in a city of the Brachmans or Brahmans, where Alexander hotly pursued them. Arrian remarks: "As they were men of spirit, a few only were taken prisoners" and most of them perished by the sword.[4] Next, Alexander assailed the main stronghold of the Malloi, situated somewhere near the boundary of the modern Jhang and Montgomery districts.[5] Here Alexander received a serious wound,[6] which spread fury and

[1] Curtius, IX, 4, *Ibid.*, p. 234.
[2] *Ibid.*, p. 235.
[3] Arrian, VI, 6, *Ibid.*, p. 140.
[4] *Ibid.*, VI 7, *Ibid.*, p. 144.
[5] *E.H.I.*, 4th ed., p. 100 and note.
[6] Arrian distinctly mentions that the accident befell Alexander among the Malloi, and not the Oxydrakai (Arrian, VI, 11, M'crindle's *Invasion by Alexander*, p. 149).

consternation among his troops, for their safety mostly depended upon his leadership and prowess. Consequently, they perpetrated a ferocious massacre of the Malloi, sparing "neither man, woman, nor child."[1] The indiscriminate slaughter of women and children was undoubtedly an act of wanton cruelty, which casts a slur on the war-code of the Greeks in India. When Alexander recovered, the submission of the Malloi became a *fait accompli*. The confederacy thus dissolved, the Oxydrakai saw no better alternative than to send ambassadors to negotiate peace with Alexander. They declared that "they were attached more than others to freedom and autonomy",[2] and that it was due to the will of the gods, and not through fear, that they had bowed to his steel.[3] Alexander appreciated their dignified bearing and entertained their leading men with marked courtesy and lavishness, which excited the jealousy of some of his own generals. Next, to impress upon these two nations that Greek authority had come to stay, Alexander appointed Philippos[4] as satrap over them. The invader then moved down the rivers until he reached the junction of the Akesines and the Indus, where he waited for Perdikkas, who during the course of his march had subdued the

Abastanoi defeated

Abastanoi or Sambastai (Skt. Ambaṣṭhas). Diodoros deposes that they were "inferior to none in India either for numbers or for bravery. They dwelt in cities in which the democratic form of government prevailed."[5] Like the other tribes, they also collected a large force consisting of 60,000 foot-soldiers, 6,000 horse and 500

[1] *Ibid.*
[2] Arrian, VI, 14, *Ibid.*, p. 154.
[3] Curtius, IX, 7, *Ibid.*, pp. 248-49.
[4] The jurisdiction of Philippos was subsequently extended much further southwards.
[5] Diodoros, XVII, Ch. CII, *Ibid.*, p. 292.

chariots to oppose Alexander, but fortune was not more favourable to them.

Subjugation of the lower Indus valley

Among other communities which submitted to Alexander during his progress to the Indus delta were the Xathroi (Kṣatri of Manu), Ossadioi (= Vasāti of the *Mahābhārata*), Śodrai (Śūdras ?) and the Massanoi; unfortunately we do not get any details about their hostilities. Alexander also subjugated a number of kings, viz., Mousikanos (lord of the Mūśikas ?), Oxykanos,[1] and Sambos (Śambhu),[2] who were too proud to acknowledge Alexander's suzerainty, even though they were mutually at war. Mousikanos had his capital at

Mousikanos

Alor (Śukkur district), and, according to Onesikritos his people were distinguished for their healthy living and longevity—their term of life extending to 130 years.[3] Some of their other characteristics have also been noted: "To have a common meal which they eat in public........, their food consisting of the produce of the chase; to use neither gold nor silver though they have mines of those metals; to employ instead of slaves young men in the flower of their age; to study no science with attention except that of medicine; to have no actions at law but for murder and outrage," for if contracts are violated one must pay the penalty for reposing too much trust on the other party.[4]

Brahmanic opposition

One interesting feature of the political situation

[1] Diodoros (*Ibid.*) calls him Portikanos. For the site of his capital, see M'crindle's *Invasion by Alexander*, p. 158, note 1.

[2] The capital of Sambos was Śindimana or Sihwan.

[3] Strabo, M'crindle's *Ancient India*, p. 41.

[4] *Ibid.*

in this part of the country was the enormous influence wielded by the Brahmans and their active participation in politics. For instance, we are told that they instigated Mousikanos and Oxykanos to revolt and shake off the ignominy of foreign thraldom. They followed their advice and lost their heads along with a large number of Brahmans. The suppression of Brahmanical opposition could not have been an easy task for Alexander, since the Brahmans were not only respected throughout the land, but they were themselves, in the words of Arrian, "men of spirit."[1] The taking up of arms by the meek Brahmans must not be regarded as a strange phenomenon or a mere figment of Greek imagination. Apart from the epic examples of such Brahman warriors as Paraśurāma, Droṇācārya, and Aśvatthāmā, we know that Kauṭilya actually refers to Brahman armies which were distinguished for their mildness towards the prostrate enemy.[2] Besides, the Hindu law-givers explicitly permit them to exchange the *Śāstra* for the *Sastra* in evil times and in defence of their country and Dharma. Thus says Manu :

शस्त्रं द्विजातिभिर्ग्राह्यं धर्मो यत्रोपरुध्यते।
द्विजातीनां च वर्णानां विप्लवे कालकारिते[3] ॥

i.e., 'The Brahmans may take up arms when they are hindered in the fulfilment of their duties, or when destruction threatens the Twice-born in evil times.' The country was menaced with such a calamity during the Macedonian avalanche, and so the Brahmans valiantly rose to defend their honour and their hearth and home.

[1] Arrian, VI, 7, M'crindle's *Invasion by Alexander*, p. 144.

[2] See Shāmaśāstrī, *Arthaśāstra*, 3rd ed., p. 373.

[3] *Manusmriti*, VIII, 348.

Pattala

Having overcome the opposition of the Brahmans and of the kings of the lower Indus valley, Alexander reached Tauala or Pattala, "a city of great note, with a political constitution drawn on the same lines as the Spartan; for in this community the command in war was vested in two hereditary kings of two different houses, while a council of elders ruled the whole state with paramount authority."[1] According to Curtius, one of its kings was named Moeres.[2]

Homeward Route

About the beginning of September, 325 B.C., Alexander finally quitted the scene of his memorable exploits. He divided the army into two sections; one was led by Nearchos by sea, and the other marched with Alexander along the southern coast of Gedrosia (Baluchistan). A part of it had, of course, already been sent under the command of Krateros through the Bolan pass. Alexander chose the most difficult and cheerless route for himself through the territories of the Arabitæ and the Oritæ, and he reached his destination after a good deal of anxiety and suffering.

Conclusion

It should be evident from the foregoing account, which is based entirely on the evidence of the Greek and Roman authors, that the progress of Alexander's arms in India was by no means easy or smooth. No doubt, some of the Indian potentates and autonomous

[1] Diodoros, XVII, Ch. CIV, M'crindle's *Invasion by Alexander*, p. 296. Pattala has been identified with modern Bahmanabad.

[2] Curtius, IX, 8, *Ibid.*, p. 256.

communities

> "bowed low before the blast,
> And let the legions thunder past."

But others fought bravely and resolutely, and this coupled with the prospect of unending wars in India even created apprehensions in the minds of the Greek veterans, who had blown off the mighty Persian forces almost like chaff. Nor did India "plunge in thought again" after the great meteor had flashed across her political skies,[1] and within a few years of Alexander's departure and death in June 323 B.C. all vestiges of Greek occupation were destroyed and swept away.[2]

Alexander's Arrangements

Alexander remained in India east of the Indus for a brief period of about nineteen months only from the spring of 326 B.C. to September 325 B.C. He was mostly busy fighting, and he could not, therefore, get time enough to consolidate his conquests. But the steps he took clearly indicate that he intended to annex the Indian provinces permanently to his empire. He posted Greek garrisons at strategic centres; appointed governors, like Philip over the region above Sind up to the lower Kabul valley, and Peithon in Sind, to exercise control over the native princes; conciliated

[1] While Alexander was on his way home, Satrap Philippos was murdered in India, and the former could do no more than direct Āmbhi of Taxilā and Eudamos, a Thracian Commandant on the Upper Indus, to take over the administration of the province.

[2] When the Macedonian empire was partitioned for the second time in 321 B.C. at Triparadeisos, Peithon had already retired to the west of the Indus, and Greek authority had all but disappeared in the Punjab and Sind, although Eudamos succeeded in holding his charge until 317 B.C.

his mighty opponent, Poros; constructed docks and harbours at Pattalene (Indus delta); and tried to explore the easiest and quickest route between India and Greece. All his arrangements and aspirations, however, came to nought when Alexander prematurely died in Babylon in June 323 B.C.

Results of the Invasion

One of the important effects of Alexander's invasion was the establishment of a number of Greek settlements in India. The army of occupation, of course, did not long survive his departure, but the cities founded by him continued to flourish. Another indirect result of this expedition was that it discredited the small state system of the Punjab, and thus helped the cause of Indian unity. It also demonstrated to Indians that there was something inherently wrong with their military organisation and strategy, and that a drilled and disciplined army, though small, could accomplish wonders in the face of odds. Lastly, it brought India into direct touch with the European world. This not only gave an impetus to trade and commerce, but also mutually influenced the development of art, thought, and literature. Some of the tangible relics of Alexander's invasion of India are imitation Athenian "owl" coins and silver drachms of Attic weight. One remarkable silver decadrachm is supposed by Barclay Head to represent Alexander on the reverse and on the obverse Poros mounted on a retreating elephant, which is being pursued by a horseman.

Society and Religion

The Greek writers yield us some interesting information on the social customs and religious beliefs of the people of those times. For instance, we learn that beauty was so highly appreciated in the kingdom of Sophytes that if any child was born defective or deformed he was killed and not allowed to grow. A handsome person was a better passport to marriage than nobility of birth. Among the Kathaians and other tribes women observed the custom of *Satī*, i.e., widows burnt themselves on their husbands' funeral pyre. In Taxilā the Greeks noted the strange custom of poor parents putting up girls for sale in the market-place, and further we are told that the dead were left to be devoured by vultures. Polygamy was another common practice among the people there.

Despite the prevalence of many queer customs, Brahmanism appears to have been the dominant religion in that part of India, and Alexander's historians narrate some unusual practices of Brahmanical ascetics like Mandanis and Kalanos (Kalyāṇa). The Brahmans commanded great respect by their learning, lofty conduct, and spirit of self-abnegation; and kings, like Mousikanos, were ready to follow their lead and direction even in political matters. Next, there were the Sarmanes or Śramaṇas, Buddhist and non-Buddhist recluses, who wore the bark of trees and lived in forests on wild fruits and roots. Indians in general worshipped Zeus Ombrios—the rain-god Indra, and Herakles, perhaps Krisṇa's elder brother Balarāma. The river Ganges was then also, as now, venerated, and certain trees were held so sacred that their defilement was considered a capital offence.

Economic Condition

The most remarkable feature of the economic situation of the times was the abundance of towns, such as Massaga, Aornos, Taxilā, 37 Glausai towns,

Pimprama, Sangala, Pattala, etc., which testified to the material prosperity of the country. Their construction, location, and fortifications give us some idea of the system of town-planning too, then in vogue.[1] Besides these towns, the material progress of the people was reflected in the presents received by Alexander in the course of his campaign. Thus, the envoys of the Oxydrakai, clad in purple and gold, are said to have brought for him a large quantity of cotton goods, tortoise shells, bucklers of ox-hide, and "100 talents of steel;" and Āmbhi of Taxilā presented to Alexander "280 talents of silver and golden crowns."

North-western India was then, as now, famous for its fine breed of oxen, of which Alexander captured 2,30,000 from the Aspasians and sent them to Macedonia for use in agriculture. He further welcomed a gift of 3,000 "fat oxen" and 10,000 sheep from Āmbhi.[2] Evidently, agriculture and cattle-breeding were important occupations of the people in the Punjab and the North-west.

In conclusion, it may be noted that one of the most flourishing crafts then was that of the carpenter, who supplied chariots for the army and carts and other vehicles for trade and traffic. Judging from the existence of several rivers in the Punjab, boat and ship-building was perhaps a prosperous industry. It is known that Alexander used a flotilla of boats for crossing the Hydaspes and a part of his troops sailed down the Indus under the command of Nearchos, and one may reasonably suppose that for this fleet the invader must have utilised native labour and materials.

[1] On this subject, see B. B. Dutt, *Town Planning in Ancient India*, (Thacker Spink & Co., 1925).

[2] See also *Hindu Civilisation*, pp. 310-11.

CHAPTER VIII

SECTION A

CANDRAGUPTA MAURYA

Ancestry

After the departure of Alexander there arose on the political firmament of India a new star that soon eclipsed the rest by its brilliance. Traditions differ regarding the antecedents of Candragupta. One account represents him as the son of the last Nanda monarch from his Śūdra concubine, Murā by name, from which was derived the surname Maurya.[1] Another[2] makes Candragupta a scion of the famous Moriya clan, a branch of the Śākyas of Pālī works, and thus the second part of the name (Maurya) appears to have been a tribal appellative. Further, certain mediæval inscriptions and the *Divyāvadāna* affirm that he was a Kṣatriya, although it is probable, as the Greek writer Justin deposes, Candragupta was born in "humble life." This expression would suggest that he was not a prince but a mere commoner without any direct title to the crown of Magadha.

Conditions Favourable to his Rise

Northern India was in a state of ferment about

[1] cf. चन्द्रगुप्तं नन्दस्यैव पत्न्यन्तरस्य मुरासंज्ञस्य पुत्रं मौर्याणां प्रथमम् । This is obviously wrong. The derivative from Murā would be Maureya.

[2] *Mahāvaṁśa*, Geiger's Translation, p. 27. According to the *Mahāparinibbāna Sutta* the Moriyas were Khattiyas or Kṣatriyas.

the beginning of the last quarter of the fourth century B.C. In Magadha the Nanda dynasty was tottering because of its base origin and the tyranny, avariciousness, and financial extortions of Dhanananda; and in the Punjab the people, divided as they were, smarted under the blows of Alexander the Great. So the political situation afforded excellent opportunities for bold spirits, and Candragupta tried his fortune by riding on the crest of the popular wave of discontent. He seems to have served at first in the Nanda army as a general or *Senāpati*. But somehow he fell out with his master, and raised the standard of revolt with the active support, and under the guidance, of that "Michiavellian Brahman" named Viṣṇugupta or Cāṇakya, who cherished a grudge against the Nanda ruler for some petty breach of social etiquette. The attempt miscarried and both of them had to flee for their life. According to the *Mahāvaṁśa-ṭīkā*,[1] the story runs that while concealed in an old woman's hut Candragupta overheard her scolding a child, who in the act of eating had burnt its fingers by beginning with the middle of a cake and not with its corners. Candragupta took lesson from this conversation, and accordingly transferred the scene of his activities to the North-west. It is alleged that he sought an interview with Alexander, when he was still in the Punjab, perhaps with a view to inducing him to advance against the Nanda king. But the boldness of his speech offended "Alexandrum,"[2] and so Candragupta had to run away for safety. With the invader's departure, the latter again emerged from his obscurity and addressed himself to the task of organising the tribes of the Punjab, which were not yet quite reconciled to the Greek yoke, as would appear from the assassination of Philip,

[1] Hemacandra's *Sthavirāvali-carita* has a similar story.

[2] Sometimes emended into "Nandrum," identified with Nanda or Dhanananda.

Satrap of the north-western provinces, soon after Alexander had left India. The precariousness of Greek authority is further evident from the fact that when he received advices of this incident, he could do no more than ask his Indian friends, Poros and Āmbhi, to carry on the administration with Eudamos to exercise general supervision over them. The premature death of Alexander in June, 323 B.C., spurred on the ambitions of Candragupta, and within a short time he succeeded in subverting the Greek garrisons, although Eudamos somehow managed to hold his charge until 317 B.C., when he quitted India to participate in the struggle between Eumenés and Antigonos.

Destruction of Nanda power and date of Accession

Having driven away the Yavanas beyond the Indus, Candragupta collected a strong force to try conclusions with the Nandas of Magadha.[1] According to the *Mudrārākṣasa*, Candragupta's chief ally was Parvataka, who has sometimes been identified with Poros. The drama gives us some idea of the complicated intrigues and conflicts of the various parties; but all accounts, Paurāṇic, Buddhist, or Jain, agree that Candragupta was able to rout the Nanda army completely.[2] The overthrow of the Yavana power and the defeat of the Nandas may be presumed to have been brought about within two or three years of Alexander's death, and so we may place

[1] Some scholars believe that the conquest of Magadha preceded the ousting of the Greek garrisons in the Punjab.

[2] The *Viṣṇu Purāṇa* says:

ततश्च नवचैतान्नन्दान् कौटिल्यो ब्राह्मणः समुद्धरिष्यति । तेषामभावे मौर्याः पृथिवीं भोक्ष्यन्ति । कौटिल्य एव चन्द्रगुप्तमुत्पन्नं राज्येऽभिषेक्ष्यति ।

It may also be noted here that the commentator Śrīdharasvāmin explains the word उत्पन्नं thus: नन्दस्यैव भार्यायां मुरासंज्ञायां सञ्जातम् ।

the accession of Candragupta in the year 321 B.C.,[1] a date in accord with the Ceylonese evidence also, according to which, as shown above, the Śaiśunāga dynasty ended in 343 B.C., and the Nandas ruled for 22 years only.

Conquests

Unfortunately, we do not get definite details of Candragupta's campaigns. The Greek writers, Plutarch and Justin, represent him as having overrun and obtained possession of the whole of India. It is no doubt an exaggeration, if taken literally, but there is ample evidence to show that besides Magadha and the Punjab Candragupta's jurisdiction extended to distant regions of India. The inclusion of Saurāṣṭra is proved by the Junāgaḍh rock inscription of Rudradāman, which refers to Candragupta's irrigational projects there and the appointment of a *Rāṣṭriya* or governor named Puṣyagupta Vaiśya. The Tamil writers, Māmulanār and Paraṇar, even allude to the Mauryan invasion of the Far South up to the Podiyil Hill in the district of Tinnevelly. Jain tradition and certain late inscriptions further testify to Candragupta's connection with North Mysore. Thus, it appears that the conquest of a large part of India is to be ascribed to him.

War with Seleukos

In the years following the death of Alexander, there was a scramble for power among his generals, and in this clash of arms Seleukos ultimately triumphed. By 305 B.C., he found his position so secure in western Asia that he thought of emulating the exploits of Alexander and of recovering the Indian territories, which

[1] Mr. N. K. Bhattasali proposes 313 B.C., on the strength of certain Jain works, as the date of Candragupta's accession (*J.R.A.S.*, 1932, pp. 273-88).

had practically been abandoned in the second partition at Triparadeisos in 321 B.C. The situation in India had, however, vastly changed since Alexander's invasion. There ruled now a monarch, whose genius had built up a mighty empire, and he was not unfamiliar with the Greek technique of warfare too. The extant text unfortunately does not make it clear whether Seleukos was worsted in a fight with Candragupta, or the combatants merely made a display of their forces and did not actually come to grips. The call had already come from the West, and so the invader was anxious to get back home and finally reckon with his rival Antigonos. Accordingly, Candragupta extracted the most favourable terms for himself, Seleukos perhaps ceding to him the satrapies of Aria (Herat), Arachosia (Kandahar), Paropanisadæ (Kabul valley), and Gedrosia (Baluchistan)[1] in exchange for just 500 elephants which played a conspicuous part in the battle at Ipsos in 301 B.C. The limits of the Mauryan empire were thus extended right up to the Hindukush, "the scientific frontier of India." Also as a mark of friendship and amity a matrimonial alliance was contracted,[2] and Seleukos deputed an ambassador, named Megasthenes, to the Mauryan court.

Megasthenes and Kauṭilya

Megasthenes and Kauṭilya are the two most important authors, whose writings throw a flood of light on the people, government and institutions of India under Candragupta Maurya. The *Indika* of Megasthenes is now

[1] Pliny VI, 69; *E.H.I.* 4th ed., App. F., pp. 158-60. See, however, Tarn, *The Greeks in Bactria and India*, p. 100. He doubts the cession of all these territories to Candragupta Maurya by Seleukos.

[2] It is not necessary to suppose that Seleukos gave the hand of his daughter to Candragupta. Any Greek princess may have been meant (see also V.A. Smith, *Aśoka*, p. 15, note 1).

lost, but happily it is still preserved in the form of quotations by later writers. Kauṭilya or Cāṇakya, is reputed to have been the minister of Candragupta. His production, the *Arthaśāstra*, is a comprehensive compendium on polity and statecraft, and it would perhaps be no overestimate of its value to say that, despite its theoretical character, it is a unique work in early Indian literature.[1]

Administration

Military organisation

Candragupta had inherited a vast army from his predecessors, but he further raised its strength to 600,000 infantry, 30,000 horse, 9,000 elephants, besides about 8,000 chariots. This formidable force was efficiently maintained by a war-office, consisting of thirty members, divided into six boards of five each. The several departments assigned to them were as follows :

Board No. I	..	Admiralty.
„ No. II	..	Transport, commissariat, and army service.
„ No. III	..	Infantry.
„ No. IV	..	Cavalry.
„ No. V	..	Chariots.
„ No. VI	..	Elephants.

The last four represented the traditional divisions of an Indian army, *viz.*, *Patti* or *Padāti*, *Aśva*, *Ratha*, and *Hasti*, which were, according to Kauṭilya, under their

[1] It is sometimes argued that the *Arthaśāstra* is a late work of the third century A.D., and belongs to the school founded by Cāṇakya. Dr. Raychaudhuri believes that though "a comparatively late work," the *Arthaśāstra* "probably existed before the second century A.D." (*Pol.Hist. Anc. Ind.*, 4th ed., p. 226).

respective *Adhyakṣas* or Superintendents.

Imperial Government

At the head of the administration was the king, who was the supreme and final authority in all matters, military, judicial, executive, and legislative. He led in war, and deliberated over plans of offence and defence with his *Senāpati* or Commander-in-chief. He received petitions from his subjects and meted out prompt justice.[1] He made high appointments, looked into the state-finances, granted audience to envoys, and collected secret information from spies. Lastly, he issued "śāsanas" or orders for the guidance of the people.[2]

The king was assisted in the discharge of his duties by a *Mantri-Pariṣad*. It was an advisory body of Ministers (*Mantris* or *Sacivas*), whose devotion to duty, integrity and wisdom had been fully tested. The various branches of administration were controlled and supervised by other high officials, *Amātyas*, *Mahāmātras*, and *Adhyakṣas*, mentioned in the *Arthaśāstra*. The traditional list of eighteen *Tīrthas* or officers consisted of the following : *Mantrin* (Minister), *Purohita* (Priest), *Senāpati* (Commander-in-chief), *Yuvarāja* (Crown-prince), *Dauvārika* (Door-keeper), *Antarveśika* (Officer in charge of the harem), *Praśātri* (Inspector-General of prisons), *Samā-*

[1] Megasthenes deposes that the king was accessible to his people even when his body was being "massaged by ebony rollers." Kauṭilya also exhorts the ruler never to cause "his petitioners to wait at the door," but to hear "all urgent calls at once and never put off" (*Arthaśāstra*, Bk. I, Ch. XIX, Shāmaśāstrī's Translation, 3rd ed., p. 38).

[2] According to the *Arthaśāstra* Bk. III, Ch. I, (Shāmaśāstrī's Trans., 3rd ed., pp. 170-71), the king could make new laws, but Gautama, Āpastamba, Bodhāyana, etc., do not recognise him as a source of law. Indeed, Manu (VIII, 336) says that a king was liable to be fined, like any other citizen, if he transgressed the established Law.

hartā (Collector-General), *Sannidhātā* (In charge of Treasury), *Pradeṣṭri* (Divisional Commissioner), *Nāyaka* (City constable), *Paura* (Governor of the capital), *Vyavahārika* (Officer in charge of transactions or Chief Judge), *Karmāntika* (Officer in charge of mines or manufactories), *Mantripariṣadādhyakṣa* (President of the Council), *Daṇḍapāla* (Police Chief), *Durgapāla* (Officer in charge of Home Defences), *Antapāla* (Frontier-Defence Officer). Among the various *Adhyakṣas* or Superintendents were those of *Koṣa* (Treasury), *Ākara* (mines) *Loha* (metal), *Lakṣaṇa* (mint), *Lavaṇa* (salt), *Suvarṇa* (gold), *Koṣṭhāgāra* (store-house), *Paṇya* (royal trade), *Kupya* (forest-produce), *Āyudhāgāra* (Armoury), *Pautava* (weights and measures of capacity), *Māna* (measurement of space and time), *Śulka* (tolls), *Sūtra* (spinning and weaving), *Sītā* (cultivation of Crown-lands), *Surā* (intoxicating liquor), *Sūna* (slaughter-houses), *Mudrā* (passports), *Vivīta* (pastures), *Dyūta* (gambling); *Bandhanāgāra* (jails), *Gau* (cattle) *Nau* (shipping), *Pattana* (ports), *Gaṇikā* (courtesans), besides those of the army,[1] trade (*Saṁsthā*), and religious institutions (*Devatā*).

Provincial Administration

The empire being vast, it was divided into a number of provinces for administrative convenience. The home-provinces were under the immediate control of the king, and, as we know from the inscriptions of Aśoka, the important provinces were governed by *Kumāras* or princes of the blood royal. Taxilā, Tośali (Dhaulī), Suvarṇagiri (Songir), and Ujjain were such seats of viceroyalties. Besides, there were feudatory chiefs, who acknowledged the suzerainty of the Emperor,

[1] The army Superintendents were those of *Patti* (Infantry) *Aśva* (Horse), *Hasti* (Elephant force), and *Ratha* (Chariots).

and rendered him military assistance in times of necessity. The bureaucracy was responsible for running the machinery of government, and its actions and movements were closely watched by overseers and spies (*cāras*). This system of espionage and counter-checks must have prevented harassment of the people in outlying parts, and kept the king posted with every kind of information.

Municipal Administration

Megasthenes gives us a detailed account of the municipal administration of Pāṭaliputra only, but it appears reasonable to infer that other great towns of the empire must have been similarly governed. We learn that the local affairs were under a commission of six boards, each consisting of five members. According to Vincent Smith, these boards were "an official development of the ordinary non-official *pancāyat*."[1]

The first board was in charge of everything pertaining to industrial arts. Besides enforcing the use of good material and fixing of proper wages, artisans were its special concern. Anybody disabling a craftsman was sentenced to death by the state.

The second board looked to the movements and needs of the foreigners. They were provided lodgings and, when necessary, medical aid also. In case of death, their remains were interred, and their belongings were handed over to the claimants. The existence of this board shows that there must have been a fairly large foreign population in the capital.

The third board was responsible for the registration of births and deaths. The collection of vital statistics was thus regarded as necessary for purposes of taxation and information of the government.

The fourth board was entrusted with trade and

[1] *E.H.I.*, 4th ed., p. 133.

commerce. It regulated the sale of commodities, and checked the use of false weights and measures. Anybody dealing in more than one article had to pay proportionately heavier taxes.

The fifth board supervised the manufacturers, who were by law, under penalty of fine, prevented from mixing old and new articles together.

The sixth board enforced the payment of tithes on goods sold. The evasion of this tax, specially perhaps if the sum involved was considerable, was visited with capital punishment. But honest default must have been treated leniently.

In their corporate capacity the municipal commissioners were expected to manage the affairs of the city, and to maintain temples, harbours, and other works of public utility.

Kauṭilya does not mention any of these boards. He contemplates a *Nāgaraka* or *Nagarādhyakṣa* as Prefect of the town, and under him were the *Sthānikas* and *Gopas*, whose jurisdictions extended to one-fourth and to a few families of the city respectively.

Pāṭaliputra

It may not be out of place here to give a brief description of the Imperial metropolis. Palimbothra, as Megasthenes calls it, situated in the country of the Prasians, was the "largest city in India," being 9½ miles (80 *stadia*) long and about 1¾ miles (fifteen *stadia*) broad. It stood on the tongue of land formed between the two rivers Erannoboas (Sone) and the Ganges. Its defences were further strengthened by a surrounding ditch, over six hundred feet (six *plethra*) wide and thirty cubits deep. Another protection was the external wall, which had 570 towers and 64 gates. There must have been similar fortifications in other big cities of the empire.

Rural Government

The village (*grāma*) was the lowest unit of administration. It was controlled by a *Grāmika* (headman) with the help of the *grāmavriddhas* or village elders. An officer in charge of five or ten villages was called *Gopa*; and above him was the *Sthānika* who looked after one-fourth of a district (*janapada*). These officers worked under the general supervision of the *Pradeṣṭri* and *Samāhartā*.

Penal Code

Both Megasthenes and Kauṭilya testify to the severity of the penal laws. Offenders were ordinarily punished with fines, varying in amount, but there were also terrible penalties. For instance, injury to an artisan, or evasion of tithes on sales, led to the award of capital sentence, and perjury was punishable with mutilation of the limbs. Kauṭilya prescribes death even for a petty theft by a government servant. We further learn that judicial torture, like whipping etc., was authorised and openly used for extracting information from criminals and suspects. These rigorous methods must have gone a long way in the prevention of crime.

Irrigation

Candragupta paid special attention to the problem of irrigation. Megasthenes speaks of officers, whose duty was to "measure the land and to inspect the sluices by which water is distributed into the branch canals, so that every one may enjoy his fair share of the benefit."[1] It was perhaps due to his solicitude for the needs of his subjects that Candragupta ordered Puṣyagupta, his governor in distant Saurāṣṭra, to dam up

[1] Bk. III, *Fragm.*, 34; see also M'Crindle, *Ancient India, Megasthenes and Arrian*, p. 86.

a mountain stream, and thus was formed a reservoir of water called Sudarśana, which proved of immense irrigational value.[1]

Sources of Income and Expenditure

Land-revenue was the main source of income. Normally the share of the crown (*bhāga*) was one-sixth of the gross produce, but the proportion perhaps varied according to place and other circumstances. Heads of income also included dues from mines, forests, customs at the frontiers, tolls and ferry duties, fees from professional experts, taxes and tithes, fines and benevolences exacted in crises. The officer, responsible for the finances and revenue-collection of the state, was the *Samāhartā*.

The money thus derived was largely spent on the maintenance of the king and his court, as well as on the army, defences of the kingdom, salaries of officers, allowances to artisans and some other classes of people, charities, religious provisions, and works of public utility like roads, irrigation, buildings, etc.

Megasthenes on Indian Castes

It is interesting to note that Megasthenes divides Indian society into seven classes or 'castes'. The first class was that of the 'philosophers', and, although numerically small, they were the most honoured. This class denoted the Brahmans and ascetics in general. The second class was composed of cultivators, who constituted the bulk of the population. The third class comprised hunters and herdsmen. The fourth class included traders, artisans, and boatmen. The fifth was that of the warriors, representing the Kṣatriyas.

[1] cf. the Jūnāgaḍh Rock Inscription of Rudradāman, *Ep. Ind.*, VIII, pp. 43, 46, l. 8.

The sixth and seventh classes consisted of secret service men and councillors respectively. Evidently, here we have got a clear instance of mal-observation on the part of the Seleucid ambassador, for the last two could in no case have formed social divisions.

The Imperial Palace

Candragupta lived in the midst of pomp and splendour. He had built for himself a magnificent palace, which stood in the centre of an extensive park, and was beautified by gilded pillars, artificial fish-ponds, and shady avenues. There was much to excite admiration, and even the palaces of Susa and Ekbatana could not vie with it. Being chiefly constructed of wood, it was not, of course, able to withstand the ravages of time and nature, but the ruins at Kumrahar, near Patna, discovered by Dr. Spooner, are supposed to represent a hundred-pillared hall of Candragupta's palace.

His Personal Life

Here the Emperor usually remained under the protection of female body-guards.[1] He was in constant dread of assassination, so that, it is said, he could not venture to sleep in the same room for two nights consecutively.[2] This is, no doubt, an exaggeration, but it certainly indicates that special pre-

[1] E.H.I., 4th ed., p. 130 and note. Strabo observes that these women were bought from their parents (XV, 55). Kauṭilya also says that "on getting up from the bed, the king shall be received by troops of women, armed with bows (*Arthaśāstra*, Bk. I, Ch. 21. *Shāmaśāstri's Translation*, 3rd ed. (1929), p. 41). cf. also प्रविश्य शार्ङ्गहस्ता यवनी (*Śakuntalā*, Act. VI, p. 224; *Vikramorvaśī*, Act V, p. 123).

[2] cf. Strabo, XV, 55. Plots to kill the king are also referred to in the *Mudrā-rākṣasa* (Act II)—Trans. H. H. Wilson in *Hindu Theatre*, II, 2nd. ed., p. 184, (London, 1835).

cautions were taken to ward off danger to the king's person. He left the palace on four occasions, when he had to undertake military expeditions, offer sacrifices, administer justice, and to go ahunting. He was keenly devoted to duty, and he received petitions, even though his body was being massaged by ebony rollers. At the time of his hunting excursions the route was marked by ropes, and it was death for any one to cross it. When the king made a public appearance he was borne in a golden palanquin, and was distinguished by his embroidered and shining apparel. He used horses or elephants also for going on journeys. He was fond of sports. He took pleasure in witnessing gladiatorial contests and fights of rams, bulls, elephants, and rhinoceroses. Another favourite amusement was ox-racing, which provided occasion for lively betting.

Candragupta's End

According to certain Jain traditions, Candragupta was a Jain, and he retired to Mysore with the Jain patriarch, Bhadrabāhu, when there broke out a severe famine in Magadha towards the close of his reign.[1] Further, Candragupta is said to have starved himself to death in accordance with the Jain rule. How far these traditions are reliable is not known, but some mediæval inscriptions also associate him with Mysore.[2] It is likely Candragupta came under Jain influences about the end of his life, and abdicated in favour of his son to practise penances. He passed away about 297 B.C. after a reign of 24 years.

[1] *Ind. Ant.*, 1892, p. 157; *Pol. Hist. Anc. Ind.*, 4th ed., p. 241.
[2] Lewis Rice, *Epigraphia Carnatica*, Vol. I, p. 34.

SECTION B

BINDUSĀRA

Candragupta's Successor

Candragupta was succeeded by his son, Bindusāra. The Greek writers call him 'Amitrachates (Athenaios) or Allitrochades (Strabo), which appears to be a corruption of the Sanskrit Amitraghāta or Amitrakhāda.

Did he Conquer the South?

Some scholars believe that the southern regions were conquered by Bindusāra, as, according to Tāranātha, he is said to have "made himself master of all territory between the eastern and western seas."[1] It is certain that Aśoka ruled as far as the confines of Mysore, and the one country he is known to have annexed to his empire was Kaliṅga. Hence the conquest of the South must be ascribed either to his father or to his grand-father. But as Candragupta's career was so brilliant, and as traditions aver his connection with Mysore, it would probably be more reasonable to credit him with this achievement also.

Revolt

Bindusāra occupied the throne during a period of stress and storm. There was revolt in Taxilā, and when Susīma, his eldest son and viceroy, could not quell the disturbance, Bindusāra transferred Aśoka from Ujjain, and the latter was fortunate in restoring order.

[1] According to Tāranātha, Cāṇaka (Cāṇakya) served Bindusāra also as Minister for a few years (*Pol. Hist. Anc. Ind.*, 4th ed., p. 243). Subsequently Khallāṭaka, mentioned in the *Divyāvadāna* (p. 372), became Bindusāra's Prime Minister.

Foreign Contact

Bindusāra maintained cordial relations with contemporary Hellenic rulers—a policy initiated by his illustrious father. A curious correspondence between Bindusāra and Antiochos I Soter reveals that the former asked his Greek friend to send him sweet wine, figs, and a philosopher. The latter replied that he was happy to forward the first two articles, but that he could not comply with the last, as the law of the land forbade any transaction of that nature. The Syrian monarch is also known to have sent an ambassador, named Deimachos, to the court of Bindusāra.

CHAPTER IX

SECTION A

AŚOKA[1]

Accession

According to the *Purāṇas*, Bindusāra ruled for 25 years, whereas the Pāli books assign to him a reign of 27 or 28 years. Assuming the correctness of the former, Bindusāra must have died about 272 B.C., when he was succeeded by one of his sons, named Aśokavardhana or Aśoka, who had served his period of apprenticeship as Viceroy both at Taxilā and Ujjain.

Disputed Succession

The Ceylonese accounts represent him (Aśoka) as wading through a pool of blood to the throne, for he is said to have made short work of all his brothers, 99 in number, except his uterine brother, Tiṣya. This story is doubted by many scholars, who detect an allusion to the existence of his brothers in Rock Edict V. But, although the epigraphic evidence is inconclusive, as it simply mentions Aśoka's solicitude for the harems of his brothers, we may well believe that the Southern version is exaggerated. Presumably, the monks were interested in emphasising the dark background of his early career to show how Aśoka, the monster of cruelty, was turned into the most gentle sovereign after

[1] See Macphail, *Aśoka*; V. A. Smith, *Aśoka*; Dr. R. K. Mookerji, *Aśoka*; Dr. D. R. Bhandarkar, *Aśoka*. I have consulted all these works with profit.

he had come under the influence of the merciful teachings of the Buddha. This much, however, may be accepted as a fact that Aśoka had to reckon against his eldest brother, Suṣīma or Sumana, before he could establish his claim to the throne. That the succession was disputed is also indicated by the interval of three or four years between Aśoka's accession and coronation, which may, therefore, be dated *circa* 269 or 268 B.C.

The Kaliṅga War

The most important event of his reign was the conquest of Kaliṅga, when he had been anointed eight years. We have ventured the surmise elsewhere that the power of the Nandas extended to this region, and hence it must have asserted its independence in the confusion accompanying their overthrow,[1] or during the disturbed reign of Bindusāra. Thus, the task of recovering it fell to the lot of Aśoka. The Kaliṅga people offered stubborn resistance, for we learn from R. E. XIII that in the conflict no less than "one hundred and fifty thousand persons were captured, one hundred thousand were slain, and many times that number died," perhaps of privation and pestilence. But nothing availed them, and their country was ruthlessly pillaged and conquered. The indescribable sufferings and atrocities of war smote the victor's conscience, and he made the solemn resolve that never again would he unsheathe the sword to enlarge the bounds of his realm.[2] The war-drum (*bherīghoṣa*) was silenced for ever, and thenceforth were heard only the reverberations of the 'Dhaṁmaghoṣa,' the call to

[1] This appears more probable. The Kaliṅgas must have developed their power, taking advantage of Candragupta's preoccupations in Northern India.

[2] Thus by his sovereign will Aśoka had long ago anticipated the Kellogg Pact, renouncing war as a policy of the State. The present World War has, however, torn this Pact to shreds.

non-violence and universal peace.

His Personal Religion

Thus a revolutionary change came over Aśoka's outlook and guiding motives of life. His mind and heart were profoundly moved by the gentle teachings of Buddhism, which he now adopted as his religion. He himself declares in R.E. XIII that "directly after the conquest of the Kaliṅgas, the Beloved of the gods became zealous in the pursuit of Dhaṁma, love for Dhaṁma, and teaching of Dhaṁma." Sometimes it is doubted if he was a Buddhist, but his attachment to Buddhism is apparent from authentic traditions as well as epigraphic evidence. In the Bhabru edict he professes devotion to the Buddhist Trinity—the Buddha, the Dhaṁma, and the Saṁgha—and recommends both the Order and the laity certain sections from the Buddhist scriptures for their recitation and meditation. In the minor pillar edict at Sarnath and its variants, Aśoka speaks almost as the Defender of the Faith, prescribing penalties for any attempts to create schisms in the church.[1] He also performed pilgrimages to Buddhist holy places like Bodhgayā (R. E. VIII) and Lumbinī (M. P. E.),[2] and abolished sacrifices and amusements which involved the slaughter of innocent animals (R. E. I.). Lastly, we learn from traditions that Aśoka built a large number of *Stūpas* to enshrine

[1] Aśoka himself, however, never renounced the world, nor ever became a monk, as supposed by some scholars on the authority of the *Divyāvadāna* and of I-tsing, who deposes that he saw a representation or image of Aśoka as a monk (*J.R.A.S.*, 1908, p. 496). And that well-known passage in M. R. E. I—"Saṁgham upayīte"—simply shows that Aśoka was drawn closer to the *Saṁgha* by his activities.

[2] Aśoka's pilgrimages to Sarnath, where the Buddha first "turned the wheel of the Law," and to Kuśinārā, the place of *Parinibbāna*, are not mentioned in his inscriptions.

the relics of the Buddha, originally deposited in eight such structures; and to further the cause of Buddhism and settle the canon the Emperor convoked a council, too, under the leadership of Moggaliputta Tissa.

Aśoka's Toleration

But though Aśoka had himself embraced Buddhism, he was by no means an intolerant zealot. On the contrary, he bestowed due honours and patronage on all the sects then prevailing. He granted cave-dwellings to the Ājīvikas, and inculcated the virtues of liberality and seemly behaviour towards the votaries of different creeds—Brāhmaṇas, Śramaṇas, Nirgranthas, etc. He believed that the followers of all sects aimed at "restraint of passions and purity of heart," and, therefore, he desired that they should reside everywhere in his empire (R. E. VII).[1] Above all, he exhorted his subjects to exercise self-control, be "bahuśruta," i.e., have much information about the doctrines of different sects, and avoid disparaging any faith merely from attachment to one's own, so that there may be a growth in mutual reverence and toleration (R. E. XII).[2] Truly, these are lofty sentiments, which may bring solace even to the modern distracted world.

His "Dhaṁma"

Owing to this catholicity Aśoka did not seek to impose his personal religion upon the people. Indeed, nowhere in his edicts does he mention the chief characteristics of Buddhism, to wit, the Four Noble Truths, the Eightfold Path, and the goal of *Nibbāna* or *Nirvāṇa*. The

[1] See, however, *Arthaśāstra* (Bk. II, chs. iv & xxxvi, Shāmaśāstrī's Trans, 3rd ed., pp. 54, 161), where Kauṭilya appears to restrict the right of the *pāṣaṇḍas* to reside in all places.

[2] See Appendix I for the English rendering of R. E. XII.

"Dhaṁma", which he presents to the world is, so to say, the essence or *sāra* of all religions. He prescribes a code of conduct with a view to making life happier and purer. He laid great stress on obedience (*suśrūṣā*) and respect (*apaciti*) for parents, preceptors, and elders. Liberality (*dānaṁ*) and proper treatment (*sampratipati*) of Brāhmaṇas, Sramaṇas, relations, friends, the aged, and the distressed, were highly commended. Sometimes (P. E. II, R. E. VII) Aśoka defines the "Dhaṁma" as comprising charity (*dāna*), compassion (*dayā*), truthfulness (*sace* or *satyaṁ*), purity (*socaye* or *saucaṁ*), saintliness (*sādhutā*), self-control (*saṁyama*), gratitude (*katamñatā* or *kritajñatā*), steadfastness (*dadhabhatitā* or *dridhabhaktitā*) and so on. Negatively, it is freedom from sin (*pāpaṁ*), which is the outcome of *kodhe* = *krodhaḥ* (anger), *niṭtūliye* or *naiṣṭhūryaṁ* (cruelty), *mānaṁ* (pride), and *Isyā* = *Irṣā* (jealousy), etc. (P. E. III). These are points common to all religions, and so Aśoka can hardly be accused of utilising his vast resources as sovereign in the interests of any particular creed. To him, therefore, goes the credit of first conceiving the idea of a universal religion, synonymous with *Duty* in its broadest sense.[1]

Peculiarities

Aśoka did not, however, give to all the current religious practices and beliefs the stamp of his recognition. In pursuance of the principle of non-injury to sentient beings (*anāraṁbho prāṇānam, avihisā bhūtānaṁ*), he did not hesitate to suppress entirely the performance of sacrifices accompanied with the slaughter of animals (R. E. I). This may have meant a real hardship to some of his people, who believed in their efficacy,

[1] Aśoka was thus much ahead of his times and the "Dhaṁma" may be regarded as the precursor of some modern reformist movements. See also Dr. R. K. Mookerji, *Aśoka*, pp. 60-76.

but Aśoka was not prepared to make any compromise on this cardinal doctrine. He also condemned certain ceremonies as trivial, vulgar, and worthless (R. E. IX). Mostly they were performed by womenfolk on occasions of births, deaths, marriages, journeys, etc. According to Aśoka, true ceremonial (*Dhaṁma-maṅgala*) consisted of proper conduct in all relations of life. Similarly, he tried to change the popular idea of gifts and conquests. He declares that there is no such gift as *Dhaṁma-dāna*, which consists of "proper treatment of slaves and servants, obedience to mother and father, liberality to friends, companions, relations, Brāhmaṇa and Śramaṇa ascetics, and abstention from slaughter of living creatures for sacrifice" (R. E. XI).

Measures for its Promotion

Aśoka propagated the "Dhaṁma" with the zeal and earnestness of a missionary, and he claims in Minor Rock Edict I that as a result of his strenuous exertions for a year, indeed for more than a year,[1] "human beings who were unmixed were caused to be mixed with gods throughout Jaṁbūdvīpa."[2] He achieved this extraordinary success on account of his well-planned measures. He exhibited "spectacles" of celestial chariots (*vimāna*), luminous balls of fire (*agi-khaṁdhāni*), and elephants (*hasti-dasanā*), representing the kinds of bliss, which the virtuous enjoyed in heaven. He believed that these shows would attract people to the path of righteousness. He himself gave up plea-

[1] Aśoka, however, informs us that "for more than two years and a half that he had been a lay-disciple (*upāsaka*), he did not exert himself well" (M.R.E. I).

[2] cf. *Iminā cu kālena amisā samānā munisā Jambudīpasi misā devehi.* The exact interpretation of this passage is beset with difficulties. What it seems to record is that Aśoka's efforts bore fruit, and people, who had no gods or were not devoted to religion, became religiously-inclined.

sure-tours (*vihāra yātras*), consisting of hunting and other diversions, and substituted for them "*Dhaṁmayātras*" to foster Dhaṁma and a spirit of liberality in the country by his precept and personal example (R. E. VIII). With the same object in view, as Aśoka tells us in P. E. VII, he "set up Dhaṁmastambhas, appointed Dhaṁma-Mahāmātas or Dhaṁma-Mahāmātras, and made Dhaṁma-sāvanas or Dhaṁma-śrāvaṇas," The appointment of Dhaṁma-Mahāmātras was an important step, for they were expected to look after both the material and the spiritual needs of the people.

Humanitarian Work

Aśoka embarked on a programme of benevolent activities to relieve the distress of man and beast. We have already referred to his prohibition of sacrificial slaughter, and R. E. I further says that he gradually eliminated the non-vegetarian items from the royal *menu*. All *Samājas*, involving meat-eating, dancing, music, etc., were strictly stopped. Similarly, P. E. V. mentions certain regulations which he prescribed in order to restrict the killing and mutilation of animals. He gave largess to ascetics, the poor, and the oppressed; and he employed superior officers (*Mukhas*) for supervising his charities as well as those of his queens and the princes. According to R. E. II, Aśoka instituted "medical treatment" of two kinds—one for human beings and the other for the lower creation—in his dominions and in those of his frontier neighbours in the South, the Coḷas, the Pāṇḍyas, the Satiyaputras, the Keralaputras, up to Tāmraparṇi (Ceylon); and also in the kingdoms of the Hellenic rulers (R. E. XIII), Aṁtiyoka or Antiochos II Theos of Syria (261-46 B.C.), Turamāya or Ptolemy II Philadelphos of Egypt (285-47 B. C.), Amtekina or Antigonos Gonatos of Macedonia (278-39 B.C.), Maga or Magas of Cyrene (300-258 B.C.), Alikasudaro or Alexander of Epirus (272-58 B.C.).[1] Wells at every half *Kos* (=one mile roughly) and rest-houses were constructed; medicinal herbs and roots, wherever they did not exist, were imported and planted. Banyan trees and mango groves were also planted for the enjoyment of man and beast (*paribhogāya paśumanuṣānaṁ*). He thus worked unceasingly for the welfare and happiness of the entire animate world, and his love and sympathy knew no bounds or barriers. He never wanted the Greeks to give up their gods "at the bidding of an alien," as supposed by Dr. Rhys Davids, but Aśoka certainly felt it his duty to send his message of peace and good-will through envoys or *dūtas*, who were also instructed to undertake philanthropic work on his behalf, so that the Emperor may obtain release from the debt he owed to creatures (*bhūtānaṁ ānaṁnaṁ gaccheyaṁ*).

The Third Buddhist Council

One of the notable events, which took place in the 17th year of Aśoka's coronation, was the convocation of the third Buddhist council[2] to resolve the differences between the various sects of Buddhism. It met at Pāṭaliputra under the presidentship of Moggaliputta Tissa (Upagupta, according to Northern texts), and after nine months' deliberations the issues were decided in favour of the *Sthaviras*. At the conclusion of the council, the President organised and dispatched evangelical missions to distant lands. For instance, Majjhāntika went to Kashmir and Gandhāra, Majjhima led the party to the Himālaya country, Mahādeva was deputed to Mahiṣamaṇḍala

[1] Alikasudaro does not appear to be identical with Alexander of Corinth (252-244 B.C.), as suggested by Bloch. The reference to the five Hellenic rulers is very important for settling problems of chronology, Asokan as well as general.

[2] The first council was called by Mahākaśyapa at Rājagriha, and the second at Vaiśālī to check some unorthodox tendencies in the Licchavi territory.

(Mysore), Sona and Uttara to Suvarṇabhūmi (Burma), Mahādharmarakṣita and Mahārakṣita were sent to Mahārāṣṭra and the Yavana country respectively, and Aśoka's son Mahendra,[1] who had become a monk, was sent along with others to Laṅkā (Ceylon). Subsequently the Emperor's daughter, Saṁghamitrā, is said to have taken there a branch of the sacred Bodhi Tree. The propagation and promotion of Buddhism in Aśoka's time must have largely been due to the zeal and perseverance of these indefatigable missionaries.

Extent of Empire

It is well known that Kaliṅga was the only conquest of Aśoka. But he had inherited an enormous empire from his predecessors, and its limits may be fixed with tolerable accuracy. On the north-west, it certainly extended to the Hindukush, for there is every reason to believe that he retained the four satrapies of Aria (Herat), Arachosia (Kandahar), Gedrosia (Baluchistan), and Paropanisadæ (Kabul valley), which were ceded to his grand-father by Seleukos Nikator. That Southern Afghanistan and the frontier regions continued to form part of Aśoka's vast realm is clear from the findspots of his rock-edicts in Shahbazgarhi (Peshawar district) and Mansehra (Hazārā district), as also from the evidence of Yuan Chwang who refers to the existence of Aśokan *Stūpas* in Kafiristan (Kapiśa) and Jalalabad.

Further, the inclusion of Kashmir is deposed by the Chinese pilgrim, Yuan Chwang, and by Kalhaṇa's *Rājataraṅgiṇī*. It may be interesting to add here that the foundation of Śrīnagara is ascribed to Aśoka, who is also credited with having built numerous *Stūpas* and *Caityas* in the valley.

[1] According to Yuan Chwang and Buddhist works in Sanskrit, Mahendra was Aśoka's brother.

The inscriptions of Aśoka at Girnar and Sopārā (Thānā district) definitively point to his jurisdiction over Saurāṣṭra and the south-western regions. Besides, we also know from the Junāgaḍh rock inscription of Rudradāman that Yavanarāja Tuṣāspa[1] was Aśoka's Viceroy in Saurāṣṭra.

In the north, Aśoka's authority extended up to the Himālaya mountains. This is apparent from his edicts, which have been found at Kalsi (Dehradun district), Rummindei and Niglīva (Nepalese Tarai). Tradition also attributes to Aśoka the foundation of Lalitapatan in Nepal, where he went with his daughter Cārumatī and her husband Devapāla Kṣatriya.

Eastwards, Bengal was comprised within his empire. Yuan Chwang noticed several Aśokan *Stūpas* in the different parts of Bengal, and according to legends Aśoka went as far as Tāmralipti (Tamluk) to see his son and daughter off to Ceylon.[2] Kaliṅga, which was the only conquest of the Emperor, was, of course, included. Here he got two edicts inscribed—one at Dhaulī (Puri district) and the other at Jaugaḍa (Ganjam district).

Towards the south, Aśoka's rock inscriptions have been discovered in Maski and Irāguḍī in the Nizam's dominions, and Chitaldroog district in Mysore. Beyond this, there were the independent kingdoms of the Coḷas, the Pāṇḍyas, the Satiyaputras, and the Kerala-putras (R. E. II).

R. E. V and XIII mention certain subject peoples, that lived in the outlying provinces. They were the Yonas, Kambojas, Gandhāras, Raṣṭika-Petenikas, Bho-

[1] *Ep. Ind.*, *VIII*, p. 46. Tuṣāspa sounds an Iranian name, although he has been called a Yavana.

[2] The inclusion of Bengal in the Mauryan Empire further receives some confirmation from the Mahāsthān (Bogra district) Pillar Inscription, engraved in Brāhmī characters of the Mauryan period (see *Ep. Ind.*, XXI, April, 1931, pp. 83 f).

jas, Nābhaka-Nābhapaṁtis, Andhras and Pārimdas or Pāladas.[1]

Lastly, the edicts contain references to some of the towns of the empire, viz., Bodhgayā, Takṣaśilā (Taxilā), Tosali, Samāpā, Ujjayinī, Suvarṇagiri (Songir or Kanakagiri), Isilā, Kauśāṁbi, Pāṭaliputra.

All these evidences indicate that the empire extended from the Hindu-Kush in the north-west to Bengal in the east; and from the foot of the mountains in the north to the Chitaldroog district in the south. It also comprised the two extremities of Kaliṅga and Saurāṣṭra. Indeed, it was of such imposing dimensions that Aśoka was fully justified in saying "mahālake hi vijitaṁ", i.e., "vast is my empire" (R. E. XIV).[2] No king in ancient India was ever master of such extensive territories.

Administration

The administrative system remained more or less the same as in the time of Candragupta Maurya. It was an absolute benevolent monarchy, and Aśoka laid special stress upon the paternal principle of government. In the second Kaliṅga Edict he says: "All men are my children, and just as I desire for my children that they may enjoy every kind of prosperity and happiness both in this world and in the next, so also do I desire the same for all men." As before, there was a council of Ministers (*Pariṣad*) to advise and help the Emperor in the business of the state (R. E. III and VI). He continued also the system of Provincial Administration. The important provinces were each under a

[1] Rapson takes them to be "border peoples" to the north-west and to the south "beyond the king's dominions" but "coming within his sphere of influence" (*Cam. Hist. Ind.*, Vol. I, p. 514).

[2] In R.E. V, Aśoka calls his Empire "*Sava pu(tha)viyaṁ.*"

prince of the blood royal (*Kumāra*). We learn from the edicts that Takṣaśilā (Taxilā), Ujjayinī, Tosali (Dhaulī), and Suvarṇagiri (Songir) were such seats of viceroyalty during Aśoka's reign. Sometimes, however, trusted feudatory chiefs were appointed to the exalted viceregal offices, as is proved by the case of Rājā Tuṣāspa, the Yavana, who had his capital at Girnar. Presumably, the Viceroys had their own ministers (*Amātyas*). At any rate, it was against the latter that the people of Taxilā revolted in the time of Bindusāra. The minor provinces were under governors, perhaps the *Rājukas* of the edicts, whereas the *Prādeśikas* probably corresponded to modern divisional commissioners. The departmental chiefs were known by the generic term *Mukhas* (P.E. VII) or *Mahāmātas*, i.e., *Mahāmātras*—the particular department being indicated by the prefix. For instance, the Mahāmātras in charge of harems, cities, and frontier administration were respectively called *Stryadhyakṣa-Mahāmātras*, *Nagaravyavahāraka-Mahāmātras*, and *Anta-Mahāmātras*. The officers of the civil service were called *Puruṣas*, and they were of high, low or middle rank. The subordinate officials in general were designated *Yuktas*.

Reforms

Aśoka introduced a number of administrative innovations for good governance. He created the new office of *Dhamma-Mahāmātas* for the temporal and spiritual weal of his subjects. They were to look after the interests of the different religious groups and the distribution of charities, and also to mitigate the rigours of justice by securing reduction in penalties or release from imprisonment on the ground of age or numerous progeny, and by preventing any undue harassment (R.E.V).

Further, Aśoka ordered his officers from the *Rājukas* and *Prādeśikas* down to the *Yuktas* to go on quinquennial or sometimes triennial tours (*anusaṁyāna*), so that they may come into direct touch with people in the countryside (R.E. III and K.R.E.I). Thirdly, he allowed the *Paṭivedakas* (Reporters) to inform him about urgent public matters at all times wherever he may be (R.E. VI).[1] Fourthly, Aśoka granted to the *Rājukas*, "set over many hundred thousands of people", independence in the award of honours (*abhihāle*) and punishments (*daṁḍe*) in order that they might discharge their duties confidently and fearlessly. They were, however, expected to maintain uniformity in penalties (*daṁḍa-samatā*) as well as in judicial procedure (*vyavahāra-samatā*) (P.E. IV). Lastly, the Emperor released prisoners on the anniversary of his coronation (P.E. V), and gave three days' respite to those sentenced to death (P.E. IV).

Society

We get some glimpses of society as constituted in Aśoka's time. It comprised religious orders like the Brāhmaṇas, Śramaṇas, and other Pāṣaṇḍas, among which the Ājīvikas and the Nirgranthas (Jains) were the most prominent. These monks and ascetics spread the truth as they conceived it, and promoted the cause of learning by instruction and discussion. Besides, there were the householders (*grihasthas*), and curiously the edicts mention all the four divisions, viz., Brāhmaṇas; soldiers and their chiefs (*bhaṭamāya*), corresponding to Kṣatriyas; *Ibhyas* or Vaiśyas (R.E.V); and slaves and servants (*dāsabhaṭaka*), i.e., Śūdras. The people were wont to perform many ceremonies to bring

[1] The *Paṭivedakas* were allowed by Aśoka to report on state matters at all times and places whether he was eating (*bhuṁjamānasa*), or in the harem (*orodhanaṁhi*), or in the ante-chamber (*gabhāgāraṁhi*), or in the royal ranch (*vacaṁhi*), or on horse-back (*vinītaṁhi*-religious study?), or in the pleasure gardens (*uyānesu*).

them good luck, and they believed in the hereafter (*paraloka* or *svarga*). Meat-eating must have undoubtedly been a common feature of society, as appears from the comprehensive regulations laid down by Aśoka for preventing slaughter of animals (P.E. V). The "upper ten" perhaps practised polygamy, if the case of Aśoka himself furnishes any analogy. The references to harems (*avarodhana*) in R.E. V would show that the segregation and restrictions upon the freedom of women-folk were then not unknown.

Monuments

Aśoka's claim to the remembrance of posterity rests not merely on his victories of "Dhaṁma", but also on his achievements in the domain of art and architecture. Tradition credits him with the foundation of two cities, Śrīnagara in Kashmir and Lalitapatan in Nepal. He also made, as noted by Fa-hian, considerable additions to the grandeur of his palace and the metropolis. He built a large number of *Stūpas* throughout his far-flung empire to enshrine the corporeal relics of the Buddha.[1] Besides, Aśoka undertook the construction of *Vihāras* or monasteries and cave-dwellings for the residence of monks. Unfortunately, however, the extant evidence of his building activities is very scanty. Far more important than the above are his monoliths, which are huge *tapering shafts of Chunar sandstone*, weighing about fifty tons, with an average height of 40 to 50 feet. They are surmounted by what is known as the Persepolitan Bell-capital, but what, in the opinion of Havell, is an inverted lotus. Other parts of these

[1] After the cremation of the Buddha's remains his ashes were shared by eight claimants, who each raised a *Stūpa* over them. These were opened by Aśoka, and, as the legend goes, he re-distributed the relics among 84,000 *Stūpas*, which he himself built for the purpose.

columns are the necking, the abacus adorned with figures, and the sculpture in the round representing any of the following animals: the lion, the bull, the elephant, or the horse. The treatment of these crowning pieces is so naturalistic, exquisite, and spirited that some scholars have stoutly maintained that it was inspired by foreign art, either Greek or Persian. The excellence of these sculptures, if compared with the earlier crude pieces like the Parkham statue, is no doubt an enigma, and it cannot be satisfactorily explained unless we assume alien influences, or that there was a sudden artistic outburst in India. Another remarkable feature of the pillars is the fine polish of their surface, which misled some observers even into the belief that they were metallic. Curiously enough, this sort of polish is not to be found in later monuments, as if the art of imparting it was lost after the time of Aśoka. On the whole, as Vincent Smith rightly remarks, "their fabrication, conveyance, and erection bear eloquent testimony to the skill and resource of the stone-cutters and engineers of the Maurya age."[1]

Edicts

The inscriptions of Aśoka[2] are a unique collection of documents. They give us insight into his inner feelings and ideals, and transmit across the centuries almost the very words of the great Emperor. These edicts, "rugged, uncouth, involved, full of repetitions" (Rhys Davids), may be divided into several classes as follows :

[1] *Aśoka*, 3rd ed., pp. 120-21.

[2] In the Edicts Aśoka uniformly calls himself *Devānam-piya Piyadasi Rājā*. It is only in the Maski version of M.R.E.I. that the name Aśoka occurs. Other records, in which it is mentioned, are the Junāgaḍh inscription of Rudradāman dated year 72=150 A.D. (*Ep. Ind.* VIII, pp. 36-49), and the Sarnath inscription of Kumāradevī (*Ibid.*, IX, pp. 319-28).

(*i*) The two Minor Rock Edicts: No. II appears at Siddapur, Jatiṅga Rāmeshwar, Brahmagiri—all in the Chitaldroog district (Mysore). No. I is found at the above-mentioned places, and also at Rūpnāth (Jubbulpur district), Sahasrām in Arrah district, Bairāṭ, near Jaipur; and Maski, Gavimaṭh, Palkiguṇḍu, Irāguḍi in the Nizām's dominions.

(*ii*) The Bhabrū Edict.

(*iii*) The Fourteen Rock Edicts, discovered at Shāhbāzgarhī (Peshawar district) and Mansehrā (Hazārā district); Girnar, near Junāgaḍh; Sopārā (Thānā district); Kalsi (Dehra-Dun district); Dhaulī (Puri district); Jaugaḍa (Ganjam district); Irāguḍi (Nizām's State).

(*iv*) The two Kaliṅga Separate Edicts at Dhaulī and Jaugaḍa in lieu of R.E. XI, XII, XIII.

(*v*) The three Cave Inscriptions at Barābar.

(*vi*) The Seven Pillar Edicts, viz., Toprā-Delhi; Meerut-Delhi; Kauśāṁbī-Allahabad; Rāmpurwā, Lauriyā-Ararāj, Lauriyā-Nandangarh (the last three being in Champaran district, Bihar).

(*vii*) The two Tarāi Edicts at Rummindei and Niglīva.

(*viii*) The Minor Pillar Edicts at Sāñchī, Kauśāṁbī—Allahabad and Sarnath.

Excepting those at Shāhbāzgarhī and Mansehrā, which are inscribed in the Kharoṣṭhī script running, like Arabic, from right to left, the rest are all engraved in the *Brāhmī lipi*, which is the parent of modern Indian alphabets and is written from left to right.

Estimate of Aśoka

Aśoka is undoubtedly one of the most striking personalities of the ancient world. He has often been likened to such great figures of history as Constantine, Marcus Aurelius, Akbar, Omar Khalif and others. The comparisons are, however, not altogether apposite. Aśoka was flowing with the milk of human kindness, and his love and sympathy embraced the whole of animate creation. He had a high sense of duty, which urged him to scorn delights incidental to his position, and live laborious days. He was ready to transact state business at all hours and places, and he directed all his resources and energies to the alleviation of the sufferings of humanity and the dissemination of the "Dhamma", as he understood it. Indeed, the welfare and happiness of his subjects in particular and men and beings in general was such a dominating passion of his life that he could never feel satisfied with his exertions or despatch of work. During his momentous reign, Art received a tremendous impetus, and Pālī or Māgadhī, in which dialect the edicts are couched, became almost the *lingua franca* of India.[1] But its political greatness suffered a severe setback. After the conquest of Kaliṅga, he suddenly brought the steam-roller of Mauryan aggression to a halt, and thus arrested the expansion of Magadha by his policy of "Dhaṁmavijaya." The military ardour of the people having cooled down, the country fell an easy prey to the onslaughts of the Indo-Bactrian invaders, who not long after descended into the plains of India.

Section B

Aśoka's Successors

Aśoka died about 232 B.C. after a long reign of forty years.[2] When the sceptre dropped from his

[1] If it be permissible to coin an expression, it may be called *lingua Indica*.

[2] Vincent Smith notes that, according to a Tibetan tradition, Aśoka passed away at Taxilā (*The Oxford History of India*, p. 116). The story, however, lacks corroboration.

mighty hands, the fortunes of the Maurya dynasty began to suffer decline. Traditions regarding his successors are discrepant, but one thing seems to be certain, that none of them rose to the stature of Aśoka. Of his sons, Tīvara alone is named in the edicts, and perhaps he predeceased his father as he is not heard of subsequently. Another, Jālauka, who was a Śaiva, appears from the *Rājataraṅgiṇī* to have become independent in Kashmir after Aśoka's death. The third, Kunāla (Suyaśas?), ruled for eight years according to the *Vāyu Purāṇa*, but in the Southern works he is passed over as a blind man. Thus our information about the sons of Aśoka is extremely vague. The *Aśokāvadāna*, on the other hand, would have us believe that on account of his lavish benefactions to the *Saṁgha* Aśoka was compelled by the ministers to abdicate in favour of his grandson Samprati (son of the blinded Kunāla[1]). Legends aver that Saṁpadī or Samprati was a great patron of Jainism who had his seat of government at Ujjain. The *Vāyu* and the *Matsya Purāṇas*, however, testify that he was preceded by another grandson of Aśoka, named Daśaratha. That the latter was an historical reality is also proved by the Nāgārjuni cave inscriptions, which record his dedications to the Ājīvikas. Vincent Smith tries to reconcile this divergent testimony by suggesting that after Aśoka there was a partition of the empire—Daśaratha getting the eastern part and Samprati the western.[2] But this view is not borne out by the evidence available, for in some Jain versions Samprati is described as the sovereign of all India, having his court at Pāṭaliputra and not at Ujjain. What, therefore, appears to us a fact is that both Daśaratha and Samprati had an historical existence, and that

[1] It is said that Kunāla, so called because of the beauty of his eyes, was blinded as a result of the jealousy and machinations of his step-mother, Tiṣyaraksitā.

[2] *E.H.I.*, 4th ed., p. 203.

the former came before the latter. The successors of Samprati were mere nonentities,[1] and during their time the Maurya power steadily waned until Brihadratha met with a tragic end at the hands of his own commander-in-chief, Puṣyamitra Śuṅga.

Causes of the down-fall of the Mauryas

When one stands by the grave of the Mauryan rule, it is inevitable to enquire what were the causes which led to its dismemberment so soon after Aśoka. Mahāmahopādhyāya H. P. Sastri[2] thought that it was entirely due to the reaction of the Brahmans against the policy of Aśoka, who had alienated them by his prohibition of sacrifices, appointment of Dhaṁma-mahāmātas to supervise morals, and his introduction of uniformity of judicial procedure and punishment, which they regarded with special aversion inasmuch as they considered it a calculated infringement of their privileged position or of the immunities they had hitherto enjoyed. These measures may have to some extent contributed to Brahmanic dissatisfaction, and it is significant that the last Maurya ruler was assassinated by a Brahman general, but there were other causes also at work. The successors of Aśoka were weaklings, and there were perhaps fissiparous tendencies in the provinces, for we know that Jālauka (*Rājataraṅgiṇī*) and Vīrasena (Tārānātha) became independent in Kashmir and Gandhāra respectively after Aśoka had passed away. The officers, who were placed in charge of outlying territories, also took full advantage of the weakness of the central government and gave loose rein to their rapacity. There was no Aśoka to check their oppression sternly, and thus discontent grew apace among the people. The vitality of the

[1] Vide Appendix II.
[2] *J.A.S.B.*, 1910, pp. 259 f.

empire was gone and when the storm burst, it was soon overwhelmed.[1]

APPENDIX I

TRANSLATION OF R.E. XII—TOLERATION EDICT

"His Sacred and Gracious Majesty the king is *honouring all sects*, both ascetics, and house-holders; by gifts and offerings of various kinds is he honouring them. But His Sacred Majesty does not value such gifts or honours as that how should there be a growth of the essential elements of all religious sects. The growth of this genuine matter, is, however, of many kinds. But the root of it is *restraint of speech*, that is, that there should not be honour of one's own sect and condemnation of others' sects without any ground. Such slighting should be for specified grounds only. On the other hand, *the sects of others should be honoured* for this ground and that. Thus doing, one helps his own sect to grow, and benefits the sects of others, too. Doing otherwise, one hurts his own sect and injures the sects of others. For whosoever honours his own sect and condemns the sects of others wholly from devotion to his own sect, i.e., the thought, "How I may glorify my own sect",—one acting thus injures more gravely his own sect on the contrary. Hence *concord alone is commendable*, in this sense that all should listen and be willing to listen to the doctrines professed by others. This, is, in fact, the desire of His Sacred Majesty, viz., that *all sects should be possessed of wide learning and good doctrines*. And those who are content in their respective faiths, should all be told that His Sacred Majesty does not value so much gift or external honour as that there should be the *growth of the essential elements; and breadth, of all sects*........."[2]

[1] See also Dr. Raychaudhuri, *Pol. Hist. Anc. Ind.*, 4th ed., pp. 293-305.

[2] See Dr. R. K. Mookerji, *Aśoka*, pp. 158-60, 232.

APPENDIX II

GENEALOGICAL TABLE OF THE MAURYAS

Candragupta Maurya (*circa* 321-297 B.C.)

Bindusāra (297-272 B.C.)

- Suṣīma or Sumana
- Aśoka (272-232 B.C.)
- Tissa
- Other sons

(Aśoka's wives-Vidiśā Devī, Padmāvatī, Asandimitrā, Kāruvākī, Tiṣyarakṣitā)

- Kunāla or Suyaśas ? (232-224 B.C.)
- Jālauka
- Tīvara

- Daśaratha (Bandhupālita ?) (224-216 B.C.)
- Samprati (Indrapālita ?) (216-207 B.C.)

(Śāliśūka or Brihaspati ?)

(Some *Purāṇas* assign him a reign of 13 years, but others ignore him altogether. Perhaps his reign was very brief and we may well suppose that it lasted a year or two only, i.e., 207-206 B.C. ?)

Devavarman or Somaśarman (*circa* 206-199 B.C.).

Śatadhanus or Śatadhanvan (*circa* 199-191 B.C.)

Brihadratha (*circa* 191-184 B.C.).

CHAPTER X

I. THE BRAHMAN RULERS

SECTION A

THE ŚUṄGAS

Subversion of the Maurya Dynasty

According to the *Purāṇas*, the Maurya dynasty was subverted about 184 B.C. by Puṣyamitra Śuṅga, who then usurped the throne.[1] The circumstances of Brihadratha's assassination are mentioned in the *Harṣacarita*, which informs us that, while reviewing the army, he was killed by his commander-in-chief.[2] Probably Brihadratha was a very weak ruler (*prajñā durbalaṁ*) and Puṣyamitra had the full support of the forces, otherwise he could not have struck down his master on the parade ground itself.

Who were the Śuṅgas?

The Śuṅgas appear to have been Brahmans. The celebrated grammarian, Pāṇini, connects them with the Bhāradvāja family, and in the *Āśvalāyana Śrautasūtra* the Śuṅgas are known as teachers.[3] Further, Tārānātha

[1] cf. पुष्यमित्रस्तु सेनानीः समुद्धृत्य वृहद्रथम् ...... ।

[2] cf. *Harṣacarita* :

प्रज्ञादुर्बलं च बलदर्शनव्यपदेशदर्शिताशेषसैन्यः सेनानीरनार्यो मौर्यम् वृहद्रथं पिपेष पुष्यमित्रः स्वामिनम् ॥ (see also *Hc. C.T.*, p. 193; *Hc.*, vi, p. 199, Bombay ed., 1925).

[3] XII, 13,5; cf. भरद्वाजाः शुङ्गाः कृताः शैशिरयः; see also *Political*

represents Puṣyamitra as a Brahman, the family priest (*purohita*) of a certain monarch; and at one place he expressly calls him a "Brahman king."[1] There was nothing incongruous in the meek and contemplative Brahmans changing the *Śāstras* for the *Śastras*, for they are permitted to adopt the arms in times of necessity (cf. Manu, VIII, 348).[2] Besides the well-known epic instances of Droṇa and Aśvatthāmā, we have the testimony of Greek writers that the Brahmans came forward to oppose Alexander when he was in the lower Indus valley. During the first quarter of the second century B.C. India was similarly threatened with foreign invasions, and Puṣyamitra arose to avert this danger.[3]

Events

(*a*) *War with Vidarbha*: The first event of Puṣyamitra's reign was his conflict with Vidarbha. According to the *Mālavikāgnimitra*, the kingdom had been newly established, and its ruler Yajñasena, who was related to the minister of the fallen Maurya, is described as a "natural enemy" of the Suṅgas. Perhaps the former had made himself independent in Vidarbha in the confusion following Brihadratha's murder, and

History of Ancient India, 4th ed., pp. 307-08. The *Divyāvadāna*, however, erroneously represents Puṣyamitra as a son of the Maurya Puṣyadharma (xxix, p. 433). Some early works, on the other hand, connected the Śuṅgas with the *Baimbikas* of the Kaśyapa *gotra* (*Pol. Hist. Anc. Ind.*, 4th ed., p. 307 & note).

[1] Trans. Schiefner, ch. xvi.

[2] See *Ante*. cf. also सेनापत्यं च राज्यं च दण्डनेतृत्वमेव च ।
सर्वलोकाधिपत्यं च वेदशास्त्रविदर्हति ॥
(*Manusmriti*, XII, 100).

[3] Illustrating Pāṇini's rule about राज्य (VI, 2, 130), Patañjali mentions ब्राह्मणराज्य as the example *par excellence*. Should this not be taken to indicate that Patañjali was living under the rule of a Brahman?

as soon as Puṣyamitra felt his position secure on the throne he demanded the allegiance of Yajñasena. The course of the tussle is obscure, but it seems Agnimitra, who was Puṣyamitra's son and Viceroy at Vidiśā, carried on hostilities with great vigour and consummate diplomacy. He won over to his side Yajñasena's cousin, Mādhavasena, and, at last, when the struggle ended, Vidarbha was apportioned between the two cousins.

(*b*) *The Yavana incursions*: During the time of Puṣyamitra, India was in the grips of serious Yavana inroads. The great grammarian Patañjali, who was a contemporary of Puṣyamitra, as we shall show presently, alludes to their operations against Madhyāmikā (Nāgarī, near Chitor) and Sāketa (Ayodhyā), for he gives the following illustrations of the use of the imperfect tense to indicate events not seen by the speaker and yet recent enough to have been witnessed by him: *Arunad Yavanaḥ Sāketaṁ* (the Greek was besieging Sāketa); *Arunad Yavano Madhyāmikāṁ* (the Greek was besieging Madhyāmikā).[1] The *Gārgī-Saṁhitā* also testifies that the "viciously valiant Greeks" reduced Mathurā, the Pañcāla country (Gangetic Doab), and Sāketa, and even reached Kusumadhvaja (Pāṭaliputra). Similarly, the *Mālavikāgnimitra* refers to the defeat of the Yavanas—perhaps their advance body—on the banks of the river Sindhu[2] by Vasumitra. We do not know exactly who was the Yavana general to attack India at this time. Some scholars identify him with Demetrios and others with Menander. According to Strabo, they were both great conquerors, and carried the Greek standards to distant lands.

[1] *Mahābhāṣya*, 3.2.111

[2] Vincent Smith thinks that this river "now forms the boundary between Bundelkhand and the Rajputana States" (*E.H.I.*, 4th ed., p. 211). Its identification with the Indus, however, appears equally plausible (*I.H.Q.*, 1925, pp. 214 f; see also *Journ. U.P. Hist. Soc.*, July, 1941, pp. 9-20).

(*c*) *The Aśvamedha sacrifice*: The performance of the *Aśvamedha* was one of the notable events of Puṣyamitra's reign. It is referred to in the *Mālavikāgnimitra*, and by Patañjali. Indeed, the latter officiated as priest in this sacrifice, as would appear from the passage—"iha Puṣyamitraṁ yājayāmaḥ" (here we are sacrificing for Puṣyamitra)—which Patañjali mentions as an instance of the use of the present tense to denote an incomplete action. The Ayodhyā inscription[1] further informs us that Puṣyamitra performed not one but two horse-sacrifices. In the opinion of Jayasval, the second *Aśvamedha* was celebrated because Puṣyamitra suffered a reverse at the hands of king Khāravela of Kaliṅga. We shall, however, show below that the contemporaneity of these two rulers is extremely doubtful.

Extent of Kingdom

Puṣyamitra's jurisdiction extended to Jalandhar and Śākala (Sialkot) in the Punjab, if we accept the testimony of the Tibetan historian, Tārānātha, and the *Divyāvadāna*. The latter also indicates that Pāṭaliputra continued to be the royal residence. Puṣyamitra's sway over Ayodhyā is proved by an inscription found there,[2] whereas according to the *Mālavikāgnimitra* his dominions comprised Vidiśā and the southern regions as far as the Narmadā. Puṣyamitra appears to have made virtually a feudal division of his extensive territories, for one version of the *Vāyu Purāṇa* states :

[1] *Ep. Ind.*, *XX*, (April, 1929), pp. 54-58. cf. कोसलाधिपेन द्विरश्वमेधयाजिनः सेनापतेः पुष्यमित्रस्य.....।

[2] Ayodhyā appears to have been a viceroyalty under *Kośalādhipa* Dhana (deva or bhūti ?), whose coins are also known. He is described in the inscription as "पुष्यमित्रस्य षष्ठेन", i.e., the sixth son of Puṣyamitra. Some scholars, however, take the expression to mean the sixth brother or descendant of Puṣyamitra.

पुष्यमित्रसुताश्चाष्टौ भविष्यन्ति समा नृपाः

i.e., all the eight sons of Puṣyamitra will rule simultaneously.[1]

Puṣyamitra's Persecutions?

According to the *Divyāvadāna*, Puṣyamitra was a persecutor of Buddhism and he is represented to have made the notorious declaration at Śākala setting a price of one hundred gold *dīnāras* on the head of every Buddhist monk.[2] Tāranātha also affirms that Puṣyamitra was the ally of unbelievers and himself burnt monasteries and slew monks. Puṣyamitra was no doubt a zealous champion of Brahmanism, but the Buddhist *Stūpas* and railings erected at Bhārhut (Nagod State) "during the sovereignty of the Śuṅgas"[3] would hardly corroborate the literary evidence regarding his ebullitions of sectarian rancour. Of course, this conclusion will have to be modified, if the above expression is not taken to refer to the time of Puṣyamitra.

Puṣyamitra's Successors

Puṣyamitra passed away in about 148 B. C. after a reign of 36 years. He was succeeded by his son, Agnimitra, who as Viceroy at Vidiśā had ample experience of the methods of government. He ruled for a brief period of eight years only, and was followed by Sujyeṣṭha or Jeṭhamitra (Jyeṣṭhamitra) of the coins, perhaps his brother. After him came Agnimitra's son, Vasumitra. In his earlier days he defeated the Yavanas, who had tried to obstruct the progress of the sacrificial

[1] cf. also पुष्यमित्रस्तु सेनानीरकारयिष्यत् वै राज्यं ।

[2] *Divyāvadāna*, ed. Cowell and Neil, pp. 433-34.
cf. यो मे श्रमणशिरो दास्यति तस्याहं दीनारशतं दास्यामि ।

[3] Cunningham, *Stūpa of Bhārhut*, plate XII, p. 128. cf. "Suganaṁ raje...." Although no name is given, it is probable Puṣyamitra is intended.

horse let loose by his grandfather. The Śuṅga dynasty consisted of ten rulers, but history has not condescended to record anything of note about the rest. One of them, the fifth named Odraka, or, as some think, the last but one called Bhāgavata, was identical with king Kāśīputra Bhāgabhadra of the Besnagar pillar inscription. It was to his court that king Antialkidas (Aṁtalikita) of Taxilā sent his ambassador Heliodorus (Heliodora), son of Dion (Diya), who calls himself a *Bhāgavata*.[1]

Śuṅga Religion, Art, and Literature

This piece of information from the Besnagar pillar inscription is important, for it proves that the Greeks were not only hurled back, but also that they thought it a wise policy to maintain friendly relations with the Śuṅgas. We further learn that Hinduism was then not so narrow and parochial in outlook, as now, and that even foreigners could find a place within its roomy fold. The Bhāgavata form of religion was then prevalent and was gaining new adherents.

Art also received an impetus, as is clear from the railings of the Bhārhut *Stūpa* erected during the Śuṅga sovereignty. Besides, it is suggested that the ivory-workers of Vidiśā were responsible for one of the exquisite gateways of Sāñchī (Foucher).

Literature must have flourished during the time of the Śuṅgas. Patañjali, a native of Gonarda, wrote his *Mahābhāṣya*, the great commentary on Pāṇini's grammar; and perhaps there were other literary celebrities, but their names have not yet been rescued from the limbo of oblivion.

[1] *J.R.A.S.*, 1909, pp. 1053-56.

SECTION B

THE KAṆVAS

Date and Circumstances of their Rise

It appears from the *Purāṇas* that the Śuṅga dynasty lasted for 112 years, and we may, therefore, believe that the Kāṇvāyanas or Kaṇvas, also Brahmans, seized power about 72 B. C. The above works and the *Harṣacarita* testify that the first Kaṇva, Vasudeva, became ruler after successfully carrying out the plot to assassinate the "overlibidinous" Devabhūti.[1]

A Minor Family

This dynasty comprised four kings only, and the total duration of their reigns is 45 years only.[2] They did not distinguish themselves in any manner whatever.

[1] cf. "In a frenzy of passion the over-libidinous Śuṅga was at the instance of his minister Vasudeva reft of his life by a daughter of Devabhūti's slave woman disguised as his queen" (*Hc. C.T.*, p. 193). cf. *Harṣacarita* (VI, p. 199, Bombay, 1925):

अतिस्त्रीसङ्गरतमनङ्गपरवशं शुङ्गममात्यो वसुदेवो देवभूतिदासीदुहित्रा देवीव्यञ्जनया वीतजीवितमकारयत् । See also Pargiter, *Dynasties of the Kali Age*, p. 71.

cf. *Viṣṇu Purāṇa*, IV, Ch. 24, 39, p. 352, Gītā Press ed.

देवभूतिं तु शुङ्गराजानं व्यसनिनं तस्यैवामात्यः कण्वो वसुदेवनामा तं निहत्य स्वयमवनीं भोक्ष्यति ।

[2] cf. *Vāyu Purāṇa*,

चत्वारः शुङ्गभृत्यास्ते नृपाः काण्वायना द्विजाः ।

APPENDIX I

Genealogical Tables

The Śuṅgas

Serial No.	Name of king	Length of reign
1.	Puṣyamitra	36 years
2.	Agnimitra	8 ,,
3.	Vasujyeṣṭha or Sujyeṣṭha	7 ,,
4.	Vasumitra	10 ,,
5.	Ādraka or Odraka	2 ,,
6.	Pulindaka	3 ,,
7.	Ghoṣa	3 ,,
8.	Vajramitra	9 ,,
9.	Bhāgavata	32 ,,
10.	Devabhūti or Devabhūmi	10 ,,
	Total	120 years

Note:—The *Purāṇas* say: "These ten Śuṅga kings will enjoy this earth full 112 years." Curiously, however, the details of the length of their reigns amount to 120 years.

APPENDIX II

The Kaṇvas or Kānvāyanas

1.	Vasudeva	9 years
2.	Bhūmimitra	14 ,,
3.	Nārāyaṇa	12 ,,
4.	Suśarman	10 ,,
	Total	45 years

SECTION C

THE SĀTAVĀHANAS

Date of Their Rise

The date of the rise of the Sātavāhanas has been a frequent source of controversy. Some scholars, relying on the Paurāṇic (*Matsya*) testimony that the Andhras ruled for about four centuries and a half, assign the beginnings of their power to the last quarter of the third century B. C. Much stress should not, however, be laid on this date, for another tradition preserved in the *Vāyu Purāṇa* mentions 300 years only as the duration of their rule. Dr. Bhandarkar, on the other hand, believes that the Sātavāhana dynasty was founded about 72-73 B. C. In his opinion the statement of the *Purāṇas* that Simuka or Śiśuka, the first Sātavāhana, "will obtain the earth after uprooting Suśarman Kaṇvāyana and what was left of the Śuṅga power,"[1] proves that the "Śuṅgabhritya" Kaṇvas ruled, like the Peshwas, simultaneously with their masters. But if this view is accepted, how are we to reconcile it with the other Paurāṇic reference that Vasudeva Kaṇva killed the last Śuṅga Devabhūti? The above passage, as Dr. Raychaudhuri points out, simply signifies that Simuka destroyed even those chiefs of Śuṅga blood, who had survived the Kaṇva *coup d'etat*.[2] Hence the fall of the Kaṇvas was brought about by the Sātavāhanas in 29 B. C. (i.e., 72 B. C.—45 years). This does not, of course, exclude the possibility that Simuka, who is said to have ruled for 23 years, ascended the throne

[1] cf. *Vāyu Purāṇa*:

काण्वायनस्ततो भृत्यः सुशर्माणं प्रसह्य तम्। शुङ्गानां चैव यच्छेषं क्षपयित्वा बलं तदा। सिन्धुको अन्ध्रजातीयः प्राप्स्यतीमां वसुन्धराम्।

[2] *Pol. Hist. Anc. Ind.*, 4th ed., p.333, to which I owe a number of suggestions.

earlier—say some time about the middle of the first century B. C.

Which Name to Apply—Andhra or Sātavāhana?

The Sātavāhanas are called Andhras in the *Purāṇas*. The latter were an ancient people, occupying the Telugu country between the Godāvarī and the Krisṇā. They are mentioned in the *Aitareya Brāhmaṇa* as beyond the pale of Aryanism, and Megasthenes gives some details of their power and wealth.[1] In the edicts of Aśoka they are included among the peoples within his sphere of influence. What happened to them after the decline of the Mauryan Empire is not known, but presumably they asserted their independence. Let us now examine the relation between the Sātavāhanas and the Andhras. The former uniformly call themselves Sātavāhana or Sātakarṇi in their epigraphic documents,[2] and the name Andhra is conspicuous by its absence. Besides, their earliest inscriptions are found in Nānāghat (Poona district) and Sāñchī (Central India). This raises a strong suspicion that the Andhras and the Sātavāhanas did not belong to the same stock. Indeed, it appears that the Sātavāhanas started from the Deccan,[3] and after a short time conquered Andhradeśa. But when they lost their western and northern territories on account of the Śaka and Ābhīra invasions, their

[1] According to Pliny, who probably quotes from the *Indika* of Megasthenes, the king of Kaliṅga maintained an army of 60,000 foot soldiers, 1,000 horsemen, and 700 elephants.

[2] The name Śālivāhana is sometimes found in literature.

[3] The homeland of the Sātavāhanas is uncertain. Dr. V.S. Sukthankar suggests the Bellary district (*Ann. Bhand. Inst.*, 1918-19, p. 21), whereas Dr. H. C. Raychaudhuri is in favour of "the territory immediately south of Madhyadeśa (*Pol. Hist. Anc. Ind.*, 4th ed., p. 342). *MM.*V.V. Mirashi, on the other hand, thinks that Berar or the region on both banks of the Waingangā was their home-province (*J.N.S.I.*, Vol. II, p. 94).

power was limited to the regions of the Godāvarī and the Krisṇā, and then they became known as the Andhras.

Origin of the Sātavāhanas

The origin of the Sātavāhanas is obscure. Some scholars connect them with the Satiyaputas of Aśokan edicts, and the *Setai* mentioned by Pliny. Others give fanciful derivations of the name.[1] Whatever the exact significance of the terms Sātakarṇi or Sātavāhana, the inscriptions of the dynasty suggest a Brahmanical ancestry. For in the Nasik inscription Gautamīputra is described as "the unique Brahman (*eka Baṁhana*) in prowess equal to Rāma (Paraśurāma)."[2] This obtains further confirmation from the fact that he is called "the destroyer of the pride and conceit of the Kṣatriyas."[3] The author of the inscription thus regarded Gautamīputra as a great Brahman, a veritable Paraśurāma.[4]

Rulers of the Dynasty

Not much is known about Simuka, the founder of the line, except that he subverted the Kaṇvas and the remnants of the Śuṅga power. He was succeeded by his brother Kanha (Krisṇa), and a Nasik inscription informs us that during his reign an inhabitant of the place had a cave made there. This clearly indicates that Krisṇa's authority was recognised in the Nasik region. The third king, Sātakarṇi, son of Simuka, appears to have been a considerable figure. According

[1] See *Kathāsaritsāgara*, VI, 87 f; Jinaprabhāsūri's *Tīrthakalpa*.
[2] *Ep. Ind.*, VIII, pp. 60, 61, l. 7.
[3] *Ibid.*, l. 5. cf. "Khatiyadapamānamadanasa."
[4] See also K.P. Jayasval, *J.B.O.R.S.*, Vol. XVI, pts. III and IV, pp. 265-66.

to the Nānāghat inscription,[1] he made extensive conquests and performed two *Aśvamedha* sacrifices. If he is identical with Sātakarṇi mentioned in an inscription on the gateway of the Sāñchī *Stūpa*, we have got epigraphic proof that Central India was an early possession of the Sātavāhanas. Next, the similarity in the scripts of the Nānāghat and Hāthīgumphā inscriptions[2] shows that it was perhaps this Sātakarṇi, whom Khāravela of Kaliṅga defied in the second year of his reign. The former's wife was Nāyanikā or Nāganikā, daughter of the Mahārathi Traṇakayiro of the Aṅgīya family, and she acted as regent during the minority of the princes Śakti-Śrī and Veda-Śrī. Then follows a period of darkness until the curtain is lifted by Gautamīputra Śātakarṇi. No doubt, the *Purāṇas* give a string of names, but unfortunately no coins or inscriptions have been discovered to corroborate them. One of these rulers, Hāla, is credited with having composed a Prakrit anthology called *Sattasai* (*Saptaśataka*). Towards the end of the first century A. D. the fortunes of the Sātavāhanas suffered an eclipse, as the Śaka Kṣatrapas wrested Mahārāṣṭra from them.

Gautamīputra Śātakarṇi

The conquerors did not, however, long enjoy the fruits of their victory, for the Dekkan was soon recovered by Gautamīputra Śātakarṇi, whose exploits are detailed in a Nasik inscription of the queen-mother, Gautamī Balaśrī.[3] He is said to have crushed the pride and conceit of the Kṣatriyas, and to have restored the observance of caste rules. He overthrew the Śakas, Yavanas, and the Pahlavas; destroyed the Kṣaharātas; and re-established

[1] *Rep. Arch. Surv. West. Ind.*, V., pp. 60 f.
[2] See R.D.Banerji, *Mem. As. Soc. Beng.*, XI, No. 3, pp. 131 f.
[3] *Ep. Ind.*, VIII, pp. 59-62.

the glory of the Sātavāhana race.[1] The above claims obtain some confirmation from the names of the various countries that were under his domination;[2] they correspond roughly to modern Gujarat, Saurāṣṭra, Malwa, Berar, North Konkan, and the region around Poona and Nasik. That he deprived the Kṣaharātas of their possessions is also apparent from the large Jogalthambī (Nasik) hoard containing silver coins of Nahapāna and his other pieces restruck by Gautamīputra Śātakarṇi He dedicated a cave at Pāṇḍu-leṇa, near Nasik, in the 18th year of his reign; and he issued another inscription in the 24th year, granting a field to certain ascetics.[3] The latter record proves that he ruled for at least 24 years.

Vāsiṣṭhiputra Śrī Puḷamāvi

Gautamīputra was succeeded by his son Vāsiṣṭhiputra Śrī Puḷamāvi in about A.D. 130. He extended the Sātavāhana sway over Andhradeśa; and he has been rightly identified with *Siropolemaiou*, whom Ptolemy calls king of Baithan or Paiṭhān (Pratiṣṭhāna), which may have been the capital of the later Sātavāhanas. It is further believed that Puḷamāvi is the Śātakarṇi, lord of Dakṣiṇāpatha, mentioned in the Junāgaḍh Rock inscription as having been twice defeated by Rudradāman.[4] We also learn that the rival's mutual relation was "not remote." Probably Puḷamāvi was the victor's

[1] *cf.* खतियदपमानमदनस सकयवनपह्लवनिस्दनस.....खखरातवस-निरवसेसकरस सातवाहनकुलयसपतिथापनकरस......

[2] Their names are as follows: Asika, Asaka, Muḷaka, Suraṭha, Kukura, Aparānta, Anūpa, Vidabha (Vidarbha), Ākarāvanti.

[3] *Ep. Ind.*, VIII, no. 5, pp. 73-74.

[4] *Ep. Ind.*, VIII, pp. 36-49.

cf. दक्षिणापथपतेः सातकर्णेर्द्विरपि निर्व्याजमवजित्यावजित्य सम्बन्धा-विदूरतयानुत्सादनात्प्राप्तयशसा—।

son-in-law, if Rapson is correct in identifying him with Vāsiṣṭhiputra Śrī Śātakarṇi, represented in a Kanheri (Thānā district) inscription to have married the daughter of Mahākṣatrapa Rudra (Rudradāman). But though the latter spared the Sātavāhana ruler, he annexed a good deal of his territories, as would appear from the list of countries, over which, according to the Junāgaḍh inscription, the Śaka Mahākṣatrapa ruled. Śrī Puḷamāvi died about 155 A. D.

Yajña Srī Sātakarṇi

Yajña Srī Sātakarṇi or Srī Yajña Sātakarṇi was the last great monarch of the dynasty. He ruled from *circa* A. D. 165 to 195—an inscription discovered at Chinna in the Kriṣṇā district being dated in the 27th year of his reign. This record as well as those found in Kanheri and Pāṇḍu-leṇa (Nasik), and the provenance of his coins, prove that his dominions extended east to west from the Bay of Bengal to the Arabian sea. Thus he regained much of the land, which the Sakas had conquered earlier; and presumably the pieces he issued in imitation of the Western Kṣatrapa coinage were meant for circulation in these regions. Further, the maritime power and activity of Srī Yajña Sātakarṇi are indicated by a coin having a two-masted ship with a fish and a conch and the legend *(Ra) ṇa Samasa sar (i) Yaña Satakaṇasa i.e., Raṇa Sāmisa Siri Yaña Sātakaṇisa* on the obverse and the Ujjaini symbol on the reverse.[1]

Yajña Srī's successors were mere nonentities. During their time the Sātavāhana power rapidly declined, and it collapsed when the Ābhīras seized Mahārāṣṭra, and the Ikṣvākus and the Pallavas appropriated the eastern provinces.

[1] *J.N.S.I.*, Vol. III, pt. I, June 1941, pp. 43-45.

The Dekkan under the Sātavāhanas

The political data that we gather from the inscriptions of the Sātavāhanas are disappointingly meagre, but, as shown by Dr. D. R. Bhandarkar, they yield us valuable information regarding the social, religious, and economic conditions of the Dekkan during their sway.[1]

Society

There were at least four classes of social divisions. The *Mahābhojas*, the *Mahāraṭhis*, and the *Mahāsenāpatis*, who controlled the *rāṣṭras* or districts, comprised the highest rank of society. The second class included officials like the *Amātyas*, *Mahāmātras*, and the *Bhāṇḍāgārikas*; such non-officials as the *Naigama* (merchant), *Sārthavāha* (head of the traders), and the *Śreṣṭhin* (chief of the trade-guild). The third class consisted of the *Vaidya* (physician), *Lekhaka* (scribe), *Suvarṇakāra* (goldsmith), *Gāndhika* (perfumer), *Hālakīya* (cultivator), etc. The fourth class comprehended the *Mālākāra* (gardener), *Vardhakī* (carpenter), *Dāsaka* (fisherman), *Lohavaṇija* (blacksmith), etc., The head of a family (*kula*) was called *Kuṭumbin* or *Grihapati*; his position was certainly one of authority.

Religion

Both Brahmanism and Buddhism prospered under the tolerant rule of the Sātavāhanas. Pious donors excavated *Caitya-grihas* (temples) or caused caves to be made for the residence (*layanas*) of the *Bhikṣus*, and also adequately provided for their maintenance by depositing money on interest with guilds. Brahmanism

[1] *Ind. Ant.*, XLVIII (1919), pp. 77 f. See also Dr. D. R. Bhandarkar's article, "Dekkan of the Sātavāhana Period," *Ind. Ant.*, XLVII. (1918), pp. 149 f.

was showing signs of vigour. Aśvamedha, Rājasūya, Āptoryāma, and other sacrifices were performed by the Royalty, and Brahmans got decent *Dakṣiṇas* or fees. The worship of Śiva and Kriṣṇa was popular,[1] and votaries of the different faiths lived in harmony. Sometimes they even gave grants to one another. Foreigners adopted either religion—Brahmanism or Buddhism—and were being assimilated into the Hindu society. Indeed, their names had become thoroughly Hinduised. Thus, in a Karle inscription two Yavanas are called Sihadaya (Siṁhadvaja) and Dharma respectively. Similarly, the Śaka Uṣavadāta is represented as a staunch Brahmanist.

Economic Conditions

Guilds (*śreṇis*) were a normal feature of the age. We learn of such organisations of corn-dealers (*dhaṁñikas*), potters, weavers (*kolika-nikāyas*), oil-pressers (*tilapiṣaka*), braziers (*kāsākaras*), bamboo-workers (*vaṁsakaras*), etc. Besides bringing members of the same craft together, they served as banks, in which money (*akṣaya nīvī*) could be invested on interest. The currency consisted of *Kārṣāpaṇas*, both silver and copper, and gold *Suvarṇas*. Each *Suvarṇa* was equivalent to 35 silver *Kārṣāpaṇa* pieces.

Trade flourished; and ships from the West, laden with merchandise, visited the ports of Broach, Sopārā, and Kalyān. The two important inland marts were Tagara and Paithān. Communications were generally good, and people freely went from one part of the Dekkan to another on business.

Literature

The Sātavāhana kings were great patrons of Prakrit,

[1] The Nānāghat inscription refers to other gods like Dharma,

which is used in all their documents. One of them, Hāla, was even the author of a Prakrit anthology called the *Sattasai* (*Saptaśataka*). About the same time Gūṇādhya is said to have written his original *Brihat-kathā* in Prakrit. Further, Mr. Allan points out that Sarvavarman produced the *Kātantra* for the benefit of an Andhra king who was "ashamed of his ignorance of Sanskrit and found Pāṇini too difficult."[1] One need not unduly emphasise these traditions. It appears rather strange, however, that the Brahman Sātavāhanas neglected Sanskrit in favour of Prakrit literature.

II. *King Khāravela of Kaliṅga*

Chronological Position

We do not know with certitude what happened to Kaliṅga after the death of Aśoka. When darkness is dispelled, we see a colossus strutting on the political stage. The Hāthīgumphā inscription on the Udayagiri hills, near Bhuvaneśvar (Puri),[2] describes the achievements of Khāravela, the third ruler of the Ceta dynasty, till the 13th year of his reign, but being undated it does not throw any definite light on his chronological setting. Some scholars think that in the 16th line the record contains a reference to the 165th year of the Maurya era; others emphatically deny this interpretation. Perhaps a clue to Khāravela's date is furnished by the similarity in the scripts of the Nānāghat and Hāthīgumphā inscriptions, and by the expression "ti-vasasata," which, as Dr. Raychaudhuri has rightly

Indra, and guardians of the four quarters—Yama, Varuṇa, Kubera, and Vāsava.

[1] *Cam. Sh. Hist. Ind.*, p. 61.

[2] *Ep. Ind.*, XX, January, 1930, pp. 71 f; see also K. P. Jayasval, *J. B. O. R. S.*, 1918 (IV), pp. 364 f; *Ibid.*, 1927 (XIII), pp. 221; *Ibid.*, 1928 (XIV), pp. 150 f.

pointed out, is used in line 6 of the latter epigraph in the sense of 300 and not 103 years from the time of Nandarāja, identified with Mahāpadma.[1] It would thus appear that Khāravela flourished some time about the third quarter of the first century B.C.

Events

Having received training in writing, mathematics, law, and finance, necessary for a crown-prince, Khāravela ascended the throne in his 24th year. He spent the first year of his reign in completing certain works of public utility. In the second year he defied the might of Śātakarṇi, and attacked the city of Muṣika.[2] The Raṭhikas and Bhojakas submitted to him in the fourth year, and in the fifth Khāravela extended a canal that had not been used for "ti-vasa-sata" since Nandarāja had brought it into the capital. The Kaliṅga monarch invaded Magadha twice—in the 8th and 12th years of his reign. The people of Magadha were terrified, and Bahasatimitra, who is said to have been then ruling at Rājagriha, was compelled to sue for peace. Nothing is known about the latter, but his name as well as the location of his capital militates against identifying him with Puṣyamitra. The successes of Khāravela overawed the Yavana general, whose name and identity are, however not quite clear.[3] The Pāṇḍyas were sub-

[1] *Pol. Hist. Anc. Ind.*, 4th ed., pp. 314-15, 337-38, 345. See *Ante* for the date of Mahāpadma.

[2] In place of Muṣikanagara, Dr. D.C. Sirkar reads Asikanagara, city of the Asikas (=Ṛṣikas of the *Purāṇas*), which he locates on the left bank of the Krisṇā (or Kañhabenna)—*J.N.S.I.*, Vol. III, pt. I (June, 1941), p. 62.

[3] The reading D(i)mi(ta)or Dimita (Demetrios), proposed by the late Prof. R. D. Banerji and Dr. K. P. Jayasval, is by no means certain (cf. line 8, Hāthīgumphā inscription, *Ep. Ind.*, XX, pp. 71 f). See also Tarn, *The Greeks in Bactria and India*, Appendix V, pp. 457-59.

dued in the 13th year after which the inscription does not tell us more about the meteoric career of Khāravela. He gave largess to the needy, and was himself a devout Jain. He excavated caves for Jain monks, and brought back from Magadha a celebrated image of the Jain *Tīrthaṁkara*, carried away earlier by Nandarāja.

CHAPTER XI

I. THE EPOCH OF FOREIGN INVADERS

Section A

THE INDO-GREEKS[1]

Revolt of Parthia and Bactria

About the middle of the third century B. C. there occurred in Central Asia two events, which were destined to have far-reaching effects on the course of Indian history. These were the defections of Parthia and Bactria from the Seleucid empire. The revolt of the former province, comprising the inhospitable regions of Khurasan and the South-East Caspian coast, which had never adopted the Greek culture, was a sort of a popular uprising headed by an enterprising chief named Arsakes.

Arsakes

The dynasty he founded about 248 B.C. lasted nearly five centuries. The rebellion of Bactria, on the other hand, was largely due to the ambitions of its own governor Diodotus, who about the same time formed designs of breaking away from the Seleucids.

Diodotus I

The land of Balkh, lying between the Hindu-Kush and the Oxus, was rich, fertile, and thickly populated; and it was regarded as an important out-post of Hellenism in the East. We do not know how far the disturbed condi-

[1] See W. W. Tarn, *The Greeks in Bactria and India*, (Cambridge, 1938); H.G. Rawlinson, *Bactria* (London, 1912); *India and the Western World* (Cambridge, 1916); *Cam. Hist. Ind.*, Vol. I, Ch. xxii, pp. 540-62.

tion of the Syrian monarchy after the death of Antiochos II Theos in 246 B. C. helped Diodotus in his

Diodotus II

undertakings, but his son, who had come to terms with his Parthian contemporary, appears to have achieved full independence. Probably Diodotus II ruled from *circa* 245 to 230 B. C. He met a violent death at the hands of an adventurer

Euthydemos

from Magnesia (-under-Sipylos ?) named Euthydemos, who seized the throne for himself. He was, however, involved in a protracted struggle with Antiochos III (*circa* 223-185 B.C.), when the latter made determined efforts about 212 B.C. to recover the lost provinces. After a long

Invasion of Antiochos III

siege of Balkh the contending parties concluded peace mainly through the good offices of a certain Teleas. The Seleucid monarch recognised the independence of Bactria, and as a mark of friendship gave the hand of his daughter to Demetrios,[1] son of Euthydemos, with whose diplomacy and dignified bearing during the course of the peace negotiations he was greatly impressed. Antiochos III then crossed the Hindu-kush in 207 or 206 B.C., and received the submission of king Sophagasenos (Subhāgasena), perhaps the successor of Vīrasena, who, according to Tārānātha, soon after Aśoka's death established his sway over Gandhāra.[2] Antiochos the Great did not, however, proceed beyond the frontiers of India, and he hastily returned homeward to attend to urgent affairs in the West. His departure thus left the Bactrian Greeks free to pursue their schemes of expansion and aggrandisement.

[1] See, however, Tarn, who says: "It is quite certain that whomever Demetrios married it was *not* a daughter of Antiochos" (*The Greeks in Bactria and India*, pp. 82, 201, n. 1).

[2] See also Tarn, *The Greeks in Bactria and India*, p. 130 and note 2; *J.A.S.B.*, 1920, pp. 305, 310.

Conquests of the Bactrian Greeks

The kingdom of Bactria rapidly grew in power under Euthydemos who appears to have subjugated a large part of Afghanistan. When he died about 190 B.C., his son Demetrios undertook foreign expeditions of greater magnitude. Crossing the Hindu-Kush about 183 B.C. he conquered a considerable portion of the Punjab; and if he is the Yavana general mentioned in the *Mahābhāṣya* and the *Yuga-purāṇa* of the *Gārgī-Saṁhitā*, he over-ran the Pañcāla country, besieged Madhyāmikā (Nāgarī, Chitor) and Sāketa (Ayodhyā), and even threatened Pāṭaliputra, perhaps in the time of Puṣyamitra. It is noteworthy that Strabo partly gives to Demetrios and partly to Menander the credit for the extension of Greek dominion in Ariana and India.[1] While Demetrios was busy with his Indian adventure, a certain Eukratides, who, according to Tarn,[2] was a general and first cousin of Antiochos IV, successfully raised the standard of revolt in Bactria with the help of the disgruntled Greek settlers, and seated himself on the throne (*c.* 175 B.C.). Demetrios could not dislodge his rival from this position, and it seems, therefore, his authority remained confined to the Greek conquests in the Punjab and Sind. For Demetrios is known in traditions as

Demetrios

Eukratides revolts

[1] cf. Strabo: "The Greeks who occasioned the revolt (i.e., Euthydemos and his family), owing to the fertility and advantages of Bactria, became masters of Ariana and India....These conquests were achieved partly by Menander and partly by Demetrios, son of Euthydemos. They overran not only Pattalene, but the kingdoms of Saraostos and Sigerdis, which constitute the remainder of the coast. They extended their empire as far as the Seres and Phrynoi." Tarn believes that Demetrios and Menander were "acting in concert," and that the latter went farther than the former (*G.B.I.*, p. 144).

[2] *G.B.I.*, pp. 195-97.

Rex Indorum, "king of the Indians"; and we also learn that he founded a town, Euthydemia, in memory of his father. Further, the town of Dattāmitrī among the Sauvīras perhaps owes its origin to Dattāmitra or Demetrios, as pointed out by Tarn on the strength of a scholion to Patañjali.[1] Demetrios was the first Greek ruler to issue bilingual coins, having legends in Greek along with the Indian language in the Kharoṣṭhī script.[2] Sometime afterwards (*c.* 165-60 B.C.) Eukratides, who had founded the city of Eukratideia, bearing his own name, in Bactria, "conquered India and became lord of a thousand cities" (Justin). Thus arose two separate Greek principalities in the East, ruled by the rival houses of Euthydemos and Eukratides. The former held eastern Punjab, with its capital at Euthydemia or Śākala (Sialkot), Sind, and the adjoining regions; and the latter was in possession of Bactria, Kabul valley, Gandhāra, and western Punjab. Coins are almost our sole evidence about these numerous princelings, and due to the meagreness of the data their ancestry, chronology and territory are often a matter of extreme doubt and difficulty. Among the descendants or successors of Euthydemos mention may be made of Agathocles, Pantaleon, and Antimachus. Perhaps Apollodotus and Menander also belonged to this line.[3] The latter is by far the most interesting figure in Indo-Greek history. Strabo says that he conquered "more nations

Division

House of Euthydemos

Menander

[1] *G.B.I.*, p. 142 and note.

[2] Some scholars, however, attribute these coins to Demetrios II (see Allan, *Cam. Sh. Hist. Ind.*, p. 64).

[3] According to Vincent Smith (*E.H.I.*, 4th ed., pp. 238-39), however, Apollodotus and Menander belonged to the family of Eukratides. For Menander, see the Bajaur inscription (*New Ind. Ant.*, Vol. II, No. 10, January, 1940, p. 647).

than Alexander." No doubt, this claim is to some extent confirmed by the wide distribution of his coins, which have been found from Kabul to Mathurā and even in places further eastwards like Bundelkhand. According to the anonymous author of the *Periplus Maris Erythraei*, Menander's coins were current along with those of Apollodotus in the markets of Barygaza (Broach) in his time (about the third quarter of the 1st century A.D.). Some scholars have identified Menander with the Yavana invader, who carried his arms as far as Madhyamikā, Sāketa, and Pāṭaliputra during the reign of Puṣyamitra.[1] Milinda or Menander was a Buddhist, and he has survived in Indian traditions. Thus, the *Miliñdapañho* preserves some of his puzzling questions on religion put to Thera Nāgasena. Indeed, according to a Siamese legend Menander even attained to Arhatship.[2] Some of his coins bear the Buddhist symbol *dharma-cakra* and the epithet "Dhramikasa," which may be regarded as an additional proof of his faith in Buddhism. The *Milindapañho* also contains a glowing account of the capital, Śākala, which abounded with parks, gardens, tanks, beautiful buildings, well-laid out streets, and strong defences. It had shops for the sale of Benares muslin, jewels, and other costly articles indicating the wealth and prosperity of the kingdom. Menander was noted for his justice, and Plutarch informs us that on his death in camp[3] there were disputes among his subjects for the possession of his ashes, over which they wanted to raise *Stūpas*. Coins yield us the names of Menander's successors—Strato I, Strato II, and others—, but nothing definite is known about them.

[1] See *Supra*.

[2] H.G. Rawlinson, *Bactria*, p. 111. See, however, Tarn, *G.B.I.*, pp. 262-68.

[3] Tarn places the death of Menander about 150-45 B.C. (*G.B. I.*, p. 226).

House of Eukratides

To turn to Eukratides; it appears he did not enjoy his conquests long. While he was returning home after his Indian expedition he was assassinated, as Justin deposes, by his son and colleague (?) who has been rightly identified with Heliocles.[1] This event happened about 155 B.C., and the unnatural youth is alleged to have gloried so much in his heinous crime that he even refused to give a burial to the dead body. Tarn, however, does not accept the tradition of parricide, or that Heliocles insulted his father's corpse.[2] He was the last Greek king of Bactria, for after Heliocles it was overwhelmed by the Śaka deluge from the steppes of Central Asia. Of the many members of his line, whose authority was confined to the valleys of Afghanistan and the Indian border-lands, history has not condescended to record anything except their names. One of them, Antialkidas, however, is known from the Besnagar pillar inscription to have sent his ambassador Heliodora or Heliodorus, son of Diya (Dion), to the court of Kāśīputra Bhāgabhadra, identified with the fifth Śuṅga monarch, Odraka, or with the last but one, Bhāgavata.[3] It is noteworthy Aṁtalikhita or Antialkidas is described as king of Taxilā, and his ambassador calls himself a *Bhāgavata*—worshipper of Viṣṇu. Most of the coinage of Antialkidas,

Heliocles

Antialkidas

[1] According to Vincent Smith, the parricide was Apollodotus (*E.H.I.*, 4th ed., p. 238). According to another story given by Justin, Eukratides was killed by the Parthians. Tarn disbelieves the version of parricide. He thinks that Eukratides was killed by "a son of one of the dead Euthydemid princes." Was he Demetrios II? (*G.B.I.*, pp. 220, 222).

[2] *G.B.I.*, p. 220. The parricide is alleged to have driven "his chariot wheels through the blood of his father" (*E.H.I.*, 4th ed., p. 238; Justin, xli, 6).

[3] See *Supra*.

like that of other Greek rulers in India, is bilingual but there is one silver issue on the Attic standard bearing his Greek legend only, "Of king Antialkidas the Victorious," which may indicate some of his military successes. The last Greek ruler of the frontier regions and the Kabul valley was Hermæus, who flourished about the second quarter of the first century A.D.[1] Hemmed in by enemies on all sides, he succumbed to the pressure of the advancing Kushans under Kujūla Kadphises. The Greek power had already been weakened by internal feuds, and so it could not withstand the inroads of these "barbarian" hordes.

Hermæus

Results of the Greek contact

Let us now consider the effects of the Greek occupation of the north-western parts of India. Did these foreign rulers influence the subsequent development of Indian institutions and polity, or were they regarded merely as brilliant commanders of armies, to be dreaded rather than imitated? Questions like these have evoked widely different answers; some emphasise the debt India owes to Hellenism, and others deny its impress altogether. As is often the case, the truth lies somewhere midway. The Greeks first came into touch with India at the time of Alexander's invasion, and whatever his intentions may have been, he could not in the midst of nineteen months' hard fighting act as a pioneer of Greek civilisation, or materially change the course of Hindu society. Indeed, the Indian revolt, following closely upon his premature death, soon obliterated all traces of Greek conquest. Then came Seleukos Nikator about 306 B.C., but he got no chance to disseminate the seeds of Greek culture on Indian soil. His arms were effectively checked on the frontiers by Candra-

[1] Tarn suggests 50 B.C. (*G.B.I.*, pp. 331, 337).

gupta Maurya, who is said to have wrested from his adversary four important satrapies corresponding to modern Baluchistan and southern Afghanistan. Neither Megasthenes nor Kauṭilya bears out that there were any Hellenic signs in the Maurya court. For the next one hundred years India enjoyed immunity from Greek incursions. In 206 B.C. Antiochos III appeared on her border-lands, but he, too, had to hurry back home after receiving the homage of a prince named Sophagasenos (Subhāgasena). The later expeditions of Demetrios, Eukratides, and Menander, which covered with intervals a period of about four decades (*c.* 190-155 B.C.), penetrated far into the interior of the country. These were not wholly transitory raids, for in the Punjab and adjacent territories they led to the establishment of Greek rule, which lasted over a century and a half. It is, however, surprising that traces of Hellenism are even here very scanty.

It appears that in the matter of coinage Indians learnt much from the Greeks. Prior to their advent rude punch-marked coins were current in India, but they introduced the practice of using regular coins, properly shaped and stamped. The Greek word *Drachma* was even adopted by Indians as *Dramma.*[1]

Further, the Greek language on coins is supposed to indicate that it was understood in the Indo-Greek dominions, but this view is not borne out by the evidence available. The introduction of the Indian legends and the use of the Kharoṣṭhī on coins would, on the other hand, prove that the masses in general did not know the Greek language at all. That this was the case is also clear from the fact that no Greek inscription has so far been discovered in India.

Turning to literature, it is alleged by St. Chrysostom (A.D. 117) that "the poetry of Homer is sung by the

[1] Is the Hindi word दाम derived from the term *Dramma*?

Indians, who had translated it into their own language and modes of expression." This is further corroborated by Plutarch and Ælian, but there is hardly any basis for such assertions except some superficial similarities between the legends of Greece and those of India. For instance, the main theme of the *Rāmāyaṇa* curiously offers a parallel to the story of the *Iliad*. Similarly, although Greek plays may have been staged in places like Sākala and other centres of Greek power, we have really no evidence to warrant the assumption that Indian drama owes much to the Greek. The term *Yavanikā* merely denoted a curtain of Greek fabric, and other resemblances also are doubtless mostly fortuitous.

In the realm of astronomy Indians were certainly indebted to the Greeks. Thus says the *Gārgī-Saṁhitā*: "The Yavanas are barbarians yet the science of astronomy originated with them, and for this they must be reverenced like gods." Indian astronomy preserves a number of Greek terms; and, of course, the *Romaka* and *Paulisa Siddhāntas* bear obvious traces of Greek influences. As to astrology, Indians had some knowledge of it, but they are said to have borrowed from Babylon the art of divining the future by means of the stars.

It is difficult to say how far these Indo-Greeks affected the development of Indian art and architecture. Not one notable piece of sculpture belonging to the period of Demetrios and Menander has so far been unearthed,[1] but the later Gandhāra school, depicting on stone scenes from the life of the Buddha, is beyond doubt inspired by Hellenic ideals. Similarly, no Greek building in India has come to light, save the unembellished walls of some houses and a temple at Taxilā with

[1] Some pieces of Greek sculpture that have come to light are "the head of a Dionysos and the child with its finger to its lips" (see also *A.S.I.*, 1914-15, pp. 13 f).

Ionic pillars and classical mouldings, dating from about the first quarter of the first century B.C. The Hellenic style preponderated in the decorative arts for a long time. It was then modified by the addition of Indian motifs.

The contact of diverse civilisations gave an impetus to trade and commerce,[1] and there began a constant flow of ideas, which produced far-reaching results in different directions. Such instances as the conversion of Heliodorus to Vaiṣṇavism, and of Menander or of Theodoros of the Swat Vase inscription[2] to Buddhism, show that the Greeks were gradually succumbing to the subtle influence of Indian faiths. Thus, when "the legions had thundered past," India "plunged in thought again" in a manner which slowly converted her military conquerors into her moral and spiritual captives. The Indianisation of the Greeks must have been, to some extent, brought about by mixed marriages also.

Section B

THE ŚAKAS AND THE PAHLAVAS

Śaka Migrations

About 165-160 B.C. there were momentous movements of nomadic tribes in Central Asia. The Yueh-chis were dislodged from their position in North-western China, and were forced to migrate westwards. In the course of their wandering they encountered the Sakas or Sse,[3] who occupied the lands to the north of

[1] cf. e.g., the display of huge quantities of Indian ivory and spices by Antiochos IV at Daphne in 166 B.C. (Tarn, *G.B.I.*, pp. 361-62). Similarly, Ptolemy II exhibited Indian dogs and cattle "in his triumph" (*Ibid.*, p. 366). Among the Greek exports to India were perhaps parchment and "good-looking virgins for concubines," as the *Periplus* attests (see *Ibid.*, p. 373).

[2] Sten Konow, *C.I.I.* II, no. 1, pp. 1-4.

[3] They were called Sakai by Greek authors. See Sten Konow, Introd, *C.I.I.*, Vol. II, pt. I, pp. xvi f.....; K.P. Jayas-

the Jaxartes (Syr Daryā). The latter, having been pushed south, swooped down on Bactria and the Parthian kingdom in the period between 140 and 120 B.C. Weakened by foreign wars and internal dissensions, the Bactrian monarchy fell an easy prey to the invasion of these hordes. Then the Śakas pressed towards the south-west, and in the struggle, which followed with Parthia, Phraates II was killed in 128 B.C., and Artabanus I lost his life a few years later in 123 B.C. Mithridates II (123-88 B.C.), however, reasserted the Parthian power, which naturally diverted the Śakas eastwards. As their expansion was impeded in the Kabul valley, where the attenuated Greek kingdom lay like a wedge, they spread themselves in the territory, afterwards called Seistan or Śakastan. Sometime later, they moved through Arachosia (Kandahar) and Baluchistan into the lower Indus country, which consequently became known as Śaka-dvīpa to Hindu writers and Indo-Scythia to Greek geographers. From this base the Śakas established their settlements in several parts of India.

I

Maues

The earliest Śaka ruler of India appears to have been Maues, who is probably identical with Moa (cf. "Moasa") of the Maira (Salt Range) well inscription,[1] and with Moga of the Taxilā plate of Satrap Patika.[2] Vincent

val, *J.B.O.R.S.*, Vol. XVI, pts. III and IV, pp. 227-316 ("Problems of Śaka-Sātavāhana History"); R. D. Banerji, *Ind. Ant.*, XXXVII (1908), pp. 25 f; *Cam. Hist. Ind.*, Vol. I, Ch. xxiii, pp. 563-92; Govind Pai, "Chronology of Śakas, Pahlavas and Kushans" *Jour. Ind. Hist.*, Vol. XIV, (1935), pp. 309 f.

[1] The Maira inscription appears to be dated in the year 58 (*C.I.I.*, II, no. VIII, pp. 11-13).

[2] Mr. Govind Pai, however, reads *māgasa*, 'of the month Māgha,' instead of *Mogasa* in the Taxilā copper-plate inscription (*Journ. Ind. Hist.*, XIV, (1935), pp. 328-38).

Smith,[1] on the other hand, regards him as an Indo-Parthian king. These two ethnic types—the Śakas and the Pahlavas (Parthians)—are no doubt constantly associated with each other in Indian literature and inscriptions, and sometimes it is even difficult to distinguish between them. The same family includes both Pahlava and Śaka names, and similarities are also found in their coinages and their systems of satrapal government. Rapson, therefore, rightly remarks that to label Maues and his successors as Śakas is "little more than a convenient nomenclature."[2] Maues (Mauakes?) was certainly a great ruler. A copper-plate, found at Taxilā,[3] which calls him "Mahārāya," proves that this region was included in his dominions. He subsequently adopted the title "great king of kings" on his coins; and their provenance and types also show that Gandhāra and other adjacent lands, formerly under the Yavanas, came under his possession. But Maues does not appear to have carried his arms far into the Punjab, and thus his kingdom lay between the remnants of the two Yavana houses in the upper Kabul valley and in eastern Punjab. The date of Maues is uncertain, as we do not know definitely to which era the year 78 of the Taxilā copper-plate is to be assigned. Dr. Raychaudhuri thinks that he ruled "after 33 B.C., but before the latter half of the first century A.D."[4] Sten Konow, on the other hand, believes that Maues began to rule in about 90 B.C.[5]

His successors

Maues was followed by Azes,[6] who maintained his

[1] *E.H.I.*. 4th ed., p. 242.
[2] *Cam. Hist. Ind.*, I, p. 568.
[3] *C.I.I.*, II, pt. I, pp. 28, 29.
[4] *Pol. Hist. Anc. Ind.*, 4th ed., p. 365.
[5] *Jour. Ind. Hist.*, 1933, p. 19. cf. Sten Konow, Notes on Indo-Scythian Chronology," *Ibid.*, pp. 1-46.
[6] Is he identical with Aya or Aja (Azes?) of the Kalawān

predecessor's conquests intact, as is clear from the continuance of his coin-types. He also restruck the coins of Hippostratus, thereby indicating that Azes extended the Śaka rule over eastern Punjab. Some believe that he was the originator of the era commencing from B.C. 58. This view is, however, not at all convincing.

According to numismatic evidence Azilises came after Azes I, although there was a period in which both were associated in the government. The former was in turn succeeded by another Azes, designated Azes II. Some scholars identify the two Azes, but better opinion takes them as separate rulers. As we shall see below, after Azes II the Śaka territories passed under the sway of Gondophernes.

II

Satraps of the North-West

In the government by Satraps, it was the usual practice of the Mahākṣatrapa to rule in association with a Kṣatrapa,[1] generally his son, who in due course succeeded to the higher position. The Taxilā copper-plate of the year 78 gives us two such names—Liaka Kusulaka and his son Patika.[2] They were Satraps, under Mahārāya Moga, of the districts of Chhahara and Chuksha, perhaps near Taxilā.

III

Satraps of Mathurā

The earliest known members of this family were

inscription dated year 134 and with that of the Taxilā silver scroll inscription dated year 136 of an unspecified era (*C.I.I.*, II, no. XXVII, pp. 70-77)? Sten Konow refers the Kalwān (near Taxilā) record of the year 134 to the Vikrama era (*Ep. Ind.*, XXI, pp. 256, 259).

[1] Kṣatrapa is the Sanskrit adaptation of the old Persian Kṣatrapāvan (governor of a province).

[2] See Sten Konow, *C. I. I.*, II, pt. I, no. XIII, pp. 23-29.

Hagāna and Hagāmasa, who appear to have for some time ruled conjointly. Their successor was probably Rañjubula or Rājuvula, called Mahākṣatrapa in the Mora (near Mathurā) inscription. He copied the coins of Strato I and Strato II, and it may, therefore, be reasonable to suppose that Rañjubula put an end to Greek rule in eastern Punjab. After him, his Kṣatrapa son, Soḍāsa, succeeded to the dignity of Mahākṣtrapa. According to the Mathurā Lion Capital inscription he was satrap when Paḍika, or Patika, identified with Patika of the Taxilā record,[1] was great Satrap or Mahākṣatrapa. So we may regard them as contemporaries. In the Amohini votive tablet inscription, Soḍāsa is called a Mahākṣatrapa, and if its date 42 (Rapson) is to be referred to the Vikrama era, he must have flourished about 17-16 B.C.[2] Not much is known about his successors.

IV

The Kṣaharātas of Mahārāṣṭra

The first known Kṣatrapa of Western India was Bhūmaka, who belonged to the Kṣaharāta family.[3] He held sway in Saurāṣṭra. The type and fabric of his coins as well as the legends on them clearly indicate that Bhūmaka preceded Nahapāna; and their insignia "arrow, discus, and thunderbolt" may be com-

[1] *Ep. Ind.*, IV, pp. 54-57. Fleet doubts the identification of the two Patikas (*J.R.A.S.*, 1913, p. 1001 and note 3). For the Mathurā Lion Capital inscription, see Sten Konow, *C.I.I.*, II, pt. I, pp. 30-49.

[2] Some scholars propose the reading 72, in which case Soḍāsa's date would fall about 15 A.D. Sten Konow refers the date to the Vikrama era (*Ep. Ind.*, XIV, pp. 139-141). Others, however, believe that Soḍāsa dated the inscription in the Śaka era. Bühler originally took the date in the Amohinī record to be 42 (*Ep. Ind.*, II, p. 199), but subsequently corrected it to 72 (*Ibid*, IV, p. 55, n. 2). Rapson prefers the former reading (*Cam. Hist. Ind.*, I, p. 576, n. 1).

[3] Is the name Kṣaharāta identical with Ptolemy's Karatai? Is it derived from the district of Chhahara?

pared with certain pieces having "discus, bow and arrow" on the reverse, issued "conjointly by Spalirises and Azes."[1]

Nahapāna

The next Kṣaharāta ruler was Nahapāna whose precise relation with Bhūmaka is uncertain. There can, however, be no doubt about the former's Śaka nationality. For his daughter bearing a Hindu name, Dakṣamitrā, was married to Uṣavadāta (Riṣabhadatta), who is expressly called a Śaka in one of his inscriptions. The records of the latter, discovered at Pāṇḍu-leṇa (near Nasik), Junnar and Karle (Poona district), show that Nahapāna was master of a large part of Mahārāṣṭra. He must have wrested this region from the Sātavāhanas. He also sent his son-in-law to help the Uttamabhadras in repelling the aggressions of the Mālayas or Mālavas. After his victory, Uṣavadāta made certain benefactions in the Puṣkara *tīrtha* (Pokhara), which may indicate the extension of Nahapāna's influence as far as Ajmer. The inscriptions of his reign are dated in the years 41 to 46 of an unspecified era. On the assumption that these dates refer to the Śaka era, although Dubreuil would assign them to the Vikrama era,[2] Nahapāna was ruling in 119-124 A.D. But if he is identical with Mambarus or Mambanos of the *Periplus*,[3] as has sometimes been supposed, he must have flourished about the third quarter of the first century A.D. It appears from the evidence of the Nasik inscription and the Jogalthambī (near Nasik) hoard of coins that the power of Nahapāna, or perhaps

[1] Dubreuil, *Anc. Hist. Dec.*, p. 17.

[2] *Ibid.*, p. 22.

[3] The capital Minnagara has been variously identified with Jūnāgaḍh (B. Indraji), Mandasor or modern Dasor (Dr. Bhandarkar), Junnar, or Dohad (Fleet); but Jayasval believed that Nahapāna ruled at Broach.

one of his successors, was crushed by Gautamīputra Śātakarṇi.[1]

IV

THE SATRAPS OF UJJAIN

Caṣṭana

The founder of this line, which exercised sway in western India for several centuries, was Caṣṭana, son of Ysāmotika. Some scholars regard him as the originator of the Śaka era beginning from 78 A.D.[2] Others deny this, but they admit that the year 52 of the Andhau (Cutch) inscriptions is to be referred to this reckoning—a theory which would fix the year 130 A.D. as a date in Caṣṭana's reign.[3] He has been identified with Ptolemy's Tiastenes of Ozene; and his coins were copied from those of Nahapāna. Caṣṭana first ruled as a Kṣatrapa, and subsequently as a Mahākṣatrapa. Was he then "a vassal of Gautamīputra," as G. Jouveau Dubreuil believed,[4] or of the Kushans?

Rudradāman

Caṣṭana's son, Jayadāman, was only a Kṣatrapa, and he died without achieving any distinction. The latter's son, Rudradāman, was, however, a great figure. His exploits are described in the Junāgaḍh Rock ins-

[1] See *Ante.* Did Gautamīputra fight Nahapāna personally, or were they separated by "a very long time"? (See also *Anc. Hist. Dec.*, pp. 24-25).

[2] Dubreuil, *Anc. Hist. Dec.*, p. 36.

[3] Caṣṭana is sometimes supposed to have ruled conjointly with Rudradāman according to the Andhau epigraphs (Dr. D.R. Bhandarkar, *Ind. Ant.*, XLVII (1918), p. 154). Dubreuil disagrees with this view, and he takes the Andhau (Cutch) inscriptions to be dated in the reign of Rudradāman (*Anc. Hist. Dec.*, p. 27).

[4] *Ibid.*, p. 37.

cription dated year 72 or 150 A.D.[1] It represents him as having won for himself the title of Mahākṣatrapa;[2] conquered the "proud" Yaudheyas; and twice vanquished Śātakarṇi, lord of Dakṣiṇāpatha, to whom his relation was "not remote."[3] That these claims were not mere boasts is also evident from the names of lands, where his authority was recognised. They included northern Gujarat, Saurāṣṭra, Cutch, the lower Indus valley, north Konkan, Māndhātā region, eastern and western Malwa, Kukura and Maru *i.e.*, parts of Rajputana, etc.[4] Some of these territories, as we have elsewhere noted, were under Gautamīputra Śātakarṇi. Thus the power of Rudradāman grew at the cost of the Sātavāhanas. Another important event of his reign was the bursting of the embankment of the Sudarśana lake. But it was rebuilt three times stronger mainly by the efforts of his Pahlava governor of "the whole of Ānartta and Surāṣṭra," named Suviśākha, son of Kulaipa. We further learn that Rudradāman himself bore the entire expenses of its repairs, and did not resort to the usual royal device of imposing additional taxation. How solicitous he was indeed for the welfare of his people !

Rudradāman's successors

Several members of the dynasty ruled after Rudradāman, but nothing of moment is known about them.[5] About the fourth decade of the third century

[1] *Ep. Ind.*, VIII, pp. 36-49.

[2] *cf.* स्वयमधिगतमहाक्षत्रपनाम्ना ।

[3] See *Ante.*

[4] *cf.* पूर्वापराकरावन्त्यनूपनीवृदानर्तसुराष्ट्रश्वभ्र (म) रुकच्छसिन्धुसौवीरकुकुरापरान्तनिषादादीनां समग्राणां तत्प्रभावाद्य—।

[5] See Rapson, *Catalogue of the Coins of the Andhra Dynasty, the Western Kṣatrapas*, etc., (London, 1908).

A.D. the fortunes of the Kṣatrapas suffered a temporary eclipse owing to the irruption of the Ābhīras under perhaps Īśvaradatta, who usurped a portion of their dominions. The family, however, soon reasserted itself, and carried on its existence amidst vicissitudes till *Saka* 31x(=A.D. 31x+78),[1] a date occurring on the coins of Rudrasiṁha III, who is perhaps identical with the Śaka sovereign, mentioned in the *Haraṣacarita* as having been killed by Candragupta Vikramāditya. The Guptas then annexed the Śaka territories, and issued silver coins of the Kṣatrapa type, substituting the Garuḍa emblem on the reverse for the Kṣatrapa symbols.

V

The Pahlavas[2]

Vonones

The history of the Indo-Parthians or Pahlavas is still obscure. But a few facts may be gleaned from coins and inscriptions. The earliest known prince of the dynasty was Vonones, who attained power in Arachosia and Seistan, and adopted the title of "great king of kings."[3] On his coins, imitated from the issues of the house of Eukratides, Vonones is associated with his brothers, Spalirises and Spalahores, and his nephew, Spalagadames. Perhaps they were his Viceroys in the conquered regions. Vonones was succeeded by Spalirises, who appears to have been the suzerain of Azes II, for on certain coins the former's name is given in Greek on the obverse and that of Azes in Kharoṣṭhī on the reverse.

Spalirises

[1] The sign x stands for the third digit, which is not clear on coins.

[2] See Sten Konow, *C.I.I.*, II, Introd., pp. xxxvii-xlix.

[3] Rapson calls Vonones "suzerain over the kingdoms of eastern Iran," and he is believed to have flourished later than the reign of Mithradates II (*C.H.I.*, Vol. I, pp. 572-73).

Gondophernes

Gondophernes (Vindapharṇa)[1] was the next and the greatest Indo-Parthian monarch. The period of his reign has been almost definitely fixed with the help of the Takht-i-Bāhī inscription, which is dated in the year 103.[2] Referring it to the Vikrama era,[3] Fleet placed the record in 45 A.D. This date represents the 26th year of Mahārāya Guduvhara's (?) rule. Hence he came to the throne in 19 A.D., and remained king at least till 45 A.D. The epigraph further proves that the Peshawar district then owned his sway. His coin-types indicate that he became master of the Śaka-Pahlava dominions both in Eastern Iran and North-western India. That he supplanted Azes II in some territories seems evident from the coins of Aspavarman, who was at first the latter's *Strategos*, but afterwards acknowledged the overlordship of Gondophernes. In Christian traditions he is called "king of India," and is connected with St. Thomas. One can hardly rely on such legends, but this much appears to be based on fact that the Apostle visited the court of Gondophares or Gondophernes and that he met there with some success in his missionary labours.[4] When the Pahlava sovereign died, his kingdom broke up and was appropriated by various princes. One of these, Pakores, probably ruled over Western Punjab and portions of Southern Afgha-

[1] Other variants of the name are Guduphara or Guduvhara, Gondophares, Guḍana (coins), etc.

[2] See Sten Konow, *C.I.I.*, II, no. XX, pp. 57-62.

[3] This attribution is doubted by some scholars. The late R. D. Banerji assigns the year 103 of the Takht-i-Bāhī inscription to the Śaka era (*Ind. Ant.*, 1908, pp. 47, 62). Dr. Vincent Smith, however, does not accept such a late date for Gondophernes. He (Smith) believes that "the stratification at Taxilā shows that Gondophares preceded Kadphises I" (*E.H.I.*, 4th ed., p. 248, note 1).

[4] For the legend of St. Thomas, see Smith, *E.H.I.*, 4th ed., pp. 245-250.

nistan. The family was overthrown by the advance of the Kushans.

Section C

THE KUSHANS[1]

Yueh-chi Movements

About the fourth decade of the second century B.C.—the year commonly accepted being 165—,the Hiung-nu, a tribe of Turki nomads, won a decided victory over the Yueh-chi, their neighbours in Kan-su in North-western China, and forced them to quit their pasture-grounds. In the course of their westward migrations, the Yueh-chi encountered in the basin of the Ili river another horde called the Wu-sun, whose chief Nan-teou-mi was killed in defending his country. Here the Yueh-chi were split into two sections. One division, deflecting southwards, settled on the Tibetan border, and came to be known as the Little Yueh-chi (Siao Yueh-chi). The main body (Ta Yueh-chi) marched onward until they came into conflict with the Śakas, who, as already noticed, were dispossessed of their lands north of the Jaxartes. But the Yueh-chi did not long remain in the usurped territory, for they were expelled by Kwen-mo, son of the dead Wu-sun chieftain, with the help of the Hiung-

[1] See V. A. Smith, "The Kushān or Indo-Scythian Period of Indian History" (*J.R.A.S.*, 1903, pp. 1-64); R. D. Banerji, *Ind-Ant.*, XXXVII (1908), pp. 35 f; Sten Konow, *C.I.I.*, II, Introd., pp. xlix-lxxxii. The usual form of the name is Kushana, but sometimes Kushāṇa is also used. Dr. F. W. Thomas took it as "a family or dynastic title" (*J.R.A.S.*, 1906, p. 203). In the Panjtar record of the year 122, however, Gushaṇa occurs as the name of a *Mahārāya* (*C.I.I.*, II, no. XXVI, p. 70). Similarly, in the Taxilā silver scroll inscription of the year 136 (*Ibid.*, no. XXVII, p. 77) Kushāṇa is simply used for the name of the sovereign, perhaps Kadphises I or Wema Kadphises (cf. "The Great King, the King of Kings, the Son of Heaven, the Kushāṇa").

nu about 140 B.C. The Yueh-chi then made their way into the Oxus valley, subjugating a prosperous and peaceful people called the Ta-hia (Bactrians) by the Chinese. The Yueh-chi gradually occupied Bactria and Sogdiana, and by the beginning of the first century B.C. they gave up their nomadic habits of life. They

The five Principalities

became divided into five principalities: Hieu-mi, Chouang-mo, Kouei-Chouang, Hi-thun, Kao-fu. Nearly a century after this division, the *Yabghu* or *Yavuga* (*Jabgou*) of the Kouei-Chouang (Kushan) defeated the other four, and thus all were united in one kingdom under the former, named K'ieou-tsieouk'io. This king (*Wang*) has been identified with the Kujūla Kadphises of

Kujūla Kadphises

coins, which afford testimony to the gradual extinction of the Greek power in the Kabul valley. For some coins have the name Kujūla Kasa in Kharoṣṭhī and Kozoulo Kadaphes in Greek along with that of Hermæus, whereas others do not bear the latter name at all. It may, therefore, be reasonable to conclude that at first the two monarchs were allied together, perhaps to resist the expanding Pahlava power, but subsequently the Kushan rule superseded the Greeks in the Kabul region. Kujūla Kadphises attacked Parthia, conquered Kipin (probably Gandhāra) and southern Afghanistan. He must have achieved these victories late in his reign after the death of Gondophernes, who ruled Peshawar in 45 A.D. according to the Takht-i-Bāhī inscription. Chinese writers state that Kujūla Kadphises lived up to the age of eighty, and accordingly his end may be placed in or about the middle of the third quarter of the first century A.D.

Vīma Kadphises

We learn from Chinese historians that Kujūla Kadphises was succeeded by his son, Yen-kao-chen, identified with the "Great King Uviama Kavthisa" or Oēmo or Wema or Vīma Kadphises of the coins.[1] He is credited with the conquest of India (T'ien-tchieou). This may not be true, if taken literally, but the wide distribution of his coins and the assumption of high-sounding titles like "the great king, king of kings, the lord of all people......," show that his authority extended east of the Indus to the Punjab and possibly also to the United Provinces. He governed his Indian possessions through a Viceroy, to whom has been attributed the large number of copper coins, usually known as the issues of the "Nameless king", which are quite common in various parts of Northern India. Lastly, it appears from the epithet, *Māheśvara*, on his coins as also from *Nandi* and the figure of Śiva on their reverse, that Vīma Kadphises was probably a devotee of the Hindu god, Śiva. Needless to comment on how soon the Kushans succumbed to their Hindu environments.

Kaniṣka

His date

Kaniṣka is indubitably the most striking figure among the Kushan kings of India. A great conqueror and a patron of Buddhism, he combined in himself the military ability of Candragupta Maurya and the religious zeal of Aśoka. Our knowledge of Kaniṣka is, however, meagre, and his chronological position unhappily still remains a puzzle to us. It is not known what his connection was with Vīma Kadphis-

[1] Also identified with Mahārāya Gushaṇa, mentioned in the Panjtar record of the year 122 (*C.I.I.*, II, no. XXVI, pp. 67-70). Sir John Marshall, on the other hand, hesitatingly identifies this king with Kadphises I (*J.R.A.S.*, 1914, p. 977). The name Uvima Kavthiṣa or Vīma Kadphises, however, occurs, if the reading is correct, in the Khalatse (Ladakh) inscription of the year 184 (?) or 187(?), *C.I.I.*, II, no. XXIX, pp. 79-81.

es. Though the possibility of a brief gap between the two sovereigns cannot be entirely ruled out, their sequence may be regarded as almost certain.[1] The coins of both Kaniṣka and Vīma Kadphises have been found together at several places (e.g., Benares, Gopālpur *Stūpa* in Gorakhpur district, Begram near Kabul), and they often display "in the field the same four-pronged symbol, and agree accurately in weight and fineness, besides exhibiting a close relationship in the obverse devices."[2] Thus the numismatic evidence and the stratification of the remains of Taxilā indicate that Kaniṣka was very close in time to Vīma Kadphises, and indeed succeeded him. With regard to the precise year of the former's accession, the choice really lies between 78 A.D., and 125 A.D., although other improbable dates, ranging from 58 B.C. (Fleet) to 248 A.D. (Dr. R.C. Majumdar), or even 278 A.D. (R.G. Bhandarkar), have been suggested for the event. Without entering here into the details of these intricate and interminable controversies, it appears to us a fairly plausible theory that Kaniṣka was the the originator of the era of 78 A.D.[3] There can be no doubt that he founded an era, since his reckoning was continued by his successors; and we do not know of any *Saṁvat*, current in Northern India, which began at the end of the first quarter of the second century A.D., the other date usually proposed for Kaniṣka's assumption of the crown.[4] Besides, if Kujūla Kadphises died about the middle of the third quarter of the first century

[1] Fleet, however, was of opinion that the two Kadphises ruled after Kaniṣka and his "immediate successors" (*J.R.A.S.*, 1903, 1905, 1906, 1913). This view was also held by Kennedy and Otto Francke.

[2] *E.H.I.*, 4th ed., p. 273 and note.

[3] The era was afterwards called the Śaka era "in consequence of its long use by the Śaka princes of Western India."

[4] For a discussion on Kaniṣka's date, see *J.R.A.S.*, 1913, 1914. Also *Ind. Hist. Quart.*, Vol. V (1929), pp. 49-80.

A.D., Kaniṣka cannot be far removed from this date, as Vīma Kadphises, having come after an octogenerian, must have ruled for a short time only.

Conquests

Kaniṣka was a doughty warrior and he won many successes in war. He annexed Kashmir to the Kushan empire, and was extremely fond of that pleasant valley. If any credence is to be given to traditions preserved in Chinese and Tibetan works, his arms penetrated as far as Sāketa and Magadha, whence he carried off a celebrated Buddhist monk named Aśvaghoṣa. Kaniṣka is also said to have successfully repulsed the attack of the Parthian king. But his most important engagements were with the Chinese; they resulted ultimately in the conquest of Kashgar, Khotan, and Yarkand. The Chinese, whose influence in Central Asia had ceased by the end of the first Han dynasty in 23 A.D., reasserted their power half a century later, and made a steady advance westward under General Pan-chao. This was naturally viewed with some concern by the Kushan monarch, who, as a mark of his equality with the Chinese Emperor, demanded the hand of a Chinese princess and adopted the title of *Devaputra* ("the son of Heaven"). Pan-chao considered it an affront to his master, and accordingly arrested the Kushan envoy. Kaniṣka then crossed the Pamir to fight against him, but suffered a severe reverse, and bought peace by paying tribute to China. A few years afterwards Kaniṣka led another expedition across the Pamirs; victory favoured him this time against Pan-yang, son of Pan-chao. The Kushan ruler thus avenged his previous defeat, and compelled a feudatory state of China to surrender hostages to him.

Hostages

The belief that they included a son of the Han Emperor does not, however, appear to be well founded. We learn that these hostages were treated with the utmost consideration, and adequate arrangements were made for their stay in the *She-lo-ka* monastery in Kapiśa (Kafiristan), Gandhāra, and at a place called Chīnabhukti in eastern Punjab, during the various seasons of the year. Here, it is said, they introduced the peach and the pear, and their memory continued to be cherished in Yuan Chwang's time in the Kapiśa monastery, where according to his biographer, Hwui-li, they had made endowments for the repairs and maintenance of the *She-lo-ka* shrine. The treasure was deposited under the foot of the image of the Great Spirit King (Vaiśravaṇa), and once a certain covetous king tried to open it, but was foiled in his attempt by portents. Yuan Chwang, however, is alleged to have succeeded in doing so after propitiating the "guardian spirit," and a part of the jewels and gold was then utilised in making necessary repairs in the building of the *Vihāra*. The remainder of the treasure was left to meet future requirements.[1]

Extent of Kaniṣka's Dominions

Kaniṣka ruled a vast empire. Outside India it certainly comprised Afghanistan, Bactria, Kashgar, Khotan, and Yarkand. Its limits in India are, however, hard to determine with precision. The inscriptions of Kaniṣka's reign have been discovered in Peshawar, Māṇikyāla (near Rawalpindi),[2] Sui Vihār (Bahawalpur State),[3] Zeda (near Uṇḍ), Mathurā, Śrāvastī, Kosambī, Sarnath; and his coins are found all over Northern India including Bihar and Bengal. Thus, it appears from these findspots and the traditions of his conquests that Kaniṣka's Indian

[1] *Life*, pp. 56-58; *E.H.I.*, 4th ed., pp. 278-280.

[2] cf. Māṇikyāla inscription of the year 18 of Mahārāja Kaṇeṣka's (Kaniṣka's) reign, *C.I.I.*, II, pt. I, no. LXXVI, pp. 145-50.

[3] cf. Sui Vihār inscription, dated year 11, of Mahārāja Rājātirāja Devaputra Kaniṣka's reign (*Ibid.*, no. LXXIV, pp. 138-41).

possessions consisted of the Punjab, Kashmir, Sind, United Provinces, and perhaps the country still further to the east and the south.

His Capital

The capital of these far-flung territories was Puruṣapura or Peshawar. It controlled the main route from Afghanistan to the Indus plains, and was, therefore, of considerable strategic importance.

His Satraps

Scarcely anything is known about Kaniṣka's administration. The Sarnath inscription dated in the year 3 or 81 A.D.(?)[1], however, gives us just a glimpse of his Satrapal system in the provinces. We learn that Kharapallāna was his Mahākṣatrapa, presumably at Mathurā, and Vanaṣpara was governing the eastern regions of Benares as Kṣatrapa. It seems reasonable to suppose that the government of other outlying parts of the realm was organised on similar lines.

Kaniṣka's Public Works

Like Aśoka, Kaniṣka was a great builder of *Stūpas* and cities. He erected in his capital a monastery and a huge wooden tower, in which he placed some relics of the Buddha.[2] Several years ago, a casket containing

[1] Formerly this was considered to be the earliest known inscription of Kaniṣka, but a few years ago another record, dated in the year 2 of his reign, was discovered, probably at Kosambī. It is now preserved in the Allahabad Museum.

[2] The Chinese pilgrim Sung-yun refers to the pagoda (*Feou-thou*) of Ka-ni-si-ka i.e., Kaniṣka (Beal, pp, ciii-civ). See also Fa-hian's *Fo-kuo-ki*, ch. XII, Beal, p. xxxii; and Yuan Chwang's *Si-yu-ki*, Bk. II, Beal, I, p. 99; Watters, I, p. 204, for the *Stūpa* of Ki-ni-kia or Kia-ni-se-kia (Kaniṣka). Alberuni also mentions that the *Vihāra* of Purushāvar was built by Kanik. It was called after him Kanika-Caitya (Sachau, Trans., Vol. II, p.11).

some fragments of bones was unearthed here. The inscription[1] on it furnishes us the interesting information that the *Stūpa* was constructed under the supervision of a Greek architect, named Agiśala or Agesilaos. Kaniṣka built a town near Taxilā,[2] and Kānispōr (Kaniṣkapura), mentioned in the *Rājataraṅgiṇī*, may also have owed its foundation to him.[3]

His Religion

Coins do not afford any clear testimony regarding the religious beliefs of Kaniṣka. If they prove anything, it is his eclecticism,[4] the tendency to honour a strange medley of Greek, Mithraic, Zoroastrian, and Hindu gods. On his coins, which, it may be incidentally noted, always bear legends in the Greek alphabet only, there figure Herakles, Serapis, the Sun and the Moon under their Greek names Helios and Selene, Miiro (Sun), Athro (Fire), Nanaia, Śiva, etc. Some rare pieces also depict the Buddha (Boddo), seated in the Indian fashion, or standing clad probably in Greek costume. On the other hand, Buddhist authors strongly affirm Kaniṣka's faith in the Buddha. They aver that in his unregenerate days Kaniṣka revelled, like Aśoka, in cruel and impious acts, and he embraced the religion of the Śākyamuni owing to feelings of profound remorse for his past misdeeds. No doubt, the main purpose of such stories is to emphasise the ennobling influence of Buddhism, which could turn base metal into shining gold, but that is no argument for disbelieving the fact of Kaniṣka's conversion. His enshrinement of the Buddha's relics

[1] See Sten Konow, *C.I.I.*, II, pt. I, no. LXXII, p. 137.

[2] Its remains are represented by Sir-Sukh.

[3] Some scholars think that it was founded by another Kaniṣka of the Ārā inscription (see *Infra*).

[4] Or, are we to conclude that these deities on coins only indicate the various forms of faiths prevailing in Kaniṣka's vast empire?

in an exquisite edifice and the convocation of a grand Buddhist Assembly further point in this same direction.

The Buddhist Council

The reign of Kaniṣka is specially important in the history of the Buddhist church, for we learn that, being perplexed in his theological studies, he convened with the permission of his teacher, Pārśvika or Pārśva, a council of 500 monks (*mahāsaṁgha*), belonging to the Sarvāstivādin school, to settle the disputed doctrines. The conference was held at Kundalavana in the delightful vale of Kashmir;[1] its deliberations were guided by Vasumitra, and in his absence Aśvaghoṣa acted as President. Their labours resulted in the compilation of the *Vibhāṣā Śāstra* and other comprehensive commentaries on the canon, which after being engraved on "sheets of red copper" were sealed and deposited in a *Stūpa*. Who knows these invaluable documents may still lie buried there, and a lucky spade may one day bring them to light?

Rise of the Mahāyāna

The appearance of the Buddha along with other deities on Kaniṣka's coins clearly indicates that Buddhism had by this time moved far away from its original moorings. While the early Buddhists regarded the Master merely as a human being, a great guide in the journey of life, he was now elevated to the position of a god, accessible to the supplications of his devotees, and

[1] cf. Yuan Chwang, *Si-yu-ki* (Beal, I, pp. 151-156; Watters, I, pp. 270-278). According to another Chinese account, the meeting place of the assembly was Gandhāra. Still another authority locates it at Jalandhar. We hear of the conference from Northern traditions only; the Ceylonese chronicles make no mention of it.

attended by "a hierarchy of Bodhisattvas" and other divinities. This led to the inculcation of the doctrine of salvation by faith in the Buddha. Of course, the old ideal of an individual seeking release for himself from the evils of transmigration still persisted, but alongside of it there emerged the conception that every one might aim at, or even rise to, Buddhahood for the deliverance of the world from tribulation. The rituals were also elaborated to satisfy the popular tastes for ceremonial. This modified Buddhism was known as the Mahāyāna, "the great Vehicle," in contradistinction to the Hīnayāna. "the little Vehicle," the name used for the primitive teaching. Although definite proof is lacking, there are reasons to believe that the former was nascent, much earlier than the time of Kaniṣka. It may have owed its origin to the "penetration of Buddhism by *Bhakti*," or to the spread of Buddhism among the masses, for they required a more catholic religion in place of the icy idealism of the Hīnayāna, which could hardly kindle the flame of their devotion. Besides, the introduction of foreign racial elements into the body politic of India, and the interaction of their civilisations, must have quickened the development of this newer Buddhism.

The Gandhāra Art

The new school found expression in a distinctive style of art. The earlier Buddhist sculptures, as known from their remains at Sāñchī and Bhārhut, portrayed scenes from the *Jātakas* and other stories connected with the Buddha, but he himself was never carved in stone. His presence was merely indicated by symbols, such as footprints, the Bo-tree, a vacant seat, or the umbrella. Henceforward, the Enlightened One is the most favourite subject for the sculptor's chisel. As most of these specimens have been found in Gandhāra, of which Puruṣapura (Peshawar) was the centre, the art has been called Gandhāran after the name of the country. Sometimes, however, it is labelled Græco-Buddhist or Indo-Hellenic, as Greek forms and technique are applied to subjects drawn from the newer Buddhism. Thus, the arrangement of the drapery follows Hellenistic examples, and in showing the Buddha artists take such liberty that his images often bear a close resemblance to Apollo. Later on, the great Teacher's figure was standardised, and it became the accepted pattern everywhere. The Gandhāra sculptures do not, of course, possess the grace and vigour of the work of the Gupta period, but they are surely not devoid of interest and charm. It is a moot point how far the art of Mathurā and Amarāvatī derived its inspiration from Gandhāra.

Kaniṣka's Court

According to traditions, Kaniṣka's court was adorned by a brilliant galaxy of intellectual celebrities and Buddhist leaders like Pārśva, Vasumitra, Aśvaghoṣa, Nāgārjuna, Caraka, Mātriceṭa, and others. These stories appear almost on a par with the legends associated with Vikramāditya. The first three are spoken of in connection with the Buddhist Council of Kaniṣka, but it is doubtful if the rest also were his contemporaries.

His death

Kaniṣka is said to have met a violent death somewhere in the north at the hands of his own people, who were tired of his incessant hard campaigns.[1] He ruled for at least 23 years, but, if he is identical with Kaniṣka of the Ārā inscription,[2] his last known date

[1] *Ind. Ant.*, vol. xxxii, 1903, p. 388; *E.H.I.*, 4th ed., pp. 285-86.

[2] See Sten Konow, *C.I.I.*, II. pt. I, no. XXXLV, pp. 126-65. cf. "Maharajasa Rajatirajasa Devaputrasa (Ka) i (sa) rasa Vajheṣka-

would be the year 41. A headless statue of the king, discovered at Māṭ in the Mathurā district, is one of his tangible relics.

Vāsiṣka

Our knowledge regarding the successors of Kaniṣka is very scanty. It appears, however, from two inscriptions, found in Mathurā and Sāñchī, that Vāsiṣka was governing these regions in the years 24 and 28. None of his coins has so far come to light, and perhaps he did not issue any.

Huviṣka

The dates of Huviṣka range from the year 31 to 60 of the era founded by Kaniṣka. Some scholars believe that the latter was followed by Vāsiṣka and Huviṣka. But this view is doubted, because an inscription, unearthed at Ārā (Peshawar district),[1] mentions a Kaniṣka, son of Vājheṣka or Vājheṣpa, as flourishing in the year 41. Now, who was this personage? He was either different from, or identical with, the great Kaniṣka. In case the former hypothesis is correct, he must have been an independent contemporary of Huviṣka, or more probably his Viceroy. If, on the other hand, the two Kaniṣkas are identified, then we shall have to suppose that: Vāsiṣka and Huviṣka were at first Viceroys of the great Kaniṣka; that Vāsiṣka predeceased him; and that Huviṣka assumed full sovereign powers after the year 41. Whichever theory is accepted, coins and inscriptions testify that Huviṣka was a powerful prince, and that he maintained the empire intact.

putrasa Kaniṣkasa Saṁbatśarae ekacapar (i) (śa) i sam 20 20 1......" i.e., "During the reign of the Mahārāja, Rājātirāja Devaputra, Kaisara Kaniṣka, the son of Vājheṣka, in the forty-first year."

[1] Sten Konow, *C.I.I.*, II, pp. 162-65, no. LXXXV; *Ep.Ind.*, XIV, pp. 130-43.

His authority was doubtless recognised in Kabul,[1] Kashmir, the Punjab, Mathurā, perhaps eastern United Provinces, but there is nothing to prove the continuance of the Kushan rule in the lower Indus valley and eastern Malwa. Huviṣka's coinage is very artistic, having excellent portraits of the king, and it is also extensive. The types include representations of Herakles, Sarapis (Sarapo); Mithra and Mao, Pharro; Skandha and Viś-ākha, and other gods, but both the name and the figure of the Buddha are absent. Huviṣka was, however, not altogether indifferent to Buddhism, for he is said to have built a Buddhist monastery and a temple at Mathurā. He also founded a town in Kashmir, called Juṣkapura or Huviṣkapura or modern Huṣkpur or Uṣkür (Zukur).[2]

Vāsudeva

The exact date of Huviṣka's death is uncertain, but an inscription records that in the year 74 of Kaniṣka's reckoning the ruling authority was Vāsudeva (Bazodeo of the coins). According to another epigraph, his last known date is 98; so that he may be credited with having reigned for 25 to 30 years. His inscriptions have been found in the Mathurā region only, and his coins mostly come from the Punjab and the United Provinces. We may, therefore, reasonably infer that the territories in the north-west and beyond, ruled by his predecessors, had slipped away from the hands of Vāsudeva. That he held sway over an attenuated kingdom appears also from the reduction in the number of his coin-types. The coins with the goddess Nanaia are extremely rare, whereas many of them bear on the reverse the figure of

[1] cf. Wardak (Khawāt *stūpa*) brass vase inscription of the year 51, *Ibid.*, no. LXXXVI, pp. 165-70; *Ep.Ind.*, XI, pp. 202-19.

[2] cf. *Rājataraṅgiṇī*, Bk. I, v. 169; Hwui-li also refers to the temple of U-sse-kia-lo (Huṣkapura)—*Life*, p. 68.

Śiva with *Nandi* (bull). The latter class of coins has generally been taken to prove that Vāsudeva belonged to the Śaiva faith. At any rate, his Sanskritised Hindu name, synonymous with Viṣṇu, attests that the Kushans were by no means averse or impervious to Brahmanical influences.

Decline of the Kushan Empire

The downfall of the Kushans began during the reign of Vāsudeva, and in course of time the empire, reared by the genius of Kaniṣka, broke up into petty principalities under princelings, some of whom bore the name Vāsudeva. They are known entirely from their coins on which are written their initials or monograms perpendicularly. According to Dr. Vincent Smith, the "Persianising of the Kushan coinage of Northern India" in the early third century A.D. indicates that the decay of the Kushan power must have been hastened by Persian invasions like the one recorded by Firishta as having been undertaken by the first Sassanian king.[1] The overthrow of these Kushan chieftains must have, however, been largely due to the rise of the Nāgas and other native dynasties, which prepared the way for the Guptas for welding Northern India eventually into one mighty empire. But the Kidāra Kushans, a branch race, established themselves in the Kabul valley and adjacent lands, and despite the fierce onslaughts of the Hūṇas in the fifth century A.D., there are traces of their survival until about the middle of the ninth century A.D.

II. *The "Dark" Interval*

After the dismemberment of the Kushan empire the history of India is mostly enveloped in darkness,

[1] *E.H.I.*, 4th ed., pp. 288-89. Ardashīr Bábagán (*c.* 225-241 A.D.) is represented as having advanced up to Sirhind from where

which hides from our view the course of events, until we emerge into the light of the Gupta epoch. Occasionally, however, a glimmer reveals the principal scenes and actors during the third and the early part of the fourth century A.D. This was a period when the Nāgas or their Bhāraśiva branch dominated a large part of Northern India.[1] According to the *Purāṇas*, their chief seats of power were Vidiśā, Padmāvatī (Padampawāyā), Kāntipurī (Kantit, Mirzapur district), and Mathurā. One of the earliest Nāga rulers was Vīrasena, who "re-established Hindu sovereignty" at Mathurā, formerly a strong Kushan centre in India. The authority and influence of the Bhāraśiva Nāgas may also be judged from the fact that the marriage of the daughter of the Bhāraśiva king, Bhavanāga, with the son of Pravarasena Vākāṭaka was considered so important as to be repeated in all the official records of the Vākāṭakas. We further learn from them that prior to this matrimonial alliance the Bhāraśivas had been "anointed to sovereignty with the holy water of the Bhāgīrathī (Ganges), which they had acquired with their valour," and they had performed no less than ten *Aśvamedha* sacrifices.[2] They were thus mighty princes, who flourished after the Kushans and maintained their influence for a long time. Later traces of Nāga rule may be found in the Allahabad Pillar inscription,[3] which mentions the defeat of Gaṇapatināga and other Nāga kings at the hands of Samudragupta. This epigraph gives us, as we shall see below, an idea

he retired after exacting a huge tribute from Jūnah (Elliot, *History of India*, VI, (Introd. to Firishta's History), pp. 557-58; *E.H.I.*, 4th ed., p. 289, n. 3).

[1] See K. P. Jayasval, *J. B. O. R. S.*, March—June, 1933, pp. 3 f.

[2] Fleet, *C.I.I.*, III, pp. 237, 241, 245, 248. cf. पराक्रमाधिगत-भागीरथ्यमलजलमूर्द्धाभिषिक्ताना दशाश्वमेधावभृथस्नानानां भारशिवानाम् ।

[3] *C.I.I.*, III, no. 1., pp. 1-17.

of the political condition of India about the middle of the fourth century A.D. It may, therefore, be reasonably supposed that some of the royal houses and autonomous clans, mentioned therein, must have risen into prominence considerably earlier. Indeed, they may have sprung up on the ruins of the Kushan power.

PART III

CHAPTER XII

I. THE IMPERIAL GUPTAS

Origin of the Guptas

When we enter upon the Gupta period, we find ourselves on firmer ground owing to the discovery of a series of contemporary inscriptions, and the history of India regains interest and unity to a large extent. The origin of the Guptas is shrouded in mystery, but on a consideration of the termination of their names it has been contended with some plausibility that they belonged to the Vaiśya caste.[1] Much stress should not, however, be laid on this argument, and to give just one example to the contrary we may cite Brahmagupta as the name of a celebrated Brahman astronomer. Dr. Jayasval, on the other hand, suggested that the Guptas were Kāraskara Jāṭs—originally from the Punjab.[2] But the evidence he relied on is hardly conclusive, as its very basis, the identification of Candragupta I with Caṇḍasena of the *Kaumudīmahotsava*, is far from certain.

Beginnings of the Gupta power

According to the genealogical lists, the founder

[1] cf. शर्मदिवश्च विप्रस्य वर्मा त्राता च भूभुजः ।
भूतिर्गुप्तश्च वैश्यस्य दासः शूद्रस्य कारयेत् ॥
Viṣṇu Purāṇa, Bk. III, Chap. 10, v. 9.

[2] *J.B.O.R.S.*, XIX (March-June, 1933), pp. 115-16. According to Jayasval, the Kakkar Jāṭs are "the modern representatives of the original community of the Guptas."

of the dynasty was a person named Gupta. He is given the simple title of Mahārāja, which shows that he was only a minor chief ruling a small territory in Magadha. He has been identified with Mahārāja Che-li-ki-to (Śrī-Gupta), who, according to I-tsing, built a temple near Mrigaśikhāvana for some pious Chinese pilgrims. It was handsomely endowed, and at the time of I-tsing's itinerary (673-95 A.D.) its dilapidated remnants were known as the 'Temple of China.' Gupta is generally assigned to the period, A.D. 275-300. I-tsing, however, notes that the building of the temple began 500 years before his travels.[1] This would, no doubt, go against the dates proposed above for Gupta, but we need not take I-tsing too literally, as he merely stated the "tradition handed down from ancient times by old men."[2]

Gupta was succeeded by his son, Ghaṭotkaca, who is also styled Mahārāja. This name sounds rather outlandish, although some later members of the Gupta family bore it.[3] We know almost nothing about him.

Candragupta I

After Ghaṭotkaca, his son Candragupta I came to the throne. Unlike his predecessors, the latter assumed the grandiloquent title of Mahārājādhirāja, and we may, therefore, regard him as the first monarch to raise the power and prestige of the dynasty. He

[1] Allan, *Catalogue of the Coins of the Gupta Dynasties*, Introd., p. xv; Beal, *J.R.A.S.*, 1881, pp. 570-71; *Ind. Ant.*, X, p. 110.

[2] Fleet does not accept the identification of Gupta with I-tsing's Che-li-ki-to (*C.I.I.*, III, p. 8, note 3). See, however, Allan, *C.C.G.D.*, Introd., p. xv. The king is called Śrī-Gupta in inscriptions. But Śrī is not an integral part of the name, and is used here only as an honorific term.

[3] cf. *e.g.*, श्रीघटोत्कचगुप्तस्य of a Vaiśālī seal(Bloch, *Arch. Surv. Ann. Rep.*, 1903-04, p. 107).

married the Licchavi princess, Kumāradevī, as is evident from the epithet "Licchavidauhitraḥ," applied to Samudragupta in inscriptions. The marriage is also attested by some gold coins, which bear on the obverse the standing figure of the king offering a ring or bracelet to his spouse with the legends Candra or Candragupta on the right and on the left Kumāradevī or Śrī-Kumāradevī; and on the reverse we have the legend "Licchavayaḥ," and the goddess (perhaps *Siṁhavāhinī* Durgā) seated on a lion. Allan believes that these coins were of a medallic nature, struck by Samudragupta in commemoration of his parents,[1] but it is likely they may be issues of Candragupta I himself.[2] His alliance with the Licchavis, who suddenly emerge now into view after several centuries of oblivion, was evidently a turning-point in the fortunes of the Guptas. Vincent Smith is of opinion that in consequence of this union Candragupta I "succeeded to the power previously held by his wife's relatives" and that he obtained possession of Pāṭaliputra.[3] The suggestion, however, appears untenable, for according to I-tsing's testimony the territories of Mahārāja Gupta must have already comprised this city. It is no less doubtful if Vaiśālī, the Licchavi capital, came under Candragupta I as a result of the marriage settlement. At any rate, a well-known passage in the *Purāṇas* proves that his authority extended to South Bihar, Prayāga, Sāketa, and the adjoining districts.[4]

He ruled from A.D. 320 to *circa* 335.[5] The reckoning which began from his accession, was carried on by

[1] *C.C.G.D.*, Introd., p. xviii.

[2] *J.A.S.B.*, Numismatic Supplement No. XLVII, Vol. III (1937), pp. 105-11.

[3] *E.H.I.*, 4th ed., pp. 295-96.

[4] *cf.* अनुगङ्गँ प्रयागँ च साकेतं मगधाँस्तथा ।
एतान् जनपदान् सर्वान् भोक्ष्यन्ते गुप्तवंशजाः ॥

[5] If, however, the Nālandā plates (*Ep. Ind.*, xxv, pp. 50-53)

his successors; and its initial year ran from February 26, 320 A.D. to March 15, 321 A.D.

Samudragupta

Candragupta I was followed by his son Samudragupta. As the latter seems to have been nominated by his father to succeed him, he may not have been his eldest son. Whatever his earlier position, Samudragupta turned out to be one of the ablest Gupta sovereigns, and by his exploits more than justified his father's selection.[1] With his ideal of war and aggrandisement, Samudragupta is the very antithesis of Aśoka, who stood for peace and piety. The former's achievements formed the subject of an elaborate panegyric composed by the court poet, Hariṣeṇa, and, strangely enough, Samudragupta chose to leave a permanent record of his sanguinary conquests by the side of the ethical exhortations of Aśoka on one of his pillars, now inside the fort at Allahabad.[2] The inscription is unhappily undated, but it is surely not a posthumous document, as supposed by Fleet.[3] It must have

Allahabad Pillar Inscription

and the Gayā plate of Samudragupta, dated years 5 and 9 respectively, are genuine, and if they refer to the Gupta era, the reign of Candragupta I must have been briefer still.

[1] Some gold coins of Kāca, closely resembling the issues of Samudragupta, have been found. Vincent Smith regards the former as a rival brother of the latter (*E.H.I.*, 4th ed., p. 297, n. 1). But in our opinion the expression "Sarva-rājocchettā" on the reverse argues in favour of their identification. Perhaps Kāca was the original or personal name, and the appellation Samudragupta was adopted in allusion to his conquests. Dr. D.R. Bhandarkar, on the other hand, takes the Kāca (Rāma?) coins to be issues of Rāmagupta (*Mālavīyajī Commemoration Volume*, 1932, pp. 204-06).

[2] Fleet, *C.I.I.*, III, no. 1, pp. 1-17.

[3] *Ibid.*, pp. 4, 10 and note 2. The passage (lines 29-30), however, only refers to Samudragupta's *fame* "having gone to the abode of (Indra) the lord of the gods."

been engraved—say about 360 A.D.—after the completion of Samudragupta's "digvijaya" and before the performance of the *Aśvamedha*, which is not mentioned in it.

Conquests

Although the account seems to follow a geographical and not a chronological order,[1] we may reasonably assume that Samudragupta must have first tried conclusions with his neighbours, the kings of Āryāvarta. Here he followed a policy of ruthless annexation, for he is said to have "violently exterminated" the following nine monarchs:

(*i*) Rudradeva (Rudrasena I Vākāṭaka?).
(*ii*) Matila : identified with Mattila of a seal found at Bulandshahr.
(*iii*) Nāgadatta : perhaps a Nāga king.
(*iv*) Candravarman : The identification is not certain. Sometimes he is considered the same as his namesake of Pokharaṇa, mentioned in the Susunia Rock inscription.[2] It is further believed that Candravarman is identical with king Candra of the Mehrauli Iron Pillar inscription (Fleet's no. 32), but this view has been doubted and appears improbable.
(*v*) Gaṇapatināga : a Nāga ruler of Padmāvatī (modern Padam Pawayā, near Narwar, in the Gwalior state).
(*vi*) Nāgasena } : Presumably both belonged to the
(*vii*) Nandin } Nāga lineage.
(*viii*) Acyuta : identical with "Acyu" of the coins discovered at Ahicchatra (Ramnagar) in the

[1] For the identification of names, see Fleet, *Ibid.*, notes; Allan, *C.C.G.D.*, Introd., pp. xxi-xxx; Smith, *J.R.A.S.*, 1897, pp. 859-910; Dubreuil, *A.H.D.*, pp. 58-61; Raychaudhuri, *Pol. Hist. Anc. Ind.*, 4th ed., pp. 447-60; D. R. Bhandarkar, *Ind. Hist. Quart.*, I, 2, pp. 250-60; G. Ramdas, *Ibid.*, I, 4. pp. 679 f; K. N. Dikshit, *Proc. 1st. Or. Con.*, I, p. cxxiv; Jayasval, *J.B.O.R.S.*, March-June, 1933, pp. 144 f.

[2] *Ep. Ind.*, XII, p. 318; *Proc. As. Soc. Beng.*, 1895, pp. 177 f.

Bareilly district.

(*ix*) Balavarman : not yet satisfactorily identified.[1]

Samudragupta next turned his arms against the "kings of the forest countries," whom he compelled "to become his servants." Their territories probably lay in Central India.

Samudragupta then undertook the difficult task of subjugating the monarchs of Dakṣiṇāpatha. They were defeated and captured, but the victor released and re-instated them, and thus won their allegiance by his magnanimity. These rulers were :

(*i*) Mahendra of Kośala (Mahākośala or the districts of Bilaspur, Raipur, and Sambhalpur).

(*ii*) Vyāghrarāja of Mahākāntāra (perhaps the wild tracts of Gondwana ?).[2]

(*iii*) Mantarāja of Korāla (Korāḍa in South India; or the Sonpur region, its capital being Yayātinagarī on the Mahānadī).

(*iv*) Mahendra of Piṣṭapura (modern Piṭhāpuram in the Godāvarī district).

(*v*) Svāmidatta of Koṭṭūra on the hill (Kothoor in the Ganjam district). According to another interpretation, the passage "Paiṣṭapuraka-Mahendragiri-Kauttūraka-Svāmidatta" signifies "Svāmidatta who had his seat at Piṣṭapur and at

[1] Dr. Jayasval regarded Balavarman as "the second or *abhiṣeka* (coronation) name of Kalyāṇavarman," ruler of Pāṭaliputra, who is mentioned in the *Kaumudī-Mahotsava*, but is "left unnamed in verse 7" of the Allahabad Pillar inscription (*J. B. O. R. S.*, March-June, 1933, p. 142). Mr. K. N. Dikshit (*Proc. 1st. Or. Conf.*, 1920, Vol. I, p. cxxiv), however, identifies Balavarman with an ancestor of Bhāskaravarman of Assam, mentioned in a Nidhanpur inscription (*Ep. Ind.*, XII, pp. 73, 76).

[2] Dr. Raychaudhuri thinks that Mahākāntāra is identical with "a wild tract of Central India, which probably included the Jaso State" (*Pol. Hist. Anc. Ind.*, 4th ed., p. 452). G. Ramdas, however, identifies it with the "Jhād-Khaṇḍ" Agency tracts of Ganjam and Vizagapatam (*I.H.Q.*, I, pt. 4, p. 684).

Koṭṭūra near Mahendragiri." But it may be questioned, as not more than one stronghold has been mentioned in case of each king in the inscription.

(*vi*) Damana of Eraṇḍapalla (Eraṇḍapalli, near Chicacole in the Ganjam district).

(*vii*) Viṣṇugopa of Kāñci (Conjeeveram, near Madras).

(*viii*) Nīlarāja of Avamukta : The Hāthīguṁphā inscription indicates that Pithūṇḍa, near Godāvarī, was the capital of the Āva country or people.

(*ix*) Hastivarman of Veṅgī (Peḍḍa-vegi in Ellore).

(*x*) Ugrasena of Pālakka (Nellore district).

(*xi*) Kubera of Devarāṣṭra (Yellamañcili in the Vizagapatam district).

(*xii*) Dhanañjaya of Kusthalapura (Kuṭṭalur in North Arcot).

According to the identifications, given above, Samudragupta's campaigns were limited to the eastern coast of the Dekkan. There is, however, nothing to support Prof. Jouveau-Dubreuil's suggestion that the invader was defeated by a confederacy of the southern kings under the leadership of Viṣṇugopa of Kāñcī, and that Samudragupta was forced to retreat homeward post-haste.[1] On the other hand, if we accept the identifications, proposed by Fleet and Smith, of Korāla, Eraṇḍapalla, Pālakka, and Devarāṣṭra with Kerala (Malabar coast), Eranḍol in Khandesh, Pālghat or Pālakkāḍu, and Mahārāṣṭra respectively, Samudragupta must have advanced as far as the Cera kingdom in the extreme south and returned to his capital by way of Mahārāṣṭra and Khāndesh.

The military activities of Samudragupta overawed the tribes and the frontier kings, who accordingly "gratified his imperious commands by paying all kinds of taxes, obeying his orders and coming to do homage."[2]

[1] *Ancient History of the Deccan* (1920), p. 61.

[2] cf. "सर्वंकरदानाज्ञाकरणप्रणामागमनपरितोषितप्रचण्डशासनस्य"

Among the frontier (*pratyanta*) states were :

(*i*) Samataṭa (south-eastern Bengal; its capital was Karmmānta or Baḍ-Kamta, near Comilla).

(*ii*) Davāka (Dacca; or the hill tracts of Chittagong and Tippera. Vincent Smith, however, identifies it with the modern districts of Bogra, Dinajpur and Rajshahi; and Mr. K. L. Barua with the Kopili valley in Assam).

(*iii*) Kāmarūpa (Assam).

(*iv*) Nepāla (Nepal).

(*v*) Kartripura (compare Katuriārāj of Kumaon, Garhwal, and Rohilkhand;[1] or Kartarpur in the Jalandhar district, as suggested by Fleet and Allan).

The tribes, which submitted to Samudragupta of their own accord, are named as follows :

(*i*) Mālavas: They are identical with the Malloi of the classical writers. By the end of the first century A.D. they migrated from the Punjab to Rajputana, and ultimately settled in the region called Malwa after them.

(*ii*) Ārjunāyanas : They were probably settled in the eastern part of Jaipur and Alwar states.

(*iii*) Yaudheyas : They lived in northern Rajputana. Their name still survives in Johiyāwār—a tract on the confines of the Bahawalpur State.[2]

(*iv*) Madrakas : They were to the north of the Yaudheyas, and their capital was Śākala or Sialkot.

(*v*) Ābhīras : Their territory (Ahirwāḍa) was between the Pārvatī and Betwā rivers in Central

[1] *J.R.A.S.*, 1898, pp. 198-99.

[2] The Yaudheyas are mentioned in an inscription discovered at Bijayagaḍh, near Bayānā, in the Bharatpur State (*C.I.I.*, III, no. 58, pp. 251-52). The author of the *Brihat-Saṁhitā* places both the Ārjunāyanas and the Yaudheyas in the northern division of India.

India.[1]

(*vi*) Prārjunas : Their seat of power was either Narsingpur or Narsingarh in C.P.

(*vii*) Sanakānīkas : They were near Bhilsa. A Sanakānīka feudatory of Candragupta II is mentioned in an Udayagiri inscription (Fleet's no. 3).

(*viii*) Kākas : They were the neighbours of the Sanakānīkas.

(*ix*) Kharaparikas : Perhaps they occupied the Damoh district, C.P., and were identical with the Kharparas of the Batihagarh inscription,[2] as pointed out by Dr. D. R. Bhandarkar.[3]

Degrees of conquests

The foregoing account shows that Samudragupta's conquests were of varying degrees. He forcibly extirpated certain kings, and annexed their dominions; others were vanquished, taken prisoners, and set free after an acknowledgement of suzerainty; and, lastly, the frontier monarchs and the tribes, being impressed by his victories, paid him homage of their own accord.

Relations with foreign powers

Thus, Samudragupta made himself master of an extensive empire, but beyond the sphere of his direct authority were the foreign potentates, who were no less anxious to be on good terms with him. We learn from a Chinese source[4] that his Ceylonese contemporary, Meghavanna or Meghavarṇa (352-79 A.D.), sent two monks to Bodhgayā on a religious mission. Meeting

[1] Some, however, locate the Ābhīras in Saurāṣtra and Gujarat, as they are often referred to in Kṣatrapa inscriptions.

[2] *Ep. Ind.*, XII, pp. 46, 47, v. 5.

[3] *Ind. Hist. Quart.*, I, (1925), p. 258.

[4] Sylvain Lèvi, *Journal Asiatique*, 1900, pp. 406, 411; V.A. Smith, *Ind. Ant.*, 1902, pp. 192-97.

with little or no hospitality there, they complained to the king on their return home that they could not obtain even a suitable accommodation. Meghavarṇa then sent a formal embassy with rich gifts to Samudragupta seeking his permission to build a monastery at that sacred site for the use of Ceylonese pilgrims. The request was, of course, granted, and soon there grew up a magnificent structure, which was known as the *Mahābodhi Saṅghārāma* in the time of Yuan Chwang. The Allahabad pillar inscription further informs us that the Daivaputra-Śāhi-Śāhānuśāhi, the Śaka-Muruṇḍas as well as the people of Siṁhala and other islands, "purchased peace by self-surrender, bringing presents of maidens, the application of charters, stamped with the Garuḍa seal, confirming them in the enjoyment of their territories."[1] Although such claims savour of rhodomontade, it appears nevertheless that the above mentioned powers were profoundly struck with the expanding fame and influence of Samudragupta, and, therefore, they thought it prudent to enlist his friendship and favour. They were evidently the representatives of the Kushans and the Śakas, who had formerly held sway over a large portion of India. It is, however, difficult to identify them definitely, or even to analyse the Sanskrit compound words. The title Daivaputra-Śāhi-Śāhānuśāhī was orginially adopted by the great Kushan emperors and after the disintegration of the empire it was divided among the princes of the smaller states according to their status. Thus, the Devaputra was perhaps located in the Punjab, and the Śāhī or Śāhīśāhānuśāhi ruled Afghanistan and the adjoining lands. Similarly, the term

[1] cf. "दैवपुत्रशाहिशाहानुशाहिशकमुरुण्डैः सैंहलकादिभिश्च सर्वद्वीपवासिभिरात्मनिवेदनकन्योपायनदानगरुत्मदङ्कस्वविषयभुक्तिशासनयाचनाद्युपायसेवाकृतबाहुवीर्यप्रसरधरणिबन्धस्य. ."
Were the people of the Malay Archipelago meant by the "dwelers of other islands"?

Saka-Murundas[1] denotes either two separate ethnic types, or simply "lords of the Śakas," if taken as one word.

The Aśvamedha sacrifice

Samudragupta is represented in the inscriptions of his successors to have revived the horse-sacrifice, which had long been in abeyance ("*cirotsannāśvamedhāhartuḥ*").[2] It must have been performed at the conclusion of his fighting days, and after the incision of the Allahabad pillar inscription, as it is not mentioned therein.[3] He distributed large sums in charity during this ceremony, and to commemorate it he issued gold coins, showing a horse standing before a sacrificial post (*yūpa*) on the obverse, and on the reverse the queen and the legend "Aśvamedhaparākramaḥ."

His personal accomplishments

Samudragupta was a versatile genius. He was proficient not only in war, but also in the sacred lore (*Śāstras*). Himself highly cultured, he was fond of the company of the learned. He is called "kavirāja", which shows that he was a poet of no mean order. Besides, he cultivated the sister art of music, and his attainments in this direction are confirmed by certain coins depicting him sitting on a high-backed couch and playing on the lute (*vīṇā*). The Allahabad pillar inscription also says that Samudragupta "put to shame

[1] On the Muruṇḍas, see *C.C.G.D.*, Introd., pp. xxix-xxx; Jayasval, 'The Muruṇḍa Dynasty,' *Mālavīyajī Commemoration Volume*, pp. 185-87.

[2] We may, however, recall here that the Bhāraśivas, Pravarasena I Vākāṭaka, and other kings had celebrated the *Aśvamedha* not very long before Samudragupta. Does the expression signify that it was restored by the latter as a full detailed Imperial rite? (see Dr. S. K. Aiyangar, *Studies in Gupta History*, pp. 44-45).

[3] See H. R. Divekar, *A.B.R.I.*, Vol. VII (1926), pp. 164-65.

the preceptor of the lord of the gods (i.e., Brihaspati) by his sharp and polished intellect and Tumburu and Nārada by lovely performances of music."[1]

His Religion

We learn from the Allahabad pillar inscription that the kings of the north-west asked for Samudragupta's charters, stamped with the Garuḍa seal. As Garuḍa is the bearer (*vāhana*) of Viṣṇu, it is clear that Samudragupta was specially devoted to this god. But his Vaiṣṇavism was by no means inconsistent with militarism—the true ideal of a Kṣatriya.

Date of his death

The exact year of Samudragupta's death is nowhere recorded, but there is no doubt he had a long reign. The earliest known date of Candragupta II being 380 A.D. according to a newly discovered inscription at Mathurā,[2] we may tentatively assume that Samudragupta ruled until about 375 A.D.

Rāmagupta

Samudragupta had several sons (cf. *bahu-putra-pautra*, *C.I.I.*, III, no. 2, pp. 20-21), and one of them named Rāma (Sarma?) gupta is believed to have succeeded him. The latter is mentioned in a lost drama by Viśākhadatta, entitled *Devī-Candraguptaṁ*, fragments of which are preserved in the *Nāṭya-darpaṇa*, a work on dramaturgy by Rāmacandra and Guṇacandra. Rāmagupta was a cowardly ruler, and it is alleged that in response to the Śaka king's demand he agreed to surrender even his wife, Dhruvadevī. But her honour was saved

[1] cf. "निशितविदग्धमतिगान्धर्वललितैर्व्रीडितत्रिदशपतिगुरुतुम्बुरुनारदादेर्विद्वज्जनोपजीव्यानेककाव्यक्रियाभिः प्रतिष्ठितकविराजशब्दस्य"

[2] See *Infra*.

owing to the intervention of her husband's brother, Candragupta, who in the guise of a woman killed the Śaka ruler. Candragupta then did away with Rāmagupta too, and ascended the throne of Pāṭaliputra with Dhruvadevī as his queen amidst the plaudits of the people. Echoes of this story also come from Bāṇa's *Harṣacarita*, the commentary on it by Saṅkarārya, and some other later authorities like the *Sriṅgāra-Prakāśa* of Bhoja, the Sanjan Plates of Amoghavarṣa[1], and the *Mujmālut-Tawārīkh*.[2] Despite these evidences, the historicity of Rāmagupta is still a matter of controversy among scholars. It is argued that the above traditions are late and have hardly any air of reality; and the absence of Rāmagupta's coins[3] as well as the complete silence of the Gupta records about him, no doubt, lend further weight to this scepticism.

Candragupta II Vikramāditya (c. 375-414 A.D.)

Accession

Candragupta, usually designated Candragupta II Vikramāditya to distinguish him from his grand-father, was Samudragupta's son by Dattadevī. Whether we take him as the immediate successor of his craven brother Rāmagupta, or of his father, as the expression "tatparigrihītaḥ" suggests,[4] Candragupta must have been a man of mature years, when he ascended the throne some time between 375 and 380 A.D.[5]

[1] *Ep.Ind.*, XVIII, pp. 248-255, verse 48.

[2] Elliot and Dowson, *History of India*, I. pp. 110-12.

[3] Dr. D. R. Bhandarkar's attempt (*Mālavīyaji Commemoration Volume*, 1932, pp. 204-06) to attribute the Kāca coins to Rāmagupta is not at all convincing. See *Ibid.*, pp. 206-11 for citations of original passages. On Rāmagupta, see also *J.B.O.R.S.*, June, 1928, pp. 223-53; March-June, 1929, pp. 134-141; March, 1932, pp. 17-36, etc.,

[4] *C.I.I.*, III, no. 12, p. 50, l. 19.

[5] The earliest known date of Candragupta II is G.E. 61=

Position of the empire

Candragupta II was spared the difficult task of building up an empire. It had already been successfully accomplished by the military genius of his father, Samudragupta, who had annexed many territories in Āryāvarta, overawed the frontier kings and tribes into submission, and made the independent powers of the North-west seek his friendship. But the Western satraps were still holding their own, and, except for a temporary eclipse by the Vākāṭakas, continued to be an important factor in contemporary politics.

The Vākāṭaka alliance

With a view to pursuing his schemes vigorously against the Śakas, Candragupta II gave the hand of his daughter, Prabhāvatī, born of Kuberanāgā, a Nāga princess, to Rudrasena II Vākāṭaka. This matrimonial alliance was a masterstroke of diplomacy as the Vākāṭaka Mahārāja "occupied a geographical position in which he could be of much service or disservice to the northern invader of the dominions of the Śaka satraps."[1]

The Śaka campaign

Having organised a strong force, Candragupta II himself advanced against the Śaka ruler of Western India. An inscription at Udayagiri, near Bhilsa, recording the dedication of a cave to Śambhu (Śiva) by his minister for peace and war, named Sāba-Vīrasena, gives us a clue to Candragupta's line of march, as the former is said to have gone there "accompanied by the king in person, who was seeking to conquer the whole world."[2]

380-81 A.D. (cf. Mathurā inscription, *Ep. Ind.*, XXI, pp. 1f).

[1] *J.R.A.S.*, 1914, p. 325.

[2] *C.I.I.*, Vol. III, pp. 35, 36. cf. "कृत्स्नपृथ्वीजयार्थेन राज्ञैवेह सहागतः"

Unhappily the epigraph is undated, otherwise we should have known the actual year of Candragupta's conflict with the Śakas. But we can fix it approximately with the help of the coins. The latest issues of the Western Kṣatrapas are those of Rudrasiṁha III, dated in the year 31x=388-97 A.D. Now, Candragupta II started a silver currency in close imitation of that of the Kṣatrapas after the occupation of their territory. The earliest date on these coins is 90 or 90x=409 or 409-413 A.D.[1] We may, therefore, reasonably suppose that the conquest took place some time between 395 and 400 A.D.[2] An allusion to this event occurs in Bāna's *Harṣacarita*, although according to its testimony Candragupta II killed his adversary by stratagem and not in an open fight. For it transmits the "scandalous tradition" that "in his enemy's city the king of the Śakas, while courting another man's wife, was butchered by Candragupta concealed in his mistress' dress."[3]

Results of the war

The defeat of Rudrasiṁha III not only resulted in the annexation of the fertile and rich regions of Malwa, Gujarat, and Saurāstra (Kāthiāwāḍ) by the victor, but it also brought the Gupta empire into direct touch with the western sea-ports. This gave a tremendous impetus to overseas commerce, and along with it there was a free flow of ideas, to and from, foreign lands. Inland trade, too, grew with the establishment of a supreme government over the greater part of Northern India, as merchants could now transport goods right across the country without having to pay customs duties at the

[1] Candragupta II died about this year.

[2] See also J. Allan, *Cam. Sh. Hist. Ind.*, p. 93.

[3] *Hc.C.T.*, p.194. cf. अरिपुरे च परकलत्रकामुकं कामिनीवेषगुप्तश्चन्द्र गुप्तः शकपतिमशातयत् ॥

frontiers of each petty state on the way. Previously, these levies hampered business a good deal; they raised the prices of articles and left little margin for profits to manufacturers and tradesmen. The most important *entrepot* at that time was Ujjain, where converged trade-routes from different directions. It also enjoyed pre-eminence as a religious and political centre, and was indeed made the second capital of the Gupta empire after Candragupta's western conquests.

Who was king Candra?

An inscription on the Iron Pillar, which stands near Kutb-Minar (Delhi), not far from the village of Mehrauli, records the exploits of a king named Candra. He is said to have vanquished a combination of his enemies in Vaṅga (Bengal); perfumed the Southern ocean by "the breezes of his prowess;" and overcome the Vāhḷi-kas,[1] traversing the seven mouths, i.e., tributaries of the river Indus (i.e., the Punjab).[2] Thus having "acquired supreme sovereignty in the world" (*aikādhirājya*), he ruled "for a long time" (*suciraṁ*). The identification of this Candra has unfortunately been a frequent source of controversy among scholars.[3] But if he is identical with

[1] According to Varāhamihira, the Vāhlikas were a northern people. Some scholars identify them with the Bāhikas of the Punjab (Basak, *History of North-Eastern India*, p. 14, n. 12), and others with the people of Balkh. It has sometimes even been suggested that the term Vāhlika was used in a general sense to signify a body of foreign invaders, like the Pahlavas, Yavanas, etc., (see Allan, *C.C.G.D.*, Introd., p. xxxvi).

[2] cf. "यस्योद्वर्तयतः प्रतीपमुरसा शत्रून्समेत्यागता-
न्वङ्गेष्वाहदवर्तिनोऽभिलिखिता खड्गेन कीर्तिर्भुजे ।
तीर्त्वा सप्तमुखानि येन समरे सिन्धोर्जिता वाह्लिका
यस्याद्याप्यधिवास्यते जलनिधिर्वीर्यानिलैर्दक्षिणः ॥

(*C.I.I.*, III, no. 32, p. 141, v. 1).

[3] R. G. Basak (*History of North-Eastern India*, pp. 13-18) and Fleet (*C.I.I.*, III, Introd., p. 12) identify Candra with Candragupta I;

Candragupta II, as seems quite probable, we have then definite evidence that the Gupta monarch firmly established his supremacy in Bengal, and destroyed the remnants of the Śaka and the Kushan power in the northwest, a task which Samudragupta could accomplish only partially.

Fa-hian's itinerary (399-414 *A.D.*)

During the reign of Candragupta II, the celebrated pilgrim, Fa-hian, came overland from China to India, enduring the hardships and dangers of the Gobi Desert and the mountainous tracts of Khotan, the Pamirs, Swat, and Gandhāra. Reaching Peshawar, he made a detour across the hills to the north and the west, entered the Punjab, passed on to places like Mathurā, Saṁkāśya, Kanauj, Śrāvastī, Kapilavastu, Kuśinagara, Vaiśālī, Pāṭaliputra, Kāśī, etc. He then proceeded to Tāmralipti (Tamluk, Midnapur district), where he embarked for Ceylon and Java on his voyage homeward.[1] Fa-hian was, no doubt, so engrossed in his quest for Buddhist manuscripts and relics that he did not even care to note the name of the emperor, in whose dominions he spent several happy years. But occasionally the pilgrim persuaded himself to write about the life of the people and the general condition of the country. Let us now consider what information we obtain from these incidental observations.

Pāṭaliputra

Fa-hian stayed in the Imperial city of Pāṭaliputra

Vincent Smith believes Candra is the same as Candragupta II (*J. R.A.S.*, 1897, pp. 1-18); R. D. Banerji (*Ep. Ind.*, XIV, pp. 367-71) and H. P. Śāstrī (*Ibid.*, XII, pp. 315-21; XIII, p. 133) equate Candra with Candravarman; whereas Dr. Raychaudhuri takes Candra to be identical with either Sadā-Candra or Candrāṁśa, "preferably the latter" (*Pol. Hist. Anc. Ind.*, 4th ed., p. 449, n. 1).

[1] See *Fo-kwo-ki* (The Travels of Fa-hian), Beal, *Buddhist Records of the Western World*, pp. xxiii-xl.

for three years, learning Sanskrit. He mentions that it had two "imposing and elegant" monasteries—one of the Hīnayāna and the other of the Mahāyāna-tenanted by six or seven hundred monks, whose learned expositions of the Law and disciplined life attracted seekers after knowledge from all parts of India. He felt amazed to see the splendour of Aśoka's palace, which was extant at the time of his visit to Pāṭaliputra, and was reputed to have been the work of superhuman agency. The wealth and prosperity of Magadha deeply impressed the pilgrim, and he says with admiration that its inhabitants "vied with one another in the practice of benevolence and righteousness." They organised a grand procession of richly adorned images of the Buddha and Bodhisattvas every year on the eighth day of the second month. These figures were carried on "perhaps twenty cars," all constructed according to a certain pattern, but differently painted and decorated. Fa-hian also testifies that "the heads of the Vaiśya families establish houses for dispensing charity and medicines." There was an excellent hospital, endowed by nobles and householders, in the capital where the poor and destitute patients were supplied food and medicine free according to their needs. Besides, rest-houses existed in large towns as well as on highways for the comforts of travellers.[1]

State of Society

The pilgrim's account gives us some glimpses of the social conditions in Madhyadeśa. It appears the bulk of the people were vegetarian, and followed the principle of *Ahiṁsā*. They had "no shambles or wine-shops in their market-places." They do not keep pigs and fowls, nor do they eat onions and

[1] *Ibid.*, ch. xxvii, pp. lvi-vii.

garlic, nor drank wine[1]—a feature which may hearten modern temperance reformers. The *Caṇḍālas* were regarded as social outcasts, being the only persons "to go hunting and deal in flesh." They lived away from the people, and when they approached a city or market they had to strike a piece of wood, so that other folk might avoid coming in contact with them.[2] Truly, this savours of untouchability, which is still an ugly blot on Hinduism.

Religious condition

Fa-hian came to India with the set purpose of collecting Buddhist manuscripts, and of visiting the sites hallowed by the memory of the Buddha. Naturally, therefore, he speaks more enthusiastically about Buddhism and the ramifications of the *Saṁgha*. It appears from his description that the faith was "flourishing" in the Punjab and Bengal, and that it was gradually gaining ground in Mathurā, where he noticed twenty establishments. But it was by no means popular in Madhyadeśa, for in each of its principal towns the pilgrim saw just one or two monasteries only, and sometimes even none. Here Brahmanism predominated, and the king was himself a devout Vaiṣṇava (*Paramabhāgavata*). The relations between the "Brahman heretics" and the Buddhists were generally cordial, and nowhere is there any hint of persecution of any religion. Indeed, we learn from inscriptions that some of the high officers of Candragupta II, like Śāba-Vīrasena and Āmrakārdava, were Śaiva and Buddhist in their persuasions.[3]

[1] This is, however, to be taken with a grain of salt.

[2] *Ibid.*, ch. xvi, p. xxxviii.

[3] An Udayagiri inscription records that Candragupta II's minister of peace and war, named Śāba-Vīrasena, excavated a cave to serve as a sanctuary of the deity Śiva (*C.I.I.*, III, no. 6, pp. 34-36). Similarly, another inscription at Sāñchī says that Āmrakārdava, a general in Candragupta II's army, made a gift of 25 *dīnāras*

Administration

Fa-hian refers favourably to the temperate climate and administration of the Middle kingdom, i.e., the territories of Candragupta II. The people were prosperous and free from poll-tax or from the shackles of overgovernment. They "had not to register their households or attend to any magistrates and their rules." The king did not impose any restrictions on the movements of his subjects. "If they desire to go, they go: if they like to stop they stop."[1] The criminal law was mild as compared to the Chinese system of the day. Offenders were fined, lightly or heavily, according to the nature of their crimes, and corporal punishments were not inflicted. It is interesting to learn that capital penalty was not awarded then, and even persons guilty of treason suffered only amputation of the right hand. The picture, however, appears to be more idealistic than realistic.

The mainstay of finance was the land revenue, amounting to a certain portion of the produce or its cash value. The royal officers were regularly paid fixed salaries. Cowrie shells formed the ordinary currency for smaller transactions, but gold "suvarṇas" and "dīnāras", mentioned in inscriptions, were also in free circulation.

It is thus clear from the above remarks of the pilgrim that the government of Candragupta II was efficient and well organised. The people enjoyed the blessings of peace, and Fa-hian travelled through Northern India without meeting with any mishap. While the conditions in general were so satisfactory, decay and desolation had overtaken some localities, like Gayā Kuśinagara, Kapilavastu, Śrāvastī, which were once

and a village to the *Ārya-Saṅgha* or Buddhist community (*Ibid*, no. 5, pp. 29-34.)

[1] *Fo-kwo-ki*, Beal's Trans., ch. xvi, p. xxxvii.

busy centres of life.

Epigraphic evidence

We must also glean a few facts from the Basārh seals[1] and other inscriptions about the working of Candragupta's empire. The king ruled with the advice and assistance of his ministers (*mantris*), whose office was often hereditary.[2] Some of them combined both civil and military functions, and they accompanied the sovereign to the battle-field. The empire was divided for the sake of administrative convenience into several provinces (*deśas* or *bhuktis*) under governors (*Uparika Mahārājas* or *Goptas*), often princes of the blood royal; and next, there were the districts (*viṣayas*) and their subdivisions. The provincial and local governments were carried on by a regular bureaucracy, and the Basārh seals give us the designations of a number of such offices, e.g., *Kumārāmātya* (counsellor of a prince; or literally, one who was a minister since boyhood); *Mahādaṇḍa-nāyaka* (chief commandant); *Vinayasthiti-sthāpaka* (censor?); *Mahā-pratīhāra* (chamberlain); *Bhaṭāśvapati* (lord of the infantry and the cavalry); *Daṇḍapāśādhikaraṇa* (office of the police chief), etc. It appears from the Damodarapur copper-plates that the head of a district (*viṣayapati*) was directly responsible to the provincial governor, and was described as "*tanniyuktaka*." "He had his headquarters in an "*Adhiṣṭhāna*," where the office ("*Adhikarana*") was located. He was assisted by a council comprising representatives of the principal local interests of the times, *viz*., the chief *Seṭh* or

[1] *Ann. Rep. Arch. Surv.*, 1903-04, pp. 101-20.

[2] The Udayagiri inscription (*C.I.I.*, III, no. 6, pp. 34-36) describes Śāba-Vīrasena, Candragupta II's minister of peace and war, as "anvayaprāpta-Sācivyo vyāpṛta-Sandhi-Vigrahaḥ." Similarly, the Karamdanda inscription (*Ep. Ind.*, X, pp. 70 f) refers to Kumāragupta I's minister, Prithvīsena, whose father, Śikharasvāmin, was himself a minister under Candragupta II.

banker (*nagara-śreṣṭhin*), chief merchant (*sārthavāha*), chief artisan (*prathama kulika*), and the chief scribe (*prathama kāyastha*). But we do not know if they formed merely an advisory body, or any specific duties were entrusted to them. Among other important functionaries were the record-keepers (*pustapāla*), who were kept informed of the title to all lands. Indeed, the authorities sanctioned "land sales only after these record-keepers had, on receipt of application from purchasers, determined the title to the land under proposal of transfer and sent in their report to the Government."[1] As before, the lowest unit of administration was the village (*grāma*), which was under the headman (*grāmika*). With the help of the *pañcamaṇḍalī* or *pañcāyat* consisting of the village elders (*grāmavriddhas*), he maintained peace and security within his jurisdiction.

Family

Besides Kuveranāgā, referred to already, Candragupta had another wife named Dhruvadevī or Dhruvasvāminī. He had at least two sons—Kumāragupta I and Govindagupta; the latter was Candragupta II's Viceroy at Vaiśālī.

Titles

The inscriptions apply to Candragupta II the epithets of Parama-bhāgavata and Mahārājādhirāja-Sri-Bhaṭṭāraka. On the coins he assumes the high-sounding titles of Vikramāditya, Vikramāṅka, Narendracandra, Siṁha-Vikrama, Siṁha-Candra, etc. He bore the name Devarāja also.[2] In some of the Vākāṭaka inscriptions he is called Devagupta.[3]

[1] *Ep. Ind.*, XV, p. 128.

[2] *C.I.I.*, III, no. 5, pp. 32, 33, l. 7.

[3] cf. Cammak plate inscription, *C.I.I.*, III, no. 55, pp. 237, 240, l. 15,

Kumāragupta I Mahendrāditya (414-55 *A.D.*)

Date of Accession

According to the Sāñchī inscription (no. 5) Candragupta II was ruling in the Gupta year 93=412-13 A.D., whereas the Bilsad inscription (no. 10),[1] dated G.E. 96=415 A.D., belongs to the time of his son and successor Kumāragupta (I) whose mother was queen Dhruvadevī. We may, therefore, suppose that the sceptre changed hands about 414 A.D.

His power

Not much is known of Kumāragupta's career, but the number and variety of his coins, as well as the wide distribution of the inscriptions of his reign, indicate that he maintained the strength and unity of the empire, which extended from Bengal to Saurāṣṭra and from the Himālayas to the Narmadā. Bandhuvarman then ruled Daśapura (Mandasor, Western Malwa) as Kumāragupta's feudatory; Cirātadatta was governor of North Bengal (Pauṇḍravardhana-bhukti); and Ghaṭotkacagupta held charge of the Airikiṇa or Eran region (Saugor district, C. P.)

The Aśvamedha sacrifice

Certain gold coins of Kumāragupta I prove that he performed the Aśvamedha sacrifice. Unhappily, inscriptions do not throw any light on his conquests, but it may be safely said that he could not have indulged in this Imperial celebration without having won some successes in war.

The Puṣyamitra war

We learn from the Bhitari pillar inscription that

[1] The numbers refer to Fleet's *C.I.I.*, Vol. III.

the last years of Kumāragupta I were seriously disturbed owing to the invasion of the Puṣyamitras, who had "developed great power and wealth."[1] Kumāragupta I himself could not take up arms against them—perhaps on account of old age or illness, and he, therefore, sent his crown-prince, Skandagupta, to avert the danger. The latter rose equal to the occasion, and after a hard struggle, in which he had to spend a whole night "on a couch that was the bare earth", he retrieved the fallen fortunes of his family.[2]

Religious condition

Like his predecessors, Kumāragupta I was a tolerant ruler. During his protracted reign numerous endowments for the maintenance of alms-houses (*sattras*) and temples were made. We also hear of the installation of the images of the Buddha and Pārśva; and among Brahmanical gods the most popularly venerated were the Sun, Śiva, Viṣṇu, and Kārtikeya, whose worship was now growing into special favour. Indeed, it appears from certain gold and silver coins of Kumāragupta I that his object of adoration was Kārtikeya rather than Viṣṇu.[3]

[1] *C.I.I.*, III, pp. 54, 55. cf. "समुदितबलकोषान्..." Fleet placed the Puṣyamitras somewhere along the banks of the Narmadā (*Ind. Ant.*, 1889, p. 228). The *Viṣṇu Purāṇa* associates the Puṣyamitras with the region of Mekala, near the source of the Narmadā (IV, 24, 17; *Pol. Hist. Anc. Ind.*, 4th ed., p. 479). Mr. Divekar, on the other hand, suggests the reading : "Yuddhyamitrāṁśca" (*A. B. R. I.*, 1919—20, pp. 99-103). If this is accepted, do the *amitras*, then, refer to Skandagupta's internal enemies ?

[2] cf. "विचलितकुललक्ष्मीस्तम्भनायोद्यतेन
क्षितितलशयनीये येन नीता त्रियामा..."

(*C.I.I.*, III, pp. 53, 55).

[3] *Ind. Hist. Quart.*, XV, no. 1, March, 1939, p. 6.

Skandagupta Kramāditya (455-67 *A.D.*)

Initial troubles

It appears that during the progress of the Puṣyamitra war Kumāragupta I died, for when Skandagupta gained victory over his enemies he went to announce it to his living mother "just as Kriṣṇa did to Devakī."[1] Indeed, the Bhitari pillar inscription explicitly says that soon after this conflict Skandagupta "placed his left foot on the royal foot-stool"[2], i.e., ascended the throne. But the course of his reign was not destined to run smooth.

Hūṇa Invasions

Close upon the heels of the engagement with the Puṣyamitras followed a greater menace to the safety of the empire; this was the onrush of the nomadic Hūṇas, who at this time began to pour down the north-western passes like an irresistible torrent. At first, Skandagupta succeeded in stemming the tide of their advance into the interior in a sanguinary contest,[3] but the repeated attacks of these savage hordes eventually undermined the stability of the Gupta dynasty. If the Hūṇas of the Bhitari pillar inscription are identified with the Mlecchas of the Junāgaḍh rock inscription, Skandagupta must have defeated them before the Gupta year 138=

[1] cf. पितरि दिवमुपेते विप्लुतां वंशलक्ष्मीम्
भुजबलविजितारिर्यः प्रतिष्ठाप्य भूयः ।
जितमिति परितोषान् मातरं सास्त्रनेत्राम्
हतरिपुरिव कृष्णो देवकीमभ्युपेतः ॥

[2] cf. "क्षितिपचरणपीठे स्थापितो वामपादः" My translation materially differs from Fleet's.

[3] cf. "हूणैर्यस्य समागतस्य समरे दोर्भ्यां धरा कम्पिता भीमावर्तकरस्य" (*C.I.I.*, III, pp. 54, 55.)

457-58 A.D., the last date mentioned in the latter record. Saurāṣṭra seems to have been the weakest point of his empire, and he was hard put to it in ensuring its protection against the attacks of his enemies. We learn that he had to deliberate for "days and nights" in order to select the proper person to govern those regions. The choice, at last, fell on Parṇadatta, whose appointment made the king "easy at heart."

The Sudarśana lake

Another great event of Skandagupta's reign was the restoration of the embankment of the Sudarśana lake, which had burst with excessive rain-fall. It had a long history behind. Candragupta Maurya first built a reservoir of water by damming a mountain stream, and the irrigational sluices were supplied during the time of Aśoka. In the year (Śaka) 72=150 A.D., Rudradāman repaired the damages caused by a severe storm.[1] Breaches again occurred in the embankment in G.E. 136=456 A.D. and Parṇadatta's son, Cakrapālita, who was governor of Girnar, rebuilt it of solid masonry at an "immeasurable cost." To commemorate the successful completion of the work, a temple of the god Cakrabhrit or Viṣṇu was constructed in G. E. 138=458 A.D.[2] No traces of the lake or of the temple are found now.

Religion

Skandagupta was himself a devout Vaiṣṇava, but he continued the tolerant policy of his predecessors.[3]

[1] Junagaḍh inscription of Rudradāman, *Ep. Ind.*, VIII, pp. 36-49.

[2] Junagaḍh Rock inscription of Skandagupta, *C.I.I.*, III, no. 14, pp. 56-65.

[3] See my paper, *Religious Toleration under the Imperial Guptas*, *Ind. Hist. Quart.*, Vol. XV, No. 1, (March, 1939), pp. 1-12

The people followed the noble example of their sovereign. The Kahaum inscription (no. 15),[1] for instance, records the erection of five stone images of the Jain *Tīrthaṁkaras* by one Madra, who is described as "full of affection for Brahmans, religious preceptors, and ascetics." Similarly, the Indor plate (no. 16)[2] registers a gift by a certain Brahman for the maintenance of a lamp in a Sun temple built by two Kṣatriyas at Indrapura (Indor, Bulandshahr district). The donor made a permanent deposit with the local guild of oil-men (tailika-śreṇī), who were to provide oil for the lamp daily out of its interest "without diminishing its original value."

Titles

Skandagupta's usual title was "Kramāditya". On some of his silver coins he bears the more famous title of "Vikramāditya" as well. It may incidentally be noted here that in the Kahaum inscription he is called "kṣitipaśatapatiḥ" or "lord of a hundred kings."

Date

According to the silver coins, the last known dates of Kumāragupta I and Skandagupta are respectively 455 and 467 A.D. Presumably, therefore, these two limits represent the duration of Skandagupta's reign.

The Later Emperors

The Gupta dynasty, no doubt, continued its existence after the death of Skandagupta, but its greatness appears to have departed. He was succeeded in about 467 A.D. by his brother or half-brother, Puragupta, born of Anantadevī. The latter's name has been recovered

[1] *C.I.I.*, III, pp. 65-68.
[2] *Ibid.*, pp. 68-72.

from the Bhitari seal inscription,[1] which, curiously enough, omits to mention Skandagupta in the genealogical list. This has led some scholars to believe that the two brothers were on terms of enmity, and that there was a partition of the empire between them after a fratricidal fight. The theory is, however, altogether untenable, since such omissions are by no means rare in ancient Indian epigraphic documents, and the available evidence conclusively proves that Skandagupta was a powerful monarch ruling over the entire Gupta dominions. On his coins Puragupta assumes the title, "Śrī-Vikramaḥ", and in the opinion of Hoernle those pieces, which have the legend "Prakāśāditya" on the reverse, are also to be attributed to him.[2] It is difficult to determine with precision the extent of his kingdom or the duration of his reign.

Narasiṁhagupta

Puragupta's successor was his son, Narasiṁhagupta, by Vatsadevī. He bore the epithet, Bālāditya, but he was not identical with the famous conqueror of the Hūṇas, as is commonly supposed. Narasiṁhagupta's rule was probably very brief.

Kumāragupta II

Narasiṁhagupta was followed by Kumāragupta, his son by Mahālakṣmīdevī. He is called Kumāragupta II to distinguish him from his great-grandfather. He was "protecting the earth" in G.E. 154= 473-74 A.D., if we identify him with Kumāragupta of the Sarnath inscription.[3] It was in his time (Mālava

[1] *J.A.S.B.*, 1889, pp. 84-105.

[2] *Ibid.*, pp. 93-94. Subsequently Hoernle ascribed these coins to Yaśodharman (*J.R.A.S.*, 1909, pp. 135-36). See, however, Allan, *C.C.G.D.*, Introd., pp. li-lv.

[3] *Ann. Rep. Arch. Surv.*, 1914-15, no. xv, p. 124.

Saṁvat 529=472-73 A.D.) that a guild of silk-weavers repaired the temple of the Sun at Daśapura, originally constructed in Mālava Era 493=436-37 A.D. during the reign of Kumāragupta I.[1]

Budhagupta

According to another epigraph from Sarnath, Budhagupta was on the throne in G. E. 157=476-77 A.D.[2] His accession may, therefore, be dated a year or so earlier. This shows that all the three rulers, whose names have been revealed to us by the Bhitari seal inscription, had very short reigns covering a period of about eight years only. What Budhagupta's relation was to this group is not clear. Yuan Chwang states that he was a son to Śakrāditya, and as in Sanskrit Śakra and Mahendra are synonyms of Indra, Budhagupta may have been a son of Kumāragupta I, who adopted the epithet Mahendrāditya. The inscriptions, discovered at Damodarapur (Dinajpur district),[3] Sarnath (Benares district), and Eran (Saugor district, C.P.)[4] demonstrate that Budhagupta's authority was acknowledged all over the country from Bengal to Central India. At that time North Bengal was under his Viceroys, Brahmadatta and Jayadatta; Eastern Malwa was governed by Mahārāja Mātriviṣṇu; and a feudatory Mahārāja, Suraśmicandra, was in charge of the territory between the Kālindī (Yamunā) and the Narmadā.

Bhānugupta

Budhagupta must have ceased ruling shortly after G.E. 195=494-95 A.D., which is his last date known from the coins (silver). He was perhaps succeeded by

[1] cf. Mandasor Stone Inscription, *C.I.I.*, III, no. 18, pp. 79-88

[2] *Ibid.*, no. XVI, pp. 125-26.

[3] *Ep.Ind.*, XV, pl. no. 3 and 4, pp. 134-141.

[4] *C.I.I.*, III, no. 19, pp. 88-90.

Bhānugupta, although their relation is uncertain. During the latter's reign, the Hūṇas wrested Malwa from the Guptas, for whereas Mātriviṣṇu was a vassal of Budhagupta, his younger brother, Dhanyaviṣṇu, acknowledged the sovereignty of Toramāṇa.[1] The Eran inscription, dated G. E. 191=510 A.D.,[2] also testifies that Bhānugupta's general, Goparāja, died in a "very famous battle", evidently while fighting against the Hūṇas. Henceforward the Gupta power steadily declined, and except a few names from coins we know nothing about the later members of the dynasty. They ruled over a small territory, comprising parts of Bihar and Bengal only. The Imperial ties were torn asunder by the provinces, which now pursued their own devices and destinies.

The Imperial Gupta Line

- Gupta (*circa* 275-300 A. D.)
  - Ghaṭotkaca (*c.* 300-319 A. D).
    - Candragupta I=Kumāradevī (319-335 A. D.)
      - Rāmagupta (?)
      - Candragupta II=Dhruvadevī (*c.* 375-414 A.D.)
        - Kumāragupta I (*c.* 414-455 A. D.)
          - Skandagupta (*c.* 455-467 A.D.)
          - Puragupta=Vatsadevī
            - Narsiṁhagupta=Mahālakṣmīdevī
              - Kumāragupta II
            - (Puragupta, Narsiṁhagupta, Kumāragupta II: *c.* 467-75 A.D.)
          - Budhagupta (*c.* 475-95 A. D.)
            - Bhānugupta (*c.* 495-510 A. D.)

[1] *Ibid.*, no. 36, pp. 158-161.
[2] *Ibid.*, no. 20, pp. 91-93.

Later coins give us the names of Viṣṇugupta Candrāditya,[1] Vaiṇyagupta Dvādaśāditya and others. Absolutely nothing is recorded about them or their interrelation.

A seal, recently discovered at Nālandā, describes Viṣṇugupta as the son of Kumāra, probably Kumāragupta II. But it is not clear when and where he ruled. I am thankful to Dr. Altekar for having drawn my attention to this seal.

CHAPTER XIII

CIVILISATION UNDER THE GUPTAS AND RISE OF NEW POWERS

SECTION A

A Glorious epoch

The period of the Imperial Guptas has often been described as the golden age of Hindu history. It comprised the reigns of a number of able, versatile and mighty monarchs, who brought about the consolidation of a large part of Northern India under "one political umbrella," and ushered in an era of orderly government and progress. Both inland and foreign trade flourished under their vigorous rule, and the wealth of the country multiplied. It was, therefore, natural that this internal security and material prosperity should find expression in the development and promotion of religion, literature, art, and science.

Religion—Brahmanism

During this epoch Brahmanism gradually came into ascendancy. This was to a large extent due to the patronage of the Gupta kings, who were staunch Brahmanists with special predilections for the worship of Visnu. But the wonderful elasticity and assimilative power of Brahmanism were not less important factors in its ultimate triumph. It won over the masses by giving common beliefs, practices, and aboriginal superstitions the stamp of its recognition; it strengthened its position by admitting the casteless foreign invaders within its roomy fold; and above all, it cut the ground—so to say—from under the feet of its great rival, Buddhism, by including the Buddha among the ten *Avatāras* and absorbing some of his noble teachings. Thus with all these new features the aspect of Brahmanism changed into what is now called Hinduism. It was characterised by the worship of a variety of deities, the most prominent then being Viṣṇu, also known as Cakrabhrit, Gadādhara, Janārdana, Nārāyaṇa, Vāsudeva, Govinda, etc. The other gods in popular favour were Śiva or Śambhu;[1] Kārtikeya;[2] Sūrya; and among the goddesses may be mentioned Lakṣmī, Durgā or Bhagavatī, Pārvatī, etc. Brahmanism encouraged the performance of sacrifices, and the inscriptions refer to some of them, such as Aśvamedha, Vājapeya, Agniṣṭoma, Āptoryāma, Atirātra, Pañcamahāyajña, and so on.

Buddhism

Buddhism was beyond doubt on the downward path in Madhyadeśa during the Gupta period, although to Fa-hian, who saw everything through Buddhist glasses, no signs of its decline were visible in the course of his wanderings. The Gupta rulers never resorted to persecution. Themselves devout Vaiṣṇavas, they followed the wise policy of holding the scales even between the competing faiths. Their subjects enjoyed full liberty of conscience, and if the case of Candragupta's Buddhist general, Āmrakārdava, is a typical instance, the high offices of the realm were open to all irrespective of creed. Without digressing into a discussion of the causes of the decay of Buddhism, it may be pertinent to observe that its vitality was considerably sapped

[1] Siva was also called Bhūtapati, Śūlapāṇi, Mahādeva, Pinākin, Hara, etc.

[2] Other names are Skanda, Svāmī-Mahāsena.

by schisms and subsequent corruptions in the *Saṁgha*. Besides, the worship of the images of the Buddha and Bodhisattvas, the growth of its pantheon, the introduction of ceremonial solemnities and religious processions, carried Buddhism so far away from its pristine purity that to the ordinary man it became almost indistinguishable from the popular phase of Hinduism. Thus the stage was well set for its eventual absorption by the latter. Even in modern times we see a striking illustration of this process of assimilation in Nepal, where, as Dr. Vincent Smith points out, "the octopus of Hinduism is slowly strangling its Buddhist victim."[1]

Jainism

The inscriptions testify also to the prevalence of Jainism, though it did not rise into prominence on account of its severe discipline and lack of royal patronage. There appears to have been a commendable concord between it and other religions. For a certain Madra, who dedicated five statues of the Jain *Tīrthaṁkaras*, describes himself as "full of affection for Brahmans and religious preceptors."[2]

Religious benefactions

With a view to gaining happiness and merit both in this world and the next, the pious generously endowed free boarding-houses (*sattras*), and gave gifts of gold or village lands (*agrahāras*) to Brahmans. They evinced their religious spirit also in the construction of images and temples where out of the interest on permanent deposits (*akṣaya-nīvī*) lights were maintained all the year round as

[1] *E.H.I.*, 4th ed., p. 382.

[2] cf. the Kahaum Stone Pillar Inscription, *C.I.I.*, III, no. 15, pp. 65-68. cf. "द्विजगुरुयतिषु प्रायशः प्रीतिमान् यः"

a necessary part of worship. Similarly, the Buddhist and Jain benefactions took the form of installations of the statues of the Buddha and the *Tīrthaṁkaras* respectively. The Buddhists built monasteries also (*vihāras*) for the residence of monks, who were provided with proper food and clothing.

Revival of Sanskrit

Side by side with the renovation of Brahmanism the use and influence of Sanskrit grew apace. An early stage in its revival was marked by the long Junāgaḍh rock inscription of Rudradāman, dated 72 (*Śaka*?) =150 A.D., but now it was uniformly given the place of honour as the official language of epigraphic documents and coin legends.[1] Even Buddhist writers of the day, like Vasubandhu and Dignāga, preferred Sanskrit to Pālī, the earlier vehicle of expression.[2]

Development of Literature

The Gupta period has generally been compared to the Periclean age in the history of Greece, or to the Elizabethan epoch in that of England. It was distinguished by a number of intellectual celebrities, whose contributions vastly enriched the different branches of Indian literature. The Gupta monarchs encouraged learning, and were themselves highly cultured. We have already noted the evidence of the Allahabad pillar inscription about Samudragupta's poetical attainments and proficiency in music. Besides, the universal tradition which associates the nine gems (*nava-ratna*) with the legendary Vikramāditya, shows what a profound

[1] It is noteworthy that the short Ayodhyā inscription (*Ep. Ind.*, XX, pp. 54-58) of the time of Puṣyamitra (*c.* 184 B.C.-148 B.C.) is entirely in Sanskrit. It is one of the earliest known inscriptions in that language.

[2] The Buddha himself did not use Sanskrit, but gave his discourses in the popular speech then current.

impression the brilliant literary coterie of Candragupta II Vikramāditya's court created in the popular mind Its most shining light was, of course, Kālidāsa, the famous poet and dramatist, who was perhaps a native of Malwa.[1] Unfortunately, his date is still open to doubt, and some scholars persist in the view that he was living in 57 B.C. But there are strong grounds to believe that he flourished in the Gupta age, and that he was a contemporary of Candragupta II or Kumāragupta I. Indeed, an allusion to the conquests of the former may be detected in the exaggerated description of Raghu's "digvijaya" in the *Raghuvaṁśa*. Another epic poem by Kālidāsa is the *Kumāra-saṁbhava*, while the *Ritusaṁhāra* and the *Meghadūta* present two excellent examples of lyrical poetry. Of his plays, we know the *Mālavikāgnimitra*, *Vikramorvaśi* and *Śakuntalā*, the last being so superb as to win the appreciation of the greatest literary critics of the world. Although eclipsed by the genius of Kālidāsa, there were many other poets of repute during the Gupta times. Hariṣeṇa and Vatsabhaṭṭi, contemporaries of Samudragupta and Kumāragupta II respectively, have left to us their compositions permanently incised on stone. Presumably to the same period belong Viśākhadatta, author of the *Mudrā-rākṣasa*; the lexicographer Amarasiṁha, who wrote the *Amarkoṣa*; the celebrated physician Dhanvantari; and the great Buddhist scholars whom we have mentioned in the preceding para. Furthermore, the Brahmans now retouched and rearranged their literature in order to bring it into harmony with the feelings of their growing followers, and strengthen their hold over them. The *Purāṇas*, which

[1] *Nagpur University Journal*, no. 5, Dec., 1939, pp. 1-22. Mr. T. J. Kedar in a learned paper on "Kālidāsa—his birthplace and date" argues that the poet flourished in the Śuṅga times and was perhaps a protégé of Bhāgabhadra or Bhāgavata. Mr. Kedar further believes that Kālidāsa was "a resident of Malwa" and was born at Devagiri.

refer to the Gupta dynasty last of all, were recast into their present form; so also was the *Manusmriti*. Other *Smritis*, like the *Yājñavalkya-smriti*, and the *Bhāṣyas* or commentaries on the *Sūtras* were written to give canonical sanction to the new changes that had taken place. Astronomy and Mathematics were assiduously cultivated; and Āryabhata (born in 476 A.D.), Varāhamihira (505-87 A.D.), and Brahmagupta (born in 598 A.D.) made remarkable contributions to the development of these branches of scientific literature. They appear to have been acquainted with Greek astronomy, for their works contain many Greek technical names.

Education

The intellectual output of the age shows that the system of education, then in vogue, must have been sound. Unhappily, however, our information on this topic is disappointingly meagre. According to inscriptions, the teachers were then known as Ācāryas and Upādhyāyas, but sometimes the title of Bhaṭṭa was also applied to the learned Brahmans. They were supported by the grant of villages and the charities of the generous public. The religious disciples, called Śiṣyas or Brahmacārins, were grouped round Śākhās and Caraṇas, i.e., Vedic schools following a particular recension of any one of the Vedas.[1] Among these recensions the inscriptions mention Maitrāyaṇīya, Taittirīya, Vājasneya, and several others. Regarding the subjects of study, we learn of the fourteen sections of science (*caturdaśavīdyā*), comprising the four Vedas, six Vedāṅgas, the *Purāṇas*, the Mīmāṁsā, Nyāya, and Dharma or Law. There are also references to the Vyākaraṇa (*Aṣṭādhyāyī*) of Śālāturīya (Pāṇini) and the *Śatasāhaśrī-saṁhitā* or the

[1] It is, however, contended that *Śākhās* and *Caraṇas* were now defunct.

Mahābhārata. In addition to these, instruction must have been imparted in the large mass of secular literature.

The catholicity of the age may further be judged from the fact that Nālandā, the great centre of Buddhist learning, was founded about the middle of the fifth century A.D. by Śakrāditya, probably Kumāragupta I, who endowed a monastery there. Additional grants to the establishment were made by Budhagupta, Tathāgatagupta, Bālāditya, and other Gupta monarchs. Nālandā followed a very comprehensive curriculum of studies, and in due course it rose to such eminence that students from all parts of India, and even from beyond its frontiers, flocked here in order to satisfy their mental and spiritual thirst.

Gupta currency

The earliest gold coins of Samudragupta (or of Candragupta I?), weighing 118-122 grains, closely follow the Kushan standard and types. The influence of foreign coinage is also proved by the use in the Gupta inscriptions of the Kushan name of *Dīnāra*, derived from Latin *Denarius*. However, in the time of Candragupta II, whose coins are of 124 to 132 grains there began a deviation from the Kushan (Roman) weight until it was given up by Skandagupta in favour of the Hindu standard of *Suvarṇa* (146 grains). After the conquest of the Kṣatrapa territories, the Guptas too issued silver coins on the Śaka standard of 32 grains, which was subsequently raised by Skandagupta to that of the *Kārṣāpaṇa*. It may be added that the copper coinage of the Guptas is very scarce, perhaps because small transactions were then made in cowrie-shells, as observed by Fa-hian.

Architecture

The Gupta rule gave a great impetus to architecture, although owing to a combination of causes the extant remains of this age are not many. Most of the Gupta edifices perished owing to the ravages of nature; some of them later provided materials for the building needs of the people; others that lay in the track of the Moslem armies fell a prey to their iconoclastic fury. Our knowledge is, therefore, limited to a few survivals only, and they too are not secular structures, but were all consecrated to religion. Dr. Vincent Smith refers to two such temples—the one at Deogadh (Jhansi district) contains fine pieces of sculpture on the panels of the walls, and the other of brick at Bhitargaon (Cawnpore district) is noted for its well-designed figures in terra-cotta.[1] We may add here that the achievements of the Gupta art are further illustrated by the Ajantā caves. No doubt, they were mostly hewn and carved out of solid rock in different periods, but there are some which were perhaps excavated during the centuries under survey, and they certainly bear eloquent testimony to the skill of Gupta engineers.

Sculpture

The discoveries at Sarnath and other places show that the plastic art reached a high level of perfection during the Gupta age. It gradually liberates itself from Gandhāran influences, and the statues of the Buddha are now characterised by decorated haloes, close-fitting transparent garments, and peculiar arrangement of the hair. Among the numerous Gupta sculptures, found at Sarnath, the most pleasing and graceful perhaps is the seated Buddha in the preaching attitude (*dharma-cakra-mudrā*). Besides depicting scenes from the Master's life, incidents from Paurāṇic mythology are treated with remarkable freshness. On the whole the work of the Gupta artists is distinguished by vitality, freedom from extravagance, and exquisite technique.

[1] *Ox. Hist. Ind.*, p. 16.

Painting

In the realm of painting also a high degree of proficiency was attained, as appears from the Ajantā (Hyderabad State) caves, whose interiors were freely decorated with frescoes. They range in date from the first to the seventh century A.D., and thus some of them fall within the scope of this period. In the opinion of a learned connoisseur the work of Ajantā is "so accomplished in execution, so consistent in convention, so vivacious and varied in design, and full of such evident delight in beautiful form and colour, " that one cannot help ranking it with the best art of the ancient world.[1] The Ajantā school further extended its operations to the caves at Bāgh in the Gwalior State, and these paintings also display high merit and infinite variety.

Metal-working

The craftsmen of the Gupta age were experts in working metals. This is evident from the discovery of several colossal copper statues of the Buddha and an iron pillar at Mehrauli near Delhi. It represents the triumph of Gupta metallurgical skill, and the wonder is that in spite of exposure for centuries to sun and rain the column has not yet rusted.

Causes of activity

We have now finished our review of the civilisation of the Gupta age. Naturally, the question arises: What were the causes of this outburst of intellectual and artistic activity? According to Dr. Vincent Smith, it was "mainly due to contact with foreign civilisations.[2]

[1] See Griffiths, *The Paintings of the Buddhist Caves of Ajantā*, p. 7.

[2] *E.H.I.*, 4th ed., p. 324. Besides China and the Western countries, India then came into intimate touch with the Malay peninsula and islands owing to the commercial and colonising

The fact that India was then in constant communication with China and the Western world may, of course, be readily accepted. For devout pilgrims, like Fahian, came to the land of the Buddha in almost a regular stream; and India on her part sent out eminent sages of the type of Kumārajīva (383 A.D.) to the celestial empire on Buddhist missions. Moreover, with the extension of the Gupta dominions to the seaports of Saurāṣṭra and Gujarat India's foreign trade with the West increased; and this led, it is believed, to a flow of ideas, which produced important reactions on the Indian mind. But the most potent stimulus to progress must have been the beneficent rule of Gupta Emperors who were men of catholic culture. It was largely due to their liberal patronage of art and learning that such brilliant and fruitful results followed.

SECTION B
THE VĀKĀṬAKAS

Their importance

One of the most powerful dynasties, ruling contemporaneously with the Guptas, was that of the Vākāṭakas. Their inscriptions and the *Purāṇas* testify that in the hey-day of their glory they dominated the entire country of Bundelkhand, Central Provinces, Berars, Northern Dekkan up to the sea, besides exercising suzerainty over their weaker neighbours.

Origin and derivation of the name

According to Dr. Jayasval, the Vākāṭakas took their rise in Bundelkhand, and they were so called from Vākāṭa, the name of a place now represented by Bāgāṭ in the Orcha State.[1] It has further been suggested

activities of her adventurous sons. The remains in Java, Combodia, Sumatra and other lands bear the impress of Gupta style and architecture.

[1] *J.B.O.R.S.*, March—June, 1933, p. 67.

that they were Brahmans, but the evidence on this point is hardly conclusive, for the term "dvija" applied to the founder of the line in an inscription at Ajantā[1] may as well mean that he was a Kṣatriya.

Prominent rulers of the dynasty

The first king of the house, which appears to have established its power about the last quarter of the third century A.D., was Vindhyaśakti. His son, Pravarasena I (Pravīra of the *Purāṇas*), was a considerable figure, as his assumption of the title *Samrāṭ* clearly indicates. He performed four *Aśvamedhas* and other sacrifices like the *Vājapeya* and *Brihaspati-sava*. His son, Gautamīputra, married the daughter of the Bhāraśiva king, Bhavanāga, but he did not ascend the throne. The next ruler was Pravarasena I's grandson, Rudrasena I, who has been identified with Rudradeva mentioned in the Allahabad pillar inscription as having suffered defeat at the hands of Samudragupta. Henceforth the Guptas became masters of Central India, and the Vākāṭaka centre of gravity shifted to the Dekkan. Rudrasena I's son and successor, Prithvīsena I, subjugated Kuntala (Northern Kanarese districts). The latter's son, Rudrasena II, signalised his reign by marrying Prabhāvatīguptā, daughter of Candragupta II by Kuberanāgā. Thus, the two families became allied together—a factor which must have materially helped the Gupta monarch in his designs against the Śakas of Western India. This matrimonial alliance is one of the fixed points in the Vākāṭaka chronology. After the death of her husband, Prabhāvatī ruled on behalf of her minor son. Then fol-

[1] Several Vākāṭaka inscriptions have been found at Ajantā and they help us much in settling the dates of certain caves. See also V.A. Smith, *J.R.A.S.*, 1914, pp. 317-38, on the Vākāṭakas of Berar; Govinda Pai, "Genealogy and Chronology of the Vākāṭakas," *Jour. Ind. Hist.*, XIV (1935), pp. 1-26, 165-204.

lowed several other kings until we come to the reign of Hariṣeṇa Vākāṭaka about the close of the fifth century A.D. He is represented to have made extensive conquests in Kuntala, Avanti (Malwa), Kaliṅga (the country between the Mahānadī and the Godāvarī), Kośala (Mahā-Kośala or eastern C.P.), Trikūṭa (perhaps Konkan), Lāṭa (southern Gujarat), and Āndhra (lying between the Godāvarī and the Kriṣṇā). If these claims have any substance, Hariṣeṇa Vākāṭaka carried his arms right across the centre of India from the western coast to the eastern Ghats. But it does not appear probable that these campaigns led to any permanent results. The Vākāṭaka power was ultimately shattered some time in the second quarter of the sixth century A.D. by the Kalacuris of the South.

Section C

THE HŪṆAS AND YAŚODHARMAN

Hūṇa movements

The Hiung-nu or the Hūṇas of Sanskrit literature and inscriptions first come into view about 165 B.C., when they defeated the Yueh-chi and compelled them to quit their lands in North-western China. In course of time the Hūṇas also moved westwards in search of 'fresh fields and pastures new'. One branch proceeded towards the Oxus valley, and became known as the Ye-tha-i-li or Ephthalites (White Huns of Roman writers). The other section gradually reached Europe, where they earned undying notoriety for their savage cruelties. From the Oxus the Hūṇas turned towards the south about the second decade of the fifth century A.D., and, crossing Afghanistan and the north-western passes, eventually entered India. As shown in the last chapter, they attacked the western parts of the Gupta dominions prior to 458 A.D., but were hurled

Attack on the Guptas

back by the military ability and prowess of Skandagupta. To use the actual expression of the Bhitari pillar inscription, he "by his two arms shook the earth, when he.... joined in close conflict with the Hūṇas."[1] For the next few years the country was spared the horrors of their inroads. In A.D. 484, however, they defeated and killed king Firoz, and with the collapse of Persian resistance ominous clouds again began to gather on the Indian horizon. The Hūṇa hordes now poured into India like swarms of locusts in terrific numbers, and caused the downfall of the Gupta empire. The leader of these renewed incursions was perhaps Toramāṇa, known from the *Rājataraṅgiṇī*, inscriptions, and coins. It is clear from their evidence that he wrested large slices of the western territories of the Guptas and established his authority as far as Central India. The conquest of this region must have been made some time after G.E. 165=484-85 A.D., when Mahārāja Mātriviṣṇu was ruling there as a vassal of Budhagupta,[2] but it was certainly a *fait accompli* within the same generation, for the former's younger brother, Dhanyaviṣṇu, dedicated an image of the Varāha incarnation of Viṣṇu in the first regnal year of Toramāṇa, and thus acknowledged his overlordship.[3] Indeed, it is likely that the "very famous battle," in which Bhānugupta's general Goparāja lost his life according to an Eran inscription dated G.E. 191=510 A.D.,[4] was fought against the Hūṇa conqueror himself. The loss of Malwa was a tremendous blow to the fortunes of the Guptas, whose direct sway did not now extend much beyond Magadha and Northern Bengal.

Toramāṇa

[1] *C.I.I.*, III, pp. 54, 55.

[2] *Ibid.*, no. 19, pp. 88-90.

[3] *Ibid.*, no. 36, pp. 158-61.

[4] *Ibid.*, no. 20, pp. 91-93.

Mihirakula

Toramāṇa was succeeded by his son, Mihirakula (-gula), who is represented in traditions as a great tyrant, taking fiendish delight in acts of brutality. According to Yuan Chwang, he (*Mo-hi-lo-ki-lo*) persecuted the peaceful Buddhists and mercilessly destroyed and plundered their *stūpas* and monasteries. He attacked king Bālāditya of Magadha, but was defeated, taken prisoner, and subsequently released. Mihirakula then sought safety in Kashmir and received a very generous treatment at the hands of its ruler. The refugee, however, misused the kindness shown to him, and by his machinations soon seized the throne of his benefactor. Mihirakula could not long enjoy the fruits of his usurpation, and within a year his death took place, heralded by portents. It is difficult to disentangle the kernel of fact from the husk of legend in the Chinese pilgrim's testimony. We do not even know with certitude who this Bālāditya was, except that he was not identical with Narasiṁhagupta Bālāditya. The latter ruled before 473 A.D. (G.E. 154), the date recorded for his successor Kumāragupta II. In that age Bālāditya was a common royal epithet and both the Deo-Baraṇārk inscription of Jīvitagupta II[1] and the Sarnath inscription of Prakaṭāditya[2] refer to a king or kings of this name. Indeed, R. D. Banerji may be right in identifying the Bālāditya of these inscriptions with the one mentioned by Yuan Chwang.[3] Whatever his other achievements, Bālāditya was certainly successful in repelling the invasion of Mihirakula.

Yaśodharman

Here we must pause to consider the information

[1] *C.I.I.*, III, no. 46, pp. 213-18.
[2] *Ibid.*, no. 79, pp. 284-86.
[3] *Prehistoric, Ancient and Hindu India*, p. 194.

we get from an inscription engraved on a pillar at Mandasor in western Malwa. It immortalises the exploits of the *Janendra* Yaśodharman who "spurning the limits of his own kingdom......conquered countries not enjoyed before even by the Guptas;......and invaded lands, which the chiefs of the Hūṇas could not penetrate."[1] Further, homage was tendered to him by chieftains from the river Lauhitya (Brahmaputra) to Mt. Mahendra, and from the Himālaya to the Western ocean. Still more important than this is the statement that the famous Mihirakula paid him obeisance "by touching his feet with the forehead."[2] The Hūṇa king must have suffered discomfiture shortly after 532-33 A.D., since another Mandasor inscription, dated in the Vikrama year 589,[3] eulogises Yaśodharman in general terms only, and does not mention anything about Mihirakula. Now the question is: How are we to reconcile the epigraphic evidence with that of Yuan Chwang? Vincent Smith's theory that Yaśodharman and Bālāditya formed a confederacy to oppose the Hūṇa invader may be original, but it is purely conjectural and cannot be relied upon. A better suggestion is that Mihirakula was routed on two separate occasions—in the direction of Magadha by Bālāditya, and in Central India by Yaśodharman, to whom should be given the credit for finally breaking the power of Mihirakula. Of course, Yuan Chwang did not wilfully distort facts. He was either misinformed, or, owing to his Buddhist prepossessions, he emphasised the achievement only of his brother-in-faith, king Bālāditya.

[1] The Mandasor inscription of Yaśodharman, *C.I.I.*, III, no. 33, pp. 146, 148.
cf. ये भुक्ता गुप्तनाथैर्न सकलवसुधाक्रान्तिदृष्टप्रतापै-
नाज्ञा हूणाधिपानां क्षितिपतिमुकुटाध्यासिनी यान्प्रविष्टा ।

[2] *Ibid.*
cf. चूडापुष्पोपहारैर्मिहिरकुलनृपेणार्चितं पादयुग्मम् ।

[3] *C.I.I.*, III, no. 35, pp. 150-58.

Death of Mihirakula

The exact year of Mihirakula's death is not known, but if he is identical with Gollas, "the lord of India", mentioned by the Alexandrian monk, Cosmas Indicopleustes, in 547 A.D., he may have continued to exercise authority over a limited territory by that date. After Mihirakula no great leader arose among the Hūṇas to reassert their hegemony. But inscriptions and literary works amply prove that for many centuries afterwards they remained a potent factor in the political situation of Northern India until they were gradually absorbed into the Hindu social polity.

SECTION D

THE KINGS OF VALABHĪ[1]

Foundation of the dynasty

The irruption of the Hūṇas, although at first checked by Skandagupta, appears to have brought to the surface the latent disruptive forces, which readily operate in India when the central power weakens, or its grip upon the remote provinces slackens. One of the earliest defections from the Gupta empire was Saurāṣṭra, where *Senāpati* Bhaṭṭāraka founded a new dynasty at Valabhī (Wala, near Bhavnagar) about the last decades of the fifth century A.D.

Origin

His ancestry is still a matter of controversy, but whether he belonged to the Maitraka tribe (modern Mers or Mehers), or the latter were the enemies of his

[1] See also N. Ray, "The Maitrakas of Valabhī," *Ind. Hist. Quart.*, Vol. IV (1928), pp. 453-74.

family[1], there is hardly any doubt that Bhaṭṭāraka was a native of the soil, and was not Iranian in origin, as believed by Vincent Smith.[2]

Growth of power

Numerous inscriptions of the dynasty have been discovered, and they are all dated in the Gupta or Gupta-Valabhī era. They do not, however, supply us much political information of value beyond yielding a string of names. The first few rulers were not absolutely independent,[3] since the founder of the line and his successor, Dharasena I, are called merely *Senāpatis*; and Bhaṭṭāraka's three other sons, named Droṇasiṁha, Dhruvasena I, and Dharapatta, who ruled successively, assume the title of Mahārāja only. But it is not clear whose suzerainty they acknowledged. Did they for some time nominally keep alive the tradition of Gupta paramountcy? Or, did they owe allegiance to the Hūṇas, who gradually overwhelmed the western and central parts of India? Step by step the power of the house grew until we come to the reign of Dhruvasena II. It was during his time that Yuan Chwang visited Valabhī, and he records about it: "The reigning sovereign was of Kṣatriya birth, a nephew of Śīlāditya, the former king of *Mo-la-po* (Mālava) and a son-in-law of the Śīlāditya reigning at Kānyakubja; his name was *Tu-lo-po-po-ta* (i.e., Dhruvabhaṭa); he was of a hasty temper, and of shallow views, but he was a sincere

Dhruvasena II

[1] The difference of opinion is due to the difficulty in the analysis of the Sanskrit compound words.

[2] *Ox. Hist. Ind.*, p. 164. Curiously enough, the Maitrakas come into prominence almost contemporaneously with the Hūṇas. Were they an allied tribe with the latter?

[3] For instance, the Maliya copperplate records that Mahārāja Droṇasiṁha was installed as king "by the paramount master in person" (*C. I. I.*, III, no. 38, pp. 165, 168).

believer in Buddhism."[1] If the Śīlāditya of this passage is identical with Śīlāditya Dharmāditya of Valabhī (*circa* 595-612 A.D.), as seems almost certain, it may then be reasonably inferred that Mālava or its western portion was added to his ancestral kingdom by conquest during his reign. We also learn that king Harṣavardhana of Kanauj attacked Dhruvasena II or Dhruvabhaṭa, who suffered some reverses in the beginning and was driven to seek the shelter of Dadda II of Broach. Ultimately the Valabhī monarch regained his power with the latter's help; it is, at any rate, certain that he occupied the throne when Yuan Chwang visited him. Having married the daughter of his quondam adversary, Dhruvabhaṭa subsequently attended Harṣa's assembly at Prayāga in the capacity of his ally and son-in-law.[2] The next ruler of Valabhī was Dhruvasena II's son, Dharasena IV. He appears to have been a mighty figure, as he assumes the full Imperial titles of Paramabhaṭṭāraka, Mahārājādhirāja, Parameśvara, and Cakravartin. One of his grants was issued in G.E. 330=649 A.D. from "the camp of victory" (*vijayaskandhāvāra*), located at Bharukaccha or Broach, which may show that he aggrandised himself at the cost of the Gurjaras, and became their overlord.[3] It was perhaps during his time that the poet Bhaṭṭi wrote his celebrated *Kāvya*.[4] The family continued to rule for more than a century after Dharasena IV, the known date of the last king, Śīlāditya VII, being G.E. 447=766 A.D. But hardly anything substantial is recorded about these later monarchs. Valabhī, of course, did not lose its importance, and in the fourth quarter of the seventh

Dharasena IV

Later history

[1] Watters, II, p. 246; Beal, II, p. 267; *Life*, p. 149.

[2] See *Infra*.

[3] See the Kheḍā (Kaira) grant : *Ind. Ant.*, XV (1886), pp. 335-40.

[4] cf. काव्यं रचितं मया वलभ्यां श्रीधरसेननरेन्द्रपालितायाम् ।

century A.D. I-tsing found it, like Nālandā, a great centre of learning in Western India. Never extending beyond Saurāṣṭra, parts of Gujarat and Mālava at the height of its glory, the kingdom thus existed for nearly three centuries, and in the end fell a prey to Arab raids from the side of Sind.

Section E

THE LATER GUPTAS OF MAGADHA

The Aphsaḍ (Gayā district) inscription of Ādityasena[1] and the Deo-Baraṇārk (Shahabad district) inscription of Jīvitagupta II[2] disclosed the existence of a line of Gupta princes, called the Later Guptas by modern historians. The founder of this dynasty was Kriṣṇagupta, but unfortunately his exact connection with the Imperial Guptas is nowhere mentioned. He and his two successors, Harṣagupta and Jīvitagupta I, must have ruled Magadha in the interval between the death of Bhānugupta and 611 (?Mālava)=554 A.D., when Kumāragupta III was reigning. We get this date from the Haraha inscription[3] for Īśānavarman Maukhari, who is represented in the Aphsaḍ inscription as having been defeated by Kumāragupta III. After this victory, the latter perhaps extended his jurisdiction as far as Prayāga, for there are indications that his funeral rites took place there.[4] The next ruler, Dāmodaragupta, was routed and killed by his Maukhari contemporary,[5] who annexed Magadha or

[1] *C. I. I.*, III, no. 42, pp. 200-08.

[2] *Ibid.*, no. 46, pp. 213-18.

[3] *Ep. Ind.*, XIV, pp. 110-20.

[4] *C. I. I.*, III, p. 206, n. 3. Of course, this argument by itself has not much force.

[5] We learn from the Aphsaḍ inscription that Dāmodaragupta, "breaking up the proudly-stepping array of mighty elephants, belonging to the Maukhari, became unconscious (and expired in the fight)" (*C. I. I.*, III, pp. 203, 206, l. 8). No doubt, the

ι large part of it. Dāmodaragupta's son, Mahāsenagupta, ιppears from the *Harṣacarita* to have then retired to ;astern Mālava, which, as the records of the Parivrājaka Mahārājas show, still acknowledged the supremacy of the Guptas.[1] Here Mahāsenagupta strengthened his position, ınd even carried his arms against Susthitavarman as far as Lauhitya (Brahmaputra).[2] His son, Devagupta, formed ın alliance with Śaśāṅka of Bengal, and advanced against Grahavarman Maukhari of Kanauj, whom he killed. The nurder was, however, soon avenged by Rājyavardhana, for he in turn vanquished and perhaps slew Devagupta. A scion of this family, named Mādhavagupta, was subsequently placed by Harṣavardhana in Magadha ıs his feudatory or Viceroy, so that he might be a bulwark against the aggressions of Śaśāṅka. Mādhavagupta's son, Ādityasena, known from the Shahpur stone image inscription[3] to have been alive in H.E. 66=672 A.D., gave a good account of himself after the death of Harṣa, and raised the dynasty to independence ınd importance. He adopted the full Imperial titles, ınd performed the Aśvamedha sacrifice. He even boastfully claims to have ruled "the earth up to the shores of the oceans." He was followed by several weak kings,[4] and with the death of Jīvitagupta II, the last ruler, the fortunes of Magadha became obscure for a short time.

conventional claim for Dāmodaragupta's victory is made here, but the outcome of the conflict was certainly against him, as he is represented to have been killed in the battle.

[1] See *e.g.*, Khoh plates of Mahārāja Saṁkṣobha, dated in the Gupta year 209 (*C. I. I.*, III, no. 25, pp. 112-116); Khoh plates of the Ucchakalpa Mahārāja Sarvanātha of the Gupta year 214 (*Ibid.*, no. 31, pp. 135-39; *Ep. Ind.*, XV, p. 125).

[2] *C. I. I.*, III, no. 42, pp. 203, 206, ll. 10-11.

[3] *C. I. I.*, III, no. 43, pp. 209-10.

[4] An inscription of one of these kings, Mahārājādhirāja-Parameśvara-Śrī-Viṣṇugupta, has recently been found at Mangraon (Buxar, Shahabad district). It is dated in the 17th year of his reign. The inscription is being edited by Dr. Altekar.

SECTION F

THE MAUKHARIS[1]

Antiquity

The Maukharis came into prominence after the decline of the Imperial Guptas, but there are indications that the name Maukhari was "possibly known to Pāṇini and also Patañjali." Their antiquity is further borne out by a clay seal, on which the legend "Mokhaliṇaṁ", i.e., "of the Mokhalis (Maukharis)", is written in Mauryan Brāhmī characters.[2]

Origin

The origin of the Maukharis is uncertain. The *Harṣacarita* derives them from Mukhara,[3] but according to the Haraha inscription they were the "descendants of the hundred sons, whom king Aśvapati got from Vaivasvata (Manu)."[4] Whoever was their progenitor, this much appears from the evidence of the Haraha inscription and the termination *varman* in all the Maukhari names that they were Kṣatriyas.[5]

Their branches

The Maukharis occupied an important place in the politics of Northern India for a long time. A line of Maukhari chiefs with the title of *Mahāsenāpati* is known from three short inscriptions, recently discovered in

[1] See my *History of Kanauj*, Ch. II, pp. 20-60.

[2] *Arch. Surv. Ind. Rep.*, XV, p. 166.

[3] *Hc.C.T.*, p. 128.

[4] *Ep. Ind.*, XIV, p. 119, verse 3.

[5] If, however, the Mauharīs of the Gayā district, who are Vaiśyas, are the modern representatives of the Maukharis, as Jayasval believed (see *The Kaveri, the Maukharis and the Sangam Age*, p. 80, n. 1), they must have in after times gone down in the social scale probably owing to loss of sovereignty or change of occupation.

the Kotah State.[1] They are dated in the *Krita* (Mālava ?) year 294=238 A.D. (?). A set of three Maukhari feudatories, perhaps of the Guptas, are mentioned in the Barābar and Nāgārjuni hill inscriptions,[2] which are inscribed in the characters of the fifth century A.D. But the most important family was that of Kanauj. The first three rulers of this branch were matrimonially allied with, and presumably in political subordination to, the Later Guptas. In the reigns of Īśānavarman and Sarvavarman there was a tug of war between the two houses with the results noted above. Īśānavarman was the first to bring the family into eminence; he "conquered the Andhras........; vanquished the Sūlikas (not satisfactorily identified)........; and caused the Gauḍas to remain within their proper realm."[3] His son, Sarvavarman, defeated the Hūṇas of the north-west as well as Dāmodaragupta.[4] Not much is known about Avantivarman. His son and successor, Grahavarman, who married Rājyaśrī, daughter of Prabhākaravardhana of Thāneśvar, was assassinated by Devagupta of Malwa. Thus ended the Kanauj line, although the Maukharis did not entirely disappear, and in the time of Ādityasena we learn of one Bhogavarman, "the crest-jewel......of the valorous Maukhari race."[5]

The Maukharis of Kanauj were staunch Brahmanists; and the rise of this new centre of political power was due to their achievements, which welded almost the

[1] See *Ep. Ind.*, XXIII, no. 7, pp. 42-52.
[2] *C. I. I.*, III, nos. 48-50, pp. 221-28.
[3] *Ep. Ind.*, XIV, pp. 117, 120, verse 13.

cf. जित्वान्ध्राधिपतिं सहस्रगणितत्रेधाक्षरद्वारणं
व्यावल्गन्नियुतातिसंख्यतुरगान्भङ्क्त्वा रणे शूलिकान् ।
कृत्वा चायतिमोचितस्थलभुवो गौडान्समुद्राश्रया—
नध्यासिष्ट नतक्षितीशचरणः सिंहासनं यो जिती ॥

[4] *C. I. I.*, III no. 42, pp. 203, 206, ll. 8-9
[5] *Ind. Ant.*, IX, pp. 171, 181, verse 13.

whole of modern U. P. and a large part of Magadha into one mighty state.

The fixed points in Maukhari chronology are 611 (? Mālava—Vikrama year)=554 A.D., mentioned in the Haraha inscription,[1] and 606 A.D., the date of Grahavarman's murder.

[1] *Ep. Ind.*, XIV, pp. 118, 120, v. 21.

CHAPTER XIV

HARṢAVARDHANA OF THĀNEŚVAR AND KANAUJ[1]

Importance emphasised by ample materials

The seventh century A.D. begins with the appearance of a remarkable figure on the political stage, and although Harṣavardhana had neither the lofty idealism of Aśoka nor the military skill of Candragupta Maurya, yet he has succeeded in arresting the attention of the historian like both those great rulers. This has, indeed, been largely due to the existence of two contemporary works, viz., Bāṇa's *Harṣacarita* and Yuan Chwang's *Si-yu-ki* or the *Records* of his travels, which are here and there supplemented by epigraphic documents[2] and the *Life of Yuan Chwang* written by Hwui-li.

Ancestors of Harṣa

According to the *Harṣacarita*, the predecessors of Harṣa were all rulers of the land of Śrīkaṇṭha (Thāneśvar). It traces the genealogy to the remote Puṣpabhūti, a devout Śaiva, but the inscriptions of Harṣa mention the names of only four of his immediate ancestors. The kingdom was founded by Naravardhana about the close of the fifth or the beginning of the sixth

[1] See my *History of Kanauj*, (Benares, 1937), pp. 61-187.

[2] See the Banskhera copper-plate (*Ep. Ind.*, IV, pp. 208-11); Madhuban C. P. (*Ibid.*, I, pp. 67-75); Sonpat copper seal (*C. I. I.*, III, no. 52, pp. 231-32), besides the Nālandā seals (*Ep. Ind.*, XXI, April 1931, pp. 74-76), and the Aihole-Meguṭi inscription of Pulakeśin II (*Ep. Ind.*, VI, pp. 1-12.)

century A.D.—the period of the Hūṇa disturbances. His grandson, Ādityavardhana, is chiefly known for having married Mahāsenaguptā, who was probably a sister of the Later Gupta monarch, Mahāsenagupta. Under Prabhākaravardhana, the kingdom grew both in territory and influence, as he is the first to be styled Mahārājādhirāja and Paramabhaṭṭāraka in the family inscriptions. The *Harṣacarita* calls him "a lion to the Hūṇa deer, a burning fever to the king of the Indus land, a troubler of the sleep of Gujarat (Gurjaras?), a bilious plague to that scent-elephant the lord of Gandhāra, a looter to the lawlessness of the Lāṭas, an axe to the creeper of Malwa's glory."[1] But we must not at once jump to the conclusion that all these states named in the above passage were actually annexed by Prabhākaravardhana. In our opinion, it is merely a poetical description of Prabhākara's greatness and might as compared with the other contemporary rulers. At the time of Yuan Chwang's visit the kingdom of Thāneśvar was not more than 7,000 *li* or 1,200 miles in circuit. Its north-western frontiers appear to have been limited by the Hūṇa territories in the Punjab, and in the north it probably extended up to the hills. In the east it was conterminous with the Maukhari state of Kanauj, and on the west and south it just covered portions of the Punjab and the Rajputana desert. Harṣa, not only inherited these paternal dominions, but also got the Maukhari throne of Kanauj owing to a combination of tragic circumstances, which we now proceed to narrate.

Early position

When the death of Prabhākaravardhana took place

[1] *Hc. C. T.*, p. 101. cf. हूणहरिणकेशरी सिन्धुराजज्वरो गुर्जरप्रजागरः गन्धाराधिपगन्धद्विपकूटपाकलः लाटपाटवपाटच्चरः मालवलक्ष्मीलतापरशुः (*Hc.*, Cal. ed., pp. 243-44).

in 605 A.D., the crown of Thāneśvar devolved on Rājyavardhana, who after fulfilling his father's commission of subduing the Hūṇas hurried back to the capital. But before he and his younger brother, Harṣa, could recover from the shock of their bereavement, they were struck by another bolt from the blue. For they received the sad news that the king of Malwa, who is identical with Devagupta of the Madhuban and Banskhera charters had attacked and killed their brother-in-law, Grahavarman, and that their sister, Rājyaśrī, had been thrown into a dungeon in Kānyakubja. The courier, named Saṁvādaka, apprised the royal brothers of the Malwa king's reported designs against Thāneśvar as well.[1] Hearing this, Rājyavardhana immediately started with his troops to repress the "unmannerly foe," and asked Harṣa to remain behind probably with a view to guarding the rear. Ill-luck was, however, dogging both the princes at every step, and soon it was young Harṣa's turn to take a plunge into the troubled waters of the political storm. After some time he learned that though Rājyavardhana had routed the Mālava army with "ridiculous ease", he was treacherously assassinated by the king of Gauḍa,[2] identified with Yuan Chwang's She-sang-kia (Śaśāṅka), who had come all the way from his distant kingdom to assist his ally, Devagupta. Having thus avenged the latter's defeat, Śaśāṅka occupied Kanauj, and in order to divert the attention of the Vardhana army, now under the command of Bhaṇḍi, the Gauḍa monarch released the widowed Maukhari queen,

[1] *Hc. C.T.*, p. 173.

[2] It is said that Śaśāṅka threw Rājyavardhana off his guard by offering to marry his daughter to him "as a token of submission and friendship," and when he was "weaponless, confiding, and alone," the Gauḍa king "despatched him (Rājyavardhana) in his own quarters" (*Hc. C.T.*, p. 178). cf. तस्मात् च हेलानिर्जितमालवानीकमपि गौड़ाधिपेन मिथ्योपचारोपचितविश्वासं मुक्तशस्त्रं एकाकिनं विश्रब्धं स्वभवन एव भ्रातरं व्यापादितमश्रौषीत् (*Hc.*, Cal. ed., p. 436).

Rājyaśrī, from detention in her own capital. After this unexpected turn in the wheel of Destiny Harṣa was "the only *śeṣa* left to support the earth", and he, therefore, ascended the paternal throne of Thāneśvar. His immediate and pressing duties were to rescue his distressed sister, relieve Kanauj from the control of Śaśāṅka, and punish him for his foul deed. To realise these objectives Harṣa advanced with a strong force, and in the course of his march concluded a perpetual treaty of friendship with his Assam contemporary, Bhāskaravarman, through the latter's messenger, Haṁsavega. Soon Harṣa met Bhaṇḍi, and learned of Rājyaśrī's release and her flight to the Vindhya forests. He made a vigorous search for her, and at last found her just when she was about to immolate herself. Harṣa then returned to his camp with his sister, and unhappily our source of information, the *Harṣacarita*, abruptly comes to an end at this stage. But, in the meantime, it seems that on the approach of Harṣa's hosts Śaśāṅka thought discretion was the better part of valour, and instead of facing an open conflict he withdrew from Kanauj, as after the Thāneśvar-Kāmarūpa (Assam) alliance he was exposed to serious danger both from the front and the rear. Bhaṇḍi had already cut off the support of the Malwa army after the defeat, and perhaps death, of Devagupta, and in the face of the new odds arrayed against Śaśāṅka strategy certainly demanded that he should beat a masterly retreat. Thus, Kanauj was left in a hopeless state of confusion, deprived as it was of its young Maukhari monarch. Should Rājyaśrī then be asked to assume the reins of government? But probably owing to her afflictions and her inclinations towards the quietist teachings of Buddhism she was herself unwilling to undertake the onerous responsibilities of rulership. In the absence of any other rightful Maukhari claimant, the ministers and statesmen of Kanauj, led by Poni, invited Harṣa to accept the crown.[1] He hesitated to agree to this tempting offer, presumably because he was not sure of the feelings and support of the people in the matter. Accordingly, he consulted the omens and the oracle Bodhisattva Avalokiteśvara, who directed him not to ascend the throne or adopt the style Mahārāja. In conformity with these instructions he assumed the royal office with the sobriquet Śīlāditya, and called himself "Kumāra". Now, this unostentatious title definitely suggests that although, according to Bāṇa, Harṣa was already king of Thāneśvar, in Kanauj he was merely charged with the duty of keeping the machinery of the government running, and that his political status there was originally no better than that of a guardian or regent. But it would appear that with the lapse of time, when he had consolidated his position and laid opposition, if any, to rest, he transferred his capital from Thāneśvar to Kanauj and became the sovereign ruler of the latter kingdom also by assuming the full Imperial titles. Thus was brought about the amalgamation of both the kingdoms, which helped Harṣa greatly in extending the sphere of his influence and authority over the numerous warring states that continually disturbed the political equilibrium of the North.

Campaigns of Harṣa

Regarding the conquests of Harṣa, we do not get any definite details. There are, of course, some vague generalities in the accounts of the admiring Yuan Chwang, e.g., "Proceeding eastward, he invaded the states which had refused allegiance; and waged incessant warfare until in six years he fought the 'Five Indias' (according to another reading: 'had brought the Five Indias under allegiance')[2]. Again, the Chinese pilgrim says: "He (Harṣa) was soon able to avenge

[1] Beal, I, pp. 210-211; Watters, I, p. 343.
[2] Watters, I, p. 343; Beal, I, p. 213.

the injuries received by his brother, and to make himself *Master of India*."[1] Further, Yuan Chwang adds: "At the present time Śīlāditya Mahārāja had conquered the nations from east to west and carried his arms to remote districts."[2] But nowhere does the worthy pilgrim mention how, when, and what kingdoms were conquered by Harṣa. It is, however, certain that the king of Valabhī, Dhruvabhaṭa or Dhruvasena II, had to bear the brunt of Harṣa's aggression. The latter won some successes in the beginning and his adversary had to seek the protection of Dadda II of Broach. With his help Dhruvabhaṭa regained his power, being on the throne at the time of Yuan Chwang's visit. This conflict could not have been a matter of indifference to Pulakeśin II, who considered himself "lord of the whole region of the south." Accordingly, a trial of strength between the two great monarchs was inevitable. The *Life* deposes that Harṣa personally took the command against *Pu-lo-ki-sha* (Pulakeśin II) of *Mo-ha-la-cha* (Mahārāṣṭra),[3] but nothing availed him, and he was repulsed with severe losses by his southern rival. The clash must have occurred prior to A.D. 634, the date of the Aihoḷe-Meguṭi inscription, in which it is mentioned with a sense of legitimate pride.

The evidence of Bāṇa, too, does not throw any clear light on the military achievements of Harṣa. Indeed, the court poet does not even inform us how his patron proceeded against the Gauḍa king, who was the immediate object of his wrath. There is hardly any doubt that Śaśāṅka evaded Harṣa's grasp, and was flourishing in all glory as late as G.E. 300=619 A.D. according to a Ganjam inscription.[4] We further learn that Harṣa, "having pounded the king of Sind, made

[1] *Life*, p. 83.
[2] Watters, II, p. 239; Beal, II, pp. 256-57.
[3] *Life*, p. 147.
[4] *Ep. Ind.*, VI, pp. 144, 146.

his wealth his own",[1] which signifies that both came into collision, and the former not only got the upper hand, but also succeeded in exacting a war tribute.

Chronology of Harṣa's campaigns

Yuan Chwang's remark that "Harṣa waged incessant warfare until in six years he had brought the five Indias under allegiance"[2] has been interpreted by some scholars to mean that all his wars were over between 606 A.D., the date of his accession, and 612 A.D. It is, however, an altogether gratuitous assumption that Yuan Chwang's six years began the very year Harṣa ascended the throne. Besides, we know that Śaśāṅka continued to hold power until A.D. 619, and so Harṣa must have conquered the eastern regions some time after—say between 620 and 625 A.D. Further, it appears from the testimony of Yuan Chwang that the engagement with Pulakeśin II took place when Harṣa had already carried his arms to "remote districts from east to west." Thus, the earliest and the latest limits may be fixed between *circa* A.D. 625 and 634 (the date of the Aihole record); and we may, therefore, take roughly the year 630 A.D. as the date of the event.[3] At this point we must explain also the other

[1] *Hc. C. T.*, p. 76.

cf. "अत्र पुरुषोत्तमेन सिन्धुराजं प्रमथ्य लक्ष्मीः आत्मीकृता"

(*Hc.*, Cal. ed., pp. 210-11).

There is another oft-quoted passage, "अत्र परमेश्वरेण तुषारशैलभुवो दुर्गाया गृहीतः करः", which has been taken to mean that Harṣa "exacted tribute from an inaccessible land of the snowy mountains"—perhaps Nepal or Kashmir. It may, however, be interpreted as "here the overlord has obtained the hand of Durgā born in the snowy mountains", which may refer to Harṣa's marriage with some hill-princess of a powerful family.

[2] Watters, I, p. 343; Beal, I, p. 213.

[3] See, however, Mr. K. C. Chattopādhyāya, *Proc. Ind. Hist, Cong.*, 1939, 3rd session, Calcutta, pp. 586-604. He places the Harṣa-Pulakeśin war between 610 and 612 A. D.

statement by Yuan Chwang that Harṣa "reigned in peace for thirty years without raising a weapon."[1] Accepting the correctness of this translation—although Beal renders it: "*After* thirty years his arms reposed, and he governed everywhere in peace"[2]—we may at once say it only shows that Harṣa soon established internal security and stability of government after the earlier confusion due to the Gupta-Gauḍa incursions. But in his foreign policy Harṣa remained an Imperialist, and the Kongoda (Ganjam district) campaign of A.D. 643 proves beyond doubt that he had to undertake military expeditions almost till the close of his momentous reign.

Extent of the Empire

It has generally been supposed from the epithet "Sakalottarāpathanātha" that Harṣa made himself master of the whole of Northern India. There are, however, grounds for believing that it was often used in a vague and loose way, and did not necessarily connote the whole of the region from the Himālayas to the Vindhya ranges.[3] A careful analysis of Yuan Chwang's account also shows that the dominions of Harṣa were much more limited in extent. The pilgrim explicitly mentions the existence of a number of states, along with their dependencies, at the time of his visit. Among them were: Kapiśa Kashmir, Jalandhar, Bairat, Mathurā, Matipura (Mandawar, Bijnor district), Suvarṇagotra country, Kapilavastu, Nepal, Kāmarūpa (Assam), Mahārāṣṭra, Broach,

[1] Watters, I, p. 343.

[2] Beal, I, p. 213.

[3] There is mention of a "Sakalottarāpathanātha" in the inscriptions of Cālukya Vinayāditya (*Ind. Ant.*, VII, pp. 107, 111; *Ibid.*, IX, p. 129), and if he is identical with one of the successors of Ādityasena in the Later Gupta line, as has been suggested, it is certain that this "Sakalottarāpathanātha" was far from being the ruler of the whole of Northern India.

Valabhī, Gurjara country, Ujjain, Bundelkhand, Maheśvarapura (Gwalior region), and Sind. These were evidently outside the pale of Harsa's jurisdiction. On the other hand, Yuan Chwang is silent about the governments of the following territories in Northern India: Kullu, Śatadru country (Sirhind), Thāneśvar, Srughna (Sugh), Brahmapura (British Garhwal and Kumaon), Govisana (modern districts of Kashipur, Rampur, and Pilibhit), Ahicchatra (eastern Rohilkhand), Bilsaḍ (Etah district), Kapittha (Sankissa), *A-yu-te* (Ayodhyā, or Aphui in the Fatehpur district), Hayamukha (Rae-Bareli and Partabgarh districts), Prayāga, Kosambī, Vishoka (?), Śrāvastī, Rāma-grāma, Kuśinagara, Vārāṇasī (Benares), Ghazipur district, Vaiśālī, Vriji country, Magadha, Monghyr, Bhagalpur, Rajmahal, Pauṇḍravardhana, Samataṭa, Tāmralipti, Karṇasuvarṇa, Orissa including modern Ganjam.[1]

Yuan Chwang's silence about the political status of all these territories perhaps indicates that they were included in the kingdom of Kanauj. That some of them were actually within the empire of Harṣa can be proved by means of independent evidence. We have already discussed that his ancestral dominions comprised Thāneśvar, the valley of the Saraswatī river, and parts of eastern Rajputana, to which he afterwards added the Maukhari kingdom of Kanauj covering almost the whole of modern U.P. and a portion of Magadha. Harṣa's authority over Magadha is also proved by his title, "King of Magadha", found in the Chinese documents bearing on his embassy. The Banskherā and Madhuban charters, recording grants of land, show that Ahicchatra and Śrāvastī formed *bhuktis* or divisions of his empire. His sovereignty

[1] For the sake of brevity I have omitted the Chinese form of names. I have critically analysed here Yuan Chwang's testimony to make my theory on this knotty and controversial topic more explicit.

over Orissa is clear from the *Life*[1]; and the fact that in his progress in East India Harṣa held his court at Kajaṅgala (Rajmahal district) furnishes another proof of the extension of his jurisdiction so far. We may, therefore, on the strength of Yuan Chwang's testimony and other epigraphic and literary records roughly define the kingdom of Harṣa in modern geographical terminology as consisting of portions of eastern Punjab, almost the whole of the present U.P. (excepting Mathurā and Matipura,), Bihar, Bengal, and Orissa including Kongoda or the Ganjam region.[2] That this was the view of Yuan Chwang also appears from the expression "lord of the five Indias", which has been explained as comprising Svarāṣṭra or the Punjab (eastern parts of the Punjab in this case), Kānyakubja, Mithilā or Bihar, Gauḍa or Bengal, Utkala or Orissa. Thus the whole evidence harmonises remarkably well, and it is high time to abandon every exaggerated notion of Harṣa's sovereignty extending up to Kashmir and Sind, Saurāṣṭra and even the far South, Kāmarūpa (Assam) and Nepal. Such a view is flagrantly opposed to the unimpeachable contemporary accounts of Yuan Chwang. These territories themselves were of sufficiently imposing dimensions, being much larger than any other individual state in Northern India; and this was the reason why the power of Harṣa made such a

[1] *Life*, p. 154. Śīlādityarāja is represented as having assigned to Jayasena, a noted Buddhist scholar, the revenue of eighty large towns of Orissa.

[2] The phenomenon of small states, almost adjacent to Kanauj, may be explained by their alliance with Harṣa at the very start of his career to escape his war-frenzy. And Harṣa, who stood in dire need of allies then, astutely tolerated their continued existence. The powers, which lay on his southern route, maintained their autonomy either by giving a passage to Harṣa's forces, or, if they had to submit to his yoke, by re-asserting themselves afterwards at his discomfiture when warring against Pulakeśin II.

deep impression upon the Master of the Law.[1]

Administration

The foregoing discussion shows that Harṣa's empire mostly extended towards the east, and naturally he could not but aspire to the control of the territories lying on this side, since the southern routes were already blocked by the mighty arms of Pulakeśin II. In those early times the Ganges was the highway of traffic linking up all the country from Bengal to "Mid India", and the supremacy of Kanauj over this vast Gangetic region was, therefore, essential for its commerce and prosperity. Harṣa succeeded in bringing nearly the whole of it under his yoke and, the kingdom having thus developed into comparatively gigantic proportions, the task of its successful governance became all the more difficult. The first thing that Harṣa did was to increase his military strength, both to keep the unsubdued states overawed and to fortify his own position against internal upheavals and foreign aggressions. Yuan Chwang writes: "Then having enlarged his territory he increased his army bringing the elephant corps up to 60,000 and the cavalry to 100,000."[2] It was thus on this large force that the empire ultimately rested. But the army is merely an arm of policy. Harṣa secured his position by other means as well. He concluded an "undying alliance" with Bhāskaravarman, king of Assam, when he started on his initial campaign. Next, Harṣa gave the hand of his daughter to Dhruvasena II or Dhruvabhaṭa of Valabhī after measuring swords with him. Thereby he not only gained a valued ally, but also an

Military strength

Alliances

[1] See my *History of Kanauj*, pp. 78-119.
[2] Watters, I, p. 343; Beal, I, p. 213.

access to the southern routes. Lastly, he sent a Brahman envoy to Tai-Tsung, the Tang Emperor of China, in 641 A.D., and a Chinese mission subsequently visited Harṣa.[1] His diplomatic relations with China were probably meant as a counterpoise to the friendship that Pulakeśin II, his southern rival, cultivated with the king of Persia about which we are told by the Arab historian Tabari.[2]

Harṣa's exertions

In an oriental despotism, the sovereign being the centre of the state, much of the success in administration necessarily depends on his benevolent example. Accordingly, Harṣa essayed the trying task of supervising personally the affairs of his wide dominions. He divided his day between state business and religious work. "He was indefatigable and the day was too short for him."[3] He was not content to rule from the luxurious surroundings of the palace only. He insisted on going about from place to place "to punish the evil-doers and reward the good." During his "visits of inspection" he came into close contact with the country and the people, who must have had ample opportunities for ventilating their grievances to him.

Civil administration

Unfortunately our data for the then existing system of government are very meagre. Probably Harṣa was assisted in the administration by an advisory council (*mantri-pariṣad*). According to Yuan Chwang, Harṣa was invited to accept the crown of Kanauj by the statesmen and ministers of that kingdom led by Poni,[4] and it is reasonable to believe that they may have continued to wield some sort of control even during the palmy days of Harṣa's power. The pilgrim even goes so far as

[1] *E. H. I.*, 4th ed., p. 366.
[2] *J. R. A. S.*, N. S. XI (1879), pp. 165-66.
[3] Watters, I, p. 344; Beal, I, p. 215.
[4] Beal, I, pp. 210-11; Watters, I, p. 343.

to assert that "a commission of officers held the land".[1] Further, owing to the large extent of territory and the scanty and slow means of communication, it was necessary to establish strong centres of government in order to keep the loosely knit parts of the empire together. The out-lying provinces were, therefore, put in charge of viceroys (*Rājasthānīya*?) or governors (*Lokapāla* or *Uparika Mahārāja*) or feudatories (*Sāmantas* or *Mahāsāmantas*). Among those of the last class was Mādhavagupta of Magadha. Besides, it appears from the *Harṣacarita* and inscriptions that the bureaucracy was very efficiently organised. Among some of these state functionaries, civil and military, may be mentioned *Mahāsandhivigrahādhikrita* (supreme minister of peace and war); *Mahābalādhikrita* (officer in supreme command of the army); *Senāpati* (general); *Brihadaśvavāra* (head cavalry officer); *Kaṭuka* (commandant of the elephant forces); *Cāṭa-bhaṭa* (irregular and regular soldiers); *Dūta* (envoy or ambassador); *Rājasthānīya* (foreign secretary or viceroy); *Uparika Mahārāja* (provincial governor); *Viṣayapati* (district officer); *Āyuktaka* (subordinate officials in general); *Mīmāṁsaka* (Justice ?), *Mahāpratīhāra* (chief warder or usher); *Bhogika* or *Bhogapati* (collector of the state share of the produce); *Dīrghadvaga* (express courier); *Akṣapaṭalika* (keeper of records); *Adhyakṣas* (superintendents of the various departments); *Lekhaka* (writer); *Karaṇika* (clerk); *Sevaka* (menial servants in general), etc.

Territorial divisions

The inscriptions of Harṣa testify that the old administrative divisions continued, viz., *Bhuktis* or provinces, which were further sub-divided into *Viṣayas* (districts). A still smaller territorial term, perhaps of the size of the present day *Tahsil* or *Taluka*, was *Pathaka*; and the *Grāma* was, as usual, the lowest unit of

[1] Beal, I, p. 210.

administration.

General features

Yuan Chwang was favourably impressed by the government, which was founded on benign principles. Families were not registered and individuals were not subject to forced labour contributions. The people were thus left free to grow in their own surroundings unfettered by the shackles of overgovernment. Taxation was light; the main sources of revenue were the traditional one-sixth of the produce and "duties at ferries and barrier stations",[1] paid by tradesmen, who went to and fro bartering their merchandise. The enlightened nature of Harṣa's administration is also evident from the liberal provision he made for charity to various religious communities and for rewarding men of intellectual eminence.[2]

Criminal administration

Owing to the well-organised character of the government the people generally lived together on good terms, and there were few instances of violent crime.[3] But the roads and river-routes were by no means immune from bands of brigands, Yuan Chwang himself having been stripped by them more than once. Indeed, on one occasion he was even on the point of being offered up as sacrifice by desperate characters. The law against crime was exceptionally severe. Imprisonment for life was the ordinary penalty for transgressions of the statute law and conspiracy against the sovereign, and we are informed that, though the offenders did not suffer any corporal punishment, they were not at all treated as members of the community.[4] The *Harṣacarita*, however, refers to the custom of releasing prisoners on joyous and festive occasions.

[1] Watters, I, p. 176.
[2] Watters, I, p. 176.
[3] Watters, I, p. 171.
[4] Ibid., p. 172.

The other punishments were more sanguinary than in the Gupta period: "For offences against social morality and disloyal and unfilial conduct, the punishment is to cut off the nose, or an ear, or a hand, or a foot, or to banish the offender to another country or into the wilderness".[1] Minor offences could be "atoned for by a money payment". Ordeals by fire, water, weighing or poison were also recognised instruments for determining the innocence or guilt of a person. The severity of the criminal administration was, no doubt, largely responsible for the infrequency of violations of law, but it must also have been due to the character of the Indian people who are described as of "pure moral principles."[2]

Glories of Kanauj

The prosperity and importance of Kanauj, so well begun during the time of the Maukharis, grew tremendously under Harṣa; and it now easily became the premier city of Northern India supplanting Pāṭaliputra, the older centre, through which the main currents of political life had flowed since the days of the Buddha. To the observant eyes of a foreigner it must have appeared a great cosmopolitan town whose inhabitants were almost equally divided between orthodoxy and heterodoxy. There were one hundred Buddhist monasteries with more than 10,000 brethren belonging to both the "Vehicles". The "Deva temples" amounted to about two hundred, and the non-Buddhists were several thousands in number. The city itself (twenty *li* or about 5 miles in length and five *li* or 1¼ mile in breadth)

[1] *Ibid.*; Beal, I, pp. 83-84.

[2] Yuan Chwang adds: "They will not take anything wrongfully, and they yield more than fairness requires. They fear the retribution for sins in other lives, and make light of what conduct produces in this life. They do not practise deceit and they keep their sworn obligations" (Watters, I, p. 171; Beal, I, p. 83).

was strongly defended by both nature and art. It was well planned, and had beautiful gardens and tanks of clear water. The houses were, on the whole, clean, comfortable and simple, or, in the words of Yuan Chwang, "sumptuous inside and economical outside". The people wore "a refined appearance", and the rich were "dressed in glossy silk attire". Praising the citizens Yuan Chwang says: "They are pre-eminently explicit and correct in speech, their expressions being harmonious and elegant, like those of the Devas, and their intonation clear and distinct, serving as rule and pattern for others."[1]

Assembly at Kanauj

Great as was Harṣa as a ruler and conqueror, he was greater still in the arts of Peace that "hath her victories no less renowned than War". One of them was the convocation of a grand assembly at Kanauj to give the utmost publicity to the doctrines of the Mahāyāna. Harṣa marched from his camp with accustomed pomp and pageantry along the southern bank of the Ganges, accompanied by Yuan Chwang and Bhāskaravarman, king of Kāmarūpa, and in the course of ninety days reached his destination. Here Harṣa was received by the "kings of eighteen countries" of the Five Indies[2] and several thousand priests belonging to the various sects, who had gathered together in response to the royal summons to join in the deliberations. Harṣa had previously ordered the construction of two thatched halls, each to accommodate one thousand persons, and a huge tower, in the middle of which was placed a golden statue of the Buddha, "of the same

[1] Watters, I, p. 153; Beal, I, p. 77.

[2] *Life*, p. 177. According to the *Si-yu-ki*, there were kings of twenty countries present (Beal, I, p. 218). The account of Harṣa's assemblies is mainly based on the *Life* and the *Si-yu-ki*.

height as the king himself." The proceedings of the assembly started with a solemn procession, and the main object of attraction was a golden statue of the Buddha, three feet high, which was carried on a gorgeously caparisoned elephant. Both Harṣa and Bhāskaravarman attended it, dressed in the guise of Śakra and Brahmā respectively. They were followed on elephants by a brilliant train of princes, priests, and prominent state officials. After the termination of the procession Harṣa performed a ceremonial worship of the image, and gave a public dinner. This being over, the conference opened with Yuan Chwang as "lord of the discussion". He dwelt on the merits of the Mahāyāna, and challenged those present to assail his arguments. But none came forward, and he remained in undisputed possession of the field for five days, when his theological rivals entered into a conspiracy to take the pilgrim's life. Getting a scent of it, Harṣa at once issued a stern proclamation threatening to behead anybody causing the least hurt to his celebrated guest.[1] The announcement had the desired effect, and for eighteen days there was none to oppose him in debate. Thus, though according to the *Life* the programme was gone through successfully to the utter confusion of all heretics and the joy of the Mahāyānists, the account preserved in the *Si-yu-ki* avers that the convocation concluded with startling incidents. The great tower suddenly caught fire,[2] and there was an attempt to assassinate Harṣa on account of his indifferent treatment of the assembled "heretics". He then got five hundred Brahmans arrested, and deported them. To the rest he extended mercy.[3]

Whichever of the two accounts may be true, it is

[1] *Life*, p. 180.
[2] Beal, I, p. 219.
[3] *Ibid.*, p. 221.

certain that the victory of Yuan Chwang in this assembly of public disputation considerably enhanced his prestige and influence over Harṣa, who honoured and reverenced him more than ever by precious gifts, but the pilgrim in a rare religious spirit respectfully declined to accept any of them.

Quinquennial distributions at Prayāga[1]

When the special assembly at Kanauj broke up, Harṣa invited Yuan Chwang to witness his sixth quinquennial distribution of alms (*Mahā-mokṣa Pariṣad*) at Prayāga at the sacred confluence of the Ganges and the Jumna. The latter, although homesick, agreed to be present at that unique function, which was attended by Dhruvabhaṭa, "king of South India", Kumārarāja (Bhāskaravarman) of Assam and other royalties, besides a vast concourse of people amounting to about 500,000—Śramaṇas, heretics, Nirgranthas, the poor, the orphans and the bereaved of the Five Indias, who had been summoned by an Imperial decree. The "Great distribution Arena" was the immense sandy plain between the rivers, and the proceedings lasted for seventy-five days, commencing with an impressive procession. The religious services were of the curiously eclectic kind, so characteristic of Hindu society and worship. On the first day the statue of the Buddha was set up in one of the temporary shrines built upon the sands, and was honoured by costly offerings and lavish distributions. On the second day the image of Ādityadeva (Sun) was worshipped and on the third day the idol of Īśvara-deva (Śiva) was offered adoration, but in each case the gifts bestowed were only half the value of those consecrated to the Buddha on the opening day. On the fourth day generous gifts were given to Buddhist monks. During the next twenty days Brahmans were the recipients of

[1] See *Life*, pp. 183-87.

Harṣa's bounty. Then ten days were spent in bestowing largess on the "heretics", i.e., Jains and members of other sects. The same number of days was reserved for giving alms to the mendicants, while it took a month to distribute charity to the poor, the orphans, and the destitute. By this time the accumulated treasures were exhausted, and then Harṣa gave away even his personal "gems and goods". Thus, he established a record in individual liberality hardly equalled in history.[1]

Yuan Chwang's departure

After the conclusion of the Prayāga assembly, Yuan Chwang took leave of Harṣa, who saw him off a long distance, and provided him with a military escort of "a king of North India called Udhita" to carry the books and images on horseback. Subsequently, Harṣa again met the pilgrim, and sent some money for the necessary expenses of his arduous journey over-land to China.[2]

Harṣa's Religion

We now pass on to a consideration of Harṣa's faith, which urged him to scorn delights incidental to his position, and work untiringly for the moral and material progress of his subjects. It may at the outset be mentioned that he did not inherit Buddhism. His three immediate ancestors were votaries of the Sun (Āditya). According to the inscriptions found at Banskhera (Shahjahānpur district) and Madhuban (Azamgarh district), Harṣa himself was a "Parama-māheśvara" or a

[1] But this sort of munificence must have been a heavy drain on the treasury. Was it, therefore, in any way responsible for the sudden collapse of the kingdom after Harṣa's death?

[2] Fa-hian, on the other hand, had preferred the southern sea-route, and returned home by way of Java or Sumatra.

devout Śaiva until at least the 25th regnal year—631 A.D. In his latter days, however, he appears to have inclined more and more towards Buddhism, perhaps due to its brilliant exposition by Yuan Chwang and the influence of his Buddhist sister Rājyaśrī. In the Kanauj assembly Harṣa even showed some partiality for the Mahāyāna by stifling free discussion and by representing Sakra and Brahmā as mere attendants on the Buddha. But it must not be understood that Harṣa ever became anything like a royal missionary of Buddhism. On the contrary, he maintained the eclectic character of his public worship, and officially honoured the Brahmanical deities of Āditya and Śiva in the Prayāga assembly. He fed the Brahmans, and gave them alms without stint.[1] Some of the activities of Harṣa, of course, bear a distinctly Buddhist flavour, e.g., his "forcible appropriation" of the tooth relic of the Buddha from Kashmir and its subsequent enshrinement in a *Saṅghārāma* in Kanauj;[2] his annual summoning of the Buddhist monks together for examination and discussion; his construction of Buddhist monasteries and *stūpas*;[3] and his prohibition of slaughter and the use of animal food under severe penalties.[4] His humanitarian services by the erection of hospices (*puṇyaśālas*) for the free supply of food and medicine to the poor and the afflicted may also have been inspired by his Buddhist ideals.[5] Thus, as a result of Harṣa's patronage there was a marked growth of Buddhism in Kanauj, though it was visibly on the wane in other countries.

General religious conditions

It is evident from Yuan Chwang's *Records* and the

[1] Watters, I, p. 344; Beal, I, p. 215.
[2] *Life*, pp. 181, 183.
[3] Watters, I, p. 344.
[4] *Ibid*; Beal, I, p. 214.
[5] *Ibid.*

Harṣacarita that Buddhism, Brahmanism, and Jainism were the principal religions in Harṣa's empire. Of these, the last was not so popular except in certain parts, viz., Vaiśālī, Pauṇḍravardhana, and Samataṭa, where the Digambaras were numerous. The Śvetāmbaras constituted its other important section. To Yuan Chwang, of course, Buddhism appeared to be in quite a flourishing condition, but it had suffered decline in several localities like Kosambi, Śrāvastī, and Vaiśālī. The monastic establishments, whose very existence depended upon the support and charity of the laity, were the centres of Buddhist life and activity. Of the two broad divisions of Buddhism, Mahāyāna and Hīnayāna, the former seems to have considerably gained ground. The pilgrim also speaks of its eighteen schools, which differed widely in their practices and claimed intellectual superiority over one another.[1] Such unseemly controversies must have weakened the cause of Buddhism and reacted in favour of Brahmanism, which had been showing signs of revival and vigour since the glorious epoch of the Guptas. Its main strongholds in Harṣa's empire were Prayāga and Vārāṇasī. Like Jainism and Buddhism, which in its Mahāyāna form encouraged the worship of the Buddha and the Bodhisattvas, Brahmanism was frankly given to idolatry. The most popular Brahmanical deities were Āditya, Śiva, and Viṣṇu, and their idols were installed in temples where they were worshipped with elaborate ceremonial.[2] The Brahmans kindled the sacrificial fire (Agni), held the cow sacred, and performed various rites to bring good luck and prosperity.[3] Another feature of Brahmanism was the multiplicity of philosophical schools and ascetic orders. Bāṇa

[1] Watters, I, p. 162.

[2] *Hc. C.T.*, p. 44.

[3] *Ibid.*, pp. 44-45; see also pp. 71, 90, 130.

mentions the followers of Kapila, Kaṇāda, Upaniṣads (Vedantins), believers in God as a creator (Aiśvara-karaṇikas), and even atheists like the Lokāyatikas.[1] Similarly, there were different classes of recluses, such as those pulling out their hair (Keśaluñcakas), Pāśupatas, Pañcarātrikas, Bhāgavatas, etc.[2] The *Life* also mentions Bhūtas, Kāpālikas, Jutikas, Sāṅkhyas, Vaiśeṣikas, etc.[3] They differed widely in their garbs, observances, and beliefs. They got their food by begging, and paid no attention whatsoever to their personal needs and comforts in the pursuit of what thay considered Truth.[4]

Harṣa's patronage of Learning

One of the claims of Harṣa to remembrance rests on his liberal patronage of learning. Yuan Chwang says that Harṣa used to earmark a fourth of the revenue from the crown lands for rewarding men of intellectual distinction.[5] According to the *Life*, he generously assigned "the revenue of eighty large towns of Orissa" to a noted Buddhist scholar, named Jayasena, who, however, thankfully declined even this tempting offer.'[6] Harṣa also made munificent endowments to Nālandā, the great centre of Buddhist learning. Its lofty structures, its inspiring instruction imparted through discussion, its comprehensive curriculum, its large assemblage of students from far and near,[7] and above all, the noble character and deep scholarship of its teachers and *alumni*, were then matters of pride to the entire

[1] *Hc. C. T.*, p. 236.
[2] *Ibid.*, pp. 33, 49, 236.
[3] *Life*, pp. 161-62.
[4] Watters, I, pp. 160-61
[5] *Ibid.*, p. 176; Beal, I, p. 87.
[6] *Life*, p. 154.
[7] According to one account, there were 10,000 students at Nālandā (*Life*, p. 112).

Buddhist world; and kings vied with one another in their liberality to equip and endow this great institution.[1] Harṣa's interest in literature is further evident from his patronage of authors like Bāṇabhaṭṭa, who wrote the *Harṣacarita*, first part of the *Kādambarī*, *Caṇḍīśataka*, etc.; Mayūra, whose chief contribution was the *Sūryaśataka*; and also Mātaṅga-Divākara, a shadowy bard.

Harṣa as author

But Harṣa was not a mere detached patron of letters. He himself appears to have wielded the pen with no less dexterity than the sword. Scholars generally ascribe to him the composition of three plays, viz., the *Priyadarśikā*, the *Ratnāvalī*, and the *Nāgānanda*. Bāṇa credits him with poetical skill of a high order;[2] moreover, several ancient writers, like Soḍḍhala (11th century A.D.)[3] and Jayadeva (12th century A.D.),[4] rank Harṣa along with other literary monarchs and even with Bhāsa, Kālidāsa, etc. Notwithstanding such references, the authorship of these plays has been a matter of doubt since quite early times. Mammaṭa, a Kashmiri writer of the 11th century, and several scholiasts of the 17th century A.D.,[5] thought that they were composed by one Dhāvaka in the name of Harṣadeva for some monetary consideration. In the face of these conflicting traditions it is difficult to be dogmatic, but as royal literati are not an unusual phenomenon in Indian history, there is nothing intrinsically improbable in regarding Harṣa as an author. This does not, however, preclude the possibility that some literary protégé of Harṣa may

[1] See H. D. Sankalia, *The University of Nālandā* (Madras, 1934).

[2] *Hc. C. T.*, pp. 58, 65.

[3] *Udayasundarī-kathā*, p. 2, C.D. Dalal & Krishnamacharya's edition (Gaekwāḍ's Oriental Series, no. 11; Baroda, 1920).

[4] *Prasannarāghava*, Act I, Stanza 22, p. 10, ed. Paranjpye & Panse (Poona, 1894).

[5] *e.g.*, Nāgojī in the *Kāvyapradīpoddyota*, and Paramānanda.

have lent an obliging hand in polishing his patron's dramas, for as the proverb has it, royal authors are only half authors.

Harṣa's death and its effects

After a momentous reign lasting for about four decades, Harṣa passed away in the year 647 or 648 A.D.[1] The withdrawal of his strong arm let loose all the pent-up forces of anarchy, and the throne itself was seized by one of his ministers, O-la-na-shun (i.e., Aruṇāśva or Arjuna). He opposed the entry of the Chinese mission sent before the death of *She-lo-ye-to* or Śīlāditya, and massacred its small armed escort in cold blood. But its leader, Wang-heuen-tse, was lucky enough to escape, and with the help of the famous Srong-btsan-Gampo, king of Tibet, and a Nepalese contingent he avenged the previous disaster. Arjuna or Aruṇāśva was captured in the course of two campaigns, and was taken to China to be presented to the Emperor as a vanquished foe. The authority of the usurper was thus subverted, and with it the last vestiges of Harṣa's power also disappeared.[2]

What followed next was only a general scramble to feast on the carcass of the empire. Bhāskaravarman of Assam appears to have annexed Karṇasuvarṇa and the adjacent territories, formerly under Harṣa, and issued a grant from his camp there to a Brahman of the locality.[3] In Magadha Ādityasena, son of Mādhavagupta, who was a feudatory of Harṣa, declared his independence, and as a mark of it assumed full Imperial

[1] According to the *Life* (p. 156), however, Śīlāditya died at the end of the Yung Hwei period (i.e., about 654-55 A.D.).

[2] See *J. A. S. B.*, VI (1837), pp. 69-70; *J. R. A. S.*, 1869-70 (N. S. IV), pp. 85-86; *Asiatic Journal and Monthly Register for British and Foreign India, China, and Australia*, 1836, pp. 220-21., etc.

[3] *Ep. Ind.*, XII, p. 66.

titles and performed the *Aśvamedha* sacrifice.[1] In the west and north-west those powers, that had lived in dread of Harṣa, asserted themselves with greater vigour. Among them were the Gurjaras of Rajputana (afterwards Avanti) and the Karakoṭakas of Kashmir, who during the course of the next century became a formidable factor in the politics of Northern India.

[1] *C. I. I.*, III, pp. 212-13.

CHAPTER XV

POST-HARṢA AND PRE-MOSLEM NORTHERN INDIA—(FROM A.D. 647 TO *c.* 1200)

SECTION A

THE KINGDOM OF KANAUJ

I—Yaśovarman[1]

After the fall of the usurper, the earliest monarch, about whom we know anything definite, is Yaśovarman. Unfortunately, his ancestry is still a mystery. The alleged connection with the Mauryas, according to certain Jain works, altogether lacks confirmation. Nor is there any proof, excepting the termination *Varman*, in support of the suggestion that he was a scion of the Maukhari house. Yaśovarman appears to have ruled from *circa* 725 to 752 A.D. He was a contemporary of Lalitāditya Muktāpīḍa of Kashmir, and has rightly been identified with I-cha-fon-mo, "king of Central India", who sent his minister Seng-po-ta to China in 731 A.D. The *Gauḍavaho*, a contemporary composition, credits Yaśovarman with extensive conquests as far as the South, but though the truth of these campaigns may be doubted, his war with the "Magahanāha" (lord of Magadha) seems to be founded on fact. The latter, who was most probably identical with Jīvitagupta II, was defeated in a hard-fought battle. Subsequently, in the year 733 A.D., Yaśovarman himself suffered a reverse at the hands of Lalitāditya of Kashmir.

[1] See the author's *History of Kanauj*, pp. 192-212.

The former's reign is memorable for the works of two great poets, viz., Bhavabhūti, author of the *Mālatī-mādhava*, *Mahāvīracarita*, and the *Uttararāmacarita*; and Vākpati, who wrote the Prakrit *Gauḍavaho*. The three successors of Yaśovarman are mere names, buried in the limbo of oblivion.

II—The Āyudhas

This dynasty comprised three kings, who ruled for a short period only. It is, however, not known how they rose to power, or what their lineage was. The first, Vajrāyudha, is casually referred to in the *Karpūramañjarī*[1], and his accession may be placed about 770 A.D. He was probably defeated by Jayāpīḍa Vinayāditya of Kashmir (779-810 A.D.). But, if the latter undertook this campaign late in his career, the vanquished Kanauj sovereign must have been Vajrāyudha's successor, Indrāyudha, who was reigning in the Śaka year 705=783-84 A.D., according to the Jain *Harivaṁśa*.[2] It was during his time that the tripartite struggle between the Kanauj monarchs, the Rāṣṭrakūṭas, and the Pālas began. Dhruva Rāṣṭrakūṭa (*circa* 779-94 A.D.) invaded the Doab, and in commemoration of his victory is said to have "added the emblem of the Ganges and the Jumna to his imperial insignia." Indrāyudha was afterwards defeated and dethroned by Dharmapāla of Bengal, who raised his protégé Cakrāyudha to the throne of Kanauj. This political arrangement was approved by nearly all the principal states then existing. But the Rāṣṭrakūṭas could not tolerate the

Vajrāyudha

Indrāyudha

Cakrāyudha

[1] III, 5[2], pp. 74, 266 (Konow and Lanman's edition).

[2] *Bom. Gaz.*, 1896, Vol. I, pt. II, p. 197, n. 2; *Ind. Ant.*, XV, pp. 141-42.

Bengal king's assumption of the supreme status in Northern India, and accordingly a trial of strength between the two powers became inevitable. The result of the conflict is preserved in the Sanjan plates of Amoghavarṣa I, which depose that both "Dharma and Cakrāyudha surrendered of themselves" to Govinda III (*circa* 794—814 A.D.), son and successor of Dhruva[1]. These depredations considerably harassed the populace and created confusion in the Doab. Nāgabhaṭa II Pratīhāra took advantage of the situation, and defeated Cakrāyudha, "whose lowly demeanour was manifest from his dependence on others."[2] After this victory Nāgabhaṭa boldly annexed Kanauj, and initiated a new line of rulers there.

III. The Imperial Pratīhāras

Origin

The Pratīhāra family, to which Nāgabhaṭa II belonged, appears to have been of foreign extraction. Indeed, the phrase "Gurjara-Pratīhārānvayaḥ", i.e., "Pratīhāra clan of the Gurjaras", occurring in line 4 of the Rajor (Alwar) inscription[3], indicates that they were a branch of the famous Gurjaras—one of those Central Asian tribes that poured into India through the north-western passes along with, or soon after, the Hūṇas during the period of political unrest following the disruption of the Gupta Empire. That the Pratīhāras belonged to the Gurjara stock is also confirmed by the Rāṣṭrakūṭa records, and the Arab writers, like Abu Zaid and Al Mas'ūdi, who allude to their fights with the Juzr or Gurjaras of the North. Besides, it is important to re-

[1] *Ep. Ind.*, XVIII, pp. 245, 253, v. 23.

[2] *Ibid.*, pp. 108, 112, v. 9.

[3] *Ep. Ind.*, III, pp. 263-67. The inscription bears the *Vikrama* date 1016=959 A.D., and records a grant of Mathanadeva, feudatory of P. M. P. Vijayapāladeva.

member that the Kanarese poet, Pampa, describes Mahīpāla as "Ghūrjararāja." The inscriptions of the Pratīhāras, on the other hand, trace their origin to Lakṣmaṇa, who acted as the door-keeper (*Pratīhāra*) of his brother Rāma.[1] This claim is further supported by Rājaśekhara, the dramatist, who calls his patron Mahendrapāla "Raghukulatilaka" (ornament of Raghu's race) or "Raghugrāmaṇī" (leader of Raghu's family). But we need not attach any special significance to these traditions or derivations, for such legendary connections are often ascribed in order to give the ruling families noble and well-known pedigrees.

Original Territories

The earliest known settlement of the Pratīhāras was at Mandor (Jodhpur) in Central Rajputana, where ruled the family of Haricandra. Then a branch advanced southwards, and established its power at Ujjain. That it was a Gurjara seat is evidenced by the Sanjan plates of Amoghavarṣa I, which refer to the Rāṣṭrakūṭa Dantidurga's subjugation of its Gurjara chief.[2] Moreover, the Jain *Harivaṁśa* expressly calls Vatsarāja king of Avanti.[3] As he has been identified on all hands with the father of Nāgabhaṭa II, we may reasonably infer that prior to the northern conquest the Pratīhāras of Kanauj were masters of Avanti.

Beginnings of power

The dynasty began well under Nāgāvaloka or Nāga-

[1] *Ibid.*, XVIII, pp. 95, 97, v. 4. According to the Gwalior inscription (*Ibid.*, pp. 107, 110, v. 3), however, Lakṣmaṇa came to be known as Pratīhāra owing to his act of repelling (प्रतिहरणविधे:) displayed against his enemies, like Meghanāda, in battle.

[2] *Ibid.*, XVIII, pp. 243, 252, v. 9.

[3] Bom., Gaz., 1896, Vol. I, pt. II, p. 197, fn. 2; see also *Ep.*

bhaṭa I, who repelled the "armies of the powerful Mlec-cha king," i.e., the Arab raiders of the western borders of India, and carried his arms to Broach.[1] The next two rulers were nonentities. The fourth, Vatsarāja, rose to great prominence by his achievements. He defeated the Bhaṇḍi clan, perhaps Bhaṭṭis of Central Rajputana, over which his supremacy was recognised. He won a victory also against the Gauḍa monarch, Dharmapāla, according to the Wani-Dindori[2] and Radhanpur grants.[3] But eventually Vatsarāja was routed by Dhruva, and was compelled to take shelter "in the centre of (the deserts of) Maru".

Nāgabhaṭa II (circa 805-33 A.D.)

Vatsarāja was succeeded by his son Nāgabhaṭa (II) about 805 A.D. In the beginning, the latter tried to retrieve the fallen fortunes of his family, but the stars were as unfavourable to him as to his predecessor, and he suffered a crushing defeat at the hands of Govinda III. Nāgabhaṭa II's preliminary attempts having thus proved abortive, he turned his attention towards Kanauj with the results noted above. The internal dissensions among the Rāṣṭrakūṭas after the death of Govinda III early in 814 A.D., no doubt, made Nāgabhaṭa II immune from the southern danger, but Dharmapāla of Bengal soon took the field against him for deposing his protégé, Cakrāyudha, and annexing the kingdom of Kanauj. The Pratīhāra monarch vanquished his adversary in a sanguinary contest at Mudgagiri (Monghyr), and grew so strong that even the kings of Andhra, Sindhu, Vidarbha and Kaliṅga sought his aid or alliance.

Ind., VI, pp. 195-96; *Jour. Dept. Lett.* (Calcutta University), Vol. X, pp. 23-25.

[1] cf. Hansot Grant, *Ep. Ind.*, XII, pp. 203, 204, l. 34.

[2] *Ind. Ant.*, XI, pp. 157, 161, l. 12.

[3] *Ep. Ind.*, VI, pp. 243, 248, v. 8.

The Gwalior inscription further represents Nāgabhaṭa II as having won victories against Ānartta (Northern Kāthiāwāḍ), Mālava or Central India, the Matsyas (of eastern Rajputana), Kirātas (of the Himālayan regions), Turuṣkas (Arab settlers of Western India),and the Vatsas (of Kosambī)[1].

Mihira Bhoja (c. 836-85 A.D.)

At the very start of his career Mihira Bhoja attempted the consolidation of the Pratīhāra power, which had received a rude shock during the feeble government of his father, Rāmabhadra. First, Mihira Bhoja re-established the supremacy of his family in Bundelkhand soon after his accession, and renewed a grant, made by Nāgabhaṭa II, which had fallen into desuetude in the reign of Rāmabhadra.[2] Similarly, Mihira Bhoja revived another in 843 A.D. in Gurjaratrā-bhūmi (Marwar) originally sanctioned by Vatsarāja and confirmed by Nāgabhaṭa II, but which had fallen into abeyance probably during the time of Rāmabhadra, and remained as such in the earlier years of Mihira Bhoja's reign even.[3] In the north, his suzerainty was certainly acknowledged up to the foot of the Himālayas, as is clear from the gift of some land to Kalacuri Guṇāṁbodhideva in the Gorakhpur district.[4] Having thus made himself the dominant power in *Madhyadeśa*, Mihira Bhoja turned to measure swords with the Pālas of Bengal, who under the vigorous rule of king Devapāla (*circa* 815-55 A.D.) had once again launched upon their Imperial schemes. The latter was a foeman worthy of his steel, and it is alleged he "brought low the arrogance

[1] *Ep. Ind.*, XVIII, pp. 108, 112, v. 11.
[2] *Ibid.*, XIX, pp. 15-19 (Barah copper-plate).
[3] *Ibid.*, V, pp. 208-13 (Daulatpura C. P.).
[4] *Ep. Ind.*, VII, pp. 85-93 (Kahla plate).

of the lord of the Gurjaras."[1] Undaunted by this effective check to his advance eastward, Bhoja next directed his energies towards the south from which side the Rāṣṭrakūṭas had so often emerged to despoil the smiling fields of Kanauj. He overran southern Rajputana and the tracts round Ujjayanī up to the Narmadā river. Then he tried his strength against the avowed enemies of his house, but was defeated some time before 867 A.D. by Dhruva II Dhārāvarṣa of the Gujarat Rāṣṭrakūṭa branch.[2] Subsequently, Mihira Bhoja even came into conflict with Kriṣṇa II (875-911 A.D.) of the main line; their wars were, however, inconclusive. There are also grounds to believe that Mihira Bhoja's arms had penetrated as far as Pehoa (Karnal district)[3] and even beyond it[4] in the west and Saurāṣṭra in the south-west.[5]

The Arab traveller, Sulaimān, writing in 851 A.D. pays a tribute to the efficiency of Bhoja's administration and the strength of his forces, specially cavalry. He was "unfriendly to the Arabs" and was regarded as "the greatest foe of the Muhammadan faith." The country was prosperous, safe from robbers, and rich in natural resources.[6]

Mahendrapāla I (*circa* 885-910 *A.D.*)

Mihira Bhoja's successor was his son, Mahendrapāla I or Nirbhayarāja,[7] who came to the throne about

[1] *Ibid.*, II, pp. 163, 165, v. 13. cf. खर्वीकृतद्रविडगुर्जरनाथदर्पम्

[2] *Ind. Ant.*, XII, pp. 184, 189, v. 38.

[3] The Pehoa inscription records certain transactions at the local fair by certain horse-dealers "in the victorious reign of Bhojadeva" (*Ep. Ind.*, I, pp. 184-190).

[4] See *Infra.*

[5] *Ind. Hist. Quart.*, V (1929), pp. 129-133.

[6] Elliot, *History of India*, Vol. I, p. 4.

[7] Other variants of his name were Mahendrāyudha, Mahiṣapāladeva, Nirbhayanarendra, etc.

885 A.D. Inscriptions prove that his most noteworthy achievement was the conquest of the greater part of Magadha and North Bengal just in the beginning of his reign. We further learn from two inscriptions found at Unā (Junāgaḍh State) that in the years 893 and 899 his authority was recognised so far away as Saurāṣṭra, where his feudatories, Balavarman and Avanivarman II Yoga, were ruling.[1] But the glory of Mahendrapāla's reign is partially dimmed by the diminution his kingdom suffered in the north-west, for a verse in the *Rājataraṅgiṇī* informs us that the territories, seized by "Adhirāja" Bhoja, were afterwards restored to the Thakkiya family during the course of Śaṅkaravarman's expeditions abroad.[2] Perhaps the pre-occupation of Mahendrapāla I in the east enabled the Kashmiri monarch (883-902 A.D.) to achieve his purpose. Whatever possessions the former might have thus lost in the Punjab, it is certain from a Pehoa inscription that the district of Karnal continued to remain under him,[3] as it had been in the reign of his predecessor.

Mahendrapāla I was a liberal patron of polite letters. The greatest literary ornament of his court was Rājaśekhara, who has left a number of works of varying merit, like the *Karpūramañjarī*, *Bāla-Rāmāyaṇa*, *Bālabhārata*, *Kāvyamīmāṁsā*, etc.

Mahīpāla (*circa* 912-944 *A.D.*)

After the death of Mahendrapāla I about 910 A.D. there were some disturbances in the kingdom. At first, his son Bhoja II came to the throne with the help of Kokalla Cedi,[4] but he was soon displaced by his half-brother, Mahīpāla, who got the support of Harṣadeva

[1] *Ep. Ind.*, IX, pp. 1-10.
[2] Vol. I, Bk. V, verse 151 (Stein, p. 206).
[3] *Ep. Ind.*, I, pp. 242-250 (Pehoa *Praśasti*).
[4] *Ibid.*, I, pp. 256, 264, v. 17; *Ibid.*, II, p. 306, v. 7.

Candella.[1] It appears that Mahīpāla was also known as Kṣitipāla, Vināyakapāla, and Heraṁbapāla. At the very commencement of his career, he had to bear the brunt of the Rāṣṭrakūṭa aggressions, since we are told in the Cambay plates of Govinda IV that Indra III "completely devastated" the hostile city of Mahodaya (Kanauj).[2] Accompanied by his feudatory, Narasiṁha Cālukya, he plundered the land as far east as Prayāga. The Pālas took advantage of this attack, which must have occurred about 916-17 A.D., and recovered some of their ancestral dominions up to the eastern banks of the river Sone.

Thus, though there were some secessions in the outlying parts of the realm, Mahīpāla soon tided over his initial troubles and resumed his father's schemes of conquest. For a magniloquent verse in the introduction to the *Pracaṇḍa-Pāṇḍava*[3] shows that his influence was felt by the Muralas (inhabitants of the Narmadā regions), Mekhalas (of the Amarakanṭak hills), Kaliṅgas, Keralas, Kulūtas, Kuntalas, and the Ramaṭhas (dwelling beyond Prithūdaka). There are, however, indications that the closing years of Mahīpāla were again seriously disturbed owing to the northern invasions of Krişṇa III Rāṣṭrakūṭa.[4] Al Mas'ūdi, who visited the valley of the Indus in *Hijrī* 303-04=915-16 A.D. and wrote an account of his travels in H. 332=943-44 A.D., bears eloquent testimony to the strength of the forces

[1] *Ibid.*, I, p. 122, l. 10.
[2] *Ibid.*, VII, pp. 38, 43, v. 19.
[3] I, 7. Carl Cappeller's edition (1885), p. 2. cf.

नमितमुरलमौलिः पाकलो मेकलानां,
रणकलितकलिङ्गः केलितटकेरलेन्दोः ।
अजनिजितकुलूतः कुन्तलानां कुठारः
हठहृतरमठश्रीः श्रीमहीपालदेवः ॥

[4] See *History of Kanauj*, pp. 267-68.

of Baüüra, evidently an Arabic corruption of the term Pratīhāra or Paḍihāra. The Arab chronicler also refers to the Rāṣṭrakūṭa-Pratīhāra enmity that was the characteristic feature of this epoch.[1]

Mahīpāla's successors (*A.D.* 944-1036?)

Mahendrapāla II, son and successor of Vināyakapāla (Mahīpāla), appears to have maintained the Pratīhāra authority intact, but the reign of Devapāla, who ascended the throne shortly before 948 A.D., was marked by the rise of the Candellas.[2] This was the signal for the decline and disruption of the empire, which continued during the time of Vijayapāla until it became divided into several powers, viz., (*a*) the Cālukyas of Anhilwāḍa (*b*) the Candellas of Jejākabhukti (*c*) the Kacchapaghātas of Gwalior (*d*) the Cedis of Ḍāhala (*e*) the Paramāras of Malwa (*f*) the Guhilas of southern Rajputana (*g*) the Cāhamānas of Śākambharī. The greatness and prestige of the Pratīhāra family was thus already gone when Rājyapāla succeeded to the throne about the last decade of the tenth century A.D. During his reign the Moslems of the North-west turned longing eyes towards the fertile plains of India. Along with other contemporary Hindu rulers, Rājyapāla took his share in the attempts of the Śāhis of Udabhāṇḍapur (afterwards Bhatinda) to stem the tide of their advance into the interior of the country.[3] He first sent a contingent in 991 A.D. to help Jayapāla against Sultān Sabuktigin, and another was despatched in H. 339=1008 A.D., when the former's son and suc-

[1] Elliot, *History of India*, Vol. I, pp. 21-23.

[2] cf. the Khajurāho inscription, *Ep. Ind.*, I, pp. 126-28, 132-133, verses 23 and 31. Yaśovarman Candella is described here as "a scorching fire to the Gurjaras" and as having "conquered the fort of Kālañjara."

[3] Briggs, Firishta (*History of the Rise of the Mohamedan Power*), Vol. I, pp. 18, 46.

cessor, Ānandapāla, was threatened by the aggressions of Mahmūd. On both the occasions the confederate armies were defeated. At last, the turn of Rājyapāla came in December 1018 A.D., but he fled across the Ganges to Bari, not being able to muster sufficient courage for a contest with Mahmūd. This pusillanimous submission of the Pratīhāra monarch enraged the Candella chief, Gaṇḍa, and he sent a force under the command of the crown-prince, Vidyādharadeva, who killed Rājyapāla and placed his son, Trilocanapāla, on the throne.[1] When Mahmūd received advices of the event he marched towards Kanauj in the autumn of H. 410=1019 A.D., and utterly routed Trilocanapāla in the engagement that followed. The latter, however, escaped death, and is known to have been alive in 1027 A.D. The last ruler of the line was perhaps Yaśaḥpāla, referred to in an inscription of the year 1036 A.D.[2]

IV. The Gāhaḍavālas

Chaotic conditions

After the dismemberment of the Pratīhāra empire, there were repeated incursions in the Gangetic Doab. In H. 424=1033 A.D. it was overrun by Ahmad Nialtigin, governor of the Punjab, who led his army right up to Benares, then in possession of Gaṅga or Gāṅgeyadeva Cedi.[3] Ample evidence exists to show

[1] *History of Kanauj*, pp. 285-87.

[2] With the decline of the Pratīhāra family of Kanauj, the Pratīhāras did not entirely fade into oblivion. We hear of Pratīhāra chiefs ruling in different localities long afterwards. cf. *e.g.*, Kureṭṭha (Gwalior State) plates of Malayavarman, dated V. E. 1207, and of his brother Nṛivarman, dated V. E. 1304 (*Prog. Rep. A. S. W. C.*, 1915-16, p. 59; Bhandarkar's list, Nos. 475 and 541). Dr. A. S. Altekar of the Benares Hindu University has also recently discovered a fragmentary inscription of Malayavarman in the Kotah State. He is editing it for the *Epigraphia Indica*.

[3] Elliot, *History of India*, Vol. II, pp. 123-24.

that the latter and his son, Karṇa (*c.* 1041-72 A.D.), also aggrandised themselves in the North. An important verse in the Basahi plate[1] further indicates that Bhoja Paramāra (*circa* 1000-1050 A.D.) made depredations in the Kanauj territory. When the "earth" was thus sorely troubled by destructive raids, a bold adventurer of the Gāhaḍavāla sept, named Candradeva, arose, and by his "noble prowess" put an end to "all distress of the people."[2]

Origin

The Gāhaḍavālas emerge into the light of history so suddenly that it is difficult to determine precisely who they were. Some scholars think that they were a branch of the famous Rāṣṭrakūṭas or Rathors. But it is significant that none of their numerous charters connects the Gāhaḍavālas with any of the well-known houses of Sūrya (Sun) and Candra (Moon), and their traditions trace them back merely to an obscure descendant of Yayāti. They are nowhere linked up with any hero of popular mythology. Does this show that they were originally an unimportant autochthonous tribe, which came into prominence as Kṣatriyas after seizing political power and championing the cause of Brahmanism?

Candradeva

It appears Candradeva founded the Gāhaḍavāla dynasty at Kānyakubja some time between 1080 and 1085 A.D. after defeating a chief named Gopāla.[3] In the inscriptions Candradeva assumes the full Imperial

[1] *Ind. Ant.*, XIV, p. 103, l. 3.

[2] *Ibid.*, XVIII, pp. 16, 18, line 4.

[3] cf. Saheṭ-Maheṭh inscription of "Gādhipurādhipa" Gopāla (*Ind. Ant.*, XVII, pp. 61-64; *Ibid.*, XXIV, p. 176; *J. A. S. B.*, LXI, extra no. 1, pp. 60f.).

titles of P. M. P., and calls himself "the protector of the holy places" of Kāśī (Benares), Uttarakośala (Fyzabad district), Kuśika (Kanauj), and Indrasthāna (Delhi).[1] Thus his jurisdiction extended almost over the whole length of the present United Provinces. There are also reasons to believe that in the east he took part in repressing the aggressive activities of Vijayasena of Bengal. Candradeva died about 1100 A.D., his last known date being 1099 A.D.

Govindacandra

Hardly anything useful to the historian is known about Candradeva's son and successor, Madanapāla. Shortly before 1114 A.D. the latter was followed by his son, Govindacandra,[2] who wielded substantial power even during his father's lifetime. As crown-prince, prior to 1109 A.D. he repulsed the Moslem expedition sent by the Ghaznavide king, Mas'ūd III (1098-1115 A.D.), under Hajīb Tughātigin.

We further learn that Govindacandra made encroachments at the expense of the decadent Pāla monarchy, and annexed portions of Magadha. This is evident from two of his grants—one sanctioning the gift of a village in the Patna district in 1126 A.D.,[3] and the second that of another village when in residence at Mudgagiri (Monghyr) in 1146 A.D.[4] He also conquered Daśārṇa or eastern Malwa.[5] In fine, he became a considerable power, and his fame spread to distant lands. He was on terms of friendship with Jayasiṁha of Kashmir (1128-49 A.D.) and Siddharāja Jayasiṁha of Gujarat (*c.* 1095-1143 A.D.), and perhaps even with the Coḷas of the South. Govinda-

[1] *Ind. Ant.*, XV, pp. 7, 8, v. 5; XVIII, pp. 16, 18, l. 4.
[2] See *History of Kanauj*, pp. 307-16.
[3] *J. B. O. R. S.*, Vol. II, pt. IV (1916), pp. 441-47.
[4] *Ep. Ind.*, VII, pp. 98, 99.
[5] *Raṁbhāmañjarī*, Bom. ed. (1899), p. 4.

candra's reign was marked by the literary efforts of his minister for peace and war, Lakṣmīdhara, who produced the *Kritya-Kalpataru* (*Kalpadruma*), one of the most important works on law, procedure, and other interesting topics.

Vijayacandra

Govindacandra was succeeded by his son, Vijayacandra, shortly after 1154 A.D. The *Prithvīrāja-Rāso* credits him with extensive victories, but not much reliance can be placed on these bardic tales. Like his father, Vijayacandra also stood as a bulwark against the aggressions of the Moslems.[1] He drove back the forces of Amīr Khusrau or his son Khusrau Malik, who had occupied Lahore after their expulsion from Ghazni by Alāuddīn Ghorī. In the east Vijayacandra maintained the Gāhaḍavāla authority intact over South Bihar, but it appears from an inscription that in the west he must have come into conflict with Vigraharāja Vīsaladeva, who wrested Delhi from his hands.[2]

Jayacandra

Vijayacandra's successor was his son, Jayacandra, whose accession took place on Sunday, the 21st of June, 1170 A.D. He is said to have attacked Yādavarāja of Devagiri, twice defeated Siddharāja of Anhilwāḍa, made eight tributary kings prisoners, and vanquished the Yavana (Moslem) ruler Sihābuddīn several times. All these bardic traditions lack corroboration, literary

[1] *Ind. Ant.*, XV, pp. 7, 9, verse 9.
cf. भुवनदलनहेलांहर्म्यहम्मीरनारीनयनजलदधाराधौतभूलोकतापः ।

[2] *J. A. S. B.*, 1886 (Vol. LV, pt. I), p. 42, v. 22. Thus the traditional belief that Delhi came in the possession of the Cāhamānas in the time of Prithvīrāja III is baseless. Anaṅgapāla Tomara is represented in popular stories as the founder of Dhil'ka or Delhi. These Tomaras were probably feudatories of the kings of Kanauj.

or epigraphic, and so they may be summarily rejected. Jayacandra's territories must have been comparatively limited in extent, as is evident from the contemporaneous existence of several strong principalities like those of the Cauhāns and the Candellas. In the east, it is, of course, clear from an inscription[1] that his authority was recognised up to the Gayā region, and Benares continued to be the second capital of the Gāhaḍavālas. Jayacandra celebrated the *Svayaṁvara* of his daughter Saṁyogitā, who was, however, carried away in the midst of the ceremonies by Prithvīrāja.

By far the most important event of Jayacandra's reign was the invasion of Sihābuddīn Ghorī. In 1191 A.D. the latter was defeated by Prithvīrāja at Taraori, and this debacle rankled in the Sultān's mind so much that the very next year he returned and completely routed and killed the Cauhān king. Jayacandra kept himself in proud isolation, thinking that the annihilation of his great rival would clear the way for his own supremacy over Northern India.[2] Little did he know that his own doom was awaiting him. In H. 590 =1194 A.D. Sihābuddīn marched towards Kanauj and met Jayacandra on the plain between Candawar and Etawah. The latter was defeated and slain, but the kingdom was not annexed. His son, Hariścandra, was allowed by Sihābuddīn to rule on his behalf. We do not know when and how Hariścandra met his end. This is, however, certain that by H. 623=1226 A.D. the Ganges-Jamuna Doab had completely passed into the hands of the Moslems. Before concluding, it may be mentioned that Jayacandra's name is memorable in the

Hariścandra

Śrīharṣa

[1] *Ind. Hist. Quart.*, Vol. V (1929), pp. 14-30; see also *Proc. As. Soc. Beng.*, 1880, pp. 76-80.

[2] The common view that Jayacandra invited Sihābuddīn Ghorī to invade India is, however, erroneous.

history of Sanskrit literature for the patronage he extended to Śrīharṣa, who wrote the well-known *Naiṣadhacarita*, *Khaṇḍana-khaṇḍa-khādya*, and other works.

Section B

NEPAL[1]

Area

The present kingdom of Nepal comprises an extensive territory along the southern slopes of the Himālayas. It is roughly 500 miles in length from Almora district on the west to Darjeeling hills on the east. But in ancient times the name Nepal was limited to the undulating plain, twenty miles long and fifteen broad, between the Gandak and Kosi rivers. Within this small area, where Kāṭhmāṇḍu and other towns are situated, the people led an isolated life, and if they had any connections with the outside world, they were mostly with Tibet and China. It was only on rare occasions that Nepal was brought into contact with India. In the middle of the third century B.C., Aśoka may have exercised control over the valley, for he is said to have gone there with his daughter, Cārumatī, and his son-in-law, Devapāla Khattiya (Kṣatriya), and built a number of *stūpas* and monasteries, besides founding the town of Lalitapatan. Again, in the middle of the fourth century A.D. the Allahabad pillar inscription represents Nepal as an autonomous frontier state, which, along with others, paid tribute to Samudragupta.[2] Our information regarding its history in the interval

Outside contacts

[1] See Sylvain Lévi, *Le Nepal* (Paris, 1905); Percival Landon, *Nepal* (London, 1928); D. Wright, *History of Nepal* (Cambridge, 1877); *Ind. Ant.*, IX, XIV, etc.; *Dy. Hist. North. Ind.*, I, Ch. IV, pp. 185-234.

[2] See *Ante*.

between Aśoka and Samudragupta is very scanty. The *Vaṁśāvalīs* or the local chronicles testify to the rule of the Ābhīras, Kirātas, Somavaṁśīs, and the Sūryavaṁśīs but their chronology is altogether unreliable. We are on firmer ground when we come to the close of the sixth and the first four decades of the seventh century A.D.—the period of the Ṭhākurī Aṁśuvarman,[1] who has been identified with Ang-shu-fa-na of Yuan Chwang's *Records*. He was the minister of the Licchavi king, Śivadeva, but after some time the former himself became the real master of the valley, as all power was concentrated in his hands. He ruled for at least forty-five years, and originated an era, which is generally believed to have begun in 595 A.D.

Aṁśuvarman

Some scholars are of opinion that Nepal came under the suzerainty of Harṣavardhana, but a critical examination of the available evidence does not confirm this view.[2] On the other hand, at this time Tibet wielded supreme influence over Nepal, whose king Aṁśuvarman married his daughter to the mighty Srong-btsan-Gampo (*c.* 629-50 A.D.).

The history of Nepal is obscure for the next two centuries, except that there was probably a restoration of the Licchavi rule and the country continued to acknowledge the supremacy of Tibet. In 879-80 A.D. a new era was started, perhaps to mark its liberation from foreign yoke. Darkness again descends upon the affairs of Nepal for another century and a quarter, but from the commencement of the 11th century the colophons of a large number of manuscripts preserved in the Durbar library and elsewhere yield us the

[1] The *Vaṁśāvalīs*, however, "antedate" Aṁśuvarman by about seven centuries (*Ind. Ant.*, XIII, p. 413).

[2] See *History of Kanauj*, pp. 92-99. cf. अत्र परमेश्वरेण तुषारशैलभुवो दुर्गाया गृहीतः करः (*Hc.*, Cal. ed., pp. 210-11).

names of a regular series of kings. They are, however, not credited with any notable achievements. Nepal's trade with India, Tibet, and China then flourished, and the people grew wealthy and prosperous. We further learn that Nānyadeva, the Karṇāṭaka chief of Tirhut, established his hegemony over Nepal some time in the first half of the twelfth century. Its subsequent history until the conquest of the Gurkhas in A.D. 1768 is devoid of any interest to the general reader.

Buddhism

Buddhism was perhaps introduced into Nepal during the visit of Aśoka, but nothing is known of the stages of its progress, or how Tāntric Mahāyāna became prevalent there. In the course of ages, however, degeneration set in, and laxity in the rules of discipline increased to such an extent that monkhood was with a good conscience reconciled with married life and pursuit of worldly avocations. The main importance of Nepalese Buddhism at present is that we see before our eyes the process by which Hinduism is gradually strangulating it. The principal Hindu deity of the land is Paśupati (Śiva).

SECTION C

THE CĀHAMĀNAS OF ŚĀKAMBHARĪ

Origin

According to the *Hammīra-mahākāvya* and the *Prithvīrāja-vijaya*, the Cāhamānas (Cauhāns) were descended from an eponymous Cāhamāna, born of the Sun. Bardic tradition, on the other hand, regards them as one of the four "Agnikulas," which probably indicates that, like the Pratīhāras, they were also of foreign extraction, and found a high place in the Hindu social polity after purification through a fire ceremony.[1]

Principal Rulers

The Cāhamānas played a prominent part on the Indian political stage for many hundred years. Of the several branches of the clan, the most important was that of Śākambharī or Sāmbhar. The Harṣa stone inscription, dated the Vikrama year 1030=973 A.D., which is the first known record of the family,[2] takes us back to Gūvaka I, a contemporary of Nāgabhaṭa II Pratīhāra, but the literary works trace the genealogy to a still earlier Vāsudeva. With regard to the kings of this line, only a few need detain us here. About the beginning of the twelfth century A. D. Ajayarāja founded the city of Ajayameru or Ajmer, and beautified it with palaces and temples. Another famous member of the dynasty was Vigraharāja IV Vīsaladeva (1153-64 A.D.). He is said to have made tributary the land between the Himālayas and the Vindhyas.[3] This is, no doubt, an exaggeration if taken literally, but an inscription found at Bijoliā (Mewar) specially credits him with the conquest of Delhi,[4] and in our opinion he must have wrested it from Vijayacandra Gāhaḍavāla.[5] Besides a successful military leader, Vigraharāja Vīsaladeva was also an accomplished poet and a patron of letters. The

Ajayarāja

Vigraharāja IV Vīsaladeva

[1] This interpretation of the 'Agnikula' legend is doubted by some scholars. They do not take it to indicate a rite of purgation, which the foreign tribes had to undergo.

[2] *Ep. Ind.*, II, pp. 116-30.

[3] *Ind. Ant.*, XIX, p. 219.

[4] *J.A.S.B.*, Lv., pt. I, (1886), p. 42, *v.* 22.

[5] See *Supra*.

Harakeli-nāṭaka, portions of which were recovered some time ago from an inscribed stone slab on the wall of a mosque named Adhāi-dīn-kā-Jhoprā,[1] professes to be his composition; while another play, the *Lalita-Vigrahārāja*, similarly discovered, was written in his honour by *Mahākavi* Somadeva. The greatest monarch of this house was Rai Pithaurā of the Moslem historians or Prithvīrāja III (1179-92 A.D.).

Prithvīrāja III

There is a strange halo of romance round his personality, which has made him the hero of many a popular song in Northern India. He was not on friendly terms with Jayacandra of Kanauj, and traditions affirm that when the latter held a *svayaṁvara* (selection of bridegroom) for his daughter Saṁyogitā, Prithvīrāja appeared just in the midst of the ceremonies and daringly carried her away. He also attacked the Candella king, Paramārdi or Paramala (1165-1203 A.D.), and occupied Mahobā and other fortresses in Bundelkhand. Another contemporary, with whom Prithvīrāja probably came into warlike collision, was Bhīma II Cālukya of Gujarat (*circa* 1179-1240 A.D.). Prithvīrāja was next called upon—being lord of the territories of Sāmbhar and Delhi—to resist the attacks of Śihābuddīn Ghorī, who was gradually advancing into the alluring plains of Hind. In the first engagement at Taroari in H. 587=1191 A.D. fortune favoured him, and the Moslem hosts were so completely overwhelmed that even Sihābuddīn was rescued with difficulty from the furious charges of the Cauhāns.[2] This rout constantly troubled the Sultān, and accordingly the very next year, in H. 588=1192 A.D., he returned to Hindustan with a re-organised force to avenge it. Prithvīrāja

[1] It is said to have been formerly a college founded by Vigraharāja.

[2] Briggs, Firishta (*History of the Rise of the Mohamedan Power*), Vol. I, p. 172.

appealed for succour to the neighbouring potentates, who responded enthusiastically to the call of their compatriot.[1] Jayacandra, however, kept himself aloof from this supreme effort against a danger that was soon to engulf him as well. In the battle that ensued, the Moslems carried "death and destruction" so desperately that by sunset there was complete confusion in the Hindu ranks. Prithvīrāja fled from the field for dear life, but was captured near the Sarsuti (Saraswatī) and killed. Ajmer was taken, and shortly after Delhi too fell into the hands of the victors. The family was not exterminated and the foresight of Śihābuddīn "delivered" the country of Ajmer to a son of Prithvīrāja "on a promise of punctual payment of a large tribute."[2] But owing to the activities of his uncle, Harirāja, this prince had to retire to Ranthambhor where a branch of the Cāhamānas ruled till its capture by Alāuddīn Khiljī in 1301 A.D. Qutb-ud-dīn, however, defeated the refractory Harirāja, and annexed the Cauhān territories.

SECTION D

SIND

Area

Sind roughly denoted the lower Indus valley from Multan down to the sea; in the west it sometimes included large portions of Baluchistan, and in the east it was bounded by the Indian desert. Our knowledge of its early history is extremely scanty, almost limited to what the Arab historians have written about it. We learn that at the time of the Arab invasions

Meagre information

[1] Briggs, Firishta, Vol. I, p. 175.

[2] *Ibid.*, pp. 177-78; see also *Tāj-ul-Maāsir* : Elliot, *History of India*, II, pp. 214, 215, 219. This son of Prithvīrāja is called Gola or Kola.

The Rāi dynasty

Sind was under the dynasty founded by the Brahman Chach. It was preceded by the Rāi family comprising five kings, who are said to have held power for 137 years with Alor (near modern Rohri) as their capital. When Yuan Chwang was travelling in India (629-45 A.D.), Sind was ruled by a Buddhist monarch of the Sūdra (*Shu-to-lo*) caste,[1] and if he was identical with Siharas Rāi, as is most probable, we get welcome light on the origin of the Rāis. Presumably it was this ruler, who came into conflict with the great Harṣavardhana.[2]

Line of Chach

After the death of the last Rāi, Sāhasī, his Brahman minister, Chach, married the widowed queen, and himself assumed the crown. During his long reign of forty years the kingdom grew in extent and authority, and is described to have abutted upon the confines of Kashmir.

Advent of the Moslems

His son, Dāhir, who succeeded Candar or Candra (Chach's brother), had to face a serious Arab invasion because he did not chastise the people of Debul for having seized a vessel carrying rich presents from the king of Ceylon to Hajjāj, governor of Iran. Muhammad ibn Kāsim led the expedition; he stormed Debul in H. 93=A.D. 712, captured Bahmanabad, and reduced Multan in 723 A.D., thus completing the conquest of Sind. This was the culmination of the Arab plundering raids, which began as early as H. 15=636-37 A.D. during the Khilāfat of Omar. Having got control of Sind, the Arabs initiated a vigorous policy of expansion, and Junaid, who was its governor under Khalifā Hishām (724-43 A.D.), was particularly active. He conquered Al Bailaman

[1] Watters, II, p. 252.

[2] *Hc. C. T.*, p. 76. cf. अत्र पुरुषोत्तमेन सिन्धुराजं प्रमथ्य लक्ष्मीः आत्मीकृता (*Hc.*, Cal. ed., pp. 210-11).

(Bhinmal?), Jurz (Gurjara kingdom of Western India), and other territories, but against Ujjain he could merely make an incursion. In this direction he was perhaps repulsed by Nāgabhaṭa I. From this time onwards the Pratīhāra kings continued to be the greatest foes of the Moslems and their faith, and this compelled the latter to seek the alliance of the Balharas (Vallabharājas), i.e., the Rāṣṭrakūṭas of Mānyakheta. It is likely the Arabs might have achieved more successes in the interior of India, if the Pratīhāras had not offered them a determined opposition. In Sind the conquerors followed a far-sighted policy of toleration.[1] No doubt, Islam spread, but Hindu temples were considered "inviolate like the churches of the Christians, the synagogues of the Jews, and the altars of the Magians." The Brahmans were even permitted to build or repair dilapidated temples. While the Arab garrisons were stationed at strategic centres, the internal administration was mostly left in the hands of the natives, who paid the land-tax (*khirāj*) and the poll-tax (*jeziyā*). The Arabs also in certain respects yielded to the subtle influences of their Indian environments. For instance, they learnt Astronomy and Mathematics from the Hindus, and translated into Arabic the work of Caraka and the fables of the *Pañca-tantra*.[2]

Results of contact

Later History

The later history of Sind is mainly of local interest.

[1] The Arab invaders evidently adopted this policy to conciliate the people and establish their authority in Sind on a firm footing. Besides, their outlook must have, to some extent, been affected by admixture of blood, which was inevitable as the conquerors did not bring women with them.

[2] *Dy. Hist. North. Ind.*, Vol. I, pp. 20-24. I have carefully and profitably utilised both the volumes, so full of useful suggestions and information, for the history of mediæval Hindu dynasties.

We learn of internecine struggles, and the rise and fall of Arab principalities like Multān and Mansūrah. In the eleventh century the Ghaznavides gradually displaced the Arabs in Sind, but it appears that the conquests of Mahmūd of Ghaznī were not so thorough in lower as in upper Sind. Accordingly, soon after his death the former region virtually asserted its independence under the Hindu Sumras, who ruled there for about three centuries, and were followed by the Sammas in the middle of the fourteenth century.

SECTION E

THE ŚĀHĪS OF KĀBUL AND THE PUNJAB

Turkī Śāhīs

After the disintegration of their empire, the Kushans did not entirely disappear from the stage of Indian history. The reference to the "Daivaputra-Śāhī-Śāhānuśāhī" in the Allahabad pillar inscription of Samudragupta has rightly been interpreted to suggest that princes of the Kushan race survived in the Punjab and the Kabul valley until about the middle of the fourth century A.D. The great Moslem scholar, Alberuni,[1] gives us a little more information. According to him, the descendants of Barhatakīn, one of them being Kanik (Kaniṣka), whom he calls Hindu Turks, ruled Kābul for sixty generations under the style *Shāhīya*, evidently a variant of the Sanskrit *Śāhī* or of the Kushan *Shah*. Alberuni may or may not be correct in stating that all these monarchs belonged to one family, or

[1] *Alberuni's India*, Eng. Trans. by Sachau, Vol. II, pp. 10-11. Abu-Rihān Muhammad, as his full name was, studied Sanskrit thoroughly, and his work contains an excellent account of the achievements of the Hindus in literature and science. He lived from A. D. 973 to 1048.

that their number was exactly sixty, but it seems probable that they were of the Kushan stock, and used the title *Shāhīya* (Śāhī). Scholars generally suppose that one of them was identical with the Buddhist Kṣatriya king of *Kia-pi-shi* (Kapiśa), mentioned by Yuan Chwang. The pilgrim's description of the royal caste does not in any way militate against this view; it only shows that by the time of his visit the foreign Kushans had become completely merged into Hindu society. We may recall here the tendency of even some of the great Kushans to adopt Hindu gods and names. Hardly anything is known of the Turkī Śāhīs except that they carried on intermittent wars with the Arab invaders from the seventh to the middle of the ninth century A.D.[1] The last member of the house, Lagatūrmān, is said to have been deposed by his Brahman minister, Kallar.[2]

Hindu Śāhīs

Having usurped the throne, Kallar became the founder of a new dynasty, which Alberuni calls "Hindu Shāhīya". Then came in succession Sāmand (Sāmanta), Kamalū, Bhīm (Bhīma), Jayapāla, Ānandapāla, Tarojanapāla (Trilocanapāla), and Bhīmapāla.[3] Coins partially confirm this list of Alberuni, but Kalhaṇa mentions some other names in connection with the wars between the Śāhīs and the kings of Kashmir. Thus, his Lallīya, who helped the Gurjara adversary of Śaṅkaravarman (883-902 A.D.), was perhaps identical with Kallar of the above group. We are further told that Prabhā-

[1] The Arab historians call these rulers Ratbīl, the connotation of which is not clear (*Dy. Hist. North. Ind.*, Vol. I, p. 71).

[2] *Alberuni's India*, Eng. Trans. by Sachau, Vol. II, p. 13.

[3] *Alberuni's India*, Eng. Trans. by Sachau, Vol. II, p. 13.

karadeva, minister of Gopālavarman (*c.* 902-04 A.D.), inflicted a crushing defeat on an unnamed "rebellious Śāhī," who has rightly been identified with Sāmand or Sāmanta. He is described as the "Śāhī of Udbhāṇḍapura," for the capital was transferred there after the capture of Kābul in H. 256=870-71 A.D. by the Saffārid Ya'qub ibn Laith. The coins of Sāmanta have been found in large numbers in Afghanistan and the Punjab; they are of the bull and horseman type, and have got the legend "Śrī-Sāmantadeva" on the obverse.[1] It is claimed in the *Rājataraṅgiṇī* that after his victory the Kashmiri minister gave the Śāhī kingdom to Toramāṇa, who was probably the same as Alberuni's Kamalū. The next ruler, Bhīma, was the maternal grandfather of queen Diddā of Kashmir, where he built a temple called Bhīmakeśava in the reign of Kṣemagupta (950-58 A.D.). Bhīma is known from his coins too.

Sāmantadeva

Jayapāla

From the time of Jayapāla onwards the Moslems exerted a continuous pressure on the Śāhīs. The latter gradually lost their territories in Afghanistan, and were even compelled to shift the capital to Bhatinda (now in the Patiala State). When Jayapāla was driven to desperation by the ever-recurring depredations of Sabuktigin, he organised a counter-attack on the enemy's dominions. The Hindu hosts were repelled, and Jayapāla had to conclude a humiliating treaty.[2] In the safety of his capital, however, he repudiated the terms of the agreement, and even went to the length of imprisoning the officers of the Sultān, who was thus naturally provoked to chastise him. Jayapāla invited the prominent Hindu states, like those of Delhi, Ajmer,

[1] Coins of this type continued to be issued for some centuries afterwards.

[2] Elliot, *History of India*, II, p. 21; Briggs, Firishta, I, p. 17.

Kālañjara, and Kanauj, to help him with men and money, but despite their response he suffered a severe reverse on the confines of Lamghan (Jalālābād district).[1] The next attack was made by Mahmūd in H. 392=1001 A.D., and the issues were again unfavourable to the Śāhī monarch. Then he felt so mortified that he handed over the cares of the kingdom to his son, Ānandapāla, and immolated himself by fire.[2] The ambitions of

Ānandapāla

Mahmūd did not, however, leave the new ruler in peace, and both came face to face in H. 399=1008 A.D. Like his father, Ānandapāla sought the support of contemporary Hindu kings, but nothing availed the confederates, and the arms of Mahmūd triumphed as usual. Six years later Ānandapāla was succeeded by Trilocanapāla, who lost against the Hammīra (Mahmūd) mainly because of the bad military tactics of his Kashmir ally. At last, Trilocanapāla was killed in H. 412=1021 A.D. and his son and successor, Bhīmapāla, met the same fate five years afterwards in 1026 A.D. Thus fighting valiantly at the gates of India against the foreign invaders, the Śāhīs vanished into nothingness, and were soon completely forgotten.

SECTION F

KASHMIR

Geographical Application of the name

The name Kashmir denoted a much more restrict-

[1] Raverty, on the other hand, thinks that the scene of the battle was the Kurram valley (*Notes on Afghanistan*, p. 321). Firishta refers to this confederacy of Hindu states (Briggs, Vol. I, p. 18), but Al Utbī makes no mention of it in the *Tarīkh-i-Yamīnī* (Elliot, II, p. 23).

[2] Firishta alludes to a custom among the Hindus that "whatever Rājā was twice overpowered by strangers, became disqualified

ed area in ancient times than is covered by the present State, which stretches from the Punjab in the south to the Pamirs in the north, and from the Tibetan border in the east to the Yarkhun river in the west. It was then, strictly speaking, applied to the upper valley of the Vitastā (Jhelum) and the tracts watered by its tributaries, although these territories were occasionally enlarged by the conquests of some of the monarchs. Being isolated from the rest of the country by huge mountain walls, Kashmir was rarely affected by the general currents of Indian history, and thus developed distinctive institutions and a culture of her own.

Early History

Our knowledge of the affairs of the valley is mainly based on Kalhaṇa's *Rājataraṅgiṇī*[1] and later supplementary chronicles.[2] But even Kalhaṇa, who completed his great work in 1150 A.D., is of little help for the period preceding the seventh century. It is certain that in the time of Aśoka Kashmir formed part of the Maurya empire, for he is credited with having built there numerous *stūpas* and monasteries, and founded the city of Śrīnagara. Indeed, Yuan Chwang goes so far as to assert that Aśoka "gave up all Kashmir for the benefit of the Buddhist church."[3] After Aśoka's death, probably it became independent under one of his sons, Jālauka. Several centuries later, Kashmir was ruled by the Kushan kings, Kaniṣka and Huviṣka, but it was

to reign" (Briggs, I, p. 38). Al Utbī gives a slightly different explanation (see Elliot, II, p. 27).

[1] *Rājataraṅgiṇī*, ed. by Durgā Prasāda, Bombay, 1892; English Translation by Sir Aurel Stein, London, 1900. See this work for detailed references. Also consult *Dy. Hist. North. Ind.*, I, Ch. III, pp. 107-84.

[2] See e.g., Jonarāja's *Dvitīya Rājataraṅgiṇī*, ed. by Peterson (Bombay, 1896).

[3] Beal, I, p. 151; Watters, I, p. 267.

outside the sway of the Guptas. Next, Mihirakula is said to have carved out a kingdom there after his expulsion from the Indian interior.

The Karkoṭaka Dynasty

Durlabhavardhana

The connected history of Kashmir begins with the extinction of the mythical Gonanda dynasty early in the seventh century, when Durlabhavardhana ascended the throne. He claimed descent from Nāga Karkoṭaka, and accordingly the family is called after the latter. Durlabhavardhana had a long reign of 36 years. He won the friendship of Harṣavardhana by giving him a prized tooth-relic of the Buddha for enshrinement in Kanauj. If the former is identical, as seems highly probable, with the prince at whose court Yuan Chwang spent two pleasant years from 631 to 633 A.D., Kashmir was then already an important state having dependencies like Siṁhapura (Ketas), Uraśā (Hazārā), Punch and Rājapura (Rajorī).

Lalitāditya Muktāpīḍa

The most powerful ruler of the line was Lalitāditya Muktāpīḍa (*circa* 724-760 A.D.), the third son of Durlabhaka. Though the account of Lalitāditya's *digvijaya* may be exaggerated, his victory against Yaśovarman of Kanauj in 733 A.D.,[1] the conquest of a portion of the Punjab and his campaigns in Tukhāristan (the upper Oxus valley) and Daradadeśa (Dardistan, north of Kashmir) are certainly founded on fact. Lalitāditya is further represented to have defeated an unnamed king of Gauḍa, and carried his arms to the land of the Bhauṭṭas (Tibetans). Lalitāditya Muktāpīḍa or Mu-to-pi of the Chinese historians also sent an embassy to the

[1] See *History of Kanauj*, pp. 204-05.

Emperor Hiuen Tsung (713-55 A.D.). It is noteworthy that at this time China wielded supreme influence in Kashmir, since according to the annals of the Tang dynasty Tchen-t'o-lo-pi-li or Candrāpīḍa, the second predecessor of Muktāpīḍa, received investiture as king from the Emperor of China in 720 A.D. Lalitāditya built Buddhist *Vihāras* at Huṣkapura and other places, and temples for Brahmanical gods—Bhūteśa (Śiva) and Parihāsa Keśava (Viṣṇu). His most famous construction was the Mārtaṇḍa temple of the Sun, whose ruins still testify to its former grandeur.

Jayāpīḍa Vinayāditya

Lalitāditya's grandson, Jayāpīḍa Vinayāditya (779-810 A.D.), was another illustrious member of the house. He defeated and dethroned a king of Kanauj who was identical either with Vajrāyudha or with Indrāyudha. But Kalhaṇa's description of the Kashmiri monarch's expeditions against Nepal and an otherwise unknown king of Pauṇḍravardhana (North Bengal), named Jayanta, reads more like fiction than sober history. Jayāpīḍa was a great patron of letters, and his court was adorned by such geniuses as Udbhaṭa, Vāmana, and Dāmodaragupta (author of the Kuṭṭanīmata). In his later years, however, Jayāpīḍa leaned towards avarice and tyranny owing perhaps to his wars and depletion of the treasury. He was followed by a number of weak rulers under whom the power of the Karkoṭakas steadily declined until about the middle of the ninth century they were supplanted by the Utpalas.

The Utpala Dynasty

Avantivarman

Avantivarman, who founded the Utpala dynasty in 855 A.D., was not in a position to embark upon any schemes of conquest, as the kingdom had suffered greatly both from economic and from political troubles during the reigns of the later Karkoṭakas. Avantivarman, therefore, took vigorous steps to improve the administration, establish internal security, and rehabilitate the state resources. The first thing that he did was to curb effectively the power of the Ḍāmaras, a turbulent class of rural aristocrats. We may next mention the vast engineering projects of his minister for public works, Suyya, whose name is preserved in the modern town of Sópur (Suyyapura). He constructed channels for irrigation, and even changed the course of the river Vitastā (Jhelum) to prevent floods, thus reclaiming extensive marshy areas for cultivation. These beneficent activities increased the prosperity of the land, so that a *Khārī* of rice could be bought for 36 *dīnāras*, whereas previously the price of the same was 200 *dīnāras*.

Avantivarman constructed and endowed temples, and gave liberal sums in charity to Brahmans. He also extended his patronage to literary men, amongst whom the most prominent was Ānandavardhana, author of the *Dhvanyāloka*. The name of Avantivarman survives in the present town of Vantpor or Avantipura.

Saṅkaravarman

After the death of Avantivarman in 883 A.D., the kingdom was convulsed by a civil turmoil, which eventually ended in favour of his son, Śaṅkaravarman. The latter reversed the peaceful policy of his father, and plunged headlong in foreign wars. He invaded Darvābhisāra (the region between the Vitastā and the Candrabhāgā), made his influence felt in Trigarta (Kangrā), and defeated the Gurjara lord, Alakhāna, who was helped by Lallīya Śāhī. Śaṅkaravarman also seized certain territories, conquered earlier by Mihira Bhoja, from Mahendrapāla I Pratīhāra, and transferred them to the Ṭhakkiya chief. Śaṅkaravarman died in 902 A.D. while returning from an expedition through the Hazārā country (Uraśā).

Śaṅkaravarman's military operations were a heavy drain on the treasury, which he tried to replenish by adopting strange methods of fiscal extortion. He even plundered the temples and levied fees on religious ceremonies. The result of this oppressive taxation was the gradual impoverishment of the people. Learning also languished under his rule for want of patronage.

Later Utpalas

The reign of Śaṅkaravarman's son, Gopālavarman, is chiefly remembered for the defeat his minister Prabhākaradeva inflicted on a Śāhī king, identified with Alberuni's Sāmand (Sāmantadeva). We further learn that the victor deposed his opponent, and placed Toramāṇa-Kamaluka (Kamalū) on the Śāhī throne. The period from the death of Gopālavarman in 904 A.D. to the end of the Utpala dynasty in 939 A.D. is largely dominated by the *Tantrins*, a close corporation of foot-soldiers, who, notwithstanding the rivalry of the *Ekāṅgas* (a kind of military police), had become so powerful as to assume the role of king-makers. This state of affairs was in no small measure due to the incapacity and avarice of the rulers themselves. For instance, the government did nothing to relieve the distress of the subjects when there occurred a severe famine in Kashmir in 917-18 A.D. in the time of the child-monarch, Pārtha. Kalhaṇa laments that while innumerable persons died of starvation and misery, the royal family cared only for its own comforts, and the ministers and *Tantrins* callously "amassed riches by selling their stores of rice at high prices." The last king but one, Unmattāvanti (937-939 A.D.), was indeed "worse than wicked". He slew his father, Pārtha, in his retreat at Jayendravihāra, and starved all his half-brothers to death. Unmattāvanti took fiendish delight in cruel and loathsome acts like getting the wombs of pregnant women cut open. Fortunately, he died soon, and with the brief reign of his supposed son, Śūravarman II, the Utpala house came to an end in 939 A.D.

The line of Parvagupta

After Śūravarman II, the Brahmans elected Yaśaḥkara, son of Gopālavarman's minister, Prabhākaradeva, as king. During his benevolent reign of nine years (939-48 A.D.), peace and prosperity returned to the country. His son and successor, Saṁgrāma, was killed in 949 A.D. by the minister, Parvagupta, who usurped the throne himself. The most interesting figure in this line was Diddā, grand-daughter of Bhīma Śāhī and daughter of the Lohara (in the Punch State) chief, Siṁharāja. She was an ambitious and energetic woman, and for nearly half a century—first as queen-consort of king Kṣemagupta (950-958 A.D.), then as regent, and lastly as ruler (980-1003 A.D.)—she was the dominant personality in the politics of Kashmir. During this period there were constant court-intrigues, but in spite of the opposition of the Ḍāmaras (land-owning nobles) and the Brahmans she maintained her authority with the assistance of Tuṅga, a Khasa of low origin, for whom she displayed excessive fondness.

The Loharas

Before her death in 1003 A.D., Diddā was successful in settling the succession on her nephew, Saṁgrāmarāja, brother of the Lohara prince, Vigraharāja. Saṁgrāmarāja (1003-28 A.D.) proved a weak king, and during the earlier part of his reign Tuṅga continued to be the real power in the state. The latter went to the help of Trilocanapāla Śāhī in 1014 A.D. against the aggression of Mahmūd, who, however, utterly routed the combined Hindu army. The Sultān made an attempt to conquer the valley in H. 412=1021 A.D. He advanced up to the foot of the hills but being unable to storm the fort of Lohkot he withdrew to Lahore. Barring brief intervals of good government, the subsequent history of Kashmir is mainly a long tale of lust, tyranny, misrule, and fiscal oppression. A land so fair was never perhaps so unfortunate in its early monarchs. One of them, Harṣa (1089-1101 A.D.), who began well as an administrator, military leader, and liberal patron of the softer arts of music and poetry, later degenerated into a profligate, cruel-hearted, and irreligious man. His extravagant expenditure and unbounded immorality soon led him into deep waters. He employed "Turuṣka" (Moslem) generals in the army, and devised a systematic policy of plundering the temples and defiling the images. He tried to squeeze money out of the people in other ways also. At last, the powerful Ḍāmaras raised the standard of revolt, and for a time anarchy prevailed in the kingdom. Ultimately Ucchala seized the throne of Kashmir. The sceptre, however, continued to change hands quickly with the result that the people almost began to groan under the weight of civil wars, misgovernment, and machinations of the aristocracy. Thus, Hindu rule dragged on in the valley till 1339 A.D., when a Moslem adventurer, Shāh Mīr, established his dynasty under the title Śrī-Saṁsdina or Shams ud dīn. It is worth remembering that during the time of the early Moslem kings the Brahmans maintained their political importance, and Sanskrit was the principal language of the realm.

CHAPTER XVI

MEDIEVAL HINDU DYNASTIES OF NORTHERN INDIA (*continued*)

SECTION A

ASSAM[1]

Extent of Kāmarūpa

The name Kāmrup (Kāmarūpa) is now applied to the central region of Assam—the district extending from Goalpārā to Gauhātī. In ancient times, however, it denoted the whole of the province of Assam as well as portions of North and East Bengal and Bhutan. The capital of this kingdom was Prāgjyotiṣapura, perhaps not far from the site of modern Gauhātī.

Legendary Rulers

Inscriptions and literature uniformly affirm that the kings of Kāmarūpa were descended from the mythical Naraka, whose son, Bhagadatta, figured prominently on the side of the Kauravas in the Mahābhārata war. Whatever the value of such traditions, there is no doubt that the people regarded the ruling family as existing from high antiquity. Even Yuan Chwang states about the middle of the seventh century that between his royal contemporary of Assam and the founder of the dynasty no less than one thousand gene-

[1] Sir Edward Gait, *History of Assam*, 2nd ed., (Calcutta, 1926); K. L. Barua, *History of Assam*; *Dy. Hist. North. Ind.*, I, Ch. V, pp. 235-70.

rations had elapsed.[1]

Early epigraphic notices

The earliest historically important reference to Kāmarūpa occurs in the Allahabad pillar inscription, which describes it as a frontier state yielding allegiance to Samudragupta. We next learn from the Aphsād inscription that the Later Gupta monarch, Mahāsenagupta, carried his arms up to the banks of the river Lohitya or Lauhitya (Brahmaputra) and defeated Susthitavarman,[2] who has rightly been identified with his Kāmarūpa namesake mentioned in the Nidhanpur plates.[3]

Bhāskaravarman

The reign of Susthitavarman's son, Bhāskaravarman, has been rendered memorable by the visit of Yuan Chwang to Kāmarūpa early in 643 A.D. The former was in constant dread of his neighbour, Śaśāṅka, king of Karṇasuvarṇa, and so he (Bhāskaravarman) formed an "unending alliance" with Harṣa at the very start of his career. Bhāskaravarman or Kumārarāja, as his second name was, attended both the assemblies of his great ally at Kanauj and Prayāga. This fact and the honour he extended to the Buddhist Yuan Chwang indicate how wide were the sympathies of Bhāskaravarman, who himself perhaps belonged to the Brahman caste. Some scholars, however, think that the pilgrim's testimony merely signifies the Brahmanical religion of the Kāmarūpa king. He is also said to have helped the Chinese mission under Wang-hieun-tse, against whom O-la-na-shun or Arjuna, the usurper of Harṣa's throne, took the field in 648 A.D. The Nidhanpur plates represent

[1] This is to be taken with a certain amount of caution.

[2] *C. I. I.*, III, pp. 203, 206, verses 13-14.

[3] *Ep. Ind.*, XII, pp. 74, 77. According to the Nidhanpur plates, the founder of the line was Puṣyavarman (*Ibid.*, pp. 73, 76).

Bhāskaravarman as a vanquisher of "hundreds of kings," and record a grant made from his camp at the capital of Karṇasuvarṇa,[1] which he must have annexed in the confusion following the death of Harṣa. Thus Bhāskaravarman continued to rule from almost the beginning of the seventh century to about its middle.

Later History

Nothing is known of the successors, if any, of Bhāskaravarman. It appears that his family was not long after overthrown by a local adventurer, named Sālastambha, who founded a new dynasty which was in turn supplanted by another early in the ninth century A.D. Barring one or two exceptions, none of these rulers exercised influence outside the limits of Assam. In the middle of the eighth century one of its monarchs named Śrī-Harṣa, father-in-law of the Nepalese Jayadeva, is said to have conquered Gauḍa, Odra (Orissa,) Kaliṅga, Kośala, and other lands.[2] Similarly, in the first half of the eleventh century another king, Ratnapāla, son of Brahmapāla, wielded considerable power. He claims to have struck awe into the hearts of the lord of the Gurjaras, the Gauḍa (Pāla) monarch, the Dākṣiṇātya ruler (i.e., Vikramāditya VI Cālukya, who invaded Kāmarūpa in the reign of his father Someśvara I), the *Keraleśa* (perhaps Rājendra I Coḷa?)[3]. the *Bāhikas* and the *Taiks* (Tājikas?)[4].

Pāla Aggressions

Kāmarūpa did not escape the arms of the ambitious

[1] *Ibid.*, also pp. 65-66.
[2] *Ind. Ant.*, Vol. IX, p. 179, l. 15.
[3] See *Infra*.
[4] *J. A. S. B.*, 1898, pp. 115-18. Do these *Taiks* refer to the Moslem raiders of Northern India under Mahmūd of Ghaznī and Ma'sūd? They did not, however, proceed farther eastward than Benares.

Pāla monarchs. According to the Bhagalpur inscription,[1] Devapāla (*c.* 815-55 A.D.) sent an expedition under his cousin, Jayapāla, who achieved some successes against the king of Prāgjyotiṣa (verse 6). Ample evidence exists to show that about the third decade of the twelfth century Assam recognised Kumārapāla's authority, and his minister Vaidyadeva enjoyed substantial power there.

Foreign incursions

One remarkable feature of the history of Kāmarūpa is that it did not succumb to the onslaughts of the Moslems in spite of their repeated attempts to subdue it, beginning with the ill-fated invasion of Tibet by Muhammad ibn Bakhtyār in H. 601 = 1205 A.D., in which he lost practically all his troops owing to the destruction of a strategic bridge by the Assamese, and ending with the attack of Aurangzeb's famous general, Mīr Jumlā, in 1662 A.D. Assam was, however, subjugated early in the thirteenth century by the Ahoms, a branch of the Shan tribe. They were masters of the land until 1825 A.D., when the British occupied it. The name Assam is probably derived from these Ahom conquerors.

Religion

Assam is the centre of both Buddhist and Hindu Tāntricism, and in popular imagination it is associated with magic and witchcraft. Its most sacred shrine is that of Kāmākhyā, near Gauhātī, where Śākta Hindus worship the female form of the Deity. The country presents an interesting example of the gradual spread of Hinduism among the aborigines and the Mongolian tribes that settled down there in the course of ages.

[1] *Ind. Ant.*, XV, pp. 305, 308, v. 6. Dr. H. C. Ray identifies the Assamese contemporary of Jayapāla with Harjara or with his son, Vanamāla (*Dy. Hist. North. Ind.*, Vol. I, p. 248).

Section B

THE PĀLAS[1]

Early history of Bengal

In ancient times the fortunes of Bengal were closely linked up with Magadha. The Nandas, who are described as rulers of the Prasii and the Gangaridai nations, probably extended their authority to the Lower Ganges valley, and so also did the Mauryas. The Kushans do not seem to have held sway over it, but the Guptas were certainly masters of Bengal. After the disintegration of the Gupta empire petty principalities grew up there, and the Harahā inscription of the Maukhari Īśānavarman even refers to the warlike activities of the "Gauḍas living on the seashore" about the middle of the sixth century A.D.[2] In the beginning of the seventh century, Bengal was ruled by Śaśāṅka, who killed Rājyavardhana of Thāneśvar and for a time occupied the Maukhari capital, Kanauj. Yuan Chwang calls Śaśāṅka king of Karṇasuvarṇa, whereas according to an inscription dated G.E. 300=619 A. D. his suzerainty was acknowledged by the Śailodbhavas of the Ganjam region.[3] "Mahārājādhirāja" Śaśāṅka was thus the sovereign of fairly extensive territories. Himself a Śaiva, he is said to have persecuted the Buddhists. After his decline or death, Bengal comprising Pauṇḍravardhana, Samataṭa, Tāmralipti (Tamluk), and Karṇasuvarṇa passed into the hands of Harṣavardhana. His

[1] V. A. Smith, "Pāla Dynasty of Bengal," *Ind. Ant.*, XXXVIII (1909), pp. 233-48; R. D. Banerji., "The Pālas of Bengal," *Mem. As. Soc. Beng.*, Vol. V, No. 3; R. C. Majumdar, *Early History of Bengal* (Dacca, 1924); H. C. Ray, *Dy. Hist. North. Ind.*, I, Ch. VI, pp. 271-390.

[2] See *Ante*.

[3] *Ep. Ind.*, VI, pp. 141 f. The exact findspot of this inscription is unknown, but it remained lying in the office of the Collector, Ganjam, for some time.

death in 647 A.D. was followed by a period of chaos and foreign incursions. Bhāskaravarman of Assam appears to have then annexed Karṇasuvarṇa; and some time in the second quarter of the eighth century Yaśovarman of Kanauj defeated the king of Magadha and Gauḍa. It was also overrun by Lalitāditya of Kashmir, Śrī-Harṣa of Kāmarūpa and other invaders. When anarchy was thus rampant in the land, the people assembled together and chose Gopāla as their monarch.

Who were the Pālas?

It is significant that the Pālas do not trace their descent from any ancient hero. We merely learn from an inscription discovered at Khalimpur that the Pāla dynasty, so called because the names of all its members had the termination—*Pāla*, sprang from one Dayitaviṣṇu, whose son was Vapyaṭa. Probably this shows that the family rose from humble beginnings, and had no illustrious ancestry. Later on, however, attempts were made to connect it with the Sea or the Sun.

Gopāla

Although the details of Gopāla's career are not known, there is no doubt that he introduced peace in the kingdom, and laid the foundations of the future greatness of his family. According to the Tibetan Lāmā, Tārānātha, Gopāla built the celebrated monastery at Otantapura (modern town of Bihar), and reigned for forty-five years. We agree, however, with Mr. Allan who remarks that "this can hardly refer to the period of his full power. His dates are probably *c.* A.D. 765-70."[1]

Dharmapāla

Gopāla's son and successor, Dharmapāla, was an

[1] *Cam. Sh. Hist. Ind.*, p. 142.

energetic personality, and the task of internal consolidation having already been accomplished by his father, he found himself in a position to undertake foreign expeditions. His most notable achievement was the defeat of Indrarāja (Indrāyudha), whom he deposed, raising Cakrāyudha to the throne of Kanauj. The settlement, thus made by the Gauḍa monarch, was "readily accepted" by the leading contemporary states of Northern India, viz., Bhoja, Matsya, Madra, Kuru, Yadu, Yavana, Avanti, Gandhāra, and Kīra.[1] Dharmapāla's wars with other contemporaries, however, appear to have been disastrous to his arms. Inscriptions record that both Vatsarāja Pratīhāra and Dhruva Rāṣṭrakūṭa (*c.* 779-94 A.D.), who could not tolerate the Imperial pretensions of Dharmapāla, routed him separately. The engagement with Dhruva perhaps took place in the Gangetic Doab, for we are told that he vanquished the Gauḍa ruler "as he was fleeing between the Ganges and the Jumna."[2] The Sanjan plates further testify that "Dharma (Dharmapāla) and Cakrāyudha surrendered of themselves" to Govinda III Rāṣṭrakūṭa (*c.* 794-814 A.D.). Finally, Dharmapāla's dreams of supremacy in the North came to nought when Nāgabhaṭa II Pratīhāra seized Kanauj from Cakrāyudha. Dharmapāla was furious at the dethronement of his protégé, but all was in vain and he suffered a reverse in a sanguinary contest with the Pratīhāra conqueror at Mudgagiri (Monghyr)[3].

Dharmapāla was a Buddhist, and he is said to have founded the famous establishment at Vikramaśīlā (Patharghata, Bhagalpur district). Its splendid temples and monasteries bore eloquent testimony to his liberality as well as to that of the other donors.

[1] *Ep. Ind.*, IV, pp. 248, 252.

[2] *Ibid.*, XVIII, pp. 244, 252, l. 14.

[3] *Ibid.*, pp. 108, 112, verse 10.

Devapāla

After a long reign,[1] Dharmapāla was succeeded by his son, Devapāla, who is rightly reckoned the most mighty Pāla potentate. Epigraphic records credit him with extensive conquests. It is stated that he "made tributary the earth" between Revā's parent (Vindhyas) and Gaurī's father (Himālayas), and "enjoyed" it even as far as Rāma's bridge in the south.[2] These are, no doubt, vain hyperboles, but the Badal pillar inscription[3] specifically claims that, owing to the sagacious advice of the ministers, Darbhapāṇi and Kedāra Miśra, Devapāla "eradicated the race of the Utkalas, humbled the pride of the Hūṇas, and scattered the conceit of the rulers of Draviḍa and Gurjara." We learn from the Bhagalpur inscription (verse 6)[4] that Devapāla's cousin, Jayapāla, was responsible for securing the submission of Utkala (Orissa) and also Prāgjyotiṣa (Assam). The Gurjara adversary of Devapāla may be identified with Mihira Bhoja (836-85 A.D.), who attempted to extend his power eastward. He met with some initial successes, but his further advance was effectively checked by the Gauḍa monarch. It appears from a copper-plate, discovered at Nālandā, that Devapāla granted five villages—four in the Rājagriha-*viṣaya* and the fifth in the Gayā *viṣaya* (district)—for "various comforts" of the *Bhikṣus* as well as for writing the "Dharmaratnas" and for the upkeep of a Buddhist monastery built there by Bālaputradeva, king of Suvarṇadvīpa

[1] According to the Khalimpur plate, it lasted for 32 years, whereas Tārānātha ascribes to Dharmapāla a reign of 64 years. We may, therefore, take the mean number forty-five as a rough approximation to truth.

[2] cf. verse 15 of the Monghyr grant, *Ep. Ind.*, XVIII, pp. 304-07.

[3] *Ep. Ind.*, II, pp. 160-67.

[4] cf. the Bhāgalpur grant of Nārāyaṇapāla, *Ind. Ant.*, XV, pp. 304-10.

and Yava-bhūmi. If the last two names are identical with Sumātrā and Jāvā, as has been suggested, we get definite evidence that the Pāla kingdom was in touch with these far-eastern islands.[1]

Besides a great conqueror, Devapāla was a patron of Buddhism, and he constructed temples and monasteries in Magadha. Thus, art and architecture received a fresh impetus, and Nālandā continued to flourish as the chief seat of Buddhist learning. The limits of Devapāla's reign may be fixed between *c.* 815 and 855 A.D.

Nārāyaṇapāla

The next monarch of note was Nārāyaṇapāla, who ruled for at least fifty-four years (*c.* 858-912 A.D.). He was born of Lajjā, a princess of the Haihaya (Cedi) race. The Bhagalpur inscription[2] records that in the 17th year of his reign he granted from Mudgagiri (Monghyr) a village in Tīra-bhukti (Tirhut) to the shrine of Śiva, and built one thousand temples in honour of the same deity. During the earlier part of Nārāyaṇapāla's reign Magadha remained under the Pālas, but several inscriptions, dated in the regnal years of Mahendrapāla I, prove that later it passed along with Northern Bengal into the hands of the Pratīhāras.[3] The occupation of these regions must have taken place soon after the latter's accession, for neither the alleged victories of his predecessor, Mihira Bhoja, nor the findspots of his inscriptions, support the view that he won any appreciable success in his eastern ventures. Thus, Magadha and Northern Bengal having come under the sway of the Pratīhāras, and with Eastern

[1] *Ep. Ind.*, XVII, pp. 310-27 (see the Nālandā copper-plate of Devapāladeva).

[2] *Ind. Ant.*, XV, pp. 304-10.

[3] See *History of Kanauj*, pp. 248-50.

Bengal under the Candras, the Pāla authority was limited to Western and Southern Bengal. But towards the close of his reign Nārāyaṇapāla took advantage of the fratricidal struggle between Bhoja II and Mahīpāla, and re-occupied Uddaṇḍapura (modern town of Bihar). When the Pratīhāras again received a shock owing to the invasion of the Rāṣṭrakūṭa Indra III in 916-17 A.D., Rājyapāla (*c.* 912-936 A.D.) probably further recovered his ancestral possessions up to the eastern banks of the river Sone.

Mahīpāla I

Mahīpāla, son of Vigrahapāla II, was another powerful prince of the line. From the findspots of his inscriptions it is clear that the Pāla power had once more revived, and that his dominions included places so widely apart as Dinājpur and Muzaffarpur; Patna, Gayā and Tippera. Mahīpāla I reconquered Northern Bengal from a "Gauḍa king" of the Kamboja family (i.e., of Mongolian origin), who had "snatched it away", presumably about the end of Gopāla II's reign. The Kamboja intruder, whose name is unknown, built a temple of Śiva in Bangad (Dinājpur district). An inscription of Mahīpāla furnishes us the Vikrama *saṁvat* date 1083=1026 A.D., one of the fixed points in Pāla chronology.[1] Its discovery at Sārnāth should not, however, be taken to indicate that this region was included in the Pāla realm. It simply records the construction of the *Gandhakuṭi*, and the repairs Mahīpāla caused to be made through the brothers, Sthirapāla and Vasantapāla, in the *Dharmarājika Stūpa* and the *Dharmacakra.* These were purely religious acts, and no political significance could be attached to them. There are also vague references in literary works to his

[1] Sarnath Stone inscription, *Ind. Ant.*, XIV (1885), pp. 139-140; see also *JASB.*, 1906, pp. 445-47; *Gauḍalekhamālā*, pp. 104-09.

conflicts with the Karṇāṭas and to the loss of Tīrabhukti (Tirhut), where Gāṅgeyadeva, identified with his Kalacuri namesake, was ruling in the Vikrama year 1076=1019 A.D.[1] But the most important event of Mahīpāla's reign was the northern incursion of Rājendra I Coḷa some time between 1021 and 1025 A.D.[2] Passing through Orissa, Southern Kośala, Daṇḍabhukti (Balasore and Midnapore districts), he is said to have conquered Raṇaśūra of Takkana-lāḍam (Southern Rāḍha, Howrah and Hooghly districts) and Govindacandra of Vaṅgāla-deśa (Eastern Bengal). The invader then turned northwards, and came to grips with Mahīpāla, whom he defeated. The Pāla king was, however, successful in checking the victor's advance beyond the Ganges. If, as the Tirumalai (North Arcot district) Rock inscription testifies, separate principalities existed in Eastern and Western Bengal, the territories of Mahīpāla must have suffered diminution during the latter part of his reign.

Nayapāla

Mahīpāla was succeeded by his son, Nayapāla, who is chiefly remembered because in his fifteenth year Viśvarūpa, his governor at Gayā, built the famous temple of Gadādhara and other smaller shrines.[3] It appears from Tibetan sources that Nayapāla was at war with Lakṣmī-Karṇa (*c.* 1041-72 A.D.) some time during his reign. They carried on the contest with varying fortunes, but when the forces of "Karṇya of the West" were being mown down the celebrated monk Dīpaṅkara Śrījñāna or Atīśa, then residing at Mahābodhi *Vihāra*, intervened and unmindful of personal risks negotiated a peace treaty between the contending parties. Although

[1] *Dy. Hist. North. Ind.*, Vol. I. p. 317.
[2] *Ibid.*, pp. 318-324.
[3] *Mem. As. Soc. Beng.*, Vol. V, No. 3, pp. 78-79.

it did not mean victory to any side, the Cedi records, strangely enough, boast of the submission of the Gauḍa monarch to Karṇa. There are, on the contrary, indications that the latter even suffered a reverse at the hands of Nayapāla's son, Vigrahapāla III, who married his adversary's daughter, Yauvanaśrī, probably after the cessation of hostilities and the restoration of friendly relations. But a disaster soon overtook the Pāla prince, for Vikramāditya, son of Someśvara I Cālukya (*c.* 1042-68 A.D.), is said to have vanquished the kings of Gauḍa and Kāmarūpa in the course of his northern incursions.[1] The death of Vigrahapāla III was followed by troublous times owing to the rivalry of his three sons, who aspired to the throne and in fact did rule successively. While they were fighting among themselves, the Varmans rose to power in eastern Bengal and the Pāla territories, which were already reduced to portions of Bihar and Northern Bengal, diminished still further. In Vārendra, a chief of the aboriginal Kaivarta tribe, named Divya or Divvoka, revolted and Mahīpāla was killed in the attempt to suppress him. The rebel leader was thus successful in establishing an independent kingdom in Northern Bengal.

Nayapāla's successors

Rāmapāla

When Rāmapāla came to the throne after the brief reign of his second brother, Śūrapala II, he found himself in a desperate plight. Besides the Kaivarta menace, he had to reckon with the recalcitrant feudatories, who had taken advantage of the misfortunes of the Pālas. According to the *Rāmacarita* of Sandhyākaranandi,[2] Rāmapāla visited them personally and by his tact and magnanimity won them over. With the help of

[1] See *Infra.*
[2] MM. H. P. Śāstrī, *Mem. As. Soc. Beng.*, III, No. 1.

these vassals and his maternal uncle, Rāṣṭrakūṭa Mathana, Rāmapāla led an army against the Kaivartas. After a preliminary reconnaissance conducted by the commander Śivarāja, the Pāla forces crossed the Ganges, defeated and captured the Kaivarta chief, Bhīma, who had succeeded his father, Divvoka. Eventually the captive was put to death, and Rāmapāla was able to recover his paternal dominions in Northern Bengal. This triumph spurred on his ambitions, and we learn that he then overran Kaliṅga and Kāmarūpa. His protection was even sought by the Yādava Varman ruler of eastern Bengal. The revival of Pāla supremacy was, however,

End of the dynasty

only temporary. Rāmapāla died after a reign of about forty-five years, and with him the strength of the dynasty also departed. In the time of his son, Kumārapāla, a revolt took place in Kāmarūpa; it was, no doubt, quelled by the minister, Vaidyadeva, but he himself virtually became independent there. The successors of Kumārapāla were weak like him, and they could not arrest the decline of the family. The feudatories gradually asserted themselves, and the rise of Vijayasena even resulted in the expulsion of Madanapāla from Northern Bengal. The authority of the Pālas was now confined to a portion of Bihar, where they maintained a precarious existence for a short period, hemmed in on the east by the Senas and on the west by the Gāhaḍavālas. The last glimpse of a Pāla ruler is afforded by an inscription, dated V.E. 1232=1175 A.D. in the fourteenth year of Govindapāla, about whom nothing else is known.[1]

Achievements of the Pālas

Thus, having ruled Bihar and Bengal with many vicissitudes of fortune for over four centuries, the Pālas disappeared from the stage of history. Scholars

[1] *J.B.O.R.S.*, December 1928, p. 534.

have not yet been able to locate their capital with certainty, but it may have been Mudgagiri (Monghyr), from where the Pāla kings issued several grants. The most powerful members of the dynasty were Dharmapāla and Devapāla; their spheres of activity and influence were much wider than the limits of their direct jurisdiction. The Pāla kingdom ultimatelv suffered decay owing to internal dissensions, revolts, and the rise of new powers. The Pālas were great patrons of art and literature. Vincent Smith has mentioned the names of two artists, Dhīmān and his son Vitapāla, who "acquired the highest fame for their skill as painters, sculptors, and bronze-founders."[1] Unfortunately no building of that age is extant, but a large number of tanks and channels dug during their rule bear witness to the interest the Pāla monarchs took in works of public utility. They were earnest followers of Buddhism, which developed newer Tāntric forms and was revivified under their patronage. Monasteries were generously endowed, being the most effective agencies for the promotion of learning and religion. One of the monks, the famous Atīśa, is known to have gone to Tibet on a Buddhist mission about the middle of the eleventh century. The Pālas were, however, by no means unfavourable towards Hinduism. They freely made gifts to Brahmans, and even constructed temples in honour of Hindu gods.

Section C

THE SENAS[2]

Origin

The Senas, who gave the death-blow to the Pāla

[1] *E. H. I.*, 4th ed., p. 417.

[2] G. M. Sarkar, "Early History of Bengal" (Sena Period), *Jour. Dept. Lett.*, XVI (1927), pp. 1-82.

power in Bengal, were probably of southern origin. It has been suggested that they carved out a principality in Rāḍha (West Bengal) in the confusion following the north-eastern expedition of Vikramāditya Cālukya, son of Someśvara I (*c.* 1042-68 A.D.).[1] The founder of the dynasty, Sāmantasena, is described as a descendant of Vīrasena, born in "the family of the moon," and as "the head-garland of the Karṇāṭa-Kṣatriyas" or of the Brahma-Kṣatriyas which term perhaps signifies that the Senas were at first Brahmans, but subsequently adopted the military profession and became Kṣatriyas.

Vijayasena

Vijayasena, grandson of Sāmantasena, brought the family into prominence during his long reign of over sixty-two years (*c.* 1095-1158 A.D.). He distinguished himself in warfare, and made many territorial acquisitions. He is represented as having "impetuously assailed" the lord of Gauḍa, who has usually been identified with Madanapāla. That Vijayasena drove out the Pālas from Northern Bengal is proved by the discovery of an inscription at Deopārā in the Rajshahi district[2] and by his grant of a village in Pauṇḍravardhana-*bhukti*, as recorded in a plate found at Barrackpur.[3] The latter document was issued from Vikramapura in the sixty-second year, which shows that some time before the end of his reign Vijayasena had extended his authority over eastern Bengal also. We are further told that his fleet once sailed "in its playful conquest of the western regions up the whole course of the Ganges;"[4] and he defeated a number of his contemporaries, the chief among them being Nānyadeva of Tirhut and

[1] See *Dy. Hist. North. Ind.*, Vol. I, pp. 331, 356.
[2] *Ep. Ind.*, I, pp. 305-15.
[3] *Ibid.*, XV, pp. 278-86.
[4] *Ibid.*, I, pp. 309-10, 314.

the kings of Kāmarūpa and Kaliṅga.[1] The last was presumably identical either with Kāmārṇava (*c.* 1147-56 A.D.) or with Rāghava (*c.* 1156-70 A.D.), for there is some evidence to believe that their father, Anantavarman Coḍagaṅgā (*c.* 1077-1147 A.D.), was on friendly terms with Vijayasena. The Sena sovereign was a devout Śaiva and a generous patron of the *Śrotriyas*. He excavated an artificial lake, and built a splendid temple of Pradyumneśvara Śiva at Deopārā.

Vallālasena

Vijayasena was succeeded by his son, Vallālasena, whose mother was Vilāsadevī, a princess of the Śūra line of Western Bengal. He did not gain any notable victories, although he was able to maintain his dominions intact. Traditions affirm that he introduced *Kulinism* and re-organised the caste-system in Bengal. There is, however, no epigraphic corroboration of these social reforms. Like his father, Vallālasena too was a Śaiva, and he is said to have compiled two well-known works, the *Dānasāgara* and the *Adbhutasāgara*, under the guidance of his preceptor.

Lakṣmaṇasena

Lakṣmaṇasena or Rāi Lakhamaniyā was the last important member of the dynasty. He is credited with extensive conquests. It is probable he may have overrun the neighbouring regions of Kāmarūpa and Kaliṅga in his earlier career, but his other martial exploits and the alleged erection of "pillars of victory" at Benares and Allahabad[2] are but empty vaunts and have no basis in fact. The Gāhaḍavālas were masters of these

[1] *Ep. Ind.*, I, pp. 309-10, 314. (Deopārā stone inscription).
[2] cf. Bakerganj inscription of Keśavasena, *J.A.S.B.*, N. S., X, (1914), pp. 97-104; Madhiānagar grant, *Ibid.*, N. S., V, (1909), pp. 473, 476, verse 11.

two cities, and it would be utterly wide of the mark to suppose that Lakṣmaṇasena wrested them from such a powerful king as Jayacandra, whose territories extended in the east at least up to the Gayā district. Besides, if the Moslem historians deserve any credence, Lakṣmaṇasena must have been an extremely craven-hearted man. For we are told that he fled from the backdoor of his palace without making even a show of resistance at the approach of Muhammad ibn Ba<u>kh</u>tyār <u>Kh</u>iljī, who, after conquering Bihar and massacring "the shaven-headed Brahmans" (Buddhist monks) probably in 1197 A.D., advanced against Nadiā towards the close of 1199 A.D. with a small force. Lakṣmaṇasena's government was evidently rotten to the core, otherwise Ba<u>kh</u>tyār would not have been allowed to press on to the capital, and take it by surprise with a party of eighteen horsemen only.[1] The Sena monarch then went across the Ganges to eastern Bengal, where he is known to have ruled until *c.* 1206 A.D. Minhāj-ud-dīn deposes that his reign lasted for eighty years, but this is certainly erroneous. There are strong grounds to place Lakṣmaṇasena's accession about 1180 A.D.[2] After his death, the Senas continued to exercise authority in eastern Bengal ("Bang") for almost another half a century, when it also passed into the hands of the Moslems.

Like many kings of antiquity, Lakṣmaṇasena encouraged the cultivation of polite letters. Among the literary ornaments of his court, Dhoyika, who wrote the *Pavana-dūta*, and Jayadeva, the celebrated author of the *Gīta-Govinda*, deserve special mention.

[1] Without unduly stressing the correctness of this figure, there can be no doubt that Ba<u>kh</u>tyār attacked the Sena capital with a small body of soldiers.

[2] Lakṣmaṇasena did not found the era of 1119 A.D., which afterwards came to be associated with his name. See also "On Lakṣmaṇasena Era," *Sir Asutosh Mookerjee Silver Jubilee Volume*, Vol. III, Orientalia, pp. 1-5.

Lakṣmaṇasena himself was something of a poet, for he is said to have completed the *Adbhuta-sāgara* begun by his father.

Section D

KALIṄGA AND ODRA[1]

Extent

The boundaries of Kaliṅga have varied from time to time. Roughly speaking, it corresponded to the coastal region between the Godāvarī and the Mahānadī. It was often distinguished from Odra, but there are indications that in its widest sense Kaliṅga denoted almost the whole of the modern province of Orissa.

Scanty Information

The history of this part of India during the period under survey is extremely obscure owing to the absence of a paramount power and the uncertainties of chronology. Among the dynasties that ruled simultaneously over portions of Kaliṅga and Odra with various ups and downs of fortune, the most important were the Keśaris of Bhuvaneśvar[2] and the Eastern Gaṅgas of Kaliṅganagara (Kaliṅgapaṭaṁ or Mukhaliṅgaṁ in the Ganjam district?). Unhappily, we do not get much authentic political information about the former. They were devout Śaivas, and immortalised their sway by constructing the magnificent temples of Bhuvaneśvar with a "profusion of decorative motifs inspired by human, animal and vegetable life". The

The artistic achievements of the Keśaris

[1] R. D. Banerji, *History of Orissa*; B. C. Mazumdar, *Orissa in the Making*; W. W. Hunter, *Orissa* (London, 1872); H. C. Ray, *Dy. Hist. North. Ind.*, I, Ch. VII, pp. 391-503.

[2] Their symbol was the lion.

great Liṅgarāja sanctuary (*c.* 11th century), which to this day stands as one of their noblest monuments, is veritably an inspired orgy of sculptural ornamentation almost unique in the world.[1] It has a high steeple tower with vertical sides except near the summit, and the pyramidal roof of the porch is loftier than that of earlier periods, but the pillars are still wanting. Perhaps it may not be amiss to mention here that the Orissan style of architecture has certain distinctive features, each temple consisting of the *Vimāna* (towered shrine), *Jagamohana* (audience chamber), *Naṭamaṇḍapa* (dancing saloon), and the *Bhogamaṇḍapa* (refectory). The last two are believed to be "somewhat later appendages." What is, however, specially noteworthy in Orissan temples is the high spire (*śikhara*) and abundance of carving.

The Eastern Gaṅgas[2]

The Eastern Gaṅgas established themselves in Kaliṅga about the beginning of the eighth century A.D. They originally belonged to Kolāhala (Kolar), and were thus a branch of the Gaṅgas of Mysore. Hardly anything is known of the earlier Gaṅgas, during whose time Kaliṅga suffered a good deal from foreign incursions. For instance, in the middle of the eighth century Śrī-Harṣa of Assam claims to have conquered Kaliṅga and Odra, and in the ninth century the Eastern Cālukya king, Vijayāditya (844-888 A.D.), overran it. Towards the last quarter of the eleventh century, however, the Gaṅga family rose to the zenith of its power under Anantavarman Coḍagaṅgā. He was so called because he was the son of Rājarāja Gaṅga by his Coḷa wife, Rājasundarī, daughter of Rājendra Coḍa. Coḍagaṅgā ruled

[1] See R. L. Mitra, *The Antiquities of Orissa*; M. M. Ganguly, *Orissa and her Remains*.

[2] See M. M. Chakravarti, "Chronology of the Eastern Gaṅga Kings of Orissa," *J. A. S. B.*, 1903, pp. 97-147.

for over 70 years, the known limits of his reign being Śaka 999 and 1069=1077-1147 A.D. Tradition ascribes to him the building of the famous temple of Purī; and he considerably extended the bounds of his realm. He defeated the king of Utkala, and is represented as having "exacted tribute from all land between the Godāvarī and the Gaṅgā." Anantavarman came into conflict with the ruler of Veṅgī also, but he was on friendly terms with his Sena contemporary, Vijayasena.[1] This did not, however, prevent the latter from attacking Kaliṅga in the time of his ally's sons, Kāmārṇava or Rāghava. Later on, it was again ravaged by Lakṣmaṇasena. Early in the thirteenth century the Eastern Gaṅgas began to be harassed by the Moslems, who continued their depredations until "Jājnagar" or Orissa finally fell a prey to their arms in the sixteenth century.

Section E

THE KALACURIS OF TRIPURĪ

Their Lineage

The Kalacuris or Kaṭacuris are said to have been the descendants of Kārtavīrya Arjuna. They were thus a branch of the great Haihaya race, which, according to traditions preserved in the Epics and the *Purāṇas*, ruled the Narmadā valley with Māhiṣmatī or Māndhātā as their capital.

Kokalla I

The Kalacuris[2] rose into prominence under Kokalla

[1] If Rāmapāla's boast of the conquest of Utkala and Kaliṅga has any substance, Coḍagaṅgā must have then bowed to his steel.

[2] Sometimes called Cedis owing to their occupation of the Cedi country. See for their history, Hīrālal, "The Kalacuris of Tripurī," *A. B. R. I.*, 1927, pp. 280-95; R. D. Banerji, "The

I, who founded a kingdom at Tripurī (modern Tewar) in Ḍahāla i.e., the Jubbulpur region. He flourished about the last decades of the ninth and the early part of the tenth century A.D. His matrimonial alliances and political activities increased the power of the family considerably. He married a Candella princess named Naṭṭādevī, and gave the hand of his daughter to Kriṣṇa II (*c.* 875-911 A.D.). We further learn from inscriptions[1] that Kokalla I gave help and protection to his Rāṣṭrakūṭa son-in-law, presumably in the latter's wars with the Eastern Cālukya ruler, Vijayāditya III of Veṅgī[2], and also to other princes like Bhoja, identified with Bhoja II, who had to contend against his half-brother, Mahīpāla, for the Pratīhāra throne.[3] Kokalla I is represented as having "conquered the whole earth" and plundered the treasures of a number of his royal contemporaries, but not much reliance can be placed on such boastful claims.

Gāṅgeyadeva

Hardly anything important is recorded of Kokalla I's successors until Gāṅgeyadeva, whose known dates range from 1019 to 1041 A.D. He assumed the title of Vikramāditya, and is even described as "conqueror of the universe" in a Candella inscription discovered at Mahobā.[4] Although this is an exaggeration, there are reasons to believe that he overran Northern India up to the Kīra country or the Kangra valley, and annexed the districts of Prayāga (Allahabad) and Vārāṇasī (Bena-

Haihayas of Tripurī and their Monuments," *Mem. Arch. Surv. Ind.*, XXIII (1931); Rājendra Singh, *Tripurī Kā Itihāsa* (in Hindi); H. C. Ray, *Dy. Hist. North. Ind.*, II, Ch. XII, pp. 738-820.

[1] cf. the Bilhari inscription, *Ep. Ind.*, I, pp. 256, 264, v. 17; and the Benares copper-plate grant, *Ibid.*, II, pp. 300, 306, v. 7.

[2] *Mem. Arch. Surv. Ind.*, No. 23, (1926), p. 5.

[3] *History of Kanauj*, pp. 255-56.

[4] *Ep. Ind.*, I, pp. 219, 222, l. 14.

res) after the downfall of the Pratīhāras. The *Tarikh-us-Subuktigin* of Al Baihaki definitely testifies that the latter place was in possession of Gaṅga (Gāṅgeya), when Ahmed Nialtigin, governor of the Punjab under Ma'sūd I (*c.* 1031-40 A.D.), invaded it in H. 424=1033 A.D.[1] Further, the colophon of a Nepalese Sanskrit manuscript of the *Rāmāyaṇa* indicates that Gāṅgeya occupied Tīrabhukti (Tirhut) some time before the Vikrama year 1076=1019 A.D.,[2] and an epigraph represents him as having vanquished the kings of Utkala (Orissa) and Kuntala (Kanarese territory) also.[3] Gāṅgeyadeva's power was, however, ultimately eclipsed by the rise of Bhoja Paramāra, who won a victory over him.

Lakṣmī-Karṇa

Lakṣmī-Karṇa or Karṇa, son and successor of Gāṅgeyadeva, was the most forceful personality among the Kalacuri rulers. He dominated Northern India during the greater part of his long reign from 1041 to 1072 A.D., and widely extended the bounds of his realm. His authority was recognised in Benares, where he erected a lofty temple of Śiva called Karṇameru;[4] and we learn of the progress of his arms so far north-west, too, as the land of the Kīras (Kangrā).[5] Thus Karṇa, like his father, must have made depredations in the North, and asserted his influence in the disintegrated Pratīhāra kingdom of Kanauj, and it is no doubt significant that the Basahī plate mentions him along with Bhoja in connection with the "earth's distress" before the rise

[1] Elliot, *History of India*, II, pp. 123-24.

[2] *Dy. Hist. North. Ind.*, Vol. II, p. 774.

[3] cf. the Goharwā plates, *Ep. Ind.*, XI, p. 143, v. 17.

[4] *Ep. Ind.*, II, pp. 4, 6, v. 13. Karṇa also built the new capital of Karṇavatī (modern Karanbel) near Tripurī.

[5] *Ind. Ant.*, XVIII, p. 217, l. 11.

of the Gāhaḍavālas.[1] Karṇa also defeated his Candella contemporary, identified with Vijayapāla or with Devavarman. In the east, the Kalacuri monarch came into conflict with both Nayapāla and his son Vigrahapāla III, and the latter appears to have got the upper hand in this trial of strength. Next, Karṇa utterly routed Bhoja Paramāra of Dhārā with the help of Bhīma I Cālukya of Gujarat (*c.* 1022-64 A.D.), and his power was even felt by the kings of Coḍa, Kaliṅga, Pāṇḍya, etc. But towards the close of his career, Karṇa met with a series of disasters. Having broken off alliance, Bhīma I worsted him, and Mālava as well regained its independence under Udayāditya. Karṇa suffered further reverses at the hands of the Cālukya Someśvara I Āhavamalla (*c.* 1042-68 A.D.) and Kīrtivarman Candella.

Karṇa's Successors

Unable to bear the burden of sovereignty, Lakṣmī-Karṇa in his last days probably abdicated in favour of Yaśaḥ-Karṇa, his son by Āvalladevī of the Hūṇa race. He (*c.* 1073-1120 A.D.) is said to have ravaged Campāraṇya (Camparan district), and "extirpated with ease" the Āndhra ruler, who has rightly been identified with the Eastern Cālukya Vijayāditya VII of Veṅgī (*c.* 1060-76 A.D.). Yaśaḥ-Karṇa could not, however, arrest the steady decline of the family fortunes. Lakṣmadeva Paramāra paid off old scores against the Kalacuris by attacking and storming their capital Tripurī. In the north, the Gāhaḍavālas established their power in Kānyakubja and Benares, and aggrandised themselves at the cost of the Cedis. Similarly, during the reign of Yaśaḥ-Karṇa's son and successor, Gayā-Karṇa, the Candella Madanavarman (*c.* 1128-64 A.D.) won some military successes, and the Ratnapura branch of the

[1] *Ind. Ant.*, XIV, p. 103. l. 3.

Kalacuris asserted its independence in South Kośala.[1] In the time of the successors of Gayā-Karṇa, who were weaklings, the Tripurī Kalacuris finally sank into insignificance.

Section F

THE CANDELLAS OF JEJĀKABHUKTI (*Bundelkhand*)[2]

Their Origin

The origin of the Candellas is shrouded in mystery. A legend attributes their descent to the union of the Moon (Candramā) with a Brahman damsel. This is obviously an absurd myth, invented for giving the clan a noble pedigree. In the opinion of Vincent Smith, however, the indications are that the Candellas sprang from the aboriginal stock of the Bhars or the Gonds, and their original seat was Maniyāgarh on the Ken river in the Chatarpur State.[3]

Beginnings of their power

The Candellas came into prominence in southern Bundelkhand under the leadership of Nannuka early in the ninth century. His grandson was Jejā or Jayaśakti, after whom the kingdom was called Jejākabhukti. It appears from traditions and epigraphic testimony that the first few princes of the dynasty were feudatories of the great Pratīhāra emperors of Kanauj. But Harṣadeva Candella enhanced the prestige and influence

[1] *Dy. Hist. North. Ind.*, II, pp. 791-92.

[2] V. A. Smith, "Contributions to the History of Bundelkhand" *J. A. S. B.*, 1881, Vol. I, pt. I, pp. 1-53; "The History and Coinage of the Candel (Candella) Dynasty of Bundelkhand," *Ind. Ant.*, XXXVII (1908), pp. 114-48; H. C. Ray, *Dy. Hist. North. Ind.*, II, Ch. XI, pp. 665-737.

[3] *Ind. Ant.*, XXXVII (1908), pp. 136-37.

of the family considerably by placing Mahīpāla (Kṣitipāla) on the Imperial throne in opposition to his brother or half-brother, Bhoja II. During the reign of Yaśovarman, the Candellas gained a larger measure of independence, and aggrandised themselves at the cost of their neighbours, viz., the Cedis, Mālavas, Kośalas, etc. According to an inscription, found at Khajuraho, Yaśovarman was "a scorching fire to the Gurjaras," and that he "easily conquered the fort of Kālañjara," one of the important strongholds of the Pratīhāras.[1] He is also said to have compelled Devapāla Pratīhāra to surrender to him a celebrated image of Vaikuṇṭha (Viṣṇu), which he subsequently set up in a stately shrine at Khajuraho.[2]

Dhaṅga

Strangely enough, however, Yaśovarman's son and successor, Dhaṅga (*c.* 950-1002 A.D.), invokes the name of the Pratīhāra king (Vināyakapāla II) as his overlord in the Vikrama year 1011=954 A.D.[3] It would, therefore, appear that like the Nizām of the Dekkan and the Nawābs of Oudh, who were virtually independent and yet nominally acknowledged the suzerainty of the great Moghul at Delhi, the Candel ruler did not all at once break off formal relations with the effete Imperial power at Kanauj, but for some time maintained an outward show of submission. Subsequently, the kingdom of Jejākabhukti saw its palmy days under Dhaṅga, for an inscription, discovered at Mhow, alleges that he attained to "supreme lordship after inflicting a defeat over the king of Kānyakubja."[4] The success of the Candellas is confirmed by the Khajuraho

[1] *Ep. Ind.*, I, p. 132, v. 23; p. 133, v. 31.
[2] *Ibid.*, p. 134, v. 43.
[3] *Ep. Ind.*, I, p. 135.
[4] *Ibid.*, pp. 197, 203, v. 3.

epigraph, wherein we are told that Dhaṅga ruled the earth "playfully acquired by the action of his long and strong arms, as far as Kālañjara, and as far as Bhāsvat situated (?) on the banks of the river Mālava; from here to the banks of the river Kālindī (Jumnā), and from here also to the frontiers of the Cedi country, and even as far as that mountain called Gopa (Gopādri), which is the unique abode of marvel."[1] The loss of Gwalior must have dealt a severe blow to the fortunes of the Pratīhāras, since thereby the Candellas got hold of a strategic position, which they could well use as a base for further encroachments. Indeed, it is likely that towards the close of his reign Dhaṅga carried his arms up to Benares, where he granted a village to a Brahman in the Vikrama year 1055=998 A.D.[2] In 989 or 990 A.D., when Jayapāla, the Śāhī king, invited prominent Hindu states to help him in resisting the aggressions of Sabuktigin, Dhaṅga, along with other potentates, promptly responded with men and money, and shared the disaster suffered by the confederate army.

Gaṇḍa

Similarly, Dhaṅga's son, Gaṇḍa, joined the coalition formed by Ānandapāla Śāhī in 1008 A.D. to repel the invasion of Mahmūd but nothing availed the Hindus and their forces were utterly routed by the Sultān. Next, Gaṇḍa sent an expedition under the crown-prince, Vidyādhara, to punish Rājyapāla of Kanauj for his pusillanimous surrender to Mahmūd about the end of 1018 A.D. The Pratīhāra monarch was, of course, slain, but when the tidings reached Ghaznī the Sultān was so enraged that he forthwith marched against

[1] *Ibid.*, pp. 124, 134, v. 45. The passage is important as showing the extent of Dhaṅga's dominions.

[2] *Ind. Ant.*, XVI, pp. 202-04.

Nanda (Gaṇḍa)[1] to repress his audacity. Thus, the opponents came face to face in *H.* 410=1019 A.D. Just at the psychological moment, however, the Candella ruler became alarmed at the intrepidity and strength of the Moslem hosts, whereupon under cover of night he 'fled with some of his baggage and equipments.'[2] In *H.* 413=1022 A.D., Mahmūd attacked the Candel territories for the second time. Having taken Gwalior in 1023 A.D., he invested Kālañjara. Again, Nanda or Gaṇḍa cowardly submitted to the invader, who thereupon gave him back the conquered forts, and triumphantly returned home with a large booty.

Kīrtivarman

The next distinguished member of this house was Kīrtivarman. He revived the power of the Candellas, which had been eclipsed in the time of his predecessors owing to the military activities of the Kalacuri kings, Gāṅgeyadeva and Lakṣmī-karṇa. Kīrtivarman himself was vanquished by the latter in the earlier part of his reign, but it appears from inscriptions and the prologue to Kriṣṇa Miśra's *Prabodha-Candrodaya*, an allegorical play in honour of Viṣṇu and the Vedānta philosophy, that the Candel ruler eventually won a decided victory over his mighty Cedi rival.

Madanavarman

Another notable figure was Madanavarman, whose known dates range from 1129 to 1163 A.D. He claims to have defeated the "lord of Gurjara," generally identified with Siddharāja-Jayasiṁha of Gujarat (*c.* 1095-

[1] Dr. H. C. Ray, on the other hand, suggests that Nanda is a mistake for Bīda (Vidyādhara) and not for Gaṇḍa (*Dy. Hist. North. Ind.*, Vol. I, p. 606).

[2] Elliot, *History of India*, Vol. II, p. 464.

1143 A.D.). An inscription, found at Mau (Jhansi district), further testifies that Madanavarman overcame the Cedi monarch (perhaps Gayā-Karṇa); exterminated his Mālava i.e., Paramāra contemporary; and forced the "king of Kāśī," probably identical with Vijayacandra Gāhaḍavāla, "to pass his time in friendly behaviour."[1]

Paramārdi

Paramārdi or Paramal of popular traditions was the last prominent Candella sovereign. He ruled from *circa* 1165 A.D. to 1203. We learn from the Madanapur inscription[2] and Cānd's *Rāso* that he sustained a reverse in 1182-83 A.D. at the hands of Prithvīrāja Cauhān who occupied Mahobā and other fortresses in Bundelkhand. But Paramārdi escaped complete annihilation, and afterwards recovered the lost ground. In *H.* 599=1203 A.D., he offered stubborn resistance to Qutb-ud-dīn Aibak during the siege of Kālañjara. Finding that the odds were altogether against him, Paramārdi capitulated, but he died before fulfilling any of the terms imposed. His minister, Ajadeva, then took up the defence; he also had, however, to surrender soon after. Qutb-ud-dīn next captured Mahobā, and put the subjugated territory under the charge of a Moslem governor. The Candellas were thus laid low, although they lingered on as petty chieftains until the sixteenth century.

Candella cities and lakes

The most important cities in the Candella kingdom were Khajurāho, Kālañjara, and Mahobā. Vincent Smith remarks: "The first-named town, with its group

[1] *Ep. Ind.*, I, pp. 198, 204.
[2] *Prog. Rep. Arch. Surv. Ind.*, 1903-04, p. 55.

of magnificent temples, may be regarded as the religious, the second, with its strong fortress, as the military, and the third, with its palace, as the civil capital."[1] The Candellas beautified Bundelkhand by constructing a large number of exquisite religious edifices and embanked lakes. One of the latter was the Madanasāgara, formed by Madanavarman at Mahobā.

SECTION G

THE PARAMĀRAS OF MALWA[2]

Who were the Paramāras ?

Tradition represents the Paramāras (sometimes called Paramaras or Powārs) as descendants of the hero Paramāra, who was created by Vaśiṣṭha out of his fire-altar at Mount Abu to rescue Nandinī, the cow of plenty, from Viśvāmitra. The probable significance of this mythical derivation from fire (agnikula) appears to be that, like the Pratīhāras and other clans, the Paramāras were also of foreign extraction, and they became fit to be admitted into the Hindu caste-system after the performance of some fire-ceremony. But it has recently been contended on the strength of a passage in an inscription, unearthed at Harasola (Ahmedabad district)[3], that "the Paramāras were members of the Rāṣṭrakūṭa race," and that they originally belonged to the Dekkan, which "once formed the home dominion of the Imperial Rāṣṭrakūṭas."[4]

[1] *Ind. Ant.*, XXXVII (1908), p. 132.

[2] See C. E. Luard and K. K. Lele, *Paramāras of Dhar and Malwa* (Bombay, 1908); D. C. Ganguly, *History of the Paramāra Dynasty* (Dacca, 1933); H. C. Ray, *Dy. Hist. North. Ind.*, II, Ch. XIV, pp. 837-932.

[3] *Ep. Ind.*, XIX, pp. 236-44.

[4] D. C. Ganguly, *History of the Paramāra Dynasty*, (Dacca, 1933), p. 9.

Early stages of their power

We have discussed elsewhere that prior to their conquest of Kānyakubja the Pratīhāras had their seat of power at Ujjayinī. This region was for a long time a veritable bone of contention between them and their inveterate enemies, the Rāṣṭrakūṭas of Mānyakheṭa (Malkhed), who conquered it during the northward incursions of Dhruva Nirupama, Govinda III, Indra III, and Kriṣṇa III. None of them could, however, hold Ujjain permanently. For there are evidences to show that some time at least in their careers the Pratīhāra kings, Nāgabhaṭa II, Mihira-Bhoja, Mahendrapāla I, Mahīpāla, and Mahendrapāla II, exercised authority over it. The Partabgarh inscription,[1] at any rate, definitely informs us that in V.E. 1003=946 A.D. the last-named had stationed one Mādhava as his "great feudatory lord and governor" at Ujjayinī, and another officer, Śrīśarman, was carrying on the affairs of state at Maṇḍapikā (Māṇḍū). Thus, Upendra or Kriṣṇarāja, the founder of the Paramāra dynasty, and his immediate successors must have been vassals of the Pratīhāras or of the Rāṣṭrakūṭas as they alternately gained ascendancy in Malwa (ancient Avanti). The first substantial figure was Sīyaka-Harsa, the known limits of whose reign are V.E. 1005=949 A.D. and V.E. 1029=972 A.D. This was a period of the decadence of the Pratīhāra monarchy, and he availed himself of it to increase his power. But Sīyaka-Harṣa's rise could not be a matter of indifference to his Rāṣṭrakūṭa contemporary; so a conflict between the two became inevitable. According to the Udepur inscription, the former "took away in battle the wealth of Khoṭṭiga,"[2] identified with his Rāṣṭrakūṭa namesake (*c.* 955-70 A.D.), who succeeded Kriṣṇa III (*c.* 940-55 A.D.). Dr.

[1] *Ep. Ind.*, XIV, pp. 176-86.
[2] *Ep. Ind.*, I, pp. 235, 237, v. 12.

Bühler has further shown that the sack of Mānyakheṭa is corroborated by Dhanapāla's *Pāiya-lacchī*, a Prakrit work.[1] Another notable victory of Sīyaka-Harṣa was over a chieftain belonging to the Hūṇa stock.

Vākpati-Muñja

Sīyaka-Harṣa was followed by his illustrious son, Vākpati *alias* Muñja, also called Utpalarāja, Śrīvallabha, or Amoghavarṣa, the last two being typical Rāṣṭrakūṭa epithets. His earliest known date is V.E. 1031 =974 A.D., and we may, therefore, reasonably conclude that he ascended the throne about a year previously. He was a doughty fighter, and is said to have vanquished Yuvarāja II, the Kalacuri ruler of Tripurī. Besides, the Udepur epigraph adds that Vākpati-Muñja made the Lāṭas, Karṇāṭas, Coḷas, and the Keralas bow to his steel.[2] He came into hostile contact with certain other ruling families also, but his greatest exploit was the defeat of the Cālukya Tailapa II no less than six times. Merutuṅga says that in the seventh campaign Vākpati-Muñja, disregarding the sane counsel of his minister, plunged headlong beyond the Godāvarī into the Cālukya dominions, and met with grief, having been taken prisoner and then killed. Dr. H. C. Ray points out that this disaster, which is confirmed by the Cālukya inscriptions, must have occurred between V.E. 1050=993-94 A.D., the last recorded date of Vākpati-Muñja, and the Śaka year 919=997-98 A.D., when Tailapa II died.[3] Vākpati-Muñja did not neglect the arts of peace as well. He excavated many artificial lakes, one of which, the Muñjasāgara, situated at Dhar (Dhārā), still preserves his name. He also built splendid temples in the principal cities of the realm. We

[1] *Ibid.*, p. 236.
[2] *Ibid.*, v. 14.
[3] *Dy. Hist. North. Ind.*, Vol. II, pp. 857-58.

further learn that he was gifted with poetic talents of a high order and liberally patronised men of letters. His court was graced by Padmagupta, Dhanañjaya, who wrote the *Daśarūpa*, Dhanika, author of the *Daśarūpāvaloka*, Bhaṭṭa Halāyudha[1], and other literary celebrities.

Sindhurāja

Certain Jain works, like Merutuṅga's *Prabandha-Cintāmaṇi*, indicate that Bhoja was the immediate successor of Vākpati-Muñja, but according to the more reliable epigraphic evidence there ruled between them the latter's younger brother, Sindhula, i.e., Sindhurāja or Navasāhasāṅka. His achievements have been immortalised by Padmagupta in the *Navasāhasāṅka-Carita*, which testifies to the success of his arms against a Hūṇa prince, and Kośala or Dakṣiṇa-Kośala (i.e., the Kalacuris of Tummāna), the Cālukyas of Lāṭa, and other neighbouring powers.

Bhoja[2]

After a short reign Sindhurāja was followed by his son, Bhoja, the most striking and versatile Paramāra ruler. He raised Dhārā, the capital, to a position of eminence, and owing to a rare combination of military ability and constructive statesmanship his influence was felt over a large part of India. An inscription calls him a *Sārvabhauma*, and in the Udepur *Praśasti* he is represented to have "possessed the earth" from the Kailāśa to the Malaya mountains.[3] This is no doubt an exaggeration, if taken literally, but ample proof

[1] Author of the *Abhidhāna-ratnamālā* and the *Mṛitasaṁjīvanī*.

[2] Prof. P. T. S. Ayyangar, *Bhojarāja* (Madras, 1931); B. N. Reu, *Rājā Bhoja* (in Hindi; Allahabad, 1932).

[3] *Ep. Ind.*, I, pp. 237-38.

exists to show that Bhoja conquered extensive territories, and his ambitions involved him in ceaseless conflicts with contemporary states. Probably he first directed his energies towards the Karṇāṭas, i.e., the Cālukyas of Kalyāṇī with a view to avenging the execution of Vākpati-Muñja. Bhoja easily defeated and slew his southern antagonist, identified with Vikramāditya V (*acc.* 1008 A.D.).[1] The Paramāra monarch's attempt to establish his hegemony over the Dekkan, however, came to nought shortly before the Śaka year 941=1019 A.D., when the Cālukya Jayasiṁha II (*c.* 1016-42 A.D.) humbled him and broke (or "put to flight") the "confederacy of Mālava."[2] Next, Bhoja is spoken of as having beaten the king of Cedi, i.e., Gāṅgeyadeva of Tripurī and two other chiefs, named Indraratha and Toggala, whose identification is uncertain. Further, it appears from the Basahī plate[3] that Bhoja made some northward depredations and for a time exercised supremacy over the land of Kānyakubja. He won a victory also against the Turuṣkas, i.e., the Moslem marauders of Northern India, but his engagements with Vidyādhara Candella and Kīrtirāja, the Kacchapaghāta prince of Gwalior, did not result in any advantage to him. Lastly, Bhoja overwhelmed the lord of Lāṭa (Southern Gujarat), identical with another Kīrtirāja,[4] and Bhīma I of Gujarat (*c.* 1022-64 A.D.). Notwithstanding these exploits, Bhoja's end was inglorious. His resources were sapped by constant wars, and besides he had to suffer the ig-

[1] Sir R. G. Bhandarkar prefers to call him Vikramāditya I (*Early History of the Dekkan* (1928), p. 140, n. 15). Some scholars, on the other hand, think that Bhoja invaded the Cālukya dominions in the time of Jayasiṁha II (*History of the Paramāra Dynasty* pp. 90-91).

[2] *Ind. Ant.*, V, p. 17.

[3] *Ibid.*, XIV, p. 103, ll. 3-4.

[4] This Kīrtirāja was the son of Goggirāja Cālukya.

nominy of a reverse at the hands of the Cālukya Someśvara I Āhavamalla (*c.* 1042-68 A.D.), who is said to have plundered Malwa and its capital, and put Bhoja to flight. The latter, however, soon returned and revived his authority. Not long after, his Jain general, Kulacandra, sacked Anhilvāḍa during the absence of its ruler on an expedition against the Moslems. This compelled Bhīma I to enter into a coalition with the great Kalacuri king, Lakṣmī-Karṇa, and the Paramāra kingdom was then vigorously attacked from two sides by the allied forces. During the progress of the war, Bhoja passed away, having ruled for "fifty-five years, seven months and three days" according to Merutuṅga. His death changed the situation entirely in favour of the confederates, who occupied the royal city of Dhārā and ravaged Malwa.

Bhoja appears to have wielded the pen with no less dexterity than the sword. Called *Kavirāja* in an inscription, he is the putative author of about two dozen works on a variety of subjects, such as medicine, astronomy, religion, grammar, architecture, *alaṁkāra* (poetics), lexicography, arts, etc. Among them, we may mention here just a few: *Āyurveda-sarvasva*, *Rājamṛigāṅka*, *Vyavahāra-samuccaya*, *Śabdānuśāsana*, *Samarāṅgaṇa-sūtradhāra*, *Sarasvatī-Kaṇṭhābharaṇa*, *Nāma-mālikā*, *Yukti-kalpataru*, etc. It is, however, doubtful if in the midst of his incessant military activities Bhoja found time to write so many books himself. Thus, the possibility cannot be ruled out that some of them, although ascribed to him, were in reality productions of the literary protégés flourishing at his court. Furthermore, Bhoja was a munificent patron of learning. He founded a college at Dhārā, where students flocked from far and near to quench their intellectual thirst. Valuable compositions have been recovered from engraved slabs of stone fixed to its walls. The "Bhoja-Śālā," as it is still popularly known, was converted into a mosque by the

Moslem masters of Malwa.

Bhoja was a devout Śaiva and also a great builder. The Udepur inscription informs us that he adorned the country with a large number of superb temples.[1] He expanded Dhārā, and built the city of Bhojpur to the south of modern Bhopal. Close by was an extensive lake dug under his orders. This noble monument of Bhoja's engineers ceased to exist early in the fifteenth century, when Shah Hussain of Māṇḍu got the embankments destroyed for the purpose of utilising its bed.

Later History of the Family

The alliance between Bhīma I and Lakṣmī-Karṇa did not survive long, for there are indications that they fell out over the division of the spoils of victory. Jayasiṁha seized this opportunity, and appealed for succour to Someśvara I Cālukya, the quondam enemy of his house. With a view to restoring the political equilibrium, the latter cleared Mālava of the army of occupation, and placed Jayasiṁha on the Paramāra throne. The new monarch's reign was brief, his recorded dates being V.E. 1112=1055 A.D. and V.E. 1116=1059 A.D. Far from achieving anything of note, his intrigues appear to have involved him in a disastrous war with the Karṇāṭas and the Cālukyas of Gujarat. Jayasiṁha's successor, Udayāditya (*c.* 1059-1088 A.D.), described as a *bandhu* (relation) of Bhoja,[2] then made an attempt to revive the fortunes of the family. He defeated Karṇa, usually identified with Kalacuri Lakṣmī-Karṇa, but who, as suggested by Dr. Ganguly,[3] may be identical with Bhīma I's son

[1] *Ep. Ind.*, I, p. 238, v. 20.

[2] Presumably Udayāditya belonged to a junior branch of the Paramāras. According to the Udepur (*Ep. Ind.*, I, pp. 232-38) and Nagpur inscriptions (*Ep. Ind.*, II, pp. 180-95), he was the immediate successor of Bhoja.

[3] *History of the Paramāra Dynasty*, pp. 127-32.

of the same name (*c.* 1064-94 A.D.). After this flicker of glory, the Paramāras gradually lost their importance and influence. The downward sliding continued during the twelfth century under a succession of weaklings, whose local conflicts and petty jealousies are devoid of any interest for the general reader. Ambitious aggressors repeatedly harassed the people of Mālava until Hindu rule itself was swept away in 1305 A.D. by the onslaught of Alā-ud-dīn Khiljī's general, Ain-ul-Mulk, who triumphantly marched into Māṇḍu, Ujjain, Dhārā and other cities.

SECTION H

THE CĀLUKYA DYNASTY OF ANHILWĀḌA[1]

Founder's ancestry and career

The Cālukya (Solaṅki) house of Anhilwāḍa or Anhil-pāṭaka, identified with modern Patan in Gujarat, was founded by Mūlarāja. Unfortunately, it is difficult with our present data to ascertain the connection between this family and the earlier Cālukyas of the Dekkan, whose origin and history will be discussed in the next chapter. Nor is there any evidence to prove that Mūlarāja was descended from the Cālukya chiefs of Saurāṣṭra (Kāthiāwāḍ) mentioned in two Unā charters—the one bearing the Gupta-Valabhī date 574=893 A.D., and the other the Vikrama year 956=899 A.D., as feudatories of Mahendrapāla Pratīhāra.[2] According to the chronicles of Gujarat, however, Mūlarāja's father was Rāji, a son of the prince of Kalyāṇakaṭaka[3] in Kanauj,

[1] *Bombay Gazetteer*, 1896, Vol. I, pts. I & II; Tod's *Annals and Antiquities of Rājasthan*, ed. by Crooke; Bayley, *History of Gujarat* (London, 1886); *Cam. Hist. Ind.*, Vol. III; H. C. Ray, *Dy. Hist. North. Ind.*, II, Ch. XV, pp. 933-1051.

[2] *Ep. Ind.*, IX, pp. 1-10.

[3] The identification of Kalyāṇakaṭaka has not yet been satisfactorily established.

and his mother belonged to the Cāvaḍa or Cāpotkaṭa line, which ruled a portion of Gujarat prior to the rise of the Cālukyas. Whatever value one may attach to the details of such traditions, this much appears clear that Mūlarāja was not a mere upstart adventurer, but had a noble parentage. It is further confirmed by inscriptions, which call his father Mahārājādhirāja. Regarding the circumstances of Mūlarāja's accession, he is said to have slain his maternal uncle and then seized the Cāpotkaṭa throne for himself. The event must have occurred about V.E. 998=941 A.D., his earliest year known from the Sāmbhar epigraph,[1] and not in 961 A.D, as asserted by some scholars on the basis of Merutuṅga's *Vicāraśreṇī*.[2] Having "acquired the Sāraswata-*maṇḍala* by the prowess of his arms,"[3] Mūlarāja began his career of aggrandisement. He defeated and killed Lakha (Lakṣarāja) of Kaccha (Cutch), and captured Graharipu, the Cūḍāsama chieftain of Vāmanasthalī (mod. Wanthali) in Saurāṣṭra. Mūlarāja also waged wars against Bārappa, the ruler of Lāṭa (southern Gujarat), Vigraharāja Cāhamāna of Śākambharī, and other rivals of lesser importance. As a devout Śaiva, Mūlarāja spent the evening of his life in religious acts, building temples and honouring the learned Brahmans. His last date recorded in a copper-plate grant is V.E. 1051=994-95 A.D., and we may, therefore, reasonably suppose that he died a year or two afterwards.

Bhīma I

The next important figure was Bhīma I, nephew of Mūlarāja's grandson Durlabharāja. Bhīma ruled

[1] *Ind. Ant.*, 1929, pp. 235, 236, v. 8.
cf. बसुनन्दनिधौवर्षे व्यतीते विक्रमार्कतः
मूलदेवनरेशस्तु चूडामणिरभूद्भुवि ।

[2] *Bom. Gaz.*, Vol. I, pt. I, p. 156.

[3] *Ind. Ant.*, VI, p. 191, ll. 6-7.

for about forty-two years from *c.* 1021 A.D. to 1063 A.D. In *H.* 416=1025 A.D. his kingdom was rudely shaken by the insatiable ambition and greed of Mahmūd, who marched across the Indian desert with a view to plundering the famous temple of Somanātha, the repository of untold riches accumulated for ages. The invader first appeared before the gates of Anhilwāḍa, but Bhīma I was so struck with terror that instead of offering resistance he sought safety in flight. Mahmūd then pressed on to Sumnat (Somanātha) and invested it. After a day's stubborn opposition, the town fell and the defenders dispersed helter-skelter. A large number of Hindus were slaughtered, the shrine was sacked and desecrated, and thus Mahmūd returned to Ghaznī in triumph with a huge booty and the broken idol, which was fixed to the steps of the *Jame-Masjid* at its entrance.

When the Sultān withdrew, Bhīma I recovered his capital and revived the Cālukya power. He vanquished the Paramāra chief of Abu, but during his campaign against the king of Upper Sind Anhilwāḍa was stormed by Kulacandra, the general of Bhoja Paramāra. This provoked Bhīma I to such an extent that he entered into a league with Lakṣmī-Karṇa Kalacuri, and the combined armies are alleged to have completely devastated Mālava. Bhoja died in the course of the struggle, and it appears the coalition was also dissolved subsequently. Hostilities broke out between the allies with the result that Lakṣmī-Karṇa suffered a reverse at the hands of Bhīma I. The Paramāras took advantage of this conflict and made Mālava free of foreign control.

Karṇa

Bhīma I was followed by his son Karṇa, who could not achieve anything substantial despite a long reign of about thirty years (*c.* 1063-93 A.D.). During this period, the power of the Paramāras once more waxed.

For Udayāditya is credited with a victory over Karṇa, and it has been suggested, as shown elsewhere, that the latter is identical with his Cālukya namesake.[1] He built numerous temples, dug tanks, and founded a city after his name, now represented by Ahmedabad.

Jayasiṁha Siddharāja

Karṇa's successor was Jayasiṁha Siddharāja, his son by Miyaṇalladevī. He was the most striking personality among the rulers of Anhilwāḍa, and he wielded the sceptre for nearly half a century—*c.* 1093 to 1143 A.D. In the beginning, the affairs of the state were managed by the Queen-mother because of the king's minority, and she did so with ability and tact. When Jayasiṁha came of age he embarked upon conquering the neighbouring territories. He defeated the Cauhāns of Nadol (Jodhpur State) and the Cūḍāsama chief of Saurāṣṭra, which was annexed. Next, Jayasiṁha carried on a protracted war with the Paramāra potentates, Naravarman and Yaśovarman. Eventually Dhārā fell, and the victor assumed the title "Avantinātha" in commemoration of the subjugation of Mālava. But his further drive against Madanavarman of Bundelkhand was not successful. Indeed, the tussle seems to have ended in favour of the Candella monarch. According to the *Prabandha-Cintāmaṇi*, Jayasiṁha was on terms of friendship with the "king of Ḍāhala" (i.e., the Kalacuri sovereign of Tripurī) and the "lord of Kāśī," presumably Govindacandra.

Like his predecessor, Jayasiṁha erected a number of religious edifices in his kingdom. Furthermore, he patronised learning, and encouraged free debates among the votaries of rival sects to inculcate the lesson of toleration. He himself was perhaps a Śaiva, but

[1] The vanquished Karṇa is, however, usually identified with Lakṣmī-Karṇa Kalacuri.

this did not prevent him from giving a place of honour at his court to the celebrated Jain Ācārya, Hemacandra.

Kumārapāla[1]

After the death of Jayasiṁha without leaving any male issue, the throne was seized by his distant relation, Kumārapāla. He was an energetic man, and having overcome all opposition to his accession he pursued a policy of active militarism. He attacked Arṇorāja, the Cāhamāna ruler of Śākambharī, and completely overwhelmed his forces. Kumārapāla also quelled the revolt of the Paramāra prince of Abu, and reasserted the Cālukya authority in Mālava, which had raised its head during his initial difficulties. He next turned his arms successfully against a chieftain of Saurāṣṭra, but his most remarkable exploit was the defeat of Mallikārjuna of Konkan.

Kumārapāla is said to have rebuilt the temple of Somanātha, and although inscriptions represent him as a Śaiva, the Jain works would have us believe that Hemacandra's brilliant exposition converted him to the tenets of Jainism. Perhaps it was due to Jain influences that Kumārapāla issued stringent orders prohibiting the slaughter of animals throughout his vast dominions.[2] His reign has further been made memorable by the scholarly labours of Hemacandra, who produced a crop of works on religion and other subjects. Kumārapāla died shortly before V.E. 1229 =1172 A.D., the earliest known date of his successor Ajayapāla.

[1] See *Kumārapāla-carita* of Jayasiṁha, ed. by Kṣāntivijaya Gaṇi (Bombay, 1926).

[2] See *Kumārapāla-pratibodha* of Somaprabhācārya (Gaekwāḍ Oriental Series, No. XIV); also *Moharājaparājaya* of Yaśahpāla (G.O.S., No. IX).

Later history of Gujarat

We do not get much valuable information regarding the later monarchs of Gujarat. The usual wars and court intrigues, of course, continued, but their repercussions were not of any far-reaching consequence. In 1178 A.D., soon after the accession of Bhīma II (Bholā Bhīma), who ruled for over sixty years, Gujarat had to face a Moslem invasion led by the Sultān of Ghor. Bholā Bhīma, however, repulsed him in a hard-fought battle. The next attempt was directed by Qutb-ud-dīn in *H.* 593=1197 A.D.; this time Anhilwāḍa was captured, but, as subsequent events proved, the occupation was only temporary. Besides, Gujarat also suffered from the inroads of the king of Mālava and the Yādava ruler of Devagiri. When the power of the Cālukyas was altogether weakened, the Vaghela family, tracing descent from a sister of Kumārapāla, reaped a rich harvest out of this opportunity and leapt into prominence. For it appears that Lavaṇaprasāda, the Vaghela minister and feudatory of Bholā Bhīma, established himself in an almost independent position in southern Gujarat, thereby reducing the latter's jurisdiction to its northern part. Gradually, the Vaghelas took Anhilwāḍa and extended their sway over the whole of Gujarat.[1] In 1297 A.D. Alā-ud-dīn Khiljī despatched thither a strong army under his generals, Ulugh Khan and Nasrat Khan. At its approach, Karan or Karandeva Vaghela turned his back and hurriedly fled from

[1] The marble temples of Dilwārā (near Mt. Abu) and Śatruñjaya, built by the brothers Vastupāla and Tejaḥpāla during the time of one of these Vaghela rulers, are famous for their elegant carvings and rich design. As observed by Vincent Smith, this class of temples is characterised by "a free use of columns carved with all imaginable richness, strut brackets, and exquisite marble ceilings with cusped pendants" (*A History of Fine Art in India and Ceylon* p. 116).

the capital, which was then plundered by the invaders. Soon they conquered other strategic points, and thus the curtain fell on Hindu rule in Gujarat.

PART IV

CHAPTER XVII

THE DYNASTIES OF THE DAKṢIṆĀPATHA

SECTION A

THE CĀLUKYAS OF VĀTĀPI (BADAMI)

Signification of the term Dakṣiṇāpatha

The geographical application of the Sanskrit name Dakṣiṇāpatha or Dakṣiṇa, of which the Dekkan represents the modern form, has not always been the same. It was often loosely used in ancient times for the whole of the Indian peninsula to the south of the Narmadā, just as Uttarāpatha vaguely designated the country to its north between the Vindhyas and the Himālayas. Generally, however, the Dekkan denotes the tableland from the Narmadā to the Krisṇā river, including Mahārāṣṭra on the west and the Telugu tracts on the east.

Early history

Southern India remained for long a dark land to the Vedic Aryans owing to the almost impassable barrier of the Vindhya mountains and the extensive forest called Mahākāntāra. During the Brāhmaṇic period,[1]

[1] It is significant that a story in the *Aitareya Brāhmaṇa* (VII, 18; *E. H. D.*, (1928), p. 10) refers to the Andhras, Puṇḍras, Sabaras, Pulindas, and Muṭibas as descendants of the sons of the Vedic seer, Viśvāmitra.

however, they crossed these natural obstacles with the object of conquest or the diffusion of their culture among the Dravidian tribes by peaceful means. Thus, the history of the trans-Vindhyan country may be said to begin with the southward migrations of the Aryan bands, although the roots of its distinctive civilisation lie embedded in a far more remote antiquity. Unhappily, we do not get much information regarding the stages of its Aryanisation. According to the epic tradition, it was the great sage Agastya, who first established a settlement beyond the Vindhya range to spread the Aryan religion, language, and institutions. Then followed a regular stream of conquerors, colonists, and missionary *Riṣis* both through the eastern and the Avanti routes until Kaliṅga, Vidarbha (Berar), Daṇḍakāraṇya (Mahārāṣṭra), and indeed the whole of the South were all widely affected by the advancing tide of Aryanism. Uncertainty hangs on the centuries leading to this result, but it may be pertinent to note that whereas the geographical horizon of Pāṇini, assigned to *c*. 700 B. C. by Dr. Bhandarkar,[1] extends only up to Kaliṅga, and the *Sūtta-Nipāta*—an early Buddhist work—mentions just a solitary hermitage of Bāvārin to the south of the Godāvarī, the commentator on Pāṇini's grammar, Kātyāyana (*circa* fourth century B.C.), knew, besides Māhiṣmat and Nāsikya (Nasik), the Coḍas and the Pāṇḍyas also. Further, the inscriptions of Aśoka unmistakably testify that in the middle of the third century B.C. his authority was recognised as far south as the Chitaldroog district in Mysore; and the kingdoms of the Coḍas, Pāṇḍyas, Satiyaputras, and the Keralaputras in the extremity of the Peninsula, and even Tāmraparṇī (Ceylon), were no longer unfamiliar regions. The barrier of isolation had been completely surmounted and the North and the entire South were now

[1] *E. H. D.*, 3rd ed., (1928), p. 16.

brought into intimate political and cultural relations. It is not clear what happened to the dominions of Aśoka across the Vindhyas after the dismemberment of the Maurya empire. When the curtain rises again, the Sātavāhanas appear on the stage and, as already shown, they imposed their sway over the greater part of the Dekkan and adjacent territories.[1] For a time, their power was eclipsed in Mahārāṣtra and western Malwa by the Śakas. Under Gautamīputra, the Sātavāhanas revived their glory, but about the middle of the third century A.D. an Ābhīra chieftain, named Īśvarasena, again wrested northern Mahārāṣtra from them. Next, we learn that the Vākāṭakas ruled Central India and a good bit of the Dekkan.[2] In its eastern portion, on the other hand, the Sātavāhanas were succeeded by the Ikṣvākus and the early Pallavas. Here also flourished such minor dynasties as the Brihatphalāyanas of Kudūra, the Sālaṅkāyanas of Veṅgīpura, and the Viṣṇukuṇḍins of Lenḍulūra (Denḍuluru, near Veṅgī),[3] which are mere names save to a few specialists.

With this rapid survey of the early history of the Dekkan, we now proceed to deal with the Cālukyas.

Who were the Cālukyas?

The origin of the Cālukyas[4] is lost in the mists of myths. According to one tradition, they sprang from the water pot of Hārīti when he was in the act of pouring out a libation; while according to another, as recorded in the *Vikramāṅkadevacarita* of Bilhaṇa, they are represented to have descended from a warrior, who was produced

[1] See *Ante*, Ch. X, Sec. C.

[2] *Ibid.*, Ch. XIII, Sec. B.

[3] See K. R. Subramanian, *Buddhist Remains in Āndhra and the History of Āndhra between 225 & 610 A.D.*, Chaps. VII-X.

[4] Other variants of the name are Cālukya, Cālikya, Calkya and Solaṅkī.

by Brahmā from the palm of his hand to rescue the world from unrighteousness. We are further told that the family originally belonged to Ayodhyā, from where it went to the South. Shorn of the fantastic, the above legends indicate that the Cālukyas were a northern Kṣatriya race[1], and that the hero Harīti was their progenitor. Vincent Smith, however, rejects this conclusion. He believes that the "Cālukyas or Solaṅkīs were connected with the Cāpas, and so with the foreign Gurjara tribe, of which the Cāpas were a branch, and it seems to be probable that they emigrated from Rajputana to the Deccan."[2] But any definite proof of this is lacking.

Their rise

The Cālukya power in the South had a modest beginning under Jayasiṁha and his son, Raṇarāga. The latter's successor, Pulakeśin I,[3] who came to the throne about the middle of the sixth century A.D.[4] was, however, a figure of some note. He made Vātāpi (modern Badami, Bijapur district) his capital, and even indulged in Imperial pretensions by celebrating an *Aśvamedha* or horse-sacrifice. The next member of the dynasty was Kīrtivarman. He defeated the Mauryas of north Konkan as well as the Kadambas of Banavāsī (north Kanārā) and the Naḷas, whose exact location is uncertain.[5] According to certain epigraphs, his arms

[1] See also Yuan Chwang's *Records* (Watters, II, p. 239), where Pulakeśin II is described as a Kṣatriya by birth.

[2] *E. H. I.*, 4th ed., p. 440.

[3] Called Satyāśraya Śrīvallabha.

[4] An inscription, recently discovered at the hill-fort of Badami, yields us the Śaka date 465=543 A.D. for Pulakeśin I, who is called therein Vallabheśvara, and is said to have performed the *Aśvamedha* sacrifice (*The Leader*, June 19, 1941).

[5] Fleet thinks that the Naḷas were the rulers of Naḷavāḍi (modern Bellary and Karnul districts). They have, however, been recently located in Southern Kośala and Bastar State (*J. N. S. I.*, Vol. I, p. 29).

penetrated right up to Bihar (Magadha) and Vaṅga (Bengal) in the north, and the Coḷa and the Pāṇḍya territories in the far south, but in the absence of any other corroboration it is doubtful if the alleged exploits are founded on fact. When Kīrtivarman died,[1] his younger brother brushed aside the minor nephews and assumed the crown himself. Apart from the vague claim of having subdued the country between the western and eastern seas, Maṅgalarāja or Maṅgaleśa is said to have taken Revatīdvīpa (modern Reḍi, Ratnagiri district) and subjugated the Kalacuris of northern Dekkan.[2] It was also during his time that an exquisite cave-temple of Viṣṇu was excavated at Badami. Maṅgalarāja's last days were clouded by court intrigues leading to a civil war. Eventually all attempts to settle the succession on his son came to nought, and he met his death while fighting against the forces of his energetic and vigilant nephew.

Pulakeśin II

The accession of Pulakeśin II did not mean the termination of his initial troubles. The struggle for the throne had engulfed the affairs of the Cālukya kingdom in such a whirlpool of chaos that the powers, reduced to subservience by his predecessors, now ventured to raise the standard of their aggressive activities. Parameśvara-Śrī-Prithvī-Vallabha-Satyāśraya, as the new monarch is styled in inscriptions, faced the storm with courage, determination, and success, and thus won for himself the place of honour in the dynastic niche. He

[1] In the opinion of Sir Ramkrishna Bhandarkar, Kīrtivarman ascended the throne in 567 A.D., and ruled for about a quarter of a century (*E. H. D.*, pp. 85-87).

[2] The two important princes of this family were Śaṅkaragaṇa and Buddharāja.

first repelled the attack of Appāyika and Govinda[1] beyond the Bhīmarathī (Bhīmā); captured Vanavāsī (in north Kanārā), capital of the Kadambas; overawed the Gaṅgas[2] of Gaṅgavāḍi (part of modern Mysore) and the Alūpas of Malabar (?); and also subdued the Mauryas of north Konkan seizing Purī, "the glory of the western sea." Next, the Lāṭas of southern Gujarat, the Mālavas, and the Gurjaras (of Bhrigukaccha ?) are said to have submitted to the might of Pulakeśin II. But his most valorous achievement was the defeat of the great Harṣavardhana of Kānyakubja,[3] whose personal command of the army proved of no avail against the Cālukya sovereign's superior strategy. With all these victories to his credit, Pulakeśin II became, as stated in the well-known Aihole-Meguṭi record dated the Śaka year 556=A.D. 634, the undisputed master of the three Mahārāṣṭrakas consisting of nine and ninety thousand villages. Furthermore, the kings of Kośala (Mahākośala) and Kaliṅga felt terror-stricken at the approach of his forces, and the fortress of Piṣṭapura (modern Piṭhāpuram) surrendered to him without

[1] Their identification is uncertain. Does the name Govinda suggest a Rāṣṭrakūṭa origin?

[2] Presumably the Gaṅga chief was identical with Durvinīta, who, according to Prof. Dubreuil, ruled from c. 605 to 650 A. D. (*Anc. Hist. Dek.*, p. 109). M. V. Krisna Rao, however, places Durvinīta's reign from *c.* 550 to 600 A.D. (*The Gaṅgas of Talkad*, p. 34).

[3] cf. "Harṣa whose lotus-feet were covered with the rays of the jewels of the diadems of hosts of feudatories prosperous with unmeasured wealth, was by him made to lose his mirth (*harṣa*) in fear, having become loathsome with his rows of lordly elephants fallen in battle"

अपरिमितविभूतिस्फीतसामन्तसेना—
मुकुटमणिमयूखाक्रान्तपादारविन्दः ।
युधिपतितगजेन्द्रानीकवीभत्सभूतो
भयविगलितहर्षो येन चाकारि हर्षः ॥

(*Ep. Ind.*, VI, pp. 6, 10, verse 23).

much opposition. The kingdom having enormously grown in dimensions, Pulakeśin II entrusted the administration of the eastern territories to his younger brother, Kubja-Viṣṇuvardhana-Viṣamasiddhi, about 615 A.D. The latter made some additions to his charge by conquests, but he does not appear to have broken away from Vātāpīpura. It was perhaps his son and successor, Jayasiṁha I, who asserted the independence of the branch house at a favourable opportunity.[1] Towards the south, Pulakeśin II measured strength with the Pallava prince, identified with Mahendravarman I, and threatened his capital Kāñcīpura (Conjeeveram).

[1] The rulers of this collateral line, known as the Eastern Cālukyas of Veṅgī, held sway, with various ups and downs of fortune, over the Āndhra country and a portion of Kaliṅga for about five hundred years. Mere possession of such a fertile and strategic territory was enough to give the family an important place in the political affairs of the Dekkan. But some of its members were also noted for their military abilities; for instance, Vijayāditya II (*c.* 799-843 A. D.) and Vijayāditya III (*c.* 844-88 A.D.) are said to have fought, and won victories, against the Rāṣṭrakūṭas, the Gaṅgas, and other contemporary powers. About the last quarter of the tenth century A.D., the kingdom of Veṅgī suffered a decline, and was overrun by Rājarāja I Coḷa. Śaktivarman (*c.* 999-1011 A.D.) partially retrieved the lost ground, but the next monarch, Vimalāditya (*c.* 1011-18 A.D.), and his successors were unmistakably under the influence of the Coḷas of Tanjore. This was partly due to matrimonial relations between the two houses, for Vimalāditya took the Coḷa princess, Kuṁdavā, as his spouse, and their son Rājarāja Viṣṇuvardhana obtained the hand of Rājendra I's daughter. The offspring of the latter union was Rājendra Coḷa II, afterwards called Kulottuṅga I. He assumed both the crowns in 1070 A.D., and having driven away his uncle Vijayāditya VII from Veṅgī, he successively appointed his sons, Rājarāja-Muṁmaḍi-Coḍa and Vīra-Coḍa, as Viceroys of that region. Thus resulted the amalgamation of the Eastern Cālukya and the Coḷa realms, and this mixed dynasty had a prosperous career for almost two centuries. Ultimately it collapsed owing to the incursions of the Kākatīyas of Warangal, the Hoysalas, and other hostile neighbours (see also D. C. Ganguly, *Eastern Cālukyas*, Benares, 1937).

When the Cālukya arms reached beyond the Kāverī, the Coḷas, the Pāṇḍyas, and the Keralas averted hostilities by their readiness to form an alliance with Pulakeśin II.

Pulakeśin II not only distinguished himself in warfare, but also cultivated the softer art of diplomacy to strengthen his position. According to the Arab writer Tabāri,[1] the former maintained friendly relations with Khusru II, king of Iran or Persia, who received from his Indian contemporary a special envoy in 625 A.D. bearing letters and presents. The Persian sovereign, too, sent an embassy to the Cālukya court, and it is generally supposed by scholars that the reception of the Persian mission is portrayed in one of the Ajantā cave paintings. This view is, however, doubted by Sten Konow.[2]

Diplomatic Intercourse

During the reign of Pulakeśin II, perhaps in the year 641 A.D., the celebrated Chinese pilgrim, Yuan Chwang, went in the course of his travels to the *Mo-ha-la-ch'a* (or t'a) country or Mahārāṣṭra. We are told that "its soil is rich and fertile; it is regularly cultivated and very productive."[3] Furthermore, "the inhabitants were proud-spirited and warlike, grateful for favours and revengeful for wrongs, self-sacrificing towards suppliants in distress and sanguinary to death with any who treated them insultingly. Their martial heroes who led the van of the army in battle went into conflict intoxicated, and their war-elephants were also made drunk before an engagement."[4] Owing to his superior forces the king of the land, named *Pu-lo-ke-she* (Pulakeśin), who was a Kṣatriya

Yuan Chwang's testimony

[1] J. R. *A. S.*, N. S., XI, (1879), pp. 165-66.
[2] *Ind. Ant.*, February 1908, p. 24.
[3] Beal, II, p. 256.
[4] Watters, II, p. 239.

by birth, treated the neighbouring powers "with contempt". Indeed, his benevolent sway is said to have extended "far and wide, and his vassals served him with perfect loyalty."[1]

Unhappy end

The last days of the great Cālukya monarch were inglorious. For the Pallavas now paid off all old scores under the leadership of Narasiṁhavarman I (*c.* 625-45 A.D.), who, after several successful campaigns, stormed the Cālukya capital, Vātāpi, in 642 A.D., and probably killed Pulakeśin II. But the resistance of the Cālukyas was not completely broken, and they soon emerged from their temporary eclipse.

Pulakeśin II's successors

Pulakeśin II was followed by his second son, Vikramāditya I, called Satyāśraya,[2] who valiantly recovered his paternal dominions from the rival house of the Pallavas by about 654 A.D. He captured Kāñcī (Conjeeveram), and is represented to have defeated three Pallava princes, Narasiṁhavarman I, Mahendravarman II, and Parameśvaravarman. Certain documents, on the other hand, credit the last-named with victories over the Cālukyas. If there be any truth in these claims, it would appear that the struggle between the two powers continued long, and fortune was, as usual, fickle in the case of either. We further learn that Vikramāditya I did not stop with the plunder of the Pallava capital; he pressed on to the extreme south and the weight of his arms was even felt by the Coḷas, the Pāṇḍyas, and the

[1] *Ibid.*

[2] Presumably, Vikramāditya I got the throne, as he was his father's favourite son (*priyatanaya*). Candrāditya, his elder brother, appears to have been given charge of some remote province; and Jayasiṁha, another brother of Vikramāditya I, was assigned the province of Lāṭa or southern Gujarat by the latter.

Keralas. In these wars he was ably assisted by his son, Vinayāditya, and grandson, Vijayāditya, both of whom afterwards became kings—the former ruling from *c.* 680 to 696 A.D., and the latter from *c.* 696 to 733 A.D. According to an inscription, Vinayāditya Satyāśraya acquired "the insignia of supreme dominion by crushing the lord of all the region of the North" (*Sakalottarāpatha-nātha*).[1] There is doubtless an element of exaggeration in this statement, for we do not know of any paramount sovereign of the North at this time, but it appears that Vinayāditya scored a military triumph against one of the successors of Ādityasena in the Later Gupta line. During the reign of Vijayāditya's son, Vikramāditya II (*c.* 733-47 A.D.), the traditional hostilities with the Pallavas continued; Nandivarman sustained a defeat and the Cālukya army entered the city of Kāñcī, where a mutilated epigraph of the victor, found in a temple, still bears witness to its occupation. Besides, the arms of Vikramāditya II are said to have been successful against other hereditary enemies, *viz.*, the Coḷas, the Pāṇḍyas, the people of Malabar, and the Kaḷabhras. Vikramāditya II was also noted for giving largess to Brahmans, and both of his Haihaya wives built two splendid fanes in honour of Śiva. In Śaka 669=747-48 A. D., Vikramāditya II was succeeded by his son, Kīrtivarman II, who too, like his predecessors, fought against the Pallavas. But perhaps owing to Pallava pre-occupations he or his father lost Mahārāṣṭra to the Rāṣṭrakūṭa chief, Dantidurga, about the middle of the eighth century A.D.[2] The main Cālukya dynasty disappeared after Kīrtivarman's reign, though the family itself was not annihilated and, as we shall see below, its scions subsequently reasserted their power.

[1] *Ind. Ant.*, IX, p. 129; VII, pp. 107, 111.

[2] cf. Ellorā plates of Dantidurga dated Śaka 663-741-42 A.D. (*Ep. Ind.*, XXV, pp. 25-31).

Patronage of Religion and Art

The Vātāpi Cālukyas were staunch Brahmanists, but they observed the golden rule of toleration. During their ascendancy, Jainism prospered in the Dekkan, specially its southern part. Ravikīrti, the Jaina author of the Aihoḷe inscription, who constructed a temple of *Jinendra*, claims to have obtained "the highest favour" of Pulakeśin II. Similarly, Vijayāditya and Vikramāditya II granted villages to well-known Jain *Panditas*. We have, however, no evidence to show in what manner Buddhism was patronised by the Cālukya monarchs. It was perhaps on the wane, although it had not become extinct, as would be clear from the following testimony of Yuan Chwang: "Of Buddhist monasteries there were above 100, and the Brethren, who were adherents of both Vehicles, were more than 5,000 in number. Within and outside the capital were five Aśoka *topes* where the Four Past Buddhas had sat and walked for exercise; and there were innumerable other *topes* of stone or brick."[1] As regards Brahmanism, the Paurāṇic deities rose into prominence, and superb structures were erected at Vātāpi (Badami) and Pattadakal[2] (Bijapur district) in honour of the Trinity—Brahmā, Viṣṇu, and Śiva; these gods were also known by a variety of names. Sometimes, temples were excavated out of solid rocks; as for instance, Maṅgaleśa signalised his reign by an architectural achievement of this description, consecrated to Viṣṇu.[3] It has

[1] Watters, II, p. 239.

[2] The Pattadakal temples, particularly their *Vimānas*, were built after the fashion of Pallava architecture.

[3] See H. Cousens, *The Cālukyan Architecture* (*Arch. Surv. Ind.*, Vol. XLII, Calcutta, 1926). The Cālukyan temple stands on an elaborately decorated base or plinth. It is polygonal, often star-shaped in plan. It is roofed by "a low pyramidal tower, surmounted by a vase-like ornament."

further been conjectured that some of the famous Ajantā cave-frescoes probably belong to the time of these early Cālukyas. Lastly, elaborate sacrifices were then in vogue, and we learn that Pulakeśin I alone performed a number of them, such as the Aśvamedha, Vājapeya, Pauṇḍarīka, etc.

Section B

THE RĀṢṬRAKŪṬAS OF MĀNYAKHEṬA (MALKHED)

Extraction of the Rāṣṭrakūṭas

It is rather a vexed question what stock the Rāṣṭrakūṭas of the Dekkan belonged to? According to later documents of the dynasty, they had sprung from the race of Yadu; and their direct progenitor was a prince called Raṭṭa, whose son, Rāṣṭrakūṭa, gave his name to the family itself. Sir Ramkrishna Bhandarkar,[1] however, takes them to be "imaginary persons", and probably he is right in placing no reliance on such traditions. Similarly, the suggestion of Fleet[2] that the Rāṣṭrakūṭas of the Dekkan were derived from the Rathors (Rāṣṭrakūṭas) of the north would not bear the least scrutiny; nor is there any substance in the belief of Burnell[3] that they were connected with the Dravidian Reḍḍis of Āndhradeśa. The most probable view is that the Rāṣṭrakūṭas of Malkhed were descended from the Raṣṭikas or Raṭhikas, who were important enough in the middle of the third century B.C. to be mentioned along with the Bhojakas and other *Aparāntas* (people of Western India) in the edicts of Aśoka.

Their original home

Inscriptions and coins indicate, as shown by Dr.

[1] *E. H. D.*, (3rd ed., 1928), p. 106.
[2] *Bom. Gaz.*, Vol. I, pt. II, p. 384.
[3] *South Indian Palæography*, p. x.

Altekar,[1] that the Raṭhika and Mahāraṭhi families occupied Mahārāṣṭra and portions of Karṇāṭaka in the capacity of feudatory rulers. Now wherefrom did the later Rāṣṭrakūṭas of Mānyakheṭa hail? Dr. Altekar locates their original home in Karṇāṭaka, and adds that their mother-tongue was Kanarese, since they encouraged and themselves used this language and script.[2] Besides, they are described in several epigraphs as "Laṭṭalūrapuravarādhīśa," i.e. "lords of Laṭṭalūra, the excellent town," which is identical with Lāṭūr—a Kanarese-speaking locality in the Bedar district, Nizām's dominions. No doubt, these are weighty arguments and militate against the assumption of some scholars that the Malkhed Rāṣṭrakūṭas were natives of Mahārāṣṭra.

Rise of the dynasty

The first few rulers of this house—Dantivarman, Indra I Pṛchakarāja, Govinda I, Karka I, and Indrarāja II—are not known to have achieved any distinction. Indeed, we do not even know definitely where their territory lay. Dr. Altekar[3] is of opinion that they held sway "somewhere in Berar", the family having migrated from its original home in Karṇāṭaka. Further, he regards them as "either the direct or collateral descendants of the Rāṣṭrakūṭa king, Nannarāja Yudhāsura, who was ruling at Elichpur in Berar in the middle of the seventh century A.D."[4] Whether one agrees or not with these suggestions, it is certain that the Rāṣṭrakūṭas of Mānyakheṭa[5] began their career of greatness under

[1] *Rāṣṭrakūṭas and their Times*, pp. 19-21. I have consulted this book with profit.

[2] *Ibid.*, pp. 21-22.

[3] *Ibid.*, pp. 11, 22, etc.

[4] *Ibid.*, p. 11.

[5] The Rāṣṭrakūṭa capital was established at Mānyakheṭa by

Dantidurga. He was the son of the Cālukya princess, Bhavanāgā, whom Indrarāja is said to have forcibly carried away in the midst of her nuptial ceremonies. The most notable exploit of Dantidurga was the subversion of the Cālukya power in Mahārāṣṭra about the beginning of the fifth decade of the eighth century A.D., as is evident from the newly-discovered Ellorā plates.[1] The Rāṣṭrakūṭa monarch also vanquished other contemporary kings like those of Kāñcī (a Pallava prince), Kaliṅga, Kośala (South Kośala), Mālava (the Gurjara-Pratīhāra ruler of Ujjain), Lāṭa (southern Gujarat, where Karka II became governor), Taṅka (not satisfactorily identified), and Śrīśaila (Karnul district). Dantidurga died without leaving a son, and consequently his paternal uncle, Kannara or Kriṣṇa I, succeeded to the throne not long before 758 A.D. Some scholars, however, believe that the former, being tyrannical, was deposed, and the omission of his name in certain grants appears to lend colour to this view. But presumably they pass over him because in relation to his successor he was only a collateral. Kriṣṇa I completed the overthrow of Kīrtivarman II Cālukya, whose authority, according to an inscription, survived in Karṇāṭaka and adjacent lands until at least 757 A.D. Kriṣṇarāja[2] is represented as having consolidated his position and assumed the Imperial title of *Rājādhirāja-Parameśvara* after crushing the proud Rāhappa. The latter was doubtless a strong opponent, but it is difficult to identify him with the extant materials. Kriṣṇa I then subdued Konkan; overran Gaṅgavāḍi (i.e., the kingdom of the Gaṅgas); and defeated Viṣṇuvardhana IV, the

Amoghavarṣa I. The earlier seat of power is unknown, although the names of Mayūrakhaṇḍi (Morkhaṇḍ, Nasik district) and 'Sooloobhunjun' (near Ellorā) have been suggested.

[1] See *Ep. Ind.*, XXV, pp. 25-31. The Ellorā plates, dated in *Śaka* 663=741-42 A.D., furnish us the earliest year for Dantidurga. Evidently he ruled the Ellorā region at this date.

[2] Kriṣṇa I is generally called Śubhatuṅga and Akālavarṣa.

Eastern Cālukya ruler of Veṅgī. Along with these military triumphs, Krișṇa I signalised his reign by constructing a magnificent temple of Śiva at Elāpura (Ellorā, Nizām's dominions). Excavated out of solid rock, the structure is indubitably, as observed by Vincent Smith, "the most marvellous architectural freak in India."[1]

Growth of Rāṣṭrakūṭa Imperialism

(*a*) *Govinda II*—Krișṇa I appears to have died shortly after 772 A.D., and was succeeded by his eldest son Govinda II Prabhūtavarṣa. As *Yuvarāja*, he had inflicted a defeat on Viṣṇuvardhana IV of Veṅgī. But when he became king, Govinda II did not win any memorable victory except against one Pārijāta. The Rāṣṭrakūṭa monarch dissipated his energies in unbridled licence and sensuality. Even the work of administration was carried on by his younger brother, Dhruva, who, taking advantage of the situation, rebelled and eventually seized the crown for himself in *c*. 779 A.D.

(*b*) *Dhruva Nirupama*—Dhruva Nirupama, also called Dhārāvarṣa and Kali or Śrī-Vallabha,[2] first dealt severe blows against his brother's allies. The Gaṅga king, Śivamāra Muṭṭarasa, was humbled and imprisoned, and his territories were annexed. Next, the Pallava sovereign of Kāñcī had to bow to Dhruva's steel. The latter then turned his eyes towards the north. He caused Vatsarāja, the Pratīhara ruler of Ujjain, "to enter upon the path of misfortune in the centre of (the deserts of) Maru"[3] which expression probably indicates that Dhruva defeated his antagonist and

[1] *E. H. I.*, 4th ed., p. 445.

[2] This epithet occurs in the Jain *Harivaṁśa*, which yields us the Śaka date 705=783-84 A.D. for Dhruva.

[3] *Ind. Ant.*, XI, p. 161; *Ep. Ind.*, VI, pp. 243-248.

drove him into the inhospitable regions of Rajputana. Dhruva also invaded the territories of the Gangetic Doab in the reign of Indrāyudha, and is said to have "added the emblem of the Ganges and the Jumnā to his Imperial insignia." It was perhaps during this raid that Dhruva met Dharmapāla in a successful encounter, and "seized the white umbrellas, the sporting lotuses of *Lakṣmī* of the Gauḍa king, as he was fleeing between the Ganges and the Jumnā".[1] Dhruva's campaign in Madhyadeśa did not, of course, result in any expansion of territory, but it clearly demonstrated that the Rāṣṭrakūṭas had now embarked upon a career of Imperialistic ambition and aggrandisement.

(*c*) *Govinda III Jagattuṅga*——Govinda III was selected by Dhruva as his successor; it is, however, uncertain if he came to the throne in *circa* 794 A.D. after his father's abdication or death. Stambha (Khambayya), governor of Gaṅgavāḍī and elder brother of Govinda III, challenged his accession, and the former's cause was espoused by a number of recalcitrant feudatories. Even Śivamāra, the released Gaṅgā king, raised his head against the new Rāṣṭrakūṭa ruler. But nothing availed the rebels and they were soon completely routed. Gaṅgavāḍī was again conquered, and Govinda III meted out a generous treatment to Stambha by reappointing him his local representative there. Next, having vanquished Dantiga (or Dantivarman), the Pallava prince of Kāñcī, Govinda III measured swords with Vijayāditya II (799-843 A.D.), the Eastern Cālukya monarch of Veṅgī, and put him to humiliation. Like his father, Govinda III was victorious against the northern powers. He defeated and successfully foiled all attempts of Nāgabhaṭa II to recover his paternal dominions of Ujjain[2] some time between 806 A.D. and

[1] *Ep. Ind.*, XVIII, pp. 244, 252; see also *History of Kanauj*, p. 214.

[2] Sanjan plates, *Ep. Ind.*, XVIII, pp. 245, 253, v. 22; see also Radhanpur grant, *Ibid.*, pp. 244, 250, v. 15.

808 A.D.[1] Govinda III, however, continued to apprehend danger from the ambitious Pratīhāra potentate, and so, according to the Baroda plates of Karkarāja, he (Govinda) "for the purpose of protecting Mālava...... caused his (Karkarāja's) arm to become an excellent door-bar of the country of the lord of Gurjaras."[2] Govinda III then directed his attention towards the Gangetic Doab, and the Sanjan plates inform us that both Cakrāyudha of Kānyakubja and Dharmapāla of Gauḍa "surrendered of themselves" to him.[3] But these victories brought him no peace. His preoccupations in the north led the Coḷas and Pāṇḍyas to form a confederacy with the kings of Kāñcī, Gaṅgavāḍī and Kerala against him. Once more the arms of Govinda III triumphed and afterwards he devoted the remaining years of his life to internal affairs of the kingdom.

Amoghavarṣa I

After the passing away of Govinda III early in 814 A.D., the crown devolved upon his son, who is known only by his epithet, Amoghavarṣa.[4] As the latter was a mere boy, Govinda III appears to have entrusted, before his death, Karkarāja-Suvarṇavarṣa of the collateral Gujarat branch with the task of running the machinery of administration. Things went on smoothly for a time, but the forces of disruption did not long remain dormant. The dissensions in the royal house affected the ministers with disloyalty, the tributary princes became rebellious, and the ruler of

[1] *History of Kanauj*, p. 232.

[2] *History of Kanauj*, p. 232; *Ind. Ant.*, XII, pp. 160, 164.

[3] *Ep. Ind.*, XVIII, pp. 245, 253, v. 23; see also *Ibid.*, VI, pp. 102, 105. cf. स्वयमेवोपनतौ च यस्य महतस्तौ धर्मचक्रायुधौ ।

[4] Sir R. G. Bhandarkar is of opinion that his proper name was Sarva (*E. H. D.*, p. 116).

Gaṅgavāḍī asserted his independence. Even Vijayāditya II of Veṅgī attacked the Raṭṭas (Rāṣṭrakūṭas) to avenge his previous discomfiture at the hands of Govinda III. Thus anarchy stalked through the land, and ultimately it led to Amoghavarṣa's deposition. The Surat grant,[1] however, indicates that some time before April 821 A D. he regained the throne, presumably owing to the efforts of Karkarāja.[2] Being still young, the position of Amoghavarṣa I long continued to be insecure, and he could not, therefore, undertake any military expedition. Of course, the Sirur (Dhārvāḍ district) charter,[3] dated Śaka 788 (A.D. 866), and other later epigraphs testify that the Cālukya monarch of Veṅgī bowed to his steel. But this must have happened rather late in Amoghavarṣa's reign, and most probably his opponent was Vijayāditya III Guṇaga (*c.* 844-88 A.D.), since there are grounds to believe that, far from submitting, Vijayāditya II (*c.* 799-843 A.D.) achieved further victories against the Rāṣṭrakūṭas about the close of his career. Next, Amoghavarṣa I is said to have extended his influence over the kings of Aṅga, Vaṅga, and Magadha; these claims, however, seem to be mere boasts without any basis in fact. In the south as well as in the north, Amoghavarṣa's arms made no progress. On the other hand, his Pratīhāra contemporary, Mihira Bhoja, overran the tracts round Ujjayinī up to the Narmadā river and perhaps beyond, and the credit for repelling this invasion goes not to Amoghavarṣa I but to his Gujarat kinsman, Dhruva II.[4]

[1] *Ep. Ind.*, XXI, pp. 133-47

[2] *Ep. Ind.*, XXI, pp. 133-47.

[3] *Ind. Ant.*, XII, pp. 216 f.

[4] *Ibid.*, pp. 184, 189. The Gujarat line was established by Indra, who was appointed governor of southern Gujarat by his elder brother, Govinda III, about the beginning of the ninth century A.D. Among the prominent members of this branch were Karka-Suvarṇavarṣa, Dhruva Dhārāvarṣa, Akālavarṣa Śubhatuṅga,

Indeed, the former proved so weak that he could not bring to book even the Gaṅga prince, who had cut asunder the Imperial ties early in his reign. This lack of martial ardour was perhaps due to Amoghavarṣa's leanings towards religion and literature. The tenets of Jainism, as expounded by his chief preceptor (*paramaguru*), Jinasena, greatly appealed to his heart and intellect; and if the *Gaṇitasārasaṁgraha* of Vīrācārya merits credence, Amoghavarṣa I openly turned an adherent of the *Syādvāda* doctrine. But he did not altogether forsake his catholic sympathies or Hindu attachments, for the Sanjan plates represent him as a devout worshipper of the goddess Mahālakṣmī.[1] Further, he has been compared to the renowned Vikramāditya in liberality and patronage of men of letters.[2] Amoghavarṣa I himself was the author of the *Kavirājamārga*, a Kanarese work on poetics; and of the *Praśnottaramālikā*, a catechism on moral principles, which, however, is sometimes attributed to Śaṅkarācārya or to one Vimala.

The last days of Amoghavarṣa I were spent mostly in religious exercises. It appears that he used to retire into solitude for short intervals to practise meditation, leaving the cares of government to the crown-prince or the council of ministers.

Lastly, it may be mentioned that Amoghavarṣa I fixed his capital at Mānyakheṭa (now Malkhed in the Nizām's dominions). We do not know with certitude whether he was the actual founder of the city, but it surely owed its prosperity and importance to him.

Dhruva II, the last three having fought against a king named Vallabha, whom Dr. Altekar has identified with Amoghavarṣa I (*Rāṣṭrakūṭas and their Times*, p. 84). The Gujarat family disappeared sometime in the last decade of the ninth century A.D.

[1] *Ep. Ind.*, XVIII, pp. 248, 255, v. 47. Amoghavarṣa is called in this verse Vīra-Nārāyaṇa.

[2] *Ibid.*, v. 48.

Amoghavarṣa's successors

The last known date of Amoghavarṣa I is 878 A.D.;[1] we may, therefore, tentatively assume that he died the same year after a protracted reign of about sixty-four years. He was succeeded by his son, Kriṣṇa II, surnamed Akālavarṣa or Śrī-Vallabha. The latter married a daughter of Kalacuri Kokalla I of Tripurī, who claims to have been a source of considerable strength to his son-in-law.[2] It was during Kriṣṇa II's time that the Gujarat Rāṣṭrakūṭa branch lost whatever power it once enjoyed. He also carried on the traditional hostilities with the Eastern Cālukya rulers of Veṅgī, Vijayāditya III Guṇaga—his contemporary for a few years—and Bhīma I (*c.* 888-918 A. D.), but the Rāṣṭrakūṭa arms met with reverses after some successes. Another figure, with whom Kriṣṇa II came into conflict, was Mihira Bhoja, and although the Barton Museum fragmentary inscription[3] would have us believe that the former had to retreat hastily to his own country, the Bagumrā plates[4], on the contrary, indicate that the Pratīhāra monarch could not make much headway against his opponent in the region round Ujjayinī. Perhaps their wars did not result in any advantage to either party.

Kriṣṇa II passed away about 914 A. D., and was succeeded by his grandson Indra III Nityavarṣa. The latter was the offspring of Jagattuṅga (who had died prematurely in the lifetime of his father) by his Kalacuri wife, Lakṣmī. Indra III proved a daring

[1] "Phālguna Śuddha 10, Śaka 799 (i.e., March, 878 A.D.) when the *Jayadhavalaṭīkā* of Vīrasena was finished." See *Rāṣṭrakūṭas and their Times*, p. 87.

[2] Bilhari inscription, *Ep. Ind.*, I, pp. 256, 264, verse 17; Benares grant, *Ibid.*, II, p. 306, verse 7.

[3] *Ep. Ind.*, XIX, pp. 174-77.

[4] *Ind. Ant.*, XIII, pp. 67, 69, v. 23; *Ep. Ind.*, IX, pp. 31, 39, v. 15.

warrior; his greatest achievement, according to the Cambay plates,[1] was the "complete devastation of that hostile city of Mahodaya" (Kanauj) in 916 or 917 A.D. He triumphantly marched through Ujjain, the veritable bone of contention between the Rāṣṭrakūṭas and the Pratīhāras, and across the valley of the "unfathomable Yamunā," accompanied by his Cālukya feudatory, Narasiṁha,[2] and overwhelmed Mahīpāla who had shortly before seized the crown from Bhoja II with the help of Harṣadeva Candella.[3] The invaders appear to have overrun the Gangetic Doab as far as Prayāga, but the campaign was in effect no more than a brilliant raid and left no permanent traces of Rāṣṭrakūṭa authority in the North.

After a brief reign, Indra III was succeeded by Amoghavarṣa II probably early in 918 A.D.[4] Then followed Govinda IV, who, instead of looking into the affairs of the state, indulged himself in sensual gratification and had thus "with his intelligence caught in the noose of the eyes of women displeased all beings".[5] He was worsted by Cālukya Bhīma II of Veṅgī

[1] *Ep. Ind.*, VII, pp. 38, 43, v. 19.

यन्माद्यद्द्विपदन्तघातविषमं कालप्रियप्राङ्गणम् ।
तीर्णा यत्तुरगैरगाधयमुना सिन्धुप्रतिस्पर्धिनी ॥
येनेदं हि महोदयारिनगरं निर्मूलमुन्मीलितम् ।
नाम्नाद्यापि जनैः कुशस्थलमिति ख्यातिं परां नीयते ॥

The temple of Kālapriya, mentioned in the Cambay plates, is probably to be identified with that of Mahākāla in Ujjayinī. It has, however, been sometimes identified with the shrine of Kālapriya in Kālpī.

[2] *History of Kanauj*, p. 260.

[3] *Ibid.*, pp. 256-57.

[4] This date will have to be set aside, if, as I am informed by Dr. Altekar, Indra III ruled for a few years more according to an inscription. I have, however, not been able to find out the exact reference.

[5] *Ep. Ind.*, IV, pp. 283, 288, v. 20. cf. सोप्यंगनानयनपाशनिरुद्ध-वुद्धिरुन्मार्गसंगविमुखीकृतसर्वसत्वः ।

(*c*. 934-45 A.D.) at the fag-end of his career, and, according to the *Vikramārjunavijaya* of the Kanarese poet, Pampa[1], even vassal chiefs like Arikeśarin II of Puligere gave much trouble to Govinda IV.

After Govinda IV his paternal uncle, Amoghavarṣa III Baddiga, ascended the throne in *c*. 936 A.D. Not much is known of him except that he was a righteous man, and was matrimonially allied to the Kalacuri Keyūravarṣa Yuvarāja I of Tripurī and the Gaṅga prince Būṭuga II, being the son-in-law of the former and father-in-law of the latter. Amoghavarṣa III ceased ruling about the beginning of 940 A.D.

Kriṣṇa III

Amoghavarṣa III's successor was his son, Kriṣṇa III, who seems to have wielded substantial power while only an heir-apparent. Among his earliest exploits was the subversion of Rācamalla, the Western Gaṅga ruler, and the enthronement of Būṭuga II in his place. We further learn from the Deoli plates that when sometime before *Śaka* 862=940 A.D., the date of the record, Kriṣṇa undertook an expedition in northern India "the hope about Kālañjara and Citrakūṭa vanished from the heart of the Gūrjara."[2] If the Gurjara of this passage is identical with the Pratīhāra sovereign, Mahīpāla, we get definite testimony regarding Kriṣṇa III's clash with the hereditary enemies of his house. Indeed, it has been suggested that the Rāṣṭrakūṭa invader wrested Kālañjara and Citrakūṭa from his northern rival. This may perhaps be true, although all that the epigraphic evidence implies is that, hearing of the victorious progress of Kriṣṇa, the Gurjara lord became so

[1] *Ep. Ind.*, XIII, pp. 328-29.
[2] *Ibid.*, V, p. 194, verse 25.

cf. दक्षिणदिग्दुर्गविजयमाकर्ण्य गलिता गूर्जरहृदयात् चित्रकूटाशा ।

panic-stricken as to lose hope of the defence and safety of two of his strategic strongholds. That Kriṣṇa III carried his arms northwards is also clear from an undated Kanarese inscription, engraved on a stone slab in Maihar State (Baghelkhand).[1] It is, of course, significant that here he assumes the full Imperial titles of Paramabhaṭṭāraka, Mahārājādhirāja, and Parameśvara, and accordingly the probability cannot be altogether ruled out that the actual occupation of any territory in Central India may have been due to some later incursion of Kriṣṇa III as king, when the power of the Pratīhāras was distinctly on the wane owing to the rise of the Candellas and other quondam feudatories.

The most notable victories of Kriṣṇa III were, however, won in the South. He occupied Kacchi (Kāñcī) and by his conquest of Tanjore earned the proud epithet of "Tañjaiyumkoṇḍa."[2] The Coḷa prince Rājāditya, son of Parāntaka I, was defeated in the famous battle of Takkolaṃ (near Arkoṇam, North Arcot district) in 949 A.D. with the assistance of his brother-in-law, the Gaṅga chief, Būṭuga II,[3] who got Banavāsī and other tracts in reward for the services rendered during the war. Kriṣṇa III thus became master of Toṇḍamaṇḍalaṁ, but he could not annex the southern portion of the Coḷa realm. He also curbed the ambitions of the Pāṇḍyas and the Keralas, and even the king of Siṁhala (Ceylon) is said to have paid homage to him. Another remarkable achievement of Kriṣṇa III was that he successfully opposed Amma II and raised his ally Bāḍapa, son of Yuddhamalla, to the Veṅgī throne.

[1] *Ibid.*, XIX, pp. 287-90.

[2] cf. the expression "Kacciyum-Tañjaiyumkoṇḍa."

[3] See the Ātakūr inscription, dated *Śaka* 872=949-50 A.D. (*Ep. Ind.*, VI, pp. 50-57). For the Coḷa version of the conflict, see the Tiruvālangāḍu plates (*A.R.E.*, V, p. 34) and the Leyden grant (*A.S.S.I.*, IV, pp. 206-07).

Downfall of the dynasty

Kriṣṇa III was the last great ruler of the Rāṣṭrakūṭa family, whose glory departed after his death in 968 A.D. During the reign of the next monarch, his brother Khoṭṭiga Nityavarṣa, the fortunes of the Rāṣṭrakūṭas sank to so low a level that their capital Mānyakheṭa was pillaged by the Paramāra Sīyaka-Harṣa of Mālava.[1] Khoṭṭiga's nephew and successor, Karka II or Kakkala, was decidedly a weak personality, although an inscription credits him with having put down a number of enemies. He succumbed to the onslaughts of the Western Cālukya Taila II or Tailapa some time in the year 973 A.D., and thus after a vigorous career of almost two centuries and a quarter, the Imperial Rāṣṭrakūṭas passed into obscurity.

The Rāṣṭrakūṭas and the Arabs

The Rāṣṭrakūṭa kings, called by the Arab travellers and chroniclers Balhara (evidently an Arabic corruption of the Sanskrit term Vallabharāja), were regarded by the latter as mighty monarchs. For instance, Sulaimān, alluding in 851 A.D. to "the long-lived Balhara," identified with Amoghavarṣa I, includes him among the four great sovereigns of the world, the other three being the Khalifā of Baghdad and the Emperors of Constantinople and China. The Rāṣṭrakūṭas maintained friendly relations with the Arabs and afforded them ample facilities for trade. This policy was doubtless due to

[1] *Ep. Ind.*, I, pp. 235, 237, v. 12.
cf. श्रीहर्षदेव इति खोट्टिगदेवलक्ष्मीं जग्राह यो युधि नगादसमप्रतापः ।
Dhanapāla also says in his *Pāiyalacchī* (v. 276) that he composed his work "when one thousand years of the Vikrama era and twenty-nine besides had passed, when Mannakheḍa or Mānyakheṭa had been plundered in consequence of an attack (made) by the lord of Mālava" (*Ep. Ind.*, I, p. 226).

the exigencies of the political situation, because the "Baüüra" or the Pratīhāra potentates of Kanauj were the inveterate enemies of both the Rāṣṭrakūṭas and the Arabs. Thus Al Ma'sūdī, writing in *H.* 332=943-44 A.D., deposes: "This Baüüra, who is the king of Kanauj, is an enemy of Balhara, the king of India." Again, he says regarding the disposition of the forces of Kanauj: "The army of the north wars against the prince of Multan, and with the Musulmans, his subjects on the frontier. The army on the south fights against Balhara, king of Mankir", i.e., Mānyakheṭa.[1] This friendship with the Arabs, no doubt, speaks well of the religious broadmindedness of the Rāṣṭrakūṭas, but at the same time it reflects their lack of political foresight.

Religious conditions

During the age of the Rāṣṭrakūṭas, Paurāṇic Hinduism, specially the worship of Viṣṇu and Śiva, grew popular in the Dekkan. The Rāṣṭrakūṭa copper-plate grants begin with invocations to both these deities, and their seal is either Garuḍa, the *vāhana* (vehicle) of Viṣṇu, or Śiva seated in an attitude of *Yoga*. We hear of the performance of Brahmanical sacrifices (for instance, Dantidurga celebrated the *Hiraṇyagarbha* at Ujjayinī) and also of *Tulādānas*, i.e., gifts of gold equal to one's weight, by the Royalty. Temples were constructed to house images, which were daily worshipped with an elaborate ritual. Unhappily, however, excepting the rock-cut shrine of Śiva at Ellorā—an architectural wonder—richly endowed by Kriṣṇa I, no other important monument of this period is extant. Besides Hinduism, other faiths also flourished. Jainism was patronised by Rāṣṭrakūṭa rulers like Amoghavarṣa I

[1] Elliot, *History of India*, Vol. I, pp. 21-23.

and Indra IV, and even Krisṇa II and Indra III are recorded to have honoured it. But Buddhism had definitely declined, and according to certain inscriptions of the time of Amoghavarṣa I its chief centre in the Dekkan was Kanherī.[1]

SECTION C

THE WESTERN CĀLUKYAS OF KALYĀṆA[2]

Tailapa's descent

According to later documents of the dynasty, Tailapa was a descendant of an unnamed uncle of Kīrtivarman II, who was ousted by the Rāṣṭrakūṭas from the sovereignty of the Dekkan. Thus, Tailapa had in his veins the blood of the Cālukyas of Vātāpi. Sir Ramkrishna Bhandarkar, however, doubts the authenticity of this pedigree.[3] He considers Tailapa to have sprung from "quite a collateral and unimportant branch" on the ground that the latter and his successors do not, like the earlier Cālukyas, claim Harīti to be their progenitor or represent themselves as belonging to the Mānavya *gotra*.

[1] *Ind. Ant.*, XIII, pp. 134-37.

[2] See R. G. Bhandarkar, *E. H. D.*, 3rd ed., Sec. xii, pp. 136-59; S. L. Katare, The Cālukyas of Kalyāṇī, *Indian Culture*, Vol. IV, No. 1, pp. 43-52; *Ind. Hist. Quart.*, Vol. XVII, March, 1941, pp. 11-34; Fleet, *Dynasties of the Kanarese Districts*. A record of *Śaka* 915=993 A.D., found at Kākhaṇdki, gives the interesting information that Tailapa ruled from Mānyakheṭa, which thus appears to have continued as capital even of the Western Cālukyas for some time (*A.S.I.R.*, 1930-34, p. 241). Perhaps the earliest mention of Kalyāṇa as capital is found in a record of 1033-34 A.D. (*A.S.I.R.*, 1929-30).

[3] *E. H. D.*, p. 136. Dr. Altekar leaves the question open (*Rāṣṭrakūṭas and their Times*, p. 128). See also Fleet's *Dynasties of the Kanarese Districts*, p. 41.

His Career

Before his dramatic rise, Tailapa was presumably a feudatory of the Rāṣṭrakūṭas.[1] He took advantage of the confusion following the sack of Mānyakheṭa by the Paramāra forces, and boldly attacked Karka II, who was either killed in the struggle or had to retire to some safer corner of the kingdom. This, no doubt, enhanced Tailapa's power and prestige, but the issues could not be finally decided until the suppression of Indra IV and other claimants to the Rāṣṭrakūṭa crown. They, too, were overthrown in the course of a few years, resulting in the revival of the Cālukya monarchy. Tailapa then conquered Lāṭa (southern Gujarat) and stationed Bārappa as governor there. Its occupation could not, however, be permanent, since the latter was driven away by Mūlarāja Cālukya of Anhilwāḍa. Tailapa also brought Kuntala or the Kanarese country under his authority, although the alleged victories over the Cedis and the Coḷas do not seem to be founded on fact.[2] His northern frontiers were constantly menaced by Vākpati-Muñja Paramāra, who, according to Merutuṅga, defeated Tailapa no less than six times. Whatever truth the story may contain, Vākpati-Muñja ultimately met with a tragic fate in this duel. It is said that, despite the remonstrances of his sagacious minister, he marched right into the enemy's territory across the Godāvarī, and was captured and eventually beheaded.[3] Thus

[1] Dr. Altekar suggests that, as a feudatory, Tailapa was probably "living somewhere in the northern portion of the state of Hyderabad" (*Rāṣṭrakūṭas and their Times*, p. 130). See, however, *Arch. Surv. Ind. Rep.*, 1930-34, pp. 224, 241. We learn from a record of A. D. 965, found at Narasalgi in the Bāgevāḍi *Taluka*, that Tailapa was an officer under Kriṣṇa III. Earlier still, in *Śaka* 879=957 A.D., Tailapa was probably governing Tārddevāḍi.

[2] Or, were they local skirmishes against minor Cedi and Coḷa chiefs?

[3] See *Ante*.

began the long drawn tussle between the Cālukyas and the Paramāras. Tailapa died in *c.* 997 A.D. after a reign of about twenty-four years.

C. 997 *A.D. to* 1042 *A.D.*

Tailapa was followed by his son, Satyāśraya. During his reign (*c.* 997 A.D.-1008 A.D.), the Coḷa hosts under Rājarāja I mercilessly carried death and destruction in the Cālukya kingdom. Satyāśraya, however, soon recovered from this terrific blow and even made some successful depredations in the south at the cost of the Coḷas. After him, his nephew Vikramāditya V[1] ruled for a short time. The latter was defeated by Bhoja Paramāra,[2] who attacked the Cālukyas to avenge the humiliation and assassination of Vākpati-Muñja. Having thus paid off all old scores, Bhoja formed plans for establishing his hegemony in the Dekkan, and with this end in view he astutely came to terms with powerful neighbours like Bhīma I of Anhilwāḍa and the Kalacuri king.[3] But an inscription informs us that the ambitions of Bhoja were frustrated shortly before *Śaka* 941=1019 A.D., when Vikramāditya V's successor, Jayasiṁha II Jagadekamalla (*c.* 1016-1042 A.D.), routed him and broke "the confederacy of Mālava". This Cālukya monarch is also represented to have gained an advantage over Rājendra Coḷa I, although Coḷa epigraphs testify to the contrary.

[1] Sir R.G. Bhandarkar calls him Vikramāditya I (*E. H. D.*, p. 140, n. 15).

[2] Some scholars identify the vanquished Cālukya prince with Jayasiṁha II.

[3] It is noteworthy that Gāṅgeyadeva Kalacuri is said to have achieved a victory over the king of Kuntala, who doubtless was a Cālukya ruler.

Someśvara I Āhavamalla (*A.D.* 1042-1068 *A.D.*)

In 1042 A.D., Jayasiṁha II Jagadekamalla was succeeded by his son, Someśvara I, whose *birudas* were Āhavamalla and Trailokyamalla. His father had already consolidated the Cālukya power, and so Someśvara I found himself in a better position to wage wars with the Coḷas and the Paramāras—the traditional enemies of his house. Taking advantage of Bhoja's depleted resources on account of constant military activities, Someśvara invaded Mālava and ravaged Māṇḍū and Dhārā. The Paramāra potentate, unable to resist fled towards Ujjain, which was also captured and plundered by the Cālukya forces. Subsequently Bhoja returned to the capital and reasserted his authority. Ominous clouds, however, again gathered fast, and Bhīma I of Anhilwāḍa (*c.* 1022-64 A.D.) and Laksmī-Karṇa Kalacuri (*c.* 1041-72 A.D.) combined against Bhoja and threatened his dominions on two sides. The latter died in the course of the struggle, and the confederates too fell out over the division of the spoils of victory. At this juncture, Jayasiṁha, who claimed the Paramāra crown after Bhoja, invoked the aid of his family's former foe, Someśvara I. The response was prompt, for any disturbance in the political equilibrium of Central India was fraught with grave danger to the Cālukyas as well. Someśvara I soon drove the allied army of occupation out of Mālava and placed Jayasiṁha on its throne. Thus amid the shifting politics of the times, the relations between the Cālukyas and the Paramāras took a friendly turn, enabling Someśvara I to carry his arms further northward. But before we refer to these incursions, let us note how he fared with his antagonists in the south. The inscriptions of the Coḷas represent that as a result of their operations the Cālukya monarch suffered considerable losses. Whatever the truth, the battle of Koppam in 1052 A.D.,[1] in which Rājādhirāja I was killed, does not, at any rate, appear to have ended in favour of the Coḷas. Indeed, Bilhaṇa, the famous author of the *Vikramāṅkadevacarita*, would have us believe that on one occasion Someśvara I even stormed Kāñcī, then an important seat of Coḷa power. In his wars he was ably assisted by his son, Vikramāditya (VI), a valiant youth. When Someśvara I became comparatively free from his southern pre-occupations, he turned his attention to the alluring Gangetic Doab, which was in a state of turmoil owing to the rapacity of successive invaders after the disintegration of the Pratīhāra empire. His forces marched right across Central India unchecked by the Candellas and the Kacchapaghātas, and the Yewur tablet[2] tells us that the king of Kānyakubja, probably identical with one of the Rāṣṭrakūṭa princes ruling there during this period of confusion,[3] being afraid of Someśvara I's might "quickly experiences an abode among the caves." This expedition of the Cālukyas and their continued progress eastward could not have been a matter of indifference to Laksmī-Karṇa Kalacuri, who seems to have exercised some sort of control over *Madhyadeśa* in the hey-day of his glory.[4] Accordingly, he tried to checkmate their advance, but all efforts were in vain and he sustained a defeat. Someśvara I's energetic son Vikramāditya (VI) overran Mithilā, Magadha, Aṅga,

[1] Koppam has been identified with Khidrāpur at the confluence of the Kriṣṇā and Pañca-gaṅgā rivers, *Ep. Ind.*, XII, pp. 296-98. For an account of the battle, see *S. I. I.*, III, pp. 29, 63, 112, etc. Curiously, the Cālukya inscriptions of the time of Someśvara I do not give us any information regarding the battle of Koppam.

[2] *Ind. Ant.*, VIII, p. 19.

cf. कन्याकुब्जाधिराजो भजति च तरसा कन्दरस्थानमादेरुद्दामो यत् प्रतापप्रसरभरभयोद्भूतिविभ्रान्तचित्तः ।

[3] *History of Kanauj*, pp. 289-90.

[4] *History of Kanauj*, p. 295.

Vaṅga, and Gauḍa, meeting with little or no opposition from the decadent Pāla monarchy. Ratnapāla of Kāmarūpa, however, beat back the Cālukya army, which then returned home by way of southern Kośala. Thus under Someśvara I, the Cālukyas grew strong and their influence was felt in remote parts of India.

Someśvara I founded a new capital at Kalyāṇa (modern Kalyāṇī in the Nizām's dominions) and made it a prosperous town. His death in 1068 A.D. came about in a strange manner. It is said that he got a malignant type of fever, and when he was past recovery he ceremoniously entered the waters of the Tuṅgabhadrā, chanting *mantras*, and drowned himself.[1]

Someśvara II Bhuvanaikamalla

In 1068 A.D., Someśvara I Āhavamalla was succeeded by his eldest son, the *Yuvarāja* Someśvara II, otherwise called Bhuvanaikamalla. The accession was quite peaceful. His younger brother, Vikramāditya, to whom should go the credit for most of the military achievements of Āhavamalla's reign, was then engaged in campaigns against the Coḷas and the country of Veṅgī. Having received the sad tidings of his father's death, Vikramāditya hurried to the capital and offered allegiance to the new sovereign. But, as we shall see below, not long after the relations between the two brothers became strained, and in consequence Someśvara II lost the throne. There is nothing to show that the latter attained any distinction; his only exploit during a rule of about eight years was a successful attack on Jayasiṁha of Mālava—a partisan of Vikramāditya.

[1] It is known as *Jalasamādhi* (*E.H.D.*, p. 144, n. 36).

Vikramāditya VI Tribhuvanamalla—(A.D. 1076-1126 A.D.)[1]

The *Vikramāṅkadevacarita* of Bilhaṇa throws some interesting light on the circumstances which raised Vikramāditya or Vikramāṅka to kingly dignity. We are told that Someśvara II Bhuvanaikamalla was tyrannical and distrustful, and this led to discontent among the people and the alienation of Vikramāditya's sympathies. The latter thereupon got away from the capital with his followers and younger brother Jayasiṁha, and repaired towards the Tuṅgabhadrā. Then passing through the land of Banavāsī (North Kanārā), Vikramāditya brought his military talents into play and subdued the ruler of Konkan, Jayakeśin by name, and other southern powers. Vikramāditya next tried conclusions with the Coḷa monarch, Vīra-Rājendra, who not only came to terms with him but also gave him the hand of his daughter. This alliance involved Vikramāditya in fresh troubles, for when confusion broke out in the Coḷa realm after the death of Vīra-Rājendra, he had to go post-haste to Kāñcī to help his brother-in-law. The latter's career was, however, cut short by Kulottuṅga I (Rājiga) of Veṅgī, who, in order to ward off Vikramāditya's expected attack, appealed to Someśvara II for succour. Vikramāditya at once took up the gauntlet and worsted both the opponents. Someśvara II was captured and ultimately deposed. Thus, Vikramāditya VI assumed the reins of government at Kalyāṇa in 1076 A.D., which is the initial year of the *Cālukya-Vikrama* era started by him.

Vikramāditya VI was doubtless the most striking personality in the dynasty. After becoming king he directed his energies more towards peace than military adventures. He promoted art and learning, and his

[1] Sir R. G. Bhandarkar styles him Vikramāditya II (*E.H.D.*, p. 148).

court attracted distinguished men from far and near. He was the patron of the celebrated Kashmiri writer, Bilhaṇa, who immortalised his master's exploits in the *Vikramāṅkadevacarita*, and also of Vijñāneśvara, author of the *Mitākṣarā*—an authoritative treatise on Hindu law. It should not, however, be understood that Vikramāditya VI's protracted reign of about half a century was marked by "victories of Peace" only; he had to unsheathe his sword time and again. Indeed, on reviving friendship with the Paramāras he soon got entangled into hostilities with the Cālukyas of Anhilwāḍa. Another storm Vikramāditya VI had to face was the revolt of his younger brother Jayasiṁha, whom he had appointed Viceroy of the Banavāsī province. But despite Jayasiṁha's intrigues and machinations, the uprising miscarried and was suppressed. Further, Vikramāditya VI curbed the inroads of the Coḷa king and of the Hoysala Viṣṇuvardhana, who challenged the might of the Cālukya monarch towards the close of his career.

Later Rulers

Vikramāditya VI's son and successor, Someśvara III Bhūlokamalla, ruled from A.D. 1126 to 1138 A.D. It is, of course, doubtful whether his alleged exploits deserve credence, but he certainly encouraged learning and himself wrote the *Mānasollāsa* dealing with topics of varied interest. Someśvara III's son, Jagadekamalla II (*c.* A.D. 1138—1151 A.D.), appears to have been a figure of some note. Having checked the encroachments of the Hoysalas, Jagadekamalla II attacked Jayavarman Paramāra and wrested a portion of Mālava. This was followed by a clash with Kumārapāla of Anhilwāḍa, who could never tolerate Jagadekamalla II's activities in Mālava. In the time of his brother, Nurmaḍi Taila, the Western Cālukya kingdom suffered considerable diminution owing to the ambitions and treasonable designs of his Kalacuri minister for war, Vijjala or Vijjana. With the assistance of some disgruntled feudatories, the latter drove away his sovereign southward and himself usurped the throne in 1157 A.D. The Western Cālukya power then remained in abeyance for almost a quarter of a century, but in 1182 A.D. Nurmaḍi Taila's son, Vīra Soma or Someśvara IV, recovered a part of his ancestral territories with Annigeri in the Dhārvāḍa district as capital. He continued to flourish at least up to 1189 A.D., after which nothing is heard of him. Presumably, he met his doom while defending his reduced dominions on two fronts against the aggressions of the Yādavas of Devagiri and the Hoysalas of Dvārasamudra.

The Kalacuri Interregnum

As mentioned above, Vijjala or Vijjana subverted the Western Cālukya authority in 1157 A.D. and initiated a new line, which had a brief existence until 1182 A.D. He belonged to the Kalacuri race, and was at first a *mahāmaṇḍaleśvara* and *daṇḍanāyaka* under Nurmaḍi Taila. Vijjala gradually strengthened his position, and by 1162 A.D. he even assumed the Imperial titles. His reign has been made memorable by Bāsava, who, besides occupying the exalted office of chief minister, played an important role in the religious history of the period. The latter was the founder of a sect, and his followers, called Vīra Śaivas or Liṅgāyatas, are still numerous in the Kanarese country and Mysore. They are ardent devotees of Śiva in the *liṅga* form and of his *vāhana* (vehicle) Nandin, and do not recognise the sanctity or infallibility of the Vedas. They have their sacred works, one of them being the *Bāsava-Purāṇa*. They do not uphold the caste-system and have got other social and doctrinal differences with orthodox Hinduism. Bāsava's creed spread rapidly, and the Jains specially began to lose ground. This was not liked by Vijjala, who was probably an adherent of Jainism. Accordingly, their relations became strained, and it is said that in some strange manner Bāsava hastened or brought about the end of Vijjala. Whatever the truth, Vijjala's son, Sovideva or Soma, tried to put down Bāsava and perhaps succeeded. The successors of Sovideva are mere names, and we hardly know anything about them. In 1182 A.D. Someśvara IV overthrew the last Kalacuri ruler, and thus the Western Cālukyas once more came into the limelight for a few years.

SECTION D

THE YĀDAVA RULERS OF DEVAGIRI[1]

Origin and growth of power

The Yādavas are said to have descended from the race of Yadu, to which belonged the great Mahābhārata hero, Krisṇa. Unfortunately, their early history is obscure, but there can hardly be any doubt that they were a feudatory family when the Rāṣṭrakūṭas of Mānyakheṭa and the Western Cālukyas of Kalyāṇa held sway in the Dekkan. After the decline of the latter, the Yādavas rose into prominence and in course of time established an extensive empire. The first noteworthy figure in the dynasty was Bhillama V, who, taking advantage of the moribund condition of the Western Cālukya monarchy as a result of the Kalacuri usurpation and the aggressions of the Hoysalas, wrested in *c.* 1187 A.D. the territories to the north of the Krisṇā from the feeble hands of Someśvara IV. Bhillama V fixed his capital at Devagiri, modern Daulatābād in the Hyderabad State, and also assumed the Imperial titles. His arms did not, however, progress much towards the south, for in or about the year 1191 A.D. he was

[1] R. G. Bhandarkar, *E. H. D.*, 3rd ed., Sec. xiv-xv, pp. 170-209; *Bom. Gaz.*, Vol. I, pt. II.

defeated, and perhaps slain, by Vīra-Ballāla I Hoysala at the battle of Lakkuṇḍi (Dhārvāḍa district). Bhillama's successor was his son, Jaitugi or Jaitrapāla I (*c.* 1191-1210 A.D.), who killed Rudradeva, lord of the Tailaṅgas (Trikaliṅgas), in a hard-fought contest, and placed the latter's nephew Gaṇapati on the Kākatīya throne. Thus, the Yādavas gradually extended their influence among their contemporaries.

Siṅghaṇa

Siṅghaṇa, son of Jaitugi I, was the most energetic personality in the Yādava line, and during his long rule from *c.* 1210 to 1247 A.D. he is represented to have conquered many lands. He routed Vīrabhoja about 1215 A.D. and annexed the Śilāhāra realm of Kolhāpur after the fall of the fortress of Parnāla or Panhala. Further, Siṅghaṇa avenged his grandfather's discomfiture by pushing his authority beyond the Kriṣṇā at the cost of Vīra-Ballāla II Hoysala. The Yādava ruler successfully tried conclusions with other opponents too, like Arjunavarman of Mālava and Jājalla, the Cedi chieftain of Chattīsgarh; and attacked Gujarat at least twice in the time of the Vaghela princes. In consequence of these military achievements of Siṅghaṇa, the Yādava kingdom grew to almost as imposing dimensions as that of the Western Cālukyas had done.

Siṅghaṇa's court was graced by Sāraṅgadhara, whose chief contribution to the literature of the day was an excellent work on music called the *Saṅgīta-Ratnākara*. A commentary on it is extant, and there are grounds to believe that it was written by the king himself.[1] Another distinguished protégé of Siṅghaṇa was Cāṅgadeva, the astronomer, who founded a college (*maṭha*) at Patna (Khāndesh district) for the study of Bhāskarā-

[1] Or, was the commentary attributed to Siṅghaṇa by one of his literary protégés?

cārya's *Siddhānta-Siromaṇi* and other astronomical treatises.[1]

Later Yādava Kings

Siṅghaṇa was succeeded by his grandson, Kriṣṇa or Kanhara (*c.* 1247-60 A.D.). It appears that he, too, came into conflict with the rulers of Mālava, Gujarat, and Konkan. Kriṣṇa was a devout follower of the Brahmanical religion, and to his reign may be ascribed the *Sūktimuktāvalī*, a collection of verses by Jalhaṇa, and Amalānanda's *Vedānta-Kalpataru*—a Vedāntic commentary.

Kriṣṇa was followed by his brother, Mahādeva (*c.* 1260-71 A.D.), who is recorded to have annexed northern Konkan from the Śilāhāras, "reduced the arrogant sovereigns of Karṇāṭa and Lāṭa to mockery," and overawed the Kākatīya queen, Rudrāṁbā. In the time of Mahādeva and Rāmacandra or Rāmarāja (*c* 1271-1309 A.D.) flourished the great Brahman minister (*mantrin*) Hemādri or Hemādpant, well known for his writings on Hindu Dharmaśāstra. His most important work is the *Caturvarga-Cintāmaṇi*, divided into four parts and an appendix. He is also said to have introduced a special form of temple architecture in the Dekkan, and perhaps invented, or made modifications in, the Moḍī script. We further learn that Rāmacandra was a patron of saint Jñāneśvara, who wrote a Marāṭhī commentary on the *Bhagavad-Gītā* in 1290 *A.D.*

Moslem invasions

It was during the reign of Rāmacandra that the Moslem army led by Alāuddīn Khiljī, then governor of Karrā, marched towards the south and suddenly invested Devagiri in 1294 A.D. Rāmacandra having

[1] *E.H.D.*, pp. 194-95.

retired to the fort, his son, Śaṅkara, advanced to his relief. But all was in vain, and Rāmacandra had to conclude a humiliating treaty, by which he stipulated to pay to Alāuddīn "600 maunds of pearls, two of jewels, 1,000 of silver, 4,000 pieces of silk and other precious articles", besides ceding Ellichpur and promising an annual tribute to Delhi.[1] It was, however, not sent regularly, and so when Alāuddin seized the throne he despatched his trusted general, Malik Kāfūr, to Devagiri in 1307 A.D. Rāmacandra was taken prisoner[2] and brought to Delhi, but Alāuddīn purchased his loyalty by releasing him. In 1309 A.D., Rāmacandra died and soon after his successor, Śaṅkara, stopped payment of tribute to Delhi. This provoked reprisals, and in 1312 A.D. Malik Kāfūr defeated and killed Śaṅkara. Thus the Yādava line came to an inglorious end. Subsequently, Rāmacandra's son-in-law, Harapāla, attempted to raise the standard of revolt against the Moslems; he was, however, crushed and barbarously flayed alive under the orders of Sultān Mubārak.

Section E

THE KĀKATĪYAS OF WARANGAL

Origin

The exact derivation of the name Kākatīya is uncertain. It has sometimes been connected with the word *Kākata* signifying 'a crow', or with the name of a local form of goddess Durgā, but these suggestions would hardly bear scrutiny. Nor is our information regarding the ancestry of the Kākatīyas more definite. Their mythical genealogy, which includes many names of Raghu's family, indicates that they probably belonged

[1] Briggs, Firishta, Vol. I, p. 310.

[2] Elliot, *History of India*, III, pp. 77, 200.

to the solar race of the Kṣatriyas. On the other hand, several inscriptions of the Nellore district distinctly state that the Kākatīyas were Śūdras.

Brief account

The Kākatīyas were at first feudatories of the Later Cālukyas, after whose decline they rose to power in Teliṅgānā and exercised authority there, with various vicissitudes, until its conquest by the Bahmani Sultān, Ahmad Shah, about 1424-25 A.D. The earlier seat of Kākatīya government was Anmakoṇḍa (or Hanumakoṇḍa), but subsequently Warangal (or Orungallu) became their capital. The first prince to bring the family into prominence was Prolarāja, one of whose records is dated in the Cālukya-Vikrama *Saṁvat* 42=1117-18 A.D. He distinguished himself in warfare against the Western Cālukyas, and ruled for a long time. After the reigns of Rudra (*acc. c.* 1160 A.D.) and his younger brother, Mahādeva, the latter's son, Gaṇapati, ascended the Kākatīya throne in 1199 A.D. He was the most mighty monarch of the line, and he continued to wield the sceptre for at least sixty-two years, as recorded in an inscription. He is represented to have successfully measured swords with the kings of Coḷa, Kaliṅga, Seuṇa (i.e., the Yādava ruler), Karṇāṭa Lāṭa, and Vaḷanāḍu. Gaṇapati was able to win these achievements owing perhaps to the weakness of the Coḷa sovereign and the confused political situation in southern India in the second quarter of the 13th century. Being without a son, Gaṇapati was succeeded by his daughter, Rudrāṁbā, in *c.* 1261 A.D. She ruled sagaciously, and it is said she assumed the male name of Rudradeva-Mahārāja. After a reign of nearly thirty years, Rudrāṁbā was followed by her grandson, Pratāparudradeva, who has been immortalised by Vaidyanātha's *Pratāparudrīya*—a work on poetics dedicated to him. Pratāparudra was the last great king of the Kākatīya dynasty, and he had to submit to the yoke of the Moslems during the destructive southern raid of Malik Kāfūr. Thenceforward the Kākatīyas began to sink into insignificance, and eventually their kingdom passed into the hands of the Bahmani Sultāns of the Dekkan. It is believed that scions of the family then migrated and founded the small principality of Bastar.

II

Section F

THE ŚILĀHĀRAS[1]

Origin

The Śilāhāras or Śilāras claim to be the descendants of the mythical Jimūtavāhana, king of the Vidyādharas, who, according to tradition, offered himself as an *āhāra* (food) to Garuḍa in place of a serpent. Whatever the value of the story, the Śilāhāras appear to have been Kṣatriyas.

History

There are three branches of the Śilāhāra family known to history. Their original home was probably Tagara or Ter. They never became an Imperial power, having been subordinate to the Rāṣṭrakūṭas, Cālukyas, or the Yādavas in turn. The oldest Śilāhāra house ruled over south Konkan from the last quarter of the eighth century A.D. to about the second decade of the eleventh century A.D. Their seat of government was at Goa and later perhaps at Kharepatan. The second family held sway over northern Konkan for roughly four centuries and a half from the beginning of the ninth century A.D. Their territory included the Thānā and Ratnagiri dis-

[1] Dr. Altekar, "The Śilāhāras of Western India" (*Indian Culture*, Vol. II, No. 3, pp. 393-434).

tricts and a part of the Sūrat district. Their chief town was Thānā, and Purī (western) was a sort of a secondary capital. The third Śilāhāra branch established its authority about the commencement of the eleventh century A.D. in Kolhāpur and the districts of Satārā and Belgaum.[1] For a time, it was also master of southern Konkan. This family enjoyed more independence, and one of its kings, Vijayārka or Vijayāditya, is said to have helped Vijjana or Bijjala in bringing about the downfall of the last Cālukya sovereign. The most notable monarch of the line was, however, Bhoja (*c.* 1175-1210 AD.), after whom the kingdom was conquered by Siṅghaṇa, the Yādava prince.

SECTION G

THE KADAMBAS[2]

Derivation

The Kadambas are described as Brahmans belonging to the Mānavya *gotra*,[3] and their family name is, curiously enough, said to have been derived from a Kadamba tree, which stood in front of their house.

History

The exact circumstances of the foundation of the Kadamba power are obscure. A tradition avers that a Brahman adventurer named Mayūraśarman took up arms on account of some fancied insult he met with in Kāñcī, the Pallava capital,[4] and established a principa-

[1] Kolhāpur or Panhala was their capital; and they were worshippers of the goddess Mahālakṣmī.

[2] See G. M. Moraes, The *Kadamba-Kula*, 1931.

[3] Although Brahmans, the Kadambas did not discourage Jainism, which, along with Śaivism, prospered under their rule.

[4] See the Talagunda inscription of Kakusthavarman (*Ep. Ind.*, VIII, pp. 24-36). cf. "There, enraged by a fierce quarrel with a Pallava horseman (he reflected): 'Alas, that in this Kali-age the

lity in Karṇāṭaka with Banavāsī as his seat of government. This happened about the middle of the fourth century A.D., when the Pallavas were menaced by the aggressions of Samudragupta in the south. The immediate successors of Mayūraśarman were almost nonentities until we come to Kakusthavarman, during whose reign the Kadamba dominion and influence grew considerably. The next noteworthy Kadamba king was Ravivarman (first few decades of the sixth century A.D.); he made Halsī (Belgaum district) his capital, and successfully fought against the Gaṅgas and the Pallavas. The rise of the Cālukyas of Vātāpi then dealt a severe blow to the ambitions of the Kadambas. Their northern territories were wrested by Pulakeśin I, and Pulakeśin II finally reduced them to subservience and insignificance. The Gaṅgas also aggrandised themselves at the cost of the southern portion of the Kadamba kingdom. The family, however, did not wholly disappear, for Kadamba princes again emerged into prominence about the last quarter of the tenth century A.D. after the decline of the Rāṣṭrakūṭas. These Kadamba branches[1] ruled various parts of the Dekkan and Konkan till almost the close of the thirteenth century A.D., but their activities were of local interest only.

SECTION H

THE GAṄGAS OF TALKĀḌ[2]

Descent

The origin of the Gaṅgas is uncertain. It is said

Brāhmans should be so much feebler than the Kṣatriya" (*Ibid.*, pp. 32, 34, vv. 11 and 12).

[1] Hangal (Dhārwāḍa district) and Goa were the main centres of the Later Kadambas.

[2] See *The Gaṅgas of Talkāḍ* by M. V. Krisna Rao (Madras, 1936).

that they belonged to the lineage of Ikṣvāku, whereas other traditions connect them with the river Gaṅgā or with the sage Kaṇva.

Short account

The kingdom of the Gaṅgas comprised the greater part of Mysore and was called after them Gaṅgavāḍi. It was founded by Didiga (Konganivarman) and Mādhava some time in the fourth century A.D. At first, the capital was Kuluvala (Kolar?), but about the middle of the fifth century A.D. it was transferred to Talavanapura or Talkāḍ on the Kāverī in the Mysore district by Harivarma. One of the notable early Gaṅga kings was Durvinīta,[1] who distinguished himself in warfare with the Pallavas. He was also an author, a Sanskrit version of the Paiśācī *Brihat-kathā* and other works being attributed to him. Another great Gaṅga monarch was Śripuruṣa (*c.* 726-76 A.D.). He not only successfully contended against the rising power of the Rāṣṭrakūṭas, but even inflicted a crushing defeat on the Pallavas at Vilardi. During the eighth and ninth centuries A.D. the Gaṅgas were greatly harassed by the aggressive activities of the Eastern Cālukyas of Veṅgī, the Rāṣṭrakūṭas of Malkhed and other neighbours. Indeed, the Gaṅga king, Śivamāra, was taken captive and his territories annexed by Dhruva Nirupama (*c.* 779-94 A.D.). In the confusion following the accession of Govinda III, Śivamāra attempted to recover his lost authority; he was, however, firmly put down and Gaṅgavāḍi remained under a Rāṣṭrakūṭa governor. The fortunes of the family were to some extent retrieved by Rājamalla (*acc. c.* 818 A.D.), but still the Rāṣṭrakūṭas continued to be a serious menace to the safety and

[1] Probably the second half of the sixth century A.D. According to Dubreuil, however, Durvinīta's date is *c.* 605-50 A.D. (see *Ante*).

integrity of the Gaṅga realm. Later on, the Gaṅgas became involved in fighting with the Coḷas, and by 1004 A.D. Talkad was captured and the Gaṅgā sovereignty extirpated. The Gaṅga line did not, of course, become extinct, for history records the existence of Gaṅga chiefs as vassals of the Hoysalas and the Coḷas.

Many of the Gaṅga princes were inclined towards Jainism. Avinīta, for instance, was brought up under the care of Vijayakīrti, and the former's son, Durvinīta, was a patron of the famous Jain *Ācārya*, Pūjyapāda. Similarly, during the reign of Rājamalla IV (*c.* 977-85 A.D.), his minister and general Cāmuṇḍarāya, a devout Jain, erected in 983 A.D. the celebrated image of Gomaṭeśvara at Śravaṇabelgola.

Section I

THE HOYSALAS OF DVĀRASAMUDRA

Name and ancestry

The Hoysalas (Poysalas) described themselves in their records as "Yādavakulatilaka" or "Kṣatriyas of the lunar race." Whatever the truth in this claim, the historical founder of the dynasty was a certain Sāla, who became noted for having struck and killed a tiger with an iron rod at the behest of a sage. It is said that this circumstance (Poy Sāla, i.e., strike, Sāla) gave to the family the name of Poysala or Hoysala.

Historical Survey

The Hoysalas emerge into prominence about the beginning of the eleventh century A.D. The early princes of this line exercised control over a small area in Mysore, and owed allegiance either to the Coḷa sovereigns or to the Later Cālukyas of Kalyāṇa. Gradually, Vinayāditya (*acc. c.* 1045 A.D.) and his son Ereyaṅga, who ably assisted the Cālukya overlord in his campaigns, increased their power, but it was not until the time of Biṭṭiga Viṣṇuvardhana (*c.* 1110-40 A.D.) that the Hoysalas attained a position of some importance in the politics of southern India. He transferred the capital from Velāpura (modern Belūr, Hasan district) to Dvārasamudra (Halebid), and made himself almost independent of his Cālukya suzerain, Vikramāditya VI, although Viṣṇuvardhana did not formally assume the Imperial titles. He is represented to have humbled the Coḷas, the Pāṇḍyas of Madurā, the people of Malabar, the Tuluvas of South Kanārā, the Kadambas of Goa, and even carried his arms towards the river Kriṣṇā and Kāñcī. Thus, Viṣṇuvardhana established his authority over an extensive territory, which included nearly the whole of Mysore and adjacent lands. In his beliefs he appears to have been originally a Jain, but after coming into contact with the celebrated *Ācārya*, Rāmānuja, Vaiṣṇavism got the chief place in Viṣṇuvardhana's affections.

The next noteworthy ruler of the house was Viṣṇuvardhana's grandson, Vīra-Ballāla I (*c.* 1172-1215 A.D.), who was the first to style himself *Mahārājādhirāja*. He signalised his reign by defeating Brahma, the general of Someśvara IV Cālukya, and also the forces of Bhillama V Yādava at the battle of Lakkuṇḍi (Dhārvāḍa district) in 1191 A.D. Vīra-Ballāla I's son and successor, Vīra-Ballāla II or Narasiṁha II, however, met with some reverses at the hands of the Yādava Siṅghaṇa, who extended his sway far beyond the Kriṣṇā. Not much is known of the subsequent Hoysala kings except that they were busy fighting with the Coḷas and the Pāṇḍyas. The last Hoysala monarch was Vīra-Ballāla III. About 1310 A.D., his kingdom was ravaged by the Moslem hosts under Malik Kāfūr, who, after plundering Devagiri, advanced against the Hoysala capital. It was sacked and the king fell a prisoner. When he was released after a brief captivity in

Delhi, Vīra-Ballāla III made an attempt to organise resistance to the Moslem invaders. But nothing availed him, and the Hoysala line came to a tragic end about the fifth decade of the fourteenth century A.D.

The Hoysalas were great builders of temples, and the numerous monuments, still extant at Halebid and other places, testify to their artistic achievements and love of religion.

CHAPTER XVIII

THE STATES OF THE SOUTHERN PENINSULA

SECTION A

Survey of early history

Not much is known of the early history of Southern India, comprising roughly the peninsula to the south of the Tuṅgabhadrā and Kriṣṇā rivers. Its population chiefly consists of what are called the Pre-Dravidian and Dravidian races. Among the former are the Minavar, the Villavar, and other cognate tribes, who represent the earliest inhabitants of the land. The Dravidians, however, are believed to be "later immigrants."[1] They had developed a higher culture, and their principal members, the Tamils, attained so dominant a position in Southern India as to give its greater part the name *Tamilakaṁ*[2] in ancient times. Then came the Aryans, and there are dim traditions of their southward movements reaching back to the age of the Vedic *Riṣi* Agastya, who is said to have established Brahmanical settlements on the distant Podiyur hill (Tinnevelly district), besides those in the Dekkan. With the influx of the Aryans, an important and vigorous element was, no doubt, introduced into the body politic of the South, but beyond superimposing

[1] *E.H.I.*, 4th ed., p. 457.

[2] Writing about the middle of the second century A.D., Ptolemy has corrupted the name *Tamilakaṁ* into *Damirike* or *Limyrike*.

their religion and to some extent their institutions, they could not essentially alter or modify the structure of Dravidian society, languages, and customs.

The traditional division of Southern India was into three kingdoms: (*a*) the Ceras or Keralas of the Malabar coast, occupying what are at present known as the States of Cochin and Travancore; (*b*) the Pāṇḍyas, whose territories included the modern districts of Madurā and Tinnevelly; (*c*) and the Coḷas, who ruled the tract to the north of the Pāṇḍya dominions up to the Pennar river along the east coast, called accordingly *Coḷa-maṇḍalaṁ*, from which is derived the English name Coromandel. The boundaries of these realms varied as their power waxed or waned in the course of their dynastic intrigues and internecine wars. There were also other petty principalities, too numerous to mention, but their chiefs maintained a precarious existence in constant dread of their stronger neighbours. It is noteworthy that none of the great southern kingdoms is referred to in Vedic literature, nor do they appear to have been known to the Sanskrit grammarian, Pāṇini.[1] But Kātyāyana, the celebrated commentator on the *Aṣṭādhyāyī*, whom Sir Ramkrishna Bhandarkar assigns to "the first half of the fourth century before Christ,"[2] was acquainted with both the Pāṇḍyas and the Coḷas. They are mentioned along with the Keralaputras (i.e., the Keralas) in the second Rock Edict of Aśoka also. Megasthenes, the Seleucid ambassador at the court of Candragupta Maurya, speaks of the Pāṇḍyan kingdom, its wealth, and the strength of its army; and the *Arthaśāstra* of Kauṭilya bears obvious evidence of familiarity with the South. Then, in the *Rāmāyaṇa* an allusion is made to the

[1] Sir R. G. Bhandarkar places Pāṇini about 700 B.C. (*E.H.D.*, 3rd ed., p. 16).

[2] *Ibid.*, p. 15.

grandeur of Madurā, the Pāṇḍya capital. Next, Patañjali (*circa* 150 B.C.) knew Kāñcī (Conjeeveram) and Kerala (Malabar); and the author of the *Periplus* (*c.* 81 A.D.) and the geographer Ptolemy (*c.* 140 A.D.) give some details regarding the principal ports and marts of the South. All these references doubtless indicate that the three kingdoms existed from a fairly remote antiquity.

The prosperity of Southern India was due to the fact that it produced spices, pepper, ginger, pearls, beryls, precious stones, and other articles of luxury, then in great demand among the peoples of the world. Thus, there grew up early a flourishing trade with western countries like Arabia, Chaldea, and Egypt, and also with the Far East and the Malay islands. We learn from the *Bible* that the "Ships of Tarshish" sent by Hiram, king of Tyre, brought for the temple constructed by the latter's mighty ally Soloman "ivory, apes, and peacocks" and "a great plenty of almug trees and precious stones" from Ophir (modern Sopārā in the Bombay Presidency).[1] Some of these commodities must have come from the South, as the Hebrew word *tuki-im* for peacock appears to be connected with the Tamil term *tokai*. Ancient Egypt also imported muslin, cinnamon etc. from Southern India, and one remarkable relic of commercial relations between the two countries is the *Oxyrhynchus Papyri*, a Greek farce on papyrus containing the story of a Greek lady who was ship-wrecked somewhere on the Kanarese coast. Likewise, the Greeks got ginger, pepper, and rice, etc. from South India, as the Greek words for them seem to have been derived from Tamil names. About 45 A.D., Hippalus, an Alexandrian merchant, discovered the phenomenon of monsoons, which made it

[1] See Rawlinson, *India* (1937), pp. 178-79.
cf. Ivory, Skt. *ibha-danta*, Hebrew *shen habbin*; Ape, Skt. *kapi*, Hebrew *koph*.

possible for mariners to cross the Arabian Sea in a much shorter time than they could do by keeping close to the coast. This gave considerable fillip to trade between South India and the Roman Empire. Pliny informs us that Roman gold to the extent of over a million sterling flowed annually into India in return for spices, pepper, pearls, beryls, tortoise-shell, aromatics, silks, and other Oriental luxuries; and this estimate can hardly be regarded as an exaggeration, considering the large finds of Roman coins of the first two centuries A.D. at several places in Southern India. To further their trade, Roman merchants are said to have established settlements at certain ports like Kāverīpaddanam (Puhār) and Muziris (Cranganore), where they even built a temple of Augustus.[1] Tamil writers also speak of "Yavana" ships visiting their ports with wine, vases, and gold, which were exchanged for the products of South India. Indeed, we are told that Dravidian rulers sometimes employed as their bodyguards "powerful Yavanas, dumb *Mlecchas*,[2] clad in long coats and armour"—so impressed were they by the smartness, prowess, and constancy of these foreigners. Thus, South India was early brought into contact with the outer world, and her people grew mighty and prosperous by their maritime and commercial activities.

Section B

THE PALLAVAS OF KĀÑCĪ[3]

Who were the Pallavas?

The origin of the Pallavas is one of the most vexed

[1] Smith, *E.H.I.*, 4th ed., pp. 462, 463, note 1. Other important trading towns in *Tamilakaṁ* were Korkai, Tondi, Bakarai, Kayal, etc.

[2] They are so described because their language being unintelligible they could express themselves only by gestures.

[3] R. Gopalan, *History of the Pallavas of Kāñcī*, Madras, 1928;

problems of ancient Indian history.[1] They find no place among the traditional three powers of Southern India, which, as mentioned above, are the Ceras, Pāṇḍyas, and the Coḷas. Accordingly, some scholars think that the Pallavas were foreign intruders, probably a branch of the Pahlavas or Parthians of North-western India. Apart from superficial similarity in names, there is, however, no evidence of any Pahlava migration into Southern India except perhaps into the Dekkan. Another theory is that the Pallavas were autochthons of the land, associated or allied with the Kurumbas, Kallars, Maravars, and other "predatory" tribes. After welding them, the Pallavas are believed to have emerged as a mighty political force. But Mr. M. C. Rasanayagam[2] holds that the Pallavas were of Coḷa-Nāga extraction, and belonged to the southern extremity of the peninsula and Ceylon. It is said that as a result of the *liaison* between Kiḷḷivaḷavan Coḷa and a Nāga princess, Pilivalai, daughter of king Vaḷaivaṇan of Maṇipallavaṁ (an island near the coast of Ceylon), a son was born to them named Iḷaṁ-Tiraiyan, who was made ruler of Toṇḍamaṇḍalaṁ by his father, and the dynasty thus founded came to be called after the name of the mother's native-place. Next, we may refer to the view put forward by Dr. Krishnaswami Aiyangar[3] that the Pallavas were known in the Sangam literature as Toṇḍaiyar, and they were descended from the Nāga chieftains, who were vassals of the Sātavāhana sovereigns. On the other hand, Dr. K. P. Jayasval[4] was of opinion that the Pallavas were "neither foreign-

Jouveau Dubreuil, *Ancient History of the Deccan* (1921); *The Pallavas*; Rev. Heras, *The Pallava Kings*; C. Minakshi, *Administration and Social Life under the Pallavas* (Madras, 1938).

[1] See R. Gopalan, *History of the Pallavas of Kāñcī*, pp. 15-27. This book has been very useful to me.

[2] *Ind. Ant.*, Vol. LII (April, 1923), pp. 77-82.

[3] *Jour. Ind. Hist.*, Vol. II, pt. I, (November, 1922), pp. 20-66 (The Origin and early History of the Pallavas of Kāñcī).

[4] *J. B. O. R. S.*, March-June, 1933, pp. 180-83.

ers nor Dravidians, but good Brahmin aristocrats from the North, military by profession", and that they were an offshoot of the Vākāṭakas. The suggestion regarding the northern affinities or affiliations of the Pallavas has probably some substance; for it is significant that their earliest charters are in Prākrit, and that they were also patrons of Sanskrit learning and culture. But their Brahmanical pedigree, despite certain traditions of their connections with Droṇācārya and Aśvatthāman, does not appear to be based on fact. Indeed, in the Talagunda inscription the Kadamba Mayūraśarman deplores the influence over Kāñcī of the "Pallava Kṣatriya," which expression doubtless indicates the Kṣatriya stock of the Pallavas.[1]

Beginnings of Pallava power

The earliest sources of Pallava history are three copper plate charters, in Prākrit,[2] assigned on palæographical grounds to the "third and fourth centuries of the Christian era."[3] They mention a set of rulers named Bappadeva, Śivaskandavarman, Buddhy (āṅkura), and Vīravarman. Whether Bappadeva was the actual founder of the Pallava power or not, there are reasons to believe that he held sway over the Telugu Andhrapatha and the Tamil Toṇḍamaṇḍalaṁ; the headquarters of the two regions were respectively Dhānyakaṭa (Dharaṇīkoṭṭa, near Amarāvatī) and

[1] *Ep. Ind.*, VIII, pp. 32, 34, v. 11, l. 4. cf. तत्र पल्लवाश्वसंस्थेन कलहेन तीव्रेण रोषित: कलियुगेऽस्मिन्नहो बत क्षत्रात् परिपेलवा विप्रता यतः। See also C. Mīnākshi, *Administration and Social Life under the Pallavas*, p. 13.

[2] (*a*) Mayiḍavolu (Guntur district) plates; (*b*) Hīrahaḍgalli plates and (*c*) Queen Cārudevī's grant found in the Guntur district.

[3] R. Gopalan, *History of the Pallavas of Kāñcī*, p. 32. I owe many suggestions and references to this book.

Kāñcī (modern Conjeeveram). His son, Śivaskandavarman, designated Dharmamahārāja, appears to have extended the kingdom, perhaps southward, for, unless justified by successful warfare, he would not have performed the *Aśvamedha*, *Vājapeya*, and *Agniṣṭoma* sacrifices. We learn from the Hīrahaḍgalli (Bellary district) plates recording his gift of a village in the Sātāhani-raṭṭa that southern Dekkan, at any rate, acknowledged his authority. Probably he was also called Vijaya-Skandavarman, but this identification is doubted by some scholars. Another important figure in early Pallava annals is Viṣṇugopa, who is mentioned in the Allahabad pillar inscription as king of Kāñcī. Being thus a contemporary of Samudragupta when he invaded the Dakṣiṇāpatha, Viṣṇugopa may be said to have flourished about the second quarter of the fourth century A.D. Unfortunately, his precise place in Pallava genealogy, or his relation with the monarchs of the Prākrit charters, is uncertain. Assuming, however, that they were his immediate predecessors, it may not be wide of the mark to date the rise of the Pallavas about the middle of the third century A.D.—the period which saw the dissolution of the Sātavāhana empire.

Pallavas of the Sanskrit Charters

Six sets of copper-plates, inscribed in Sanskrit, reveal the names of a number of Pallava princes—some mere *Yuvamahārājas* and more than a dozen of them kings who ruled roughly from the middle of the fourth to the last quarter of the sixth century A.D. These epigraphs give the regnal year of the donor, and are not dated in any known era, but on palæographical considerations they have been rightly ascribed to the fifth and sixth centuries A.D. Their object is merely to record gifts of land to pious Brahmans and shrines, and they throw little light on political events. It is not at all clear whether the sovereigns of the Prākrit and Sanskrit grants belonged to different branches or were directly connected, and even the chronology and order of succession of the latter group, are "far from settled." Nor do we get any definite information regarding the limits of their territory, or the founder of the line. Of course, this much we know that Vīrakurca or Vīrakurcavarman was the first to come into prominence after his marriage with a Nāga princess. Another noteworthy point about these Sanskrit charters is that they were issued from royal camps. Accordingly, it has been argued that Kāñcī had slipped from the grips of the Pallavas, presumably owing to a Coḷa incursion in the days of Karikāla, and they had to retire to the Nellore district.[1] The Velūrpāḷayam plate inscription[2] is even supposed to testify that the recapture of Kāñcī took place in the time of king Kumāraviṣṇu. The theory of a Coḷa interregnum is, however, open to objections; for, chronological difficulties apart, it is significant that the records of the Pallavas themselves nowhere give any indication of their loss of Kāñcī.

The Great Pallavas

With the last quarter of the sixth century A.D., we enter upon the most glorious epoch of Pallava history, and happily the materials, too, at our disposal yield us comparatively more data. A new Pallava dynasty was then founded by Siṁhaviṣṇu, also known as Siṁhaviṣṇupottarāyan and Avanisiṁha. He extended his sway up to the Kāverī at the cost of the Coḷas, and is further said to have defeated the Pāṇḍyas, Kaḷabhras, and the Mālavas (people of Malanāḍu?) in the course of his

Siṁhaviṣṇu.

[1] Venkayya, *A.S.R.*, 1906-07, p. 224.

[2] *S.I.I.*, II, pp. 503 f.

southern expeditions. He was probably a devotee of Viṣṇu.

Mahendravarman I

Siṁhaviṣṇu was succeeded by his son, Mahendravarman I or Mahendra-Vikrama, about the beginning of the seventh century A.D. A few years after his accession there began a deadly and long-drawn struggle between the Pallavas and the Cālukyas for supremacy in the South. Pulakeśin II claims in the Aihole inscription[1] to have vanquished "the lord of the Pallavas who had opposed the rise of his power" and made him "conceal his valour behind the ramparts of Kāñcīpura, enveloped in the dust of his armies." Pulakeśin II wrested from his opponent the province of Vengī, which was put in charge of his younger brother, Kubja-Viṣṇuvardhana-Viṣamasiddhi. As shown elsewhere, the latter's successors, designated the Eastern Cālukyas of Vengī, subsequently became independent of the Imperial house of Vātāpi (Bādāmi). The Kasakkuḍi plates,[2] on the other hand, depose that Mahendravarman I was victorious at Pullalūr (modern Pallur, Chingleput district). Although the enemy is not named, it is likely we have got a reference here to the Pallava monarch's success in driving back his Cālukya adversary when he attempted a thrust on Kāñcī itself.

Mahendravarman I originally professed Jainism, and was not well disposed towards other faiths. But about the middle of his reign, or earlier still, he abjured Jainism and turned a staunch Śaiva through the influence of Saint Appar. After Mahendravarman I's conversion, the Jains fell into disfavour, and Śaivism markedly

[1] *Ep. Ind.*, VI, pp. 6, 11, v. 29. cf. आक्रान्तात्मबलोन्नतिं बलरजः सञ्छन्नकाञ्चीपुरप्राकारान्तरितप्रतापमकरोद्यः पल्लवानां पतिम् ।

[2] S.-I. *I.*, Vol. II, part 3, p. 343.

revived and spread owing to the missionary activities of Saints Appar and Tirujñāna-Sambandar. Mahendravarman I appears to have been tolerant of other forms of Brahmanism. It is said that he constructed a rock temple in honour of Viṣṇu on the bank of a tank, called after him, in Mahendravāḍi (North Arcot district).[1] The Maṇḍagappattu inscription[2] further informs us that Mahendravarman I dedicated a shrine to Brahmā, Īśvara, and Viṣṇu, and that it was built without bricks, mortar, metal, and timber. Thus, Mahendravarman I introduced into Southern India the practice of hewing temples out of solid rocks. Indeed, one of his many *birudas* or epithets[3] was *Cettakāri* or *Caitya-kāri*, i.e., the builder of *Caityas* or temples. They were distinguished by certain peculiarities, specially cubical pillars. These rock-cut temples have been discovered at various places, such as Dalavaṅur (South Arcot district), Pallavaraṁ, Siyyamaṅgalaṁ, Vallaṁ (Chingleput district).

Mahendravarman I also gave a fillip to the arts of painting, dancing, and music; and the musical inscription at Kuḍumiyamalai in Pudukotta State is believed to have been incised at his instance. Besides, he is the reputed author of the *Mattavilāsa-prahasana*, a burlesque, which affords an interesting glimpse into the revelries and religious life of the Kāpālikas, Pāśupatas, Śākyabhikṣus, and other sects.

Narasiṁhavarman I

After the death of Mahendravarman I, his son Narasiṁhavarman I ascended the Pallava throne about the beginning of the second quarter of the seventh century A.D. He is one of the most striking personalities among the Pallava potentates. According to the

[1] *Ep. Ind.*, IV, pp. 152-53.
[2] *Ibid.*, XVII, pp. 14-17.
[3] See *History of the Pallavas of Kāñcī*, p. 90.

Kurram plates,[1] he successfully repulsed the onslaughts of Pulakeśin II Cālukya, who is said to have advanced almost up to the gates of Kāñcī. Not content with this achievement, Narasiṁhavarman I despatched a strong force under the command of his general, Siru Toṇḍa, nicknamed Paranjoti, against Vātāpi (Bādāmi). It was stormed in 642 A.D., and Pulakeśin II appears to have been killed while heroically defending his capital. For the next thirteen years Cālukya authority remained in abeyance, and Narasiṁhavarman I assumed the title of Vātāpikoṇḍa in commemoration of this great victory. Another epithet of his was Mahāmalla, which occurs in a fragmentary epigraph, discovered at Vātāpi, and written in letters of about the middle of the seventh century A.D.[2] Further, we learn that he sent two naval expeditions to Ceylon in support of Mānavamma, a claimant to its throne, who as a refugee at the court of Narasiṁhavarman I had rendered him loyal service. The first could not achieve any permanent results, and so the Pallava ships had again to set sail from the port of Mahābalipuram. This time Mānavamma's position became secure, and the invasion created such a profound impression on popular mind that it was long remembered like Śrī Rāmacandra's conquest of Laṅkā. Narasiṁhavarman I not only distinguished himself in warfare; he was also noted for his architectural activities. He is credited with the construction of several rock-cut temples in the Trichinopoly district and Pudukotta. Their general plan is almost similar to those excavated by Mahendravarman I except that the façades are more ornamental and the pillars, too, look more proportionate and elegant. Narasiṁhavarman I Mahāmalla founded, and called after his name, the town of Mahābalipuraṁ or Mahāmalla-

[1] *S. I. I.*, Vol. I, p 52.
[2] *Ind. Ant.*, IX, p. 99.

puraṁ, which he beautified by shrines like the Dharmarāja Ratha belonging to the group now known as the Seven Pagodas.

In Narasiṁhavarman I's reign, the celebrated Chinese pilgrim, Yuan Chwang, visited Kāñcī about the year 642 A.D. and stayed there for some time. According to him, the country, of which *Kin-chi-pu-lo* (Kāñcīpura) was the capital, was known as *Ta-lo-pi-ch'a* (Draviḍa). It was 6,000 *li* in circuit. "The soil is fertile and regularly cultivated, and produces abundance of grain. There are also many flowers and fruits. It produces precious gems and other articles. The climate is hot, the character of the people courageous. They are deeply attached to the principles of honesty and truth, and highly esteem learning; in respect of their language and written characters, they differ but little from those of Mid-India. There are some hundred of *Sanghārāmas* and 10,000 priests. They all study the teaching of the Sthavira (*Chang-tso-pu*) school belonging to the Great Vehicle. There are some eighty Deva temples, and many heretics called Nirgranthas."[1] Yuan Chwang says that the Tathāgata often came to this country to preach the Law, and Aśoka raised *stūpas* here to commemorate sacred sites. The pilgrim further informs us that the famous Buddhist teacher, Dharmapāla, hailed from Kāñcīpura.

Parameśvaravarman I

After the brief and uneventful reign of Mahendravarman II, who succeeded his father Narasiṁhavarman I about 655 A.D., Parameśvaravarman I acceeded to the throne. During his time the old enmity between the Pallavas and the Cālukyas revived, and, as usual, both sides claim victories for themselves. It is stated in the

[1] Beal, *Buddhist Records of the Western World*, Vol. II, pp. 228-29.

Gadval plates[1] that Vikramāditya I Cālukya captured Kāñcī, laid low the line of Mahāmalla,[2] and carried his arms up to Uragapura (Uraiyur, near Trichinopoly) on the river Kāverī. The Pallava records, on the contrary, represent Parameśvaravarman I as having put to flight, at the battle of Peruvaḷanallur in the Lalguḍi Tāluk of the Trichinopoly district, the army of Vikramāditya I, who had "only a rag" left for covering himself. The evidence being conflicting, it may be reasonably presumed that neither of the antagonists was able to have a decided advantage over the other. Parameśvaravarman I was a devotee of Śiva, and he built a number of temples in his realm in honour of that deity.

Narasiṁhavarman II

About the last decade of the seventh century A.D. Parameśvaravarman I died, and the sceptre passed on to his son, Narasiṁhavarman II Rājasiṁha. His reign was marked by peace and prosperity, and his chief title to fame is the building of the well-known Kailāśanātha or Rājasiṁheśvara temple. The Airāvateśvara at Kāñcī and the so-called Shore temple at Mahābalipuraṁ have also been attributed to him. Narasiṁhavarman II was a patron of men of letters, and it is believed that the great rhetorician Daṇḍin flourished at his court.

Narasiṁhavarman II was succeeded by Parameśvaravarman II, about whom we do not get much information from the sources available.

[1] *Ep. Ind.*, X, pp. 100-06.
cf. कृतपल्लवावमर्द्दं दक्षिणदिग्युवतिमात्तकाञ्चीकः ।
यो भृशमभिरमयन्नपि सुतरां श्रीवल्लभत्वमितः ॥
(*Ibid.*, pp. 103, 105, v. 4).

[2] *Ibid.*, pp. 103, 105, v. 5. cf. यो राजमल्लशब्दं विहितमहामल्लकुलनाशः ।

Nandivarman and his successors

When Parameśvaravarman II died about the second decade of the eighth century A.D., the kingdom was involved in civil war, each claimant making a bid for the throne. It appears from the testimony of the Kasakkuḍi plates and the sculptural representations inside the Vaikuṇṭhaperumal temple at Kāñcī that the people eventually chose as king a popular prince named Nandivarman, son of Hiraṇyavarman, who was a descendant of a brother of Siṁhaviṣṇu. During the reign of Nandivarman there was a renewal of the Pallava-Cālukya animosity. It is said that Vikramāditya II Cālukya invaded the Pallava territories shortly after coming to the throne in A.D. 733, and took their capital Kāñcī. Nandivarman, however, soon recovered the lost ground, and drove away the enemy. The Pallava monarch had also to contend against other powers, specially of the South, like the Dramiḷas (Tamils), the Pāṇḍyas, and a Gaṅga chief, who may be identified with Śripuruṣa (*c.* 726-76 A.D.). In his wars Nandivarman was ably assisted by his general Udayacandra. Further, it is alleged that Nandivarman suffered a reverse at the hands of Dantidurga, a prince of the Rāṣṭrakūṭa dynasty, which supplanted the Cālukyas of Vātāpi (Bādāmi) in the Dekkan about the middle of the eighth century A.D.

Nandivarman ruled for at least sixty-five years according to an inscription discovered at the Ādivarāha temple at Mahābalipuraṁ. He bore the epithet Pallavamalla, and was a Vaiṣṇava by faith. He is credited with having built a number of religious edifices.

Nandivarman's successor was Dantivarman, his son by queen Revā, probably a Rāṣṭrakūṭa princess. It is believed that she was the daughter of Dantidurga, who, after the cessation of warlike relations with Nandivarman Pallavamalla, married her to him. But in spite of this alliance, Govinda III is recorded to have attacked Kāñcī about the year 804 A.D., and vanquished its ruler Dantiga (Dantivarman). The latter, whose reign lasted a little over half a century from *circa* 776 to 828 A.D., also measured swords with the Pāṅdyas—the traditional opponents of his house. So did his successors, Nandi (*c.* 828-51 A.D.) and Nripatuṅgavarman (*c.* 851-76 A.D.). The last important sovereign of the line was Aparājitavarman (*c.* 876-95 A.D.), who, having allied himself with the Gaṅga prince, Prithvīpati I, inflicted a crushing defeat about 880 A.D. on the Pāṇḍya monarch, Varaguṇa II, in the battle of Śrī Puṟambīyam near Kumbhakoṇam. These conflicts went on until the Pallava power received its deathblow by the arms of the Coḷa king, Āditya I, who overwhelmed Aparājitavarman and annexed Toṇḍamaṇḍalaṁ. Thus, the once mighty Pallava kingdom ceased to exist as a factor in the politics of the South. Some other minor princes are, no doubt, known from inscriptions, but their position in the Pallava genealogy is uncertain.

Administration

In the course of their rule for about seven centuries, the Pallavas left an indelible impress on the administration, religion, literature, and art of the Tamil country. Let us now consider each of these aspects in brief:

At the head of the government was the king, called in inscriptions Mahārāja and Dharmamahārāja. He was assisted by a body of ministers or councillors (*rahasyādikadas*) in the disposal of state business, and his orders were drawn up by his private secretary. As in the Maurya and Gupta administrations, there was a regular hierarchy of officials, civil and military. Thus, in a Pallava inscription the king is said to have sent greetings to the princes (*rājakumāra*), rulers of district (*raṭṭika*), chief *Madambas* (customs officers), local prefects (*deśā-*

dhikata)........the free-holders of the various villages (*gāma-gāmabhojaka*)........ministers (*amaccha*), guards (*arakhadikata*), *gūmikas* (captains, or forest-officers?), *dūtikas* (messengers?), spies (*sanjarantakas*), and warriors (*bhaḍamanuṣas*). The territory of the empire was divided into provinces (*rāṣṭras* or *maṇḍalas*), which were governed by princes of the blood royal or by scions of noble and distinguished families. Other smaller divisions were *koṭṭaṁs* and *nāḍus* having their own officers. Regarding the organisation of the village (*grāma* or *gāma*), which was the lowest and most important unit of administration, we do not get much information from the early Pallava records, but during the time of the later Pallavas the village *Sabhā* with the various committees for the management and upkeep of gardens, temples, public baths, tanks, etc., so characteristic of rural life under the Coḷas, appears to have existed. Besides, the *Sabhā* exercised judicial functions and acted as the trustee of public endowments. There was an efficient system of irrigation and land-survey. The village boundaries were properly marked, and full details of arable and fallow lands were collected for revenue purposes as well as for making grants to pious and learned Brahmans. Taxation was elaborate, and we are told that the king laid claim to eighteen kinds of dues (*aṣṭādaśaparihāras*) from the village people. Some idea of these exactions may be had from the exemptions enumerated in inscriptions. For instance, the Hīrahaḍagalli plates refer to the immunity granted from the taking of sweet and sour milk and sugar......from taxes...... forced labour......grass and wood......vegetables and flowers, etc. The Taṇḍantoṭṭam plates also give freedom from the following taxes : duty on oil-press and looms, *uḷaviyakūli*, the fee on marriages, *ureṭṭu* fee on potters, *taṭṭukāyam*, duty on toddy-drawers and shepherds, fee on stalls, brokerage fee, *tirumugakkāṇaṁ*, royalty paid for the manufacture of salt; the good cow, the good bull, *vattināḷi*, fee on baskets of grain exposed for sale in the market, areca-nuts exposed for sale in the shops, etc.[1] Thus, the resources of the people were fully tapped and harnessed in the interests of administration, which was well organised.

Literature

During the rule of the Pallavas there was considerable literary activity, and Sanskrit enjoyed royal patronage. Barring a few, all the early Pallava inscriptions are in that language, and even in the later ones, where Tamil is used, the *praśasti* portions are in Sanskrit of a high order. Kāñcī, the capital, seems to have been a recognised centre of learning and culture from quite early times.[2] Hither came the famous Buddhist dialectician, Digṅāga, to satisfy his intellectual and spiritual thirst, and about the middle of the fourth century A.D. the Brahman Mayūraśarman, who founded the Kadamba line, is said to have completed his Vedic studies here. The Vedic colleges were then located in temples endowed by the rich and the devout. Further, Siṁhaviṣṇu (last quarter of the sixth century) is represented as having invited the great poet, Bhāravi, to his court, and it is believed that Daṇḍin, the celebrated writer on poetics, lived in the reign of Narasiṁhavarman II Rājasiṁha (end of the seventh century A.D.). Among other contemporaries of Daṇḍin, we may mention Mātridatta. One of the Pallava kings, Mahendravarman I, was himself probably an author of repute. To him has been attributed a burlesque named the *Mattavilāsa-prahasana*. Some scholars are also of opinion that "the Sanskrit plays published recently in Trivandrum as Bhāsa's were abrid-

[1] *S. I. I.*, Vol. II, pp. 530-31.

[2] See also V. R. R. Dikshitar, "A Hindu University at Kāñcī," (*Dr. Krishnasvāmi Aiyangar Commemoration Volume*, 1936, pp. 304-07).

gments, made during this period, of earlier works of Bhāsa and Śūdraka for being staged at the Pallava court."[1] Whatever the truth, the Pallava monarchs were certainly patrons of men of letters.

Religion

According to Yuan Chwang, the country, whose capital was Kāñcīpura, had "some hundred of *Saṅghārāmas* and 10,000 priests. They all study the teaching of the Sthavira (*Chang-tso-pu*) school belonging to the Great Vehicle."[2] He further deposes that Dharmapāla, the well-known Buddhist teacher, hailed from Kāñcīpura. Thus, Buddhism was not decadent in the Pallava kingdom; indeed, some of the early princes of the family were votaries of this faith. Similarly, Yuan Chwang refers to the existence of "many Nirgranthas." Mahendravarman I was himself originally a Jain, and he turned a Śaiva through the influence of Saint Appar. The latter and Tirujñāna-Sambandar zealously carried on their missionary activities in the South with the result that Buddhism and Jainism declined, and there was a marked revival of Śaivism. Many of the Pallava monarchs were profound devotees of the god Śiva. But they were also tolerant of Vaiṣṇavism, which flourished because of the efforts of the Aḻvars (Vaiṣṇava saints).

Art

The religious revival of the period gave an immense impetus to the architectural activities of the Pallava princes. Their edifices are doubtless among the noblest monuments in South India. We see in them three or four distinct types. Those found at Dalavanur (South Arcot district), Pallavaraṁ, Vallaṁ (Chingleput

[1] R. Gopalan, *History of the Pallavas of Kāñcī*, p. 159.
[2] See *Ante*.

district) represent a new style, initiated in South India by Mahendravarman I. They are excavated out of solid rocks, and are distinguished by circular *liṅgaṁs*, peculiar forms of *dvārapālas*, *prabhātoraṇas*, and cubical pillars.[1] To the second stage belong the temples constructed by Narasiṁhavarman I Mahāmalla. His earlier shrines at Pudukotta and Trichinopoly district are rock-cut like those of Mahendravarman I except that they have more ornamental façades and pillars of better proportions. Subsequently, Narasiṁhavarman I Mahāmalla built *Rathas* as the Dharmarāja, carved from a single granite boulder, at Mahābalipuraṁ. Then followed the structural temples of brick and stone, or of both, with lofty towers rising in tiers. The best specimens of these are the Kailāśanātha at Kāñcī and the so-called Shore temple of the Seven Pagodas group. One noteworthy feature of some shrines is that they are adorned by beautiful life-like images of Pallava kings and their queens. The evolution and development of Pallava architecture continued until the rise of a new style called after the great Coḷas.

SECTION C

THE COḶAS

Derivation

The name Coḷa has sometimes been taken to mean 'hoverer' from the Tamil root 'cūḻ' (to hover), whereas others connect it with Sanskrit 'cora' (thief) or Tamil 'colaṁ' (millet), or with the word 'Kōla', which "in the early days designated the dark-coloured pre-Aryan population of Southern India in general."[2] Whatever the value of these suggestions regarding the origin

[1] *History of the Pallavas of Kāñcī*, p. 92.

[2] K. A. Nīlakanta Śāstrī, *The Coḷas*, p. 24. I have studied both the volumes with great profit.

of the name, there is hardly any doubt that, like the Pāṇḍyas and the Ceras, the Coḷas were indigenous to the South, although in later literature and inscriptions they are ascribed a mythical descent from the Sun.[1]

Their territory and towns

The traditional *Coḷa-maṇḍalaṁ* or the kingdom of the Coḷas lay north and south between the two rivers, Pennar and Vellaru (Vellar), and roughly comprised the modern districts of Tanjore and Trichinopoly and a portion of the Pudukotta State. These limits considerably varied as the power of the Coḷas developed or declined in the course of dynastic conflicts. Among the capitals, we know of Uragapura (Uraiyur, near Trichinopoly), Tanjuvur (Tanjore), and Gangaikoṇḍa-Coḷapuraṁ; and their most important port was Kāverī-paddanam (Puhār), situated at the mouth of the Kāverī river (northern branch), from where the Coḷas carried on a brisk trade with the outside world.

Early history

The Coḍas or Coḷas, as rulers, are known to have existed from remote antiquity. They have been mentioned by the grammarian, Kātyāyana (*circa* 4th century B.C.), and in the *Mahābhārata*. According to II and XIII Rock Edicts of Aśoka, which are the earliest historical documents to refer to the Coḍas, they were a friendly power in the South beyond the pale of Mauryan suzerainty. Next, the *Mahāvaṁśa* throws some light on the relations between Coḷa-rattha and Ceylon, for we learn that about the middle of the second century B.C. a Coḷa named Elāra conquered the island and ruled there for a fairly long period. The *Periplus* (*circa*

[1] *Ibid.*, p. 38. In some inscriptions an eponymous Cola also finds mention (see *Ibid.*, p. 140).

81 A.D.) and the *Geography* of Ptolemy (*circa* middle of the second century A.D.) further give us some information regarding the Coḷa country and its inland towns and ports. Then the *Saṅgam* literature, assigned with a good deal of plausibility to "the first few centuries of the Christian Era," testifies to the rule of several Coḷa princes, some of whom appear to be mere legendary models of charity and justice. Others, however, may probably be historical figures, although any attempt to settle their chronology and order of succession is baffling in the extreme. One of them was Karikāla, son of Iḷañjeṭcenni. It is said that the Coḷa kingdom gained greatly both in territory and in influence under him, his most notable achievement being the defeat of the Pāṇḍya and the Cera kings and a number of minor chieftains, allied with them, in the battle of Veṇṇi (Kovil-Veṇṇi, near Tanjore). Passing down the stream of time, we come to Perunarkiḷḷi, alleged to have celebrated the *Rājasūya*; and Koccenganan, who, like Karikāla, is the subject of many a legend. About the third or fourth century A.D. the Coḷas suffered an eclipse owing to the rise of the Pallavas and the aggressions of the Pāṇḍyas and the Ceras. Of course, the Coḷas continued to exist, but for the next few centuries they were of no consequence, bowing low before almost every blast. Towards the close of the fourth decade of the seventh century A.D. we are told by Yuan Chwang that "the country of *Chu-li-ye* (Cūlya or Coḷa) is about 2400 or 2500 *li* in circuit, and the capital is about 10 *li* round. It is deserted and wild, a succession of marshes and jungle. The population is very small, and troops and brigands go through the country openly. The climate is hot; the manners of the people dissolute and cruel. The disposition of men is naturally fierce; they are attached to heretical teaching. The *Saṅghārāmas* are ruined and dirty as well as the priests. There are some tens of Deva temples, and many

Nirgrantha heretics."[1] The country, thus described by the Chinese pilgrim, corresponds, according to Dr. Vincent Smith, with "a portion of the Ceded districts, and more specially with the Cuddapah district."[2] Whether one agrees with this identification or not, it is doubtless noteworthy that Yuan Chwang maintains silence regarding its ruler. Presumably, this was because the Coḷa chief then wielded little power, and was perhaps only a feudatory of the Pallava sovereign. The fortunes of the Coḷas were indeed now completely enveloped in darkness. But when the Pallava monarchy declined about the middle of the ninth century A.D., the sun of Coḷa glory once again shone on the political horizon of the South.

The Imperial Coḷas

Vijayālaya

The greatness of the Coḷas was revived by the dynasty founded by Vijayālaya, whose exact relation to the earlier Coḷas is unfortunately unknown. He began his rule shortly before 850 A.D. in the neighbourhood of Uraiyur, probably as a vassal of the Pallava king. It is believed that Vijayālaya captured Tañjāvūr or Tanjore[3] from the Muttaraiyar chiefs, who were partisans of the Pāṇḍya monarch, Varaguṇavarman.

Āditya I

Vijayālaya was succeeded by his able son, Āditya I, about 875 A.D. He considerably enhanced the power

[1] Beal, *Buddhist Records of the Western World*, Vol. II, p. 227.

[2] *E.H.I.*, 4th ed., p. 483.

[3] Vijayālaya made Tañjāvūr or Tañjāpurī (Tanjore) the chief city of the Cola realm, although after the conquest of the Pallava territories Kāñcī became "a sort of subsidiary capital." Subsequently, Rājendra I built the new capital of Gaṅgāpurī or Gaṅgaikoṇḍa-Coḷapuraṁ.

and prestige of the family, for he overthrew the Pallava Aparājitavarman and brought Toṇḍamaṇḍalaṁ under his sway about 890 A.D. Āditya I is also represented to have conquered Kongudeśa and taken Talkāḍ, the seat of the Western Gaṅgas. Āditya I was a votary of Śiva, in whose honour he built several temples.

Parāntaka I

When Āditya s son, Parāntaka I, ascended the throne, the Coḷa realm comprised almost the entire eastern country from Kalahasti and Madras in the north to the Kāverī in the south, and during his long reign from 907 A.D. to 953 A.D. he extended it still further. First, he annexed the territories of the Pāṇḍya king, Rājasiṁha, who had to flee for safety to Ceylon; and to commemorate this exploit Parāntaka I adopted the title of "Maḍuraikoṇḍa." The Coḷa conqueror then turned his arms towards Ceylon, but the raid proved abortive. He next "uprooted two Bāṇa kings and conquered the Vaiḍumbas."[1] Parāntaka I finally swept away all traces of Pallava power, and pushed his authority up to Nellore in the north. This rapid expansion of the Coḷa kingdom, however, did not bring him peace. In the last decade of his reign, disruptive tendencies manifested themselves, and he was involved in a terrible conflict with Kriṣṇa III Rāṣṭrakūṭa. Although some late Coḷa inscriptions credit Parāntaka I with having repulsed his mighty rival, a consideration of the available evidence would show that Kriṣṇa III won a decided victory over the Coḷa forces with the help of the Gaṅga prince, Būtuga II. Indeed, it appears that the Rāṣṭrakūṭa invader seized Kāñcī and Tanjore, and assumed the proud epithet of "Tanjaiyunkoṇḍa." Ṛājāditya, the eldest son of Parān-

[1] *S. I. I.*, II, no. 76, v. 9; *The Coḷas*, p. 150.

taka I, was killed in the battle of Takkolaṁ (North Arcot district) in 949 A.D.,[1] and Kriṣṇa III is alleged to have marched triumphantly even up to Rameśvaram. Whether the latter claim is true or not, there is hardly any doubt that the Coḷas received a disastrous blow, and that they took some time to recover from it.

Parāntaka I performed several charitable sacrifices; and being a devout Śaiva, like his father, he gave impetus to the erecting of religious edifices, and himself covered the Śiva temple of Cidambaram with gold.[2]

Period of obscurity

With the death of Parāntaka I in 953 A.D. the history of the Coḷas for the next three decades is much confused. Scholars differ in their opinions considerably regarding the interpretation of facts, but it seems that after him ruled his two sons, Gaṇḍarāditya and Ariñjaya, and that the latter was followed by his son, Sundara Coḷa, who was in turn succeeded by Āditya II Karikāla and Uttama Coḷa. They were weaklings, and except for the usual family intrigues and wars with neighbours, their reigns are not relieved by any important event.

Rājarāja I (c. 985-1014 A.D.)

With the accession of Sundara Coḷa's son, Rājarāja I, who was known by a variety of titles such as Mummaḍi-Coḷadeva, Jayangoṇḍa, Coḷa-mārtaṇḍa etc., began the most glorious epoch of the Coḷas.[3] He inherited a dis-

[1] cf. the Ātakūr inscription, dated in the Śaka year 872=949-50 A.D. (*Ep. Ind.*, IV, pp. 50-57). Takkolam is about six miles to the south-east of Arkoṇam in the North Arcot district (*Ibid.*, IV, p. 331, n. 3).

[2] *The Coḷas*, p. 164.

[3] According to Kielhorn, Rājarāja I ascended the throne between the 25th June and the 25th July 985 A.D. (*Ep. Ind.*, IX, p. 217).

organised and an attenuated kingdom, but by his ability, prowess, and military skill he soon built it up again, and raised himself to a position of supremacy in the South.

One of the earliest exploits of Rājarāja I was the subjugation of the Ceras, whose fleet he destroyed at Kandalur. Then he took Madurā and captured the Pāṇḍya king, Amarabhujaṅga. Rājarāja I also conquered Kollam and the fortress of Udagai in the Western Ghats and Malai-Nāḍu, identified with Coorg. At this time, the affairs of Ceylon having fallen into confusion, he invaded the island and annexed its northern part, which became a Coḷa province under the name, Mummaḍi-Coḷa-Maṇḍalaṁ. Next, he subdued Gaṅgavāḍī and Nolaṁbapāḍī, constituting the bulk of Mysore. The ever-expanding power and influence of Rājarāja I could not be a matter of indifference to his Western Cālukya contemporary, and so a trial of strength between the two was inevitable. Whatever the truth in Tailapa's claim (referred to in an inscription dated 992 A.D.) to have vanquished the Coḷas, his successor Satyāśraya, at any rate, fared badly against Rājarāja I, who is alleged to have captured Raṭṭapāḍi and devastated the Cālukya territory. Satyāśraya (*c.* 997-1008 A.D.) was, no doubt, stunned by the terrific onslaught, but he did not take long to recover and hurl back the Coḷa advance. Rājarāja I then overran the Eastern Cālukya country of Veṅgī. Śaktivarman (*c.* 999-1011 A.D.) tried to stem the rising tide of Coḷa aggression, but his younger brother and successor, Vimalāditya (1011-18 A.D.), recognised the overlordship of Rājarāja I, who as a mark of friendship gave him the hand of his daughter, Kundavvai (Kuṁdavā). We are further told that the conquests of Rājarāja I included Kaliṅga and "the old islands of the sea numbering 12,000", which have been generally identified with the Laccadives and the Maldives. This, if true, doubtless speaks highly of the effectiveness of the Coḷa fleet. Thus, Rājarāja I made himself master of almost the whole of the present Madras Presidency, Coorg, parts of Mysore and Ceylon, and other islands. These were indeed remarkable achievements, and place Rājarāja I among the foremost warriors and empire-builders of ancient India.

Rājarāja I's claim to fame rests also on the beautiful Śiva temple which he constructed at Tanjore. It is called Rājarājeśvara after his name, and is specially noted for its huge proportions, simple design, elegant sculptures, and fine decorative motifs. On the walls of the temple is engraved an account of Rājarāja's exploits, and but for this fortunate circumstance we should not have known all the details of his career.

Rājarāja's Śaivism was by no means intolerant of other creeds. He endowed and built some temples of Viṣṇu too. Besides, it is said that he granted a village to the Buddhist *Vihāra* at Negapatam, constructed by Śrī-Māra-Vijayottuṅgavarman, the Śailendra king of Śrī-Vijaya and Kaṭāha beyond the sea in the Malay peninsula.

Rājendra I Gaṅgaikoṇḍa (*c.* 1014-44 *A.D.*)

After the death of Rājarāja I, the sceptre passed to his worthy son, Rājendra I, who had shared the burden of government with the former during the closing years of his reign. Indeed, the regnal years of Rājendra I are counted from 1012 A.D., when he was formally declared *Yuvarāja*.[1] He proved a chip of the old block, and by his military valour and administrative talents he raised the Coḷa empire to the pinnacle of glory. Already in the time of his father, Rājendra I had won renown as a warrior by his successful attacks on Iḍituṟaināḍu (Raichur district), Banavāsī (north Kanārā), Koḷḷippākkai

1 This event took place approximately between the 27th March and the 7th July A. D. 1012 (*Ep. Ind.*, IX, p. 217).

(Kulpak), and Maṇṇaikkadakkam (perhaps Mānyakheṭa or Malkhed). He had thus carried his arms across the Tuṅgabhadrā right into the heart of the Cālukya territory. A few years after coming to the throne, probably about 1017 A.D., he annexed the whole of Ceylon, its northern part having been previously conquered by Rājarāja I. The following year he *re-asserted* the Coḷa supremacy over the kings of Kerala and the Pāṇḍya country, and appointed his son, Jaṭāvarman Sundara, Viceroy of these territories with the title, Coḷa-Pāṇḍya. Further, Rājendra I maintained his hold on the "many ancient islands" (probably the Laccadives and Maldives), which had been conquered earlier by his father Rājarāja I. Rājendra I also came into conflict with the Western Cālukya monarch, Jayasiṁha II Jagadekamalla (*c.* 1016-42 A.D.). The Cālukya records represent the latter as having got the better of his Coḷa adversary, but the Tamil *praśasti*, on the other hand, avers that Jayasiṁha II "turned his back at Musangi (or Muyangi) and hid himself."[1] Whatever may have been the final issue, this much seems certain that Jayasiṁha II continued to be master of the country up to the Tuṅgabhadrā. Next, Rājendra I directed his arms towards the North, and his armies marched triumphantly as far as the Ganges[2] and the dominions of Mahīpāla, the Gauḍa sovereign. We are told in the Tirumalai (near Poḷūr, North Arcot district) inscription[3] that Rājendra I subjugated Odda-Viṣaya (Orissa); Kosalaināḍu (Southern Kosala); Dharmapāla of Taṇḍabutti (Daṇḍa-bhukti, probably the districts of Balasore and a portion of Midnapore); Raṇaśūra of Takkana-lāḍaṁ (South Rāḍha); Govindacandra

[1] *S.I.I.*, II, pp. 94-95. Muśangi or Muyaṅgi has been identified with Uccangīdrug in the Bellary district (*Ibid.*, p. 94, n. 4; *Ep. Ind.*, IX, p. 230).

[2] See also R. D. Banerji, Rājendra's Ganges expedition, *J.B.O.R.S.*, XIV (1928), pp. 512-20.

[3] *Ep. Ind.*, IX, pp. 229-33.

of Vaṅgāladeśa (Eastern Bengal); Mahīpāla, the Pāla ruler (*c.* 992-1040 A.D.); Uttira-lāḍaṁ (North Rāḍha). As this northern incursion is mentioned in the Tirumalai inscription dated in the 13th year of Rājendra I's reign and has been omitted in the Merpāḍi inscription of the 9th year,[1] one may reasonably suppose that it took place some time between 1021 and 1025 A.D.[2] It was doubtless an audacious campaign, and to commemorate it he adopted the title of Gaṅgai-koṇḍa.[3] But the invasion did not yield any permanent results except that some minor Karṇāṭa chieftains settled in Western Bengal, and Rājendra I imported into his kingdom a number of Śaivas from the banks of the Ganges. The Coḷa monarch's achievements were not limited to land only; he possessed a powerful fleet, which gained successes across the Bay of Bengal. It is said that he vanquished Saṁgrāmavijayottuṅgavarman, and conquered Kaṭāha or Kadāraṁ and other places in Farther India. Presumably, the expedition was undertaken not merely to satisfy Rājendra I's ambitions, but to further commercial intercourse between the Malay peninsula and South India. After this almost uninterrupted career of conquest and aggrandisement, Rājendra I sheathed the sword. His subsequent reign was, however, not entirely peaceful. Revolts occurred in Kerala and the Pāṇḍya realm, but they were effectively suppressed by the crown-prince, Rājādhirāja, who also claims to have successfully fought against the Western Cālukya ruler, Someśvara I Āhavamalla.

Rājendra I founded a new capital called after him Gaṅgai-koṇḍa-Coḷapuraṁ, identified with modern Gangākuṇḍapuraṁ. It boasted of a magnificent palace and a temple adorned with exquisite granite sculptures, but

[1] *S. I. I.*, Vol. III, pt. I, 1899, pp. 27-29.

[2] *Dy. Hist. North. Ind.*, Vol. I, p. 318.

[3] Among other *birudas* of Rājendra I were Vikrama-Coḷa, Parakeśarīvarman, and Vīra-Rājendra, etc.

unfortunately these edifices and works of art have altogether perished owing to the pitiless operations of both man and nature. In the vicinity of the new city, Rājendra I also excavated an immense artificial tank, which was filled with water by channels from the Kolerun and Vellar rivers. It is said that the lake and the embankments were destroyed by a hostile force, and its bed is now a thick forest.

Rājādhirāja I (c. 1044-52 A.D.)

Rājendra I was succeeded by his son, Rājādhirāja I, in 1044 A.D. He had been associated with his father's administration since 1018 A.D. in the capacity of *Yuvarāja*, and had distinguished himself in warfare as well. When he came to the throne, Rājādhirāja I had to face many troubles, but all opposition was soon laid low. He subdued the Pāṇḍya and Kerala kings, who were in league with the rulers of Laṅkā (Ceylon) named Vikkamabāhu, Vikkamapāṇḍu, Vīra-Sālamegha, and Śrī-Vallabha-Madanarāja. Presumably, it was to celebrate his victories over these adversaries that Rājādhirāja I performed the *Aśvamedha* sacrifice. He also fought with the Western Cālukya monarch, Someśvara I Āhavamalla (*c.* 1042-68 A.D.). At first, fortune appears to have favoured the Coḷa sovereign,[1] but eventually in the famous battle of Koppam he lost his life in May, 1052 A.D.[2]

Rājendra (deva) II (c. 1052-63 A.D.)

Rājādhirāja I having been killed, his younger brother,

[1] It is said that Āhavamalla "became afraid, incurred disgrace, and ran away" (*S.I.I.*, III, p. 112).

[2] This date is known from the Maṇimaṅgalam inscription of the fourth year of Rājendra II's reign (*Ibid.*, III, 58); see also *Historical Inscriptions of Southern India*, (Madras, 1932), p. 72.

Rājendra II Parakeśarī, was proclaimed king on the battlefield itself. During his time, the war between the Coḷas and the Cālukyas continued, and both sides, as usual, claim victory for themselves. Indeed, the Coḷa inscriptions state that Rājendra II pressed on to Kolhāpur (Kollāpuram) and planted a *Jayastambha* there;[1] while Bilhaṇa, author of the *Vikramāṅkadevacarita*, represents Someśvara I to have stormed even Kāñcī, then an important Coḷa centre. In the face of these conflicting accounts, what seems to be the truth is that none of the contending parties could decidedly succeed against the other. One thing, however, is clear that Rājendra II maintained the Coḷa empire intact.

Vīra-Rājendra (c. 1063-70 A.D.)

In 1063 A.D., Rājendra II was followed by his younger brother, Vīra-Rājendra Rājakeśarī, who carried on the traditional hostilities with the Cālukyas. We are told that he inflicted a crushing defeat on Someśvara I Āhavamalla in the battle of Kūḍal-Saṅgamam (Kurnool district), near the confluence of the Kriṣṇā and Tuṅgabhadrā rivers.[2] Subsequently, the latter is said to have resolved upon again trying conclusions with the victor at the same spot, but it is not known what happened to prevent him from appearing on the scene. An effigy of the cowardly Someśvara I was then put up, and Vīra-Rājendra subjected it to disgrace. The Coḷa monarch next turned his energies towards Veṅgī, where affairs had gone wrong with his ally Vijayāditya VII owing to the activities of the Western Cālukya prince, Vikramā-

[1] See the Tirukkoyilūr (South Arcot district) inscription (V. Rangacharya, *Inscriptions of the Madras Presidency*, Vol. I, p. 227, no. 851).

[2] See the Tiruveṇgāḍu inscription (*S.I.I.*, III, 193). Another view makes Kūḍalsangamam "a confluence of the Tuṅga and Bhadrā rivers."

ditya (afterwards Vikramāditya VI), younger son of Someśvara I. Vira-Rājendra engaged the Western Cālukya forces not far from modern Bezwāḍā, and, having vanquished them, crossed the Godāvarī and overran Kaliṅga and Cakka-Koṭṭam. Veṅgī was thus reconquered and Vijayāditya VII was restored to his former dignity. Further, Vīra-Rājendra curbed the Pāṇḍya and Kerala princes, who attempted to re-assert themselves; and he foiled all efforts of Vijayabāhu of Ceylon to extend his authority and drive away the Coḷas from Siṁhaladvīpa. Vīra-Rājendra is alleged to have sent an expedition against Kadāram or Śrī-Vijaya too, but the details, which led to it, are obscure. Lastly, we learn that when Someśvara II Bhuvanaikamalla succeeded Someśvara I Āhavamalla in 1068 A.D., Vīra-Rājendra again made some incursions in the Western Cālukya territory. The latter also came into clash with Vikramāditya, who, having quarrelled with his elder brother Someśvara II, left Kalyāṇa, the capital, and repaired towards the Tuṅgabhadrā. Ultimately, friendship was established between the belligerents; Vīra-Rājendra gave the hand of his daughter to the Cālukya prince, and espoused his cause.

Adhirājendra (*c.* 1070 *A.D.*)

After the death of Vīra-Rājendra in 1070 A.D., his son, Adhirājendra, occupied the throne. He appears to have served his apprenticeship as heir-apparent for three years, but his actual rule was very brief. There was confusion in the kingdom, and despite the aid of his brother-in-law, Vikramāditya (VI), Adhirājendra could not hold his own, and was killed.

Kulottuṅga I (*c.* 1070-1122 *A.D.*)[1]

Adhirājendra probably did not leave any issue to

[1] See K.A. Nilakanta Śāstrī, *The Colas*, Vol. II (Part I), Mad-

succeed him. Accordingly, the crown devolved on Rājendra II, whose title to it was based on close matrimonial relations between his house and that of the Colas. For Vimalāditya of Veṅgī (*c.* 1011-18 A.D.) had married the daughter of Rājarāja I Cola, named Kuṁdavā (Kundavvai), and their son Rājarāja Viṣṇuvardhana had won Rājendra I Cola's daughter, Ammaṅgadevī, as his spouse. But of this union was born Rājendra II Cālukya, called afterwards Kulottuṅga I, who had himself obtained the hand of Madhurāntakī, daughter of Rājendradeva II Cola. It would thus appear that Kulottuṅga I had more of Cola than Cālukya blood; and although there are no grounds to believe that he was adopted into the Cola family, the failure of the main line as well as the confusion that prevailed about the time of Adhirājendra's death certainly helped him to make good his claim to the Cola crown. Presumably, Kulottuṅga I first settled accounts at Veṅgī with his uncle, Vijayāditya VII, and then assumed power in the Cola country on the 9th of June, 1070 A.D.[1] Thus, Kulottuṅga I united the two kingdoms of the Eastern Cālukyas of Veṅgī and the Colas of Tanjavur (Tanjore). The Western Cālukya prince, Vikramāditya, tried to undo this amalgamation, perhaps at the instigation of Someśvara II Bhuvanaikamalla, who himself wanted to put his gifted younger brother out of the way somehow, but the attempt miscarried. Having secured his position and restored order in the Cola realm, Kulottuṅga I appointed his son Rājarāja-Muṁmaḍi-Coḍa to govern Veṅgī. The latter assumed charge of his office on the 27th of July, 1076 A.D., but gave it up a year after. Then his brothers, Vīra-Coḍa (1078-84 A.D.) and Rājarāja-Coḍa-

ras, 1937. The latest known inscription belongs to the fifty-second year of Kulottuṅga's reign (*Ibid.*, pp. 49, 61).

[1] *Ep. Ind.*, VII, p. 7, n. 5. "On Dates of Cola kings," see *Ibid.*, pp. 1-10; VIII, pp. 260-74; IX, pp. 207-22.

gaṅga (1084-89 A.D.), successively served as Viceroys of Veṅgī. Henceforth it became the seat of a princely Viceroy. Kulottuṅga I next brought to book the recalcitrant Pāṇḍya and Kerala chieftains and other feudatories in the south. He is also said to have successfully measured strength with his Paramāra contemporary of Mālwā, and Kaliṅga fell a prey to his arms twice. Kulottuṅga I himself led the first expedition some time prior to his 26th regnal year to counteract the designs of the Western Cālukya Vikramāditya VI, whereas the second, undertaken about 1112 A.D. against the Eastern Gaṅga king, Anantavarman Coḍagaṅgā (*c.* 1077-1147 A.D.), was dispatched under the command of Kulottuṅga's trusted general, Karuṇākara Toṇḍaimān. There are, however, grounds to believe that Kulottuṅga I did not exercise any power across the seas, and that he had to suffer the loss of Gaṅgavāḍi or Southern Mysore towards the close of his reign owing to the aggressions of the Hoysala chief, Biṭṭiga Viṣṇuvardhana (*c.* 1110-40 A.D.), who was independent of his aged Cālukya suzerain, Vikramāditya VI, in all but name.

Kulottuṅga I introduced certain reforms in the internal administration of the kingdom. Of these the most important was that he got the land re-surveyed for taxation and revenue purposes.

The reign of Kulottuṅga I was further marked by religious and literary activity. Himself a devout Śaiva by faith, he is recorded to have made grants to the Buddhist shrines at Negapatam. But he was not favourably disposed towards the great Vaiṣṇava teacher, Rāmānuja, who was, therefore, compelled to leave Śrīraṅgam, near Trichinopoly, and seek the protection of Biṭṭiga Viṣṇuvardhana Hoysala in Mysore. Among the literary figures that flourished in the time of Kulottuṅga I, we may specially mention Jayagondan, author of the *Kaliṅgattupparani*, and Adiyarkkunallar, who wrote a commentary on the *Śilappadhikāraṁ*.

Successors of Kulottuṅga I

After a long reign of about half a century, Kulottuṅga I passed away some time in 1122 A.D.[1] and was succeeded by his son, Vikrama Coḷa, surnamed Tyāgasamudra, who had held the Viceroyalty of Veṅgī. He was probably a Vaiṣṇava, and it is believed that during his time Rāmānuja returned from Mysore to the Coḷa country. Vikrama Coḷa (*c.* 1118-33 A.D.)[2] and his immediate successors, Kulottuṅga II (*c.* 1133-47 A.D.), Rājarāja II (*c.* 1147-62 A.D.), and Rājādhirāja II (*c.* 1162-78 A.D.), were all weaklings, under whom the power of the Coḷas rapidly declined. The Hoysalas of Dvārasamudra now emerged as a considerable factor in the politics of the South, and the rulers of Ceylon, Kerala, and the Pāṇḍya kingdom boldly attempted to shake off their (Coḷa) allegiance. Indeed, the Coḷa authority had fallen so low that the Ceylonese king even ventured to interfere in Pāṇḍyan affairs on behalf of one of the claimants to its throne, although eventually Rājādhirāja II was able to overcome all opposition and settle the succession in favour of his protégé. The next monarch, Kulottuṅga III (*c.* 1178-1216 A.D.),[3] had also to face an internal turmoil in the Pāṇḍya realm, and we learn that he marched in triumph to Madurā, and hurled back the advancing tide of the Ceylonese incursions in the peninsula. But despite these minor successes, the day of Coḷa ascendancy was soon drawing to a close. In the reign of Kulottuṅga III's son and

[1] The latest known date of Kulottuṅga I's reign is the year 52 (*The Coḷas*, Vol. II, pt. I, pp. 49, 61).

[2] Vikrama Coḷa's accession took place about the end of June, 1118 A.D. (*Ep. Ind.*, VII, pp. 4-5). For a few years he appears to have ruled jointly with his father (*The Coḷas*, p. 61.)

[3] *Ep. Ind.*, VIII, p. 260. Kielhorn says that Kulottuṅga III began his reign "between (approximately) the 6th and 8th July A.D. 1178, and Rājarāja III between (approximately) the 27th June and the 10th July 1216."

successor, Rājarāja III (*c.* 1216-52 A.D.), Tanjore itself was sacked by Māravarman Sundara Pāṇḍya I (*c.* 1216-38 A.D.), and the former was reduced to such dire straits that he had to appeal to Vīra Ballāla II or Narasiṁha II Hoysala (*acc.* 1215 A.D.) to come to his succour and rescue him from captivity. About this time, another chieftain named Kopperuñjiṅga, belonging to the Pallava stock, rose into prominence at Sendamaṅgalam (South Arcot district), and he, too, is said to have taken Rājarāja III prisoner. The Hoysala prince again intervened, and after defeating Kopperuñjiṅga set Rājarāja III free. Thus, the fortunes of the Coḷas were already tottering, and when there ensued a civil strife between Rājarāja III and Rājendra III in 1246 A.D., the Hoysalas of Dvārasamudra, the Kākatīyas of Warangal under the energetic rule of Gaṇapati (*c.* 1199-1261 A.D.), and the Pāṇḍyas of Madurā freely aggrandised themselves at the cost of the decadent Coḷa monarchy. Indeed, it was in the time of Rājendra III, who first ruled jointly with his rival Rājarāja III from 1246 A.D. to 1252, and afterwards independently until 1267 A.D., that the final blow to the hegemony of the Coḷas was given by Jaṭāvarman Sundara Pāṇḍya (*c*, 1251-72 A.D.). He claims to have overrun a large part of their territory, and seized Kāñcī. He overawed other contemporary chiefs also, and as a mark of his superior might and position assumed the title of Mahārājādhirāja. Rājendra III was unable to arrest the rot, and by 1267 A.D., owing to internal troubles and the rise of the Pāṇḍyas and other feudatory powers, the empire suffered complete disintegration, and the Coḷas sank into obscurity.

Administration of the Coḷas[1]

The King and his officers

The inscriptions of the Coḷas prove that their system of administration was highly organised and efficient. The emperor was the pivot on which turned the whole machinery of the state. He discharged his onerous duties and responsibilities with the advice and help of ministers and other high officers. His verbal orders (*tiruvākya-keḻvi*) were drafted by the Royal or Private Secretary. It is believed that in the days of Rājarāja I and his son the Chief Secretary (*Olaināyakam*) and another functionary (*Perundaram*) had to confirm the royal orders before they were communicated to the parties concerned by the despatch-clerk (*Viḍaiyādhikāri*). Finally, the local governors scrutinised the orders before they were registered and sent to the Department of Archives for preservation.

Territorial divisions

The kingdom (*rājyaṁ* or *rāṣṭraṁ*) was divided into a number of provinces (*maṇḍalaṁ*), the most important of which were under the charge of Viceroys. Generally, the viceroyalties were conferred on princes of the blood or on scions of noble families. Some of the provinces were formed of such principalities as had been annexed by the Coḷa Imperialists. Besides, there were the territories of the vassal princes, who paid tribute and rendered service to the suzerain in times of need. The provinces were subdivided into divisions (*koṭṭams* or *valanāḍu*), and the other units of administ-

[1] See Dr. S. Krishnasvami Aiyangar, *Ancient India*, pp. 158-190; Prof. K. A. Nīlakanta Śaśtrī, *Studies in Coḷa History and Administration*, pp. 73-162; *The Coḷas*, Vol. II, pt. I, pp. 210-462. To these works, I owe several references and suggestions.

ration in the descending scale were the districts (*nāḍus*), unions or groups of villages (*kurraṁs*) and the village (*grāmaṁ*).

Assemblies

There is ample evidence to show that these divisions had their own popular assemblies during the period of Coḷa ascendancy. First, we hear of the assembly of the people of a whole *maṇḍalaṁ* in connection with the remission of certain taxes on land under its jurisdiction.[1] Next, inscriptions refer to the *Nāṭṭar*, assembly of the people of a *nāḍu* (district), and *Nagarattār*, i.e., "assembly of the mercantile groups which went by the generic name *Nagaraṁ*." These two terms perhaps corresponded to the *Janapada* and *Paura* respectively. Unfortunately, however, the details of their constitution and working are unknown. Besides, local administration was greatly facilitated by the existence of guilds or *śreṇīs*, *pūgas*, and such other autonomous corporate organisations in which persons following the same craft or calling banded themselves together.[2] Turning to the assemblies of villages, some had what were called *Ūr*. They were mere congregations of local residents to discuss matters without any formal rules or procedure. Then there was the *Sabhā* or *Mahāsabhā*—an assembly of Brahman villages (*Brahmadevas*)—about which our information is copious indeed. It would appear from epigraphic documents, particularly from those found at Uttaramerūr (about 50 miles S.W. of Madras), that these village assemblies, subject to the supervision and general control of Imperial officers designated *Adhikārins*, enjoyed almost full powers in the management

[1] See Nīlakanta Śāstrī, *Studies in Coḷa History and Administration*, p. 79.

[2] See Dr. R. C. Majumdar, *Corporate Life in Ancient India*; Dr. R. K. Mookerji, *Local Government in Ancient India.*

of rural affairs. They were the proprietors of village lands, both tilled and untilled. Since agriculture was their chief concern, they acquired lands by fresh clearings and afforded all protection to the cultivator from molestation. They gathered taxes, and resumed lands in case of non-payment. But unnecessary strictness in the collection of the customary dues was avoided. Often the asssembly alienated or sold land for religious purposes without reference to the central government or its local representative. Further, it received deposits in cash or gifts of land to administer them as charitable trusts. The *Sabhā* seems to have acted also as a sort of guardian of the village morals. It was invested with some authority to mete out justice and award suitable punishments to offenders. Through *maṭhas* the assembly probably made provision for the education of village children both in Sanskrit and Tamil. The number of the members of the *Sabhā* cannot be precisely ascertained; presumably, it depended upon the importance and the area of the village. The meetings of the assembly were held in a temple, or a public hall, if there was any, or under an umbrageous tamarind or some other tree. To look after various affairs of common interest, the *Sabhā* had smaller committees. Thus, we learn of committees for general management (*pañca vāra vāriyam*), tanks (*ēri vāriyam*), gardens, fields, temples, charities, justice, gold (*poṉ vāriyam*), etc. For election to these bodies elaborate rules were devised. Each village was divided into wards (*kuḍumbas*), and the eligibility or otherwise of a person for membership was determined on a consideration of certain qualifications or disqualifications based on one's age, learning, character, mode of living, relations, social status, etc. A member was elected for one year only. The method of election was simple; tickets of all candidates were first thrown and thoroughly mixed up in a pot, from which they were drawn, one by one, by a boy. The successful names were then announced to the people by the priest-arbitrator. If any member of a committee was ever adjudged guilty of an offence, he was at once removed from office. Everybody was expected to be above board, and so to conduct himself as to be an example to others. Accounts were kept with meticulous care, and they were regularly checked by accountants. Any kind of tampering, embezzlement, or defalcation was severely dealt with.[1]

Land-survey

The government carried out land-survey operations periodically. They were correct to the lowest fraction, and a record of holdings was maintained. In the earlier period, rods of 16 and 18 spans were used for purposes of survey but subsequently the foot-print of Kulottuṅga I became the unit of linear measure.

Sources of Revenue (Āyam)[2]

The state derived its income mainly from land-revenue, which normally amounted to one-sixth of the gross produce. Variations, if any, from this rate depended upon the quality of land and water facilities.[3] Sometimes remissions were granted in case of floods or famine. The royal dues were collected by the village assemblies, and were paid either in cash or in kind or in both. The unit of grain then was a *kalam* (about three maunds), and the current coin was the gold *Kaśu*. An inscription enumerates numerous imposts such as those on looms (*tari irai*), oil-mills (*śekkerai*),

[1] See also *The Coḷas*, Vol. II, pt. I, Ch. XVIII.

[2] *Ibid.*, Ch. XIX.

[3] To increase the income of the State forests and waste-lands were steadily reclaimed.

trade (*seṭṭirai*), goldsmiths (*taṭṭārpāṭṭam*), animals, tanks, water-courses (*Oḻukkunīr pāṭṭam*), salt-tax (*uppāyam*), tolls (*vaḻi āyam*), weights (*idaivari*), bazaars (*aṅgāḍipāṭṭam*), besides other exactions, whose connotation is not at all clear.[1] It would thus appear that the government tapped almost every conceivable source of revenue to fill its coffers (*tālam*).

Expenditure

The chief items of expenditure were the royal household, maintenance of the civil and military administration, planning and laying-out of cities (e.g., Gaṅgaikoṇḍacoḷapuraṁ), construction of temples, roads, irrigation channels, and other works of public utility.

Army and Navy

The Coḷa emperors had at their command highly trained land forces and an effective fleet, which respectively made possible the brilliant victories of Rājarāja I and Rājendra I against the neighbouring powers and their overseas conquest in the Indian ocean and the Malay peninsula. The Coḷa army was divided into sections according to the arms used and to whether they were mounted or not. Thus, there were "the chosen body of archers (*villigaḷ*)," footsoldiers of the bodyguard (*vaḷperṟa kaikkōlar*), "infantry of the right-hand (*vēḷaikkārar of the valangai*)," "chosen horsemen" (*kudiraiccevagar*), elephant corps (*ānaiyāṭkal, kuñjiramallar*), etc. The army was garrisoned in different localities in cantonments called *kuḍagams*, where discipline was enforced and military training given. Some *Senāpatis* were Brahmans, known as Brahmādhirāja.

[1]See Dr. S. Krishnasvami Aiyangar, *Ancient India*, p. 180.

The Coḷas as builders

(*i*) *Irrigation works*—Like the Pallavas, the Coḷas undertook vast irrigational projects. Apart from sinking wells and excavating tanks, they threw mighty stone dams across the Kāverī[1] and other rivers, and cut out channels to distribute water over large tracts of land. One of the most remarkable achievements belongs to the time of Rājendra I. He dug near his new capital, Gaṅgaikoṇḍacoḷapuraṁ, an artificial lake, which was filled with water from the Kolerun and Vellar rivers. Its embankments were sixteen miles in length, and it was provided with stone sluices and channels. One can imagine what untold benefits this reservoir must have conferred on the poor peasant.

(*ii*) *Roads*—The Coḷas also constructed "grand trunk roads", which served as arteries of commerce and communication. Their existence must have indeed greatly facilitated the rapid movements of the Coḷa forces during military expeditions. Troops were stationed at regular intervals along important roads, and public ferries were provided across rivers.

(*iii*) *Cities and Temples, etc.*—The Coḷas built cities and beautified them with magnificent palaces and temples. The latter were in those days the centres of village or city life. It was there that the people found spiritual solace, and listened to the solemn recitations of the sacred texts. Further, they served as schools for the study of the Vedas, Purāṇas, Epics, Dharmaśāstras, astronomy, grammar, and other sciences. There kings and nobles performed religious ceremonies, and gave largess to the destitute and the needy. On festivals and joyous occasions dramas were also staged in temples and people amused themselves with dancing and singing.

[1] Thus, the Tiruvāḍuturai inscription (110 of 1925) refers to the raising of the banks of the Kāverī by Parakeśarī Karikāla Cōḷa.

Their Art

The chief features of Coḷa temples are their massive *vimānas* or towers and spacious courtyards. In later Dravidian structures, however, the central towers are dwarfed by richly carved *gopuraṁs* or gateways, which dominate the landscape for miles around. In the great temple of Śiva, called Rājarājeśvara after the name of its builder Rājarāja I, at Tanjore, the *vimāna* or tower is about 190 feet high, rising like a pyramid upon a base of 82 feet square in thirteen successive storeys. It is crowned by a single block of granite, 25 feet high and about 80 tons in weight. What infinite labour and engineering skill it must have required to be placed in position! Another elegant, if less imposing, edifice at Tanjore of about the 10th or 11th century A.D. is in honour of the god Subrahmaṇya. Similarly, Rājarāja I's valorous son and successor, Rājendra I, erected a splendid temple at his new capital, Gaṅgai-koṇḍa-Coḷapuraṁ (Trichinopoly district). Its immense proportions, huge *liṅgaṁ* of solid granite, and delicate carvings are specially striking. The Coḷas encouraged plastic art, and the metal and stone images cast in their time are exquisitely executed and display a wonderful vigour, dignity, and grace. It may be added that some Coḷa temples at Tanjore and Kāḷahasti contain beautiful portrait images of royal personages, like those of Rājarāja I and his queen Lokamahādevī, and of Rājendra I and his queen Coḷamahādevī.

Religion

As already noticed, the Coḷa emperors were worshippers of Śiva,[1] but they were by no means intolerant

[1] The names Īśāna, Śiva, and Śarva Śiva in the inscriptions of Rājarāja I and Rājendra I bear testimony, as pointed out by Prof. Nīlakanta Śaśtrī (*The Coḷas*, Vol. II, pt. I, p. 221), to the "North Indian connections of the Śaivism of the Coḷa court."

of other faiths then prevailing. Indeed, Rājarāja I, an ardent Śaiva himself, built and endowed temples of Viṣṇu, and made gifts to the Buddhist *Vihāra* at Negapatam.[1] The Jains also appear to have pursued their persuasion in peace and harmony. The Śaiva Kulottuṅga I, who, too, is recorded to have granted a village to a Buddhist *Vihāra*, was, on the other hand, unfavourably inclined to the illustrious Vaiṣṇava reformer Rāmānuja. Accordingly, the latter had, for a time, to leave Śrīraṅgam and retire to the Hoysala dominions in Mysore; he returned when Vikrama Coḷa reversed his father's attitude towards him. Such instances of persecution were, however, rare, and generally Vaiṣṇava Āḷvars and Śaiva Nayanmars were free to preach and disseminate their doctrines. Further, it is noteworthy that there are scanty references (except in the poems of the *Saṅgam* period) to the performance of Vedic sacrifices by Coḷa kings. Indeed, the solitary allusion to the *Aśvamedha* occurs in the records of Rājādhirāja. Perhaps greater stress was then laid on *Dāna* (gift) than on *Yajñas* or sacrifices. Brahmans were given largess, and temples were richly endowed.

Section D

THE PĀṆḌYAS OF MADURĀ[2]

Origin

It is a baffling problem, indeed, as to who were the Paṇḍyas, and what is the exact significance of their name. Legends are unhappily at variance. According to some, they were the descendants of the mythical three brothers

[1] See the Leyden grant.

[2] See Prof. K. A. Nīlakanta Śāstrī, *The Pāṇḍyan Kingdom*, (London, 1929). I have found the book very useful. "On dates of Pāṇḍya kings," see *Ep. Ind.*, VII pp. 10-17; VIII, pp. 274-83; IX, pp. 222-29.

of Korkai, who respectively founded the Pāṇḍya, Coḷa, and the Cera kingdoms. Other traditions connect them with the Pāṇḍavas of the North or with the Moon. Do these apparently conflicting stories imply that, although the Pāṇḍyas belonged to the Dravidian stock, a claim to kinship with epic heroes was advanced when the Aryans had established themselves and their religion and institutions in Southern India?

Pāṇḍya Land

The Pāṇḍyas ruled the southern extremity of the Indian peninsula along the east coast. Their kingdom, no doubt, expanded or shrivelled as the king happened to be strong or weak. Normally, however, the Pāṇḍya country comprised the present districts of Madurā, Ramnad, and Tinnevelly. Its capital was Madhurā (Madurā), the "Mathurā of the South;" and Korkai (Tinnevelly district) at the mouth of the Tāmraparṇī river was its chief commercial port in early times. Afterwards, owing to a gradual change in the land formation of the coast, it decayed, and Kayal, a few miles further down the river, became the emporium of trade.

Early glimpses

The Pāṇḍya kingdom was of high antiquity. Kātyāyana (*c.* 4th century B.C.) probably refers to it in his commentary on Pāṇini's *Aṣṭādhyāyī*, and the *Rāmāyaṇa* of Vālmīki speaks of the wealth of the Pāṇḍya capital. According to a somewhat confused statement in the *Mahāvaṁśa*, prince Vijaya of Ceylon is said to have married a Pāṇḍya princess shortly after the *parinibbāna* of the Buddha. Next, in the *Arthaśāstra* of Kauṭilya[1]

[1] *Arthaśāstra*, Bk. I, Ch. XI; Eng. Trans., 3rd ed. (1929), p. 76.

mention is made of a special kind of pearl, called Pāṇḍyakāvaṭaka, obtainable in Pāṇḍyakāvaṭa (a mountain in the Pāṇḍya country); and Megasthenes transmits to us some curious bits of information that females governed the Pandaian nation,[1] and that they bore children at the age of six years[2]. He further deposes that Herakles had only one daughter named Pandaia, and "the land in which she was born, and with the sovereignty of which he (Herakles) entrusted her, was called after her name, Pandaia, and she received from the hands of her father 500 elephants, a force of cavalry 4,000 strong and another of infantry consisting of about 130,000 men."[3] Whatever the value of the testimony of Megasthenes, it is certain that in II and XIII Rock Edicts of Aśoka the Pāṇḍyas are described as an independent people on the southern frontiers of his empire. Coming down the stream of time, we are told in the Hāthīgumphā inscription (line 13) that Khāravela of Kaliṅga humbled the Pāṇḍya king and obtained from him "horses, elephants, jewels, rubies, as well as numerous pearls." An allusion to a Pāṇḍya king also occurs in the writings of Strabo,[4] who says that "king Pandion" sent an embassy to the great Roman emperor, Augustus Cæsar, about 20 B.C. Then in the *Periplus* and the *Geography* of Ptolemy we hear of the Pandinoi with their capital Modoura (Madurā) and other cities and trading centres.

Obscure centuries

The data available for the history of the Pāṇḍyas until about the beginning of the seventh century A.D.

[1] McCrindle, *Ancient India as described by Megasthenes and Arrian* (1926), Frag. lvi. B., p. 161.

[2] *Ibid.*, Frag. li, p. 115. This is altogether absurd.

[3] *Ibid.*, Arrian, viii, p. 206.

[4] Bk. XV, Ch. 4, 73.

are meagre in the extreme. The Saṅgam works—the *Śilappadikāraṁ*, the *Maṇimekalai*, and other anthologies—assigned on plausible grounds to "the early centuries of the Christian Era," of course, yield us a few names of kings, but they throw no light on their chronology or achievements, being more concerned with the portrayal of the religious and social life of the period. One of these rulers, Neḍunjeḷiyan, appears to have greatly increased the prestige of the Pāṇḍyas by overpowering a formidable league of his enemies at Talaiyālaṅgānam (modern Talai-ālam-kādu, Tanjore district). The next three centuries or so after the close of the Saṅgam age are utterly enveloped in darkness. Presumably, the Pāṇḍyas first lapsed into obscurity owing to the rise of the Pallavas; at any rate, later, in the sixth century A.D., their country was occupied by the Kaḷabhras.[1] The intruders were, however, overthrown, and Pāṇḍya power revived, by Kaḍungōn about the close of the sixth century A.D. or the commencement of the seventh.

Period of Growth

Thus, Kaḍungōn initiated what has often been termed the "Age of the First Empire." Unfortunately, not much is known of him, but there are grounds to believe that either he or his son, Māravarman Avaniśūlāmaṇi, came into conflict with Siṁhaviṣṇu, who was about this time laying the foundations of Pallava greatness. The next notable Pāṇḍya king was Arikeśarī Māravarman (*circa* middle of the seventh century A.D.), identified with Neḍumaran or the legendary Kun Pāṇḍya. Originally a Jain, it is believed that he afterwards turned an ardent champion of the Saiva faith under the influence of Saint Tirujñānasambandar. During the reign of Arikeśarī Māravarman and his

[1] *The Pāṇḍyan Kingdom*, pp. 48-49, note 1.

successors, Koccaḍayan Raṇadhīra (*circa* close of the seventh or the beginning of the 8th century A.D.), Māravarman Rājasiṁha I, and Neḍunjaḍayan Varaguṇa I (*c*. 765-815 A.D.), the Pāṇḍya kingdom continued to expand on all sides at the expense of the Coḷas, the Keralas, and other neighbours. The last two appear to have fought with some success against Nandivarman Pallavamalla. Further, Neḍunjaḍayan completed his father's conquest of Kongudeśa (modern Coimbatore and Salem districts) and annexed Venāḍa (South Travancore). His son and successor, Śrī-Māra-Śrī-Vallabha (*c*. 815-62 A.D.), distinguished himself by defeating the king of Ceylon[1] as well as a combination of the Pallavas, Gaṅgas, and the Coḷas, etc. at Kuḍamukku (Kumbakonam). The struggle with the Pallavas, however, went on till the time of Aparājitavarman, who, with the help of the Gaṅga chieftain Prithvīpati I and perhaps of Āditya I Coḷa also, gained a decisive victory over the Pāṇḍya monarch, Varaguṇavarman or Varaguṇa II, about 880 A.D. in the battle of Śrī-Purambīyam (Tiruppurambīyam), near Kumbakonam. Besides this heavy blow, the Pāṇḍyas had now to face another serious complication in the political situation of the South owing to the rise of the Coḷas. It is said that Māravarman Rājasiṁha II, having allied himself with the ruler of Ceylon, attacked Parāntaka I (*c*. 907-53 A.D.) to curb the Coḷas, but he was repulsed and routed with considerable loss. The victor then seized the Pāṇḍya territories, and in commemoration of this exploit assumed the title of "Maduraikoṇḍa." Māravarman Rājasiṁha II fled to Ceylon, from where he tried to regain his position. All his efforts, however, came to nought.

[1] The Ceylonese, on the other hand, make counter-claims of their own success in their records.

Coḷa Suzerainty

Thus the Pāṇḍya kingdom lost its independence, and it had to suffer the Coḷa yoke from about 920 A.D. to the commencement of the thirteenth century. Of course, the ruling family was not extirpated, and from time to time its scions made attempts to throw off the Coḷa suzerainty. The battle of Takkolam (949 A.D.), in which Krisṇa III Rāṣṭrakūṭa gave a rude shaking to the Coḷas, furnished one such opportunity, but the uprising headed by Vīra-Pāṇḍya was put down. The rebel prince was then captured and killed. Similarly, Rājarāja I (*c.* 985-1014 A.D.) had to overcome the opposition of Amarabhujaṅga and subjugate the Pāṇḍya country again. Troubles, however, recurred soon, and accordingly Rājendra I (*c.* 1014-44 A.D.) appointed his son, Jaṭāvarman Sundara, Viceroy there with the title of Coḷa-Pāṇḍya. The Pāṇḍya territories thus became a mere province of the Coḷa empire. But despite this direct control, the Pāṇḍyas, along with the Ceras and the Singhalese, held aloft the banner of revolt, and successive Coḷa monarchs were hard put to it to suppress them. Indeed, by the time of Rājādhirāja II (*c.* 1162-78 A.D.) the Coḷa grip was so loosened that the king of Ceylon felt bold enough to intervene in Pāṇḍyan affairs, taking the side of Parākrama and his son Vīra, although the other claimant to the throne, Kulaśekhara, had got the support of the Coḷa suzerain. The dispute was, no doubt, ultimately decided in favour of the latter's protégé. Nevertheless, it clearly demonstrated that the Coḷas could no longer be considered the sole arbiters of South Indian politics. The last flicker of Coḷa power we see when Kulottuṅga III (*c.* 1178-1216 A.D.) beat back the Ceylonese and occupied Madurā to afford protection to Kulaśekhara's successor, Vikrama-Pāṇḍya. After this event, the Coḷas sank fast into insignificance, and the Pāṇḍyas gradually regained much of their lost glory and importance.

Renewed prosperity

The accession of Jaṭāvarman Kulaśekhara in 1190 A.D. may be regarded as a turning-point in the fortunes of the Pāṇḍyas. From now on, their recovery began, and for a century or more they dominated the political stage in Southern India. The materials for the period, usually called the "age of the second Pāṇḍya empire," are ample enough; but the recurrence of similar names and the phenomenon of several princes ruling contemporaneously over different parts of the kingdom constitute a frequent source of chronological or genealogical difficulties. Indeed, some foreign writers have even observed that there were "five crowned kings" of the "great province of Ma'bar." The belief in their "co-regency" has, however, no basis in fact, for it has been rightly maintained that they were local chiefs governing certain territories as feudatories.

During the reign of Jaṭāvarman Kulaśekhara's successor, Māravarman Sundara Pāṇḍya I (*c.* 1216-38 A.D.), the Coḷas had to recede further into the background. For he overran their dominions and pillaged and burnt the towns of Tanjore and Uraiyur. The Coḷa king, Rājarāja III (*c.* 1216-52 A.D.), at first took to his heels, but having submitted afterwards he was reinstated on the throne. He revolted again but was promptly put down. It appears that on both the occasions Māravarman Sundara Pāṇḍya I could not adopt any extreme measures against Rājarāja III owing to the intervention of Narasiṁha II Hoysala, who is described in an epigraph as the "displacer of Pāṇḍya and establisher of the Coḷa kingdom." This active interference of Narasiṁha II, who himself is alleged to have advanced against Śrīraṅgam, was inevitable, since any accession of strength to the Pāṇḍyas was fraught with danger to the Hoysalas as well. In the time of Māravarman Sundara Pāṇḍya II (*c.* 1238-51 A.D.), the Coḷa-Pāṇḍya-Hoysala relations remained almost unchanged. The next ruler, Jaṭāvarman Sundara Pāṇḍya (*c.* 1251-72 A.D.), was, however, a vigorous personality, and he raised the Pāṇḍyas to the pinnacle of their power. He finally crushed Coḷa authority in the South, occupied Kāñcī, and subdued the Cera country, Kongudeśa, and Ceylon. Besides, he chastised the Hoysaḷas under Vīra-Someśvara by storming the fortress of Kannanur-Koppam. He also defeated the Kākatīya Gaṇapati (*c.* 1199-1261 A.D.) of Warangal and Kopperuñjiṅga, the Pallava chieftain of Sendamaṅgalam. Thus, these victories resulted in a rapid extension of Jaṭāvarman Sundara Pāṇḍya's rule over a large portion of Southern India up to Cuddapah and Nellore in the north; and to mark this supreme position he assumed the grandiloquent title of Mahārājādhirāja-Śrī-Parameśvara.[1] In his wars and administration, Jaṭāvarman Sundara Pāṇḍya was, for the greater part of his reign, associated with another prince named Jaṭāvarman Vīra Pāṇḍya; and from 1268 A.D., i.e., a few years before Jaṭāvarman Sundara Pāṇḍya's end, Māravarman Kulaśekhara is said to have begun his rule. Similarly, we hear of other kings during the time of the latter. Foreign observers erroneously believed that they were ruling independently of one another; but, as already remarked, they were perhaps only feudatories of the Imperial power at Madurā. This system of subordinate rulers was a noteworthy feature of Pāṇḍya government, and its adoption was presumably due to the immense growth in the extent of the kingdom. On becoming the supreme monarch in 1271 A.D. after the death of Jaṭāvarman Sundara Pāṇḍya, Māravarman Kulaśekhara won some military successes, especially in Malaināḍu (Travancore country) and Ceylon. He also built a palace

[1] Jaṭāvarman Sundara Pāṇḍya is recorded to have given largess on occasions of the many sacrifices that he performed; and he also richly adorned and endowed the temples of Cidambaram and Śrīraṅgam.

at Jayangoṇḍaśolapuraṁ, which proves beyond doubt that the Coḷas had now vanished into nothingness. Towards the close of the thirteenth century (1293 A.D.), the Venetian traveller, Marco Polo, visited the South, and he throws interesting light on the king, the court, and the life of the common people. He further speaks admiringly of its accumulated riches, pearls, and its extensive trade in precious stones and other articles of luxury. The observations of Marco Polo are in many respects corroborated by the Moslem writer, Wassaf. According to the latter, "Kales Dewar, the ruler of Ma'-bar enjoyed a highly prosperous life, extending to forty and odd years." The last days of Kales Dewar, identified with Māravarman Kulaśekhara, appear to have been tragic. There was a fratricidal struggle between his illegitimate son, Vīra Pāṇḍya, and the legitimate Sundara, both of whom were "co-rulers" with their father since 1296 A.D. and 1303 A.D. respectively. It is alleged that Māravarman Kulaśekhara was murdered, and Sundara sought the aid of Alāuddīn Khiljī. Whatever the truth, it is clear that the dispute between the two brothers furnished a golden opportunity to Malik Kāfūr, the Sultān's intrepid general, and he boldly led an expedition to Madurā in 1310 A.D. and plundered and looted it of its wealth. This Moslem incursion, of course, introduced another complication in Southern India, but it did not mean any advantage to either of the contending brothers. They miserably dragged on their existence for some time more. Alāuddīn Khiljī again despatched a strong force under Khusru Khan a few years afterwards, and the Cera king, Ravivarman Kulaśekhara, and the Kākatīyas of Warangal also took advantage of the prevailing confusion to aggrandise themselves. Thus, weakened by all-sided aggressions, the "second Pāṇḍya empire" soon broke up and became a thing of the past, although we continue to hear of scions of the Pāṇḍya line for long. The Moslem governor of Madurā cut himself adrift of Delhi about 1330 A.D. His independence was, however, short-lived, and ultimately the Hindu kingdom of Vijayanagar wrested power in the South.

APPENDIX

Yuan Chwang's testimony

The indefatigable Chinese pilgrim, Yuan Chwang, who went to Southern India in 640 A.D., gives us the following description of *Mo-lo-kiu-ch'a* or Malakūṭa, identified with the Pāṇḍya country: "The temperature is very hot. The men are dark-complexioned. They are firm and impetuous in disposition. Some follow the true doctrine, others are given to heresy. They do not esteem learning much, but are wholly given to commercial gain. There are the ruins of many old convents, but only the walls are preserved, and there are few religious followers. There are many hundred Deva-temples, and a multitude of heretics, mostly belonging to the Nirgranthas."[1] We thus get an account of the land, character of the people, and of their religious persuasions about the middle of the seventh century A.D. It would appear that Brahmanism was then prosperous, and the Jains, too, were numerous; but Buddhism had rather fallen in popular favour.

SECTION E

THE CERAS

Their origin and territory

The Ceras or Keralas belonged to the Dravidian stock. Their kingdom, which constituted one of the three traditional divisions of Southern India, roughly

[1] Beal, *Buddhist Records of the Western World*, Vol. II, p. 231.

corresponded to the modern district of Malabar and the States of Travancore and Cochin. Sometimes it included also the Kongu region, i.e., the district of Coimbatore and the southern portion of Salem. The western coast of the Cera realm had some fine natural ports like Muziris (modern Kranganur) at the mouth of the Periyar river, and Vaikkarai, from where in ancient times flowed a large volume of trade in spices and other precious articles to foreign lands. Indeed, Muziris attracted Roman merchants and businessmen in such considerable numbers that they even built here a temple of Augustus. There was also, it seems, an old Jewish colony, and a Cera king, Bhāskara Ravivarman, is recorded to have given a charter to them about the beginning of the tenth century A.D.

History

Very little is known of the history of the Ceras. The earliest reference to them occurs in II Rock Edict of Aśoka, which mentions the Keralaputas or Keralaputras along with the Coḍas (Coḷas) and the Pāṇḍyas as a frontier power (in the south). The next definite historical allusion to the Ceras is found in the *Periplus* and in the accounts of the geographer, Ptolemy. But unfortunately our knowledge of their political history is extremely scanty until we come to the time of Senguttuvan, whose exploits have been immortalised in the celebrated Tamil classic, *Śilappadikāraṁ*, written by his own monk-brother, Ilangovadigal. It is believed that Senguttuvan was a contemporary of Neḍunjeḷiyan Pāṇḍya and of Karikāla Coḷa's grandson. Whatever the value of this alleged synchronism, Senguttuvan appears to have been a powerful monarch, and to have won several victories against his neighbours, although the statement that he carried his arms right up to the Himālayas has hardly any air of reality. His successor had to wage wars with the Coḷas and the Pāṇḍyas, who at one time even captured him, but ultimately he managed to escape. For the next few centuries after this event, the Ceras fade away from our view. When the curtain rises again about the commencement of the eighth century A.D., we find the Cera king engaged in a fight with Pallava Parameśvaravarman. During the latter part of this century, the Cera rulers had to face the aggressions of the Pāṇḍyas, especially of Māravarman Rājasiṁha I and Neḍunjaḍayan Varaguṇa I (*c.* 765-815 A.D.), who conquered Kongudeśa and Venāḍa (South Travancore). With the Coḷas, however, the relations of the Ceras were friendly, and both Parāntaka I (*c.* 907-53 A.D.) and his namesake are said to have taken Cera princesses as their queens. About the end of the tenth century, the Cera-Coḷa relations deteriorated, for Rājarāja I (*c.* 985-1014 A.D.) subjugated the Cera ruler and destroyed their fleet at Kandalur. The supremacy of the Coḷas was re-affirmed by Rājendra I Gaṅgaikoṇḍa (*c.* 1014-44 A.D.); indeed, they continued to dominate the Cera country until the beginning of their decline in the twelfth century A.D., when Vīrakerala succeeded in asserting his independence. In the thirteenth century A.D., the revival of Pāṇḍya power, specially under Jaṭāvarman Sundara Pāṇḍya (*c.* 1251-72 A.D.), again reduced the Ceras to subservience. But the sack of Madurā in 1310 A.D. by Malik Kāfūr, the ever-victorious general of Alāuddīn Khiljī, gave a paralysing blow to the Pāṇḍyas; and Ravivarman Kulaśekhara, who had ascended the Cera throne in 1299 A.D., at once seized this opportunity and freely aggrandised himself at the cost of the Pāṇḍyas as well as of the effete Coḷas. His aggressive activities were, however, arrested by the Kākatīya king, Rudra I. After Ravivarman Kulaśekhara, none of his successors is known to have achieved any distinction; and thus the Ceras, as a power, disappear from the historian's view about this time without ever having risen to Imperial position in Southern India.

CHAPTER XIX

INTRODUCTORY

Section A

POLITICAL CONDITION OF NORTHERN INDIA

The year 711 A.D. did not witness the foundation or collapse of any mighty power in India. Nevertheless, it is generally regarded as an important point in its history. For it marks the descent of the Arabs on Sind under the command of the intrepid Muhammad Ibn Qāsim, who seized Daibul and subverted the dynasty of the Brahman Chach. Although the Arabs had commenced their plundering raids, by land and sea, on the Indian frontier and coastal regions as early as *Hijrī* 15=636 A.D. during the Khilāfat of Omar, it was in 711-12 A.D. that they first gained a real foothold in a corner of India—Sind. The Arab Moslems now appeared like a tiny speck of cloud on the Indian political horizon, but three centuries later dark clouds in the form of the Afghan or Turkish hordes of Mahmūd of Ghaznī, gathered thick on it, and burst upon the fertile plains of India. The storm blew fierce and strong for some time, and then it subsided leaving its trail of destruction and desolation. Towards the last decades of the twelfth century the political sky again became overcast; the gloom deepened, and there swept over Northern India the deluge of Śihābuddīn Ghorī's invasions. Its onrush was so terrific that by 1206 A.D., when Qutb-ud-dīn was proclaimed Sultān of Delhi, all the Hindu states in Northern India were engulfed in one common ruin. But the South escaped the blast of the Moslem onslaughts for over a century more. It also was overwhelmed by the raging tempest in 1310 A.D., the date of the sack of Madura by Malik Kāfūr. Thus the Moslem authority, which made modest beginnings in Sind, took no less than six centuries to establish itself over the whole land. During all this period, however, the thunders of the Moslem invaders were not constantly heard. There was a long interval of over three centuries between the Arab conquest of Sind and the depredations of Mahmūd of Ghaznī, and of about 170 years between the latter and the invasions of Śihābuddīn Ghorī; and after his success South India remained unaffected for about a century more. Thus, though the Moslems came in waves at widely separated points of time, the expansion of their sway in India forms the most arresting feature of the period under survey. From the very early days of their advent in Sind and Western India, whether as traders or conquerors, the Moslems became an important factor in the body politic. They were believers in a highly militant faith, which uncompromisingly emphasised the oneness of God and the brotherhood of man. It would, therefore, be interesting to enquire what attitude the victorious Arabs adopted towards the polytheistic, idol-worshipping and caste-ridden natives of the soil. According to Al Bilāduri[1], the Arab rulers of Sind from the very start followed a wise policy of toleration and they considered the *Budd* of the Hindus inviolate like "the churches of the Christians, the synagogues of the Jews and the altars of the Magians." Not only that, the Arab conquerors sometimes even permitted the Brahmans to rebuild demolished or dilapidated temples. The Hindu rulers on their part, particularly Balharā of Mankir, i.e., the Rāṣṭrakūṭa king

[1] *Kitāb Futūh-al-Buldān*, pt. II, p. 221.

of Mānyakheṭa, afforded all protection and safety to Moslem traders[1] and allowed them complete freedom of worship. Says Al Maśūdi[2], "Of all the kings of Sind and India, there is no one who pays greater respect to the Musulmans than the Balharā. In his kingdom Islam is honoured and protected." Similarly Al Istakhrī[3] and Ibn Haukal[4] testify to the existence of Jāma Masjids in several cities, where the Muhammadan precepts were openly observed. The first contacts between the Moslem newcomers and the Hindus were thus informed by a commendable spirit of toleration and broadmindedness. Unfortunately, however, the harmony of their relations was rudely disturbed in later times by the excesses of wars, economic exactions, and occasional ebullitions of fanaticism or iconoclasm. It then developed into a thorny problem, but it is beyond my province here to indicate how liberal and farsighted Moslem monarch, attempted to tackle it.

The next noteworthy feature of our period is that Kānyakubja (Kanauj) continued to be the dominant power in Northern India. Indeed, it may aptly be described as the pivot of our history during these centuries. It first emerges into importance in the sixth century A.D. under the Maukharīs, to whom should go the credit for shifting the political centre of gravity there after the decline of Pāṭaliputra. Kanauj saw its palmy days during the momentous reign of Harṣa, who extended the kingdom upto eastern Punjab in the west and Bengal and Orissa in the east. His death in 647 A.D., however, plunged its affairs into darkness for almost three quarters of a

[1] Elliot, *History of India*, Vol. I, p. 88.

[2] *Ibid.*, p. 24.

[3] *Ibid.*, p. 27.

[4] *Ibid.*, p. 34.

century. When the footlights are switched on again about 725 A.D., we see another remarkable figure strutting on the political stage. Yaśovarman is represented in the *Gauḍavaho* as a *digvijayī*, but whatever allowance we make for hyperbole his success against the king of the Gauḍas and Magadha at any rate appears to be based on truth. His successors were weaklings, and the Āyudhas too did not achieve anything of note. With the appearance of the Pratīhāras on the scene about the beginning of the ninth century, Kanauj once more recalled the splendours of Harṣa's regime, and under the great Mihira Bhoja and Mahendrapāla I they held sway over territories as widely apart as eastern Punjab, Gorakhpur region, Magadha, North Bengal, Bundelkhand, Ujjain, and Saurāṣṭra. These Pratīhāras of Kanauj, and earlier Ujjain also, were the greatest bulwarks in India against Arab encroachments in the eighth and ninth centuries A.D. After the dismemberment of the Pratīhāra empire there was an anarchical interlude in the fortunes of Kanauj. It lasted from the time of Mahmūd Ghaznavī's destructive raids to about the last decades of the eleventh century, when the Gāhaḍavālas rose into ascendancy there. They tried to revive its lost glories, and Kanauj re-imposed its authority over Magadha and other adjacent lands. But the days of its grandeur came to an end when Jayacandra suffered a signal defeat at the hands of Śihābuddīn Ghorī in 590 *Hijrī* or 1194 A.D.

It must not, however, be supposed from what has been said above that the supremacy of Imperial Kanauj remained undisturbed and unchallenged throughout the centuries under consideration. Time and again the war-drums sounded, and aspirants to overlordship and military renown turned greedy eyes towards the *Mahodayaśrī*. The Kashmīrī sovereigns first attempted to snatch it. We learn that Yaśovarman was humbled by Lalitāditya Muktāpīḍa (*c.* 724—60 A. D.), and either Vajrāyudha or Indrāyudha had to bow to the steel of Jayāpīḍa Vinayāditya (*c.* 779—810 A.D.). Then followed the invasions of Dhruva Rāṣṭrakūṭa (*c.* 779—94 A.D.) and the Gauḍa king, Dharmapāla. The latter even dethroned Indrāyudha and installed in his place Cakrāyudha[1] with the approval of contemporary powers like the Bhoja, Matsya, Madra, Kuru, Yavana, Avanti, Gandhāra and Kīra kings[2] who were naturally interested in any political settlement concerning the premier state of Northern India. But Dharmapāla's pretensions to play the suzerain at Kanauj led to hostilities with Govinda III Rāṣṭrakūṭa (*c.* 794—814 A.D.), who vanquished him and his protege, Cakrāyudha[3]. When Govinda III got engrossed in internal troubles, Nāgabhaṭa II Pratīhāra availed himself of this opportunity, and swooping down on Kānyakubja boldly seized it from Cakrāyudha[4]. The victor could not, however, feel secure in his new possession without successfully measuring swords with Dharmapāla of Magadha and Gauḍa, whom he then routed[5] in a sanguinary contest at Mudgagiri (Monghyr)[6]. Such were the kaleidoscopic changes in the political fortunes of Kanauj, now the acknowledged seat of Imperial power. Thus, during the major part of the eighth century and the early ninth it was veritably the cynosure of the eyes of all military adventurers and enterprising potentates. In consequence of their ambitions the kingdom was

[1] *Ind. Ant.*, XV, pp. 305, 307.
[2] *Ep. Ind.*, IV, pp. 248, 252.
[3] *Ibid.*, XVIII, pp. 245, 253.
[4] *Ibid.*, pp. 108, 112, v. 9.
[5] *Ibid.*, v. 10.
[6] *History of Kanauj*, p. 233.

repeatedly overrun, the populace suffered greatly from their depredations, but each time it rose like the proverbial phoenix on its ashes. Although after the Pratīhāra conquest, a stable government was inaugurated and Kanauj was again on the high road of Imperialism, the fierce struggles with Gauḍa and the Dekkan continued intermittently. Indeed, the tripartite clash between the kings of Kānyakubja, the Pālas of Bengal, and the Rāṣṭrakūṭas of the Dekkan is a notable feature of this period. It was grimly carried on from bleeding sire to son. We thus learn that the Rāṣṭrakūṭa rulers—Dhruva Nirupama (*c.* 779-94 A.D.), Govinda III (*c.* 794-814 A.D.), Krisṇa II (*c.* 878-915 A.D.), Indra III (*c.* 915-18 A.D.) and Krisṇa III (*c.* 940-68 A.D.)—invaded Northern India, and that each of the great Pratīhāra monarchs—Nāgabhaṭa II (*c.* 805-33 A.D.), Mihira Bhoja (*c.* 836-85 A.D.), Mahendrapāla I (*c.* 885-910 A.D.), and Mahīpāla (*c.* 912-44 A.D.)—were engaged in a trial of strength with their respective Pāla contemporaries–Dharmapāla (*c.* 770-815 A.D.), Devapāla (*c.* 815-55 A.D.), Nārāyaṇapāla (*c.* 858-912 A.D.), and Rājyapāla (*c.* 912-36 A.D.). It was probably in the time of Mahendrapāla I that the authority of Kanauj was pushed right upto North Bengal, but the Pālas did not lose heart and they are known to have made determined efforts to recover their territories in Bengal and Magadha from the Pratīhāras. The Gāhaḍavālas also in their turn directed their gaze towards the east ; they did not, however, succeed much beyond the limits of Magadha. The antagonism between Gauḍa and Kānyakubja had become almost traditional. Travelling up the stream of time from the reigns of Yaśovarman and Harṣa, we find that Īśānavarman Maukharī (*c.* middle of the sixth century) was the first to have fought with the Gauḍas "living on seashore"[1]. The kings of Kānyakubja naturally attempted to control the lower course of the Ganges, because it was in those days the highway of commerce and communication, linking up the most fertile tracts of Madhyadeśa and Bengal ; and it was, therefore, essential for the economic prosperity of the kingdom that they should exercise supremacy over this vast Gangetic area. Similarly, it was not for political reasons only but also for the mastery of south-western trade-routes and sea-borne commerce that the great Pratīhāra rulers, mentioned above, expanded their sway towards Saurāṣṭra and waged many a war to maintain their grip over Malwa or the Ujjain region.

About the middle of the tenth century A.D., and not in 916-17 A.D., as generally supposed, the mighty fabric of the Pratīhāra Empire began to crack under the strain of continual wars, Rāṣṭrakūta Kriṣṇa III's invasion, and the rise of the Candellas. This brought to the surface the latent fissiparous forces, which are ever ready to operate whenever the hold of the Central power weakens. The process of disintegration continued rapidly until the Kanauj Empire became divided into several powers, viz., (1) the Candellas of Jejākabhukti; (2) the Kacchapaghātas of Gwalior; (3) the Cedis of Ḍāhala; (4) the Paramāras of Malwa ; (5) the Cāhamānas of Sākambharī ; (6) the Guhilas of southern Rajputana ; and (7) the Caulukyas of Anahilwāḍa.

In the north-west, there were independent principalities already existing. The Turkī Ṣāhīs of Kabul and Udbhāṇḍapura ruled upto the midle of the ninth century, when Lāgaturmān, the last king, was deposed by his Brahman minister, Kallar. The latter's usurpation initiated the regime of the Hindu Ṣāhīs, among whom Jayapāla and Ānandapāla are best

[1] *Ibid.*, XIV, pp. 117, 120, v. 13.

known for valiantly defending the gates of India against Sultān Sabuktigin and Mahmūd. The last member of the dynasty, Bhīmapāla, also was killed fighting against the Ghaznavide invader in 1026 A.D. The remnants of the Śāhī house then sought shelter in the Lohara court of Kashmir, and the Punjab passed into the hands of the Moslem conquerors. Throughout the period under survey Kashmir escaped foreign domination, and was left free to the designs and devices of its own rulers—the Karkoṭakas (*c.* 631—855 A.D.), the Utpalas (*c.* 855—939 A.D.), the successors of the Utpalas (*c.* 939—1003 A.D.), the Loharas (*c.* 1003—1171 A.D.), and the successors of the Loharas (*c.* 1171—1339 A.D.). The native rulers continued to rule till the year 1339 A.D., when a Moslem adventurer, Shāh Mīr, seized the crown under the title, Śrī Samsdina or Shams-ud-dīn. In the east, the Pālas maintained their existence amidst vicissitudes from *c.* 765 A.D. to about the middle of the 12th century, for the last glimpse of a Pāla prince, the shadowy Govindapāla, is afforded by an inscription, dated "gata-rājye caturdaśa saṁvatsare" in Vikrama year 1232=1175 A.D. But after the expulsion of Madanapāla from Northern Bengal by the Senas the Pāla kingdom had become greatly attempted, being mostly confined to the Patna and Monghyr regions in Bihar. The Senas first came into prominence about the middle of the eleventh century, but under Vijayasena (*c.* 1095—1158 A.D.) they rose into complete ascendancy in Bengal and even aggrandised themselves at the cost of the neighbouring states of Kāmarūpa (Assam) and Kaliṅga (Orissa). In 1199 A.D., however, the advance of Muhammad ibn Bakhtyār Khiljī on Nadia struck terror into the heart of Lakṣmaṇasena, and, as alleged by Minhājuddīn, he fled post haste across the Ganges to eastern Bengal, where he ruled until 1206 A.D. Whatever the truth of this story, the frontier administration of Lakṣmaṇasena must have been hopelessly rotten, otherwise the invader would not have been allowed to press on so easily right upto the capital. Western Bengal now fell under the Moslem yoke and in the next half a century or more Bang or eastern Bengal, where the Sena family had taken refuge, too followed suit. Further eastward was Assam, which was neither ever drawn into the main currents of Indian politics, nor was subjugated by the Moslems, although attempts were made by Muhammad ibn Bakhtyār Khiljī in *Hijrī* 601=1205 A.D., and later by Aurangzeb's famous general, Mīr Jumlā, in 1662 A.D. Coming to Kaliṅga on the south-eastern coast, it was from about the beginning of the eighth century under the sway of the Eastern Gaṅgas, and one of the most striking personalities of the dynasty was Anantavarman Coḍagaṅgā (*c.* 1077—1147 A.D.). The Moslem incursions began in Orissa early in the thirteenth century, but it did not succumb to their onslaughts until the sixteenth century.

With this bird's eye view of the states that flourished in our period in the extreme ends of India, let us revert to survey rapidly the powers that asserted themselves on the decay of the Pratīhāra Empire. The Candellas of Jejākabhukti (Bundelkhand) first arrest our attention early in the ninth century, and in the course of the tenth Yaśovarman and Dhaṅga (*c.* 950—1002 A.D.) considerably enhanced the prestige of the dynasty. In 990 A.D. Dhaṅga is said to have joined the coalition formed by Jayapāla Śāhī to resist the aggressions of Sabuktigin, and his son, Gaṇḍa, too promptly responded to the call of Ānandapāla Śāhī in 1008 A.D. for repelling Mahmūd of Ghaznī. Gaṇḍa even punished Rājyapāla Pratīhāra of Kanauj for his cowardly surrender to Mahmūd by sending a force against him under the command of the crown-prince, Vidyādharadeva, about the end of 1018 A.D., but when his own turn came to fight with the Sultān the Candella ruler showed his back twice—first in 1019 A.D. and the second time in 1022-23 A. D. The Candella power then revived under Kīrtivarman and Madanavarman (c. 1128-64 A.D.). In 1203 A. D., however, Paramārdi or Parmal was overwhelmed by Qutbuddīn Aibak. Without being detained by the Kacchapaghātas and the Guhilas, who never played any noteworthy part in the history of our period, we now pass on to the Cedis of Ḍāhala. They first emerge into view prominently about the last decades of the ninth and the beginning of the tenth century. Under Gāṅgeyadeva (c. 1019-41 A.D.) and Lakṣmīkarṇa (c. 1041-72 A.D.) the Cedi house reached the zenith of its glory, and they carried their arms to Madhyadeśa and other lands. However, sometime in the last quarter of the twelfth century the Cedis sank into insignificance. The next great ruling family were the Paramāras of Malwa, among whom Bhoja (c. 1010-55 A.D.) was the most versatile and commanding personality. Owing to his martial ability and constructive genius his influence was felt far and wide and his capital, Dhārā, almost rivalled the past splendours of Kanauj. The later Paramāra rulers were weak ; accordingly their importance waned considerably in the latter part of the eleventh century. This downward sliding continued during the next two centuries until the conquest of Malwa by Alāuddīn Khiljī's general, Ainul Mulk, in 1305 A.D. As regards the Cāhamānas, several branches of the clan are known to have ruled for a long time, but the most prominent was that of Sākambharī (Sambhar), which has been immortalised by the exploits of Prithvīrāja III or Rai Pithaurā of the Moslem historians. His wars with

Śihābuddīn Ghorī and romance with Saṁyogitā, daughter of Jayacandra of Kanauj who was his rival for supremacy in Northern India, form the subject of many a striking song and legend. Prithvīrāja was defeated by Śihābuddīn Ghorī, captured and killed. Sometime after, Quṭbuddīn annexed the Cāhamāna territories, although the family maintained its existence at Ranthambhor till 1301 A.D., when it capitulated to Alāuddīn Khiljī. The mention of Jayacandra leads us to refer here to the Gāhaḍavāla dynasty, which seized power in Kānyakubja and Benares sometime between 1080 and 1085 A.D. after dispelling the anarchy that prevailed in the Doab since the time of Mahmūd's raid. The Gāhaḍavālas dominated Madhyadeśa till the year 1194 A.D., when Śihābuddīn Ghorī vanquished Jayacandra in a bloody battle and killed him. Lastly the Caulukya dynasty of Anahilwāḍa was founded by Mūlarāja I, whose earliest known date is 941 A.D. In 1025 A.D., during the reign of Bhīma (*c.* 1021-63 A.D.), Mahmūd made a serious inroad on Gujarat and sacked the temple of Somanātha, famed for its accumulated riches. But the kingdom prospered again in the time of such great monarchs as Jayasiṁha Siddharāja (*c.* 1093-1143 A.D.) and Kumārapāla (*c.* 1143-72 A.D.). The Moslems subsequently made many attempts to capture Anahilwāḍa. In 1178 A.D. Sultān Śihābuddīn of Ghor descended on it, but was foiled by Bhīmadeva II. However, in 1197 A.D. Quṭbuddīn stormed it; again the occupation proved only temporary. Ultimately, it was reduced in 1297 A.D. by Alāuddīn Khiljī's generals, Ulugh Khan and Nasrat Khan, who soon conquered other strategic strongholds also in Gujarat.

The foregoing account gives in bare outline the political condition of Northern India from the ninth to the close of the twelfth century, and how step by step the steamroller of Moslem aggression levelled down the various states. It would be evident that all of them did not end their careers by 1206 A.D., and despite the establishment of the Sultanate at Delhi some, at any rate, continued to exist till long afterwards. It was not a walk-over either for the invaders in each case. Jayapāla, Ānandapāla and Bhīmpāla, the Śāhī kings, resisted the arms of Sabuktigin and Mahmūd at the very gates of India; Bhīmadeva II repulsed the attack of Śihābuddīn on Anahilwāḍa; and Prithvirāja III Cāhamāna and Jayacandra fought bravely with the Ghorī Sultān, and indeed the former even defeated his adversary once in *Hijrī* 587=1191 A.D. In their epigraphic documents Bhoja Paramāra and Govindacandra and Vijayacandra Gāhaḍavāla are respectively represented as having won victories against the Turuṣkas and Hammīra. Of course, there were craven-hearted rulers also, like Rājyapāla Pratīhāra of Kanauj, Gaṇḍa Candella and Lakṣmaṇasena, who sought safety in pusillanimous submission to the invaders. The Hindu princes made no attempts to come together for averting the common danger. Firishta, no doubt, refers to the confederacies of the kings of Delhi, Ajmer, Kālañjara and Kanauj, formed by both Jayapāla and Ānandapāla but his testimony cannot be implicitly relied upon, for the contemporary historian, Al Utbi, makes no mention of these leagues in the *Tārikh-i-Yamīni*. Each power pursued its own course, utterly unmindful of what was happening to the other. They indulged in their petty rivalries even when the enemy was knocking at their doors. Jayacandra, for instance, kept himself in proud isolation, even though Prithvīrāja III was engaged in a death-grapple with Śihābuddīn Ghorī. Indeed some rulers, like Gaṇḍa Candella, showed greater stomach for fighting against their royal compatriots rather than against the foreign invader. They felt bound by no common bond, and recognised no other loyalty except to their own selfish interests and parochial tendencies. Thus, though the country remained under indigenous rule till the close of the twelfth century, the mutually repellent Hindu states thwarted the growth of the sentiment of a common nationality.

Section B

RISE AND FALL OF KINGDOMS IN SOUTHERN INDIA

We have so far been moving in the labyrinthic maze of North Indian history. Let us now turn to take a peep into the main trends of the history of Southern India. As in the North, a number of dynasties played their role on the political stage of Southern India during the period under review. They were : (1) the last few rulers of the early Cālukya dynasty of Vātāpi (Badami); (2) the Eastern Cālukyas of Veṅgī (*c.* 615-1070 A.D.); the Rāṣṭrakūṭas of Mānyakheṭa or modern Malkhed (*c.* 740-973 A.D.); (4) the Western Cālukyas of Kalyāṇa (*c.* 973-1189 A.D.); (5) the Yādavas of Devagiri (*c.* end of the 8th century to 1318 A.D.). Besides these, such minor ruling houses also come into our view as the Silāhāras of Kharepaten and Thana, the Later Kadambas of Hangal and Goa, the Kākatīyas of Warangal, the Gaṅgas of Talkāḍ (*c.* 4th century to 1004 A.D.), and the Hoysalas of Dvārasamudra (11th century to the middle of the 14th). In the distant South, there ruled the Pallavas of Kāñcī (*c.* middle of the 3rd century to 890 A.D.), the Coḷas of Tañjavūr (*c.* middle of the 9th century to 1267 A.D.), the Pāṇḍyas of Madura, and the Ceras of Malabar. This multi-state system naturally provided ample scope for the rapacity of ambitious dynasts. Accordingly, their legions were constantly on the move, and the boundaries of kingdoms shrank or expanded. More often, however, they merely carried on raids, which left no marks save the horrid scars of bloody warfare.

We learn that the early Cālukyas of Vātāpi and the Pallavas of Kāñcī waged wars with unvarying relentlessness but with varying fortunes. The struggle was continued by the Rāṣṭrakūṭas, who stepped into the shoes of the early Cālukyas. Dantidurga Rāṣṭrakūṭa won successes against Nandivarman Pallava, and Dhruva Nirupama (*c*. 779-94 A.D.) and subsequently in 804 A.D. his son, Govinda III (*c*. 794—814 A.D.), also humbled Dantivarman Pallava. But despite these defeats the Pallavas maintained their power until 890 A.D., when it received its death-blow at the hands of Āditya I Coḷa (*c*. 875—907 A.D.). During the last quarter of the 8th and the greater part of the ninth century successive Pallava rulers, viz., Dantivarman (*c*. 776—828 A. D.), Nandi (*c*. 828—51 A.D.), Nripatuṅgavarman (*c*. 851—76 A.D.) were engaged in their traditional hostilities with the Pāṇḍya monarchs, Neduñjaḍayan Varaguṇa (*c*. 765—815 A.D.) and Śrī-Māra-Śrī-Vallabha (*c*. 815—62 A.D.); and Aparājitavarman Pallava (876—95 A.D.) distinguished himself by inflicting a crushing defeat on Varaguṇa II Pāṇḍya in 880 A.D. in the battle of Śrī Puraṁbīyam, near Kumbakonam. In the Dakṣiṇāpatha, the Rāṣṭrakūṭas of Mānyakheṭa dominated the political stage from about the middle of the eighth century to the last quarter of the tenth. Apart from their incursions in Northern India, which we shall refer to presently, the Rāṣṭrakūṭas were fighting with their southern neighbours, specially with the Gaṅgas of Talkāḍ and the Eastern Cālukyas of Veṅgī. Thus, both Krisṇa I Rāṣṭrakuṭa (*c*. 757—72 A.D.) and Dhruva Nirupama (*c*. 779—94 A.D.) are represented as having vanquished the Eastern Cālukya ruler Viṣṇuvardhana IV (*c*. 764—99 A.D.); and Govinda III (*c*. 794—814 A.D.) and Amoghavarṣa I (*c*. 814—78 A.D.) successfully measured swords with Vijayāditya II of Veṅgī (*c*. 799—843

A.D.). Amoghavarṣa I also warred with Vijayāditya III Guṇaga (*c.* 844—88 A.D.), who, as also Bhīma I of Veṅgī (*c.* 888—918 A.D.), had further to bow to the steel of Kriṣṇa Rāṣṭrakūṭa (*c.* 878—914 A.D.). This record of successes was, however, broken by the sensual Govinda IV, for he was worsted by Bhīma II of Veṅgī (*c.* 934—45 A.D.). The Rāṣṭrakūṭa power reached its zenith in the time of Kriṣṇa III (*c.* 940—68 A.D.), whose most notable exploit in the South was the occupation of Kāñcī and Tanjore and the defeat of the Coḷa prince, Rājāditya, in the famous battle of Takkolam (near Arkonam, North Arcot district) in 949 A.D. He annexed Toṇḍamaṇḍalaṁ, but he could not seize the southern portion of the Coḷa realm. He also curbed the ambitions of the Pāṇḍyas, the Keralas, and the kings of Siṁhala. After Kriṣṇa III's death, the Rāṣṭrakūṭas suffered decline; the capital, Mānyakheṭa, was sacked by Sīyaka-Harṣa Paramāra in the time of Khottiga Nityavarṣa ; and ultimately Karka II succumbed to the onslaughts of the Western Cālukya Tailapa in 973 A.D. This new dynasty, founded by Tailapa and known to historians as the Western Cālukyas, became a considerable power during the eleventh and twelfth centuries, and it was, therefore, inevitable for them to come into conflict with the Coḷas of Tañjavūr and the Paramāras of Malwa, who could never tolerate any serious disturbance in the political equilibrium of the South. Thus Vākpati-Muñja Paramāra (*c.* 974-95 A.D.) is said to have defeated Tailapa (*c.* 973—97 A.D.) no less than six times, which made him so overconfident that the seventh time he plunged headlong into the Cālukya country across the Godāvarī. This at once gave an advantage to Tailapa and Vākpati-Muñja was captured and beheaded. In the time of Satyāśraya (*c.* 997-1008 A.D.) the Cālukya dominions were overrun by the Coḷa armies under Rājarāja I (*c.* 985-1014 A.D.). Though overwhelmed for a time, Satyāśraya recovered from the shock, but his nephew and successor, Vikramāditya V (*c.* 1008-16 A.D.), received another blow from Bhojadeva Paramāra (*c.* 1010-55 A.D.). The next monarch, Jayasiṁha II Jagadekamalla (*c.* 1016-42 A.D.), however, routed Bhoja and broke the "confederacy of Malwa." It is further alleged that the Western Cālukya ruler got the better of Rājendra Coḷa I (*c.* 1014-44 A.D.). Coḷa records, on the other hand, make counter claims. In the time of Someśvara I Āhavamalla (*c.* 1042-68 A.D.) the Western Cālukya dynasty reached the summit of its power. Besides achieving victories in Northern India, which we shall mention presently, he ravaged Malwa and compelled Bhoja Paramāra to seek safety in flight. But when the latter's successor, Jayasiṁha I (*c.* 1055-60 A.D.), invoked his aid to ward off the combined attack of Bhīma I of Anahilwāḍa (*c.* 1022-64 A.D.) and Lakṣmī-Karṇa Kalacuri of Ḍāhala (*c.* 1041-72 A.D.), Someśvara I forgot all old rivalries and immediately extended help to the Paramāra prince. The allied army of occupation was driven out of Malwa, and the relations between the traditional opponents—the Western Cālukyas and the Paramāras—now took a friendly turn. In his wars with the Coḷas, Someśvara I seems to have won a preponderance over Rājādhirāja I in 1052 A.D. in the battle of Koppam, although Coḷa testimony is to the contrary. Next, Vikramāditya (VI), in the course of his adventures before he assumed the crown in 1076 A.D., came into clash with the Coḷa monarch, Vīra-Rājendra (*c.* 1063-70 A.D.), who concluded peace with him, cementing it with the marriage of his daughter. Towards the close of Vikramāditya VI's reign the Hoysalas of Dvārasamudra under Bittiga Viṣṇuvardhana (*c.* 1110-40

A.D.) entered on a career of aggrandisement, but they were afterwards curbed by Jagadekamalla II (*c*. 1138-51 A.D.), who also successfully contended against Jayavarman Paramāra and Kumārapāla of Anahilwāḍa (*c*. 1143-72 A. D.). Thus amid the shifting politics of the times, the Western Cālukya power was eclipsed in 1157 A.D. by the Kalacuri usurpation of Vijjala or Vijjana, but after a short flicker again it finally faded to nothing in 1189 A.D. owing to the aggressions of the Yādavas of Devagiri and the Hoysalas of Dvārasamudra. The Yādavas now definitely came into prominence and wrested the territories to the north of the Kistna from the feeble hands of the Western Cālukya Someśvara IV. But the Yādavas had now to reckon with the Hoyasalas, for from the time of Bittiga Viṣṇuvardhana (*c*. 1110-40 A.D.), who is said to have humbled the Coḷas, the Pāṇḍyas, the Keralas, the Tuluvas of South Kanara, the Kadambas, etc., they had grown powerful. In the conflict that ensued Bhillama V Yādava was killed in 1191 A. D. by Vīra Ballāla Hoysala (*c*. 1172-1215 A. D.) in the battle of Lakkundi. This defeat was, however, subsequently avenged by Singhaṇa Yādava (*c*. 1210-47 A.D.), who pushed his authority beyond the Kistna at the cost of the Hoysala Vīra Ballāla. About the close of the twelfth century Jaitugi Yādava (*c*. 1191-1210 A.D.) killed Rudradeva and placed Gaṇapati on the Kākatīya throne. Under the latter (*c*. 1199-1261 A.D.), the Kākatīyas of Warangal too saw their utmost rise, for he claims to have successfully encountered the kings of Coḷa Kaliṅga, Seuna (Yādava), Karṇāta, Lāṭa, and Valanāḍu. The internecine wars among the Yādavas, the Hoysalas, the Kākatīyas, the Coḷas and the Pāṇḍyas continued in the thirteenth century until all of them, except the Coḷas whose empire had disintegrated by 1267 A.D., were caught in the all-consuming conflagration of Malik Kāfūr's southern campaign. Whatever resistance, those effete and mutually warring powers offered, proved of no avail, and he triumphantly marched on to the southern extremity of the peninsula, occupying Madura, the Pāṇḍyan capital, in 1310 A.D. The sack of Madura gave a paralysing blow to the hegemony of the Pāṇḍyas; and the Cera ruler, Ravivarman Kulaśekhara (acc. 1299 A.D.), and other feudatories seized this opportunity to aggrandise themselves at their cost. The Pāṇḍya kingdom, though of high antiquity, first began to expand in the eighth century as a result of the conflicts of Koccadayan Raṇadhīra (*c.* beginning of the 8th century A.D.), Māravarman Rājasiṁha I and Neḍunjaḍayan Varaguṇa I (*c.* 765-815 A.D.) with the Coḷas and the Keralas (Ceras). During the greater part of the ninth century, however, the Pāṇḍyas were constantly engaged in warfare with the Pallavas, who under Aparājitavarman gained a decisive victory over Varaguṇa II Pāṇḍya in 880 A.D. in the battle of Śrī Puraṁbīyam, as noted elsewhere. About this time the Coḷas too had leapt into importance, and Māravarman Rājasiṁha II Pāṇḍya tried to curb them, but he suffered a crushing defeat at the hands of Parantaka I Coḷa (*c.* 907-53 A.D.). The suzerainty of the Coḷas was recognised, and thus from 920 A.D. to the commencement of the thirteenth century they were masters of the Pāṇḍya land. Of course, from time to time, specially after the battle of Takkolam 949 A.D., in which the Coḷas received a rude shaking from the arms of Krisṇa III Rāṣṭrakūṭa, the Pāṇḍyas made attempts to shake off the Coḷa yoke, but they did not achieve any success. Indeed, in the reign of Rājendra I Coḷa, the Pāṇḍya country was reduced to a mere province of the Coḷa empire. The accession of Jaṭāvarman Kulaśekhara in 1190 A.D., however, marks a turning point in the fortunes of the Pāṇḍayas, and his reign (*c.* 1190-1216 A.D.) has accordingly been described as the beginning of the "age of the Second Pāṇḍya Empire." In the thirteenth century the Pāṇḍyas reached the pinnacle of their glory. Māravarman Sundara Paṇḍya (*c.* 1216-38 A.D.) burnt and pillaged Tanjore and Uraiyur during the reign of Rājarāja III Coḷa (*c.* 1216-52 A.D.), and Jaṭāvarman Sundara Pāṇḍya (*c.* 1251-72 A.D.) gave the final blow to Coḷa authority. The latter also won successes against Vīra Someśvara Hoysala, Gaṇapati Kākatīya (*c.* 1199-1261 A.D.) and the Ceras, and thus extended his suzerainty over the greater part of southern India upto Cuddapah and Nellore in the North. By the time of Māravarman Kulaśekhara, the last notable Pāṇḍya sovereign, who built a palace at Jayangoṇḍasolapuraṁ, nothing was left of the once mighty Coḷa power. It had gone the way of all flesh after a long and fairly prosperous career of about four centuries. Of course, the Coḷas are known to have existed as rulers from remote antiquity, but their Imperial greatness dates only from the reign of Āditya I Coḷa (*c.* 875-907 A.D.), who conquered Kongudeśa and Talkād, and also annexed Toṇḍamaṇḍalaṁ after overthrowing Aparājitavarman Pallava in 890 A.D. Next, Parantaka I (*c.* 907-53 A.D.) completely swept away all vestiges of Pallava power, and established his overlordship over the Pāṇḍya territory after the flight of Māravarman Rājasiṁha II to Ceylon. But Parantaka I's ambitions received a rude check, when he was routed by Krisṇa III Rāṣṭrakūṭa in 949 A.D. in the famous battle of Takkolam. Rājarāja I (*c.* 985-1014 A.D.) then gave a fillip to Coḷa Imperialism. He subjugated the Ceras, destroying their fleet at Kandalur, and brought to book Amarabhujañga Pāṇḍya. Rājarāja I also imposed his sway over

Malai-nāḍu (Coorg) and Nolaṁbapāḍi and Gaṅga-vādi, which constituted the bulk of Mysore. Thus, with the capture of Talkāḍ in 1004 A.D., the Western Gaṅgas, whose kingdom had been founded about the fourth century A.D., and who had been greatly harassed during the eighth and ninth centuries by the Eastern Cālukyas of Veṅgī and the Rāṣṭrakūṭas of Malkhed, lost their sovereignty for ever. The waxing strength of the Coḷas brought them into conflict with the Western Cālukyas, and although Tailapa (*c.* 973-97 A.D.) claims a victory over them, his son, Satyāśraya (*c.* 997-1008 A.D.), appears to have fared badly against Rājarāja I. The latter also overran the Eastern Cālukya territory in the time of Śaktivarman (*c.* 999-1011 A.D.), whose successor, Vimalāditya (*c.* 1011-18 A.D.), at any rate acknowledged the Coḷa suzerainty. Thus, Rājarāja I made himself master of almost the whole of the present Madras Presidency, Coorg, and a large part of Mysore, and his arms even penetrated the islands of the Indian Ocean. In the reign of his son, Rājendra I (*c.* 1014-44 A.D.), the Coḷas reached the high water-mark of their power. He placed the Pāṇḍya land under a Coḷa Viceroy, and re-asserted the supremacy of his house over the Ceras. Indeed, from now the Coḷas dominated the Cera country until the beginning of their decline in the twelfth century, when Vīrakerala declared his independence. As we shall show below, Rājendra I led an expedition in northern India, and had to his credit overseas conquests too. The old antagonism between the Coḷas and the Western Cālukyas continued in his time and in that of his successors, and, as usual, both sides claim victories for themselves in their records. Thus, Rājendra I came into conflict with Jayasiṁha II Jagadekamalla (*c.* 1016-42 A.D.); and Rājādhirāja I (*c.* 1044-52 A.D.), Rājendra (deva) II (*c.* 1052-63 A.D.), and Vīra-Rājendra (*c.* 1063-70 A.D.)

warred against Someśvara I Āhavamalla (*c.* 1042-68 A.D.). It is said that in the battle of Kuḍal Saṁgamam (Kurnool district) the Western Cālukya monarch suffered a reverse at the hands of Vīra-Rājendra, who also reconquered Veṅgī and restored it to Vijayāditya VII (*c.* 1061-76 A.D.). In 1070 A.D., when Adhirājendra died without leaving any issue, Rājendradeva II of Veṅgī, born of Aṁmaṅga-devī, daughter of Rājendra I Gaṅgaikoṇḍa, ascended the Coḷa throne with the title Kulottuṅga I. Thus he united the two crowns of the Eastern Cālukyas and the Coḷas. By 1076 A.D. he drove away his uncle, Vijayāditya VII, from Veṅgī, and placed under princely Viceroys. Kulottuṅga I (*c.* 1070-1122 A.D.) suppressed the recalcitrant Kerala and Pāṇḍya chieftains, fought successfully with the Paramāra prince of Malwa, and sent two expeditions against the Eastern Gaṅga king, Anantavarman Coḍagaṅgā (*c.* 1077-1147 A.D.),—the first, led by himself, was before the 26th year of his reign, and the second in 1112 A.D. Kulottuṅga I's successors were weaklings, and during their rule the Coḷa fortunes rapidly declined. The Hoysalas of Dvārasamudra had now emerged as a considerable factor in the politics of southern India, and the rulers of Ceylon, Kerala and the Pāṇḍya country boldly attempted to shake off the Coḷa yoke. Under Māravarman Sundara Pāṇḍya (*c.* 1216-38 A.D.) and Jaṭāvarman Sundara Pāṇḍya (*c.* 1251-72 A.D.), the Pāṇḍya kingdom also was launched on a career of aggrandisement. Thus, its strength having been sapped by internal weakness, revolts, and the aggressions of neighbouring powers, the Coḷa empire disintegrated and vanished into nothing by 1267 A.D.

It has been remarked that the veil of secrecy hung over the South in ancient India except when an enterprising sovereign of the North, like Candragupta

Maurya, Samudragupta, or Harṣavardhana, lifted it by the force of his arms. Whatever the case in the earlier age, during the period under review, at any rate, southern India did not remain a backwater, but its affairs often got mingled with the main currents of north Indian history. The kings of the South even turned the tables now against the North, and overran it many a time with their invincible hosts. Thus, Dhruva Nirupama (*c.* 779-94 A.D.), having defeated Vatsarāja Pratīhāra of Ujjain, harried and despoiled the Gangetic Doab in the reign of Indrāyudha and "added the emblem of the Ganges and the Jamuna to his Imperial insignia." It was perhaps during the same campaign that Dhruva "seized the white umbrellas, the sporting lotuses of Lakṣmī of the Gauḍa king (Dharmapāla) as he was fleeing between the Ganges and the Jumna."[1] Similarly, Govinda III (*c.* 794-814 A.D.) triumphantly marched upto the Himalayas receiving the submission of Dharma (Dharmapāla) and Cakrāyudha[2] ; and Amoghavarṣa (*c.* 814-78 A.D.) is said to have extended his influence over the kings of Aṅga, Vaṅga and Magadha. It appears, as has been pointed out by Dr. N. Venkataramanyya,[3] from the testimony of Guṇabhadra, the Jain author of the *Uttarapurāṇa*, who refers to the (war) elephants of Krisṇa II (*c.* 878-915 A.D.) drinking the waters of the Ganges, that towards the close of his reign, perhaps in the time of Bhoja II, this Rāṣṭrakūṭa ruler also aggrandised himself in Northern India. The next terrific attack on Madhyadeśa was made by Indra III Nityavarṣa (*c.* 915-18 A.D.), who advanced through Ujjain,

[1] *Ep. Ind.*, XVIII, pp. 244, 252.

[2] *Ibid.*, pp. 245, 253.

[3] *Proc. Ind. Hist. Cong.*, 6th Session (1943), pp. 163-70.

then the bone of contention between the Pratihāras and the Rāṣṭrakūṭas, and "completely devastated that hostile city of Mahodaya"[1] in the year 916 or 917 A. D. Shortly before Śaka 862=940 A.D. Kriṣṇa III (*c.* 940-68 A.D.) also, as *Kumāra* or crown-prince, led an expedition in Northern India, and on his approach the Gurjara-Pratīhāra ruler became so panic-stricken that he lost all hope of the defence of his two best strongholds, Kālañjara and Citrakūṭa. Someśvara I Āhavamalla (*c.* 1042-68 A.D.) was another monarch of the Dakṣiṇāpatha, who directed his attention northwards after setting accounts with his southern neighbours. His forces marched across Central India unchecked by the Candellas and the Kacchapaghātas, and afraid of his might the king of Kānyakubja is represented as having "quickly experienced an abode among caves"[2]. Someśvara I Āhavamalla won a preponderance against Lakṣmī-Karṇa Kalacuri too. We are further told that the Western Cālukya prince, Vikramāditya, overran Mithila, Magadha, Aṅga, Vaṅga, Gauḍa, meeting with little or no opposition. The last great invasion of the North was by Rājendra I Gaṅgaī-koṇḍa (*c.*1014-44 A.D.), who sometime between 1021 and 1025 A.D.,[3] advanced right upto the Ganges subduing Odda-viṣaya (Orissa), Kosalaināḍu (Southern Kosala), Dharmapāla of Taṇḍabutti (Daṇḍabhukti, Balasore and a part of Midnapore district), Raṇaśūra of Takkana-lādaṁ (South Rāḍha), Govindacandra of Vaṅgāla-deśa (Eastern Bengal), Mahīpāla-the Pāla ruler (*c.* 992-1040 A.D.), and Uttiralāḍaṁ (North Rāḍha)[4]. Thus, though these kings of Southern India were despoiling the

[1] *Ibid.*, VII, pp. 38, 43, v. 19.
[2] *Ind. Ant.*, VIII, p. 19.
[3] See *Dynastic History of Northern India*, Vol. I, p. 318.
[4] cf. Tirumalai Inscription, *Ep. Ind.*, IX, pp. 229-33.

smiling plains of the North, it is strange that the powers of Northern India could not pay off their scores any time during the centuries under survey.

Another noteworthy feature of the history of the South in our period is that some rulers maintained strong naval forces, and their conquests were not limited to the mainland only but extended overseas also. Besides the two naval expeditions of Narasiṁhavarman Pallava to Ceylon in the middle of the seventh century A.D., we learn that Parāntaka I (*c.* 907-53 A.D.) invaded Ceylon, where Māravarman Rājasiṁha II Pāṇḍya had taken refuge after his defeat. The raid, however, proved abortive. Rājarāja I (*c.* 985-1014 A.D.) next invaded Ceylon, and annexed its northern part as a province of the Coḷa Empire. He further conquered "the old islands of the sea numbering 12000", which have generally been identified with the Laccadives and the Maldives. The whole of Ceylon was ultimately annexed by Rājendra I Gaṅgaīkoṇḍa (*c.* 1014-44 A.D.) about 1017 A.D. His powerful fleet also gained successes across the Bay of Bengal, for he is said to have vanquished Saṁgrāmavijayottuṅgavarman and conquered Katah or Kadāraṁ and other places in further India. It is likely that the expedition was undertaken not merely to feed fat the ambitions of Rājendra I, but also to promote and strengthen commercial relations between Southern India and the Malay Peninsula. Lastly, Vīra-Rājendra (*c.* 1063-70 A.D.) tried to repeat the exploits of Rājendra I in Kadāraṁ or Śrī-Vijaya ; the details, which led to this adventure, are, however, obscure.

SECTION C

RELIGION AND SOCIETY

We have now got a glimpse of the fascinating panorama of events, which unfolds itself during the early medieval period. Of course, our view is to some extent blurred by the multiplicity of actors and the rapidity of their movements. Scenes change swiftly; empires rise and fall ; and dynasties appear and disappear into the limbo of oblivion. The clash of arms and ambitions is truly bewildering. Accordingly, we would like to turn away from the splendours and tragedies of our history, and take a peep into the state of religion, society, polity, economic life, literature, and art. Was it a period of all-round stagnation and decadence ? Or, do we see any sidelights of progress ? Questions like these had better be answered by facts themselves. The first point to strike us is that Buddhism was no longer an active force in India. But it certainly lingered on in some localities. We learn that in the course of his itinerary Yuan Chwang (*c.* 629-45 A.D.) saw "some hundred of *Saṁghārāmas* and 10,000 priests" in Kāñcī. They studied the teaching of the Sthavira school and belonged to the Mahāyāna. It may, therefore, be reasonably presumed that Buddhism may have survived in the Pallava kingdom long after the visit of Yuan Chwang. Its existence in the South is also proved by the gifts made by Rājarāja I Coḷa, an ardent Śaiva, to the Buddhist *Vihāra* at Negapatam, and by those of Kulottuṅga I to another Buddhist *Vihāra*. In the Dekkan its chief centres were Kampilya (Sholapur district), Dambal (Dharvad district), and Kanheri (Thana district)[1]. When the Moslems first came to Sind in the beginning of the eighth century, they found there a fairly large population of Buddhists. The Pālas were, of course, patrons of Buddhism, and they generously endowed Buddhist monasteries in Bengal and Magadha, where it may be traced up to the time of Bakhtyār Khiljī's invasion. But here Buddhism had moved far away from its original moorings. Indeed, the new *Tāntric* forms, which it had developed, had transformed it almost beyond recognition. The monks were, however, still fired with missionary zeal, and as an instance we may mention the famous Dīpañkara Srījñāna, called by Tibetans Atisa, who is known to have gone beyond the frontiers of India to Tibet about the middle of the eleventh century to spread the light of his faith. Unlike Buddhism, the Jain church appears to have gained in strength in some parts of India. In the Dekkan it was honoured by certain early Cālukya kings and by Rāṣṭrakūṭa rulers like Amoghavarṣa I, Indra IV, Kriṣṇa II and Indra III. Many of the Western Gaṅga kings also were favourably disposed towards it. Leaving aside Avinīta and Durvinīta, who flourished prior to our period, and who respectively patronised the Jain Ācāryas, Vijayakīrti and Pūjyapāda, we know that it was during the reign of Rājamalla (*c.* 977-85 A.D.) that his minister and general, Cāmuṇḍarāya, a devout Jain, erected the celebrated image of Gomateśvara at Śravaṇa Belgola in 983 A.D. The great Bittiga Viṣṇuvardhana Hoysala (*c.* 1110-40 A.D.) was originally a Jain in his beliefs, but was converted to Vaiṣṇavism later in life by Ācārya Rāmānuja. Under the Coḷas, who were staunch Śaivas, the Jains continued to pursue their tenets in peace. Describing Mo-lo-kiu-ch'a (Mala-

[1] *Ind. Ant.*, XII, pp. 134-37.

kūṭa) or the Pāṇḍya country in 640 A.D. Yuan Chwang refers to "a multitude of heretics mostly belonging to the Nirgranthas"[1]. Similarly, he mentions "many Nirgranthas" living in the kingdom of Kāñcī. Accordingly, it may be supposed that there must have been a fairly good Jain population in the Pallava and Pāṇḍya realms in the succeeding centuries. But Jainism had its most notable triumphs under Kumārapāla Caulukya (*c.* 1143-72 A.D.), who drew inspiration from the great Ācārya Hemacandra. It is believed that as a result of the latter's preaching and encyclopaedic learning Jainism rapidly spread in Gujarat, Kāthiāwāḍ, Kaccha, Rajputana, and Malwa. In the North, however, its influence remained very limited for lack of royal patronage. Here as well as in Southern India the dominant faith was Brahmanism or Paurāṇic Hinduism, and princes and the common people alike venerated the Brahmanical gods. Among these, the most prominent were Viṣṇu and Śiva, who were known by a number of other names also[2]. The pantheon further included Brahmā, Sūrya, Vināyaka or Dāmodara (Gaṇeśa), Kumāra Skanda, Svāmī-Mahāsena or Kārtikeya, Indra, Agni, Yama, Varuṇa, Marut, and goddesses like the divine Mothers (Mātṛkas), Bhagavatī or Durgā, Śrī (Lakṣmī), besides a host of minor deities. Many of them still command popular allegiance, and thus modern Hinduism may be said to have taken shape by this period. As now, there was no exclusiveness in worship. For instance, the Rāṣṭrakūṭa inscriptions

[1] Beal, *Buddhist Records of the Western World*, Vol. II, p. 231.

[2] Thus Viṣṇu was called Vāsudeva, Cakradhara, Govinda, Nārāyaṇa, Gadādhara, Mādhava, Janārdana etc. Other names of Śiva were Śambhu, Hara, Mahādeva, Bhūtapati, Paśupati, Śūlapāṇi, Maheśvara, Pinākin, Tripurāntaka, etc.

begin with invocations to both Śiva and Viṣṇu, and the Gāhaḍavāla kings made grants after having performed adoration to Sūrya, Śiva, Vāsudeva (Viṣṇu), and after having sacrificed to the fire. Members of the same ruling family not unoften paid homage to different gods. This was specially the case with the Pratīhāra princes[1]. Indeed, royal eclecticism had sometimes a wider range, for an inscription, represents Jayacandra as becoming the disciple of a Buddhist monk namd Śrīmitra "with a pleasing heart and an indescribable hankering"[2]. We further learn that Govindacandra Gāhaḍavāla and Rājarāja I Coḷa and Kulottuṅga I granted villages to Buddhist *Vihāras*. This must have doubtless promoted a spirit of toleration and concord among the votaries of the various competing sects. Persecution and sectarian animosity were, therefore, not much in evidence then. An instance to the contrary is, of course, furnished by the aforesaid Kulottuṅga I, whose disfavour compelled the great Vaiṣṇava reformer, Rāmānuja, to leave Śrīraṅgaṁ and retire to the Hoysala dominions. His return was made possible only when Vikrama Coḷa reversed his father's attitude towards him. Generally, however, the Coḷas and other rulers of the South were tolerant of all creeds, and Vaiṣṇava Aḷvars and Śaiva Nayanmārs were free to preach and propagate their doctrines. These religious teachers infused new life and vitality in the current beliefs and practices by their precept and example. South India also produced during this period such towering personalities as Kumārila Bhaṭṭa, Śaṅkarācārya, Rāmānujācārya, and Madhvācārya, who have left an indelible impress on Hindu religion and philosophy by their moral

[1] *History of Kanauj*, p. 290.
[2] *Ind. Hist. Quart.*, V (1929), p. 26, v. 10.

fervour and intellectual grandeur. Lastly, it may be noted that Vedic sacrifices do not appear to have been the vogue then. In the inscriptions of the Rāṣṭrakūṭas, however, there are references to the performance of *Hiraṇyagarbha ceremony and Tulādānas.* A Coḷa inscription of the time of Rājādhirāja I (*c.* 1044-52 A.D.) also contains a solitary allusion to the *Aśvamedha.* Probably greater stress now began to be laid on *Dāna* (gifts) than on *Yajñas* (sacrifices) with their intricate and cumbersome details. On the other hand, the great Moslem scholar, Alberuni (*c.* 970-1039 A.D.), writing in 1030 A.D., explains their discontinuance as follows : "The sacrifices differ in duration, so that only he could perform certain of them who lives a very long life; and such long lives do no longer occur in this our age. Therefore most of them have been abolished, and only few of them remain and are practised now-a-days"[1].

Caste-distinctions (*varṇas*) formed the steel-frame of society then, as now. According to Ibn Khurdadba, who died in *Hijrī* 300=912 A.D., there were seven castes, viz., (a) Sabkufria or Sabakferya, (b) Brahma, (c) Katariya, (d) Sudariya, (e) Baisura, (f) Sandalia, (g) Lahud. These are also mentioned by Al Idrīsi (end of the 11th century), but the last he calls Zakya. There can be no doubt that (b), (c), (d), (e) and (f) respectively stand for Brahman, Kṣatriya, Śūdra, Vaiśya, and Cāṇḍāla; and (a) perhaps denotes Satkṣatriyas[2]. The identification of (g) is uncertain. Alberuni, however, says that from the very beginning the Hindus had only four castes, viz., (i) Brahman, (ii) Kṣatriya, (iii) Vaiśya, and (iv) Śūdra. Evidently his observation is based on what he had learnt from Hindu

[1] Sachau, *Alberuni's India,* Vol. II, p. 139.

[2] *Rāṣṭrakūṭas and their Times,* pp. 318-19.

Smritis, for it is well-known that by this time society was split up into numerous sub-divisions and mixed castes. This is borne out by the later *Smritis* and Kalhaṇa, who refers to 64 sub-castes. The formation of minor castes was due to illegitimate unions, or to the abandonment of hereditary occupations and the adoption of a new calling or craft. Besides the four main castes, Alberuni mentions eight classes of *Antyajas*, and Hāḍi, Doma (Ḍomba), Cāṇḍāla, and Badhatau (*sic*), who were not reckoned amongst any caste. They were occupied with dirty work, and had to live outside towns and villages. Our period thus had its untouchables, who were considered almost beyond the pale of society. Alberuni observes that men of the four castes "lived together in the same towns and villages, mixed together in the same houses and lodgings"[1], but it was tabooed for persons of different castes to sit and eat together[2]. Such restrictions were naturally inexplicable to him, and he notes with obvious regret that the institution of caste "is the greater obstacle which prevents any approach or understanding between Hindus and Muslims"[3]. Socially, therefore, the two communities could not come near each other in Alberuni's time. It is, however, interesting to know that reconversions to Hinduism from Islam were possible. Devala, writing after the Moslem conquest of Sind, permits reclamation of those who had been forcibly converted within a period of twenty years ; and Brihadyāma prescribes certain *prāyaścittas* for the purpose. Al Bilāduri (died 892-3 A.D.) laments over the fact that "the people of India had returned to idolatry

[1] Sachau, *Alberuni's India*, Vol. I, p. 101.

[2] *Ibid.*, p. 102.

[3] *Ibid.*, p. 100.

excepting those of Kassa"[1]. Al Utbī also refers to the case of Nawas Shāh, an Indian prince, who, having embraced Islām, subsequently "held conversations with the chiefs of idolatry respecting the casting off the firm rope of religion from his neck"[2]. Among the Hindus, the ascendancy of the Brahmans was fully established. They were distinguished by their *gotras* and *pravaras*, although surnames, now in use, were then gradually coming into vogue. Provincial labels had not yet arisen ; however, in an inscription the composer of the grant calls himself "Nāgara-Jñātīya Brāhmaṇa"[3]. The Brahmans were honoured by members of other castes by gifts and personal reverence. According to Al Maśūdī and Al Idrīsi, the Brahmans abstained from taking flesh and lived a life of piety and earnest endeavour. Ibn Khurdadba also deposes that they did not take wine or fermented liquors. They practised Yoga[4], and pursued the study of the Vedas, which they did not allow to be committed to writing, but learnt by heart. Further, they studied the eighteen Purāṇas, Smritis, and philosophical treatises on Sāṁkhya, Nyāya, Vaiśeṣika, Mīmāṅsā etc., the Epics, and those dealing with the exact sciences like Grammar, Metrics, Astronomy, Astrology, Mathematics, and Medicine, etc.[5]. In fine, they were the repositories of all learning and sacred lore. The Brahmans taught the Vedas to the Kṣatriyas. "The latter learnt it, but were not allowed to teach it, not even to a Brahman." Regarding the Vaiśya and the Śūdra, Alberuni says that they "are not allowed to hear it, much less to

[1] Elliot, *History of India*, Vol. I, p. 126.
[2] *Ibid.*, Vol. II, pp. 32-33.
[3] *Ep. Ind.*, III, 123.
[4] *Ind. Ant.*, XVI, pp. 174, 175.
[5] Sachau, *Alberuni's India*, Vol. I, pp. 130-9.

pronounce and recite it. If such a thing can be proved against one of them, the Brahmans drag him before the magistrate, and he is punished by having his tongue cut off"[1]. These invidious distinctions and disabilities were a blot on the society of the day, and they must have damped the arduour of the masses for the existing order of things. It is no wonder, therefore, that the Moslem invaders, fired as they were by a new message of universal brotherhood, succeeded in planting their standards in India, despite the numerical superiority of the Hindus over them.

Caste-pretensions also expressed themselves in the growing disapprobation of inter-caste marriages. Alberuni notes that though *anuloma* marriages were permissible the Brahmans in his time "never married any woman except one of their own caste"[2]. Ibn Khurdadba, on the other hand, informs us about Western India that Brahmas (Brahmans) took the daughters of Katarias (Kṣatriyas). History has undoubtedly preserved some instances of such marriages. We learn that Rājaśekhara (end of the ninth century and first quarter of the tenth) married a Kṣatriya lady, Avantisundarī by name, belonging to the Cāhamāna clan ; and Saṁgrāmarāja, a king of Kashmir, gave the hand of his sister to a Brahman. It appears that among Royalty, at least, marriages with persons of different persuasions were not prohibited. For Govindacandra Gāhaḍavāla is known to have married Kumāradevī, an ardent Buddhist. Early marriages were perhaps prevalent during this period. Thus says Alberuni : "The Hindus marry at a very young age; therefore the parents arrange the marriage of their sons"[3]. The "upper ten", at any

[1] *Ibid.*, I, p. 125; II, p. 136.

[2] *Ibid.*, II, pp. 155-56.

[3] *Ibid.*, II, p. 154.

rate, practised polygamy, and divorce was not a recognised custom. If a woman lost her husband, she could not remarry. She had either to remain a widow, or become a *Satī*. In Kashmir it was a common practice, though not so in the Dekkan. Probably the custom of *Satī* then obtained in royal families only, and did not prevail among the masses as in later times. There are grounds to believe that *Purdah* had yet to establish itself. Abu Zaid observes : "Most of the princes of India, when they held a court, allow their women to be seen by the men who attend it, whether they be natives or foreigners. No veil conceals them from the eyes of visitors"[1]. The position of women was, on the whole, not bad. Some of them distinguished themselves by their intellectual attainments. Rājaśekhara refers to female poets, and his own wife, Avantisundarī, was a very talented lady. Maṇḍaṇa Miśra's wife is said to have baffled even the great Śaṅkarācārya by her brilliant intellect. Līlāvatī was deeply proficient in Mathematics. Our period also boasts of some women rulers like Didda of Kashmir (*c.* 980-1003 A.D.) and the Kākatīya queen, Rudrāṁbā (*c.* 1261-90 A.D.). In the Western Cālukya records there are references to queen-governors too. Thus Mailādevī, one of the wives of Someśvara I Āhavamalla governed the province of Banavāsī in 1053 A.D., and Lakṣmīdevī, the *agramahiṣī* of Vikramāditya VI, held charge of 18 *agraharas* in A.D. 1095. A less pleasing aspect of society was the existence of slavery, if we are to believe the testimony of Vijñāneśvara, the protege of Vikramāditya VI (*c.* 1076-1126 A.D.) and author of *Mitākṣarā*, who refers to fifteen kinds of slaves and how they could purchase their freedom. Pilgrimages

[1] Elliot, *History of India*, I, p. 11.

to holy places (*tīrthas*) like Vārāṇasī (Benares), Mathurā, Pukar (Puṣkara) etc., were then in vogue among the Hindus. They also celebrated certain days of the year as festivals, and observed fasts (*vratas*) to gain merit. Thus we may trace to our period certain practices, which in later day Hindu society received considerable emphasis.

SECTION D

ADMINISTRATION AND ECONOMIC CONDITION

Having got a picture, dim though it is, of the religious and social life of the people, let us consider the system of government under which they lived. It may at the outset be remarked that the governments set up during this period, were fairly well organised. This would be clear from the fact that notwithstanding the shocks of intermittent wars and sometimes of disputed successions the rule of the Pālas, the Coḷas, and the Eastern Cālukyas lasted about four centuries, and that of the Pratīhāras, the Rāṣṭrakūṭas, and the Western Cālukyas for over two centuries each. In those days of scanty and slow means of communication it was remarkable indeed that they could hold together extensive territories for such long periods. The machinery of administration was more or less the same in all cases except that its parts or constituents varied with the century or with the locality. The names of the functionaries changed but not their functions. As before, the kingdom (*rājya*) was divided for administrative convenience into a number of provinces (*bhukti*, *bhūmi*, *maṇḍala* or *maṇḍalaṁ* of the South), which were in turn subdivided into divisions (*viṣaya* or *bhoga*; called *kottaṁs* or *valanāḍu* in the South). The other units of administration in the descending scale were the districts (*adhiṣṭhāna* or *pattana*; called *nāḍu* in the South), groups of villages (*pattala* or *agrahāra*, i.e., modern *tahsil*; called *kurraṁ* in South Indian records), and lastly the village (*grāma* or *grāmaṁ*). There existed a host of officials-high or low-, central, provincial and local, to carry on the administration. Sometimes the distinction between civil and military functionaries was not quite marked. It would not be pertinent to our purpose to enumerate them here, and we, therefore, content ourselves with merely indicating a few broad features of the polity of the period. The first striking point is the utter absence of non-monarchical governments. The last glimpse that we get of autonomous or oligarchic clans is from the Allahabad pillar inscription of Samudragupta. Now they had become a thing of the past, completely submerged under the rising tide of monarchism[1]. It was a hereditary monarchy, and there was no question of electing the ruler. Of course, we learn that about the middle of the eighth century Gopāla was chosen or acclaimed king by the people of Bengal, who were sorely distressed on account of the anarchical conditions then prevailing ; and in 939 A.D., after the death of Śūravarman II, Yaśaḥkara was elected as ruler of Kashmir by an assemblage of Brahmans, but these exceptions do not prove the rule. Generally the eldest son succeeded his father, who anointed him *yuvarāja* in his own lifetime. If, however, the younger one was abler, the claims of the eldest son were passed over, as happened in case of Stamba (Khambayya) when Dhruva Nirupama nominated Govinda III to the throne. Such preferences not unnaturally led to wars between the brothers. Sometimes half-brothers, like Bhoja II and Mahīpāla, also contended against cach other for the crown. In case the king was a minor, a near relation acted as regent. Not unoften it led to court intrigues and

[1] It is noteworthy that there is no reference to non-monarchical governments in South India records of the earlier period also.

disturbances in the kingdom. During this age royalty lived amidst pomp and splendour, and their absolutism was fully established ; and though *mantrins* and *amātyas*-ministers and counsellors-are heard of, there does not appear to have been any regular *mantripariṣad* of earlier days to advise and guide the king and serve as a sort of check on his arbitrariness. Indeed, the records of our period seldom refer to consultation with the ministry before the king embarked on a new venture. In order to retain their position, which devolved on them often by virtue of descent, and gain the favour of their all-powerful masters, the ministers thought it prudent to play to their tune, and Kalhaṇa alludes to such puppets in the history of Kashmir. But instances of such ministers also are not unknown who commanded the respect of their kings by their sagacity, integrity and devotion. Thus, in a record the Yādava ruler, Kriṣṇa, compares his ministers to his own tongue and right hand[1].

Feudatories (*Sāmantas* or *Mahāsāmantas*) were a prominent feature of polity. Of course, they existed from much earlier times, for conquerors mostly followed the policy of non-annexation of territory, advocated by Manu and Kauṭilya. About the middle of the ninth century Al Sulaimān too observes : "When a king subdues a neighbouring state in India he places over it a man belonging to the family of the fallen prince, who carries on the government in the name of the conqueror. The inhabitants would not suffer it to be otherwise"[2]. Attempts were, no doubt, made from time to time by Imperialistic powers

[1] *Ind. Ant.*, XIV, p. 69.

[2] This policy of non-annexation was a source of weakness to the Central authority, for recalcitrant feudatories were ever seeking opportunities to raise the standard of revolt.

to annex the territories conquered and put them under princes of the blood royal. Thus the Rāṣṭrakūṭas tried to absorb Gaṅgavāḍī and in the reign of Kriṣṇa III even Toṇḍamaṇḍalaṁ, and the Coḷas also adopted a similar policy regarding Kerala and the Pāṇḍya land, but success in each case was short-lived. Feudatories rendered the suzerain personal attendance, and helped him in military undertakings. The Kanarese poet, Pampa, tells us that Narasiṁha Cālukya accompanied his overlord, Indra III, in his northern campaign, and the records of the Pālas, the Pratīhāras and other ruling families preserve numerous instances of feudatories participating in their wars. For this purpose they maintained a certain number of troops, and it appears that the paramount powers, specially of Northern India for the Coḷas had at their command effective land and naval forces, began to rely now on these levies to such an extent that they sometimes even neglected to keep their standing armies in proper strength and efficient condition. Thus, we see the growth of *a sort* of feudal system, which subsequently became a bane, contributing in no small measure to the disruption or weakness of the suzerain authority.

The records of southern India throw considerable light on the existence and working of village assemblies during our period. Under the Coḷas they were the most characteristic feature of rural life in the South, although they have been referred to in later Pallava inscriptions also. Unfortunately, however, they do not find any mention in North Indian records. It is hardly necessary here to detail the functions of the *Mahāsabhā* or *Sabhā* of a South Indian village, but suffice it to say that subject to the supervision and general control of Imperial officers it enjoyed full powers in the management of rural affairs. For purposes of efficiency it was divided into various subcommittees, which were severally responsible for the upkeep and improvement of temples, tanks, public baths, gardens, fields, etc. There were elaborate rules devised for election to these bodies. A member was elected for one year only, and his eligibility or otherwise for membership was determined on a consideration of certain qualifications based on one's character, learning, social status, etc.

The maintenance of law and order is one of the primary duties of the State, and there are grounds to believe that however aggressive kings were in their foreign relations they were anxious to preserve peace and security within their kingdoms. Thus Al Sulaimān (851 A.D.), writing about the Pratīhāra Empire of Bhoja observes : "There is no country in India more safe from robbers." This would appear a great tribute indeed to the excellence of the Pratīhāra administration, if we remember that while travelling in Madhyadeśa during Harṣa's reign more than two centuries earlier Yuan Chwang was troubled by bands of brigands.

The State also undertook public works of utility to promote the prosperity of the people. The Coḷas constructed grand trunk roads, which served as arteries of commerce and communication, besides facilitating the movements of armies. Further, they sank wells, excavated tanks, threw mighty dams across the Kāverī, and cut channels to supply the irrigational needs of the cultivators. With this object in view Rājendra I dug near his capital, Gaṅgaikoṇḍacoḷapuraṁ, an artificial lake which was filled with water from the Koḷerun and Vellar rivers. Similarly, the Candellas and the Paramāras constructed a number of embanked lakes, like Madanasāgara at Mahobā and Muñjasāgara at Dhar. In Kashmir, Suyya, minister of Avantivarman (*c.* 855-83 A.D.), provided channels for irrigation. He even changed the course of the Vitasta (Jhelum) to prevent floods, and thus reclaimed vast marshy lands for cultivation. As a result of this, people became economically more prosperous in Kashmir, for a *khārī* of rice could be bought for 36 *dīnāras*, whereas previously the price of the same was 200 *dīnāras*. These beneficent measures clearly indicate that during this period kings did not simply minister to their whims and warlike proclivities but they also kept the well-being of the silent masses in view.

The stability and usefulness of the administration depended upon a sound system of taxation. We learn of many kinds of taxes, regular and occasional, from the records of North as well as South India, and it appears from their comprehensive nature that almost all conceivable sources of income were tapped by the government. The capacity to pay these numerous taxes, benevolences and fines also indirectly throws light on the economic condition of the people. Of course, the mainstay of finance continued to be the land-revenue, which perhaps varied according to the quality of the land, irrigational facilities, and the needs of the state[1]. It was usually paid in kind, but sometimes partly in cash also by instalments. Inscriptions at the Rājarājeśvara temple show that in the *Tamilakaṁ* the land tax was realised in paddy. Land was periodically surveyed with meticulous care, and a record of holdings was maintained. This was specially done by the Colas. The State also derived income from trade, and in this connexion it may be mentioned that the Coḷa fleet helped them considerably in their overseas commercial intercourse. Other sources of State income were waste lands, trees,

[1] The expression षड्भाग in connection with the land tax is not to be interpreted literally. In practice the king probably took as much as he needed without unduly oppressing the subjects.

mines, salt, treasure trove, etc. The State also recognised the system of forced labour. Economic life was organised on the basis of crafts. Persons following the same occupations formed themselves into guilds or corporations for regulating their business. There are numerous references to them in the records of our time. Each guild had its chief, and its members in their corporate capacity made gifts to temples, etc. These guilds sometimes acted as banks where money could be deposited at a certain rate of interest. They were free to administer their internal affairs, and the State did not meddle much with them. Besides organising society, they were of great benefit to the State, inasmuch as they certainly fostered a law-abiding spirit.

Section E

LITERATURE AND ART

Literature shows considerable development during our period. It was, however, not of a high order. There were a number of rulers, who were not only patrons of the polite letters, but who were themselves proficient in the Muses. Indeed, it appears that they could wield the pen with no less dexterity than the sword. Thus, the *Harakeli-Nāṭaka*, portions of which were recovered from an inscribed stone slab at Ajmer, is attributed to Vigraharāja Vīsaladeva Cāhamāna. Vallālasena compiled the *Dānasāgara* and the *Adbhuta-sāgara*, and the unfinished portion of the latter is said to have been completed by Lakṣmaṇasena. Vākpati-Muñja is described as having been gifted with poetic talents of a high order, and the great Bhoja Paramāra is the putative author of about two dozen works on a variety of subjects, such as medicine, astronomy, religion, grammar, architecture, poetics, lexicography, arts, etc. Among his productions, we may mention a few : *Āyurveda-sarvasva*, *Rājamrigāṅka*, *Vyavahāra-samuccaya*, *Śabdānuśāsana*, *Samarāṅgaṇa-Sūtradhāra*, *Saraswatī-Kaṇṭhābharaṇa*, *Nāma-mālikā*, *Yukti-Kalpataru*, etc. Amoghavarṣa I Rāṣṭrakūṭa wrote the *Kavirāja-mārga*, a Kanarese work on poetics, and the *Praśnottaramālikā*, which is, however, sometimes ascribed to Saṅkarācārya or to one Vimala. The *Mānasollāsa*, dealing with topics of varied interest, was probably the work of the western Cālukya, Someśvara III (*c*. 1126-38 A. D.), and Mathematics was assiduously cultivated by the Eastern Cālukya, Vinayāditya III Guṇaga. There were authors among the Gaṅga and Pallava sovereigns also. It is, however, likely that some of the kings, mentioned above, may have been helped in their compositions by their literary proteges. Princes extended their patronage to men of genius and literary merit, who have vastly enriched the literature of the period by their labours. We may enumerate here in tabular form some of the works by way of illustration :

SANSKRIT

Poetry	*Author*	*Name of work*
	Kavirāja	Rāghavapāṇḍavīya
	Jinasena	Pārśvābhudaya-kāvya
	Śrī-Harṣa	Naiṣadha-carita
	Maṅkha	Śrīkaṇṭhacarita
	Jayadeva	Gīta-govinda
	Dhoyika	Pavana-dūta
	Saṅdhyākara-naṅdi	Rāma-carita
	Bilhaṇa	Vikramāṅka-deva-carita
	Padmagupta	Navasāhasāṅka-carita
	Hemacandra	Dvāśraya-kāvya
	Somadeva	Kīrti-kaumudī
	Jayānaka	Prithvīrāja-vijaya
	Kalhaṇa	Rājataraṅgiṇī

It may be noted that the last seven are of historical importance too.

In 1037 A.D. Kṣemendra produced the *Brihat-Kathāmañjarī*, a translation in Sanskrit prose of Gūṇāḍhya's Paiśāchī *Brihat-Kathā*, which was also rendered into the *Kathāsaritsāgara* by Somadeva about the third quarter of the eleventh century.

Poetics	*Author*	*Name of work*
	Rājaśekhara	Kāvyamīmāṅsā
	Ānandavardhana	Dhvanvāloka
	Mammaṭa	Kāvyaprakāśa

	Dhanañjaya	Daśarūpa
	Dhanika	Daśarūpāvaloka
	Bhoja	Sarasvatī-Kaṇṭhābharaṇa
	Hemacandra	Kāvyānuśāsana
	Vaidyanātha	Pratāparudrīya
Drama	Bhavabhūti	Mālatīmādhava, Mahāvīra-carita, Uttara-rāma-carita
	Rājaśekhara	Bālarāmāyaṇa, Bālabhārata, Viddhasāla-bhāñjikā
	Dāmodara	Hanuman-nāṭaka
	Krisṇa-Miśra	Prabodha-candrodaya
	Somadeva	Lalitavigraha-rāja
Dictionary	Halāyudha	Abhidhāna-ratna-mālā
	Hemacandra	Abhidhāna-cintāmaṇi
	Yādava-bhaṭṭa	Vaijayantī-koṣa
	Maheśvara	Viśva-prakāśa
Philosophy	Kumārila	Commentary in three parts-Ślokavārttika, Tantravārttika, and Tuptika
	Maṇḍana Miśra	Mīmāṅsānukramaṇī Vidhiviveka
	Vācaspati Miśra	Nyāyakaṇika Tattvabindu Sāṁkhya-tattva-kaumudī
	Śaṅkarācārya	Commentaries on the Upaniṣads, Gītābhāṣya, Brahma-sūtra-bhāṣya, Upadeśasahaśrī, Ātmabodha
	Rāmānuja	Śrībhāsya on the Brahma sūtra, Gītābhāṣya,

		Vedāntasāra
	Udayana	Kusumāñjali
	Madhvācārya	Tattvasaṁkhyāna
		Śārasaṁgraha
	Hemacandra	Pramāṇa-mīmāṅsā.

Besides the above, there were a number of other commentaries and sectarian literature produced.

Astronomy	Āryabhaṭa II	Ārya Siddhānta
	Bhoja	Rājamrigāṅka
	Bhāskarācārya (1150 A.D.)	Siddhāntaśiromaṇi

Prithūdaka Svāmī wrote a commentary on Brahmagupta's *Brahmasphuṭa-Siddhānta*, and *Cāṅgadeva*, who flourished under Siṅghaṇa Yādava founded a *maṭha* at Patna (Khandesh district) for the study of Bhāskarācārya's *Siddhānta-Śiromaṇi*.

Astrology	*Author*	*Name of work*
	Bhaṭṭotpala	Commented on Varāhamihira's works, Horāśāstra
	Haraśakīrti Surī	Jyotiṣasāroddhāra
	Śrīpati (1039A.D.)	Ratnamālā
Mathematics	Mahāvīrācārya (ninth century)	Gaṇitasārasaṁgraha
	Śrīdhara (born in 991 A.D.)	Triśati
	Bhāskarācārya	Līlāvatī Bījagaṇita
Law	Medhātithi (9th cent.) Govindarāja (11th cent.)	Commentary on the Manusmriti
	Vijñāneśvara (11th century)	Mitākṣarā (commentary on the Yājñavalkya Smriti)
	Lakṣmīdhara	Smritikalpataru
	Hemādri or Hemādpant	Caturvarga-Cintāmaṇi

	Halāyudha (12th century)	Brāhmaṇasarvasva
Politics	Somadeva	Nītivākyāmrita
	Hemacandra	Laghu Arhannīti
	Bhoja	Yukti-Kalpataru
	Caṇḍeśvara	Nītiratnākara
Āyurveda	Vāgbhaṭa	Aṣṭāṁgasaṁgraha
		Aṣṭāṁgahridaya-saṁhitā
	Mādhavakara	Rugviniścaya
	Vrinda	Siddhiyoga
	Cakrapāṇidatta (*c.* 1060 A.D.)	Cikitsāsāra-saṁgraha
	Śārṅgadhara	Śārṅgadhara-Saṁhitā
Music	Śārṅgadhara	Saṁgīta-Ratnākara
Grammar	Śakaṭāyana (9th cent.)	Śakaṭāyana-Vyākaraṇa
	Hemacandra	Haima Vyākaraṇa
	Kramadīśvara (12th cent.)	Saṁkṣiptasāra

Prakrit

Vākpatirāja	Gauḍavaho
Rājaśekhara	Karpūramañjarī
Bhoja	Kūrmaśataka
Hemacandra	Kumārapāla-carita (Prakrit Dvāśraya-Kāvya)
	Kālakācāryakathā
	Prabandha-Cintāmaṇi
Somaprabhā	Kumārapāla-prabodha
Dhanapāla	Bhayasayattakahā
	Paiyalacchi (Koṣa)

Kanarese

Amoghavarṣa	Kavirājamārga
Pampa	Pampabhārata

Tamil

Jayagoṇḍan	Kaliṅgattupparani
Adiyarkkunallar	Commentary on Śilappadhikāraṁ.

It would be evident from the above list, which is only illustrative and not exhaustive, that, though the volume and range of works was large, the literature produced during this period consisted mostly of commentaries and digests etc., and was lacking in originality.

As regards Art, it was undoubtedly a fruitful age, as would be apparent from the numerous temples that are extant. They are among the most exquisite edifices ever raised in India, representing all the styles of architecture. The famous temples of Orissa, specially those of Bhuvaneśvar (Puri district), are superb specimens of the "Indo-Aryan style" in its most advanced stage of development. Each temple consists of the *vimāna* (towered shrine), and the *jagamohana* (audience chamber), besides the *naṭa maṇḍapa* (dancing saloon) and the *bhogamaṇḍapa* (refectory) ; the last two, however, are perhaps later appendages. The Orissan temples, the best example of which is the great Liṅgarāja shrine of Bhuvaneśvar (11th century), are characterised by an abundance of decorative motifs, inspired by human, animal and vegetable life ; and by lofty spires, surmounted by *amalakas*, commanding the landscape for miles around. Curiously enough, the sun-temple at Konarak abounds in indecent representation, and it is an interesting, though baffling, problem to explain this phenomenon. Another place, where several excellent structures still stand, is Khajurāho in Bundelkhand. It was lavishly beautified by the Candellas, and the Kandarya Mahādeva temple (10th or 11th century) there presents another fine example of the "Indo-

Aryan" type. One is simply enthralled by its beautiful statuary and decoration. During this period there flourished in Kashmir a style of architecture, which had certain distinctive peculiarities, and its most typical example is the Mārtaṇḍa temple, built by Lalitāditya Muktāpīḍa sometime in the second quarter of the eighth century. The Jains also were great builders, and their temples have generally the octagonal dome, and are decorated with subjects drawn from Jain mythology. In the North they are of the "Indo-Aryan style," and in Southern India of the Dravidian. The best specimens of their architectural activity are the famous temples of Dilwara (Mt. Abu) and Śatruñjaya (Palitana). Those built by one Vimala and by the brothers, Tejaḥpāla and Vastupāla, on Mt. Abu are most remarkable for their elegant carvings and rich design. The temples of Vātāpi (Badami) and Pattadakal (Bijapur district) are built on the Cālukyan or Dekkani style, and do not, strictly speaking, come in our period. In this type, the temple stands on an elaborately decorated base or plinth and it is polygonal, often star-shaped in plan. The Dekkani style was probably derived from the Dravidian, but in course of time it developed on independent lines. Some good specimens of this type are those of Belur in Mysore, built by Bittiga Viṣṇuvardhana (*c.* 1110-40 A.D.), and the Hoysaleśvara temple at Halebid (end of the 12th century), which, though incomplete, is "unsurpassed by any Indian temple in both its structural and its decorative features.[1]" Sometimes temples in the Dekkan were hewn out of solid rock. As an instance, we may mention the magnificent temple of Śiva at Elāpura (Ellora), excavated by Krisṇa I Rāṣṭrakūṭa (*c.* 757-72 A.D.), which has been regarded as "the most

[1] *Antiquities of India*, pp. 244-45.

marvellous architectural freak in India." The Pallavas gave an immense impetus to art, and the temples at Dalavanur (South Arcot district), Pallavaraṁ, Vallaṁ (Chingleput district), as well as the Rathas, like the Dharmarāja at Māmallapuraṁ, the Kailāśanātha at Kāñcī, and the Shore temple of the seven Pagodas group stand today as noble monuments of their artistic genius. But they belong to a period slightly earlier than the one we are directly concerned with. The Coḷas carried on the architectural traditions of the Pallavas, and erected a number of edifices in the South. The Dravidian temples were marked by the square *vimāna*, *maṇḍapa*, *gopuraṁ*, halls with elaborate columnation, conventional lions (*yāḷis*) for ornamentation, the use of the bracket and of compound columns, etc.[1] In later structures the central towers are dwarfed by exquisitely carved *gopuraṁs* gateways rising to a great height. The temple of Śiva at Tanjore, called Rājarājeśvara after the name of its builder, Rājarāja I (*c.* 985-1014 A.D.), may be taken as a splendid example of Dravidian architecture. Its lofty *vimāna* or tower rises like a pyramid upon a base of 82 feet square in thirteen successive storeys. It is crowned by a massive piece of granite, 25 feet high and about 50 tons in weight, and one can well imagine what a tremendous amount of labour and engineering skill it must have called forth to be placed in position. Among other noteworthy Coḷa temples are those of Tanjore, Kalahasti, and Gaṅgaikoṇḍacoḷapuraṁ. The Coḷas also encouraged plastic art, and the stone and metal images executed in their time are full of dignity, charm and grace. Thus some of the most beautiful monuments of our country, that have survived the wear and tear of time, belong to our period, and they reflect great credit on their builders.

[1] *Ibid.*, p. 242.

GENERAL BIBLIOGRAPHY

Note—This Bibliography has been prepared specially with a view to stimulating research. We have accordingly indicated here the literature on such subjects also as have not been discussed in the present volume.

IMPORTANT ORIGINAL SOURCES

The Vedas:

Rigveda Saṁhitā, ed. by Th. Aufrecht (Bonn, 1877); recent ed. Svādhyāya Maṇḍala (Aundh, V. E. 1996); Yajurveda, Taittirīya Saṁhitā, ed. by A. Weber (Berlin, 1871-72); Yajurveda, Kāṭhaka Saṁhitā, ed. by L. V. Schroeder (Leipzig, 1900-11); Yajurveda, Maitrāyaṇīya Saṁhitā, ed. by L.V. Schroeder (Leipzig, 1881-86). Yajurveda, Vājasneyī Saṁhitā, ed. by A. Weber (London, 1852); Svādhyāya Maṇḍala ed. (Aundh, V. E. 1984); Sāmaveda Saṁhitā, ed. by Thomas Benfey (Leipzig, 1848); Svādhyāya Maṇḍala ed. (Aundh, V. E. 1996); Atharvaveda Saṁhitā ed. by S. P. Pandit (Bombay, 1895-8); Svādhyāya Maṇḍala ed. (Aundh, V. E. 1995).

The Brāhmaṇas:

Aitareya Brāhmaṇa, ed. by Th. Aufrecht (Bonn, 1879); ed. and trans. by Haug (Bombay, 1863); Kauṣītakī (Sānkhāyana), ed. by Lindner (Jena, 1887); Pañcaviṁśa, ed. by Vedāntavāgīśa (Calcutta, 1869-74); Śatapatha, ed. by A. Weber (London, 1855); Taittirīya, ed. by N. Godbole (Poona, 1898); Gopatha, ed. by R. L. Mitra and H. Vidyābhūṣaṇa, (Calcutta, 1872).

The Āraṇyakas:

Aitareya Āraṇyaka, ed. by A. B. Keith (Oxford, 1909); Sānkhāyana Āraṇyaka, ed. by A. B. Keith (Oxford, 1909); Taittirīya Āraṇyaka, ed. by H. N. Apte (Poona, 1898).

The Upaniṣads:

Brihadāraṇyaka Upaniṣad, ed. by O. Böhtlingk (Leipzig, 1889); Kāṭhaka Upaniṣad, ed. by H. N. Apte (Poona, 1889); Chāndogya Upaniṣad, ed. by Böhtlingk (Leipzig, 1889); Muṇḍaka

Upaniṣad, ed. by Apte (Ānandāśrama Skt. series, 1889); Other Upaniṣads also have been edited with commentaries in the Ānandāśrama Sanskrit series (Poona, 1895). For translations of the Upaniṣads, see F. W. Max Müller, Sacred Books of the East Series, Volumes I and XV.

The Sūtras:

(a) *Śrauta Sūtras*

Sānkhāyana Śrauta Sūtra, ed. by Hillebrandt (Calcutta, 1888); Āśvalāyana Śrauta Sūtra, ed. by R. Vidyāratna (Calcutta, 1864-74); Lātyāyana Śrauta Sūtra, ed. by Ānandacandra Vedāntavāgīśa (Calc., 1870-72); Āpastamba Śrauta Sūtra, ed. by R. Garbe (Calc., 1882); Kātyāyana Śrauta Sūtra, ed. by A. Weber (London, 1855).

(b) *Grihya Sūtras*:

Sānkhāyana Grihya Sūtra, ed. by H. Oldenberg (Indische Studien, XV); Āśvalāyana Grihya Sūtra, ed. by A. F. Stenzler (Leipzig, 1864); Gobhila Grihya Sūtra, ed. by F. Knauer (Dorpat, 1884); Pāraskara (Vājasneya) Grihya Sūtra, ed. by A. F. Stenzler (Leipzig, 1876).

(c) *Dharma Sūtras*:

Āpastamba Dharmasūtra, ed. by Bühler (Bom. Skt. series, 1892, 1894); Baudhyāyana Dharmasūtra (also called Dharmaśāstra), ed, by E. Hultzsch (Leipzig, 1884). Gautama Dharmasūtra, ed. by A. F. Stenzler (London, 1876) Vaśiṣṭha Dharmasūtra, ed. by A. Führer (Bombay, 1883).

The Dharma-Śāstras:

Mānava Dharmaśāstra, ed. by J. Jolly (London, 1887); Viṣṇu Dharmaśāstra, ed. by J. Jolly (Calc., 1881); Nārada Smriti, ed. by J. Jolly (Calc., 1885); Yājñavalkya Smriti, ed. by A. F. Stenzler (Berlin, 1849); Brihaspati Smriti, Ānandāśrama Skt. series, Poona; Dharmaśāstra Saṁgraha, ed. by J. Vidyāsāgara (Calc., 1876).

The Epics:

Vālmīki Rāmāyaṇa, ed. by P. C. Roy (Calcutta, 1881-82); North-Western Recension, ed. by Bhagvad Datta, (Lahore, 1931); Mahābhārata, ed. by P. C. Roy (Calcutta, 1882); trans.

by the same (Calc. 1883-96); Śrimanmahābhāratam, based on South Indian texts, ed. by Krisṇacārya (Bombay, 1906).

Works Based on the Epics :

Rājaśekhara's Bāla-Rāmāyaṇa, ed. by Govindadeva Śāstrī, (Benares, 1869); Pracaṇḍa-Pāṇḍava or Bāla-Bhārata, ed. by Durgā Prasāda and Parab (Bombay, 1887).

Purāṇas :

Agni Purāṇa, ed. by R. L. Mitra (Calcutta, 1873-79); Brahma Purāṇa, ed. by H. N. Apte (Poona, 1895); Matsya Purāṇa, Ānandāśrama Skt. series (Poona, 1907); Vāyu Purāṇa, Ānandāśrama Skt. series (Poona, 1905); Viṣṇu Purāṇa, ed. by J. Vidyāsāgara (Calcutta, 1882); trans. by H. H. Wilson (London, 1864-70); Bhāgavata Purāṇa, ed. by Nityasvarūpa Brahmacārī (Brindāvana, 1916-17); Bhaviṣya Purāṇa, (Bib. Ind., 1910); Padma Purāṇa, ed. by V. N. Mandalika (Poona, 1894); Brahmāṇḍa Purāṇa, Śrivenkateśvara Press (Bombay, 1906).

Nīti and Arthaśāstras :

Kauṭilya's Arthaśāstra, ed. by Shamasastri (Mysore, 1909); trans. by Shamasastri, 3rd. ed. (Mysore, 1929); Kāmandakīya Nītisāra, ed. by Gaṇapati Śāstri (Trivandrum, 1912); Śukra Nītisāra, ed. by Gustav Oppert (Madras, 1882); Mitra Miśra's Vīramitrodaya, Chowkhambhā Skt. series, Benares; Bhoja's Yuktikalpataru, ed. by Īśvaracandra Śāstrī (Calcutta, 1917); Nīlakaṇṭha's Nīti-Mayūkha (Benares, 1880).

Works on Exegesis and Grammar :

Yāṣka's Nirukta, ed. by R. Roth (Gottingen, 1852); Pāṇini's Aṣṭādhyāyī, ed. by Böhtlingk (Leipzig, 1887); Kātyāyana's Vārttikas; Patañjali's Mahābhāṣya, ed. by Kielhorn, 3 vols. (Bombay, 1880-85); Jayāditya and Vāmana's Kāśikāvritti, 2nd ed. (Benares, 1898).

Works on Astronomy :

Sūrya-Siddhānta, ed. and trans. by Whitney (JAOS., VI); The Āryabhatīya, ed. with Comm. by Kern (Leyden, 1874); Varāhamihira's Brihat-Samhitā, ed. by S. Dvivedī (Benares, 1895-97); Varāhamihira's Horā-Śāstra, trans. by C. Iyer (Madras, 1885); Pañca-Siddhāntikā, ed. and trans. by Thibaut and Dvivedī (Benares, 1889); Gārgī Samhitā.

Works on Medicine :

Caraka Saṁhitā, ed. by J. Vidyāsāgara, 2nd ed. (Calc., 1896); Suśruta Saṁhitā, ed. by J. Vidyāsāgara, 3rd ed. (Calc., 1889); Vāgbhaṭa's Aṣṭāṅgahridaya, ed. by A. M. Kunte (Nir. Sag. Press, 1891).

Works on Philosophy :

Sāṅkhyakārikā, ed. in Benares Skt. series (1883); Sāṅkhyasūtras, trans. by Garbe (Calcutta, 1888-92); Mīmāṅsā Darśana, ed. with comm. of Sabarasvāmin (Calc., 1887); Brahma Sūtras, ed. in Ānandāśrama Skt. series (1890-91); Vedānta-Sūtras, trans. by Thibaut in S. B. E., XXXIV; Nyāya Sūtras, Vizianagaram Skt. series (Benares, 1896); Vaiśeṣika Darśana, ed. with Comm. (Calc., 1887); Sarvadarśana Saṁgraha, ed. by T. Tarkavācaspati (Calc., 1872).

Lexicons :

Amarakoṣa, ed. with Maheśvara's Comm. (Bombay); Halāyudha's Abhidhānaratnamālā, ed. by Aufrecht (London, 1861); Hemacandra's Abhidhāna-Cintāmaṇi, ed. by Böhtlingk and Rieu (St. Petersburg, 1847); Śabdakalpadruma (Calc., 1889); Keśava's Kalpadrukoṣa (GOS., XLII, 1928); Yadavaprakāśa's Vaijayantī, ed. by Gustav Oppert (1893).

Historical Romances and other Works :

Bāṇa's Harṣacarita, ed. by J. Vidyāsāgara (Calc., 1892); also by Führer (Bombay, 1909); trans. by Cowell and Thomas (London, 1897); Bāṇa's Kādambarī, ed. by Parab (Bombay, 1896); also by Peter Peterson (Bombay, 1900); trans. by Ridding (London, 1896); Kalhaṇa's Rājataraṅgiṇī, ed. by Durgā Prasāda (Bombay, 1892); trans. by Sir Aurel Stein (London, 1900); also by R. S. Pandit (Allahabad, 1935); Jonarāja's Dvitīya Rājataraṅgiṇī, ed. by Peterson (Bombay, 1896); Maṅkha's Śrīkaṇṭhacarita, ed. by Durgā Prasāda and K. P. Parab (Bombay, 1900); Vikramārjuna-Vijaya or Pampa-Bhārata, ed. by Lewis Rice, (Bangalore, 1898); Padmagupta's Navasāhasāṅkacarita, ed. by Islampurkar, Bom. Skt. series (Bombay, 1895); Bilhaṇa's Vikramāṅkadevacarita, Bom. Skt. series, No. 14; Sandhyākaranandi's Rāmacarita (Mem. As. Soc. Beng., III); Jayaratha's Prithvīrāja-Vijaya, ed. by S. K. Belvalkar (Bib. Ind.); Prithvīrāja Rāso, ed. by S. S. Das (Benares, 1904); Rāso-Sāra, ed. by S. S. Das (Benares, 1904); Nayacandra's Rambhāmañjarī; Bhāsa's Svapnavāsadattā, ed. by Gaṇapati Śāstri,

Trivandrum Skt. series; Subandhu's Vāsavadattā, ed. by F. E. Hall (Calc., 1859); Kālidāsa's Mālavikāgnimitra, ed. by S. P. Pandit (1889); Kālidāsa's Meghadūta, ed. by Hultzsch (London, 1911); Kālidāsa's Abhijñāna Śākuntala, ed. by M. R. Kale (Bombay, 1894); Kālidāsa's Raghuvaṁśa, ed. by Stenzler (1832); Later editions by S. P. Pandit and others; Viśākhadatta's Mudrārākṣasa, ed. by Hillebrandt (Breslau, 1912); also ed. by Telang (Bombay, 1893); Bhavabhūti's Mālatī-Mādhava, ed. by R. G. Bhandarkar (Bombay, 1905); Bhavabhūti's Mahāvīracarita, ed. by F. H. Trithen (London, 1848); Bhavabhūti's Uttararāmacarita, ed. by S. K. Belvalkar, P. V. Kane etc.; Harṣa's Ratnāvalī, Nirṇaya Sāgara Press (Bombay, 1885); Harṣa's Nāgānanda, ed. by R. D. Karamkar, 2nd ed., (Bombay, 1923); Harṣa's Priyadarśikā, ed. by Nariman, Jackson, and Ogden (Columbia Uni. series, 1923); Śūdraka's Mricchakaṭikā, ed. by J. Vidyāsāgara (Calc., 1891); Daṇḍin's Daśakumāracarita, ed. by P. Banerji (Calcutta, 1888); Rājaśekhara's Karpūramañjarī, ed. by Konow and Lanman (Harvard Oriental series, 1901); Rājaśekhara's Viddhasālabhañjikā, ed. by B. R. Arte (Poona, 1886); also by J. Vidyāsāgara (Calc., 1883); Kāvyamīmāṅsā, ed. by C. D. Dalal and R. A. K. Śāstri (GOS., No. 1, 1916); Mammaṭa's Kāvyaprakāśa, ed. by Jhalkīkara (Bombay, 1921); trans. by G. Jhā (1925); Nāgoji's Kāvyapradīpodyota, ed. by D. Chandorkar (Poona, 1898); Śārṅgadhara Paddhati, ed. by Peterson (Bom. Skt. series, No. 37); Vallabhadeva's Subhāṣitāvalī, ed. by Peterson (Bombay, 1886); Śriharṣa's Naiṣadhacarita, ed. by Śivadatta (Bombay, 1919); Krisṇa Miśra's Prabodha-Candrodaya, ed. in the Nirṇaya Sāgara Press (Bombay, 1898); Soḍḍhala's Udayasundarī Kathā, ed. by C. D. Dalal and Krisṇamacārya (GOS., No. 11 Baroda, 1920); Prasannarāghava, ed. by Paranjpye and Panse (Poona, 1894); Somadeva's Kathāsaritsāgara, ed. and trans. by Brockhaus, (Leipzig, 1839, 1862-66); also ed. Bomb., 1889; trans. by C. H. Tawney in Bibl. Ind., 1880-87; Kṣemendra's Brihatkathāmañjarī, ed. and trans. by Sylvain Lévi in *Journal Asiatique*, 1886; Kathākoṣa, trans. by C. H. Tawney from Skt. MSS (London, 1895); Bhartihari's Nīti and Vairāgya Śatakas, ed. and trans., Bombay, 1898; Pañcatantra, ed. by Kielhorn and Bühler, Bom. Skt. series, Trans. (Trichinopoli, 1887); Siṁhāsanadvātriṁśikā, ed. by J. Vidyāsāgara (Calc., 1881).

Buddhist Works:

Dīgha Nikāya, ed. by Rhys Davids and J. E. Carpenter (P.T.S., London, 1890-1911); Aṅguttara Nikāya, ed. by R. Morris and

E. Hardy (*Ibid.*, 1885-1900); Majjhima Nikāya, ed. by V. Trenckner and R. Chalmers (*Ibid.*, 1888-99); Saṁyutta Nikāya, ed. by Léon Feer and Mrs. Rhys Davids (*Ibid.*, 1884-1904); Khuddaka Nikāya; Vinaya, ed. by H. Oldenberg (London, (1879-83); Dhaṁmapada, ed. by Sūriyagoḍa Sumangal Thera (P. T. S., London, 1914); Jātakas, ed. by Faüsböll (London, 1877-97); Āryaśūra's Jātakamālā, ed. by Kern (Boston, 1891); trans. by J. S. Speyer (London, 1895); Dīpavaṁśa, ed. and trans. by H. Oldenberg (London, 1879); Mahāvaṁśa, ed. and trans. by W. Geiger (P. T. S., London, 1908, 1912); Milindapañha, ed. by V. Trenckner (London, 1880); trans. by Rhys Davids (Oxford, 1890-94); Lalita-Vistara, ed. by Lefmann (Halle, 1902-08); Mahāvastu, ed. by Senart (Paris, 1882-97); Divyāvadāna, ed. by E. B. Cowell and R. A. Neil (Cambridge, 1886); Sanskrit Buddhist Literature of Nepal, by R. L. Mitra (Calcutta, 1882); Mañjuśrīmūlakalpa, ed. by Gaṇapati Śāstrī (Trivandrum, 1925).

Jain and other Works :

Ācārāṅga sūtra, (Āgamodaya Samiti, Surat); Sūtrakritāṅga, (Āgamodaya Samiti, Surat); Samavāyāṅga, (Āgamodaya Samiti, Surat); Uttarādhyayana, (Āgamodaya Samiti, Surat); Bhagavatī Sūtra, (Āgamodaya Samiti, Surat); Bhadrabāhu's Kalpasūtra, ed. by H. Jacobi (Leipzig, 1879); Hemacandra's Sthavirāvalicarita, ed. by H. Jacobi (Calcutta, 1891); Hemacandra's Pariśiṣṭaparvan, ed. by Jacobi; also by Jain Dharma Prasāraka Sabhā, Bhavnagar; Merutuṅga's Prabandha-Cintāmaṇi, ed. by Jinavijaya Muni (Śāntiniketan, 1933); trans. by C. H. Tawney (Calc., 1899); Prabhācandra's Prabhāvakacarita, ed. by H. M. Śarmā, (Bombay, 1909); Rājaśekhara's Prabandha Koṣa, (Singhī Jain series, Calc.,); Jinaprabhāsūrī's Tīrthakalpa, (Singhī Jain series, Calc.,); Vākpatirāja's Gauḍavaho, ed. by S. P. Pandit (Bombay, 1887); Dhanapāla's Pāilacchi, ed. by Bühler (Gottingen, 1879); Hemacandra's Kumārapālacarita, ed. by S. P. Pandit (Bombay, 1900); Somaprabhācārya's Kumārapāla-pratibodha (GOS., No. XIV); Jain Harivaṁśa.

Some South Indian Works :

Maṇi-Mekhalai in its historical setting by S. K. Aiyangar (London, Luzac and Co.); The Śilappadikāram by V. R. R. Dikshitar (Oxford, 1939); Puṛanāṇuru; Periyapurāṇaṁ; Nandikkalambakaṁ; Jayangoṇḍār's Kaliṅgattu-pparani; Rājarājasoḷan-Ulā; Kulottuṅgaṉ-Piḻḻaittamil; Buddhamitra's Virasoḻiyaṁ; Coḷavaṁśacaritaṁ.

Moslem Works :

Kitāb-ul-Hind by Alberūnī, trans. by E. C. Sachau (London, 1914); Tārīkh-i-Firishta (N. K. Press, Lucknow, 1905); John Briggs, History of the Rise of the Mahomedan Power in India; Sir H. M. Elliot and John Dowson, History of India as told by its own Historians, Vols. I-III, specially see extracts from: Chach-nāma by Mohamed Ali Abū Bakr Kūfī; Sulaimān's Silsilat ut-Tawārīkh; Al Maśūdī's Murūj ul-Zahab (Paris, 1861); Al Utbī's Tarīkh-i-Yamīnī, ed by Alī and Sprenger (Delhi, 1847); Niẓāmuddīn's Tabaqāt-i-Akbarī, trans. by B. Dey, (Bib. Ind. new series, No. 1383); Minhājuddīn's Tabaqāt-i-Naṣīrī, trans. by H. G. Raverty (London, 1881); Ibn Asīr's Kāmil ut-Tawārīkh (Elliot, Vol. II); Hasan Niẓāmī's Tāj ul Maasir (Elliot, Vol. II); Mīr Khond's Rauẓat uṣ-Ṣafā (Lucknow, 1874); Khond Mīr's Ḥabīb uṣ-Siyar (Bombay, 1857).

Translations of Chinese Works :

James Legge, A Record of Buddhist Kingdoms being an account of the Chinese monk Fa-hian's travels (Oxford, 1886); Herbert A. Giles, Record of the Buddhist Kingdoms (Trübner and Co., London); Samuel Beal, Buddhist Records of the Western World (Kegan Paul, London); Samuel Beal, Hwui-li's Life of Hiuen Tsang (London, 1911); Samuel Beal, The Travels of Fa-hian (*Fo-kwo-ki*); Thomas Watters, On Yuań Chwang's Travels in India—(*Si-yu-ki*)—two vols. (London, 1904); J. Takakusu, A Record of the Buddhist Religion as practised in India and the Malay Archipelago (Oxford, 1896).

Gazetteers :

Imperial Gazetteer of India; Provincial Gazetteer Series; District Gazetteers.

Works on Chronology :

C. Mabel Duff, The Chronology of India (Westminster, 1899); Sītā Nath Pradhan, Chronology of Ancient India (Calcutta, 1927); A. Cunningham, Book of Indian Eras (Calcutta, 1883); L. D. Swamikannu Pillai, The Indian Ephemeris; B. G. Tilak, Vedic Chronology and Vedāṅga Jyotiṣa (Poona, 1925); N. Jagannadha Rao, The Age of the Mahābhārata War (Madras, 1931); T. S. N. Śāstri, The Age of Śaṅkara (Madras, 1916); K. N. Śivarāja Pillai, The Chronology of the early Tamils (Madras, 1932);

Works on Geography :

S. N. Majumdar, M'crindle's Ancient India as described by Ptolemy (Calcutta, 1927); S. N. Majumdar, Cunningham's Ancient Geography of India (Calcutta, 1924); W. H. Schoff, Translation of the *Periplus Maris Erythraei*; N. L. Dey, Geographical Dictionary of Ancient India (Calcutta, 1927); B. C. Law, Geographical Essays (London, 1937); Mark Collins, Geographical Data of the Raghuvaṁśa and the Daśakumāracarita (Leipzig, 1907).

Works on Epigraphy :

G. Bühler, Indische Palæographie (Strassburg, 1896); Indian Palæography, Eng. Trans. by J. F. Fleet in *Ind. Ant.*, 1904, Appendix; G. H. Ojhā, Prācīna-lipi (in Hindi); A. C. Burnell, Elements of South Indian Palæography (London, 1878); Epigraphia Indica; Epigraphia Carnatica; Reports of the Archæological Survey of India; Numerous inscriptions have been edited in other Journals also, mentioned in the list of abbreviations; A. C. Woolner, Aśoka Text and Glossary (Oxford Uni. Press, 1924); D. R. Bhandarkar, Inscriptions of Aśoka (Calcutta, 1920); E. Senart, Les Inscriptions de Piyadasi (Paris, 1881, 1886); E. Hultzsch, Corpus Inscriptionum Indicarum, Vol. I (Oxford, 1925); Sten Konow, Corpus Inscriptionum Indicarum, Kharoṣṭhī Inscriptions (Calcutta, 1929); A. M. Boyer, E. J. Rapson and E. Senart, Kharoṣṭhī Inscriptions (Oxford, 1920); J. F. Fleet, Corpus Inscriptionum Indicarum, Vol. III (Calcutta, 1888); Robert Sewell and Krishnaswami Aiyangar, The Historical Inscriptions of Southern India (Madras Uni. Hist. Series, No. V, 1932); V. Rangacharya, Inscriptions of the Madras Presidency, 3 vols. (Madras, 1919); South Indian Epigraphy; South Indian Inscriptions; Lewis Rice, Mysore and Coorg from the Inscriptions; C. R. Krisnamacarlu, Bombay-Karṇāṭaka Inscriptions; (Madras, 1940); Burgess and Indraji, Inscriptions from the cave temples of Western India (Bombay, 1881); Hīrālal, Descriptive lists of Inscriptions in C. P. and Berar (Nagpur, 1916); J. Vogel, Antiquities of Chamba State (Calcutta, 1901); N. G. Majumdar, Inscriptions from Bengal (Rajshahi, 1929); see *Gauḍalekhamālā*; A. P. Banerji Śāstri, Early Inscriptions of Bihar and Orissa (Patna, 1927); B. M. Barua, Old Brāhmī Inscriptions in Udayagiri and Khaṇḍagiri Caves (Calcutta, 1929); B. M. Barua, Barhūt Inscriptions (Calcutta, 1926).

Works on Numismatics :

E. J. Rapson, Indian Coins; E. J. Rapson, Catalogue of the Coins of the Andhra Dynasty, the Western Kṣatrapas, the Traikūṭaka Dynasty and the Bodhi Dynasty (London, 1908); C. J. Brown, The Coins of India, Heritage of India Series (Calcutta, 1922); C. J. Brown, Catalogue of Coins in the Provincial Museum, Lucknow, Vol. I (Oxford, 1920); V. A. Smith, Catalogue of Coins in the Indian Museum, Calcutta, Vol. I (Oxford, 1906); Pt. B. B. Bidyābinod, Supplementary Catalogue of the Coins in the Indian Museum, Non-Muhammadan Series (Calcutta, 1923); V. A. Smith, Andhra History and Coinage (Leipzig, 1902); Sir A. Cunningham, Coins of Mediæval India (London, 1893); Sir A. Cunningham, Coins of the Indo-Scythians, Śakas, and Kushans, Sir A. Cunningham, Later Indo-Scythian Coins; Percy Gardner, The Coins of the Greek and Scythic Kings of Bactria and India (London, 1886); R. B. Whitehead, Catalogue of Coins in the Punjab Museum, Lahore, Vol, I, Indo-Greek Coins (Oxford, 1914); John Allan, Catalogue of the Coins of the Gupta Dynasties and of Śaśāṅka, King of Gauḍa (London, 1914); Durgā Prasāda, Observations on the silver punchmarked coins of ancient India and their age (Benares, 1931); Durgā Prasāda, Classification and significance of the symbols on the silver punch-marked coins of ancient India (Numismatic Supplement, May, 1935); D. R. Bhandarkar, Carmichael Lectures on ancient Indian Numismatics (Calcutta, 1921); S. K. Chakraborty, A Study of Ancient Indian Numismatics (Calcutta, 1931); R. D. Banerji, Prācīna Mudrā, in Hindi, (Benares, V. E. 1981); Elliot, Coins of Southern India (London, 1885).

Classical Sources and Works based on them :

Herodotus, History, ed. by C. Hude, 2nd ed. (Oxford, 1913-14); trans. by G. Rawlinson (London, 1860); also by G. C. Macaulay (London, 1904); Pliny, Naturalis Historia, ed. by C. Mayhoff (Leipzig, 1892-1909); Strabo, Geographica, ed. by A. Meineke (Leipzig, 1866-7), trans. by H. C. Hamilton and W. Falconer (London, 1854-7); J. W. M'crindle, Ancient India as described in Classical Literature (Westminster, 1901); J. W. M'crindle, Ancient India as described by Megasthenes and Arrian (Calcutta, 1906); J. W. M'crindle, Ancient India—Its Invasion by Alexander the Great (Westminster, 1896); J. W. M'crindle, Ancient India as described by Ktesias the Knidian (Calcutta, 1882); S. N. Majumdar, M'crindle's Ancient India as described by Ptolemy (Calcutta, 1927); *Periplus*

Maris Erythraei, ed. by Fabricius (Leipzig, 1883); trans. by W. H. Schoff (London, 1912); Arrian, *Anabasis*, ed. by A. G. Roos (Leipzig, 1907); Arrian, *Indica*, ed. by R. Hercher (Leipzig, 1885); both trans. by E. J. Chinnock(London, 1893); Rooke, Arrian's History of Alexander's Expedition; E. A. W. Badge's Translation of the Life and Exploits of Alexander; W. W. Tarn, The Greeks in Bactria and India (Cambridge, 1938); H. G. Rawlinson, Intercourse between India and the Western World (Cambridge, 1916); H. G. Rawlinson, Bactria (London, 1912); H. G. Rawlinson, Foreign Influences in the Civilisation of Ancient India—900 B. C. to 400 A.D.; E. Pococke, India in Greece (London, 1852); Gauraṅga Nath Banerjee, Hellenism in Ancient India (Calcutta, 1920); Gauraṅga Nath Banerjee, India as known to the Ancient World (Calcutta, 1921); Baij Nath Puri, India as described by early Greek writers (Allahabad, 1939).

Tibetan Authorities:

Tārānātha, Trans. by F. A. Schiefner (St. Petersburg, 1869).

Histories of Indian Literature:

F. W. Max Müller, History of Ancient Sanskrit Literature, 2nd ed. (London, 1860); A. Weber, History of Indian Literature, 2nd ed., (London, 1882); Frazer, A Literary History of India (London, 1907); A. A. Macdonell, A History of Sanskrit Literature (London, 1928); A. B. Keith, A History of Sanskrit Literature (Oxford, 1928); A. B. Keith, Classical Sanskrit Literature (Heritage of India series); A. B. Keith, The Sanskrit Drama (Oxford, 1924); M. Winternitz, A History of Indian Literature, Vol. I (Calcutta, 1927); and Vol. II (Calc., 1933); Herbert H. Gowen, A History of Indian Literature (New York, 1931).

Works on Pre-historic India:

A. C. Logan, Old Chipped Stones of India (Calcutta, 1906); P. T. Srinivasa Ayyangar, The Stone Age in India (Madras, 1926); Panchanan Mitra, Pre-historic India (Calcutta, 1923); Bruce Foote, Catalogue of Pre-historic Antiquities in the Government Museum, Madras (1901); Bruce Foote, Notes on the Ages and Distribution of Indian Pre-historic Antiquities (Madras, 1916); P. C. Bagchi, Lévi's Pre-Aryan and Pre-Dravidian India (Calcutta, 1929); A. P. Banerji Śāstri, Asura India (Patna, 1926); V. Rangacharya, Pre-Musalman India, Vol. I (Madras); Sir John Marshall, Mohenjo-daro and the

Indus Civilisation, 3 volumes, (Probsthain & Co., London); E. J. H. Mackay, Further Excavations at Mohenjo-daro, two volumes, (Govt. of India Press, 1937, 1938); E. J. H. Mackay, The Indus Civilisation (London, 1935); K. N. Dikshit, Prehistoric Civilisation of the Indus Valley (Madras, 1939); Madho Sarup Vats, Excavations at Harappa, two volumes (Govt. of India Press, 1940); L. A. Waddell, The Indo-Sumerian seals deciphered (London, 1925); G. R. Hunter, The Script of Harappa and Mohenjo-daro (Calcutta, 1932).

Works on Political History etc.

E. J. Rapson, Ancient India (Cambridge, 1916); E. J. Rapson, The Cambridge History of India (Cambridge, 1922); Allan and Dodwell, The Cambridge Shorter History of India (Cambridge, 1934); F. E. Pargiter, Ancient Indian Historical Tradition (London, 1922); F. E. Pargiter, The Purāṇa Text of the Dynasties of the Kali Age (Oxford, 1913); V. Rangacharya, History of Pre-Musalman India, Vol. II; H. C. Raychaudhuri, Political History of Ancient India, 4th ed. (Calcutta, 1938); Ratilal N. Mehta, Pre-Buddhist India (Bombay, 1939); C. V. Vaidya, Epic India (Bombay, 1907); B. C. Law, Some Kṣatriya Tribes of Ancient India (Calcutta, 1924); B. C. Law, Kṣatriya clans in Buddhist India (Calcutta, 1922); B. C. Law, Historical Gleanings (Calc., 1922); H. K. Deb, Udayana Vatsarāja (Calcutta, 1919); Rhys Davids, Buddhist India (London, 1903); V. A. Smith, Early History of India, 4th ed. (Oxford, 1924); V. A. Smith, The Oxford History of India (Oxford, 1920); E. B. Havell, The History of Aryan Rule in India (London, mcmxviii); A. F. R. Hoernle and H. A. Stark, A History of India, 2nd ed. (Cuttack, 1904); M. Prothero and S. C. Vidyābhūṣaṇa, History of India, Bk. I, (London, 1915); E. B. Cowell, The History of India, Hindu Period; W. H. Moreland and A. C. Chatterjee, A Short History of India (London, 1936); Adolf Waley, A Pageant of India (London, 1927); C. S. Srinivasacari and Ramasvami Ayangar, A History of India (Madras, 1934); A Somayajulu, The Ancient History of India (Madras, 1935); Panchanan Raya, A Historical Review of Hindu India, 300 B. C. to 1200 A. D. (Delhi, 1939); R. D. Banerji, Pre-historic, Ancient, and Hindu India (Blackie and Son, 1934); H. G. Rawlinson, Indian Historical Studies (London, 1913); R. Sathianathaieyer, A College Text-book of Indian History (Madras, 1940); N. N. Ghosh, Early History of India (Allahabad, 1939); D. R. Bhandarkar, Carmichael Lectures on the Ancient History of India (Calcutta,

1918); J. N. Samaddar, The Glories of Magadha, 2nd ed. (Calcutta, 1927); J. J. Monahan, The Early History of Bengal (Oxford, 1925); R. K. Mookerji, Aśoka (Macmillan & Co., 1928); R. K. Mookerji, Men and Thought in Ancient India, (Macmillan & Co., 1924); Rev. Macphail, Aśoka; V. A. Smith, Aśoka, 3rd ed. (Oxford, mcmxx); D. R. Bhandarkar, Aśoka, 2nd ed. (Calcutta, 1932); P. L. Bhargava, Chandragupta Maurya (Lucknow, 1935); K. P. Jayasval, History of India—150 A. D. to 350 A. D. (Lahore, 1933); K. P. Jayasval, An Imperial History of India (Lahore, 1934); K. P Jayasval, Problems of Śaka-Sātavāhana History (Patna, 1931); R. G. Bhandarkar, A Peep into the early History of India (Bombay, 1920); R. D. Banerji, The Age of the Imperial Guptas (Benares, 1933); R. G. Basak, The History of North-Eastern India (Calcutta, 1934); J. J. Modi, The early History of the Hun and their inroads in India and Iran; E. A. Fires, The Maukharīs (Madras, 1934); T. G. Aravamuthan, The Kāverī, the Maukharis, and the Sangam Age (Madras, 1925); M. L. Ettinghausen, Harṣavardhana (Louvain, 1906); K. M. Panikkar, Śrī Harṣa of Kanauj (Bombay, 1922); R. K. Mookerji, Harṣa (Rulers of India Series, Oxford, 1926); C. V. Vaidya, History of Mediæval Hindu India, Vol. I (1921), Vol. II (1924), Vol. III (1926); A. S. Altekar, History of Benares (Benares, 1937); N. N. Ghosh, Early History of Kauśāṁbī (Allahabad, 1935); R. S. Tripathi, History of Kanauj to the Moslem Conquest (Benares, 1937); H. C. Ray, Dynastic History of Northern India, Vol. I (Calcutta, 1931); H. C. Ray, Vol. II (Calcutta, 1936); Crooke, Tod's Annals and Antiquities of Rājasthān (Oxford Uni. Press, 1920); D. C. Ganguly, History of the Paramāra Dynasty (Dacca, 1933); P. T. S. Ayyangar, Bhojarāja (Madras, 1931); C. E. Luard and K. K. Lele, Paramāras of Dhar and Malwa (Bombay, 1908); K. R. Subramanian, Buddhist Remains in Andhra and Andhra History (Madras, 1932); V. G. Bakhle, Sātavāhanas and the contemporary Kṣatrapas; D. C. Sircar, The Successors of the Sātavāhanas in Lower Deccan (Calcutta, 1939); D. C. Sircar, Successors of the Sātavāhanas in the Eastern Deccan (Calcutta, 1935); D. C. Ganguly, The Eastern Cālukyas (Benares, 1937); W. W. Hunter, Orissa (London, 1872); B. C. Mazumdar, Orissa in the Making; R. D. Banerji, History of Orissa (Calcutta, 1930); E. A. Gait, History of Assam, 2nd ed. (Calcutta, 1926); B. L. Barua, History of Kāmarūpa; Daniel Wright, History of Nepal (Cambridge, 1877); Sylvain Lévi, Le Nepal (Paris, 1905); Percival Landon, Nepal (London, 1928); R. G. Bhandarkar, Early

History of the Dekkan, 3rd ed. (Calcutta, 1928); J. Dubreuil, Ancient History of the Deccan (Pondicherry, 1920); K. V. Subrahmanya Iyer, Historical Sketches of Ancient Dekhan (Madras, 1917); J. F. Fleet, The Dynasties of the Kanarese Districts (Bombay, 1899); Ranjit S. Satyāśraya, Origin of the Cālukyas (Calcutta, 1937); A. S. Altekar, The Rāṣṭrakūṭas and their Times (Poona, 1934); B. A. Saletore, Ancient Karṇāṭaka, (Poona, 1936); George M. Moraes, The Kadamba-Kula (Bombay, 1931); M. V. Krishna Rao, The Gaṅgas of Talkāḍ (Madras, 1936); Lewis Rice, Mysore; Bayley, History of Gujarat (London, 1886); W. Wilberforce-Bell, The History of Kāthiāwāḍ, (London, 1916); A. S. Altekar, A History of important Ancient Towns and Cities in Gujarat and Kāthiāwāḍ (Bombay, 1926); Robert Sewell, A Forgotten Empire (London, 1900); Iśvarī Prasāda, History of Mediæval India (Allahabad, 1925); R. C. Majumdar, The Arab Invasion of India (Dacca, 1931); M. Nazim, Mahmud of Ghaznā (Cambridge, 1931).

Works on South Indian History:

S. Krishnasvami Aiyangar, Ancient India (Madras, 1911); S. Krishnasvami Aiyangar, The Beginnings of South Indian History (Madras, 1918); S. Krishnasvami Aiyangar, Some Contributions of South India to Indian Culture (Calcutta, 1923); S. K. Aiyangar and Honry, Ancient India and South Indian History and Culture (Poona, 1941); R. Gopalan, History of the Pallavas of Kāñcī (Madras, 1928); Rev. H. Heras, The Pallava Genealogy (Bombay, 1931); Rev. H. Heras, Studies in Pallava History (Madras, 1933); Rev. H. Heras, The Origin of the Pallavas (Bom. Uni. Journ., January, 1936); J. Dubreuil, The Pallavas; C. Minakshi, Administration and Social life under the Pallavas (Madras, 1938); D. C. Sirkar, The early Pallavas (Lahore, 1935); K. A. N. Śāstri, The Coḷas, Vol. I (Madras, 1925); K. A. N. Śāstri, The Coḷas, Vol. II, pt. I (Madras, 1937); K. A. N. Śāstri, Studies in Coḷa History and Administration (Madras, 1932); K. A. N. Śāstri, The Pāṇḍyan Kingdom (London, 1929); K. G. Sesha Aiyar, Cera Kings of the Sangam Period (London, 1937); V. Kanakasabhai Pillai, The Tamils Eighteen Hundred Years Ago (Madras, 1904); T. R. Sesha Iyengar, Dravidian India (Madras, 1925); V. R. R. Dikshitar, Studies in Tamil Literature and History (London, 1930);.

Works in Hindi:

Jayacandra Vidyālaṁkāra, Bhāratīya Itihāsa kī Rūparekhā

(Prayāga, V. E. 1985); J. Vidyālaṁkāra, Bhāratabhūmi aur uske Nivāsī (Punjab, V. E. 1988); Jayacandra Vidyālaṁkāra, Itihāsa Praveśa (Allahabad, 1941); Bisheshwar Nath Reu, Bhārata ke prācīna Rājavaṁśa; Gaṅgā Prasad Mehta, Prācīna Bhārata (Kāśi, 1933); Shyām Bihārī and Sukadeo Bihārī Miśra, Bhāratavarṣa kā Itihāsa (Prayāga, V. E. 1986); Shyām Biharī and Śukadeo Biharī Miśra, Buddhapūrva Bhāratīya Itihāsa (Prayāga, V. E. 1986); Śrī Sampūrṇānanda, Āryon kā ādi deśa (Allahabad, V. E. 1997); Śrī Sampūrṇānanda, Saṁrāṭ Aśoka; Satyaketu Vidyālaṁkāra, Maurya Sāṁrājya kā Itihāsa (Prayaga, V. E. 1985); Gaṅga Prasad Mehta, Candragupta Vikramāditya (Prayāga, 1932); Vāsudeva Upādhyāya, Gupta Sāṁrājya kā Itihāsa (Prayāga, 1939); Śrī Sampūrṇānanda, Saṁrāṭ Harṣavardhana (Bombay, V. E. 1977); Gaurīshankar Chatterji, Harṣavardhana (Prayāga, 1938); Lala Sitaram, Ayodhyā kā Itihāsa (Prayāga, 1932); Rajendra Singh, Tripurī kā Itihāsa; Bisheshwar Nath Reu, Rāṭhoron (Rāṣṭrakūṭon) kā Itihāsa (Jodhpur, 1933); Bisheshwar Nath Reu, Rājā Bhoja (Prayāga, 1932); Chandragupta Vidyālaṁkāra, Brihattara Bhārata (Gurukula Kāngri, 1939); Gaurī Shankar Ojhā, Madhyakālīn Bhāratīya Saṁskriti (Prayāga, 1928); Dvivedī Abhinandan Grantha (Kāśī, V. E. 1990); Bhāratīya Anuśīlana Grantha (Prayāga, V. E. 1990).

Works on Polity :

J. J. Anjaria, The Nature and Grounds of Political Obligation in the Hindu State (Longmans, Green & Co., 1935); H. N. Sinha, Sovereignty in Ancient Indian Polity (London, 1938); K. P. Jayasval, Hindu Polity (Calcutta, 1924); Benī Prasāda, Theory of Government in Ancient India, post-Vedic, (Allahabad, 1927); Benī Prasāda, The State in Ancient India (Allahabad, 1928); K. A. Nilakantan, The Theory of pre-Muslim Indian Polity (Madras, 1912); A. K. Sen, Studies in Hindu Political Thought (Calcutta, 1926); N. C. Bandyopādhyāya, Development of Hindu Polity and Political Theories (Calcutta, 1927); N. N. Law, Studies in Ancient Hindu Polity (Calcutta, 1914); N. N. Law, Aspects of Ancient Indian Polity (Oxford, 1921); N. N. Law, Inter-State Relations in Ancient India (Calcutta, 1920); P. N. Bandyopādhyāya, International Law and Custom in Ancient India (Calcutta, 1920); S. V. Viswanātha, International Law in Ancient India (Longmans, Green & Co., 1925); P. C. Basu, Indo-Aryan Polity (London, 1925); P. N. Banerji, Public Administration in Ancient India (Macmillan & Co., 1916); D. R. Bhandarkar, Some aspects of ancient

Hindu Polity (Benares, 1929); V. R. R. Dikshitar, Hindu Administrative Institutions (Madras, 1929); V. R. R. Dikshitar, The Mauryan Polity (Madras, 1932); B. K. Sarkar, The Political Institutions and Theories of the Hindus (Leipzig, 1922); U.K. Trivedī, The Constitutional Theory of Hindu Law (Bombay, 1913); R. C. Majumdar, Corporate Life in Ancient India (Calcutta, 1922); R. K. Mookerji, Local Government in Ancient India (Oxford, 1920); N. B. Pavgee, Self-Government in India, Vedic and post-Vedic (Poona, 1918); U. Ghoshal, A History of Hindu Political Theories (Calcutta, 1923); U. Ghoshal, A History of Hindu Political Theories (Calcutta, 1923); K. V. Rangasvami Aiyangar, Some Aspects of Ancient Indian Polity, 2nd ed. (Madras, 1935); Shamasastri, Evolution of Indian Polity (Calcutta, 1920); Shamasastri, Eng. trans. of Kauṭilya's Arthaśāstra, 3rd ed. (Mysore, 1929); M. N. Dutt, Śāntiparvan, Eng. trans.(Calcutta, 1903).

Works on Economic Conditions :

S. K. Das, Economic Life in Ancient India (Calcutta, 1925); M. A. Buch, Economic Life in Ancient India (Baroda, 1924); N. C. Bandhyopādhyāya, Economic Life and Progress in Ancient India (Calcutta, 1925); Prannāth, A Study in the Economic Condition of Ancient India (pub. by Royal As. Soc., London); K. V. Rangasvami Aiyangar, Aspects of Ancient Indian Economic Thought (Benares, 1934); J. N. Samaddar, Lectures on the Economic Condition of Ancient India (Calcutta, 1922); Mrs. C. A. F. Rhys Davids, Economic Conditions in Ancient India (*Economic Journal*, Sept., 1901); N. S. Subba Rao, Economic and Political Conditions in Ancient India, being an Analytical Study of the Jātakas (Mysore, 1911); U. N. Ghoshal, Contributions to the History of the Hindu Revenue System (Calcutta, 1929); U. N. Ghoshal, The Agrarian System in Ancient India (Calcutta, 1930); Rādhāraman Gangopādyāya, Agriculture and Agriculturists in Ancient India (Calcutta, 1932); U. N. Bagchi, The Law of Minerals in Ancient India (Calcutta, 1926); Binode Bihari Dutt, Town-Planning in Ancient India (Calcutta, 1925).

Works on Education :

S. K. Das, The Educational System of the Ancient Hindus (Calcutta, 1930); D. C. Sarkar, Educational Ideas and Institutions in Ancient India, circa 15th to 10th century B. C. (Patna, 1928); N. N. Mazumdar, A History of Education in Ancient India (Macmillan & Co., 1916); A. S. Altekar, Education in

Ancient India (Benares, 1934); F. E. Keay, Indian Education in Ancient and Later Times (Oxford, 1938); V. P. Bokel, The History of Education in India (Bombay, 1925); H. D. Sankalia, The University of Nalanda (Madras, 1934).

Works on the Position of Women :

B. S. Upādhyāya, Women in Rigveda, 2nd ed. (Benares, 1941); A. S. Altekar, Position of Women in Hindu Civilisation (Benares, 1938); C. Bader, Women in Ancient India (London, 1925); Indra, Status of Women in Ancient India (Lahore, 1941); B. C. Law, Women in Buddhist Literature.

Works on Religion and Culture :

H. D. Griswold, The Religion of the Rigveda (Ox. Uni. Press, 1923); A. Kaegi, The Rigveda, Trans. by R. Arrowsmith, (Boston, 1886); M. Bloomfield, The Religion of the Veda (New York, 1908); A. A. Macdonell, Vedic Mythology (Strassburg, 1897); A. A. Macdonell and A. B. Keith, Vedic Index of Names and Subjects, two volumes, (London, 1912); Z. A. Ragozin, Vedic India (London, 1895); E. W. Hopkins, The Religions of India (Boston, 1895); E. W. Hopkins, The Great Epic of India (New York, 1901); J. Barth, History of Religions in India (London, 1882); R. G. Bhandarkar, Vaiṣṇavism, Śaivism and minor Religious Systems (Poona, 1928); Sir Charles Eliot, Hinduism and Buddhism (London, 1921); T. W. Rhys Davids, Buddhism (London, 1877); Paul Dahlke, Buddhism (London, 1927); R. S. Copleston, Buddhism, Primitive and Present (London, 1908); Paul Carus, The Gospel of Buddha (Chicago, 1895); E. H. Brewester, The Life of Gotama the Buddha (London, 1926); W. W. Rockhill, The Life of the Buddha (London, 1884); Hermann Oldenberg, Buddha, trans. by Hoey (London, 1882); E. J. Thomas, The Life of Buddha (London, 1927); Réne Grousset, In the footsteps of the Buddha (London, 1932); A. K. Coomarasvamy, Buddha and the Gospel of Buddhism; J. H. C. Kern, Manual of Indian Buddhism (Strassburg, 1896); W. M. McGovern, A Manual of Buddhist Philosophy (London, 1923); A. B. Keith, Buddhist Philosophy in India and Ceylon (Oxford, 1923); Th Stcherbatsky, The Conception of Buddhist Nirvāṇa (Leningrad, 1927); N. Dutt, Early History and Spread of Buddhism (Luzac & Co., London, 1925); N. Dutt, Aspects of Mahāyāna Buddhism (Luzac & Co., 1930); N. Dutt, Early Monastic Buddhism (Calcutta, 1941); Barodia, History and Literature of Jainism (Bombay, 1909); Jagmander Lal Jaini, Outlines of Jainism (Cambridge,

1916); P. C. Nahar, An Epitome of Jainism (Calcutta, 1917); M. Bloomfield, The Life and Stories of the Jaina Savior Pārśvanātha (Baltimore, 1919); Mrs. Sinclair Stevenson, The Heart of Jainism (Ox. Uni. Press, 1915); Bühler, The Indian Sect of the Jains; Amulyacandra Sen, Schools and Sects in Jaina Literature (Calcutta, 1931); C. L. Shah, Jainism in North India (Longmans, Green & Co., 1932); M. S. R. Aiyangar, Studies in South Indian Jainism; S. Radhakrishnan, Indian Philosophy (Great Britain, 1929); Deussen, System des Vedānta (Leipzig, 1883); Garbe, Philosophy of Ancient India (Chicago, 1897); F. W. Max Müller, Six Systems of Indian Philosophy (London, 1899); T. C. Hodson, The Primitive Culture of India (London, 1922); A. C. Das, Rigvedic Culture (Calcutta, 1925); A. C. Das, Rigvedic India (Calcutta, 1927); R. C. Dutt, A History of Civilisation in Ancient India (London, 1893); R. K. Mookerji, Hindu Civilisation (Longmans, Green & Co., 1936); S. Radhakrishnan, The Heart of Hindustan (Natesan & Co., Madras, 1932); S. Radhakrishnan, Hindu View of Life (George Allen, & Unwin, London, 1927); Broja Sundara Roy, Aims and Ideals of Ancient Indian Culture (Calcutta, 1938); P. K. Acharya, Elements of Hindu Culture; M. M. Kunte, The Vicissitudes of Aryan Civilisation in India (Bombay, 1880); N. N. Law, Studies in Indian History and Culture (Calcutta, 1925); R. C. Majumdar, Outline of Ancient Indian History and Civilisation (Calcutta, 1927); A. A. Macdonell, India's Past (Oxford, 1927); L. D. Barnett, Antiquities of India (London, 1913); R. K. Mookerji, The Fundamental Unity of India (Longmans, Green & Co., 1914); F. Max Müller, India, What can it teach us? (London, 1892).

Works on Social Conditions:

P. T. S. Aiyangar, Life in Ancient India in the Age of the Mantras (Madras, 1912); V. M. Apte, Social and Religious Life in the Grihya Sūtras (Ahmedabad, 1939); S. C. Sarkar, Some Aspects of the Earliest Social History of India (London, 1928); Ratilal N. Mehta, Pre-Buddhist India (Bombay, 1939); Richard Fick, The Social Organisation in North-East India in Buddha's Time (Calcutta, 1920); N. C. Sengupta, Sources of Law and Society in Ancient India (Calcutta, 1924); Julius Jolly, Hindu Law and Customs (Calcutta, 1928); H. C. Chakladar, Social Life in Ancient India (Calcutta, 1929); Chandra Chakraberty, A Study in Hindu Social Polity (Calcutta, 1923); B. K. Sarkar, Positive Background of Hindu Sociology (Allahabad, 1921); R. C. Hazra, Studies in Paurāṇic Records on

Hindu Rites and Customs (Dacca, 1940).

Works on Art and Architecture :

James Fergusson and J. Burgess, History of Indian and Eastern Architecture (London, 1910); E. B. Havell, Ancient and Mediæval Architecture of India; J. Fergusson and J. Burgess, The Cave-temples of India (London, 1880); A. Foucher, The Beginnings of Buddhist Art (London, mcmxvii); James Burgess, Buddhist Art in India (London, 1901); J. Vogel, Buddhist Art in India, Ceylon and Java (Oxford, 1930); A.V.T. Iyer, Indian Architecture; P. K. Acharya, Architecture of Mānasāra (Ox. Uni. Press); A. Rea, Pallava Architecture; J. C. French, The Art of the Pāla Empire of Bengal (Oxford, 1928); R. L. Mitra, Antiquities of Orissa (Calcutta, 1875); M. M. Ganguly, Orissa and her Remains; N. K. Bose, Canons of Orissan Architecture (Calcutta, 1932); Henry Cousens, The Architectural Antiquities of Western India (London, 1926); H. D. Sankalia, The Archæology of Gujarat and Kāṭhiāwāḍ (Bombay, 1941); Ramcandra Kak, Ancient Monuments of Kashmir (London, 1933); P. N. Bose, Principles of Indian Śilpaśāstra (Lahore, 1926); T. A. Gopinatha Rao, Elements of Hindu Iconography (Madras, 1916); Benoytosh Bhattacharya, The Indian Buddhist Iconography (Oxford Uni. Press, 1924); A. K. Coomarasvamy, Elements of Buddhist Iconography (Harvard, 1935); B. C. Bhattacharya, The Jaina Iconography (Lahore, 1939); Ludwig Bachhofer, Early Indian Sculptures, (Paris, mcmxxix); J. Burgess, The Gandhāra Sculptures (London, 1895); A. C. Martin, Iconography of Southern India; O. C. Ganguli, Southern Indian Images; Krishnasastri, South Indian Images of Gods and Goddesses (Madras, 1916); V. A. Smith, A History of Fine Art in India and Ceylon, ed. by K. De B. Codrington (Oxford, 1990); A. K. Coomarasvamy, A History of Indian and Indonesian Art; Rai Krishnadas, Bhāratīya Mūrtikalā (Kāśī, V. E. 1996); E. B. Havell, A Handbook of Indian Art (London, 1927); E. B. Havell, Ideals of Indian Art (London, 1920); E. B. Havell, Indian Sculpture and Painting (London, 1908); F. H. Andrews, The Influences of Indian Art (London, 1925); See also *Catalogues* of various Museums and *Guides* to historical sites like Sāñchī, Taxilā, Nālandā, etc.

Painting :

Percy Brown, Indian Painting (Heritage of India series); A.K. Coomarasvamy, Indian Drawings; Stella Kramrisch, A survey of Painting in the Deccan (London, 1937); Griffiths, The Paintings of the Buddhist Caves of Ajantā, 2 vols., (London, 1896-97); G. Yazdani, Ajantā (Hyderabad, 1933); J. Marshall, The Bagh Caves in Gwalior State (London, 1927); Rai Krishnadas, Bhārata kī Citrakalā (Kāśī, V. E. 1996).

Works on the Aryans :

Isaac Taylor, The Origin of the Aryans (London, 1889); Gordon Childe, The Aryans (London, 1926); H. H. Bender, The Home of the Indo-Europeans (Oxford, 1922); B. G. Tilak, The Arctic Home in the Vedas (Poona, 1903); Lacchmi Dhar Kalla, The Home of the Aryans (Delhi, 1930); Nagendra Nath Ghose, The Aryan Trail in Iran and India (Calcutta, 1937).

Works on Ethnography and Castes :

Baines, Ethnography (Strassburg, 1912); W. Crooke, The Tribes and Castes of the North-Western Provinces and Oudh (Calcutta, 1896); Elliot, Races of the North-Western Provinces and Oudh; J. A. Anderson, Peoples of India (Cambridge, 1913); H. H. Risley, The People of India, 2nd ed. (London, 1915); R. P. Chanda, The Indo-Aryan Races (Rajshahi, 1916); E. Thurston and Rangachari, The Castes and Tribes of Southern India (Madras, 1909-10); M. Senart, Origin of Caste; S.V. Ketkar, The History of Caste in India.

Miscellaneous Works :

N. K. Dutt, The Aryanisation of India (Calcutta, 1925); P. Bose, Indian Teachers of Buddhist Universities (Adyar, Madras, 1923); S. C. Das, Indian Pandits in the Land of Snow (Calcutta, 1893); R. K. Mookerji, A History of Indian Shipping and Maritime Activities (Longmans, Green & Co. 1912); P. C. Chakravarti, The Art of War in Ancient India (Dacca, 1941); G. T. Date, The Art of War in Ancient India (Oxford, 1929); Gustav Oppert, On the Weapons, army organisation and political Maxims (London, 1880); Rama Prasad Das Gupta, Crime and Punishment in Ancient India (Calcutta, 1930); H. H. Wilson, Theatre of the Hindus (London, 1871); G. A. Grierson, The Linguistic Survey of India; B. G. Tilak, The Orion (Poona, 1893).

Works on Greater India :

R. C. Majumdar, Ancient Indian Colonies in the Far East—Champa—(Lahore, 1927); R. C. Majumdar, Suvarṇadvīpa

(Dacca, 1937); P. Bose, The Indian Colony of Champa (Adyar, Madras, 1926); P. N. Bose, The Hindu Colony of Cambodia (Adyar, Madras, 1927); Bijan Roy Chatterji, Indian Cultural Influence in Cambodia (Calcutta, 1928); Bijan Roy Chatterji, India and Java, pt. I, 2nd ed. (Calcutta, 1933); Bijan Roy Chatterji, Indian Culture in Java and Sumatra (Calcutta, 1927); Himansu Bhushan Sircar, Indian Influences on the Literature of Java and Bali (Calcutta, 1934); A. J. Bernet Kempers, Cultural Relations between India and Java (Calcutta, 1937); H. G. Quaritch Wales, Towards Angkor; P. C. Bagchi, India and China (Calcutta, 1927); N. P. Chakravarti, India and Central Asia (Calcutta, 1927); U. N. Ghoshal, Ancient Indian Culture in Afghanistan (Calcutta, 1928).

Modern Dictionaries :

N. L. Dey, Geographical Dictionary of Ancient India (Calcutta, 1927); P. K. Acharya, A Dictionary of Hindu Architecture (Oxford Uni. Press); W. Winternitz, A Concise Dictionary of Eastern Religions (Oxford, 1910); Dowson, Hindu Classical Dictionary (London, 1888); Monier-Williams, Sanskrit-English Dictionary, 2nd ed., (Oxford, 1899); Woollastan, English-Persian Dictionary.

Journals etc. :

See the list of Abbreviations; *Add:* Calcutta Review, Calcutta; Calcutta Oriental Journal, Calcutta; The Journal of Oriental Research; Proceedings of the Oriental Conferences; Memoirs and Transactions of the Royal Asiatic Society, London; Journal of the Bombay Branch of the Royal Asiatic Society, Bombay; Indian Culture, Calcutta; Journal of the Greater India Society, Calcutta; Bulletin of the Deccan College Research Society, Poona; New Indian Antiquary, Bombay; Numismata Orientalia; Annual Bibliography of Indian Archæology; Mysore Archæological Survey Reports, Mysore; Baroda Archæological Survey Reports, Baroda; Asia Major; Vienna Oriental Journal, Vienna; Journal of the American Oriental Society, New York; Bulletin of the School of Oriental Studies, London; Journal Asiatique; Ariana Antiqua; Indische Alterthumskunde; Gottingische Gelehrte Anziegen; Zeitschrift der Deutschen Morgenlandischen Gesellschaft.

INDEX OF NAMES

E

U

V

Z

ADDENDA

P. 175, *note*: See p. 182, Appendix II, for the names of Aśoka's queens. That Aśoka was a polygamist appears from traditions and the Queen's edict, in which there occurs a reference to his second wife (cf. 'dutīyāye deviye'), Kāl (r) uvāki, mother of Tīvala (Tīvara).

P. 176, *note* 1: An idea of the immense difficulties, that the engineers of Aśoka had to face in transporting these pillars to distant places, may be had from Shams-i-Sirāj, who gives us a vivid desciiption of how Sultān Firoz Shah removed one of these columns from the village of Toprā (Ambala district, Punjab) as a trophy to Delhi. We are told that the earth at its base was first carefully dug, and it then fell gently over on the bed of silk-cotton prepared for it. Next, it was thickly encased in reeds and raw-skins to prevent any damage and was raised on to a carriage with 42 wheels specially constructed for the purpose. A stout rope was fastened to each wheel, and it was drawn by two hundred men at a time. Thus, the carriage with the full weight of the pillar was pulled by 8,400 men (42×200). When the carriage reached the bank of the Jumna, the monolith was very "ingeniously transferred" to large boats collected there. It was then safely conducted to Firozabad and set up near the Jami Masjid with infinite skill and labour. Sultān Firoz Shah is represented to have removed another Aśokan pillar also from the vicinity of the town of Mirath (Meerut). Both these columns still stand near Delhi on the Kotla and the Ridge respectively (see Elliot, III, p. 350; Smith, Aśoka, 3rd ed., pp. 121-23; Bhandarkar, Aśoka, 2nd ed., pp. 215-17).

P. 210, *note*: That the Yavanas influenced the development of Indian astronomy is obvious from a number of Greek terms preserved in the works of Indian astronomers. Thus, in Varāha Mihira's *Horā-Śāstra*, we have such names for the signs of the Zodiac as *Āra* (*Ares*), *Heli* (*Hēlios*), *Jyau* (*Zeus*). Among other terms may be mentioned *kendra* for *kentron*, *jāmitra* for *diametron*. At a later period, however, Indians made a great advance in astronomy, and probably taught it to the Arabs.